The Papers of
George Washington

The Papers of
George Washington

W. W. Abbot and Dorothy Twohig, *Editors*

Philander D. Chase, *Senior Associate Editor,* and
Beverly H. Runge, *Associate Editor*

Mark A. Mastromarino, Frank E. Grizzard, Jr.,
Beverly S. Kirsch, and Debra B. Kessler, *Assistant Editors*

Confederation Series

3

May 1785–March 1786

W. W. Abbot, *Editor*

UNIVERSITY PRESS OF VIRGINIA

CHARLOTTESVILLE AND LONDON

This edition has been prepared by the staff of
The Papers of George Washington
sponsored by
The Mount Vernon Ladies' Association of the Union
and the University of Virginia
with the support of
the National Endowment for the Humanities and
the National Historical Publications and Records Commission.

THE UNIVERSITY PRESS OF VIRGINIA

First published 1994

Library of Congress Cataloging-in-Publication Data
(Revised for vol. 3)
Washington, George, 1732–1799.
  The papers of George Washington.   Confederation
series.
  Includes bibliographical references and indexes.
  Contents: 1. January–July 1784—2. July 1784–May
1785—3. May 1785–March 1786.
  1. Washington, George, 1732–1799—Archives.
2. Presidents—United States—Archives.   3. United
States—History—Confederation, 1783–1789.
I. Abbott, W. W. (William Wright), 1922–   .
II. Twohig, Dorothy.   III. Confederation series.
IV. Title.
E312.7   1992   973.4'1'092   91-3171
ISBN 0-8139-1348-9 (v. 1)
ISBN 0-8139-1506-6 (v. 3)

Printed in the United States of America

For
Lawrence William Towner (1921–1992)

Contents

NOTE: Volume numbers refer to the *Confederation Series*.

Illustration

Editorial Apparatus

Transcription of the documents in the volumes of *The Papers of George Washington* has remained as close to a literal reproduction of the manuscript as possible. Punctuation, capitalization, paragraphing, and spelling of all words are retained as they appear in the original document. Dashes used as punctuation have been retained except when a dash and another mark of punctuation appear together. The appropriate marks of punctuation have always been added at the end of a paragraph. When a tilde is used in the manuscript to indicate a double letter, the letter has been doubled. Washington and some of his correspondents occasionally used a tilde above an incorrectly spelled word to indicate an error in orthography. When this device is used the editors have corrected the word. In cases where a tilde has been inserted above an abbreviation or contraction, usually in letter-book copies, the word has been expanded. Otherwise, contractions and abbreviations have been retained as written except that a period has been inserted after an abbreviation when needed. Superscripts have been lowered. Editorial insertions or corrections in the text appear in square brackets. Angle brackets ⟨ ⟩ are used to indicate illegible or mutilated material. A space left blank in a manuscript by the writer is indicated by a square-bracketed gap in the text [   ]. Deletion of material by the author in a manuscript is ignored unless it contains substantive material, and then it appears in a footnote. If the intended location of marginal notations is clear from the text, they are inserted without comment; otherwise they are recorded in the notes. The ampersand has been retained and the thorn transcribed as "th." The symbol for per (℔) is used when it appears in the manuscript. The dateline has been placed at the head of a document regardless of where it occurs in the manuscript.

Since GW read no language other than English, incoming letters written to him in foreign languages generally were translated for his information. Where this contemporary translation has survived, it has been used as the text of the document and the original version has been included either in the notes or in the CD-ROM edition of the Papers. If there is no contemporary translation, the document in its original language has been used as the text. All of the documents printed in this volume, as well as other ancillary material (usually cited in the notes), may be found in the CD-ROM edition of Washington's Papers (CD-ROM:GW).

Individuals usually are identified only at the first appearance of their names. The index to each volume of the Confederation Series indicates where an identification may be found in earlier volumes.

A number of letters to and from Washington have been printed, in whole or in part, out of their chronological sequence, usually in footnotes. All of these letters are listed in the table of contents with an indication where they may be found in this or another volume.

Symbols Designating Documents

AD   Autograph Document
ADS   Autograph Document Signed
ADf   Autograph Draft
ADfS   Autograph Draft Signed
AL   Autograph Letter
ALS   Autograph Letter Signed
D   Document
DS   Document Signed
Df   Draft
DfS   Draft Signed
LS   Letter Signed
LB   Letter-Book Copy
[S]   Signature clipped (used with other symbols: e.g.,
        AL[S], Df[S]

Repository Symbols and Abbreviations

Arch. Aff. Etr.   Archives du Ministère des Affaires Etrangères, Paris
                  (photocopies and microfilm at Library of Con-
                  gress)
CD-ROM:GW   See "Editorial Apparatus"
CSmH   Henry E. Huntington Library, San Marino, Calif.
CaQMM   McGill University, Montreal
CtHi   Connecticut Historical Society, Hartford
DLC   Library of Congress
DLC:GW   George Washington Papers, Library of Congress
DNA   National Archives
DNA:PCC   Papers of the Continental Congress, National
            Archives
DSoCi   Society of the Cincinnati, Washington, D.C.
ICHi   Chicago Historical Society

MH	Harvard University, Cambridge, Mass.
MHi	Massachusetts Historical Society, Boston
MdHi	Maryland Historical Society, Baltimore
MiDbGr	Greenfield Village and the Henry Ford Museum, Dearborn, Mich.
MnHi	Minnesota Historical Society, Saint Paul
NBLiHi	Long Island Historical Society, Brooklyn, N.Y.
NIC	Cornell University, Ithaca, N.Y.
NN	New York Public Library, New York
NNMM	Metropolitan Museum of Art, New York
NNPM	Pierpont Morgan Library, New York
NSarNP	Saratoga National Historical Park, Saratoga Springs, N.Y.
NbO	Omaha Public Library, Omaha, Nebr.
NcD	Duke University, Durham, N.C.
NhD	Dartmouth College, Hanover, N.H.
NjMoNP	Washington Headquarters Library, Morristown, N.J.
NjP	Princeton University, Princeton, N.J.
PEL	Lafayette College, Easton, Pa.
PHC	Haverford College, Haverford, Pa.
PHi	Historical Society of Pennsylvania, Philadelphia
PPAmP	American Philosophical Society, Philadelphia
PPRF	Rosenbach Foundation, Philadelphia
PU	University of Pennsylvania, Philadelphia
PWacD	David Library of the American Revolution, Washington Crossing, Pa.
RG	Record Group (designating the location of documents in the National Archives)
R-Ar	Rhode Island State Archives, Rhode Island State Library, Providence
RPB	Brown University, Providence, R.I.
RPJCB	John Carter Brown Library, Providence, R.I.
Vi	Virginia State Library and Archives, Richmond
ViHi	Virginia Historical Society, Richmond
ViMtV	Mount Vernon Ladies' Association of the Union
ViU	University of Virginia, Charlottesville

Short Title List

Adams, *Works of John Adams.*   Charles Francis Adams, ed. *The Works of John Adams, Second President of the United States: With a Life of the Author, Notes and Illustrations.* 10 vols. Boston, 1850–56.

ASP, Claims. Walter Lowrie et al., eds. *American State Papers: Documents, Legislative and Executive, of the Congress of the United States.* 38 vols. Washington, D.C., 1832–61.

Bartlett, *R.I. Records.* John Russell Bartlett, ed. *Records of the State of Rhode Island and Providence Plantations in New England.* 10 vols. Providence, 1856–65.

Betts, *Jefferson's Garden Book.* Edwin M. Betts, ed. *Thomas Jefferson's Garden Book, 1766–1824.* Philadelphia, 1944.

Biographical Dictionary of the Maryland Legislature. Edward C. Papenfuse et al., eds. *A Biographical Dictionary of the Maryland Legislature, 1635–1789.* 2 vols. Baltimore and London, 1979.

Boyd, *Jefferson Papers.* Julian P. Boyd et al., eds. *ThePapers of Thomas Jefferson.* 24 vols. to date. Princeton, N.J., 1950—.

Brown, "Dismal Swamp Canal." Alexander Crosby Brown. "The Dismal Swamp Canal." *American Neptune: A Quarterly Journal of Maritime History,* 5 (1945), 203–21.

Burnett, *Letters.* Edmund C. Burnett, ed. *Letters of Members of the Continental Congress.* 8 vols. 1921–36. Reprint. Gloucester, Mass., 1963.

Butterfield, *Adams Diary and Autobiography.* L. H. Butterfield et al., eds. *Diary and Autobiography of John Adams.* 4 vols. Cambridge, Mass., 1961.

Butterfield, *Adams Family Correspondence.* L. H. Butterfield, ed. *Adams Family Correspondence.* 6 vols. to date. Cambridge, Mass., 1963—.

Cartmell, *Shenandoah Valley Pioneers.* T. K. Cartmell. *Shenandoah Valley Pioneers and Their Descendants.* Winchester, Va., 1909.

Diaries. Donald Jackson and Dorothy Twohig, eds. *The Diaries of George Washington.* 6 vols. Charlottesville, Va., 1976–79.

Exec. Journals of Virginia Council. H. R. McIlwaine, Wilmer L. Hall, and Benjamin Hillman, eds. *Executive Journals of the Council of Colonial Virginia.* 6 vols. Richmond, 1925–66.

Ferguson, *Morris Papers.* E. James Ferguson et al., eds. *The Papers of Robert Morris.* 7 vols. to date. Pittsburgh and London, 1973—.

Fitzpatrick, *Writings of Washington.* John C. Fitzpatrick, ed. *The Writings of George Washington from the Original Manuscript Sources, 1745–1799.* 39 vols. Washington, D.C., 1931–44.

Gambrill, "John Beale Bordley." Olive Moore Gambrill, "John Beale Bordley and the Early Years of the Philadelphia Agricultural Society." *Pennsylvania Magazine of History and Biography,* 66 (1942), 410–39.

Griffin, Boston Athenæum Collection. Appleton P. C. Griffin, comp. *A Catalogue of the Washington Collection in the Boston Athenæum.* Cambridge, Mass., 1897.

Hening.   William Waller Hening, ed. *The Statutes at Large; Being a Collection of All the Laws of Virginia from the First Session of the Legislature, in the Year 1619.* 13 vols. 1819–23. Reprint. Charlottesville, Va., 1969.

Hindle, *Pursuit of Science.*   Brook Hindle. *The Pursuit of Science in Revolutionary America, 1735–1789.* New York, 1956.

House of Delegates Journal, 1781–1785.   *Journal of the House of Delegates of the Commonwealth of Virginia; Begun and Held in the Town of Richmond, in the County of Henrico, on Monday, the Seventh Day of May, in the Year of Our Lord One Thousand Seven Hundred and Eighty-One.* Richmond, 1828.

Humphreys, *Life of Putnam.*   David Humphreys. *An Essay on the Life of the Honourable Major General Israel Putnam.* Boston, 1819.

Idzerda, *Lafayette Papers.*   Stanley J. Idzerda, Robert R. Crout, et al., eds. *Lafayette in the Age of the American Revolution: Selected Letters and Papers, 1776–1790.* 5 vols to date. Ithaca, N.Y., 1977—.

JCC.   Worthington C. Ford et al., eds. *Journals of the Continental Congress.* 34 vols. Washington, D.C., 1904–37.

Kappler, *Indian Treaties.*   Charles Joseph Kappler, ed. *Indian Affairs: Laws and Treaties.* 7 vols. Washington, D.C., 1903–41.

Kennedy, *Biography of a Colonial Town.*   Jean de Chantal Kennedy. *Biography of a Colonial Town: Hamilton, Bermuda, 1790–1897.* Hamilton, Bermuda, 1963.

Lasseray, *Sous les treize étoiles.*   André Lasseray. *Les Français sous les treize étoiles (1775–1783).* 2 vols. Paris, 1935.

Ledger A.   Manuscript Ledger in George Washington Papers, Library of Congress.

Ledger B.   Manuscript Ledger in George Washington Papers, Library of Congress.

Ledger C.   Manuscript ledger in Morristown National Historical Park, Morristown, N.J.

"Letters of James Rumsey."   "Letters of James Rumsey." *Maryland Historical Magazine* 32 (1937), 10–28, 136–55, 271–85.

Mason, *Reminiscences of Newport.*   George Champlin Mason. *Reminiscences of Newport.* Newport, R.I., 1884.

Meade, *Henry.*   Robert D. Meade. *Patrick Henry.* 2 vols. Philadelphia and New York, 1957–69.

Memoir of Richard Henry Lee.   Richard H. Lee. *Memoir of the Life of Richard Henry Lee.* 2 vols. Philadelphia, 1825.

Miner, *Goddard.*   Ward L. Miner. *William Goddard, Newspaperman.* Durham, N.C., 1962.

Mitchell, *Beginning at a White Oak.*   Beth Mitchell. *Beginning at a White Oak . . . : Patents and Northern Neck Grants of Fairfax County, Virginia.* Fairfax, Va., 1977.

Morgan, *Naval Documents.*   William James Morgan et al., eds. *Naval Documents of the American Revolution.* 9 vols. to date. Washington, D.C., 1964—.

Papers, Colonial Series.   W. W. Abbot et al., eds. *The Papers of George Washington: Colonial Series.* 8 vols. to date. Charlottesville, Va., 1983—.

Papers, Confederation Series.   W. W. Abbot et al., eds. *The Papers of George Washington: Confederation Series.* 3 vols. to date. Charlottesville, Va., 1992—.

Rice and Brown, eds., *American Campaigns of Rochambeau's Army.* Howard C. Rice, Jr., and Anne S. K. Brown, eds. *The American Campaigns of Rochambeau's Army, 1780, 1781, 1782, 1783.* 2 vols. Princeton, N.J., 1972.

Rutland, *Mason Papers.*   Robert A. Rutland, ed. *The Papers of George Mason, 1725–1792.* 3 vols. Chapel Hill, N.C., 1970.

Rutland and Rachal, *Madison Papers.*   Robert A. Rutland, William M. E. Rachal, J. C. A. Stagg, et al., eds. *The Papers of James Madison.* [1st series]. 17 vols. Chicago and Charlottesville, Va., 1962–91.

Syrett, *Hamilton Papers.*   Harold C. Syrett et al., eds. *The Papers of Alexander Hamilton.* 27 vols. New York, 1961–87.

Tatsch, *Freemasonry in the Thirteen Colonies.*   J. Hugo Tatsch. *Freemasonry in the Thirteen Colonies.* New York, 1929.

Wilkinson, *Bermuda in the Old Empire.*   Henry C. Wilkinson. *Bermuda in the Old Empire: A History of the Island from the Dissolution of the Somers Island Company until the End of the American Revolutionary War: 1684–1784.* London, New York, and Toronto, 1950.

The Papers of George Washington
Confederation Series
Volume 3
May 1785–March 1786

From Armand

dr General   Bretagne—la Rouerie this 19 may 1785—

permit me to remember to your mind one of your most faithfull servant,[1] I would have done it sooner but knowing that your Exellency would be pleased in the good treatment I should receive from the court, I waited untill the final settlement of my rank & Command in our army—but although nothing is perfected on that head, I can not deny to myself any longer the pleasure of discharging my duty towards your Exellency.

Ever since I am in france I have been tourmented by the hard Necessity of playing the Courtier at versailles & paris, happily I was unwell almost all that time, by which means I had some hours & even some days of liberty. I met with a favorable welcome from the ministre & all men in power; without giving me the trouble to ask personnally what employment I desired to have in our army, they offered me a legionary corps & a pleasing arrangment for the rank—but as no regiment can be given unless there is a vancancy by the annual promotion in the army or the death of some Colonels, & the politicks of Europe bending alternatively on war & peace have hindred the promotion to take place untill octobre next, I am still as far advanced as I was the first day of my arrival at Court, exept that I have acquired a load of polite Compliments & of these friends, which not being able to bear any longer, for it increased dayly, I have retired to my Country seat where I intend to remain untill some of our great men, for small affairs, are pleased to order me towards them; the Corps which is destined to me consist of four hundred mounted and six hundred dismounted, there are six of thoses Corps in france & without doubt they are the best in orders of our army & the most agreable for a soldier who has served under your command, for being destined to the duty on the lines, they offer more opportunity to be active & usefull.

our great politicians having, since the last european war, turned altogether their thoughts towards the best way of curling their periwig & shaping their breeches, we are not little embarrassed on the choice of a commandier in chief if we wishes to have a good one, but as things are such that the talents of all the pretenders to that post are near about of the same merite, we certainly shall not be beaten in Case of war for the want of half dozen or many hundred more of them. however we have mr le Mchl de Broglio, but his brother, who never left him in the scrape, being dead, people are not disposed to engage their fortunes nor even their words, which is very little in europe, as security for his good doings. prince de Conde of the royal familly is mentioned & in some measures appointed to the Command of the grand army should there be war; he Commanded a separate army of 25000 chusen men in Germany last european war & has done very well; he is of a serious charactere, Brave, pretty well learned in military affairs & much beloved from our army: I shall be Glad to serve under him, he was allways good to me & has received my friend schaffner with a great deal of kindness.[2]

mr de maillebois, as your Exellency may have heard, is in the united provinces at the head of their army, although envious may be at this time his private ennemys, they allow him to have military talents, some much, others less, all of them agreable to the measure of their own claime to merite in that line; but I must do him the justice to say, that, almost every one do him the injustice of believing him dishonest. the emperor of Germany has one of the largest & best disciplined army that has been known subject to one prince, it consists of *280000* foots 55000 cavallery & 45000 light cavalry—half of it is at the utmost the ⟨*illegible*⟩ which his revenues permit him to keap, he is of course under the necessity to subsist them to the expences of his neighbours or to disband them, he is extremely backward to any accomodation with holand—it is almost certain that Russia will act with him—on the other side holand has very near no standing forces. we have great many regiment, but regiments alone Can not make an army—from that general view & some others circumstances too tedious perhaps for your Exellency to be related here I have never since the dispute begone, altered my thoughts that we would have war this or next summer; there is, at this instant, a great talk of it, but from our not being so well prepared for it as wise people could wishes, many persons in our country, who go to mass & think our men in high post uncapable of an imperfection in their politicks, are most certain we shall have no war. if ever there is one in america either against Certain neighbours whose gold is much more in repute than their charactere, or any other, & your Exellency take again the command, I request you to Consider me as inlisted amongs your followers. whatever may at that time be my rank & fortune I shall leave all behind to go to the man I respect & love the most in the world—I have the honor to be with thoses sentiments dear general your most obdt hble st

armand

I beg the favour of lady washington to accept here of my best respects.

ALS, DLC:GW.

1. Armand (Charles Armand-Tuffin, marquis de La Rouërie; 1750–1793), wrote GW most recently on 18 May 1784 shortly before he returned to France, and he next wrote to GW, about his marriage, on 20 Jan. 1786. Armand was commander of the Partisan Legion, or Corps, at the close of the Revolutionary War.

2. Louis-Joseph de Bourbon, 8th prince de Condé (1736–1818), emigrated after the fall of the Bastille in 1789. After Condé raised his antirevolutionary army in 1791, Armand served as one of his officers until his death in 1793. Victor-François, 2d duc de Broglie (1718–1814), was made a marshal of France for his services in the Seven Years War. In July 1789 he commanded the troops at Versailles protecting the king, but before the end of the year he had emigrated. George Schaffner was the major in Armand's legion in America.

Letter not found: from Châteaufort, 19 May 1785. On 15 June GW wrote the chevalier de Châteaufort: "By the Post I had the honor to receive the letter which you did me the favor to write to me on the 19th of last month."

To Christopher Richmond

Sir,   Mt Vernon 19th May 1785.

Your letter of the 10th not getting to my hands 'till the 15th, I had no opportunity of writing to you before the meeting of the subscribers on the 17th, at which I exhibited the list you sent me, which was received & acted upon.[1]

Agreeably to the Laws of the two States, the subscription books ought to have been at that meeting; after which all subscriptions are to be made with the President & Directors. If it should have happened therefore, that any names have been entered on your Books subsequent, & in addition to the list you sent me; it would be proper for such subscribers to enter their names as the Law directs in the Book to be opened by the Directors, in order to give validity to their subscriptions & to prevent disputes[2]—this, I presume, may be done by letter. I am &c.

G: Washington

LB, DLC:GW.

1. For the meeting of the Potomac River Company in Alexandria on 17 May, see GW to Thomas Johnson and Thomas Sim Lee, 18 May, and particularly note 1 of that document.

2. See Richmond's letters to GW of 10 and 27 May.

To Nathanael Greene

My Dr Sir,   Mount Vernon 20th May 1785.

After a long & boisterous passage, my Nephew G.A. Washington returned to this place a few days since, & delivered me your letter of the 25th of April.

Under the state of the case between you & Capt: Gun, I give it as my decided opinion that your honor & reputation will not only stand perfectly acquited for the non-acceptance of his challenge, but that your prudence & judgment would have been condemnable for accepting of it, in the eyes of the world: because if a commanding officer is amenable to private calls for the discharge of public duty, he has a dagger always at his breast, & can turn neither to the right nor to the left without meeting its point; in a word, he is no longer a free Agent in office, as there are few military decisions which are not offensive to one party or the other.

However just Capt: Guns claim upon the public might have been, the mode adopted by him (according to your accot) to obtain it, was to the last degree dangerous. A precedent of the sort once established in the army, would no doubt have been followed; & in that case would unquestionably have produced a revolution; but of a very different kind from that which, happily for America, has prevailed.[1]

It gives me real concern to find by your letter, that you are still embarrassed with the affairs of Banks: I should be glad to hear, that the evil is likely to be temporary only—ultimately, that you will not suffer. From my Nephews account, this man has participated of the qualities of Pandora's box, & has spread as many mischiefs. How came so many to be taken in by him? If I recollect right, when I had the pleasure to see you last, you said an offer had been made you of backlands, as security or payment in part for your demand—I then advised you to accept it—I now repeat it. you cannot suffer by doing this, altho' the lands may be high rated. If they are good I would almost pledge myself that you will gain more in ten years by the rise in the price, than you could by accumulation of interest.[2]

The Marqs de la Fayette is safe arrived in France, & found his Lady & family well. From his letters, those of the Chevr de la Luzerne, Count de Rochambeau & others to me, dated between the middle & last of Feby, I think there will be no war in Europe this year, but some of the most intelligent of these writers are of opinion that the Emperial Court & Russia, will not suffer matters to remain tranquil much longer. The desire of the first to annex the Dutchy of Bavaria to its dominions in exchange for the Austrian possessions in the Netherlands, is very displeasing, it seems, to the military powers, which added to other matters may kindle the flames of a general war.

Few matters of domestic nature are worth the relation; otherwise I might inform you, that the plan for improving & extending the navigation of this river has met a favourable beginning. Tuesday last was the day appointed by Law for the subscribers to meet—250 shares were required by law to constitute and incorporate the company: but, upon comparing the Books, it was found that between four & five hundred shares were subscribed. What has been done respecting the navigation of James river I know not—I fear little.

This State did a handsome thing, & in a handsome manner for me; in each of these navigations they gave me, & my heirs forever, fifty shares: but as it is incompatible with my principles, & contrary to my declarations, I do not mean to accept of them. But how to refuse them, without incurring the charge of disrespect to the Country on the one hand, and an ostentatious display of disinterestedness on my part on the other, I am a little at a loss: time & the good advice of my friends must aid me, as the Assembly will not meet 'till Octor, & made this gratuitous offer among, if not the last act of the last Session, as if they were determined I should not resolve what to do from the *first* impulse. Mrs Washington joins me in every good wish for you, &

with sentiments of attachment & regard, I am my Dr Sir Yr affte friend &c.

G: Washington

LB, DLC:GW. The ALS was offered for sale by Parke-Bernet in its catalog of the John Gribbel collection, item 774, 30–31 Oct. and 1 Nov. 1940.

1. In his letter of 25 April, General Greene gives a full account of his refusing Capt. James Gunn's challenge to a duel arising out of Greene's disciplining of Gunn when Gunn was under his command.

2. For Greene's financial difficulties deriving from his dealings during the war with John Banks & Co. for army supplies, see Greene to GW, 29 Aug. 1784, n.2.

From John Harvie

Sir   Land office [Richmond] May 20th 1785

When I last Wrote to you I did not Recollect of any Survey being in the Land office for the Round Bottom, except the One upon which your Grant Issued[1] but upon looking over the Caveat Book, I find a Survey for this Tract of Land return'd by the Heirs of Michael Cresup decd—and claim'd under a Certificate for Settlement made in the year 1771—Van Swearingen enter'd a Caveat against their Survey, which Caveat was dismiss'd during the Sessions of the last General Court, wherefore a Grant will shortly issue to the Heirs of Cresup—as you have already a title to this Land I should Suppose a Subsequent Grant cannot Effect your Right—yet perhaps it may be well for you to enter a Caveat against a Grant issueing to them upon this Survey—as it may hereafter prevent a tedious discussion of your Title in a Court of Chancery—if you choose to take this Step, you will be pleas'd to Transmit me your Instructions by the next post setting forth your Causes for Caveat—and the Law makes it necessary that you should make Oath before some Magistrate that you enter the Caveat with design to recover the Land for yourself and not in Trust for the Heirs of the sd Cresup—the General Intention of this Oath is to prevent friendly Caveats from being enter'd in the Land Office.[2] I have the Honour to be Sir yr most Obt & Very H. Servt

John Harvie

ALS, DLC:GW.

1. Harvie, who was in charge of the Virginia Land Office, wrote GW on 13 May. See note 4 of that document, regarding GW's Round Bottom tract.

2. See GW to Harvie, 31 May, which GW intended as a caveat to bar a grant issuing to the heirs of Michael Cresap for the Round Bottom tract.

To William Fitzhugh

Dr Sir, Mt Vernon 21st May 1785.

Mr Boulton delivered me your letter of the 13th, last evening; I thank you for sending him to me. I have agreed with him to finish my large room, & to do some other work; & have no doubt from the character given of him by you, that he will answer my purposes, as he has no one now to lead him into temptation, and will be far removed from improper associates, unless he is at much pains to hunt them: it may therefore be expected that he will avoid the rock he has split upon lately.[1]

I thank you sincerely my good Sir, for the offer of such of your imported articles as you have not an immediate call for; and will take any proportion which will be most convenient for you to share, of the Spirit of Turpentine—oil & paints of all sorts —Lead—Sash line & pullies—of the different sorts & sizes of nails, as also the two plate brass Locks, if Mr Boulton upon examination, shall think they will answer my room—& of the Glass 8 by 10. The large kind of glass does not suit my sashes (which are all made)—& a marble slab (indeed two) I am already provided with.[2]

I have promised to send my waggon (a cover'd one with lock & key) to Colo. Plater's, or some landing above, for Mr Boulton's tools: all, or such part of the articles as I have enumerated & you can spare, & the waggon can bring in addition to the Tools, may accompany them; & the cost & charges of them shall be paid to your order. Mrs Washington & the family join me in offering respectful compliments to, & best wishes for you & your Lady, & with very great esteem & regard, I am Dr Sir &c.

G: Washington

P.S. 'Ere this, I was in hopes of having had it in my power to have offered the service of a Jack, or two, of the first race in Spain, to some of your mares, if you should be inclined to breed mules—but they are not yet arrived—another year, & I shall be happy to do this.[3] G. W——n

LB, DLC:GW.

1. Richard Boulton entered an agreement on this day to do work for GW, but he never returned. The agreement between Boulton and GW, written by George Augustine Washington and signed by both, provided for Boulton to "finish the large room at the north end of the said Washingtons dwelling House (Mount Vernon) in a plain and elegant manner; either of Stucco, Wainscot, or partly of both . . . new cover the whole of the said House, or such parts thereof as will make the same tight . . . [to] give a Cieling to the Piazza of plain Wainscot—Do the necessary work of a Green House—And such other Jobs as may be . . . required . . ." (DLC:GW).

2. See note 2 in Fitzhugh's letter to GW, 13 May.

3. For a discussion of the Spanish jacks that GW was expecting, see William Carmichael to GW, 3 Dec. 1784, n.1.

From Thomas Johnson

Sir.   Fred[eric]k [Md.] 21 May 1785.

I shall forward your Letter of the 18 Inst. to Mr Lee[1] I have no Opportunity of consulting him as to the place or Hour of Meeting: as it can make very little Difference to him or me and Alexandria will be most convenient to you and the other Gent. I propose to meet there at 10 OClock and shall write Mr Lee accordingly—I much wished to have been at the Meeting the 17th if I could have attended I should have endeavoured to excuse myself being under promise to attend at Williamsburgh next Month in the Fœderal Court and having a private Interest to adjust with the Company at the Great Falls I now agree to act as a Directer imagining that the Great Falls will not be an immediate Object but if I am mistaken in that or my Attend-[an]ce at Williamsburgh will in any degree delay the Execution of the Work I shall chearfully make Room for some Body else who can attend and act with propriety. I am sir with great Truth & Respect Your most obedt Servant

Ths Johnson

ALS, DLC:GW.

1. See GW to Thomas Johnson and Thomas Sim Lee, 18 May.

To Jacquelin Ambler

Sir, Mount Vernon 22d May 1785.

I had the honor to receive your favor of the 12th in time for the meeting; and in consequence of the power given me by you, represented the State on the 17th inst.

I have the pleasure to inform you that the subscriptions (including those in behalf of the two States) amounted to upwards of four hundred shares; consequently the company became legally constituted & incorporated—a president & Directors were chosen—& the business, we persuade ourselves, will be advanced as fast as the nature of it will admit.[1] I have the honor to be &c.

Go. Washington

LB, DLC:GW.

1. For the meeting of the Potomac River Company, see GW to Thomas Johnson and Thomas Sim Lee, 18 May, n.1.

To Burwell Bassett

Dear Sir, Mount Vernon 23d May 1785

It would have given me much pleasure to have seen you at Richmond; and it was part of my original plan to have spent a few days with you at Eltham whilst I was in the lower parts of the Country; but an intervention of circumstances not only put it out of my power to do the latter, but would have stopped my journey to Richmond altogether had not the meeting, the time, and the place been of my own appointing. I left company at home when I went away who proposed to wait my return—among whom a Mr Pine, an Artist of eminence, came all the way from Philadelphia on purpose for some materials for an historical painting which he is about, and for which he was obliged to stay till I got back; which I did, after an absence of eight days only.[1]

My Nephew Geo. Auge Washington is just returned from his peregrination—apparently much amended in his health, but not quite free from the disorder in his Side. I have understood that his addresses to Fanny were made with your consent—& I now learn that he is desirous, and she is willing, to fulfil the engagement they have entered into; and that they are applying to you for permission to do so.

It has ever been a maxim with me, through life, neither to promote, nor to prevent a matrimonial connection, unless there should be something, indispensably requiring interference in the latter. I have always considered Marriage as the most interesting event of ones life. The foundation of happiness or misery. To be instrumental therefore in bringing two people together who are indifferent to each other, & may soon become objects of disgust, or to prevent a union which is prompted by the affections of the mind, is what I never could reconcile with reason, & therefore neither directly, nor indirectly have I ever said a syllable to Fanny, or George, upon the Subject of their intended connection: but as their attachment to each other seems of early growth, warm, & lasting, it bids fair for happiness. If therefore you have no objec⟨tion,⟩ I think, the sooner it is consummated the better.[2]

I have just now informed them both (the former through Mrs Washington) that it is my wish they should live at Mount Vernon.[3]

It is unnecessary I hope to say how happy we should be to see you, her Brothers, & any of her friends—who can make it convenient, and are disposed—at this place, on this occasion. All here join in best wishes for you, and with very sincere esteem and regard I am—Dear Sir Yr Affecte friend and Obedt Hble Servant

Go: Washington

ALS (photocopy), DLC:GW; LB, DLC:GW.

1. For GW's attendance at the meeting of the Dismal Swamp Company in Richmond on 2 May, see GW to Thomas Walker, 10 April 1785, n.1.

2. Bassett wrote GW on 1 June expressing his approval of the match between his daughter and GW's nephew.

3. George Augustine Washington and Frances (Fanny) Bassett were already living at Mount Vernon, and they continued to live there after their marriage on 15 Oct. 1785.

Memorandum of Agreement with Joseph Davenport

[Philadelphia, 23 May 1785]

Memorandum of an Agreement made & enter'd into by Robert Lewis & Sons of Philadelphia, for & in behalf of his Excellency George Washington Esquire of Mount Vernon in the State of Virginia of the one part, and Joseph Davenport of the County of Burlington in the State of New-Jersey of the other part,[1] Witnesseth, that the said Davenport shall immediately proceed with his Family to a Mill near Mount Vernon the property of General Washington, where & by whom he is to be employ'd as a Miller & Cooper for the space of two whole Years, to commence the first day of June next, in the terms & conditions herein after specified—to wit, He is directly on his arrival at said Mill to take upon him, & perform the business of a Miller in all the branches of Manufacturing Wheat into Suprfine, or common Flour in a Workman-like manner, as well as attending to the Country or Grist-Work, at all times & Seasons as the said General Washington may require & direct; at the same time carefully Superintending & directing such Workmen, either white-men or Negroes, as may be employ'd under him; to keep fair & honest Accounts of all Monies reciev'd & paid by him, as well as of all Grain & other Articles which may be brought in, or deliver'd out of said Mill, rendering those Accounts to his employer as frequent as may be required: He is also to attend to the running Gears, & every part of the said Mill, securing Gudgeons, putting in Coggs & Rounds, & such other Jobs as are usual & customary for Millers to do in Pennsylvania, & New-Jersey, but does not engage to execute the Work of a MillWright: He likewise promises to Superintend the Business of a Cooper's Shop, situate near the said Mill, to urge the Coopers who are, or may be employ'd therein to perform their Work in the best manner, & prevent as much as possible the waste of Staves, Heading, & Hoop-Poles: And he further engages to do the duty of a Master-Cooper in said Shop at all times, when Water may be scant, or Business slack, or when his constant attendance is not absolutely necessary in the said Mill; and so alternately, to do & perform the duty of both Miller & Cooper in the best manner for the Interest &

advantage of his employer, according to the custom of Pennsylvania, New Jersey, or Virginia.

And in consideration of those Services, the said Robert
Lewis & Sons, engage on the part of his Excellency General
Washington, to furnish the said Joseph Davenport with the fol-
lowing privileges, & payment of Money—vizt—a comfortable
Dwelling House & Garden near the said Mill, plentifull keeping
for one Cow, a sufficient quantity of Fire Wood, deliver'd in due
Season at the door, during the said term of two Years, six hundred weight of good Pork, or equivalent in Beef & Pork, as the
said Davenport may prefer, deliver'd to him in Killing time each
Year, (or this present Season when he may want it)—to raise
Poultry for his own Family use, feeding them on Screenings, &
other Offal of said Mill, free of cost, but under no pretence whatever to sell any; & besides those privileges, the said Davenport
is to receive the sum of two hundred Dollars in Silver or Gold,
in quarterly payments or sooner if demanded. He is to be supply'd with as much Flour, Midlings, Corn &ca—out of the said
Mill, as will support his Family from time to time as occasion
requires, charging himself for the same at such rates & prices as
those Articles may be sold to others for Cash. And it is further
agreed by & between the said parties, that in case either of them
should think proper to discontinue or dissolve this Agreement,
he shall be at Liberty to do it, at the expiration of one Year,
giving the other three months previous Notice in Writing: For
the true & faithfull performance of every part of this
Agreement, each party hereby binds himself to the other under
the penalty of one thousand Dollars to be paid by the party not
complying, to the party complying—Witness our Hands & Seals
in Philadelphia this 23rd day of May 1785.

Sealed & deliver'd   Joseph Davenport
in the presence of   Robt Lewis & Sons
Edward Lane
Daniel Smith

DS, DLC:GW.

1. For GW's negotiations with Robert Lewis & Sons culminating in the hiring of Davenport to replace William Roberts as a miller for the mill at Mount
Vernon, see Robert Lewis & Sons to GW, 5 April 1785, nn.1 and 2.

To John Swan

Sir,   Mt Vernon 23d May 1785.

The *little* share I had in the administration of Colo. Colville's Estate, & the time which has elapsed since I had *any* concern at all with the Affairs of it, render me very incompetent to give the information you require.[1]

Mr John West deceased was the principal acting Executor of the will of Colo. Colvill, & the revd Mr West of Baltimore is the executor of John, & has I am told taken much pains to adjust the papers of his brother & the business of that Estate: from him therefore you may probably obtain more precise information of the assets, & of the Claimants therefor under the wild devisses of the will, than is in my power at this time to give you.[2]

All I recollect of the matter is, that the devises to certain persons in England, relations of the Testator, were so indefinite, & stirred up such a multitude of claims, that it was adjudged necessary for the safty of the Executor when the surplus Estate (if any) should be ascertained, to deposit the same in the hands of the Chancellor to be disposed of to the rightful owners upon due proof of their identity before him. What may have been the surplus, if the accots have been finally settled; what has been done with it, or under what predicament it may have been placed by the Laws of this Government, I have it not in my power, without a good deal of research, to inform you; not having been able to look into this business any more than into that which more immediately concerns my own, since my return to private life: for eight years previous to it, it is well known I could not. I am Sir &c.

                                            G: Washington

LB, DLC:GW. The letter is headed: "Majr John Swan."

1. See Swan to GW, 13 May.

2. John West, Jr., who died in 1777, was an executor of the estate of his wife's uncle, Thomas Colvill. For a general description of the long-drawn-out efforts of the executors to settle the Colvill estate, see the notes in GW to John West, Jr., December 1767; see also GW to Tankerville, 20 Jan. 1784, n.1. The Rev. William West (1739–1791), rector of St. Paul's in Baltimore, denied having any knowledge of the Colvill papers (see Tench Tilghman to GW, 30 May).

To Tench Tilghman

Dear Sir,   Mount Vernon 23d May 1785

The last Post brought me your letter of the 14th, inclosing one of the 30th of April from Mr Hollyday.[1] As soon as it is in my power to refresh my memory by having recurrance to my Papers, I will write you, or Mr Hollyday, more fully on the subject of the legacy in Colo. Colvils Will to Miss Anderson; or person under whom she claims; for, strange as it may seem, it is nevertheless true, that I have not been able since my retirement, to arrange my Papers, or to attend, in the smallest degree, to my private concerns. The former, from the hurry with which they have been removed from Book cases into Trunks, & sent off to escape the ravages of the enemy, when their Vessels have appeared, are in great disorder. I allotted the last Winter for the adjustment of all these matters; but never could command as much time as even to *enter* upon the business; and every matter and thing which respects the latter, are in the situation I left them ten years ago.[2]

The numberless applications from Officers of the several lines of the Army for Certificates of Service—recommendations—Copies of Orders—references of old matters, with which I ought not to be troubled—in addition to other corrispondencies in which my situation has involved me, confine me more to my writing Desk than I ever was at any period of my life; and deprives me of necessary exercise. These, with other causes, have produced the effect I have mentioned; which I feel more sensibly, as the business of others, with which I have been concerned, is involved; and is now undergoing the same suspension, as my own.

For sometime past I have been (unsuccessfully) endeavouring to get a single man of good character, and decent appearance (for he will be at my Table & with my Company) to ease me of this burthen; and if you could recommend one of this description, who would not expect high wages (for these I cannot afford) I should be obliged to you for so doing. To suit me, he must be a person of liberal education—a Master of composition—& have a competent knowledge of Accts; for I have those of ten years standing, and the intermediate transactions, to overhaul & adjust.[3]

Will you ever come to see me? You may be assured that there are few persons in the World, whose visits would give more sincere pleasure at Mount Vernon than yours. Nothing could encrease the satisfaction of it more, than bringing Mrs Tilghman with you; to whom, and to yourself, Mrs Washington joins in every good wish with Dr Sir, Your Most Affecte Frd and Obedt Hble Servt

Go: Washington

P.S. Upon second thoughts, it occurs, that the Revd Mr West of Baltimore, can do all that is necessary for Miss Anderson, without any Agency of mine; at least may determine with precision what ought to be done. He is the Executor of his Brother, Mr John West—who was the *principal* acting Executor of Colo. Thos Colvil—and has been, I am informed, assiduously employed, lately, in adjusting the concerns of that Estate.[4]

As I shall not write to Mr Hollyday until I can do it more to the purpose than at present, I will rely upon your communicating what is herementioned, to him.

I am in want of two inch pine Plank—the Man who is engaged to work for me, & who came lately from Baltimore,[5] says he saw a good deal at that place, of the Eastern white Pine, which appeared to him to be seasoned and fit for my uses. If any Vessel should becoming round to Alexandria, and you could send me from two to 500 feet of it, you would oblige me. Yrs G. W——n

ALS, PHi: Gratz Collection; LB, DLC:GW.

1. See also GW to John Swan, this date.

2. GW was soon to hire William Shaw as his secretary, and after Shaw came to work for him in August he was seldom if ever without a secretary and often one or more clerks. It seems certain, however, that it was not until the 1790s that GW was able to get far along with his long-held objectives of organizing his pre- and post-Revolutionary papers and of entering copies of many of his own letters of the 1780s in letter books.

3. On 30 May Tilghman recommends a young man named W. Falconer, but nothing comes of this.

4. See note 2 in GW to John Swan, this date.

5. GW is referring to Richard Boulton. See GW to William Fitzhugh, 21 May, n.1.

From William Minor

Sir   Alexandria 24th May 1785

The proposition that your Excellency was pleased to make of Leaving to Some Gentlemen the Matter I laid before you on Saturday the 21st Instant in Regard to my Claim against you on Account of Lawrence Posey—is perfectly agreeable to me.[1] I wish I had had presence of mind to have asked your Excellency to have Appointed Some Gentlemen to do the Business when I was at your Place—but I did not know that I Cou'd Stay So Long as I have done—If your Excellency will be pleased to nominate any two Gentlemen in Alexandria, and let me name a third, I will be Satisfied with their Determination—I am not Acquainted with any Gentlemen in this County, but Mr George Minor & Captn Moss, at whose House I shall Stay a day or two Longer[2]—Or if the Hble Gentleman who will deliver you this will do the Business for us, his Determination Shall be perfectly agreeable to Sir your Excellency's Most Obedt and Most hble Servt &Ca

                                          Wm Minor

ALS, DLC:GW.

1. In the summer of 1772 John Posey was released from jail in Queenstown on Maryland's Eastern Shore where he had been held for failure to pay his debts. Posey then returned to Virginia for several months. While he was away in Virginia, a Queenstown tavern keeper took in Posey's son, St. Lawrence Posey, and put him to work tending bar—on orders of his father according to another Queenstown tavern keeper, Francis Baker, or because the boy fell ill, according to John Posey. Posey returned to Queenstown after 14 Oct. 1772 and rescued his son from the tavern barroom, after St. Lawrence had lived and worked at Minor's tavern, according to John Posey, for only about three months. See John Posey to GW, 25 May 1771, n.5; see also Francis Baker to GW, 15 Dec. 1772, and Posey to GW, 9 Aug. 1773. Evidently Minor went to Mount Vernon on 21 May to demand that GW pay him for other expenses he incurred while St. Lawrence Posey was in his care for several months in 1772. For GW's denial of any obligation to pay Minor anything, see GW to Minor, 27 May 1785.

2. John Moss and George Minor gave up their seats on the Fairfax County court in June 1789 when they became inspectors at the tobacco warehouse in Alexandria, the town where both lived.

To Robert Lewis & Sons

Gentn   Mount Vernon 25th May 1785.

In consequence of your letter of the 5th of last month, I discharged Wm Roberts from my Mill. It now is, & has been for some time past without a Miller; & as Mr Davenport from your Accot would be ready to take charge of it in about three weeks (now seven), & not yet come, nor any reason given why he has not; I am apprehensive of some disappointment.

If this is the case I should be glad to know it as soon as possible. One Baker, who referred to you for a character, & was employ'd by Colo. Biddle at his Mill at George town, has applied to me; but considering myself under engagement, I gave him no encouragement. A person who writes the enclosed letter has also offered, but I have given him no answer. Some others have likewise made application, but as I depended upon Devenport I asked for no character nor enquired into their qualifications. If Devenport should have disappointed me, would Baker answer my purpose? Would reynolds do better? Or have you any other in view which you think preferable to both?[1] I am sorry to give you so much trouble with my affairs but hope you will excuse it. I am Gentn Yrs &c.

                                        G: Washington

LB, DLC:GW.

1. Neither Baker nor Reynolds has been identified. Joseph Davenport arrived within the week.

Letter not found: from Edward Newenham, 25 May. On 25 Nov. GW wrote Newenham: "I have been favored with your letters of the 3d of March, 25th of May."

To David Parry

Sir,   Mt Vernon 25th May 1785.

I have had the honor, lately, to receive your favor of the 18th of July last year.[1] For the politeness with which your Excellency was pleased to receive my Nephew G: A. Washington, & for the distinguished marks of attention which you shewed him whilst he was in the Island of Barbadoes (for which he retains a grateful sense) I feel myself exceedingly obliged, & should be happy in opportunities to convince your Excelly of the impression they have made on me.

My Nephew, after a peregrination thro' many of the W. India Islands—spending some time in Bermuda, & the winter in Charleston (So. Carolina) returned home a few days ago, a good deal *amended* in his health, but not perfectly restored to it. I have the honor to be &c.

G: Washington

LB, DLC:GW.

1. GW wrote to the governor of Barbados on 25 April 1784 on behalf of his nephew, George Augustine Washington, who was going to the West Indies for his health; on 18 July 1784 David Parry wrote GW that he was pleased to have made the acquaintance of GW's nephew.

From William Grayson

Dear Sir: New York May 27th 1785.

The Ordinance for the disposal of the Western territory was pass'd three days ago, & I take the earliest oppertunity of inclosing you a copy.[1] I have the honor to be with the highest respect yr Affect. fd & Most Obd. Sert

William Grayson

ALS, DLC:GW.

1. The Land Ordinance of 1785 for dividing the Northwest Territory into townships to be divided into lots of 640 acres for sale was passed on 20 May (*JCC*, 28:375–81). See also Richard Henry Lee to GW, 3 May 1785, and the references in note 2 of that document.

From Robert Johnston

Sir   Edinburgh 27th May 1785

The High Character you have so Justly aquired for the Love of your Country, and the desire that your Fellow Citizens may do Justice to mankind, has prompted me to Write you on a subject that very much concerns me, and a very numerous Family. Mr Charles Turnbull of Virginia died in 1782 (who probably you would know)[.] so long ago as 1756 he sent his sister my Mother in Law a will leaving her a fourth part of his whole Estate real or personal his Nephew Mr Robert Turnbull who lived with him for some time has taken possession of his whole Estate without giving his Relations in Scotland any account whatever.[1] I have annext a copy of the Will wherein he says "If I die either without making a Will or with a Will this Letter entitles you to a Fourth of my Estate real or personal."[2] Now Mr Robert Turnbull says his Uncle conveyd almost his whole Estate to him and his heirs Three Years before his Death.[3] I wrote to him for Copies of these papers so long ago as November 1783 a Copy of which Letter I have annext[4] and to which he has never made me a reply. I was recommended to Mr Benjamin Waller of Williamsburg to whom I sent a Power of Attorney and a Notorial Copy of the Will. he wrote that from old age he had declined business and recommended a Mr Tazwell my last Letter desiring him to make the necessary enquiries is dated Novr 1783 since which I have never heard a word on the subject out of Compassion for a Large family may I beg of you to Cause the necessary enquiries to be made so as we may get what we may be found entitled to from a relation who had every inclination to serve his Sister whom he dearly Loved, and advise me what I ought to do.[5] I believe a Relation of yours marricd a Mr Walker, a Scots Clergyman who died in Holland some years ago his son who married a near Relation of mine is now in Holland on a visit to his Stcp Mother.[6] with the Greatest Esteem I am Sir Your most hble Sert

Robt Johnston
Mercht

ALS, DLC:GW.

1. Before the Revolution Charles Turnbull became a prosperous and respected merchant in Petersburg, Virginia. In 1768 he was made one of the managers of the famous William Byrd lottery. In 1782, the year of Charles Turnbull's death, his nephew Robert Turnbull reported owning eighty-one slaves in Dinwiddie County.

2. It probably was not a copy of a formal will to which Johnston was referring, but rather to the enclosed copy of a letter from Charles Turnbull to his sister, dated at Appomattox River, 7 Feb. 1756, which states: "This Letter of this date the 7th Feby 1756 entitles you to one fourth part of my Estate real or personal to be for your use, and to be divided amongst your Children, and their heirs for ever As my Brother Thomas & the Revd Mr Robert Wallace my Brother in Law Judge proper" (DLC:GW).

3. In the copy of a letter from Robert Turnbull to Johnston of 29 July 1783 (misdated 1785), Turnbull told Johnston that his uncle wrote the letter of 7 Feb. 1756 to his sister (see note 2) before he was married "or indeed had any intention of Settling in this Country by his marrying here [in 1759]. . . . it is

natural to Suppose that his intentions respecting his Estate would alter and that they did so will appear by the Conveyance of almost the whole of his Estate to me . . . about three years before his Death" (DLC:GW). Turnbull went on to say that he would provide Johnston with a copy of his uncle's deed conveying his property to him and reported that Charles Turnbull made no will and left no children.

4. In his letter of response, 25 Nov. 1783 (the enclosed copy also misdated 1785), Johnston wrote Robert Turnbull that Charles Turnbull sent in 1768 to his brother Robert Turnbull in Scotland a deed binding himself to pay for the board and keep of their sister and her daughter. Johnston demands a copy of the deed by which Charles Turnbull conveyed his property to his nephew Robert, declaring it unlikely that Charles Turnbull would have done such a thing and thereby leave himself dependent on the charity of his nephew. Johnston concludes with an assertion that Charles Turnbull's sister and her children were in any case entitled to one-fourth part of Turnbull's estate (DLC:GW; see Robert Turnbull [the elder] to GW, this date). No response to either Johnston's or Turnbull's letter has been found.

5. Henry Tazewell (1753–1799) was a lawyer and the son-in-law of the Williamsburg lawyer Benjamin Waller. Tazewell had moved from Brunswick County to Williamsburg and in 1785 became a judge of the state's General Court. He served in the United States Senate from December 1794 until his death.

6. Neither the Rev. Mr. Walker nor his wife has been identified.

To William Minor

sir,   Mt Vernon 27th May 1785

My objection to paying your account when here—was, now is, &, whether it is done or not, will be—that it comes neither under the letter nor spirit of my letter to Mr Baker. My object was to give Lawce Posey a years schooling, to fit him for some of the better occupations of life: to do this, I agreed to pay his board also, both of which together, I was inform'd would amount at the free school, to £17—Md Curry. What followed? Why he neither went to the School, nor boarded with the person under whose care he was intended to be put—*this by your own confession*. Is it just, is it reasonable then that I should look *back* to expences which had been incurred previous to the date of my letter; or even *forward* to what might be incurred, if the end which I had in view was not to be answered by it? If the Child did not go to the school nor derive the benefits which were intended him from it, could it be supposed I meant to pay for his board without; when his fathers House & eye were more proper than any other? Might he not as well have been at home with his father, as at any other place idle? Upon these grounds it was & under this state I repeat it, that if there is a disinterested man upon Earth, who will say I ought to comply with your request, I will do it:[1] & you may have the chusing of him or them; for it does not suit me to go from home on this business. I am &c.

G. Washington

LB, DLC:GW.

1. It was when John Posey returned to Queenstown, Md., in October or November 1772 after several months in Virginia and removed his son St. Lawrence from William Minor's tavern (see Minor to GW, 24 May 1785, n.1) that he probably had with him the missing letter from GW to Francis Baker in which GW offered to pay the cost both of St. Lawrence's board at Mr. Baker's house, or tavern, and of his schooling at the free school in Queenstown. Posey did not give the letter to Baker, but GW did soon assume the responsibility of paying for St. Lawrence's board and schooling (see John Posey to GW, 9 Aug. 1773, Francis Baker to GW, 26 Mar. 1774, and Cash Accounts, November 1774). Even Minor, perhaps, came to see the absurdity of his asking GW to pay for expenses which were incurred by St. Lawrence even before GW made his offer to pay for his schooling and at a time when St. Lawrence in fact was not going to school.

From Christopher Richmond

Sir   Annapolis 27th May 1785

I had the honor of receiving your Letter of the 19th this day. Since I transmitted the List John Allen Thomas has subscribed for two Shares. I will take the first opportunity of informing him of what is further to be done by him, in order to the having his subscription established. I have the Honor to be your Excellencys obedient humble servt

Chrisr Richmond

ALS, DLC:GW.

From Robert Turnbull

[Sprouston near Kelso, Scotland]
Honourable Sir   May 27th 1785.

The greatness and dignity of your character for the virtues of a Patriot will command the Veneration of future ages; and those graces that adorn, and render aimiable your private life encourage and embolden me to address you in an affair, in which I am much interested. Tho I trust I have a mind above the Love of money, yet as old age is approaching; for I have been above forty two years a Minister of the Gospel, the just debt due to me by my deceased brother when recovered would be most convenient; just as I hope you will be convinced, by the perusal of my deceased brothers letter to me, which I have transcribed and inserted in this.[1] The only favour Good Sir I have to request of you, is to recommend to me some man of business in Virginia, to recover by the Law of that country, this Lawful and just debt. How happy for mankind were there a free and open intercourse among the nations and all men were treated as brethern. I have wrote two letters to my nephew Robert Turnbull in Virginia who has succeeded to the whole of my Brothers estate, on what foundation I am quite uncertain (but it can never exclude the payment of a just debt) for he has not had the civility to answer my letters, neither had he the Humanity to notify to me the death of my brother. I had rather be poor with that virtue, than be possessed of the greatest riches. My residence is at Sprouston near Kelso North Britain. I am with the highest esteem your most humble Servant

Robert Turnbull

ALS, DLC:GW.

1. See Robert Johnston to GW, and notes, this date. At the bottom of his letter, Robert Turnbull adds an excerpt from a letter that his brother Charles Turnbull wrote to "Dear Brother Robie" from "Virginia. Park Hall. Dinwiddie County. 6 February 1768." In the excerpt, after expressing his pleasure that their "dear Sister Stevenson" and her daughter had chosen to live with Robert "at Sprouston," Charles Turnbull wrote his brother: "You may make this letter binding on my estate after I am no more of this lower world, that whatever you are or has been in advance for my sister on her daughters Board, cloaths, or for any thing else . . . you shall be refunded or repaid two pounds for one pound Sterling . . . ." Robert Turnbull made this notation at the end of the excerpt: "There is more in the letter but it does not relate to my claim on [his

nephew] Robert Turnbull. My claim at a very moderate computation amounts to more than one thousand pounds sterling."

From Charles-Guillaume-Frédéric Dumas

Sir,   at the Hague May 28th 1785

Since full nine years I have the honor to be a Servant, as unexpectedly called as scrupulously loyal to the United States in this Country, I wanted only a proper occasion for paying your Excellncy directly my share in the admiration which Mankind owes to your Virtues. Now it presents itself with the most charming grace, my eagerness in taking it up, will not, I hope, appear unseasonable.

Favoured with the benevolence of his Excy the Marquis De Verac Embassador of the French Court at the Hague (as I was formerly, and still am with that of his worthy predecessor the Duque de La Vauguyon now at Madrid), he has contrived, and perfectly succeded, to surprize me in the most delicate and noble way, by sending me the fine brazen Bust of your Excellency on an elegant Pedestal, with a card directing it "to Mr Dumas from a friend of the United States." The bearer had vanish'd away; but I went immediately to tell his generous Principal, that happier than Diogenes, I was favoured with the Image of a Man living, and coming without a lanthorn to acknowledge the Man that favoured me with it.[1]

I look now on myself, Sir, as being the *Flamen* in this Country of your Glory, and boast of my room as being the Sanctuary, where are introduced your homagers, the friends of Civil Liberty, Equality and true Greatness.[2] Your Excellency's most obedient, humble and respectfull Servant

C.w.f. Dumas

ALS, DLC:GW; ADf, Algemeen Rijksarchief, The Hague, Netherlands; copy, DLC:GW. The copy is in Dumas's hand and has been docketed by GW.

Charles-Guillaume-Frédéric Dumas (1725–1796), who was born of French parents in Germany and had been living in The Hague since 1756, was an agent in Holland during the American Revolution for both the United States and France. At this time he was the unofficial chargé d'affaires there for the United States. For details of his career, see GW to Gouverneur Morris, 28 Nov. 1788, n.3; see also Dumas to GW, 13 June 1789.

1. Charles-Olivier de St. George, marquis de Vérac (1743–1828), was minis-

ter to St. Petersburg from 1779 until recalled in 1784 to become ambassador to Holland, where he remained until 1789. Paul-François de Quélen de Stuer de Caussade, duc de La Vauguyon (1746–1828), was ambassador to the United Provinces when in January 1784 he became ambassador to Spain. He continued as ambassador in Madrid until 1789.

2. GW acknowledged on 3 Oct. from Mount Vernon the receipt of Dumas's letter: "Your letter of the 28th of May from the Hague, does me great honor.

"The expression of it is too flattering for me not to regret that my merits fall far short of the compliment you have made me.

"I shall consider it however as a mark of your politeness whilst I have the honor of assuring, you of the esteem and respect with which I am—Sir Your Most Obedt & most Hble Servt Go Washington" (ALS, private donor; LB, DLC:GW).

Letter not found: from Richard Henry Lee, 29 May 1785. On 22 June GW wrote Lee: "I stand indebted to you for your favors of the . . . 29th of last month."

From William Goddard

Sir,   Baltimore, May 30th 1785.

As the Manuscript Papers of General Lee, after his decease, came into my hands, I have been induced from several motives to arrange & prepare them for publication. The General in his Life time requested it from me, & my Profession as a Printer & Bookseller made it an object of interest worthy my attention. But as I cannot be ignorant of some unhappy differences which subsisted between Your Excellency & General Lee, I have thought proper to acquaint your Excellency with my conduct in this Business.[1]

Influenced by no party consideration, & altogether devoid of any sinister Intention of exalting one Character at the Expence of another, I have taken care to suppress many passages that might be offensive, in the General's Pieces & Correspondence—while it was my duty to preserve what was useful in military & political knowledge, I took the liberty to suppress such Expressions as appeared to be the Ebullitions of a disappointed & irritated mind; so that, I flatter myself, your Excellency will be convinced of the Candor of my Intention in the Execution of the work. Inclosed I have sent a Copy of the Title Page, & the Proposals are now preparing for the Press; in a few

Weeks I purpose to send them to your Excellency;[2] and in the mean time, should esteem it a favour to hear, as soon as convenient, from your Excellency, whether this has come safe to your hands, & whether Your Excellency has any particular request, respecting the said Work. I am with the greatest Deference, & Esteem, Your Excellencys Most obedient & humble Servant

Wm Goddard

ALS, DLC:GW.

The fiery William Goddard (1740–1817) had come to Baltimore in 1773 from Philadelphia and at this time was publishing with his sister, Mary Katherine Goddard, the *Maryland Journal*. In its issue of 6 July 1779, the *Journal* printed Charles Lee's "Some Queries, Political and Military," twenty-five pointed questions about the conduct of the war by Congress and GW. The "Queries" of the court-martialed general brought out a Baltimore mob that confronted Goddard and forced a recantation, which Goddard in turn promptly repudiated. The long-term consequence of this episode was that Goddard and General Lee became fast friends. Lee visited the Goddards in Baltimore in September 1782 on his way to Philadelphia, where he died on 20 Oct., leaving one-sixth of his American estate to Goddard. Goddard married Abigail Angell of Providence, R.I., in May 1786. In 1792 he retired to Providence, and lived there until his death (Miner, *Goddard*, 168 *et seq.*; see also Sidney Lee to GW, 23 May 1784, n.3).

1. It is not known exactly how the papers of Gen. Charles Lee came into the hands of his friend William Goddard. Goddard's plans to publish the papers did not reach fruition (see Goddard to GW, 14 June 1785, n.1). Goddard's partner in 1785, Edward Langworthy, took with him copies of some of Lee's letters when his partnership with Goddard was terminated, and in 1792 he used them in his *Memoirs of the Life of the Late Charles Lee, Esq.*, published in London. The original papers remained in possession of Goddard's descendants, and in the 1870s the New-York Historical Society printed four volumes of the papers, before they all disappeared (ibid., 175–76).

2. Goddard enclosed the proposed title page, written in his hand, and on 14 June he sent GW a printed title page as part of his prospectus of a projected three-volume work. The title page reads: *Miscellaneous Collections from the Papers of the late Major General Charles Lee: consisting of 1st—Pieces on various political & military Subjects. 2d.—Letters to the General from several Persons of the first Character, both in Europe & America. 3d.—Letters from the General to his Friends in Europe, before the late War; and also to the principal American Characters, both civil & military, during his command in the Continental Army. To which are prefixed Memoirs of His Life. The whole will contain a great & useful Variety of military & political Knowledge, and in a striking manner elucidate the Abilities & decisive Conduct of this great and experienced Officer. In three Volumes.*

neque
Si Chartae fileant, quod benefeceris
Mercedem tuleris—Hor[ace]

For Goddard's prospectus, see note 1 in his letter to GW of 14 June. For GW's reaction to Goddard's planned publication, see GW to Goddard, 11 June.

From Tench Tilghman

Dear Sir   Baltimore 30th May 1785.

I have had the honor of receiving your letter of the 23d I shall communicate so much of the Contents, as respect Colonel Colvils Legacy to Miss Anderson, to her Uncle Mr Hollyday. I have applied to the Revd Mr West on this Business. I find him intirely unacquainted with such parts of his Brothers affairs as relate to his Executorship to Colo. Colvils Estate. Matters must therefore remain as they are, untill you can find leisure to look into these things yourself.[1]

It gives me pleasure to think I have met with a young Man, who will probably answer your purposes. He came over to take charge of a seminary in your State, in the County of Prince William. The plan fell through, and Mr Falconer, the Gentleman in question, is left to seek a livelyhood in this Country. He had actually embarked for Charleston when your letter came to my hands—I heard of him, and have prevailed upon him to suspend his purpose, untill I could make you acquainted with his Talents and Expectations—His person is pleasing—His manners and address diffident, but by no means awkward—His Age not more than 25—In the dead Languages—Natural Pholosophy—and the practical Branches of Mathematics he is said to be highly accomplished—of course he must be sufficiently master of Figures to answer your purpose as an Accomptant. He tells me he understands French eno' to translate a letter. His hand writing, of which I inclose you a specimen, is not of the best, but it may be mended with a little care and attention. Those with whom he has been acquainted since his short residence here, speak of him in such a manner, that they have really prepossessed me in his favor. The terms on which he came over to this Country were £100 S[terlin]g ⅌ ann: and every thing found him except Cloathing. He is, however, so fully sensible of the advantages that would result to him from living with you a year or two, and being so happy as to gain your confidence and Esteem, that I am certain he would abate considerably if you could not make it convenient to allow him so much. I think he might be engaged for £100 Currency.

I send this letter under Cover to Colo. Fitzgerald, with a desire that he will dispatch it by a Messenger on Thursday. If you can return an answer by the same Messenger, it may reach me by saturdays Stage.[2] I take the liberty of hurrying you, because Mr Falconer wishes to prosecute his Charleston plan if he should not go to you.

How much you flatter me, my dear General (for by that name I must ever be allowd to call you) by your kind invitation to visit you. My circumstances require a close attention to Business, and I am, on that account, cheifly confined to the limits of this Town. I often wish for a good pretence to go as far as Alexandria or George Town. Once there I should not fail to pay my Respects at Mount Vernon. If I ever find time to make a jaunt of pleasure—Mrs Tilghman will assuredly be of the party. She joins in sincerest Compliments to Mrs Washington and yourself with Dear Sir Yr most affect: humble Servt

Tench Tilghman

I shall send your white Pine plank by the first oppertunity.

ALS, DLC:GW.

1. See also GW to John Swan, 23 May.

2. The "specimen" of W. Falconer's handwriting that Tilghman enclosed is a letter from Falconer to Tilghman dated 31 May. GW received from John Fitzgerald in Alexandria Tilghman's letter with its enclosure on Thursday, June 2. Replying that he could not afford to pay what Falconer was likely to expect, GW went on to describe in detail what he would require of a secretary. In his letter to Tilghman, Falconer expressed an interest in Tilghman's suggestion made the night before of the possibility of his "being employed" by GW. "Having regularly obtained the Degree of Master of Arts in a University of Great Brittain," Falconer wrote: "I was sent into America to be rector of an Academy, in consequence of an application from the Trustees thereof to the President of the said University. But want of unanimity among those interested effected the dissolution of the Academy; which is the cause of my being at present unemployed" (DLC:GW). Falconer assured Tilghman that he could supply his diploma from the university and a certificate of his good character. Tilghman, however, decided that Falconer would not fit the bill, which ended the matter (see Tilghman to GW, 4 June).

To John Harvie

Sir,   Mount Vernon 31st May 1785.

I am informed that a patent (in consequence of a Certificate from Commrs appointed to enquire into, & decide upon Claims for settlement of the Western Lands) is about to issue to the heirs of Michl Cresap, from the Land Office of this Commonwealth, for a tract of land on the river Ohio formerly in Augusta County, now commonly called & distinguished by the round bottom:[1] against granting which to the heirs of the said Cresap, I enter a Caveat for the following reasons; First, because this Land was discovered by me in the month of Octor 1770, & then marked; which was before, as I have great reason to believe, the said Cresap, or any person in his behalf had ever seen, or had the least knowledge of the tract. Secondly, because I did at that time, whilst I was on the Land, direct Captn (afterwds Colo.) Willm Crawford to survey the same for my use, as a halfway place on stage between Fort Pitt & the 200,000 acres of land which he was ordered to survey for the first Virginia regiment agreeably to Govr Dinwiddie's Proclamation of 1754. Thirdly, because consequent of this order he made the survey in the month of [   ] the year following for 587 acres, & returned it to me accordingly:[2] and equally certain I am that it was made before Ml Cresap or any person in his behalf had ever stretch'd a chain thereon, knew of, or, as I have already observed, had taken a single step to obtain the land. Fourthly, because subsequent of this survey; but previous to any claim of Cresaps, a certain Dr Brisco possessed himself of the Land, & relinquished it, after I had written him a letter in the words contained in the inclosure No. 1.[3] Fifthly, because upon the first information I received of Cresaps pretentions, I wrote him a letter, of which No. 2 is a copy.[4] Sixthly, because it was the practice of Cresap, according to the information given me, to notch a few trees, & fell as many bottoms on the river above the Little Kanhawa as he could obtain purchasers, to the disquiet & injury of numbers. Seventhly, Because the Commrs who gave the certificate under which his heirs now claim, could have had no knowledge of my title thereto, being no person in that District properly authorised, during my absence, to support my claim. Eighthly, Because the survey, which was made by Colo. Crawford, who was legally appointed by the Masters of Wm & Mary College for the purpose of surveying the aforesaid 200,000 acres, is expressly recognized & deemed valid by the first section of the Act, entitled an Act—*see the Act*—as the same was afterwards returned by the surveyor of the county in which the Land lay.[5] Ninthly & lastly, Because I have a Patent for the said Land, under the seal of the said Commonwealth signed by the Goverr in due form on the 30th day of Octor 1784; consequent of a legal Survey made the 14th of July 1773 as just mentioned, & now of record in the Land Office.

For these reasons I protest against a Patent's issueing for the Land for which the Commissioners have given a Certificate to the Heirs of Mr Cresap so far as the same shall interfere with mine: the legal & equitable right thereto being in me.

If I am defective in form in entering this Caveat, I hope to be excused, & to have my mistakes rectified. I am unaccustomed to litigations; & never disputed with any man, until the ungenerous advantages which have been taken of the peculiarity of my situation, & an absence of eight years from my country, has driven me into Courts of Law to obtain common justice. I have the honor to be &c.

G: Washington

LB, DLC:GW.

1. Harvie informed GW on 20 May of the intentions of the heirs of Michael Cresap to apply for a grant of the Round Bottom tract. See Harvie to GW, 5 Aug., nn.2, 3.

2. William Crawford wrote GW on 2 Aug. 1771 that he had run a survey of the tract which came to be known as Round Bottom. GW found it necessary to have Crawford resurvey the tract in 1774 (see GW to Thomas Lewis, 17 Feb., 5 May, and William Crawford to GW, 8 May, 20 Sept., and 14 Nov. 1774). GW has an asterisk after the word "survey" in his third point and at the bottom of the page is the following passage: "This survey is either in the hands of the county Surveyor of Augusta, or with my Agent in the Westn Country: it is not to be found among my papers; tho' I am sure of the fact, & will procure it if necessary."

3. See GW to John Briscoe, 3 Dec. 1772.

4. See GW to Michael Cresap, 26 Sept. 1773.

5. The first section of "An Act for adjusting and settling the titles of claimers to unpatented lands under the present and former government, previous to the establishment of the commonwealth's land office," enacted in 1779, pro-

vided that "all surveys of waste and unappropriated land made upon any of the western waters before the first day of January, in the year 1778 . . . by any county surveyor commissioned by the masters of William and Mary college" would be valid if properly made and registered (10 Hening 35–50).

From Burwell Bassett

Dear Sir   Wilton 1 June 1785
    Your favour of the 23 of may is now before me I most sincearly return you my thanks for the offer you made Fanny[.] Majr Washington had my permisson to pay his addresses to Fanny & from my long acquantance with him I have no reason to alter the good opinion I ever entertain of him I think myself they had better put of there intended marriage till they return from the springs where I intend going up with Fanny the last of this month but if Mrs Washington should be of a different opinion, & Fanny health will permit of her being married I then shall have know objection to it, I will endeavour to be at M. Vernon about the 25 of this month,[1] I must beg you'll present my best Complements to Mrs Washington I am Dear Sir yr affect. Freind & Obt Hble Servt

Burl Bassett

ALS, DLC:GW.
    1. Bassett arrived at Mount Vernon with his sons Burwell (1764–1841) and John (1766–1826) on 22 June. Bassett himself left on 8 July; the two younger Bassetts left the next day with George Augustine Washington for the springs in Botetourt County. George Augustine Washington and Fanny Bassett were not married until October (see note 3, GW to Bassett, 23 May).

From William Augustine Washington

Dr Sir   Blenheim [Westmoreland County] June 1st 1785
    Your Esteem'd favr by Mr Blane, I recd and was particularly attentive in collecting of the Holly Berrys, agreeable to your request, wch I trust has got safe to hand[1]—I have been industrious in inquiring for some *Wild Goose* & Swans for you, at length I have procured these Geese, which I now send you, the one with a tame Goose for a Mate is a present from Mr McCarty to you, who desired me to inform you that the Wild Goose has been

much attatch'd to his Mate for these three Years past, for wch reasin he sends you the tame Goose, least the Wild one should leave you, as he can fly perfectly well[2]—I shall indeavour to procure you some *Swans* this Winter—By the Bearer you will receive a Gross of ⟨Hues⟩ Crabb Cyder, wch you will much oblige me by accepting 'tho not so good as I could wish, from the management of my Cyder last fall being left intirely to the Negroes, from the Loss of both my Overseers.

This fall I shall direct a Hogshead to be put up in the best manner for you—Mrs Washington joins me in our Loves to you & Mrs Washington—and believe me to be Dr Sir Your Sincerely Affectionate

Wm Augt. Washington

ALS, CSmH.

William Augustine Washington (1757–1810) was the son of GW's half brother Augustine Washington, who died in 1761, and the husband of Jane Washington, the daughter of GW's brother John Augustine Washington.

1. GW's letter has not been found; Blane may be Thomas Blane (Blaine) of Westmoreland county.

2. GW noted in his cash accounts for 4 June the payment of eighteen shillings for "Freight Cyder & 3 Wild Geese from Capt. W. Washington" (Ledger B, 203), but see also GW's diary entry for 19 May (*Diaries*, 4:141). Daniel McCarty (d. 1795) of Pope's Creek was a near neighbor of William Augustine Washington.

From Rochambeau

Paris June the 2th 1785.

I come, my Dear Général, of taking leave from Doctor franklin. I could not See without being moved to pity that respectable man at eighty years old, with a very sharp and weighty cause of sickness, having the courage to undertake So a long voyage to go and die in the bosom of his native country. it will be impossible to him, at his coming-back in america, to go and visit you, but I told him that you would certainly come and see him, and that I had always hear'd you speaking of him in the best terms and having a great consideration for his respectable character. he will have a great joy to see you again; and I Should be very happy if I could enjoy of the Same pleasure.[1]

it has been presented yesterday to the King, my Dear Général, two pictures to put in his closet which have been done by an Excellent painter, one representing the siege of york and th'other the defile of the British army between the american and french armies.

Mr le Marshal de segur promis'ed me Copies of them which I will place in my closet on the right and left Sides of your picture—besides that they are Excellent paintings, they have been drawn, both by the truth and by an excellent design done by the young Berthier whom was deputed quarter-master general at the said siege.[2]

The peace between the Emperor and the holland is not yet settled and suffers obstacles and delays but it appears certain that it will have no war in Europe for this subject. it remains to be known what shall happen if the King of Prussia or the Elector of Bavaria, comes to die—the young Pitt maintains himself in a great majority by his wisdom, his moderation, virtue and talents. Don't you find that the Count de chatham was the greatest Minister that the England have had to make conquests, and that the son Should have been much more wiser than him to Conserve them? adieu, my Dear Général, I am ready to depart for going to Calais where I shall remain four months in my command. I Shall be very glade if I receive good news of your health. my respects to Mad[am]e Washington and be well Convinced of my inviolable and respectful attachment with which I have the honour to be My Dear General Your most obedient and very humble servent;

le cte de Rochambeau

ALS, DLC:GW.

1. Benjamin Franklin landed in Philadelphia on 14 September. GW wrote Franklin a formal letter of welcome on 25 Sept. before receiving Franklin's letter of 20 Sept., which GW answered on 26 September.

2. Louis-Nicolas Van Blarenberghe (1716–1794) painted for Louis XVI the "Seige" of Yorktown in 1784 and the "Surrender" in 1785, both of which remain at the royal palace at Versailles. Rochambeau's copies, dated 1786, hang at Chateâu de Rochambeau. The paintings were based upon drawings by Louis-Alexandre Berthier (1753–1815), a young captain in Rochambeau's army at Yorktown and later Napoleon's first marshal of France. The marquis de Ségur was minister of war. Rochambeau's portrait of GW was done by Charles Willson Peale. See Rice and Brown, eds., *American Campaigns of Rochambeau's Army*, 2:161–64.

To Tench Tilghman

Dear Sir,   Mount Vernon June 2d 1785

As your letter of the 30th Ulto did not reach me until late this afternoon, and the Post goes from Alexaa at 4 Oclock in the morning, I have scarcely a moment (being also in company) to write you a reply.

I was not sufficiently explicit in my last. The terms upon which Mr Falconer came to this Country are too high for my finances—and (to you, my dear Sir, I will add) numerous expences. I do not wish to reduce his (perhaps well founded) expectations; but it behoves me to consult my own means of complying with them.

I had been in hopes, that a young man of no great expectations, might have begun the world, with me, for about fifty of Sixty pounds Virga Curry pr Ann.—but for one qualified in all respects to answer my purposes, I would have gone as far as Seventy five—more would rather distress me.

My purposes are these. To write Letters agreeably to what shall be dictated. Do all other writing which shall be entrusted to him—Keep Accts—Examine, arrange, & properly methodize my Papers, which are in great disorder. ride, at my expence, to do such business as I may have in different parts of this, or the other States, if I should find it more convenient to send, than attend my self, to the execution thereof. And, which was not hinted at in my last, to inetiate two little children (a girl of six, & a boy of 4 years of age, descendent's of the deceased Mr Custis, who live with me, and are very promising) in the first rudiments of education. This to both parties, would be mere amusement, because it is not my wish that the Children should be confined.

If Mr Falconer should incline to accept the above stipend in addition to his board, washing & mending, and *you* (for I would rather have *your opinion* of the Gentleman than the *report* of a thousand others in his favor) upon a close investigation of his character, Temper, & moderate political tenets (for supposing him an English man, he may come with the prejudices, & Doctrines of his Country) the sooner he comes, the better my purposes would be promoted.[1]

If I had had time, I might have added more, but to you it would have been unnecessary. You know my wants—you know my disposition—and you know what kind of a man would suit them. In haste I bid you adieu. With assurances of great regard & sincere friendship, I am—Dr Sir Yr Affecte Hble Servt

Go: Washington

ALS, NN: Lee Kohns Collection; LB, DLC:GW.

1. See note 2 in Tilghman to GW, 30 May; see also Tilghman to GW, 4 June.

From Michael Jenifer Stone

Sir   Charles County Maryland.   June 3d 1785

I hereby authorise and request you as president of the Potomac Company to Subscribe for me two Shares to the before mentioned Copartnery; Or to consider me (if consistent with the regulations of the Company) as an Adventurer to the amount of two Shares.

I take the liberty to observe, that I have long agoe earnestly desired the exhibition of the present Scheme—and would have Subscribed forth with, but that the Company's Books were kept at a considerable distance from my home—and I was not informed 'till lately that I could become a Partner by Letter Signifying my consent. I hope I am not too late. And if I am considered as a partner I hereby oblige Myself my Heirs Executors and Administrators to pay to the President and directors of the Potomac Company or to Such person as they shall authorise to receive the amount of two Shares in the Said Company in Such manner as the President and directors shall require.[1] I am your most obedient

M. J. Stone

ALS, NIC.

Michael Jenifer Stone (1747–1812) of Charles County, Md., was a lawyer and political figure in Maryland.

1. See GW's response of 15 June.

From Richard Boulton

Sir   St Marys County St Inegoes [Md.], June 4th 1785

I am sorry to inform your Excellency that my Affairs in St Marys are in such a situation that it is at this time Intierly out of my power to serve your Excellency or comply with my Agreement, for Reasons I will hearafter mention.

On my return from your Excellencies to St Marys, I ware under the Disagreeable nicessity of Offering a number of my Tules for Sail to Discharge a number of considerable Debts due from me to my Creditors. But Money being Scarce & the Tules not salible in our County which I offerd, Rendered my sail of no Use towards Satisfying my Creditors. In consiquence of which & thier hearing of my Agreement with your Excellency, and my intention of muving out of the State to Serve you, have sot them all on me, I have heard of several Rits being out against me, which I expect dailey to be served, the consiquence of which will be that I must Inavoidable goe to Joal.[1]

Having wayed every Sircumstance minutely find it intierly out of my power to Serve your Excellency, Therefore intierly Relying on your Excellencyes linety & Goodness hoping youl Excuse my non complyance with my Agreement with you, as numbers of Others have s[o] universally expearencd.

As I apprehend Collo. Wm Fitzhugh recommended me to you as an Able Workman, I thought proper to right him a state of my Affairs and let him no it is out of my power to comply with my Agreement with you. From your Excellencies most Obt Hble Sert

Richd Boulton

ALS, DLC:GW.

1. William Fitzhugh denied that Boulton's excuse had any validity (Fitzhugh to GW, 4 July). For the agreement into which Boulton had entered with GW, see GW to Fitzhugh, 21 May, n.1.

From Holtzendorf

Sir   Nymegen [Holland] June the 4th 1785.

This Letter will come to your hands by favour of Colonel Senf, who is returning to america very soon. I thought it incumbent to me to take that opportunity in order to renew to you, Sir, my most grateful thanks for all the marks of Benevolence you shewed to me during my Stay under your Commands in th' American Army. the satisfaction about my military Character, as well as the Regrets about my Leaving the said service, you was pleased to manifest even by your laest Letter, I was honoured with in answer of that by wich I informed you of my returning to France,[1] make me hope you will be glad to learn, that I Stay as yet in the Service of the united States of Holland, having been granted by the General Count de Maillebois with a Place of Lieutenant Colonel in the Legion which he is raising for this Service.

I'll allways regret sincerely, that circumstances did not allow my terminating with you, Sir, a war by yourself so gloriously ended; for, the French Regiment, I was from, though destinated in the year 1780 to go to america with the corps of army of the G[ener]al Rochembeau, which became one of them of his 2nd Division, that could not be carried over for want of vessels, I was obliged to see myself disappointed of that hope. I'm the more sorry as I believe I would have been granted with the admission to your association of Cinsinnatus, which favour would have flatterd me particularly, as I would have considered it not only as a recompense of my zeal I shewed, you Know sir, whilst I Served your own country, but of the real hopes, Even the unjustice, I proved by the particular Illwill of Mr Lovel, whose influence prevented their good intensions to me, as well as the fulfilling of one of their Resolveds, which I Keep in original, and according to which I should be indemnified.

Will you, Sir, give me leave to beg your influence about both them Subjects? If you think it possible, I should be very happy to be honoured with the admission to your association of Cinsinnatus. for the rest, it would be indeed an act of justice and Even of honour to congress to fulfill a resolved they gave in favour of myn in the beginning of 1778.[2]

this new mark of your Benevolence, Sir, shall increase the gratitude consecrated to you for ever, with which I have the honour to remain very respectfully Sir your most obedient humble servant

Lewis Casimir Baron de holtzendorff
Lt Coll of the Legan of maillebois
in garrison at Nymegen

ALS, DLC:GW.

The service in America of Louis-Casimir, baron de Holtzendorf of Prussia, was brief. In response to his letter of 16 Aug. 1777 from Philadelphia, GW wrote Holtzendorf on 18 Aug. that he was attaching him to Gen. Nathanael Greene's division as a lieutenant colonel. On 30 Dec. 1777, dissatisfied with his treatment, Holtzendorf presented a memorial to Congress making a number of extraordinary demands and asking permission to return to France (DNA:PCC, item 41). Congress voted on 31 Jan. that Holtzendorf might "have liberty to depart for France" and on 21 Feb. voted to give him the funds to do so (*JCC*, 10:105, 188). Holtzendorf entered the Dutch service in 1785.

1. When Holtzendorf asked GW for a certificate of his conduct, GW wrote him on 3 Feb. 1778: "I shall be always ready, Sir, to declare that you uniformly supported a good character during your stay in the Army under my command, and that it is to be regretted that the Nature of your Post did not afford you a favorable opportunity of displaying your military talents." Christian Senf, an engineer who returned to Europe after the war, came back to America in 1785 and visited Mount Vernon 11–14 June 1786, when he delivered this letter.

2. GW replied to Holtzendorf from Mount Vernon on 31 July 1786: "Sir, The letter of the 4th of June 1785 which you was pleased to address to me by Colo. Senf, has very lately been put into my hand; in answer to which I have the honor to observe, that having divested myself of an official character & retired to private life, I can have no agency whatever in matters of a public nature. This, I thought, had been made known extensively enough by the manner of my resignation & retirement. The want of being acquainted with these facts seems however, to have involved some gentlemen at a distance in unnecessary & unavailing applications. All therefore, that I have it in my power to advise you on the two objects of your letter, is, that application for admittance into the Society of the State in whose line the officer served, or, if the Officer was a foreigner, to the Society in France; and that with respect to pecuniary claims, recourse must be had either to the Paymaster General, or Secretary for the Department of War. With due consideration & regard I have the honor to be &c. G: Washington" (LB, DLC:GW). The copyist spelled Senf's name "Serf."

From John Jebb

Sir   Parliament Street [London] 4 Jun. 1785.

The Bearer, a Gentleman of whose abilities in his profession, as well as of whose attachment to the Cause of freedom I have a very favourable opinion, mentioning to me his intention of revisiting Virginia, his native Country,[1] I felt a strong inclination to testify that high regard & veneration, in which I have ever held your exertions in support of the rights of your Countrymen & of Human nature—Thank Heaven! the glorious Struggle has been crownd with full success—and later posterity will with gratitude acknowledge the share which under providence you have had in establishing the liberties of Mankind.

Our Europe groans under the lash of Tyranny Civil & Religious, & as yet scarcely feels the wish for freedom. I feel for the present inattention of my Countrymen to the noblest objects—but I trust that our English spirit will revive ere long, & emulate the great example of their Transatlantic Brethren, reforming our government & assuming a character the reverse of that we have too long sustained.

Notwithstanding the representations of the interested, I own I look to Ireland with prophetic expectation.

That in the full perception of every blessing which approving Heaven can bestow you may long enjoy the fruits of your many labours in the Cause of Public Virtue is the fervent wish of y[o]ur obedt Servt

John Jebb

ALS, DLC:GW.

Dr. John Jebb (1736–1786), a clergyman, in 1775 gave up his living to become a medical doctor in London. As a liberal theologian and political writer, he advocated in particular prison reform, the reform of Parliament, and universal suffrage.

1. The "Bearer" was probably Dr. William Baynham who was returning to Virginia after sixteen years abroad. See George William Fairfax to GW, 23 June 1785, n.6.

From Edmund Randolph

Dear sir   Richmond June 4. 1785.

I entered upon the execution of my promise to Major Washington without delay; but the paper being lengthy cannot be compleated for this post. You will be so good as not to expect it, until the next week. I shall fortify it with as many authentications, as the situation of our public records will permit.[1] I am Dear sir yr obliged and affectionate friend & servant

Edm: Randolph

ALS, DLC:GW.

1. GW's correspondence with Randolph in the summer of 1785 (see Randolph to GW, 9, 17, 29 July, 8 Aug., 2 Sept., and GW to Randolph, 30 July, 13 Aug.) deals almost exclusively with GW's attempts to secure documents to bolster his claims to the Millers Run (Chartiers Creek) tract in Pennsylvania on which unauthorized settlers were living. Because most of GW's letters to Randolph are missing, the documents that he is seeking cannot always be identi-

fied. Precisely what George Augustine Washington asked for on behalf of GW is not known, but almost certainly it was for a copy of some document relating to the conflicting claims to the Millers Run land, and it may have been to the "copy of the proclamation" that Randolph enclosed in his letter of 9 July. For a rundown on the dispute over the Millers Run tract, see the editorial note, Thomas Smith to GW, 9 February.

From Tench Tilghman

Dear Sir   Baltimore 4th June 1785
    Your favor of the 2d reached me this day—which was as soon as I expected your answer—Had your terms been agreeable to Mr Falconer, I do not think he would have suited all the purposes for which you wanted him—He is more a Man of letters than a Man of Business—and altho' he might have managed your Correspondencies, I do not apprehend he would have made much hand of your Business abroad. The tutorage of the Children was a matter which he would not have wished to have undertaken—Having had no personal acquaintance with this Gentleman myself, I could not have answered for his temper or political principles.
    I should imagine young Men of as good Education as this Country generally affords, and of respectable families also, might be found, who would be ambitious of the post you want filled. Their time would be profitably and agreeably passed, and I may add, without flattery, they could not carry with them into the World a better recommendation than that of General Washington. I shall still be upon the lookout for you, and shall occasionally mention those Characters that fall in my way, untill I find you are supplied.
    I sent you a few days past by the Alexandria packet, addressed to Colo. Fitzgerald, 357 feet of 2 Inch white pine plank[1]—@

22/6 ⅌Ct	£4.3.9
Carriage on Board	3
Maryland Currency—	£4.6.9

You cannot make me happier than by giving me oppertunities of convincing you how sincerely I am Dear Sir Your most affect: & very humble Servt

                                           Tench Tilghman

ALS, DLC:GW.

1. GW wrote Tilghman on 23 May asking him to secure this lumber to be used by Richard Boulton. In an entry dated 30 June in his cash accounts, GW notes owing Tilghman £3.14.6 Virginia currency for the planks (Ledger B, 203).

To James Rumsey

Sir,　　　　　　　　　　　　　　　　Mt Vernon 5th June 1785.

Your letter of the 10th of March came safe, but not in a short time after the date of it. The reason which you have assigned for giving me an order on Mr Ryan, is perfectly satisfactory. I wish that that or any other expedient would have extracted from him what he owes you. From the accot given of his circumstances & conduct, I fear you have incurred a bad debt with the manager of the Theatre.[1]

As the Car[ria]ge house you was to build for me, was in such forwardness at the date of the above letter, & as you expected to have had it raised by the first of May last; I am very well satisfied with the advance it has made, & that it should continue, provided you can make it convenient to wait a while for your money; but I should be wanting in candor were I to give you assurances of speedy payment. The Kitchen & stable I would gladly have finished as soon as possible & what ever the cost of them amounts to, I will settle for without delay.[2]

It gives me much pleasure to find by your letter that you are not less sanguine in your Boat project, than when I saw you last; and that you have made such further discoveries as will render them of greater utility than was at first expected: you have my best wishes for the success of your plan.[3]

Inclosed are the proceedings of the Directors of the Potomac navigation—I pray you to have them set up at some public place. If the manager advertised for, can come *well* recommended, liberal wages will be given him.[4] It were to be wished that the following qualities could be readily combined in the same person—integrity—Abilities—indefatigable industry—& if he has not experimental knowledge of this particular kind of work, at least that he may be possessed of a genius which may soon fit him for it.

Mr Ryan's Note is enclosed,[5] & I am with great esteem, Sir, &c.

G: Washington

LB, DLC:GW. GW wrote Rumsey on 2 July that he had sent this letter "under cover to my brother in Berkely," Charles Washington.

1. For Dennis Ryan's "bad debt," see GW to Alexander Henderson, 20 Dec. 1784, n.1, and references.

2. See Rumsey's discouraging report on the progress he was making on GW's house at Bath in Berkeley County, 24 June 1785. For even worse reports about what Rumsey did and did not do in building the house at Bath, see George Lewis to GW, 25 Aug. 1786, and Jean Le Mayeur to GW, 28 Aug. 1786; see also Rumsey to GW, 5 Sept. 1786.

3. For Rumsey's mechanical boat, see GW's certificate for James Rumsey, 7 Sept. 1784, Rumsey to GW, 10 Mar. 1785, and GW to Rumsey, 31 Jan. 1786.

4. This copy of the minutes of the meeting of the president and directors of the Potomac River Company, 30–31 May, is included in DNA: RG 79, Records of the Potomac Co. and the Chesapeake and Ohio Canal Co., item 159: "At a Meeting of the President and Directors of the Potowmack Company in Alexandria on Monday the 30th Day of May 1785 were present Genl George Washington President Geo. Gilpin John Fitzgerald Thomas Sim Lee and Thomas Johnston Directors[.]

"George Gilpin administered the Oath of Office prescribed by the Acts of Assembly of Virginia and Maryland to George Washington, John Fitzgerald, Thomas Sim Lee and Thomas Johnston, and John Fitzgerald administered the Oath of Office to George Gilpin.

"William Hartshorne of Alexandria appointed Treasurer under the Allowance of three ⅌ Cent, he giving Bond in the Penalty of ten thousand Pounds Sterling with two good and sufficient Securities, such as this Board shall approve.

"It is the Opinion of this Board that it is the most eligible to employ two sets of Hands, one of them in opening and improving the Navigation from the great Falls to Payne's Falls and the other from the upper part of the Shanadoah Falls to the highest place practicable on the North Branch.

"That each Sett of Hands consist of 50 Men to be under the general Direction of one skilful person who shall have a proper Assistant as well as three Overseers with each Party.

"Adjourned till tomorrow.

"May 31st present as Yesterday.

"Mr John Potts Junr of Alexandria appointed Clerk to this Board, to be paid twenty one Shillings Sterling for each Day he shall attend this Board, besides his reasonable Expences when he occasionally attends out of Alexandria and thereby incurs an extraordinary Expence.

"By the President and Directors of the Potowmack Company, May 31st 1785

"Ordered, that the Proprietors of the said Company pay into the Hands of

William Hartshorne Treasurer of the said Company on each Share five pounds
Sterling on or before the fifteenth Day of July next and also the further Sum
of two pounds ten shillings Sterling on or before the first Day of October next.

Go: Washington P.

Ths Johnston

Thos S. Lee

George Gilpin

John Fitzgerald

"Four hundred and three of the five hundred Shares in the Potowmack
Company having been subscribed Books are now opened at Mr William Hart-
shornes Treasurer in Alexandria to recieve the first Subscriptions that may be
offered to make up the ninety seven remaining Shares.

"Ordered, that Advertisements be inserted in the Alexandria, Baltimore
and some one or more of the Philadelphia Papers giving Notice that this Board
will meet at Alexandria on the first Day of July next to agree with a Skilful
Person to conduct the opening and improving the Navigation of the Potowmack River from the great Falls to Payne's and from the upper part of the
Shanadoah to the highest place practicable on the North Branch, and also to
agree with two Assistants and overseers—Also that liberal wages will be given
to any Number not exceeding one hundred good Hands with provisions and
a reasonable Quantity of Spirits; that a further Encouragement will be given
to such as are dextrous in boring and blowing Rocks in which Service a proportion of the Men will be employed and that the Conductor of the Work or
some other person authorised will attend at Seneca on the third Day of July
next and at Shanadoah on the sixth Day of July next to contract with the Men
who may offer for this Service.

"Ordered, That the Clerk write a Letter to Captn Abraham Sheppard of
Sheppards Town requesting him to contract for the building two very strong
Boats for the Use of the Company each to be thirty five feet long, Eight feet
wide or upwards and not less than twenty Inches deep in the common Manner
of the Flats used at the Ferries on Potowmack above Tide Water.

"That a like Letter be written to Col: Josias Clapham to contract for the
building two other such Boats as above.

"It is the Opinion of this Board that a View and Examination of Potowmack
River by the President and Directors assisted by the Conductor of the Work
may promote the great End of the Institution of the Potowmack Company and
therefore they resolve to proceed in such View and Examination immediately
after the general Meeting in August next."

The advertisement was printed in a number of newspapers. See, for example, the issue of 9 June of the *Virginia Journal and Alexandria Advertiser.*

5. See note 1 of GW to Alexander Henderson, 20 Dec. 1784, and references.

To David Stuart

Dear Sir,   Mount Vernon 5th June 85.

The celebrated Mrs Macauly Graham, & Mr Graham her Husband, are here on a Visit. As I wish to shew them all the respect I can, I should be glad if you, Mrs Stuart & your Sister, would come to morrow or next day, and dine with us.[1] I am—Dr Sir Yr Obedt & Affecte Hble Ser⟨vt⟩

Go: Washington

P.S. Come tomorrow if convenient.

ALS (photocopy), R-Ar.

1. Catharine Sawbridge Macaulay Graham, the historian, and her husband William Graham arrived at Mount Vernon on 4 June for a ten-day visit. See *Diaries*, 4:148–53, *Virginia Journal and Alexandria Advertiser*, 9 June, and Richard Henry Lee to GW, 3 May 1785, n.3. Stuart came to dinner on 7 June, without either his wife Eleanor Calvert Custis Stuart or his sister Ann Stuart, and "stayed all Night" (*Diaries*, 4:149).

From Thomas Freeman

Redstone [Pa.]

May it Please your Excellency,   June 9th 1785

I had the favour of yours dated the 11th May on the 28 of the same and shall Endeavour to comply with the Contents,[1] I should have wrote before but expect you out this spring, in regard to the Lands on the Ohio & Kanhawa I Advertised Imediately as you left this last fall as Extensively as oppertunity offered, but had but few Applicants and not one of them would Agree to Settle on any of the Lands agreeable to my Instructions nor do I think that any of the Lands will Rent on the Terms at Present, there being so extensive a Country to Settle, the Applicants in general gave this as their reason and also the Rents too High they alow that for little more than Two Years Rent they can Patent the same Quantity of Land, there is but one thing that at present seems to favour the Settling the Kanhawa Lands and that in my opinion is Mr Lewis Building a Town at the Mouth thereof,[2] I thought surely to have had a Tenant on the Great Meadows but am disappointed Mr Johnson who was about taking it when you was out here was the Person whom I cheifly depended on Indeed I ventured to make him an Offer of one Year more than what you thought was Sufficient for making repairs & Buildings but it would not do, so that in short I have not one Place Occupyed more than when you was out last fall.[3]

I have also taken what care and Industry I could to get the Mill Rented on some Terms but cannot, I have had Thomas Maire in her on the share but she scarcely goes at all and keeps falling down, I am forced as the last expedient to Advertise for Undertakers and shall have the meeting the first of next Month, tho' from Circumstances am of Opinion I shall not get any to undertake it; I have made what Enquiry amongst workmen I conveniently could what the rebuilding & Repairs would amount to, and they are various being from 250£ to 600£ if when I meet there should be none Offer for less than Six five four or three Hundred I shall do nothing in it untill I hear further from you as I am Convinced that the Money will never be made by the Mill before new repairs will be wanting again.[4]

The Tract of Land Lying in this County[5] is Settled as when you left it save that William Tyler moved away this Spring and I have got in his place one John Craig I have demanded the Rents as I thought due from the different Tenants but they deny there is any due on Account of your making a new Contract, that they agreed with you in taking the late Leases on this footing that all arrears whatever was done away before they agreed to take their Leases on the Present time & Rent, I should have tryed the matter with them but Expected you out here yourself, some of them have already advised With a Lawyer, however I intend to try it with them Imediately, I expect to see Mr Smith in Beeson Town next Term, (and I hope by that time to give him some Information relating the Lands in Washington County,) as far as I can understand by others the Tenants in general on this Land will remove of this fall or next spring.

I understand by Mr Simpson that he cannot stay on the present Rent the Seasons being difficult and the Rent so high, however he says if he should remove he will give timely notice that any Person may have time to Seed down this fall all his Corn Ground and other Grounds that may be desired for Seeding by the Person coming on the Place, he likewise request you will be kind Enough to write how the Public accounts stand that you look for him & John John[son] and wether they will be good against their Bonds.[6]

The above is as near the State of your Affairs in this quarter as Possible, The Hay is all unsold but about 1200 lb. the Corn all on hand but 4 Bushells, the wheat likewise, the Rye I took myself I thought I could by getting it distilled sell it, but there is no Market this Season at all, however I shall make out Pay for the Rye at any rate, what Corn was made by the Mill I Sold, the greater part, which does not amount to thirty Bushells, this is a disagreeable but true Return.

If your Interest & Inclination should lead you to this Country any time this Season I should be happy in seeing you, if not I beg your Assistance in a Line or two if you should wish any thing done Contrary to my Present Proceedings.

I heartily Congratulate you on your safe Return from this Quarter last fall had you Proceeded on your Tour down the River I believe it would have been attended with the most dreadfull Consequences the Indians by what means I can't say had Intelligence of your Journey and Laid wait for you, Genl Wilkinson fell in their Hands and was taken for you and with much difficulty of Persuasion & Gifts got away this is the Common Report, & I believe the Truth.[7]

I Received a Letter from Mr Richd J. ⟨Waters⟩ falls of Ohio dated 18th April 1785 which says the Southern Indians are more troublesome than ever and Commit daily the most horrid barbarities on the defenceless outsettlers from Garrissons I doubt this will turn out a dreadfull summer of Carnage and destruction, People are so careless & hardy, that the Savage is tempted to do what his natural Ferocity would not prompt him to. &ca.

Several small Companys have this spring gone down the River to make Improvements on the Indians Side and have met with a Repulse, one small Party of five went up Hohockin four of which Returned two of them much wounded & the one Missing they are assured is killed, another Company of Eight went up the Scioto four of which Returned, only, and it is said Several other small Companys have shared the same fate.[8] I have the Honour to be with the Greatest Respect your Excellency's most Obedient Humble Servt

Thomas Freeman

ALS, DLC:GW.

1. Letter not found, but see GW to Freeman, 11 April, and 16 Oct., n.4.

2. When in Pennsylvania in September 1784, GW made the Pennsylvanian Thomas Freeman superintendent of all of his "affairs on the Western Waters in the State of Pennsylvania & Virginia." In his letter of 23 Sept. 1784 appointing Freeman, GW gave him full instructions for renting extensive holdings on the Ohio and Great Kanawha, the tract at Washington's Bottom in Fayette County, Pa., which had been under the management of Gilbert Simpson, Jr., and the 234–acre holding at Great Meadows in Westmoreland County, Pennsylvania. When he wrote his second letter to Freeman, dated 11 April 1785 (see note 1), GW gave him the additional responsibility of securing a renter for the Round Bottom tract, a grant for which GW had secured in October 1784. The Millers Run (or Chartiers Creek) tract, GW's land under dispute in Washington County, Pa., absorbed much of GW's attention in 1785 and 1786, and Freeman's role was largely to give what aid he could to Thomas Smith who as GW's attorney was seeking to eject the people who had settled on the Millers Run land (see Smith to GW, 9 Feb. 1785, editorial note). For later references to Thomas Lewis's plans to build a town at the mouth of the Great Kanawha, see GW to Samuel Purviance, Jr., 10 Mar. 1786, and GW to Thomas Lewis, 25 Dec. 1787.

3. In his letter of 23 Sept. 1784, GW wrote this about his holdings at Great Meadows: "There is a house on the premises—arable land in culture, & meadow inclosed . . . its being an excellent stand for an Inn-keeper, must render it valuable." On 22 Sept. GW wrote Freeman telling him to offer the Great Meadows tract to Jonathan Johnson for $100 per annum subject to certain conditions. In a letter to Tobias Lear, 30 Nov. 1786, GW wrote that at times there had been tenants on the tract but that he had never received any payment for rent. See GW to John Lewis, 14 Feb. 1784, n.2.

4. This was the mill at Washington's Bottom in Fayette County, Pa., that Gilbert Simpson built at great cost to GW. Israel Shreve leased the mill and 600 acres of the Washington's Bottom tract from 1787 until 1794 when he bought all 1,644 acres (see source note, Shreve to GW, 22 June 1785).

5. Freeman is referring to the Washington's Bottom tract in Fayette County, Pennsylvania.

6. Gilbert Simpson continued to live for a time on one of the farms at Washington's Bottom after GW terminated their partnership. For Simpson's decision to leave, see Freeman to GW, 27 July 1785, but see also GW to Freeman, 16 Oct. 1785.

7. GW returned from Pennsylvania in early October after deciding that Indian unrest made it imprudent for him to go down the Ohio River as planned in order to visit his lands on the Great Kanawha. James Wilkinson (1757–1825) made his first trading venture into the Ohio country in 1784, but no record of the young adventurer's having been mistaken for GW and held by the Indians has been found.

8. By the Treaty of Fort McIntosh of 21 Jan. 1785, the United States set the Ohio as a boundary line, affirming that the land beyond the Ohio River should

be held by the Indian tribes and withdrawing protection from any American settlers who encroached.

To William Carmichael

Sir,   Mt Vernon 10th June 1785.

It is with grateful pleasure I sit down to acknowledge the receipt of your favour of the 25th of March covering a triplicate of your letter of the 3d of December (which is the first that has been received), & a copy of the Count of Florida Blanca's note to you.[1]

I feel myself under singular obligation to you sir, as the mean of procuring two Jacks of the first race, to be sent me; but my gratitude for so condescending a mark of esteem from one of the first crowned heads in Europe, calls for a better expression than I have, to make suitable acknowledgements to His Catholic Majesty; especially too as his Majesty's very valuable present was accompanied by a sentiment of approbation which cannot fail of making a lasting impression on my mind, & of becoming very dear to my remembrance.

It is to you Sir, I must stand further indebted for the manner of making known in terms most acceptable, the high sense I entertain of the Kings goodness. The Jacks are not yet arrived, but I hope they soon will, & the accot which you mean to transmit, of the mode of treating them for the propagation of mules, will be equally necessary & acceptable, for my management of them.[2]

Mr Gardoqui is safely arrived at Philada—I have not had the honor of paying my compliments to him; but, as well for the respect I owe his sovereign, & his own great merit, as on acct of your recommendation of him, I shall be happy in every opportunity which shall offer of shewing him all the attention in my power.

Great Britain, viewing with eyes of chagrin & jealousy the situation of this Country, will not, for some time yet if ever, pursue a liberal policy towards it; but unfortunately *for her* the conduct of her ministers defeat their own ends: their restriction of our trade with them, will facilitate the enlargement of Congressional powers in commercial matters, more than half a century wou'd otherwise have effected. The mercantile interests of this Country are uniting as one man, to vest the fœderal Government with ample powers to regulate trade & to counteract the selfish views of other nations: this may be considered as another proof that this Country will ever unite in opposition to unjust or ungenerous measures, whensoever or from whomsoever they are offered. I have the honor to be &c.

G: Washington

LB, DLC:GW.

1. GW received only the third copy of Carmichael's letter of 3 Dec. 1784, which Carmichael included with his letter of 25 Mar. 1785. Floridablanca's letter to Carmichael is dated 24 Nov. 1784 and is printed above as an enclosure in Carmichael's letter to GW of 3 Dec. 1784.

2. For the jacks presented to GW by the king of Spain, see Carmichael to GW, 3 Dec. 1784, n.1.

From Patrick Henry

Dear Sir.   Richmond June 10th 1785

You may remember that when you were at this place, I informed you my Son in Law Mr Fontaine was in Carolina, & that when he returned I would let you know the Situation, in which the Lands near the so. End of the dismal swamp, were. By the best Intelligence I can collect there is near pasquotank River, a few Miles from the Bridge, a pretty considerable Quantity of Swamp now vacant Say 6,000 Acres. Mr Fontaine has located a large Tract, near 10,000 acres I think, for himself & his Friends, of which I am to have abt 1/6th. I beleive that which is to be had now is of the same quality or value.

The Terms on which the vacant Grounds are taken up, are 10£ per hundred payable in Cash or Certificates for specie Debts due from the State. These Certificates are to be had for half a Dollar for one pound—The other Charges are low. I mean the Entrytakers, Surveyors & Secretarys Fees.[1]

I find the Lebanon Company hold their Lands higher than I informed you. Lands near thiers & not better, nor perhaps so good, are at a Dollar per Acre. I suppose a Hope of seeing a navigable Canal to Virga somewhere in that Neighbourhood, has enhanced them.

Mr Andrews & Mr Ronald two of our Comrs for viewing & reporting the proper place for the Canal, have been with me lately. The former, who has spent much Time in traversing that Country is of Opinion, the most proper Direction for the Canal is thro' the dismal Swamp—If you would wish to know the Substance of the Report I shall certainly give it you when it comes in.[2]

It will give me great pleasure to render you any acceptable Service. If I can serve you in Carolina or elsewhere, I beg you will command me without any Reserve. With sincere Attachment I am dear sir your affectionate humble Servant

P. Henry

ALS, DLC:GW.

1. John Fontaine (1750–1795), of Henry County, was married to Patrick Henry's daughter Martha. GW promptly declined the invitation to participate in the scheme of Fontaine and Henry to acquire Dismal Swamp land in North Carolina, but among Henry's extensive landholdings at his death was that in North Carolina held in partnership with Fontaine, George Elliot, and Bartholomew Dandridge (Meade, *Henry*, 2:316).

2. GW was a leading figure in efforts dating back to the 1760s to develop the Great Dismal Swamp, and he was keenly interested in the report being prepared on the feasibility of the Elizabeth River Canal. See GW to Henry, 24 June, 30 Nov. 1785, and Henry to GW, 11 Nov. 1785, especially note 2, and 18 Jan. 1786. See also Thomas Walker to GW, 24 Jan. 1784, for a brief description of GW's involvement in the Dismal Swamp Company, and see the resolution of the Virginia assembly printed as Enclosure III in James Madison to GW, 9 Jan. 1785. Robert Andrews and David Meade made the report to the assembly on the proposed Elizabeth River Canal, which is printed in note 2 of Henry's letter of 11 November. Andrews, Meade, and William Ronald, like GW, were all members of the Dismal Swamp Company.

To Willing, Morris, & Swanwick

Gentn,   Mt Vernon 10th June 1785.

No such person as Mr Lang being in my employ, & having no knowledge of such a character *myself*, I detained the letter to him until I could make some enquiries of others: these proving fruitless, you will receive under cover, the letter which was committed to my care. with esteem I am, Gentn Yrs &c.

G: Washington

LB, DLC:GW.

John Swanwick (1740–1798) had been a clerk in the firm of (Thomas) Willing & (Robert) Morris before becoming a partner in the Philadelphia firm in September 1783. The forwarded letter has not been identified.

To William Goddard

sir,   Mt Vernon 11th June 1785.

On the 8th inst: I received the favor of your letter of the 30th of May: In answer to it I can only say, that your own good judgement must direct you in the publication of the manuscript papers of Genl Lee—I can have no request to make concerning the work.

I never had a difference with that Gentleman but on public ground, & my conduct towards him upon this occasion, was such only, as I conceived myself indispensably bound to adopt in discharge of the public trust reposed in me. If this produced in him unfavourable sentiments of me, I yet can never consider the conduct I pursued, with respect to him, either wrong or improper; however I may regret that it may have been differently viewed by him, & that it excited his censure and animadversions. Should there appear in Genl Lee's writings anything injurious or unfriendly to me, the impartial & dispassionate world, must decide how far I deserved it from the general tenor of my conduct.[1]

I am gliding down the stream of life, & wish as is natural, that my remaining Days may be undisturbed and tranquil; & conscious of my integrity, I would willingly hope that nothing would occur tending to give me anxiety; but should anything present itself in this or in any other publication, I shall never undertake the painful task of recrimination—nor do I know that I shall even enter upon my justification.

I consider the communication you have made as a mark of great attention, & the whole of your letter as a proof of your esteeem. I am &c.

                                        G: Washington

LB, DLC:GW.

1. See Goddard to GW, 30 May, and notes 1 and 2 of that document.

From George Walton

Sir,   Savannah, 11 June, 1785.

I recollect, that, in the autumn of 1776, when the armies which contended for the Empire of the new Hemisphere viewed each other on the peninsula of Haarlem, you spoke to me particularly of Capt. McKay, who, in a former war for the same object, had shared the dangers and glory of some critical situations with your Excellency. This worthy and respectable old gentleman, now makes a tour to the Northward; and I think principally to pay his respects to the man whom he has such just and honorable cause to remember.[1]

It gives me, too, the oppertunity of congratulating you, tho late, upon the happy, perfect and splendid close of the war which the fates imposed upon you to conduct thro' Superior difficulties. And, as it will be always, no doubt, a high gratification to your feelings, to See the effects of the Revolution prosperous and in order, it also gives me the occasion to assure you, that, whatever may have happened, or later calumnies taken place, this State is in the most flourishing condition, and its government, in all its departments, in system, harmony and efficiency. In viewing its advantages the mind opens into expansity.[2]

I beg, Sir, my particular respects to Mrs Washington. With regard to yourself, we were flattered, some time ago, with seeing you this way: whenever that shall take place, none will be more happy than, Sir, Your most obedient, and very humble Servt

Geo. Walton

ALS, PHi: Gratz Collection.

1. George Walton (c.1750–1804) arrived in Philadelphia in June 1776 as a delegate to the Continental Congress from Georgia and served until October 1777. The *Virginia Journal and Alexandria Advertiser* noted on 1 Dec. 1785: "DIED: In this Town, on his way to Mount-Vernon, JAMES MACKAY Esq; of the State of Georgia, a Native of Scotland." James Mackay, who was an officer in Georgia under James Oglethorpe in the 1730s and 1740s, became captain of one of the South Carolina independent companies in 1749, and he and his company were with GW at the capitulation of Fort Necessity in 1754 (see *Papers, Colonial Series*, 1:passim).

2. Walton at this time was chief justice of Georgia, having triumphed over his bitter political enemy, Gen. Lachlan McIntosh.

From Barbé-Marbois

Sir, Newyork June 12th 1785.

I beg leave to trouble your Excellency about the request of Msr de Corny a gentleman who in the character of a commissary general preceeded the French army in the year 1780. the ⟨5⟩th of June of the Same year congress resolved *that a brevet commission of lieutenant of Cavalry be granted to Msr Louis Ethis de Corny*. Msr de Corny has been Since employed in the service of both armies either here or in france to procure & forward their Supplies: he now is commissary general of the Suiss infantry in france.[1] he informs me that he is desirous to be a member of the cincinnati Society in the State where your Excellency reside, & he has Send to me his quota of the Subscription according to his rank: I take the liberty to Send to you his bill—due Mr Wadsworth for the amount. you'll excuse me, sir for troubling you about this affair: I would not have done it if I had had the honour to be acquainted with the officers of the Society in Virginia.[2]

According to very late intelligence from Europe the Emperor —impressed with the danger of staying alone of his party, seems desirous to compromise the matter. there is little doubt but we Should Support the Dutch in case they were attacked.

Mr Gardochi is not yet arrived. Congress are uncertain what reception to make to him—as his character of a *Chargé des affaires plenipotentiaire* is a novelty in the diplomatic Style. There is no doubt, however that he will be made an Envoy as soon as the States Shall have resolved to Send one to Spain.

The governor of georgia informed the delegates of the States that there has been an encounter between the Spaniards at fort natchez & the inhabitants there, & that persons have been Killed on both Sides.[3]

No determination about the 2d Treaty with the indians. Congress cannot come to a resolution as to the funds: there are eight States & two half States who are for providing all necessary expences; but it is Said Some individuals are opposed to this measure from private motives.[4] With great respect, I have the honour to be sir your Excellency's Very humble obedient servant

De Marbois

I have been told that Msr de Corny on advice of Some of the members of the society in france has taken the insignia of the order, as they Saw no doubt of his being a member in consequence of his commission.

ALS, DLC:GW.

François Barbé-Marbois (Barbé de Marbois) had been French chargé d'affaires in Philadelphia since June 1784.

1. Dominique-Louis Ethis de Corny (1736–1790) held a commission in the American army in 1781 and 1782.

2. GW responded to this letter on 21 June, promising to attend to the matter for Corny promptly, but he did not write George Weedon about Corny until 23 July. Weedon wrote GW on 10 Aug. that he had taken care of it.

3. See Gov. Samuel Elbert (1740–1788) to President of Congress, 5 May 1785 (DNA:PCC, item 73).

4. Barbé-Marbois is referring to Congress's passage on 6 June of the resolution: "That the commissioners instructed to hold a treaty under the resolutions of the 18 of March last, with the western tribes of Indians, at post St. Vincent, on the 20 day of June, for the purpose of obtaining from them a cession of lands, be, and they are hereby authorized and directed, to avail themselves of the disposition of the Indians and the funds committed to their charge, to make such cession as extensive and liberal as possible" (*JCC*, 28:431).

From Alexandre de Gubian

My General   Marseilles 13th June 1785

I take the liberty of giving you an account of my Services, for to beg of Your Excellence to Grant me, what my Companions have obtain'd; Having been embarked aboard the King's Ship, the Scipion, In the Army of Mr the Compte de Grasse, Whilst we were in the Chessapeak, That General gave me charge of the Correspondence, with the Camp, by the Back River, & I Continued in that Situation, all the time of the Siege. After the Capitulation of York; I had the Honour of carrying you, with a Boat of the Back River, aboard the Ville de Paris, with Monsr de Rochambeau, the Marquiss de la fayette, Mr Laurence, the Comte Chatus, & the Comte De la Valle.[1]

I have been Sufficiently happy, to have Saved from the Hands of Our Ennemy's, a Brigantine of your Nation, Bound to Port au Prince, during the time I Commanded an advice Boat of the Kings, The St Louis Station'd at St Dominique Destined to Conduct the Ships of your Nation, Spanish & French, from the Cape, or Mole of St Nicolas, to Port au Prince. If I Could be Sufficiently happy, Great Genl that these little Services, could make me obtain of you the Honourable Cross of St Singnatus, It would be adding those Marks of Distinguish'd Honour, of a Good Officer, of which you have been, the True Pattern.[2] I am with the most Profound Respect—My General Your Very Humble & Very Obedt Servant—

Alexander De Gubian
formerly Lieutenant of Marselle Frigatte

Translation, DLC:GW; ALS, in French, DLC:GW.

Gubian may have been the *lieutenant de frégate* aboard *Le Scipion* in de Grasse's squadron listed as "Gubriant" (*Les combattants français de la guerre américaine, 1778–1783* [Paris, 1903], 112).

1. In an entry in his diary for 21 Oct. 1781, two days after Cornwallis's capitulation, GW wrote: "Set out for the Fleet to pay my respects, & offer my thanks to the Admiral" (*Diaries*, 3:433).

2. GW responded in these terms from Mount Vernon on 20 Nov.: "I have had the honor to receive your favor of the 13th of June from Marseilles. If the right of admitting Members into the order, or Society of the Cincinnati rested with me, I should be happy in adding to its number a gentleman of your merit. But as this is not the case, & as a Society is established in France, at the head of which the Counts de Estaing & Rochambeau are placed—to examine the pretentions of gentlemen of your nation—I beg leave to refer you to it, where I am persuaded your services & merits will have the weight they deserve" (LB, DLC:GW).

From William Goddard

Sir, Baltimore, June 14th 1785.

I have now the Honour to present you with a Copy of the proposals, for publishing Miscellaneous Collections of General Lee's Papers, agreeable to my last.[1] I hope it will come safe to your hands; and am most respectfully, Your Excellency's most obedient & very humble Servant

William Goddard

ALS, DLC:GW.

1. Goddard enclosed his printed *Proposals for Printing by Subscription* of Charles Lee's papers, dated 10 June 1785 at Baltimore. The prospectus included the statement that the three volumes would be sent to the press "as soon as a competent Number of Subscribers can be obtained." The price was to be one guinea, one-half guinea to be paid upon subscription and the other one-half upon delivery of the volumes. The *Proposals* notes: "The most difficult Task the Editors met with in collecting and arranging these posthumous Papers, arose from their Desire of not giving Offence to such Characters as had

been the Object of the General's Aversion and Resentment. Unhappily his Disappointments had soured his Temper; the Affair of *Monmouth*, several Pieces of Scurrility from the Press, and numerous Instances of private Slander and Defamation, so far got the better of his Philosophy, as to provoke him in the highest Degree, that he became, as it were, angry with all Mankind.

"To this exasperated Disposition we may impute the Origin of his *Political Queries*, and a Number of satirical Hints, thrown out both in his Conversation and Writing, against the Commander in Chief. Humanity will draw a Veil over the involuntary Errors of Sensibility, and pardon the Sallies of a suffering Mind, as its Presages did not meet with an Accomplishment. General *Washington*, by his Retirement, demonstrated to the World, that Power was not his Object; that *America* had nothing to fear from his Ambition; but that she was honoured with a Specimen of such exalted Patriotism, as could not fail to attract the Attention and Admiration of the most distant Nations." Subscriptions were to be paid at Goddard's printing shop in Baltimore or to the printers Frederick Green at Annapolis and George Richards at Alexandria (*Maryland Journal* [Baltimore], 15 July 1785). Not enough people subscribed to make publication feasible.

From William Minor

Sir   Alexandria. 14th June 1785
Your Letter of the 27th May was Duly recd am perfectly Satisfied with your Generous offcr of Leaving this Affair to any Disinterested person whom I may Choose. I have Laid my Papers before Several But Cannot get any Gentl[ema]n to give an Opinion in Writing about the Matter. they Say ware your Excellency to ask it of them they wou'd Gladly do what they thought wright but not Otherwise. but it Seems to be the General Oppinion of all that I have Spoke to that in Justice & Humanity I ought to Receive Something. at Least the difference between Six pounds Nineteen shillings & Sixpence[,] the Sum you pay Baker[,] and Seventeen pounds. as I was Brought into this Expence intirely in Consequence of your Letter—I cannot think your Excellency bound to pay Any thing More but am Satisfied the Articles of Cloathing was furnish'd at my Own Risque. but at the Same time for a Motive as I then thought to Oblige you. I shall be Satisfied with this Sum. Or if your Excellency will be Pleased to Say who you wou'd be willing to Leave the Matter too & Signify the Same to him or them. I will Lay my Papers & your Letters before them. & get a Decided Opinion in Writing, which I will deliver or Cause to be deliver'd to your Excellency, which Shall Put a

final end to this Bussiness.[1] Your Condecending to give me an immediate Answer will Conferr a great Obligation on sir, your Excellencys mo. Obedt & mo. hble servt

Wm Minor

ALS, DLC:GW.

    1. See GW to Minor, 16 June.

To Châteaufort

Sir,   Mount Vernon 15th June 1785.

    By the Post I had the honor to receive the letter which you did me the favor to write to me on the 19th of last month, together with those of the Chevr De la Luzerne & the Baron de Viominel. I pray you to be assured Sir, that I shall have great pleasure in seeing you at this Seat on your way to Charleston. Your own merit is sufficient *alone* to entitle you to every attention from me; but the letters above mentioned, bring with them the force of Law.[1] I have the honor to be &c.

G: Washington

LB, DLC:GW.

    1. Châteaufort's letter has not been found, but on 5 Sept. 1785 GW acknowledged the receipt of Vioménil's letter enclosed in Châteaufort's and the receipt of letters from La Luzerne dated 20 Dec. 1784, 15 Feb. 1785, and 25 Mar. 1785. La Luzerne's letter of 20 Dec. 1784 is a letter introducing the chevalier de Châteaufort, who was coming to America as French consul for the Carolinas and Georgia; this is presumably the letter to which GW is referring here. On 5 Sept. 1785 GW responds to Vioménil's missing letter in this way: "Every occasion which presents you to me, & assures me of your health, cannot fail to give me pleasure: your letter therefore by Mr de Chateaufort did me honor & was flattering; & I should have been very happy in an opportunity of testifying to that Gentleman the respect I wished to shew to your recommendation & his own merits; but being longer delayed with Congress than he expected, added to the heat of the weather; he found it more convenient to pass from Philada to Charleston by water, than by Land; by which means I had not the honor of seeing him" (LB, DLC:GW).

To Robert Howe

Dr Sir,   Mount Vernon 15th June 1785.

A few days ago Mr Sitgreaves gave me the pleasure of receiving your letter of the 4th of May. It is the only one I recollect to have had from you since my return to private life.

It gives me pleasure to hear that Congress have dealt honorably by you, & mean to do more; it is devoutly to be wished that they could do the same by all the Officers whose meritorious services & sufferings have a just claim upon their gratitude, & call loudly for their exertions.

As you are at the source of intelligence, any thing I could say respecting foreign matters, would only be a reverberation of intelligence; & few things occur of a domestic nature worthy of recital. Mrs Washington is in tolerable good health & joins me in Compliments & best wishes for you, Mr Lots family, & others of our old acquaintance.[1] I am Dr Sir &c.

G: Washington

LB, DLC:GW.

1. In July 1777 GW had his headquarters at the house of Abraham Lott "8 Miles East of Morris Town" (GW to Daniel Morgan, 26 July 1777).

From Battaile Muse

Honourable Sir   June 15th 1785

I was so unfortunate Some time ago as to Loose Mr Whiting Replevey Bonds due you—since which I have obtained a replevey Bond for £199.8.0 with Interest there on from the Twenty fifth day of December Last[.] Mr Whiting has Promised to Confess a Judgement in Berkeley Court next Tuesday on my staying Execution untill September[.] the sheriff of Berkeley Mr James Crane has Promised to Pay the Money in September Next —you may be assured that I will recover the Money for you as soon as Possable.[1] I am sir your Most Obedient Humble servant

Battaile Muse

ALS, DLC:GW.

1. In the issue of the *Virginia Journal and Alexandria Advertiser* of 5 May, Battaile Muse entered a notice dated 3 May that the evening before there had "DROPPED from my servant's horse, at the Bridge near the Church, about

eight o'clock last evening, a pair of black SADDLE-BAGS with an iron lock, which contained a number of bonds, receipts, and other papers in a red pocket-book . . ." He noted: "Among the number of bonds there are two replevy bonds, given by Mr. Henry Whiting to His Excellency George Washington, one for £.159 8s. the other for £.50."

To Samuel Powel

Dear Sir,   Mount Vernon 15th June 1785.

I have been honoured with your favour of the 25th of April, but have not yet had the pleasure to see Doctr Moyes—On the 22d Instt I shall look for him—I pray you to be assured that, it is unnecessary for you to apologize to me for the introduction of any Gentleman of whom you entertain a favourable opinion; for, such as you may conceive to be worthy of my civilities, will always meet a ready reception at Mount Vernon.[1]

I shall now, my good Sir, give you a little trouble.

A Gentleman whose person, whose name, and whose character are equally unknown to me, has written me the inclosed letter; to which, as yet, I have made no reply. The work, if well executed, would unquestionably be valuable; & ought to be encouraged: but the abilities of the Author I am a stranger to; and it has been too often found, that similar attempts by persons whose reputations are not established in the literary world, are either founded in ignorance—or end in imposition. to encourage the first, or give sanction to the latter, would be alike disagreeable to me. I would beg therefore, if it is not likely to be attended with much trouble, that you would be so obliging as to give me your own, and the Sentiments of others on the Author, & his performance; that I may be enabled to decide properly with respect to his request.[2]

My respectful Compliments & best wishes, in which Mrs Washington join, are presented to Mrs Powel, and yourself. I am—Dear Sir Yr Most Obedt Hble Servt

G: Washington

ALS, ViMtV; LB, DLC:GW.

1. Powel wrote GW on 25 April introducing Dr. Henry Moyes (Moyse). See note 1 of that document.

2. The enclosed letter was from Charles Vancouver to GW, 10 May 1785.

See Powel's response to GW, 24 June, and GW's letter of 30 June to Vancouver declining to allow him to dedicate his proposed publication to him.

To Edmund Richards

Sir,   Mt Vernon June 15th 1785.
Your letter of the 1st of Feby from Plymouth Dock, came safe.[1] In explicit terms I assure you, that the information which I suppose you must have received respecting a Will, & the Plantations of a Mr Richd Richards, is without the smallest foundation. I never heard of the man, his Will, or the Estate which you say was left in my hands, until your letter reached me: equally unacquainted am I with Lawyer Haines or Lawr Briton, consequently can give you no satisfaction in any of the matters requested of me.

If any such event as you speak of ever did happen with any of my name, it is unknown to me—it is not in my power therefore to give you any clue by which you may pursue your enquiries, or I would do it with pleasure. I am &c.

G: Washington

LB, DLC:GW.
1. See also GW's correspondence with Richard Thomas, an attorney in Charleston, S.C., regarding Richards's claims: Richard Thomas to GW, 13 Aug. 1785, GW to Thomas, 5 Dec. 1785, and Thomas to GW, 10 Dec. 1785, 25 July 1786.

To Michael Jenifer Stone

Mount Vernon 15th June 1785
I have ⟨re⟩ceived your letter of the 3d Instt, and have sent it to Mr Hartshorne the Company's Treasurer for Entry—he being authorized by the Board of Directors to receive Subscriptions until the deficiency is made up.

The 15th of next ⟨Mon⟩th, or before, the Sum of five pounds on each share ⟨is⟩ to be paid to the Treasurer, and on or before the first day of October next, the further Sum of Fifty shillings on each share is likewise to be paid to him.[1] I am Sir Yr Most Obedt Servt

Go: Washington

ALS, owned (1990) by Mrs. Robert B. Carney, Washington, D.C.

1. See the minutes of the meeting of the president and directors of the Potomac River Company printed in note 4, GW to James Rumsey, 5 June.

To William Minor

Sir,   Mt Vernon 16th June 1785.

Your letter of the 14th is this moment delivered to me. Moral obligations, or the obligations of humanity are equally binding on all men: if motives of humanity therefore induced me to bestow a years schooling on Lawce Posey, & to effect it I was willing to incur the expence of a years board also; the same motives might have induced you, without making a charge of it against me, to have acted a similar part in other respects by the boy; for sure I am, my connexion with him was not stronger, nor legal nor honorary obligation greater on me than on any other mans to excite them. Schooling, I reiterate in this letter, as I urged in my former, was my object; consequently, if he did not go to the Free school in Queen Anne, (the place designed) as you yourself acknowledged to me, nor to any other School—for what purpose let me ask was I to pay £17? Was not his Fathers house, if time was to be misspent, the best place for him to waste it in? Can it be supposed I ever had it in contemplation to board him out for the purpose of idleness? If then the conditions of my letter to Mr Baker were never complied with, as you candidly confessed to me they were not when here, where is the justice of requiring £17—or an iota of it from me, when the compensation was expressly stipulated? But I will be done. I am too much engaged in company & in business to go further into the detail of this matter.

If Genl Robardeau (whom you mentioned to me yourself in a former letter) will be so obliging as to undertake to determine the point, I shall be perfectly satisfied with his decision. I shall expect however that both this letter, & my former to you which was directed to his care, and such papers as you exhibited to me, will be laid before him—one of which certified that Lawce Posey was not at the Free school: another, in effect that your charge was antecedent to the date of my letter to Mr Baker—& a third, from Capt. Posey to you, which will serve to proove that he was a House-Keeper at Rovers-delight (as he call'd his place) at the time you want me to pay you for the boy's board, & when he was not at school, nor ever derived the benefit which was the object of my benevolence.[1] I am Sir—&c.

G: Washington

LB, DLC:GW.
1. See Minor to GW, 24 May, n.1, and Daniel Roberdeau to GW, 17 June. GW's most recent letter to Minor is dated 27 May.

From Daniel Roberdeau

Alexandria June 17th 1785

The request you made of me in a letter to Wm Minor I instantly obeyed as a command, and have now the happiness to inform your Excellency, that the last Evening I convinced him of his indecency in making any demand of you, particularly in refusing your generosity in the offer of a ballance to which he had no claim, but from that principle, and for which he would consider himself obliged.[1] I am much more obliged by this opportunity afforded of testifying my ready obedience to your commands, as an obligation conferred, which will be heightened by every intimation of your pleasure whenever and however the occasion may offer of signifying the ineffable regard I have for your Person and Character, as a pepper corn of acknowledgment of the obligations by which I am bound ever to be Your Excellencys most grateful and obedient humble Servant

Daniel Roberdeau

ALS, DLC:GW.
1. See GW to William Minor, 16 June.

To Henry Knox

My dear Sir   Mount Vernon 18th June 85

I am quite ashamed to be so long deficient in acknowledging the receipt of your favors of the 24th & 29th of March, and 5th of May; but an intervention of circumstances (with the enumeration of which I shall not trouble you) have prevented it.

It gave me great pleasure to hear of your appointment as Secretary at War—without a complimt, I think a better choice could not have been made—and though the Salary is low, it may, under the circumstances you mention, be considered as auxiliary.

Inclosed is a certificate of Service for Major Sergeant, of whose worth I have a high opinion; but for want of a more competent knowledge of the time of his entering the line of the Army, and of the Commissions he has borne, I could not be more particular.[1]

At any time this Summer, the Limestone would be useful to me; but the sooner it comes the greater benefit I shall derive from it, as the Walls for which I want it, are now in hand.[2]

The sentiment which you have dropped respecting the appropriation of the shares which were intended for me, by the Assembly of this State, in the Navigations of the Rivers Potomack & James, is very pleasing; and would give me great pleasure to see it reallized.

For want of a competent view of the designs of Congress respecting the Western Territory; and not knowing how matters stand with Great Britain, respecting the Posts of Detroit & other places at present occupied by British Garrisons, on the American side of the Line; I feel an unfitness to answer your question respecting such Posts as may be proper for the purposes mentioned; but under the ideas I hold at prest, I am inclined to think that if Garrisons are to be established within the limits & jurisdiction of any of the 13 States, that Fort Pitt, or Fort McIntosh, which ever shall be found most convenient and in best repair, would suit very well for a Post of deposits; from whence *all* the others should be supplied. and as it is my opinion that great part of the Fur & Peltry of the Lakes (when we shall have free access to them) will be transported by the Cayahoga and big beaver Creek, a Post at the Mouth of, or at some convenient Port on the former, must be eligable. The spot marked Miami Village & Fort in Hutchins's Map, I have always considered as of importance, being a central point between Lake Erie, Lake Michigan, & the river Ohio; communicating with each by Water. To these the Falls of the Ohio, or some more convenient spot for the lower settlements, may be added. Whether this chain embraces territory enough, whether it goes far enough to the Southward to afford protection to the back parts of Virginia the Carolinas and Georgia—or whether these are objects which are meant to be comprehended, are for those who are more behind the Curtain than I am, to determine. My opinion of the matter is, that I have described a sufficient extent of Country to answer all our *present* purposes; beyond which, neither Settlements nor Locations of Land ought to be admitted; because a larger would open a more extensive field for Land jobbers & Speculators—Weaken our Frontiers—exclude Law, good government, & taxation to a later period—and injure the union very essentially in many respects. At the conflux of the Great Kanhawa & Ohio, a Post might be established so as to answer benificial purposes. Indeed it is the opinion of many, that it is a more eligable place than Pittsburgh. In time, if the Navigation of the Kanhawa should be extended, & an easy communication opened with James River, it may be so; but in the present state of things, considering the Settlements about the latter, & the sources from whence proceed all the Supplies of that Country, it certainly is not. As a protection of the River—& the movements thereon, it is desirable.

If I am right in my principles some such distribution as the following may not be ineligable for the 700 men which are ordered to be raised.

	Men
At Fort Pitt, Fort McIntosh, or the Mouth of big Beaver (being in the vicinity of a thick settlemt only—	100.
Cayahoga, from whence a Detachment might occupy the Carrying place between that water & big Beaver; being on the line, & most exposed, should have	200.
Miami Fort or Village, and Dependences—D[itt]o D[itt]o	200
At the Falls of the Ohio, or some spot more convt & healthy, on that river	150.
At the Conflux of the Great Kanhawa & Ohio for security of the River—protection of Trade, & covering emigrants	50
Total	700.

Mrs Macauly Graham and Mr Graham, and others, have just left this, after a stay of about 10 days. A Visit from a Lady so celebrated in the Literary world could not but be very flattering to me. Mrs Washington joins me in best wishes for yourself, Mrs Knox and family; with great truth & sincerity I am My dear Sir Yr Most Obedt & Affecte Hble Servt

Go: Washington

ALS, MHi: Knox Papers; LB, DLC:GW.

1. GW's certificate for Winthrop Sargent is dated 18 June. It reads: "I certify that Major Winthrop Sergeant, lately an Officer in the line of Artillery and Aid de Camp to Major General Howe, has served with great reputation in the Armies of the United States of America. That he entered into the Service of his Country at an early period of the War, and during the continuance of it, displayed a zeal, integrity & intelligence which did honor to him as an Officer, & Gentleman" (owned [1991] by Mr. Joseph Rubinfine, West Palm Beach, Fla.).

2. For Knox's attempts to secure lime for GW, see GW to Knox, 5 Jan. 1785, n.6.

From Robert Hanson Harrison

Dr Sir,   Nanjemoy [Md.] June 20th 1785

After returning home last week, the difficulties of your situation presenting themselves very strongly to me, I cast about in my mind for a person who might relieve you in some degree from the load of business which oppresses you.[1] The result was, I could not recollect one I thought would suit. I saw a friend of mine two or three days after, whom I asked if he was acquainted with such a character as I described. He obligingly told me he would reflect upon the subject—that he was going to por-tobacco, and if he could think or hear properly of One, that he would mention him to me. I now inform your Excellency that it has been reported to me, that Mr Wm Briscoe, who will have the honor of presenting this, and who is desirous of being of your family, is a discreet, diligent, sensible and amiable Young gentleman—of a good country grammar education—and possesses besides, a pretty good knowledge of Accounts & book-keeping.[2] I have had myself but a slight acquaintance with Mr Briscoe, by reason of my absence & our being since I came here, some distance apart, and therefore cannot undertake to say that he would answer your Excellency's views; but from the little opportunity I have had of being acquainted with him, he has appeared sensible & gentlemanny, and from the favourable sentiments entertained of him by Others, who have had it in their power to know him, I should hope, should he become one of your family, that he would prove agreable to your Excellency and contribute in no inconsiderable degree to your relief & ease. From Mr Briscoe's youth, he may not have been much employed in Letter writing, but if he possesses the education and diligence it is said he does, he may be able in a little time, to take a good deal of the drudgery in common cases off your hands.

Before I conclude I would mention that Mr Briscoe stands distantly related to myself & more nearly still to Mrs Harrison; but I would willingly hope that your Excellency, from your knowledge of me, will be persuaded, should You & Mr Briscoe agree—and he unfortunately not answer your expectations, that these considerations of themselves had not the least operation in my mind upon the present occasion, and that it is my most earnest wish that they may not have any sort of influence upon your own conduct with respect either to taking or continuing him in your service. I write of him from the knowledge & report of others, more than from any knowledge I possess of him myself—and I introduce him to the honor of your acquaintance, not because he is connected with me; but because he is well spoken of, and as a character that may serve your Excellency pretty well, which seems to be much his wish. I pray You to present me most respectfully to Mrs Washington—Miss Basset & the Major —and to believe that I am Dr Sir, with the truest attachment and respect Yr friend & Hb. servt

Rob: H: Harrison

ALS, DLC:GW.

1. Robert Hanson Harrison (1745–1790), at this time living in Nanjemoy, Charles County, Md., spent the weekend of 11 to 13 June at Mount Vernon.

2. When William Briscoe arrived on 23 June with Harrison's letter, GW told Briscoe he would take "8 or 10 days to give him a definitive answer" (*Diaries*, 4:155). Two days before, Thomas Montgomerie of Dumfries had written GW recommending William Shaw, the man he ended up hiring as his secretary instead of Briscoe. See GW to Harrison, 3 July.

Letter not found: to Benjamin Stoddert, 20 June. Stoddert on 21 June wrote GW: "I am honored with your favor of yesterday."

To Barbé-Marbois

Sir,   Mount Vernon June 21st 1785.
The last Post brought me the honor of your favor of the 12th—I am made happy by occasions which induce you to write to me—and shall take pleasure in rendering Mr De Corney any

service in my power. I will immediately inform myself of the name, & residence of the Treasurer of the Society of the Cincinnati of this State, and transmit Mr De Corney's Bill on Colo. Wadsworth, to him.

I am greatly obliged to you, Sir, for the several communications of your letter—I wish disagreeable consequences may not result from the contentions respecting the Navigation of the River Mississippi—The emigrations to the Waters thereof, are astonishingly great; and chiefly from a description of people who are not very subordinate to Law & good Government. Whether the prohibition from the Court of Spain is just or unjust—politic or otherwise; it will be difficult to restrain a people of this class from the enjoyment of natural advantages. It is devoutly to be wished that Mr Gardoqui would enter into such stipulations with Congress as may avert the impending evil, & be mutually advantageous to both nations.

After the explicit declarations of the Emperor, respecting the Navigation of the Scheldt, and his other demands upon Holland, he will stand I think, upon unfavorable ground;[1] for if he recedes, his foresight & judgment may be arraigned—and if he proceeds, his ruin may be involved. But possibly I am hazarding sentiments upon a superficial view of things, when it will appear, ultimately, that he has had important objects in view, and has accomplished them.

I take the liberty of addressing the inclosed letter to your care & to assure you of the respect and esteem with which I have the honor to be, Sir, Yr Most Obedt Hble Sv⟨t⟩

Go: Washington

ALS, owned (1991) by Mr. Kenneth W. Rendell, Inc., Wellesley, Mass.; LB, DLC:GW.

1. As an example of how GW's clerks often changed GW's language, usually not for the better, Bartholomew Dandridge years later when making the letterbook copy expanded GW's "he will stand I think, upon unfavorable ground" to read: "it should seem I think, as if he stood in a predicament not very desirable."

From Thomas Montgomerie

Dear Sir   Dumfries 21st June 1785

It was not long after I parted with you at Mount Vernon, that I recollected a person (but a few days arrived in this Country) who I think would suit you in the character you mentioned—His name is Mr William Shaw[1]—his Father a Clergyman, not many miles distant from the place of my nativity, well connected and very universally and deservedly respected—he has a large family and to my knowledge they have all turned out well—I was several times in Company with this Young man (who has been used in good Company) when last in Britain, and he is of pleasant conversation and manners—He had an opportunity from his fathers attention and a public education to improve himself in literature, and I believe he is sufficiently informed—He has been bred to business, and was engaged for two or three years in an active business in Canada He is now come out to this Country with a view of pursuing that line, with letters of strong recommendation to me from several of my friends—I have inquired a little into his views and advantages, and am inclined to think he would accept of proposals from you.

When you did me the honor to mention this matter to me at Mount Vernon, I confess I had no Idea that I would have named a person to you equally qualified as Mr Shaw, in fact I did not expect to have had it in my power to name one at all.

If you wish to make any inquiries, or to have any other information than what I have now given, I beg you will state them, it will give me very great pleasure in any way to serve you. If you wish to see and converse with Mr Shaw I can promise he shall wait on you—I have the honor to be with sentiments of regard Dear Sir Your most Obt Humbe Servt

Thos Montgomerie

ALS, DLC:GW.

1. Thomas Montgomerie had dinner at Mount Vernon on Sunday, 19 June. Upon receiving this letter from Montgomerie, GW promptly entered negotiations with William Shaw. He offered Shaw the position of his secretary, and Shaw accepted, beginning work at Mount Vernon on 26 July and remaining for a little over a year. See GW to Montgomerie, 25, 30 June, Montgomerie to GW, 28 June, 1 July, William Shaw to GW, 4, 12 July, and GW to Shaw, 8 July 1785.

From Benjamin Stoddert

Sir   George Town [Md.] 21st June 1785.

I am honored with your favor of yesterday, inclosing an order on Col. Hooe for £70:8:6, for the account forwarded to Col. Charles Washington for cash & goods furnished your Nephews.[1]

I first began to supply them upon the Death of their Guardian Mr Nourse, without any authority, merely because at that time no other person could be instructed to do it, and was far from having any view to advantage in the transaction, & indeed, neither expected, nor wished to continue supplying them longer than 'till arrangements could be made for their accomodation by the Gentleman upon whom the care of them devolved. Under such circumstances, it gives me not a little pain, that the articles in my account should appear to be overcharged, as thence may be inferred an imputation which I am very happy in knowing myself incapable of meritting.[2]

The Young Gentlemen now board with Mr Wm Bailey of this Town, who has a Store—being continually under his Eye, he can much better Judge than I can, what will be really necessary for them—like all Boys, they are apt to want too much—I hope you will approve of my having requested him to accomodate them in future—he agrees to supply what goods they may have, at 125 ₴Ct Maryland, on the cost, something more than 75 in Virga which is lower than I retail goods.[3] I have the honor to be with very great esteem Yr Excellency's most Obedt Servt

Ben Stoddert

ALS, DLC:GW.

Benjamin Stoddert (1751–1813) was a merchant in Georgetown, Md., across the Potomac from Alexandria, in partnership with Uriah Forrest (1756–1805).

1. Letter not found. See Cash Accounts, June 1785 (Ledger B, 203).

2. James Nourse, guardian of GW's nephews George Steptoe Washington and his brother Lawrence Augustine Washington, died in October 1784.

3. For GW's reaction to placing his nephews in the house of William Bailey, see GW to Stephen Bloomer Balch, 26 June. See also GW to William Bailey, 2 August.

To William Grayson

Dr Sir,   Mount Vernon, 22d June 1785.

Since my last to you I have been favored with your letters of the 5th—27th & [   ] of May,[1] & beg your acceptance of my thanks for their enclosures, & for the communications you were pleased to make me therein.

I am very glad to find you have pass'd an Ordinance of Congress respecting the sale of the Western Lands: I am too well acquainted with the local politic's of individual States, not to have foreseen the difficulties you met with in this business; these things are to be regretted, but not to be altered until liberallity of sentiment is more universal. Fixing the Seat of Empire at any spot on the Delaware, is in my humble opinion, demonstrably wrong: to incur an expence for what may be call'd the *permanent* seat of Congress, at this time, is I conceive evidently impolitic; for without the gift of prophecy, I will venture to predict that under any circumstance of confederation, it will not remain so far to the Eastward long; & that until the public is in better circumstances, it ought not to be built at all. Time, too powerful for sophistry, will point out the place & disarm localities of their powers: In the meanwhile let the widow, the Orphan & the suffering Soldier, who are crying to you for their dues, receive *that* which can very well be rendered to them.

There is nothing new in this quarter of an interesting nature, to communicate, unless you should not have been informed that the Potomac navigation proceeds under favourable auspices: At the general meeting of the subscribers in May last, it appeared that upwards of 400 of the 500 shares had been engaged—Many more have been subscribed since—a Board of Directors have been chosen—proper characters & Labourers advertized for, to commence the work in the least difficult parts of the river, 'till a skillful Engineer can be engaged to undertake those which are more so; & it is expected the work will be begun by the 10th of next month. With great esteem & regard I am &c. &c.

G: Washington

LB, DLC:GW.

1. The letter for which GW left blank the day of the month is printed above under the date of 4 May.

From Lamar, Hill, Bisset, & Co.

Sir,   Madeira, 22d June 1785
We have had an order by us from our Henry Hill of Philadelphia ever since November 1783, to ship you a Pipe of fine old Wine for your own use,[1] by any good Vessel bound to Alexandria in Virginia; but none having from that period to the present offered, & being likewise without expectations of any casting up, beg to know if we may send it to Norfolk, where we have a very careful friend, (Doctor James Taylor) who from that place will forward it to you in the most eligible manner.[2] We have the honor to be—Sir Your most obedient humble Servants
                                        Lamar Hill Bisset & Co.

LS, DLC:GW.
    GW began using the wine export company of Hill, Lamar, & Hill to ship him wine from Madeira in 1760 after his marriage to Martha Custis.
    1. Henry Hill (1732–1798), a merchant in Philadelphia and a director of the Bank of North America, was a partner in the Madeira firm of Lamar, Hill, Bisset, & Company. Henry Hill first corresponded with GW regarding wine from Madeira on 22 June 1773. At one time during the Revolution, in 1777, GW had his headquarters in Hill's house.
    2. For GW's receipt of the "Pipe of fine old Wine" and reference to further correspondence regarding it, see Lamar, Hill, Bisset, & Co. to GW, 20 Aug. 1785, n.1. James Taylor began practicing medicine in Norfolk in 1766 and had a long and distinguished career in that place.

To Richard Henry Lee

Dear Sir,   Mount Vernon 22d June 1785.
I stand indebted to you for your favors of the 3d 7th & 29th of last month,[1] & feel myself exceedingly obliged to your Excellency for the communications, & inclosures therein.
It gives me pleasure to find that *an* Ordinance of Congress has passed respecting the Western Territory. A little longer delay of this business, & I believe the Country would have been settled, maugre all that could have been done to prevent it. As it is, I am not clear that the same respect will be paid *now* to this Ordinance, that would have been at an earlier period; before men began to speculate in Lands No. Wt of the Ohio, and to obtrude themselves thereon.

From the general tenor of my letters, from very respectable & intelligent characters in France, as late as the end of March, it should seem most likely that the dispute between the Emperor & Holland will be settled without Bloodshed; and that the former will scarcely be able to effect the exchange of his dominions in the Netherlands for the Dutchy of Bavaria; among other reasons, because the Duke Deux Ponts Nephew & heir to the Elector, is opposed thereto. But notwithstanding, the state of politics, & temper of some of the formidable powers of Europe are such, as to place War at no very remote distance.

I have just parted with Mr, & Mrs (Macauly) Graham; who after a stay of about ten days, left this in order to embark for England, from New York. I am obliged to you for introducing a Lady to me whose reputation among the Literati is so high, and whose principles are so much, & so justly admired by the friends to liberty and of mankind. It gave me pleasure to find that her sentimts respecting the inadequacy of the powers of Congress (as also those of Doctr Price) coincided with my own.[2] Experience evinces the truth of these observations; and the late movemcnts of thc mcrcantilc intcrcst cxhibits a recent proof of the conviction it is working in the popular mind. but is is unfortunate for us, that evils which might have been averted, must be first felt; and our National character for wisdom, justice & temperance, called in question before we can govern the political Machine.

The plan for improving and extending the Navigation of the River Potomack is in a promising way—inclosed I do myself the honor of sending you the printed proceedings of the Board of Directors. Mrs Washington joins me in complimts, & every good wish for you, and with great esteem, regard, & respect I am— Dear Sir Yr Most Obedt & Affecte Hble Servt

Go: Washington

P.S. Colo. Wm Brent died two or three days ago. Your Son Ludwell, was well at our Court yesterday.[3]

ALS, PPAmP: Lee Papers; LB, ViHi: Lee transcripts; LB, DLC:GW.

    1. Lee's letter of 29 May has not been found.

    2. Lee sent GW on 16 Jan. a copy of Richard Price's *Observations on the Importance of the American Revolution and the Means of Making It a Benefit to the World* (London, 1784).

    3. The estate of Col. William Brent, Jr., of Stafford County, was inventoried

in 1786. Ludwell Lee (1760–1836) visited Mount Vernon with his father in
November 1785.

To John Rumney, Jr.

Dr Sir,   Mt Vernon 22d June 1785.

I stand indebted to you for two letters, one of the 8th of September—the other of the 9th of Feby—the first should not have
remained so long unacknowledged, but for the expectation I
had of the second—the second led me to expect a third, upon
the receipt of which I meant to give you but one trouble by replying to them all at the same time.

Permit me to thank you Sir, for your attention to my Commissions: the joiner arrived safe, & I believe will fully answer your
description & expectation of him; he gives great satisfaction, &
seems well satisfied himself. The expence of his passage, & your
advance to him, has been paid to Mr Sanderson.[1]

I delayed making choice of either of the samples of Flag
Stone, until I had seen the Irish marble, & was made acquainted
with the cost of it; but as it is not yet arrived, & I like the whit-
est & cheapest of the three samples wch you sent me by Capt.
Atkinson, I request the favor of you to forward by the first opportunity (with some to spare in case of breakage or other accidents) as much of this kind as will floor the Gallery in front of
my house, which within the margin, or border that goes round
it, & is already laid with a hard stone of the Country, is 92 feet
7½ inches, by 12 feet 9¼ inches.

Having given the exact dimension of the floor or space which
is to be laid with flag-stone, I shall leave it to the workman to
procure them of such a size (not less than one foot square—&
all of one size) as will answer best, & accord most with the taste
of the times. I take it for granted that 7½d. or 8d. is the price
of the white Stone in the prepared state in which it was sent, &
that shipping charges & freight only, are to be added to the Cost:
if a rough estimate of the latter had been mentioned, it would
have been more pleasing, as I could then have prepared accordingly.

I am at a loss to determine in what manner these dressed
Flags can be brought without incurring much expence, or being

liable to great damage: to put them in Cases will involve the first; & to stow them loose, the other may be sustained; unless great care is used in the stowage, which is rarely to be found among Sailors, or even Masters of Vessels. If the Flags are well dressed, a little matter will chip the edges, and break the corners; which would disfigure the work & be hurtful to the eye. I will give no direction therefore on this head—your own judgment on the spot shall dictate; at the same time I have but little doubt, if they are placed in the hold of the Ship with hay or straw to keep them from rubing, of their coming free from damage.

I will soon follow this letter with a remittance from hence, or draft upon London for a sum to enable you to discharge the undertaker.[2] In the mean while let me pray you to hasten the execution & the Shipping of them, as my Gallery is very much in want. With great esteem & regard I am Sir, &c.

G: Washington

LB, DLC:GW.

1. Rumney had asked GW to deduct from the salary of Matthew Baldridge the amount Rumney had advanced Baldridge and to pay it to Rumney's business associate in Alexandria, Robert Sanderson. See Rumney to GW, 9 Feb., nn 4 and 6.

2. GW sent on 18 Nov. 1785 a bill of exchange drawn on Wakelin Welch of London. See GW to Rumney, 18 Nov. 1785 and 15 May 1786.

From Israel Shreve

Dear Sir   Burlington State of New Jersey 22nd June 1785

I have been told you hold large tracts of Land upon the Waters of the Ohio Either upon the great Kanhawa or Licking Creek or both, since the Peace I with several others have an Inclination to become Adventureers to the back Country some where in that Quarter—have long Wated to hear the Determination of Congress respecting the Sale of the Lands in the New States, but had no Idea of such a plan as they have Fixed, the Land no Less than a Dollar ℔ Acre, and then take it by guess and how long before this plan is carried into Execution cannot be known, I am no Speculator hold no Cirtifecates but for my own Services which I have kept with a vew of Purchaceing Land. Whether it would not be your Advantage to sell about ten Thousand acres at a Moderate price to be paid for in final Settle Notes Includeing Interest due thereon, to be Immediately Setled with good farmers from New Jersey, which I will engage to do, If you should Incline to Oblige me with such a purchace Adjoining the Ohio River where the Land is good well Watered and one or more good Mill Scites thereon please to Send me a Draft of the Tract So that I can find it—I have the Maps of the Country and should chuse to see it and Call upon you on my return and Confirm the Bargain. I was Bred a farmer and am Determined If life and health Permits to go some where Back to settle and have thought If you could oblige me it would be an Advantage to you in Selling or Improveing your Adjoining Land, however this I Leave for you to Determine.[1] I am Sir with Great respect your Excellencys Most Obedient Servent

Israel Shreve

P.S. My son that was in the Army with me is a good Surveyor and will go with me to settle in that Country.[2] I. Shreve.

If you incline to Sell please to send me the price and Quantity you will part with. I.S.

ALS, DLC:GW.

Israel Shreve (1739–1799) was lieutenant colonel of the 2d New Jersey Regiment from November 1775 to November 1776 and was thereafter, until 1 Jan. 1781, its colonel. Shreve first attempted in 1787 to buy Washington's Bottom on the Youghiogheny River in Fayette County, Pa., but he succeeded only in leasing the 600-acre portion of the tract with the mill on which Gilbert Simpson, Jr., had lived until September 1785 (Shreve to GW, 5, 12 Mar., 7 April 1787, 29 June 1794; see also GW to Simpson, 13 Feb. 1784, source note and nn.1 and 2, and GW to Thomas Freeman, 23 Sept. 1784). After Shreve approached GW on 29 June 1794 about buying the 600-acre tract at Washington's Bottom where he was living, GW on 14 Jan. 1795 agreed to sell to Shreve all 1,644 acres of the Washington's Bottom tract for £4,000 Pennsylvania currency. The sale was completed on 31 July 1795, and the extensive correspondence for the following three and one-half years between GW and Shreve and between GW and James Ross, GW's Pennsylvania agent, relates to Shreve's failure to make prompt and regular payments. In his last letter to Shreve, dated 10 Jan. 1799, GW reluctantly agreed once more to delay foreclosing on Shreve's bond.

1. See GW's response of 15 July in which he declares his Ohio and Great Kanawha lands not for sale.

2. Shreve's son John served in the 2d New Jersey Regiment from 25 July 1776 to May 1780, reaching the rank of lieutenant.

From George William Fairfax

My Dear Genl,   [near Bath] June 23d 1785.

By the receipt of your favor of Feby 27th I am well convinced of what I have long suspected, that your Letters to me, and mine to you are stoped, whether at the Post Office or by private Persons, I cannot guess, this I know, that you are looked upon as the most capable, and therefore the most dangerous Enemy on this side the Water, and that I am known to be such on this, as far as my abilities, and contracted power goes. For the reasons above given, I must request that your Excellency will enclose the Letters you do me the honor to write, to Mr Athawes, if they come by a London Ship, if to Bristol, be pleas'd to send them to Mr Benjn Pollard, Mercht at Norfolk, in which case I hope to get them safe. Be assured my good Sir, I have address'd you so frequently since the Peace, that I was apprehensive of being thought troublesome, and supposed my Letters being unnoticed proceeded from that cause.[1] I believe Mrs Fx and I have blotted some Quire of paper to our Virginia friends, which has not been received, as the Letters has not been answer'd. I am very sorry my Packet enclosing the Countess's Letter miscarried:[2] also that one I wrote intreating the favor of your countena[n]ce, to poor Mr Pine, the ingenious painter & designer of the Print, of the great revolution, in which you had so Principal and active a part, did not get to hand; I informed you that Mr Pine was my near neighbour while he resided at Bath, that He was a Man of merit, had ever been the stanchest Friend to the American cause and the liberties of mankind, that from that reason only, he had lost his business and friends, and was obliged to leave England, tho' acknowledged to be the best Portraite painter in it. from my own knowledge, I said, that it was his earnest wish to have your Person in the place of Herorick Virtue, could your likeness have been procured, while the Picture was painting. I wrote to you, and Colo. Fielding Lewis several times, to beg that a miniature one might be sent or even a profile for that purpose. Poor Pine has a very worthy Woman to Wife and six daughters, all highly accompld in their professional Art. he is now in Philadelphia, Mrs Pine, and one Daughter, just gone over to him. If you would be so good to write a line to some of your friends in Pensylvania in his favor, it would be doing a charity, and I should esteem it as an additional favor confired upon me. I cannot quit the subject without adding that He merits every favor, from all true Americans.[3] Mrs Fairfax, and I are extremely obliged, by your very friendly and polite Invitation to Mount Vernon, which it is impossible for us to think of accepting. do you good Sir, consider our time of Life, it's much too late in it, to enter upon Building and improveing a Place of residence, as well as Emerging into the fatigue of a large Family, and keeping, or entertaining so much Company, as would be expected of a Man of my nominal fortune, for I can call it no other. The conviction of the Expediency of contracting business, and retireing from the busy Wor[l]d, induced Us, as soon as the Peace was concluded, to take a House in the Country about eight Miles from Bath. it is situated, in a plesant Vale, in a beautiful hilly Country, and surrounded by dairy-Farms, so that We have abundance of sweat Meadows to look upon, wherever we turn, those are enclosed with quick Hedges and many of them filled with fine Sheep and Cows, which altogether cons[t]itutes as perfect an Arcadia as ever Poet's fancy formed, here we enjoy sweat Air, much composure, and time for contemplation, which We esteem the first of terrestial blessings. The American War (as it's called here) humbled Us into the dust, and I trust totally eradicated the weeds of vanity and ostentation. We live in an humble, neat and comfortable way, have a Chaise and pair, have only two Men and two Women Servants, have every necessary of Life brought to our door, our Garden produces the sweetest Vegitables I ever tasted, and the Flowers and Shrubs employ me, and delight my old Woman. In short We enjoy the constant feast of content, and would not change situations with any Crown'd head, upon earth.

I blush to think, that the States should allow You to take the drudgery of regulating those Voluminous Accots. Fy, fy upon it, why should you my good Sir decline to accept the Compt that your Country, and all the world judge you so well merit; you must not come hither to look for such an instance of self denial. I believe it will be harder to find such a one, on this side the Atlantic, than it was for me to convince the People here, that you served all the War without Pay or Emolument. I will do my best to procure and send you a Buck and a doe of the best kind next Spring. Mrs Fairfax bids me say She will take care to send the

Seeds of many kind of Shrubs that She thinks is not in Virginia. when you inform that Your Hot House is ready to receive the Plants, We will also send many kind of Myrtles and Geraniums if possible from Bristol, and if we could borrow Fortunatus's Cap, we would take a flight to see Cincinatus cultivating them in high delight. this is our Stile, you know a Flower was ever S. Fxs hobby, and at Bath we meet with the produce of all the World in that way.

I am sorry, and ashamed to reflect upon the trouble I have given you upon the business of Mrs Bristows and my Paper, which is not now an object of consequence, I having settled that matter as far as I could here.[4] gladly would I have evaded Mrs Bristows application, but it was not to be done. sufferers will leave no Stone unturned, where interest is concerned, in vain did I plead your having no part in the Civil affairs, your multiplicity of business, &c. She was the importunate Widow that would be heard.

Before the communication was stoped between Us, & You I wrote to request, that you would accept the blue damask Furniture out of Belvoir House, and then petitioned, that you would remove the two Pictures in the Dining-Room to Mount Vernon, and keep them for me, till opportunity offer'd to send them over, whether Lord Dunmore, stoped that Letter, or if you received it, I never heard, but if those Pictures did escape the Flames, I would be much obliged to you, to have them well cased up, and send them to Mr B. Pollard Mercht at Norfolk, with directions to forward them to me at Bath by one of Mr Spans Ships, and could wish them to be addressd to Mr Span at Bristol for safety.[5]

This my dear Sir, I hope you will receive from the hand of Mr William Baynham, a young Gent. of a most worthy Character, held in the highest Esteem by all that know him in Scotland, where he lived many years, prosecuting his Studies in Surgery. also in London, where I understand he was in considerable practice some time past, but the love of his Country was so prevalent, as to make him forego those advantages, when He had acquired the nec[e]ssary Professional knowledge, by attending the Hospitals, and every other close application to business. I never heard a young Man better spoke off for good Conduct, assiduity, and capasity. therefore it is with much pleasure, I comply with his request of introducing him to the *Glorious General*. those are his own words.[6] Your pathetic discription of the Ruin of Belvoir House produced many tears & sighs from the former Mistress of it, tho' at the first hearing of the Fire, she felt no shock. the Peace, which she hoped, would place her Friends in safety and happiness, had extinguished every sentiment except that of gratitude to Heaven for their deliverance.

Adieu my Dear Genl we pray God to preserve you, and Dear Mrs Washington, long in health and happiness. I am Your sincere friend, and Affecte Humbe Servant

Go. Wm Fairfax

ALS, DLC:GW.

1. The two old friends succeeded in renewing their correspondence in 1783 when Fairfax wrote GW on 26 Mar. in praise of his role in winning his country's independence, and GW wrote a long letter in response on 10 July. See GW to Fairfax, 27 Feb. 1785, n.2. Samuel Athawes was a prominent London merchant in the Virginia trade to whom Fairfax had consigned tobacco before the war.

2. For the countess of Huntingdon's letter of 20 Mar. 1784, see doc. III in Lady Huntingdon's Scheme for Aiding the American Indians, 20 Dec. 1784, printed above.

3. Fairfax's earlier letter introducing Robert Edge Pine is dated 23 Aug. 1784. See also his letter of 10 June 1784.

4. For "the business of Mrs Bristows," see GW to Benjamin Harrison, 14 June 1784, n.1, and GW to Mary Bristow, 15 June 1784. For "my Paper" relating to the payment of quitrents to Lord Fairfax, see Fairfax to GW, 23 Aug. 1784, and note 1 of that document, and GW to Fairfax, 30 June 1785.

5. Fairfax wrote GW on 10 Jan. 1774 to instruct him to sell the contents of the house at Belvoir, and at the sale held on 15 Aug. 1774, GW bought goods and furnishings. See Francis Willis, Jr., to GW, 2 June 1774, and notes, and GW to Fairfax, 10–15 June 1774, n.25. On 2 Mar. 1775 Fairfax wrote GW giving him the blue damask furniture, which remained unsold. GW wrote Fairfax on 30 June 1786 that this furniture from Fairfax's "blue room" had been moved to Mount Vernon during his absence in the war, but the pictures were "left standing at Belvoir; and, unfortunately, perished with the house."

6. GW wrote in his diary on 5 Dec. 1785: "When I returned home, wch. was not until past three Oclock found a Doctr. Baynham here—recommended to me by Colo. Fairfax of England" (*Diaries*, 4:244). William Baynham (1749–1814) of Caroline County, Va., had been abroad since 1769. On his return he settled in Essex County where he had a distinguished career as a surgeon.

To Richard Boulton

Mr Boulton,   Mount Vernon 24th June 1785.

Your letter of the 4th inst: never reached me until Monday last. I do not enter into agreements, but with an intention of fulfilling them; & I expect the same punctuality on the part of those with whom they are made: you must therefore perform your's with me, or abide the consequences.

The reason which you assign for not coming, is futile & can have no weight with your creditors; your property & your labour are all the means with which you can satisfy them; a mortgage or bill of sale of the first; & an order on me by way of security of the latter as your wages shall arise, is all they can desire (if your Tools are unsaleable) & these are in your power to give them.

You know the purposes for which I engaged you, & that they are important & urgent: that I waited a considerable time after Colo. Fitzhugh had recommended you to me, without applying elsewhere, for your answer; that near a month more has elapsed since our agreement took place; that the season is now far advanced, & workmen consequently so much engaged as not to be procured: In the mean while, the roof of my house yields to every rain, & the furniture in no part of it is secure from the injuries which result therefrom. These reasons, will fully justify my holding you to the engagement we have entered into, & I expect you will enter upon the performance of it without further delay, I am &[c].

G: Washington

LB, DLC:GW.

Letter not found: from Thomas Corbin, 24 June. GW wrote Corbin on 8 July: "Yesterday afternoon I had the honor to receive your favor of the 24th of June."

To Patrick Henry

Dr Sir,   Mount Vernon June 24th 1785.

The letter which your Excellency did me the honor to write to me on the 10th inst. came duly to hand, & calls for my particular acknowledgments; & my grateful thanks for your obliging offers.

Altho' I conceive that the sunken Lands lying on Albermarle sound, & the waters emptying into it, will in time become the most valuable property in this Country; yet when I reflect further, that it will require a considerable advance to reclaim & render them fit for cultivation, & in the mean time that they may be subjected to expences; I believe it would be most adviseable for me, in my situation not to add to my present expenditures; but I am as much obliged by your friendly offer to serve me in this matter, as if they had actually been rendered.

If your Excellency could make it convenient to give me the substance of the report of the Comm[ission]ers, respecting the place & manner which are thought best for a cut between the waters of Elizabeth river & those of North Carolina, I should think myself obliged:[1] the improving & extending the inland navigation of the Waters of this Country, are in my judgment very interesting to the well being & glory of it, & I am always pleased with any accounts which seem to facilitate those important objects. With great esteem, regard & respect I am Dr Sir &c. &c.

G: Washington

LB, DLC:GW.
   1. See Henry to GW, 11 Nov. 1785, n.2.

From Samuel Powel

Dear Sir   Philadelphia June 24. 1785.

I am honored with your Favor of the 15th Inst. & beg you to accept my best Thanks for your polite Attention to my Introduction of Dr Moyes to your Notice, as well as for your Permission of doing the like, in future, for any Gentleman whom I may conceive to be worthy of your Civilities—Of this Permission, however highly I may estimate it, be assured that I shall ever avail myself with great Delicacy.

I am now to endeavor to give you such Information relative to the Business you have mentioned, as I have been able to obtain; & could wish that my Enquiries had been attended with such Success as to enable me to form a decisive opinion, equally removed from misleading you in a Point of Delicacy, or unwillingly & unintentionally, prejudicing the Applicant in your good Opinion.

The Result of my Enquiries, as gathered from the Communications of various Persons, who appeared to me most likely to be acquainted with the Author as well as with the Merits of his intended Publication, amounts to this. That they are entire Strangers to the Man &, equally so, to the Merits of his work, except as far as may be judged from the Specimen already published. They conceive it to be a Compilation taken, chiefly, from Dr Goldsmith's animated Nature, & the Lectures publickly delivered in this City by Dr Moyes, which it is said, & I believe truly, were taken down, in short Hand, by this Gentleman; & this Opinion, I believe, is well founded. If these are the Materials he has selected for his Work, I do not think that any Thing very new, correct, or instructive can be contained in it; & allow me to say, that I think the Work will derive more Honor from your Name, than the Dedication will reflect back on you—Dr Moyes may, probably, have given you much fuller Information on this Subject than I can, if you have ever made it a Topic of Conversation. I am told he was so much hurt by it as even to have consulted Mr Wilson whether an Action would not be against any Person who should publish his Lectures without his Permission; not, perhaps, adverting to the Distinction between giving them to the World as the Lectures of Dr Moyes, or giving the Substance of them without a Name, which last any Person had a Right to do after they once became the property of the public by being publickly delivered.

I shall without Scruple, declare to you, that from the Specimen which Mr Vancouver has sent me, as well as from the best Information that I can obtain, I shall decline becoming a Subscriber, as I do not expect that Knowlege will be much advanced by his Work.

Inclosed I return Mr Vancouver's Letter.[1] Mrs Powel begs Leave to add her Comps. & unfeigned good Wishes for Mrs Washington & yourself, to those of, Dear Sir, Your most obedt humble Servt

Samuel Powel

ALS, DLC:GW.

1. Charles Vancouver's letter of 10 May has not been found, but see GW to Vancouver, 30 June. James Wilson (1742–1798) was at this time a prominent lawyer and public figure in Philadelphia.

From James Rumsey

Sir   Bath June 24th 1785
I had the honor of Receiving your favour of the 5th Inst. with the Inclosures and am happy To find that you Excuse my Imprudence Respecting Mr Ryans note. But the following acount I fear will give you Sum Disapointment the number of houses I undertook was four yours included that was Large[.] the Stuff for the hole was Sawed But from the Badness of the Roads ocationed by So much Rain the greatest part of it Lay at the mill untill the Begining of April when Unfortunately the Sawmill took fire in the night and was not Discovered untill next Day By which time the mill was Intirely Consumed with a great part of the plank and Scanting this Stroke put it Intirely out of my power to proceed with your Large house[1] and notwithstanding my Outmost Exertions at Other mills to get the Stuff nesasary It has put me So far back that I shall Be under the Disagreeable Nesesaty of Disapointing at Least One of the three gentlemen that I have Obligated with for the present Season But I have prepared him a house Should he Insist on being furnished with one, I Should have gave you this Information much Sooner but I Saw your brother Coln. John Washington at april Court and he Said he would Inform you of It as he went home perhaps he Did not See you or multiplisity of Business may have Caused it to have Sliped his memmory.[2] I have got my Boat nearly Done the Mechenery Excepted. Inclosed I Send a Letter for you and the Directors of the potomack Company and if you pleas be kind anough to Read it and have it Dilivered or Suppresed as you may think best I Can only add that Should I have the honour of an apointment I will Exert myself to the Outmost of my power to afect the Business. your Small houses are nearly done the Chimney Seller &C. will be Very Compleat, their will be Sum money comeing To me and I am Sorry I am under the nesesaty of Requesting the favour of you to answer the first Draft towards

my share of the potomack navegation I am Sir your Sincere
freind and Very hbe Servt

James Rumsey

ALS, DLC:GW.
    1. For further information on Rumsey's building of a house for GW at Bath,
in Berkeley County, see the references in note 2 of GW's letter of 5 June.
    2. For another instance of John Augustine Washington's forgetfulness, see
the tale of the greatcoat and the book in John Augustine Washington to GW,
17 July 1785.

Letter not found: to William Fitzhugh, 25 June. Fitzhugh wrote GW on
16 July: "I had the Honor of your favor of the 25th Ulto."

To Thomas Montgomerie

Dear Sir,   Mount Vernon 25th June 1785.
    In the evening of yesterday, I was favored with your letter of
the 21st; & thank you for your early & friendly attention to the
enquiry I made of you.
    I do not now recollect whether I was so explicit as perhaps I
ought to have been in communicating all the purposes for which
I wanted an assistant: they are these.
    A Gentleman who can compose a good letter from the heads
which shall be given to him; do all other writing which shall
be entrusted to his care; keep Accounts; examine, arrange &
properly methodize my papers (which from hasty removals into
the interior country, are in great disorder); ride, at my expence,
to do such business as I may have in different parts of this, or
the other States, if I should find it more convenient to send than
attend myself to the execution therof; & occasionally to devote
a *small* portion of time to inetiate two little Children (a Girl of
six, & a boy of four years of age, descendants of the decd Mr
Custis who live with me & are very promising, and whom I
would not wish to confine) in the first rudiments of Education.
    A fit person who inclines to accept these employments, will
live as I do—be company for those who visit at the House—have
his washing & mending found him, & such wages as we can
agree upon; which I must be candid in declaring can not be
high, as my finances & expenditures will not admit of it.
    If you think Mr Shaw competent to these ends & find him

disposed to be employed for them, I wish to know it by the return of the Post, as there are others offering. If he would write to me, or to you upon this subject, the letter in the latter case to be enclosed to me, I could form some judgment of his hand writing & diction: he will please to signify the lowest wages which he will take per Ann: or quarterly—If he chooses a personal interview, which perhaps may be more agreeable, I should be glad to see him here, with some samples of his writing. With great esteem &c. I am

G: Washington

LB, DLC:GW.

To Stephen Bloomer Balch

Sir,   Mt Vernon 26th June 1785.
My Nephews are desireous of going to the Dancing School in George town kept by Mr Tarterson (I think his name is)—and as it is my wish that they should be introduced into life with those qualifications which are deemed necessary, I consent to it. Sometime ago I expressed my approbation of their learning French, & a wish that when you had got your House in order to receive them, they might again board with you: Altho' I have no occasion [to doubt] the care, attention and kindness of Mr Bailey to them, I conceive they can board at no place so eligably as at their Preceptors; for it is my wish that their morals as well as educations may be attended to; & tho' I do not desire they should be deprived of necessary & proper amusements, yet it is my earnest request that they may be kept close to their studies.[1]
I am Sir &c.

G: Washington

LB, DLC:GW.
    Stephen Bloomer Balch (1747–1833), a native of Harford County, Md., and a graduate of Princeton College, founded the first Presbyterian church in Georgetown in 1780 and remained its pastor until his death.
    1. GW placed his nephews George Steptoe Washington and Lawrence Augustine Washington in Balch's academy in Georgetown, Md., in October 1784. See GW to David Griffith, 29 Aug. 1784, n.1, and Benjamin Stoddert to GW, 21 June 1785. Before leaving Georgetown at the end of November, the boys did board part of the time with the merchant William Bailey (see GW to Bailey, 22 Nov.).

From Samuel Fraunces

Sir   New York June 26 1785

I rec'd yours pr Governor Clinton—and can but say I receive the greatest Honor in your kind Acceptance of the Grottesque Work.[1]

I know not in what manner to apologize to your Excellency for my boldness in enclosing Mr Whites Letter in this, but my reliance on your goodness so often experienced—My Circumstance has obliged me to quit the City and dispose of my House—I have put some dependance in the State's Assistance but find it Vain—I cannot either Collect in my debts so as to Clear me from the World—under this Situation I have made bold to beg your Excellencys favor in recommending the enclosed—Mr White perhaps you may be acquainted with and it will be of the greatest weight, as their is upwards of five hundred and Fifty pounds due me from the Estate of Gen. Lee—Mr White has the Acct from Col. Hamilton—The enclosed is open with a request to direct favors to me under cover to the Governor who will kindly forward any[2]—I must again beg pardon for my Assurance but your Excellency may believe me I am forced thro Necessity and therefore reassume the hope of being once more relieved thro' your Excellency's goodness. I have the Honor to remain with the utmost respect to your lady and self Your Excellencys Most Obedient and very humble Servant—

                                        Samuel Fraunces

Mrs Fraunces and family desire their respect to you and your Lady.

ALS, DLC:GW.

1. In his letter to GW of 5 Mar. 1785, Gov. George Clinton of New York refers to having sent GW "a Glass case with Wax or Grotto work, presented by Mr Francis to Mrs Washington." GW probably enclosed a missing letter to the New York tavern keeper in his letter to Clinton of either 5 or 20 April.

2. Mr. White was the lawyer Alexander White whom Sidney Lee in England had retained to settle the American estate of her brother, the late Gen. Charles Lee. See Sidney Lee to GW, 23 May 1784, n.3, and 5 April 1785. GW wrote White on behalf of Fraunces on 14 July and received a letter from White on 26 July explaining the delay in paying the claims of General Lee's creditors.

From Thomas Montgomerie

Dear Sir   Dumfries 28th June 1785

Your favor of the 25th I duely received—I communicated the contents to Mr Shaw, who seems to have no objection to the line of duty you lay down, except that of being considered as a preceptor, and I believe except in the name he would take a pleasure in giving every assistance in forwarding your wishes with respect to the two little Children—He does not wish to engage for any certain time, and he means in this respect you should be equally at liberty—this desire does not proceed from an intention speedily to change his situation, he expects to be happily situated, and to give you satisfaction—He declines naming a sum in consideration of services, he wishes to leave this with yourself; however on a personal interview, in case matters are otherwise agreeable to you, this matter may be understood—Mr Shaw would have waited upon you this week at Mount Vernon, but I am informed of a good deal of Compy that will be at your House[1]—Should you not engage with any other person in the mean time, and incline to see him, he will wait upon you any day next week you will please to name—a line by Sundays post will be obliging—I have the honor to be with great regard Dr Sir Your most Obed. & very Humbe Servt

Thos Montgomerie

ALS, DLC:GW.

1. According to GW's diary, those staying the night of 28 June at Mount Vernon included Evan Edwards of Pennsylvania, Charles Phillips of the West Indies, Col. Josias Hawkins of Charles County, Md., Col. William Booth of Westmoreland County, Va., GW's brother Charles Washington, his brother-in-law Burwell Bassett and Bassett's sons Burwell, Jr., and John, all in addition to the permanent inhabitants: GW, Mrs. Washington, Fanny Bassett, George Augustine Washington, and Mrs. Washington's grandchildren, Eleanor Parke Custis and George Washington Parke Custis.

To William Blake

Sir,   Mt Vernon 30th June 1785.

By my Nephew I had the honor to receive your favor of the 20th Mar: accompanied with some plants & Seeds of the Palmetto royal, for which I pray you to accept my sincere thanks;

the former are not only alive yet, but look vigorous; & the latter (being sowed) are vegitating, & appearing above ground—I shall nurse them with great attention.

It would give me great pleasure to visit my friends in So. Carolina: but when, or whether ever it may be in my power to accomplish it, is not, at this moment, in my power to decide. I have the honor to be &c.

G: Washington

LB, DLC:GW.

To George William Fairfax

My Dr Sir,   Mount Vernon 30th June 1785.

When I wrote you in Feby last, I intended to have followed it with a letter of earlier date than the present; but one cause succeeding another, has prevented it 'till now.[1]

I proceeded to a diligent search for the paper requested in your favor of the 23d of August last year, & after examining every bundle, & indeed despairing of success, it occurred to me that your Accot with Lord Fairfax might afford some clue by which a discovery of it might be made; & in looking in your ledger for an index, I found the receipts pasted on the cover of the Book. Having a call to Richmond the latter end of April, I took the receipts with me intending to leave them in the hands of the Attorney General; but it being his opinion there would be no occasion for them, I brought them back, & restored them to the place from whence I took them: the enclosed are copies of those receipts, which I meant should supply the place of the originals, had they pass'd from me to the Attorney.[2]

I have not yet received the Pictures which you were so obliging as to send me by Mr Bracken; but have some prospect now of getting them, as Colo. Bassett who left this lately & who expects to be up again in Octor to the marriage of his Daughter who lives with us, with a son of my brother Charles (who acted as an Aid de Camp to the Marqs de la Fayette from the year 1780, to the close of the War) has promised to bring them.[3] Altho' I have been so long deprived of the copy, I have lately had the plea[sure] of seeing the original in the hands of the designer & executioner Mr Pine, who spent three weeks with me in May last.

Mr Pine has met a favorable reception in this Country; & may, I conceive, command as much business as he pleases; he is now preparing materials for historical representations of some of the most important events of the War; & if his choice and the execution is equal to the field he has to display his talents in, the peices (which will be large) will do him much credit as an artist, & be interesting for America & its friends as a deposit for their posterity.[4]

The information which you have given of the disposition of a certain Court coincides precisely with the sentiments I had formed of it from my own observations upon many late occurrences, and from a combination of circumstances. With respect to ourselves, I wish I could add, that as much wisdom had pervaded our Councils; as reason & common policy most evidently dictated; but the truth is, the people must *feel* before they will *see*; consequently, are brought slowly into measures of public utility. Past experience, or the admonitions of a few, have but little weight—where ignorance, selfishness & design possess the major part: but evils of this nature work their own cure; tho' the remedy comes slower than those who foresee, or think they foresee the danger, attempt to effect. With respect to the commercial system which G: B: is pursuing with this Country, the Ministers, in this as in other matters, are defeating their own ends, by facilitating those powers in Congress which will produce a counter action of their plans, & which half a century without, would not have invested that body with. The restriction of our trade, & the additional duties which are imposed upon many of our staple commodities, have put the commercial people of this Country in motion; they now see the indispensible necessity of a general *controuling* power, and are addressing their respective Assemblies to grant this to Congress. Before this every State thought itself competent to regulate its own Trade, & were verifying the observations of Lord Sheffield; who supposed we never could agree upon any general plan: but those who will go a little deeper into matters, than his Lordship seems to have done, will readily perceive that in any measure where the Fœderal interest is touched, however wide apart the politic's of individual States may be, yet as soon as it is discovered they will always unite to effect a common good.

The Subscriptions for improving & extending the inland navigation of Potomac, have filled very fast: A Company is incorporated—a President & Directors are chosen—a Dividend of the money will soon be paid in, & the work will begin about the first of August. We still want a skilful Engineer—a man of practical knowledge to conduct the business; but where to find him we know not at present: In the meanwhile, the less difficult parts of the river will be attempted, that no time may be lost in effecting so important & salutary an undertaking.

Our course of Husbandry in this Country, & more especially in this State, is not only exceedingly unprofitable, but so destructive to our Lands, that it is my earnest wish to adopt a better; & as I believe no Country has carried the improvment of Land & the benefits of Agriculture to greater perfection than England, I have asked myself frequently of late, whether a thorough bred *practical* english Farmer, from a part of England where Husbandry seems to be best understood & is most advantageously practiced, could not be obtain'd? And upon what terms? The thought having again occurred to me, whilst I was in the act of writing this letter, I resolved as a more certain & eligible mode of having the questions determined, to propound them to you—That a man of character & knowledge may be had for *very high wages* there can be no doubt—money we know will fetch any thing, & command the service of any man; but with the former I do not abound. To engage a man upon shares as the Overseers of this Country are, might be productive of much discontent to the employed; for we could scarcely convey to a good English Farmer a just idea of the wretched condition of our Lands—what dressings they will require, & how entirely our system must be changed to make them productive: & if we do not, disappointment and continual murmurings would be the consequence. It follows then that the only means by which we can think of obtaining one, must be to give standing wages; for what then my good Sir, do you think a sober, industrious & knowing Farmer might be had to take charge of one of our Plantations—say, of ten labourers? Or to bring the matter nearer to his own conception of things—A Farm of about 200 or 250 acres of cleared Land, to be stocked with a competent number of Plows—black Cattle—Sheep & hogs?

When I speak of a knowing Farmer, I mean one who understands the best course of Crops; how to plough—to sow—to mow—to hedge—to Ditch & above all, Midas like, one who can convert every thing he touches into manure, as the first transmutation towards Gold: in a word one who can bring worn out & gullied Lands into good tilth in the shortest time. I do not mean to put you to the trouble of actually engaging one, but I should be obliged to you for setting on foot the enquiry, & for communicating the result of it to me; because I could not receive your answer in time for the next year; the autumn being, as you well know, the season at which our Overseers are engaged, & our plans for the ensuing Crop must be formed. These enquiries, as you will readily perceive, are pointed to a Farmer of the midling class; which more than probably, would best answer my purpose: but, if it could be made convenient to you to extend your enquiries further; permit me to ask if one of a higher order could be had? And upon what terms? I mean for a Steward.

It may not in this place be amiss to observe to you that I still decline the growth of Tobacco; & to add, that it is my intention to raise as little Indian corn as may be: in a word, that I am desirous of entering upon a compleat course of husbandry as practiced in the best Farming Counties of England. I enquire for a man of this latter description with little hope of success—1st because I believe one who is compleatly fit for my purposes, wou'd be above my price; & 2dly because I have taken up an idea that an English steward is not so much a farmer, as he is an Attorney or an Accomptant; because few of the Nobility & Gentry having their Estates in their own hands—stand more in need of a Collector who, at the same time that he receives the rents, will see that the Covenants of the Leases are complied with, repairs made &c. &c., than of a Farmer. In this however I may be mistaken. One thing more & then I will close this long letter: if from your own observation, or from good information you should fix your eyes upon men of one or both of these descriptions—& could ascertain his or their terms (leaving me at liberty to accede to them or not, within a reasonable time for an intercourse by letter)—I had rather he or they should be personally known to you; or their characters well ascertained by a friend in whom you can confide; because what you or such a person would say of them, I could rely upon: but how often do we find recommendations given without merit to deserve them—founded in a disposition to favor the Applicant, or want of resolution to refuse Him—oftentimes indeed, to get rid of a dependant who is troublesome or injurious to us, upon what are *called* decent terms. A man in the character of a Steward (if single, & his appearance equal to it) would live in the House with me & be at my table, in the manner Lund Washington was accustomed to do, who is now married and a House Keeper tho' still attending my business. The common Farmer would live on the Farm which would be entrusted to his care.[5]

I have lately had the pleasure of receiving your favor of the 19th of March, & to learn by it that Mrs Fairfax & you have enjoyed better health than usual, last winter: a continuance of it Mrs Washington & I most sincerely wish you.

I have not yet seen Mr Thos Corbin; he sent your letter under cover a few days ago with assurances of making me a visit as soon as he had recovered from a slight indisposition. He appears from your account to have been very ill treated by his brother Dick—but the latter I understand has not been behind him in charges to some of his friends in this Country, who think Thos in the wrong.[6] Mrs Washington joins me in most affectionate regards, & in every good wish for you & Mrs Fairfax—With much truth I am Dr Sir &c. &c.

G: Washington

P.S. I thank Mr Heartley for the compliments he sent me thro' you, & for his other polite attentions to me; & pray you to make mine acceptable to him whenever a proper occasion offers. I did not know of your Nephew's intended trip to England or I would most assuredly have written to you by so good an opportunity.[7]

G: W——n

LB, DLC:GW.

1. GW wrote Fairfax on 27 February.

2. Fairfax wrote GW on 23 Aug. 1784 asking him to search "my Papers (if they remain in your hands) for the Lord Proprietors discharge, for all arrears of Quitrents." Fairfax, in fact, wrote GW shortly before sailing for England in 1773 about leaving this particular document with GW (Fairfax to GW, 5 Aug. 1773; see also Fairfax to GW, 23 Aug. 1784, n.1, and 23 June 1785, n.4).

3. Fairfax wrote GW on 10 June 1784 that he was sending by the Rev. John

Bracken "two Prints," one for GW and one for Martha Washington. In his letter of 23 Aug. 1784 Fairfax goes on to describe the prints and to identify Robert Edge Pine as "the ingenious Allegorical designer and executor" of the "fine press Print, expressive of the great Oppressions and Calamities of America." See also George Augustine Washington to GW, 3 Feb. 1786.

4. For a description of Pine's large project, see Francis Hopkinson to GW, 19 April 1785. See also the comments of others in note 1 of that document.

5. GW's extended and eloquent statement here of his views of and aspirations for farming practices at Mount Vernon and in America at large led directly to the English farmer James Bloxham taking up residence at Mount Vernon in 1786. It also led to the initiation of a fruitful correspondence between Arthur Young, the noted agriculturalist in England, and GW, the agricultural experimenter and reformer at Mount Vernon. See particularly Fairfax to GW, 23 Jan. 1786, and Arthur Young to GW, 7 Jan. 1786. See also GW's Agreement with James Bloxham, 31 May 1786 (DLC:GW), and *Diaries*, 4:315.

6. For the Corbin affair, see Fairfax to GW, 19 Mar. 1785, n.1. See also Fairfax to GW, 23 Jan. 1786.

7. David Hartley sent GW his respects through Fairfax on 19 March. Bryan Fairfax's son Thomas was visiting in England (see George William Fairfax to GW, 23 Jan. 1786).

To the Countess of Huntingdon

My Lady   Mount Vernon June 30th 1785

In the last letter which I had the honor of writing to you, I informed Your Ladyship of the communication I had made to the President of Congress, of your wishes to obtain Lands for a number of Emigrants in the Western territory; as a means of civilizing the Savages, and propagating the Gospel amongst them.[1]

In answer, he informed me that Mr Henry—the Governor of this State—had laid your Ladyships Letter and Plan (which were addressed to him) before Congress in a clear, & ample manner; but his private opinion of the matter was, that under the pressure of debt to which this Fund was to be appropriated; and the diversity of sentiment respecting the mode of raising it, that no discrimination would, or indeed could be made, in favor of Emigrants of any description whatever. I waited however a considerable time to know the result of Mr Henry's reference, before I would give your Ladyship the trouble of another letter on this Subject; but hearing nothing more of the matter, and having had the enclosed resolution, & Ordinance sent to me by the

President himself, as the result of their long, and painful deliberation on the mode of disposing of the Western Lands; I will delay no longer to express my concern that your Ladyships humane & benevolent views are not better seconded.[2]

The resolution & Ordinance herewith enclosed (on which I shall make no comment), will give the terms, and point out the mode by which the Lands belonging to the Union, are to be obtained. In other words, how difficult it is for foreigners to know when, or where, to apply for them.[3] With the highest respect and Consideration I have the honr to be Yr Ladyships Most Obt & Most Hble Servt

Go: Washington

ALS, Chestnut College, Cambridge, England; LB, DLC:GW.

1. GW wrote Selena Hastings, the countess of Huntingdon, on 27 February. See also Lady Huntingdon's Scheme for Aiding the American Indians, 20 Dec. 1784, printed above.

2. GW wrote to Richard Henry Lee on 8 Feb. about the countess's scheme, and Lee wrote GW on 27 Feb. of Congress's negative reaction to it.

3. For GW's views on the Land Ordinance of 1785, see GW to William Grayson, 25 April 1785.

To Thomas Montgomerie

Dr Sir,   Mount Vernon 30th June 1785.

I received your favor of the 28th, last night. I was under promise when I wrote to you on the 25th of giving an answer to an application which had been made to me, in a few days before, which are now nearly expired: that I may be decisive on it, I should be glad to know precisely what Mr Shaw would expect for his services if he comes to me; for altho' I cannot as I observed in my last, afford to give high pay on the one hand, so neither would I, by any means, leave it indifinite on the other: whatever stipulations I enter into, shall be strictly complied with; which will leave no cause for discontent—I am the more explicit in these declarations because I am apprehensive that higher pay is expected from me than I can afford to give. Mr Shaw undoubtedly has set a value upon his (those wch are to be rendered) services—he knows what he has received for former services; It is not reasonable to expect that any Gentleman will lessen his prospects by coming to me, nor do I desire it—I do not expect them for less than he can obtain elsewhere; but if my means will not enable me to give as much, I must do without, or get one less capable of assisting me.

Another thing in Mr Shaw's proposals is not very agreeable to me: if a Gentn does not engage with me for *some fixed time*, I may in a month—nay less, be put to a greater non-plus than ever, which would be inconvenient, & perhaps injurious to me—short engagements & early notice of discontinuance might answer the purpose of Mr Shaw, & remove my difficulties.

That matters may be reduced to a certainty, & I enabled to give the answer above alluded to, in time, I send this by a special messenger. I am obliged to attend the Board of Directors in Alexandria tomorrow; but whether I shall be detained there longer is at present uncertain; I should be glad therefore if it is convenient to see Mr Shaw here this evening, or on Saturday—or at Alexandria tomorrow—when upon a little conversation we can readily determine whether our purposes can be reciprocally answered.[1]

He will not, indeed cannot, be considered in the light of a preceptor—because this, as I observed in my last, is only occasional & secondary. I am &c.

G: Washington

LB, DLC:GW.
1. See William Shaw to GW, 4 July.

From Thomas Montgomerie

Dear Sir   Dumfries 30th June 1785

Mr Shaw will wait upon you at Mount Vernon on Saturday; should your business detain you in Alexa. till the evening of that day, you will find him there on your return home—He does not at any rate mean to leave you in a short time, and at no period untill you can provide yourself agreeably.[1]

I have urged him strongly to name a sum in lieu of services, but I cannot get him to do it—He says it is no consideration to him for the present He does not expect such wages as he could obtain in business, he came into the Country with an intention of entering into business, but he thinks there may be hereafter a more favorable juncture; and it appears to me from conversing with him, that should he answer your purposes and expectations, he may still thereafter be equally servicable to you and employ his money in that line—you need be under no difficulty of making him some small offer in consideration of Wages or expences—I am with very great regard Dr Sir Your most obt Hume Se⟨rvt⟩

Thos Montgomerie

ALS, DLC:GW.
   1. For William Shaw's visit to Mount Vernon, see Montgomerie to GW, 1 July, and Shaw to GW, 4 July.

To Charles Vancouver

sir,   Mt Vernon 30th June 1785.
   Your favor of the 10th of last month came safely to hand.[1]
   You do me much honor by proposing to inscribe a work (of which you sent me a specimen) to my special patronage & protection: but tho' willing to give every support to the encouragment of literature & useful knowledge, which may be within my sphere of action; yet, on the present occasion I must beg leave to decline the honor of having your labors dedicated to me.[2] With chearfulness I will follow the subscriptions (wch I presume must 'ere this, be pretty well advanced) of Gentn of my acquaintance; & with a proper sense of the distinction meant for me—I am &:

G: Washington

LB, DLC:GW.
   1. Letter not found.
   2. See GW to Samuel Powel, 15 June, and Powel to GW, 24 June.

To William Washington

Dear sir,   Mount Vernon 30th June 1785.
   My nephew delivered me your letter of the 21st of April. For the kind attention shewn him by Mrs Washington & yourself he entertains a grateful sense, & I offer you my sincere thanks, which I should be glad to renew to you both, in person at this place. He enjoys a tolerable share of health, but is gone to (what

are called in this Country) the Sweet Springs, to obtain a better stock to fit him for the pleasures, & duties too, of a matrimonial voyage, on wch he is to embark at his return.

I would thank you my good Sir, for the Acorns, Nutts, or seeds of trees or plants not common in this Country; but which you think would grow here, especially of the flowering kind: the best method, I believe, to preserve those which are apt to spoil by withering & drying, & from worms, is to put them into dry Sand as soon as they are gathered; this retains the moisture in them, and vegitative properties, without sprouting. Mrs Washington joins me in best respects to you & your Lady, & I am with truth & affection, Dr Sir—&c.

G: Washington

LB, DLC:GW.

From Thomas Montgomerie

Dear Sir   Dumfries 1st July 1785
    This will be delivered you by Mr William Shaw[1]—I have told you he has been warmly recommended to me, and from my acquaintance with him I am inclined to have a good opinion of him; but I beg you not entirely to depend on the opinions I may have formed, but to examine and discover if his abilities and information are equal to what you would expect or desire—If you are satisfied on these points, I think I can answer you are safe in every other—I hope my recommendation will not be considered as a motive to take a person into your service who is not adequate to your objects—In no event can it be a disappointment to Mr Shaw, in the event of his giving you satisfaction I consider his situation a very desirable one—I beg you to make my compliments acceptable to Mrs Washington and I have the Honor to be with great regard Dr Sir Your most Obt Huml. Servt

Thos Montgomerie

I have taken the liberty to send by Mr Shaw 27 Dblewoons 53 half Joes and 4 Dollars, making in all £250—which I request you to deliver Mr Lund Washington[2]—It is all good weight, for in fact all this money came out of the Treasury—The balance of the money for the flour shall be ordered very soon—It will be obliging if you or Mr Washington will acknowledge the receipt of this money by return of Mr Shaw. T.M.

ALS, DLC:GW.

1. William Shaw spent Saturday night, 2 July, at Mount Vernon. In his letter to GW of 4 July, Shaw reveals the nature of their conversation and spells out his terms for accepting an offer to become GW's secretary.

2. GW enters in his cash account £250 from Montgomerie on 2 July "on Accot of Flour" (Ledger B, 203).

From George William and Sarah Cary Fairfax

My Dear Sir   Writhlington near Bath 2d July 1785.

Tho' I did myself the honor of filling more than one sheet of Paper in answer to your Excellencys last favor, very recently, by the hands of Doctor Baynham,[1] Yet as my very worthy friend Doctor Ruston came from London to Bath, and from thence hither, on purpose to desire to be introduced to some of our friends in Virginia where He and his family are unknown; I trust you will excuse the liberty I take of assuring you, that he is not only a good American by birth, but also in sentiments, his Lady and Father in law, Mr Fisher, very worthy Gents: highly esteemed by all that know them, in short I believe them to be such a family, as will be an acquisition to any Country, or neighbourhood. And Mrs Fx and self will be much obliged to You and Mrs Washington to mention their worth to your acquaintance, that they may meet with the reception they so well merit.[2] We are my Dear Sir and Madame, with every sentiment of Affectionate regard your faithful friends &c. &c.

G. Wm and S. Fairfax

LS, in George William Fairfax's hand, DLC:GW.

1. Fairfax wrote GW on 23 June in answer to GW's letter of 27 February.

2. The Fairfaxes wrote an almost identical letter on this date to Mrs. Fairfax's brother Wilson Miles Cary (DLC: Ruston Papers). Thomas Ruston of Chester County, Pa., studied medicine in the University of Edinburgh and had been practicing in England since receiving his degree in 1765. After his return to Philadelphia in 1785, he speculated in land with Robert Morris and ended up in jail for debt in 1796. GW does not record in his diaries a visit from Dr. Ruston, but he did dine with Ruston in Philadelphia during the Federal Convention in 1787.

From Guéniot

My Lord   Avallon in Bourgoyne 2d July 1785

The Heroes of the War, are those who are the Authors of the Peace. Without Victory there would not have been any Peace; If you had not made the American People, a Nation of Heroes, You had not received any other Peace, but what had been given you; a New Fabius; You have known how to Conquer without Drawing the Sword, & Your Hands, My Lord, have the uncommon advantage of Being Victorious without being imbrued with Blood. what inexhaustible Subject for the Poets, I have tried to Join myself, in the General Voice, for to Sing your Pacifick Victory's & I have Seen France & All Europe applauding my Songs, Since they can Assist, to Shew to Posterity your Name! The Heroes of Former times would not be known If it was not for the Assistance of the Muse. At Present the Muse themselves have need of a Celebrated Name, for to make themselves known, Your Name My Lord, is for mine, a Certain Passport, & as often as any One will Read the Name of Washington in my Verses, It will be Sufficient I Flatter myself, to render them immortal. But in Waiting for that immortality, very uncertain for my Muse, She languishes, in the Trouble, & in the Missfortune, of Being So Bold, My Lord, as to recommend her to your Noble Mind? before that it Can be immortal, It must live, & not be So unhappy as to Die, I have Chargd Madle Deon, my Compatriote & my Friend to Send you, My Lord, Some Copy's of that Ode upon the Peace, & I have Desir'd her to write her Recommendation, with mine I am

Gueniot Med.

Translation, DLC:GW; ALS, in French, DLC:GW.

Guéniot, a medical doctor turned poet, was born and died (c.1802) in Avallon. In addition to the *Ode sur la paix* referred to in this letter, Guéniot was the author of the *Ode sur l'abolition de la servitude dans les domaines du roi, par Louis XVI* and *Ode sur l'électricité*.

To James Rumsey

Sir,   Mt Vernon, 2d July 1785.

Early in last month I wrote you an answer to your letter of
March 10th—and sent it under cover to my brother in Berkely,
who happened at that time to be from home: the presumption
is however, that you have received it 'ere this, and I shall not
trouble you with a repetition of the sentiments therein contained.[1]

In that letter I enclosed you a hand Bill of the proceedings of
the Board of Directors, containing an Advertisement of their
want of a Manager, two Assistants, some Overseers, and a number of Labourers; requesting that it might be exposed at some
public place in the County where you live:[2] those of the two first
descriptions were required to meet the Directors at Alexandria
on Yesterday; but whether the notice was too short, or that characters who are competent to the business are difficult to be met
with, I shall not take upon me to determine; but none appearing
with such testimonials of their abilities, industry & integrity, as
the board conceived indispensably necessary for their justification—no agreement was made, but the 14th inst: appointed for
them & others, to produce such, of their qualification for this
business.

As I have imbibed a very favorable opinion of your mechanical abilities, and have had no reason to distrust your fitness in
other respects; I took the liberty of mentioning your name to
the Directors, & I dare say if you are disposed to offer your services, they would be attended to under favourable circumstances: but as this is a business of great magnitude, and good
or ill impressions in the commencement of it will have a powerful effect on the minds of the Adventurers, & on the public opinion; and as the Directors are no more than Trustees of the Company, & of consequence must proceed circumspectly; Candour
obliges me to observe to you, as I believe some of those who will
meet for the purpose of appointing a Manager & Assistants have
only a superficial acquaintance with you, that it might be well, if
you incline to offer your services, to bring some letters or other
credential of your industry &c.—& if these were to come from
members of the Company they would have the greater weight.

Colo. Gilpin (one of the Directors, & who is the bearer of this letter) is on his way to the Falls of Seneca & Shenandoah; & it would be fortunate if he shou'd meet with you in this trip.[3] I am &c.

G: Washington

LB, DLC:GW.

1. GW wrote Rumsey on 5 June. Charles Washington lived in Berkeley County.

2. See note 4 in GW to Rumsey, 5 June.

3. The minutes of the meeting on 1 July of the president and directors of the Potomac River Company, GW in attendance as president and George Gilpin and John Fitzgerald as directors, read: "A number of persons having applied to act as Directors Assistants &c: in the Potowmack Navigation, but this Board being of Opinion that none of the Applicants are equal to the Superintendance of the Business, and that none of them have brought sufficient Credentials of their Abilities and Integrity to be employed in the Subordinate Departments adjourned the Meeting to Thursday the 14th Inst: when the Board is again to sit at this place; and in the meantime Colo. Gilpin at the request of the Board undertakes to meet the Workmen at Seneca and Shanadoah agreeable to Advertisement in order to agree with them, & fix a Time when they shall come prepared to begin the Work" (DNA: RG 79, Records of the Potomac Co. and the Chesapeake and Ohio Canal Co., item 159). See also George Gilpin to GW, 10 July.

To Robert Hanson Harrison

Dear Sir: Mount Vernon, *July* 3, 1785.

In the interval between your leaving this and the arrival of Mr. Briscoe, Mr. Montgomery, of Dumfries, recommended a young man whom he thought would answer my purpose; and being desired to speak to him, he accepted my offer, and will be with me in the course of a few days.[1] Had it not been for this, the good character given of Mr. Briscoe by you and others would have induced me, without hesitation, to have accepted of his services. I thank you very sincerely for the ready and early attention you paid to my inquiries. To assure you of the great esteem and regard I have for you is unnecessary, because you must be convinced of it; I shall only add, therefore, that I am, very affectionately, your obedient and obliged humble servant,

GEORGE WASHINGTON.

Printed in *ASP, Claims*, 1:852.

1. Harrison was at Mount Vernon on 11 June, and William Briscoe arrived there on 23 June with Harrison's letter of 20 June (*Diaries*, 4:151, 155). Thomas Montgomerie's letter is dated 21 June. See note 1 in Montgomerie's letter.

From John Rumney, Jr.

Sir   W[hite]haven [England] 3d July 1785

By the Casar I did myself the Pleasure of writing you, at same Time sent you Patterns of Flags made in this Country—which I hope you recd.[1] By this Opportunity of the Ship Peggy, I send you the Patterns of three Irish Flags, which have but lately recd. you had the Particulars of them before & you can easily distinguish them. One of the Kilkenny Marble, one of the black Stone of the Country & one of Portland Stone, They seem to give the Preference to the Black Stone, rather than the Marble the latter is easily defaced. In my opinion the black Flag from the Isle of Man will answer your purpose best. I shall wait your Determination & upon receiving your Instructions, shall endeavour to execute them in the best Manner. I hope the Young Man I sent you out would give entire Satisfaction, which I should be very glad to hear. I cannot meet with a Bricklayer that would suit you, if you are not allready furnish'd with one, please at some Opportunity to mention it & I shall use my Endeavours to procure you one.

In a Letter from my Father lately, he requests his sincere thanks to you for your very polite & genteel Letter to him.[2] Pray present my best respects to Mrs Washington & Family. I am with the greatest respect Sir Your mo. obt & hble Servt

John Rumney

ALS, DLC:GW. "℗ Peggy Captn Tyndall" is written on the cover.

1. GW wrote to Rumney on 22 June to acknowledge Rumney's letters of 8 Sept. 1784 and 9 Feb. 1785. Rumney here is referring to the latter.

2. Only one letter from GW to John Rumney, Sr., that of 5 July 1784, has been found.

From William Fitzhugh

Dear General   Millmont [Md.] July 4th 1785—

I had the Honor of your favor by Mr Bolton of the 21st of May—It came to me One month After date, Coverd by one from Him, informing me of his Contract to do your Business, but that his Creditors takeing Alarm at His going out of the state, had threatn'd to Sue him, & that he was Inform'd, some had Actually taken out writs against him—in consequence of which he had written to the care of Colo. Hooe of Alexandria Adviseing you that it woud not be in his power to Comply with His Contract[1]— I have not seen Bolton, but am Inform'd he has been drunk The Greatest Part of the time since His return from Virga—I was at Colo. Platers yesterday, who says that Bolton, Immediately on his return acknowledged his Contract, and at the same time De-clar'd he had no Intention to Comply with it—The Colo. is of oppinion that the Excuse he offers is without foundation, & that he has no other reason for disappointing you, than his un-willingness to seperate from His Idle & Drunken Associates Here—I am Extreamly Sorry that I recommended so Intemper-ate and Imprudent a Man to You—He is certainly one of the first Workmen on this Continent, & the most Capable of Per-forming the Business you wanted in an Elegant Manner—I did flatter myself that freed from an Idle Family, & distant from Worthless Associates—He wou'd compleatly Answer Your Pur-pose—But His Conduct on the present Occasion has convinc'd me, that He was unworthy of Attention—& I now wish your Ex-cellency to have no dependance on him.

I shall be Happy in Supplying the Several things you want for Building, & amongst them will venture to send the Brass Spring Locks or hinges unless you forbid it—on a presumption that they will Answer your Purpose—as I do not Expect Boltons ad-vice—you shall have the Crown Glass 8 Inches by ten, & a divi-dend of the other materials you mention—you say nothing of Hinges—I presume you have got the list of materials sent by Bolton[2]—As from Boltons Conduct you will have no occasion to send for His tools, wou'd it not be convenient to Send the Wag-gon for the Building Materials, which I Suppose will weigh Near or upwards of 800 Ct—or wou'd you rather take the Chance of an opportunity by Water? Shou'd the first be prefer'd, I have spoke to Colo. Plater to give your Servant an Immedeate Passage to me, & I will dispatch my boat with the materials to His Seat, where the Waggon may wait.

I Purpose going to Annapolis the 15th Inst. & shall return in a Week—and be at Home until the middle of September—And If not the Goods shall be Pack'd—ready for dispatch when Call'd for.

Be pleas'd to acept my thanks for your very friendly Offer of the Service of your Jacks next Spring in case they shou'd Arive, & will Accept it for two of my Mares. Mrs Fitzhugh Joins with me in respectful Complts & best wishes to you your Lady & Family. I have the Honor to be with every Sentiment of respect & Esteem Your Excellencys Affectionate & Oblig'd Humle Servt

Willm Fitzhugh—

P.S. The grass seeds and corn you were so kind to give me have been attended to—of the Guinea Grass not a seed has vegetated—the Orchard Grass is in growth & promises to be very valuable. the Corn is Also flattering. yrs W.F.

ALS, DLC:GW. Fitzhugh sent the letter to the care of John Fitzgerald in Alexandria (Fitzhugh to GW, 16 July).

1. See Richard Boulton to GW, 4 June.
2. See Fitzhugh to GW, 13 May, n.2.

From William Shaw

Dear Sir   Dumfries 4th July [17]85.

I have embraced the first opportunity of writing you my Sentiments, upon the Subject we were Speaking of at Mount Vernon.[1] In the first Place, as to Wages, I hope your Excellency will not think Fifty Pounds Stg ℀ Annum with Bed, Board, Washing &c. too great a Demand, as I Can Assure you I have refus'd much greater offers, but Preferr Staying with you, for a less Sum, as it will entitle me to be in Better Company, & a Genteeler line of Life; & Secondly as to the Time, I Shall Stay with you, I cannot at Present name, But Shall think myself always obligd to give you a Sufficient Notice, before I leave you, So as to enable you to look out for another Person Capable for doing your Bussiness, & Shall not part with you untill you have found one, &

lastly Shall expect to have it in my Power to come down to Dumfries, or any other Place at a Small dist. for a Day or Two, when your Bussiness does not interfere, which I Shall always look upon, not only as my duty, but interest to attend to; These, Sir, are my Sentiments upon the Subject, which I hope will Coincide with yours, & you will please let me know ℔ return of Post,[2] if they are So, & I Shall wait upon you Some time next week, as Bussiness will not allow me to Come Sooner, But Should you wish me before that time, I Shall Leave my own affairs unsettled, & wait upon you, & Believe me to be with respect Your Excellency's Mo. Obet servt

William Shaw

N.B. You will excuse this Confus'd letter, as it is wrote in haste, the Stage Being just going off, & Please let the Ladies know that there are Black & White Sattin Shoes here, & if they Wish any to Send their Measure, & I Shall do myself the Pleasure of getting them. Yours &c. W.S.

ALS, DLC:GW.
1. Shaw was at Mount Vernon on 2–3 July.
2. GW wrote Shaw on 8 July accepting Shaw's terms.

Letter not found: from Clement Biddle, 5 July. On 27 July 1785 GW wrote Biddle: "Your letter of the 5th. came duly to hand."

Letter not found: to William Hartshorne, 5 July. On this date Hartshorne wrote GW that he had received "your favor of this morning."

From William Hartshorne

Sir   Alexandria July 5th 1785
   Your favor of this morning[1] I recd with a Bill of Excha. for £20 Stg enclosed which I am willing to take myself 40 ℔ Ct that being the rate at which I bought lately and I believe is the Currt Exchange—at which rate it shall be Passed to Col. Washingtons Credit, unless you think more can be had, if so I shall do my endeavor to sell them for the most they will fetch—The Bills shall not be remitted before the 15th. The £20 Stg shall be immediately placed in the Potomac Companys fund and the remr

accounted for with Col. Washington towards his next payment, or in any other way he pleases.[2] I am very Respectfully Yours

Wm Hartshorne

ALS, DLC:GW.

1. Letter not found.

2. This relates to William Augustine Washington's payment on the requisition made on all shareholders in the Potomac River Company. See William Augustine Washington to GW, 10 July 1785, and the minutes of the meeting of the president and directors of the Potomac River Company, 30–31 May, when the requisition was adopted (GW to James Rumsey, 5 June, n.4).

From Samuel Powel

Dear Sir   Philadelphia July 5. 1785.

I wrote to you on the 24th of last Month, in Answer to the Enquiries you requested me to make, & enclosed the Paper which lead you to make them. I do not find any Reasons to induce me to change the Sentiments I then gave, tho' I should most readily have done so, had subsequent Information convinced me that they were erroneous.[1]

Dr Moyes, who passed thro' this City a few Days since, confirms me in the Opinion that the Work in Question is a mere Compilation. He regretted much that the Heat of the Weather agreed so ill with his Health as to oblige him to seek the Influence of a more northern Climate, & prevented him the Honor of paying his Respects to you, which, however, he flatters himself he shall be able to do before he leaves the Continent. Mrs Macaulay too, left us about Ten Days since, on her Way for New York. She appears to be much pleased with her Journey to Virginia.

Mrs Powel, who begs Leave to join me in the best Wishes for yourself & Mrs Washington, requests the Favor of you to deliver the enclosed Letter to your Nephew.[2] I am, with real Respect, Dear Sir Your most obedt humble Servt

Samuel Powel

ALS, DLC:GW.

1. GW had already taken Powel's advice and written Charles Vancouver conveying his refusal to grant permission for him to dedicate his book to GW. See GW to Vancouver, 30 June, and GW to Powel, 19 July.

2. Bushrod Washington became acquainted with Powel and his wife, Eliza-

beth Willing Powel, when he went to Philadelphia in 1782 to study law under James Wilson.

From Samuel Powel

Sir   Philadelphia July 5. 1785
   The Society for promoting Agriculture, lately established in this City, having done themselves the Honor of electing you a corresponding Member, have charged me with the Care of communicating the same to you. It is with particular Pleasure that I fulfill this Injunction, & doubt not that you, after having so eminently contributed to the Establishment of the Independence of our Country in the Field, will, chearfully, become a Member of a Society whose Views are solely directed to the Increase of it's Advantages, by cultivating one of the most usefull Arts of Peace.[1]
   In Conformity to the Directions of the Society, I have enclosed its Address to the public, & also a summary View of a Course of Crops &ca written by a Mr Bordely of Maryland.[2] I have the Honor to be Sir Your most obedt humble Servt
                                                      Samuel Powel

ALS, DLC:GW.
   1. The Philadelphia Society for Promoting Agriculture composed of twenty-three members living in or about Philadelphia was founded in February 1785. At its first meeting on 1 Mar., Samuel Powel was elected president of the society and served until his death in 1793. As the stated purpose of the society was "the promoting a greater increase of the products of land within the American states," it sought to add honorary, or corresponding, members like GW from other states and from abroad (Gambrill, "John Beale Bordley," 419).
   2. John Beale Bordley (1727–1804) of Maryland, the first vice president of the Philadelphia Society for Promoting Agriculture, published in Philadelphia in 1784 *A Summary View of the Courses of Crops, in the Husbandry of England & Maryland* . . . .

Letter not found: from Peter J. Van Berckel, 5 July. On 22 Aug. GW wrote Peter J. Van Berckel: "The letter which your Excellency did me the honor to write to me on the 5th of last month, came to this place."

To Tench Tilghman

DEAR SIR: [Mount Vernon 6 July 1785]

By Mr Go[u]v'r Morris I send you two Guineas and an half, which is about the cost of the plank you were so obliging as to send me by the Baltimore Packet.[1] Please to accept my thanks for your attention to that matter, and the assurances of the sincere esteem and regard with which. I am, Dear Sir, Y'r Most Obed't and Affect'd Hble. Serv't,

Geo. Washington.

Printed in John Heise catalog no. 3, item 164, 1968.

1. Tilghman wrote GW on 4 June that he had sent by the packet 357 feet of plank to John Fitzgerald for GW at a charge of £4.6.9 Maryland currency. GW fails to note in his cash accounts the payment of the two and one-half guineas to Tilghman. Gouverneur Morris was at Mount Vernon from 5 to 7 July. Morris had been in Virginia prosecuting a lawsuit for Robert Morris to collect a debt from Carter Braxton.

From Middleton Balt

Sir   George Town [Md.] 7th July 1785

By this will Informe you of a Brother in Law of minc who has been bred a Military Enginere in the Tower of London and may Probably understand Something of inland navigation I am Desirous to Know from his Excey and the Directors Whether Such a person would meet with Encourgemt In the proposd Undertaking to render Potomac River navigable and Also what Incouragemet He might meet with from the Gentlemen Directers Heare If Such a Gentlemem Should Be wanting I will Immediately Wrighte him in the Jerseys and what he Knowes Conserning this Buisiness, He is a Compleat Drafsman And if wanted will p[r]oduce a Carector to Satisfacton. I Am Gentlem. Your Most Obt Hubl. Servt

Middleton Balt

ALS, NjMoNP: Smith Collection. The letter is addressed to GW and the directors of the Potomac River Company.

To Thomas Corbin

Sir,   Mount Vernon 8th July 1785.

Yesterday afternoon I had the honor to receive your favor of the 24th of June; covering a letter from Colo. Fairfax of Bath, dated in Mar: last.[1] The latter speaks of the injurious treatment you have met with, & of the aspersion of your character in England—for which I am exceedingly sorry; but as he draws no conclusion, & your letter is silent, I am a little at a loss to discover the tendency of the information of them to me;[2] & therefore shall only add that whenever it is convenient & agreeable to you to come into this part of the Country, I shall be glad to see you at this place—& that, I am Sir—&c.

G: Washington

LB, DLC:GW.

1. Corbin's letter has not been found, but see George William Fairfax to GW, 19 March. Both letters were brought to Mount Vernon on 7 July by Corbin's steward.

2. See note 1 in Fairfax to GW, 19 March.

To William Shaw

Sir,   Mount Vernon 8th July 1785.

Your letter of the 4th I receiv'd on the 6th. Altho' the sum stipulated is above the mark I had prescribed myself yet, in consideration of the good character given of you by Mr Montgomerie—the idea I entertain of your knowledge of Accots, & the hope that you may answer my purposes in other respects; I accede fully to the terms of your letter, with this condition only— that in payment of this sum, Dollars shall be estimated at four & six pence Sterling, & other Gold & Silver coin (currt in this Country) in that proportion. This is the legal difference of exchange of it, and will render it unnecessary for either of us to enquire into the rise or fall, to ascertain the value of any payment.

I do not request you to come hither before the time mentioned in your letter; but should be glad if you would not exceed it. With esteem & regard, I am &c.

G: Washington

LB, DLC:GW.

Letter not found: to William Grayson, 9 July 1785. GW wrote in his diary on 9 July that on that day he wrote and gave Arnold Henry Dohrman a letter to Grayson (*Diaries*, 4:163).

To Richard Henry Lee

Dear Sir,   Mount Vernon July 9th 1785.

Mr Dohrman who does me the honor of presenting this letter to your Excellency, is represented to me as a Gentleman of great merit; and one who has rendered most benevolent & important Services to the injured Sons of America, at a period when our Affairs did not wear the most favorable aspect.

He has some matters to lay before Congress which he can explain better than I. the justice due to which, & his sufferings, need no advocate; but I take the liberty nevertheless of introducing him to your countenance & civilities.[1] With great respect, esteem & regard I am, Dr Sir Yr Excellys Most Obt & Affecte Hble Servt

Go: Washington

ALS, DNA:PCC, item 78. Written on the cover: "favd by Mr Dohrman." The letter is docketed: "Letter—Genl Washington—in favr of Mr A: H: Dorhman."

1. See Patrick Henry to GW, 4 April 1785, and note 1 of that document. GW also wrote on this date a letter of introduction to Samuel Chase, the text of which reads: "I take the liberty of introducing Mr. Dohrman to your friendly notice and civilities. He is represented to me as a gentleman of great merit, and one who, at an early period of the war, (when our affairs were rather overshadowed,) advanced his money very liberally to support our suffering countrymen in activity [captivity].

"He has some matter to submit to Congress, which he can explain better than I. I am persuaded he will offer nothing which is inconsistent with the strictest rules of propriety, and, of course, that it will merit your patronage" (*ASP, Claims*, 1:512).

From Edmund Randolph

Dear sir   Richmond July 9. 1785.

With this you will receive a copy of the proclamation, authenticated by the register's seal.[1] I was indeed hopeful to add the testimonials of the state: but the lieutenant governor, not being in town nor expected until the departure of the post, I thought it adviseable rather to send the inclosed, than delay you. I believe that this will answer your purpose; but for fear of cavil, I will forward by the next post an act of the Lt Govr, declaring Mr Harvie to be register, & that his official proceedings are intitled to full faith and credit.[2] I am Dear sir with the sincerest regard yr affte friend & serv.

Edm: Randolph

ALS, NhD.

1. The royal Proclamation of 1763 halting settlement in the transmontane West also provided that the veterans of the French and Indian War would be given the right to claim land in the West. See Thomas Smith to GW, 14 July, and Randolph to GW, 4 June 1785, n.1.

2. Beverley Randolph was lieutenant governor of Virginia. Edmund Randolph forwarded the certificate in his letter to GW of 17 July.

Letter not found: to James Wilson, 9 July 1785. GW wrote in his diary on 9 July that on that day he wrote and gave to Arnold Henry Dohrman a letter to Wilson (*Diaries*, 4:163).

From George Gilpin

Dr sir   Sunday July 10th 1785

on Sunday the 3d of this month I went within one mile of the Seneca falls it then rain'd very fast which prevented me from going nearer, on monday the 4th I went to Mr Gideon Moss's who lives the nearest to the Falls of any person on the Virginia Side and who Issued provisons to the hands that workd under Johnston & Clapham last year, I then Crossed over the river Just above the falls to the maryland Side and went down to Where the huts was in which the people lived last fall and then to a Mr Goldsborougs at whoes house Johnston & Clapham lodged When they attended the works I found no person at any of these places who wanted to engage immediately one person who had been At mr Goldsborougs on the 1st day of the month by mistake Went away he wanted work and Said he understood blowing rocks Mr moss and others informd me that they thought hands might be procured after harvest but they ware all employd in gathering their Grain and Hay; I left a Short advertizment at those places and Some Others I then View'd the falls on both Sides and then Went to Shenandoah I arvied at harpers ferry on the 5th in the evening.

on the 6th it was near 12 oclock before I Could procure an Express to Bath a few labourers Came but they did not want to enter to work there was one old dutchman who Came very drunk, I informed them of the 8th day of august as the day on which their wages would begin if they appeard and would go to work—from what I Could gather from a number of gentlemen that assembled there that labourers may be had I believe anough for our porpose and 40/ Virginia Curry is about the price, the reason assignd why more did not appear was that their harvest is great and all the labourers employd I wrote a letter to Goverr Johnston and one to Goverr, S. Lee and Sent them I wrote a few Advertizements Sent one to Fredericks Town and Some to other places I viewd the falls on both Sides and got Whate Intelligence I Could Concerning the river and then waited at Capt. Breadys till Friday evening when Mr Rumsay Came we had Some Conversation about the navigation of poto-mack in which he informd me that he would be down on the 14th he gave me a letter for you which the bearer will deliver to you as also one from a Member of the Company a Colonel Hunter in favor of Mr Rumsay.[1]

I have Sent a State of the falls in the river as they now appear and have taken the liberty to make a few remarks on them, if your Excellency Should not have by you notes of this nature Sufficient Already they may be of Service & if you Should they Can be distroyd I thought it my duty to give you the best infor-mation I Could, I am with due Esteem your Excellencys Most Obt Servt

George Gilpin

ALS, MnHi. GW docketed the letter: "Colonl Gilpin's Letter & Observns 10th July 1784."

1. James Rumsey's letter has not been identified. Moses Hunter was a mem-ber of the Potomac River Company. For the possible identity of Bready, see John Sedwick to GW, 8 Aug. 1785, n.1.

From Thomas Jefferson

Dear Sir   Paris July 10. 1785.

Mr Houdon would much sooner have had the honour of at-tending you but for a spell of sickness which long gave us to despair of his recovery & from which he is but recently recovered.[1] he comes now for the purpose of lending the aid of his art to transmit you to posterity. he is without rivalship in it, being employed from all parts of Europe in whatever is capital. he has had a difficulty to withdraw himself from an order of the Empress of Russia, a difficulty however which arose from a desire to shew her respect, but which never gave him a moment's hesitation about his present voyage which he considers as promising the brightest chapter of his history. I have spoke of him as an Artist only; but I can assure you also that, as a man, he is disinterested, generous, candid, & panting after glory: in every circumstance meriting your good opinion. he will have need to see you much while he shall have the honour of being with you, which you can the more freely admit as his eminence and merit gives him admission into genteel societies here. he will need an interpreter. I supposed you could procure some person from Alexandria who might be agreeable to yourself to perform this office. he brings with him a subordinate workman or two, who of course will associate with their own class only.

On receiving the favour of your letter of Feb. 25 I communicated the plan for clearing the Patowmac, with the act of assembly, and an explanation of it's probable advantages, to mr Grand, whose acquaintance & connection with the monied men here enabled him best to try it's success. he has done so, but to no end. I inclose you his letter.[2] I am pleased to hear in the mean time that the subscriptions were likely to be filled up at home. this is infinitely better, and will render the proceedings of the companies much more harmonious. I place an immense importance to my own country on this channel of connection with the new Western states. I shall continue uneasy till I know that Virginia has assumed her ultimate boundary to the Westward. the late example of the state of Franklin separated from N. Carolina increases my anxieties for Virginia.

The confidence you are so good as to place in me on the subject of the interest lately given you by Virginia in the Patowmac company is very flattering to me. but it is distressing also, inasmuch as, to deserve it, it obliges me to give my whole opinion. my wishes to see you made perfectly easy by receiving those just returns of gratitude from our country, to which you are entitled, would induce me to be contented with saying, what is a certain truth, that the world would be pleased with seeing them heaped on you, and would consider your receiving them as no deroga-tion from your reputation. but I must own that the declining them will add to that reputation, as it will shew that your motives have been pure and without any alloy. this testimony however is not wanting either to those who know you or who do not. I must therefore repeat that I think the receiving them will not in the least lessen the respect of the world if from any circumstances they would be convenient to you. the candour of my communi-cation will find it's justification I know with you.[3]

A tolerable certainty of peace leaves little interesting in the way of intelligence. Holland & the emperor will be quiet. if any thing is brewing it is between the latter & the Porte. nothing in prospect as yet from England. we shall bring them however to decision now that mr Adams is received there. I wish much to hear that the canal thro the Dismal is resumed.[4] I have the hon-our to be with the most perfect esteem & respect Dr Sir your most ob⟨edie⟩nt & most humble servt

Th: Jefferson

ALS, DLC:GW.

1. Jefferson wrote GW on 10 Dec. 1784 of Houdon's intended mission to Mount Vernon. In addition to this letter from Jefferson, Houdon brought with him to Mount Vernon on 2 Oct. 1785 letters from Lafayette and Charles Da-mas. GW's letter from Lafayette in Paris, dated 9 July 1785, reads: "My dear General, this letter Will Be delivered By the Celebrated M. Houdon who is Going for Your Statue to America—Nothing But the love of glory and His Respect for You Could induce Him to Cross the Seas, as His Business Here far Exceeds His leisure, and His Numerous and qualified friends make Him very Happy at Home—those Circumstances I mention—as a farther Recom-mendation to Your Attentions—as I am writing By the Same opportunity I will only add a tribute of the tender love, and Grateful Respect I Have the Honour to be With My dear General Your Lafayette" (PEL). Lafayette's other letter to GW by Houdon is dated 14 July 1785.

The text of the undated letter from Damas reads: "I do myself the honour to take this opportunity to present my dutys to your Excellency. after having enjoyed your Kindness during the time I have been under your Command in America, I always remember it with the greatest pleasure and gratitude. give me leave to introduce and reccommend to your Excellency Mr houdon—the best Sculpter in Paris. the greatest Character of our age will welcome the most distinguished talent in its Kind. he Wishes to have the favour of making your bust. the most glorious employment of his parts shall be to have drawn a faith-ful picture of your Excellency, and to bring back to france his true image, where our hearts are grieved to be so far distant from the original that we will love and admire forever" (DLC:GW). GW acknowledged Damas's letter from Mount Vernon on 5 Dec. 1785: "I had the honor to be favor'd with your letter by Mr Houdon, & thank you for your kind recollection of, & for the favorable sentiments you have expressed for me.

"The moments I spent with the army of France in this country, are amongst the most pleasing of my life, & I shall ever remember with grateful sensibility, the polite attentions of all the officers who composed it—& of none more than yours" (LB, DLC:GW).

2. There is no translation in GW's papers of the enclosed letter to Jefferson from Ferdinand Grand, the French banker for the United States in Paris, and it may be that GW remained ignorant of its content. Grand wrote from Paris on 8 July 1785: "Monsieur Je me Suis ⟨ouvré⟩ avec Empressement des moyens de trouver des fonds pour le projet dont vous m'aves fait part—relativement á La Potowmac, parce que jaurois été Infiniment flaté de pouvoir Contribuer en quelque Chose au Succés dun Etablissement qui doit ajoutet un nouveau rayon à la Gloire de Mr Wasington, mais malheureusement les Circonstances me favorisent si mal que je ne puis me permetre de Vous Laisser entrer en quelques Esperances, non Seulement par la repugnance quont toujours nos Capitalistes pour les ⟨placements loinestains⟩, mais aussy par une autre raison qui n'est pas trop bonne á dire mais il n'en est pas moins vray—qu'il sest ⟨*illegible*⟩ icy depuis quelques temps un Esprit de jeu qui sest Emparé de touttes les ⟨Tetes⟩ au point que Chacun veut faire fortun dans autant ⟨d heures⟩ que nos Peres y mettoyent d'⟨oeuvres⟩ on Se ⟨jette sur⟩ nos fonds ⟨oublies⟩ qui présént plus que tout autre Employ a La Cupidité, voila pourquois La moitie des Terres du Royaume Sont á vendre ⟨Linterett⟩ qu⟨ils⟩ rendent ne Suffit plus au Sence actuel lon quitte ainsy le Sollide pour Courrir apre la fumée, cette Esquisse de nos Illusion ne doit pas passer en Amerique ou l'on nous prendroit pour de fols & n'est que pour vous faire voir qu'il faut tourner vos vues d'un autre Coté Il Servit bien a souhaiter que LAmerique Seulle ⟨puit S⟩e Suffère á elle meme pour le projet; [   ] S'il me servit doux davoir des meilleures raisons á vous donner de Limpossibilité que je trouve à faire des E⟨mprunts icy⟩ à present, Il me le servit bien d'avantage de pouvoir faire quelque Chose d'agreable á monsr Wasington & á vous monsieur . . ." (DLC:GW).

3. Well before Jefferson wrote this, GW had decided what to do about the gift of stocks in the James River and Potomac River companies. See, particularly, GW to William Grayson, 25 April, and to Nathanael Greene, 20 May.

4. See GW to Jefferson, 26 Sept., n.2.

From William Augustine Washington

Dr sir   Blenheim [Westmoreland County] July 10th 1785
    Your favour by Francis Herbert together with a Gross of Bottles came safe to hand[1]—I thank you for the information, of the demand of 5 Pr Ct upon each Share, from the Proprietors

of the Potomck Company; I have for some time past waited with impatience, for an opportunity to Alexandria, by which I might contrive my quota, but none offering, have determined to send my servant as far as your house with the Money, and have to request the favour of you to contrive it to Mr Hartshorn.[2] Jenny joins me in our sincere Loves to you & Mrs Washington, concludes me Dr sir Your Sincerely Affe

Wm A. Washington

ALS, ViMtV.

1. Letter not found. Francis Herbert has not been identified.

2. For earlier references to William Augustine Washington's payment of the requisition due from Potomac River Company shareholders, see William Hartshorne to GW, 5 July. There is this notation below Washington's signature:

Memm of Money sent—

10 half Joes	£24. 0.0
1½ Guineas	2. 2.0
2 Dollars	12.0
	£26.14.0

From William Shaw

Dear Sir   Dumfries 12th July [17]85.

Your letter of the 8th Inst. Came duly to hand, & am Sorry you think the Sum mentioned in my last, above what you intended giving. But I Still leave you at liberty, & wish, that you will reward me, only as my Services may deserve. I am Sorry that I Cannot be with you, So Soon as I intended, as Bussiness obliges me to be at Fredricksburgh, the end of this Week, & Beginning of next, which will Detain me a few days longer, But Shall be up as Soon as it is in my power. Till then I remain Your Excellency's Mo. Obedt Servt

William Shaw

ALS, DLC:GW.

From Catharine Sawbridge Macaulay Graham

New York July 13. 1785

The intemperate heat of the air which prevailed on the morning when we parted with our illustrious friends accompanied us during the whole of our journey from Mount Vernon to New York.[1]

When I arrived in this city I found my self too much indisposed to embrace so early as inclination prompted, the honor Sir of obeying the most obliging command you could have laid on me.

When we address ourselves to characters so eminently distinguished Sir as yours we wish to describe the impressions which very extraordinary virtues never fail to make on the candid mind. There are some scenes however too lively for painting to do justice too in the representation, and some sentiments too strong even for Oratory to express.

The voice of flattery has so often swelled moderate virtues into all the magnitude of excellence which speech can convey to the immagination, that we in vain search in the language of panigeric for some arrangement of words adequate to that superiority of praise which is due to the first character in the world—My present feebleness obliges me for the present to desist from the arduous undertaking especialy as I know the delicacy of your mind makes you as backward to meet applause as you are forward to deserve it. You must however give me leave to say that you above all the human race seem happily distinguished in the privilege of preserving and encreasing the esteem of mankind through the opportunity of a more intimate and correct knowledge of your character and talents.

The more attentively Sir you are examined by the inquisitive mind the more it finds, that the voice of fame tho noted for exaggerating the puny merit of mortals into a gigantic form of virtue has in your case even lessened truth; and whilst we contemplate with an exalted admiration the grand features of your public character we indulge with delight those softer sentiments of friendship which your domestic and private virtues are so well calculated to inspire. With impressions such as these Sir you may immagine that the virtues of the Great Hero of the Western World, the benevolence of Mrs Washingtons temper with that polite and captivating attention with which she exercises the virtues of hospitality to all the numerous visitors which resort to Mount Vernon are the favorite topicks of conversation on which we have dwelt ever since we have had the honor of being entertained under your roof. These topicks are fortunately universally pleasing.

That Heaven may long preserve that mode of existence in which so many bright, useful, and aimable qualities, are united, and that it may long preserve to you Sir, every pleasing circumstance which marks the felicity of the present day is the sincere wish Of Your Most Obliged And Most Humbe Servnt

Cath. Macaulay Graham

Mr Graham joins me in best respects to yourself and to Mrs Washington, for whom our wishes for a long succession of happy years are most sincerely offered; we beg to be remembered to Major Washington, and Miss Basset, and that you will present our love to the very young Lady and Gentleman.

ALS, MH: Sparks Papers.

1. On 14 June, the day Mrs. Graham left Mount Vernon, GW recorded in his diary: "Mercury at 78 in the Morning—80 at Noon And 80 at Night" (*Diaries*, 4:153).

From Thomas Johnson

Gent.   Fredk [Md.] 13 July 1785

Mr Richardson Stewart, who waited on you at the last Meeting, intends to present himself again at the next. I believe I mentioned him at the former Meeting as a very ingenious Man, of a strong mechanical Turn, sober and active, and as I had heard used to conduct those under him well—he has not been practiced in clearing Rivers one who had and earned a Character would undoubtedly justly claim a preference of any other— whether a chief Conductor of the Work answerable to the Ideas we entertained of such a One can be got or not Mr Stewart will too probably stand on a Footing with those who may offer for either End. If he is favoured with Time and a private Conversa[tion] he will explain himself on the Subject of breakg the Rocks and removing the Fragments, the most material immediate Objects, so as to enable you to form your own Idea of him in that Part; indeed he has mentioned to me a way of drilling them that I have neither seen practiced or before heard of—One of my Brothers, and they all have the Success of the Undertaking much at Heart, has more Acquaintance with Mr Stewart than I have, he has several Times mentioned him to me as a Man of whom we may entertain good Expectations in every View, and unless he is excluded by others who have been practiced in the very kind of work and are unexceptionable on other Accounts I should gladly see him employed either above the Great or Shannadoah Falls.[1]

My present State of Health will not permit me to attend now with Convenience, else as our preperation is not so forward as we hoped and expected I would have waited on you, though I still flatter myself that we may be ready by the Time Men can be worked to Advantage for the Water keeps up unusually high. I am Gent. Your most obedt Servt

Th. Johnson

ALS, PHi: Gratz Collection. The letter is directed to the "President & Directors of the Potomack Company."

1. The minutes of the meeting held in Alexandria on 14 July when James Rumsey was named superintendent of the works and Richardson Stewart the assistant manager were as follows:

"At a Meeting of the president and Directors of the Potowmack Company held on this Day and at this place pursuant to Adjournment from the 1st Inst:

were present

Genl George Washington	pt
George Gilpin	Directors
John Fitzgerald	

who after examining the following Accounts produced against the said Company allowed the same to be just and directed payment of them to be made by the Treasurer to this Company.

George Richards	£ 9.12
Philip Marsteller	2.14
Josiah Watson & Co.	30.
Wm Hartshorne & Co.	6.14
John Hartshorne	1. 5
Wm Abbot	66. 5
	£116.10

"appointed Mr James Rumsey principal Superintendant of the work for effecting which this Company was instituted under an Allowance or Salary of two hundred pounds Virginia Currency ℔ Ann: inclusive of all Expences he may incur, and Mr Richardson Stewart one of the Assistant Managers under an Allowance or Salary of One hundred and twenty five pounds Virga Currency inclusive of all his Expences—No other person appearing who produced sufficient Testimonials of Capacity and Integrity to fill the place of the other Assistant Manager the Board did not proceed to the Appointment but directed it to be made by Mr Rumsey the principal Conductor.

"It was also ordered by the Board that the Men when employed in the work should recieve their wages once in every two weeks and that a Ration should be as follows

"1 lb. Salt pork or 1¼ lb. Salt Beef or 1½ lb. fresh Beef or Mutton—1½ lbs. Flour or Bread and 3 Jills Rum ℔ day" (DNA: RG 79, Records of the Potomac Co. and the Chesapeake and Ohio Canal Co., item 159).

To William Fitzhugh

Dear Sir,   Mt Vernon 14th July 1785.

Your favor of the 4th came to me on the 12th: at the time of writing it you could not have received my letter dated in the latter part of June, covering one for Richard Boulton—not knowing how, otherwise, to get one to him, I took the liberty of addressing it to your care.[1]

In that letter I informed him, that if he did not immediately enter upon the execution of his Contract, I would put the penalty thereof in force: but from the abandoned course in which he seems to have engaged, from your last letter; & his unwillingness to forsake his Associates in drunkeness; I do not choose (altho' the disappointment occasions me the loss of a summer) to be concerned with him, lest his bad example should have an unfavorable influence upon my workmen, of which I have several. I beg therefore, if my letter to him has not been forwarded, that you would be so obliging as to destroy it.

As I am not in immediate want of the Articles which you were so good as to offer me, I had rather take the chance of a water conveyance round, than to send my waggon to Colo. Platers: but as this may not happen soon, & it is unreasonable to keep you out of the cost of them; if you will ascertain the quantity & price of such as you can best spare, I will pay the amount to your order at any time. The brass-spring Locks & hinges, & any other hinges—the mortice locks & furniture—the Glue, & Painter's brushes, or such part of each as you can most conveniently dispense with, may be added to my former list.[2]

The Guinea-grass seeds which I sowed proved as defective as yours; but my Nephew who arrived after I had the pleasure of your company at this place, brought me a small quantity from Bermuda—some of which I sowed & part has vegitated: if it prospers & is worth cultivating, I will supply you with a little of it to put you in stock—he speaks of it in very favourable terms, but is doubtful of the Climate. Mrs Washington joins in complimts & best wishes for Mrs Fitzhugh & yourself with Dr Sir &c. &c.

G: Washington

P.S: I address this letter to you at Annapolis in consequence of the information of your intention to be there about the middle of this month. G: W——n

LB, DLC:GW.

1. GW's letter to Fitzhugh of 25 June, covering his letter to Richard Boulton of 24 June, has not been found. Fitzhugh reports on 16 July having received the letters only two days before.

2. See GW to Fitzhugh, 21 May.

From Lafayette

Targuemines on the french fronteer
My dear General   july the 14th 1785

Before I leave the borders of france, I wish once more to Remind you of your absent friend, and to let You Hear that I am well and just Begining my German travels—I Have Been lately Visiting Some french towns where I Spoke grat deal about American trade, and fully Answered the views I Had the Honour to Communicate in a former letter[1]—Now I am on my way to *the deux ponts* where Resides our friend the future elector of Baviera, to *Cassel* where I will See Again the Hessian Regiments, to *Berlin* where I am told lord Cornwallis is also going—from there I will wait on the King of prussia on His Grand Maneuvres in *Silesia*—Visit *Saxony*—See the *austrian Camps in Bohemia*—pay my Respects to the Emperor at *Vienna*—Return to *Berlin*, where grand Maneuvres are to take place at the end of September—and after I Have on My Way examined all the fields of Battle, I will Return through *Holland* and Be again in paris By the Middle of october This letter, my dear General, goes with our old friend doctor franklin who, I Hope, will Be Received with that Respect He So much deserves—it will Be forwarded By His Grand Son a very deserving Young Man who wishes Being introduced By me to You, and whom I Beg leave to Recommend to Your Attentions. He Has Been much employed in public Service—got Nothing By it—and as the doctor loves Him Better than Any thing in the world, I think He ought to Have the Satisfaction to See Him Noticed By Congress—You will oblige me to let them know that I spoke to You My Mind about it.[2]

You Remember an idea which I imparted to you three years ago—I am Going to try it in the french Colony of Cayenne—But will write more fully on the Subject in my other letters.[3] Nothing New Now in the political world—war is far at a distance—adieu, my Beloved General, my most affectinate Respects wait on Ms Washington—Remember Me to the young ones—to my aid George—to M. lund—all our friends, and particularly to Ms Stuart—You Know My Heart, my dear general, and I Need not adding the assurances of the filial love, Respect, and gratitude I Have the Honour to Be with Your devoted friend

Lafayette

Gouvion is going with me and Has the Honour to present His Respects to You.

ALS, PEL.

1. Lafayette may be referring to his letter of 13 May when he writes GW about "Some proposals for a Contract about Whale oils."

2. See the letters to GW from Benjamin Franklin and William Temple Franklin dated 20 Sept. and GW's responses dated 26 September. See also GW to Benjamin Franklin, 25 Sept., printed as note 1 in Franklin to GW, 26 September.

3. Lafayette wrote GW on 5 Feb. 1783 proposing that the two of them "Unite in Purchasing a Small Estate Where We May try the Experiment to free the Negroes, and Use them only as tenants. Such an Exemple as Yours Might Render it a General Practice" (Idzerda, *Lafayette Papers*, 5:90–93). Lafayette on 7 June 1785 instructed his attorney to buy for him estates in French Guinea with the proviso that the owner would "neither sell nor exchange any black" (ibid., 330). He wrote GW on 6 Feb. 1786 that for ₶125,000 he had bought "a plantation in the Colony of Cayenne and am going to free my Negroes in order to Make that Experiment which you know is my Hobby Horse."

To Thomas Smith

Sir, Mt Vernon, 14th July 1785.

Your letter of the 9th of Feby was long on its passage to me; but my answer would not have been delayed 'till now, had not much time been spent in obtaining the several enclosures herewith sent you: a very necessary voucher however, viz.—the British Kings proclamation, properly authenticated, forbiding the settlement of the Western Lands, in defiance of which the Defendants took possession of the Land which was surveyed for military service, is not yet come to hand—but shall be sent as soon as it does.[1]

The signature to Poseys Bond has the best proof of the hand writing I can obtain without incurring much trouble & expence: there are numbers in this part of the Country, where he formerly lived, who are well acquainted with his hand writing; but these are far removed from the Executive of the State, or any of the judges of the Supreme Court of this Commonwealth. To me, I confess the proof seems unnecessary; for in my judgment there can be no higher evidence of the authenticity of the Bond, than the recognition of it in the Grant which was made in consequence; & which, if I mistake not, expressly declares that it is granted to me as Assignee of John Posey; consequently this Government must have been satisfied of the legality of the Assignment, & such as would warrant the Patent granted me thereon.[2]

I transmit you the Act of our Assembly passed in the session of 1779, properly authenticated, in which is included all the Law relative to the present subject: in this you will find upon what footing settlement & pre-emption rights are placed; & what are the requisites necessary for rendering them valid.[3] It is very certain the Defendants have not taken those necessary steps pointed out by the Law, in order to give them a title by settlement or pre-emption: they knew that the Land had been surveyed for me; that it was always called mine; that one Cabbin if no more was built upon it when they came there, & they were repeatedly forewarned from settling themselves there during the life of Mr Crawford. Being thus apprized that their claim was contested, they should have submitted it to the decision of the Commissioners sent out to that Country for the special purpose of adjusting all such disputed titles; & altho' the jurisdiction of these Commissioners only extended to unpatented Lands, yet such a submission was necessary on the part of the Defendants, that they might obtain Certificates & act agreeably to the direction of the Law: as they failed to do this, I conceive they have precluded themselves from getting up a title by occupancy at this day: I say they failed to make this submission; because as

I was never summoned to litigate their Claim, any proceeding therein without such a process would have been illegal.

I expect that one objection to my title will be, that this Land was not surveyed by a County Surveyor, but only by one invested with a special commission for surveying the 200,000 acres which were given as a bounty to the 1st Va regiment. But you will find that my case comes fully within the first Clause of the Law;[4] & as this Survey was covered with a Military warrant, such as is mentioned in the Act—no person could more legally have made it than Mr Crawford. I will observe here, that at the time this survey was *returned* to the Office—Mr Crawford was Deputy surveyor to Mr Lewis.[5] You will observe by a subsequent clause in the Law, that all locations made by Officers and Soldiers upon the Lands of actual settlers, shall be void; but this cannot operate against me for several reasons: in the first place it is confined merely to Locations, & cannot extend to Patents; secondly, admitting that my survey was made lawfully, then it is evident that instead of being intruded upon—the Defendants themselves were the intruders; and thirdly, setting my survey & Patent out of the question, I was the prior occupant and entitled to at least 1400 acres, admitting only one Cabbin to have been built; altho' I believe, & Capt. Crawford in letters which I left with you expressly declares it, there were more; so that whichever way you view their title, it appears to be defective. From what cause I know not, but I believe Capt. Posey's warrant is dated subsequent to the return of the Survey made by Mr Crawford, and if I remember right the recital in the Patent which you have makes this appear: I apprize you of this lest any handle should be made of it by your Opponents.

The only difficulty which can arise in the prosecution of the ejectments, in my conception (if my *legal* title shou'd be thought insufficient, which I scarcely think possible) is to prove the *extent* of my improvement before the Defendants took possession of the Lands, & the warnings wch they received afterwards to quit it. Colo. Crawford who transacted my business in your County, or his Brother Val. could have placed these matters in a clear point of view, as I dare say many others are able to do, if I knew who to fix upon & how to come at them; but never having an idea that it was necessary, & the removal of persons &c., may give some trouble.[6]

To ease you as much as I am able of this, I have in a paper enclosed, put down the ground & supports of my title under all circumstances as they have occurred to me; & the plea which I suppose will be urged in behalf of my Opponents in opposition thereto.[7]

I feel myself under great obligation to Mr Wilson for signifying a readiness to serve me in this suit—because I am satisfied motives of friendship more than those of interest were at the bottom. His attendance in Congress must now render this impracticable if it were ever so necessary; but to me the case seems so clear & self evident, that I think nothing more is necessary but to state facts: however, as you understand the decision of your Courts better than I do, I leave it wholly to yourself to call in assistance or not, & from whom you please. I should be glad to know when you think the cause will come to issue: if I could be morally certain of the time & nothing of greater importance should happen to prevent it, I would be in the Western Country at that time. I am &c.

G: Washington

P.S: Since writing the above I have received an attested Copy of the Proclamation alluded to in the body of this letter, which with the letter enclosing it, from our Attoy General, I send.[8] On a cursory reading of it, (for I was obliged to enclose it almost in the same instant I received it) it may be doubted, I think, whether military Locations beyond the sources of the rivers running into the Atlantic, do not come under the general restriction: to remove this objection, if it should be made, I will endeavor to obtain an attested copy of an order of the Governor & Council of this Dominion, recognizing the right of the Troops of this State, to Lands under the aforesaid Proclamation; & directing surveys thereof to be made on the Western Waters; tho' I fear it will be difficult to come at, as I have understood that the records of the privy Council had fallen into the hands of the Enemy, or were otherwise lost.[9] G: W——n

LB, DLC:GW.

1. See Edmund Randolph to GW, 9 July. Smith did not receive this letter from GW for some time and did not answer it until 17 November.

2. John Posey transferred to GW his right to claim 2,000 acres under the royal Proclamation of 1763, and it was under Posey's right that GW secured a

patent to most of the Millers Run tract. See Bond of John Posey, 14 Oct. 1770, printed above. GW was to discover later that Posey's warrant was dated as late as 25 Nov. 1773 (GW to Smith, 28 July 1786).

3. "An Act for adjusting and settling the titles of claimers to unpatented lands under the present and former government, previous to the establishment of the commonwealth's land office" (10 Hening 35–50).

4. GW is probably referring to the provision on the second page of article 1 of the act cited in note 3: "that all officers and soldiers, their heirs or assigns under proclamation warrants for military service, having located lands by actual surveys made under any such special commission [as William Crawford's], shall have the benefit of their said locations, by taking out warrants upon such rights, resurveying such lands according to law, and thereafter proceeding according to the rules and regulations of the land office."

5. For Crawford's appointment in 1774 as deputy surveyor to Thomas Lewis in Augusta County, see GW to Thomas Lewis, 17 Feb., 5 May 1774, and William Crawford to GW, 8 May 1774.

6. See the discussion of the Millers Run controversy in editorial note, Smith to GW, 9 Feb. 1785.

7. GW's memorandum is quoted in the editorial note cited in note 6.

8. See note 1.

9. See Randolph to GW, 29 July, n.1, for the order of the Virginia council regarding the claiming of western land under military rights.

To Alexander White

Dear Sir,   Mt Vernon 14th July 1785

Mr Fraunces's letters to you & to me, the last of which I also enclose for your perusal, are so expressive of his wants as to render it unnecessary for me to add ought, on the occasion of them.[1]

He has been considered (tho' confined within the british lines) as a friend to our cause: It is said he was remarkably attentive to our prisoners in the City of New York; supporting them, as far as his means would allow, in the hour of their greatest distress: this it is which lead both Governor Clinton & myself to countenance & support him; & is the cause I presume of his applying, thro' me, to you—& must be my apology for giving you the trouble of this letter.

With respect to his demand against the Estate of Genl Lee, I know nothing; his letter, to the best of my recollection, is the first intimation I ever had of his being a Creditor; the propriety & justice therefore of the Claim must speak for themselves, &

will no doubt have their due weight: the *time* of payment seems interesting to him.

The subject of this letter reminds me of an accot of my own against Genl Lee's Estate, which I put into your hands at the Springs last year.[2] With great esteem I am &c.

G: Washington

LB, DLC:GW. When acknowledging this letter on 26 July, White identifies it as a letter of the "16th instant."

1. Samuel Fraunces enclosed a letter to White in his letter to GW of 26 June, which see. For White's role as attorney to settle Gen. Charles Lee's estate in America on behalf of Lee's sister, Sidney Lee, see Sidney Lee to GW, 23 May 1784, n.3, and 5 April 1785. See also White to GW, 26 July 1785.

2. White promises on 26 July to pay GW as soon as possible. GW must have seen White in September 1784 when on his way to Pennsylvania GW stopped at Bath in Berkeley County to view James Rumsey's model of a self-propelled boat.

From Darrot

General   Tobago 15th July 1785

Allow me the honor of recalling myself to your remembrance, and asking the news of you. Tho I have frequent opportunities by your Countrymen, who touch at this isle, (of which I am Governor) of learning this; yet I cannot resist the desire I have, of paying my respects to you, and solliciting a continuation of the kindnesses with which you loaded Coll Darrot while he had the honor of serving under you—My fears of being troublesome to you, have hitherto prevented me from making you this acknowledgement; which I assure you has been a real punishment to me—I shall be particularly happy, General, if you will continue your kindness to me so far, as to inform me of the news with you, and whether it will be agreeable to you, that I should profit occasionally of the opportunities of writing to you—If the little isle of Tobago furnishes any productions that would be agreeable to you, the Governor, who is, and will always be at your service, will take a pleasure in executing your commissions—If Mrs Washington recollects Col'l Darrot, who was with his regiment of Hussars to pay his respects to her, he begs permission to offer his respects to her.[1] I have the honor to be with the most respectful attachment—Your very Hble Sert

Le Darrot

Translation, in the hand of David Stuart, DLC:GW; ALS, in French, DLC:GW, transcribed in CD-ROM:GW.

René-Marie, vicomte de Darrot (d'Arrot; 1754 [or 1749]–1821), came to America in 1780 as a colonel of Lauzun's legion in Rochambeau's army. Darrot was made governor of Tobago on 19 July 1783 and remained in the French West Indies until returning to France in about 1802.

1. See GW to Darrot, 25 Sept. 1785.

To Israel Shreve

Sir,   Mt Vernon 15th July 1785.

Your letter of the 22d of June came safely to hand.

I have no Lands in the Western Country which I incline, at this time, to make actual sale of. Between the two Kanhawa's on the banks of the Ohio, I hold (bounded by the river, & of rich bottom with good Mill Seats) about 10,000 Acres of as valuable land as any in that region; and on the Gt Kanhawa, from near the mouth upwards, I have about 30,000 acres more of equal quality with the first mentioned; all of which I have offered on Leases, for 21, 999, or 10 years, renewable forever, on encreasing rents; on certain conditions which were published in Claypoole's paper in March or April of last year, & may easily be resorted to.[1]

As I have not disposed of these lands yet, I presume the terms are thought too high; but as I know the situation & convenience of them, & that the quality of the soil is inferior to none in all the Western Territory, I do not incline to make any change in my terms, unless I am in a manner compelled to it by taxation, which (however inconvenient it may be to myself) I wish to see heavily laid on, that the Officers & Soldiers, & other public creditors may receive their just dues. I am &c.

                                                    G: Washington

LB, DLC:GW.

1. See GW's advertisement of his western lands printed as an enclosure in a letter to John Witherspoon, 10 Mar. 1784.

From William Fitzhugh

Dear General   Millmont [Md.] July 16th 1785 Saturday

I had the Honor of your favor of the 25th Ulto Covering one for Mr Bolton—It did not come to Hand until last thursday Evening. & I yesterday sent Boltons L[ette]r to Colo. Platers, in hopes of obtaining His Answer to forward Herewith from Annapolis—where I Expect to be on Monday next & to return Home at the end of the Week.[1]

My address of last week in Answer to your favor of the 21st of May, went by a Gentleman Immediately to Alexandria,[2] who promis'd to deliver it to Colo. Fitzgerrald so that I have no doubt of its getting to hand, but lest it shou'd not, it may be necessary to repeat that your Excellency Shall have the Crown Glass 10 Inches by 8—& a dividend of the Other Materials—Nails—Oil, Paint—Glew, Sash Lines & Pullies—&c. as noted in your Letter of the 21st of may. And directly on my return from Annapolis about this day week, they Shall be divided—pack'd, & ready for your Call, at my Old Settlement of Rousby where they have remain'd as they were Imported—If you Shou'd find it convenient to Send Your Waggon to Colo. Platers, tho for a light Load, it perhaps may be most Elegible for the Safety & Security of the Goods—I have spoken to the Colo. who will be happy in the Accommodation of your Servants & hands, & has promis'd to give me Immediate Notice of their Arival at His House—When I will Send my Boat directly with the Materials to his landing—If you shou'd rather approve the Chance of a Water Passage the Goods Shall be ready for it at Rousby Hall.[3]

The distress I feel for your disappointment—the disagreeable Situation of your House, & Boltons Infamous conduct—leaves me really at a Loss what to say on the Subject—cou'd I have foreseen that the Man had been Capable of Acting as he has done, I wou'd sooner have parted with my right hand than recommended Him to you. I knew him to be an Excellent Workman, & perfectly Qualify'd to Finish Your Large Room in the most Elegant Manner, And tho at times Imprudent & adicted to Liquor—Expected that when Seperated from his Idle & disorderly Connections, He wou'd Have perform'd to Your perfect Satisfaction—& I hope your Excellency will do me the Justice to believe that those were the only motives which Induced me to recommend Him to You. I wish I had never seen him—He is an unworthy Man, & deserve to be prosecuted to an example, And If he has any friends who will risque their Character, in the Countenance or Support of Such Improper Conduct, they will perhaps, or at least ought to Pay the damage.[4]

Mrs Fitzhugh & my Son William Join with me ⟨in⟩ respectful Complts & best Wishes to you your Lady and Family. I have the Honor to be with perfect, Respect & Esteem Yr Excellencys Affect. & Oblig'd Hle Sert

Willm Fitzhugh

ALS, DLC:GW. See note 4.

1. GW's letter to Fitzhugh has not been found. The letter to Richard Boulton is dated 24 June. No "Answer" from George Plater has been identified.

2. See Fitzhugh's letter of 4 July.

3. See GW to Fitzhugh, 14 July.

4. Fitzhugh wrote to GW from Annapolis on 19 July: "I did Expect Boltons Answer to your Letter to send herewith, but he told my servant who demanded it that it requir'd time of Consideration—I do not believe He intends to give any—He has I am told undertaken several Pieces of Work in St Marys County" (DLC:GW)

From John Tucker

Dear Sir   Barbados July 16, 1785

The sensible pleasure I feel at being Personally known to you, has Induced me to send you the Inclosed Dissertation on the Revolutions of States and Empires. It is the performance of a Worthy Clergyman of this Island; a Gentleman of a most amiable Character, and who I have the Happiness of being Intimately acquainted with.

As this Treatise Breaths Liberal sentiments, Favourable to the Future Happiness and Prosperity of my Country; so I please my self it will not only meet with Your Approbation, but also with the Approbation of all America.[1]

Inclosd I send you a Letter Mr Bowcher wrote to me on the Subject; and to which I beg leave to Refer you by which you will find he has under Contemplation a Code of Laws respecting the future Prosperity and Happiness of America.[2]

This Worthy Gentleman has a Numerous Family, and the Living of his Parish does not admit him to make that Provision for them that his Friends wish him the Power of doing, a Circumstance that has in some Measure Induced many of his Friends to undertake the disposal of these Treatises, and as I have the pleasure of being of the Number, so I shall by the first Vessel to Norfolk, send to Mr Thos Newton and to Mr Wm Pennock at Richmond One Hundred Copies to be disposed of at a Dollar Each; so that should this Gentlemans Sentiments Coincide with your Ideas, Permit me, Sir, to request the Favor of your Countenance in the Disposal of them; An Obligation that I shall be Happy to make you any return for in this Island. I am, Believe me, Dear Sir, Your very Obedt hum. Servt

John Tucker

ALS, DLC:GW.

This is most likely John Tucker of St. George, Bermuda, the son of Chief Justice John (Jacky) Tucker of Bridge House and the brother of two influential assembly members, Henry Tucker of Somerset and Speaker James Tucker. Partners of the privateer and merchant firm, Jennings, Tucker and Company, this prominent family actively supported the American cause and flourished during the Revolution (Wilkinson, *Bermuda in the Old Empire*, 192; Kennedy, *Biography of a Colonial Town*, 27–28). GW may have met Tucker during his visit to Barbados in 1751.

1. GW's copy of the sixteen-page treatise, *A Dissertation on the Revolutions of States, and Empires, with Some Considerations on the Blessings of Peace, and the Evils of War*, printed in Barbados in 1785 "for the Author," the Rev. Robert [Francis] Boucher, is in the Washington Collection of the Boston Athenæum (Griffin, *Boston Athenæum Collection*, 29–30).

2. In Robert Boucher's letter to Tucker, dated 6 June 1785, which Tucker enclosed in his letter to GW, Boucher expresses his gratitude for Tucker's offer "to inclose a Copy of my Treatise to His Excellency Genl Washington." He went on to say that it would give him "a sensible Pleasure, & confer the highest Honor, to be known tho' only in a literary Point of View to so illustrious a Personage equally renowned with the most celebrated Worthies of Antiquity, unrivalled by any Patriot, or Hero, of the present Age & whose Memory will be perpetuated thro' the loud Trump of Fame, with distinguished Lustre to the latest Posterity." Boucher explained that his treatise had begun as a sermon and expressed his chagrin that GW would find it "shockingly stopped, misspelt in some Places, & erroneous in the Application of great & small Letters," because of the inexperienced printer (ibid.).

To Michael Hillegas

Sir,   Mt Vernon 17th July 1785.

The enclosed packet contains necessary & valuable papers, in a Suit which I have depending in Washington County in the State of Pennsylva., under the management of the Gentn to whom they are directed. Mr Smith requested me (tho' by a circuitous rout) to address them to your care, & he should be certain of getting them: this must be my apology for the trouble I am giving you, & for which I hope to obtain your excuse.[1]

The sooner the packet could be sent, by a *safe* hand, the better, as some of the papers point to evidence which may require time to obtain—& all of them want consideration. With esteem & regard, I am &c.

G: Washington

LB, DLC:GW. The ALS copy of this letter was listed in *American Book Prices Current*, 56 (1950), 557.

1. See the editorial note in Thomas Smith to GW, 9 Feb. 1785, and GW to Thomas Smith, 14 July. Michael Hillegas, who held the position of United States treasurer, lived in Philadelphia.

From David Humphreys

My dear General   Paris July 17. 1785

I cannot permit M. Houdon to depart for Mt Vernon without being the bearer of a line from me. I am very happy Mr Jefferson has been able to procure him to make the voyage, because I am persuaded he will be able to transmit an excellent likeness of you to the remotest ages. He is considered as one of the ablest statuaries in Europe & has performed some capital peices for the Empress of Russia. I hope Congress will also employ him to make the Equestrian Statue which they have voted for you. His having once taken a perfect likeness will facilitate very much the execution of it. The likenesses may likewise be multiplied to any number. Not only the present but future generations will be curious to see your figure taken by such an Artist. And indeed, my dear General, it must be a pleasing reflection to you amid the tranquil walks of private life to find that history, poetry, painting, & sculpture will vye with each other in consigning your name to immortality.[1]

As I know you never found me guilty of adulation on any occasion, I am confident you will not believe me capable of flattery in the present instance, even if I were to express in still stronger terms the interest I feel in your reputation. Be assured the advocates of your fame are very numerous in Europe, and that they wish for the honour of human nature & the benefit of mankind to see it placed in a just & candid point of view. Since my arrival in France I have become acquainted with a circle of noble & literary Characters who are passionate admirers of your glory; and since my last letter to you I have been strongly urged by some of them to undertake to write either your life at large; or if I had not leisure & materials for that work, at least a sketch of your life & character—I have answerd "were I master of my own time & possessed of adequate abilities, there is no task I would more willingly impose upon myself—but with a consciousness of these defects, nothing but a fear that the work would ultimately devolve upon still worse hands could ever induce me to attempt it." This makes me wish still more devoutly my dear General (after you shall be eased of the drudgery of business by the assistance of a Secry as you propose) that you would yourself rescue the materials from the unskillfull & prophane into which they will one day or another inevitably fall.[2]

Some of my acquaintances here who had seen a little Poem of mine solicited for copies in such a manner as to make a publication of it necessary—it has also be[en] reprinted in London & occasioned the author to be the subject of many news paper paragraphs—tho the sentiments & discriptions were not calculated to please English readers: yet their criticisms, as far as I am able to learn, have been sufficiently favourable as to the merits of the composition—I have the honour of forwarding a copy herewith.[3]

The certainty of peace & the consequent dearth of news & politics leave me nothing to say on these subjects—in the mean time I find myself here in circumstances agreeable enough for a man of moderate expectations. My publick character puts it in my option to be present at the King's Levee every tuesday, & after the Levee to dine with the whole Diplomatique Corps at the Cte de Vergennes—It is curious to see forty or fifty Ambassadors, Ministers or other strangers of the first fashion from all the nations of Europe assembling in the most amicable manner &

conversing in the same language; what heightens the pleasure is their being universal men of unaffected manners & good dispositions—there is none of them more civil to us than the Duke of Dorset, with whom I often dine, & who is the plainest & best bred Englishman I have seen at Paris.

The Marquis la Fayette has just set off for Prussia—he is as much the favourite of the Americans here as in America—With my most respectful Complts to Mrs Washington & the family I have the honour to be my dear Genl Your sincere friend & hble Servt

D. Humphreys

ALS, DLC:GW; ADfS, MH: Autograph file.

1. For the arrangements made by the Virginia legislature to have Houdon create a statue of GW, see doc. I in Virginia Assembly and George Washington, 15 May–15 July 1784, and note 1 of that document. See also Thomas Jefferson to GW, 10 July.

2. For Humphreys' earliest reference to GW's biography, or rather autobiography, see his letter to GW of 15 July 1784.

3. When in 1790 he published *The Miscellaneous Works of Colonel Humphreys* (New York), Humphreys gave first place to his "little Poem" of 466 lines, entitled "Address to the Armies of the United States." Preceding the poem in his *Works* are extracts from reviews by English and French critics and a letter about the poem from Chastellux, whose translation of it was published in France. Humphreys also included in the volume a preface to the poem and an "Argument." He composed the poem in 1782 and published it in 1785 under the title of "Address to the Armies of the United States of America" (ibid., 5–29). Calling GW "O first of heroes, fav'rite of the skies," Humphreys ends his panegyric with these lines:

> THE foe then trembled at the well-known name;
> And raptur'd thousands to his standard came.
> His martial skill our rising armies form'd;
> His patriot zeal their gen'rous bosoms warm'd:
> His voice inspir'd, his godlike presence led,
> The Britons saw, and from his presence fled.

From Thomas Jefferson

Sir   Paris July 17. 1785.

Permit me to add, what I forgot in my former letter, a request to you to be so kind as to communicate to me what you can recollect of Bushnel's experiments in submarine navigation during the late war, and whether you think his method capable of being used successfully for the destruction of vessels of war. It's not having been actually used for this purpose by us, who were so peculiarly in want of such an agent seems to prove it did not promise success.[1] I am with the highest esteem Sir Your most obedt & most humble servt

Th: Jefferson

ALS (letterpress copy), DLC: Jefferson Papers. Jefferson sent the letter by Houdon.

1. On this day, Jefferson wrote Ezra Stiles: ". . . a man in this city has invented a method of moving a vessel on the water by a machine worked within the vessel. . . . It is a screw with a very broad thin worm . . . and may be literally said to screw the vessel along: the thinness of the medium and it's want of resistance occasions a loss of much of the force. The screw I think would be more effectual if placed below the surface of the water. I very much suspect that a countryman of ours, Mr. Bushnel of Connecticut is entitled to the merit of a prior discovery of this use of the screw" (Boyd, *Jefferson Papers*, 8:298–301; see also Jefferson to Hugh Williamson, 6 Feb. 1785, ibid., 7:641–43). See GW to Jefferson, 26 Sept., n.5, for David Humphreys' description of David Bushnell's submarine action.

From Edmund Randolph

Dear sir   Richmond July 17. 1785.

The inclosed certificate will, I believe, authenticate the acts of Mr Harvie in his official character, to the fullest extent.[1] This is the earliest moment, in which I could procure it. I am Dear sir with great truth yr affectionate friend & serv.

Edm: Randolph

ALS, NhD.

1. The certificate has not been found, but see Randolph to GW, 9 July.

To Tench Tilghman

Dr Sir   Mt Vernon 17th July 1785

By Mr Gouverr Morris I sent you the amount of the cost of plank, which you were so obliging as to send me from Baltimore.[1]

The packet enclosed with this, for Mr Hilligas contains necessary & valuable papers for Mr Thos Smith, in a suit I have been obliged to commence in Washington County, State of Pennsylva., against sundry persons who taking adavantage of my absence & peculiar situation during the War, possessed themselves of a tract of Land I hold in the vicinity of Fort Pitt; for which I have a Patent, obtained in legal form, ever since the year 1774, and for which I am now compelled to bring ejectmts.

Mr Smith requested these papers to be sent to him under cover to Mr Hilligas as a certain mode of conveyance; but as much time has elapsed in obtaining them; as some of the papers point to evidence which may not readily be come at; as the Suit may come forward at the Septr term, & as the channel of conveyance pointed out by him is very circuitous; I should be much obliged, if *good* opportunities frequently offer from Baltimore to Carlisle, by your stripping off the address to Mr Hilligas, and forwarding the enclosure as directed to Mr Smith.[2] With much truth & sincerity I am &c. &c.

G: Washington

LB, DLC:GW. The ALS was advertised in *American Book Prices Current*, 9 (1903), 716.

1. See GW to Tilghman, 6 July.
2. See GW to Michael Hillegas, 17 July, and GW to Thomas Smith, 14 July.

From John Augustine Washington

My dear Brother   Bushfield 17th July 1785

Previous to my setting off to Mt Vernon and Alexandria the last time I was up, a great Coat of yours that you had been kind enough to lend my son Corbin when he was last at your House, and a book that my Wifes maid the time before the last that she was there had put up supposing it to be her Mistreses, as she had one in the Chariott to read on the road, was carefully sowed up in a bundle and deliver'd to me, but I forgot both and brought them back, this is the first safe opportunity by Mr Carters Vessel that has since offered to send them.[1]

I thought you seem'd undetermined when I saw you last in case both your Jack Asses came in safe, where you should fix one of them—if you should be of opinion that Berkley would be as adventagious as any other place, I would gladly take him to my plantation where I have a very carefull manager, he should be well taken care of at my expence for the prevelidge of putting my own Mares to him—the price for the season for other Mares to be fixed by your self and the money recd and paid to you, provided no Credit is given, if Credit is given Security shall be taken, but in my opinion the plan of Credit would be improper, what principally put this thought into my head was that the more Mules there was in the part of the Country where a Man lived or had property the better chance he would have to purchase if he can not raise fast enough for himself, and I am so well convinced from experience of there great utility that I would wish to have nothing else for plantation use—the foregoing proposicion is only made in case you should Judg it expedient, for otherwise I would not wish it—this family Join me in love and best wishes for you my Sister and the Family at Mt Vernon. I am my dear Brother Your very Affe & Obt

John Auge Washington

ALS, NNMM: William Smith Collection on deposit, New York Public Library.

1. John Augustine Washington came out to Mount Vernon on 18 June from Alexandria, "having gone to that place by Water," and went back to Alexandria on 20 June (*Diaries*, 4:154). "Mr Carters Vessel" may have been that of his neighbor Robert Carter (1728–1804) of Nomini Hall.

From John Paul Jones

Sir,   Paris July 18th 1785.

I avail myself of the departure of Mr Houdon to transmit to your Hands two sets of Certificats in favor of Captain Stack and Captain McCarty, who in consequence of their Service under my Orders pray to be admitted as Members of the Society of Cincinnatus.[1] Although Count de Rochambeau has made difficulties about giving those Officers his Certificate to support their pretentions, I am persuaded that you will, from the very honorable testimony I now transmit you, think they have deserved the gratification they ask; which I shall consider as a favor confered on me by the Society. If their prayer is granted, the Diplomas may be sent to Mr Jefferson or Colonel Humphreys, who know their address.

I beg Pardon, if this mode of Application is irregular, and I beseech you support the Object of the Certificates, if you think they deserve your protection. I am, wishing you perfect Happiness, Sir, your most obedient & most humble Servant

Paul Jones

ALS, PHi: Gratz Collection.

1. Edward (Edmund) Stack and Eugene McCarthy were sublieutenants in a French regiment in 1779 when Jones secured for them brevet commissions of lieutenant of marines in the United States service. Both were serving aboard the *Bonhomme Richard* when it engaged the *Serapis* off the coast of England in September 1779. The virtually identical certificates written for the two men by Jones and the supporting statements endorsed by Jones, from David Humphreys, d'Estaing, Saint-Simon-Montbléru, and Lafayette, are in DLC:GW. See GW's response of 25 Nov. 1785.

From Noah Webster

Sir   Baltimore July 18th 1785

If the request I am now to make should need any apology but such as will naturally be suggested by its own importance, I am sure it will find it in your candour. The favourable reception of my grammatical publications in the northern States, has induced me to offer them for sale in the Southern; and I am happy to find they meet with the approbation of those literary Gentlemen, with whom I have conversed on my tour to Charleston. The performance may possibly appear, at first thought, trifling; & yet as containing the rudiments of our native language, the foundation of our other scientific improvements, it doubtless ought to be considered as extremely important.[1] If you, Sir, view it in the latter point of light & have taken the trouble to examine the general plan & execution, your name, as a patron of the Institute, would be very influential in introducing it to notice in these States. I should be very unhappy to make any request, a compliance with which would require the least sacrifice from so distinguished a character; but if it can be done, consistently with the sentiments of your heart & the delicacy of your feelings, the addition of your name, Sir, to the catalogue of patrons, will, I vainly hope, be a continuation of your public utility—& will certainly be esteemed a singular favour conferred on one who is anxious to improve the literature & advance the prosperity of this country.[2] I have the honour to be Sir, with the highest respect, your most obedient most humble Servant

Noah Webster jun.

P.S. I shall probably remain here till October.

ALS, DLC:GW.

1. Noah Webster (1758–1843) had recently published his *Grammatical Institute of the English Language*. He visited Mount Vernon in May, spending the night of 20 May there. On 15 Sept. he began advertising in the *Virginia Journal and Alexandria Advertiser*: "*Webster's Grammatical Institute, In THREE PARTS.*"

2. See GW's response, 30 July. See also the correspondence regarding the possibility of Webster's becoming GW's secretary: Webster to GW, 16, 18 Dec. 1785, 31 Mar. 1786; GW to Webster, 18 Dec. 1785, 17 April 1786.

From William Jackson

Dear General,   Philadelphia July 19. 1785.

I am directed by the Pennsylvania State Society of the Cincinnati to inform you, that the diplomas which were signed by you, and intended for our State Society, were lost in the transmission from Mount Vernon to Baltimore—and I am likewise directed to request that you would be pleased to point out such mode, as may be most acceptable to yourself, to obtain the recovery of them.

It would seem from the circumstance of a diploma being found in the possession of a person, committed to Baltimore gaol for theft, that the packet had formed a part of his plunder—although, when questioned on the subject, he would give no satisfactory information.

Perhaps an advertisement in the news-papers, offering some reward for the restoration of them, might answer a good purpose—and prevent designing persons from making an improper use of them—But the Society submit the mode, and means of carrying it into effect, entirely to the President General's opinion.[1] With ardent wishes for your happiness—and, with the most respectful and affectionate esteem—I am, my dear General, Your much obliged and most obedient Servant.

W. Jackson

ALS, MdHi.

William Jackson (1759–1828), who was later to become secretary of the Constitutional Convention and, from 1789 to 1791, GW's secretary, was at this time secretary of the Pennsylvania Society of the Cincinnati, in which capacity he was writing.

1. For the loss of the diplomas intended for the Pennsylvania members of the Society of the Cincinnati, see Otho Holland Williams to GW, 20 April, and the references in note 1 of that document.

From Battaile Muse

Honourable Sir   Berkeley County July 19th 1785

I wrote to you some Time ago respecting the Debt due you by Mr Henry Whiting[.] Least the Letters Fail'd I have to inform you that I expect to receive the money from the Sheriff in this County the Last week in Septr.[1] When received I shall waite on you Immediatly I shall endeavour to Collect the money and be at Mount Vernon before the middle of October next. I am Sir your Obedient Humble servant

Battaile Muse

ALS, DLC:GW.

1. For the successful efforts of GW and his land agent, Battaile Muse, to collect the arrears in rent from GW's former tenant, Henry Whiting, see GW to Muse, 3 Nov. 1784, n.3.

To Samuel Powel

Dear Sir,   Mount Vernon 19th July 1785.

Consequent of your first letter respecting Mr Vancouver, & his proposed publication, I wrote to him, and declined the honor of his dedication—I thank you for your second Acct of his performance, which confirms me in the propriety of the measure.[1]

It would have given me pleasure to have seen a Gentlemn of Doctr Moyes[']s eminence; and I shall hope for the endulgence of it when he returns from Carolina. I am not less pleased at hearing that Mrs Macauly Graham was satisfied with her journey Southward, considering the extreme heat in which it was made & her unfitness to encounter it.

I pray you, Sir, to offer my best respects to Mrs Powel & to assure her that great care shall be taken of her letter to my

Nephew; who lives at present in Fredericksburgh. Mrs Washington unites in compliments & best wishes for your Lady & self with Dr Sir Yr Most obedt & very Hble Servant

Go: Washington

ALS, ViMtV.

1. Powel wrote GW about the unsavory reputation of Charles Vancouver on 24 June and 5 July (first letter); GW's letter to Vancouver is dated 30 June.

To Samuel Powel

Sir   Mount Vernon 19th July 1785.

The honor which the Society for promoting agriculture, lately established in the City of Philada, have done me by electing me an honorary member, is highly pleasing & flattering to me; the strongest assurances of which I pray you, at the next meeting, to communicate with my respectful compliments to the Society: Accept at the same time Sir, my acknowledgement of the flattering expression, with which you have accompanied the certificate of my election.

No measure, in my opinion, will be more conducive to the public weal than the establishment of this Society, if the purposes of it are prosecuted with spirit. Much is it to be wished that each State would institute similar ones; & that these Societies when formed would correspond regularly & freely with each other. we are not only in our infancy of agricultural improvment; but in this State the farmers are pursuing an unprofitable course of Crops, to the utter destruction of their Lands.

I am obliged to the Society for its address to the public, & for the summary of a course of crops by Mr Bordely: the latter I had before received from the author, who was so obliging as to send me several copies immediately after the publication thereof.[1] I have the honor to be &c.

G: Washington

LB, DLC:GW.

1. See Powel to GW (second letter), 5 July, n.2.

From Arthur St. Clair

Dear Sir   Philad[elphi]a July 21st 1785

This is accompanied by a Letter from the State Society of the Cincinnati which was written to you more than a Year ago, and by some inadvertance of the under Secretary was never forwarded.[1] I am very sorry that it has so happened, because it would have been some satisfaction to you to have known, at an early period, that this State Society had come into the proposed Alterations—It was not however without great Reluctance the first Institution was parted with; yet it was happy that it was parted with, for the Prejudices against the Society have since entirely subsided, and, if the paper Medium that has been introduced in this State can be supported, We are in the receipt of the Interest of our Funds. I have very often the Pleasure to hear of your Excellency and never fail to enquire after You with all the earnestness of Freindship and Affection. I request You to present my best Respects to Mrs Washington and to believe me ever with the greatest Respect and Esteem Dear Sir Your most obedient Servant

Ar. St Clair

ALS, DLC:GW.

1. The letter "written to you more than a Year ago," dated 9 July 1784, is in the hand of William Jackson and was signed by St. Clair. See enclosure.

Enclosure
From Arthur St. Clair

Sir,   Philadelphia July 9. 1784

The circular letter from the General Society of the Cincinnati addressed to the several State Societies on the 15th of May 1784 has been received,[1] and laid before the Society of this State, and they have at their annual meeting held on the 5th of July, and continued by adjournment, agreed to accept the Institution, as altered and amended, that accompanied the said letter: But Sir, it is their opinion that the ground of the Society has been too much narrowed, and that without some farther alterations, the Society itself must necessarily, in the course of a few years, reach its final period. they have therefore directed me to lay before the General Society, the following additions and amendments, which they wish may take place, and which, they, with great deference are of opinion would not only tend to render the Institution more permanent, but more extensively useful.[2] I have the Honor to be with the greatest Respect Sir Your most obedient and very humble Servant,

Ar. St Clair
President of the State Society of Pennsylvania

LS, in William Jackson's hand, DLC:GW.

By oversight, this letter was not sent to GW until over a year after it was written, at which time St. Clair enclosed it in his letter to GW of 21 July 1785. Writing from Mount Vernon on 31 Aug. 1785, GW responded in these terms: "The letter which you did me the honor to write me in behalf of the Society of the Cincinnati of the State of Pennsylvania, has been received. The Additions & amendments proposed by it shall be laid before the General society at its next meeting" (LB, DLC:GW).

1. The circular letter is included as Appendix V in General Meeting of the Society of the Cincinnati, 4–18 May 1784, printed above.

2. St. Clair noted at the bottom of this letter these "additions and amendments": "That this be added to the 2nd Section.

"'And where any vacancy or vacancies are occasioned by the death or expulsion of any member or members belonging to any of the State Societies such State Society shall have power to fill said vacancy or vacancies at the annual meeting next, after such vacancies may happen, or some subsequent meeting.'

"The second Clause of the 4th section, after each State:

"add 'The expences of which to be borne from the State funds respectively, and that on all questions, each State shall have but one vote.'

"Section 10h after the words 'Widows and Orphans' add 'and their distressed descendants.'"

To John Fitzgerald

Dear Sir,   Mount Vernon July 23. 1785.

If there is any ship in the Port of Alexandria by which the enclosed Letters could receive a *proper* conveyance, you would much oblige me by giving them a passage—if not, by returning them.[1]

If I do not hear from my Lawyer in the Western Country before the first of August, it will be out of my power to proceed with the Directors (from the General meeting) to the Survey of the River. If my Suit should come to a hearing at the September term, wch he thought highly probable, occurances, of which he is to advise me, may indispensably call for my attendance at the Tryal—To perform both journeys, I cannot ⟨do⟩ nor would it be prudent for me, to put it out of my power, by absence on the one, to avoid the other; as the decision of the Court *may* make a difference of between £3500 and £4000 to me for which I can sell the Land in dispute if I establish my right to it; of which there can be no doubt, if justice prevails, and the title is as clearly delineated as the case will admit of.[2] I mention this matter in time, from a hope, that similar causes may not interfere to produce the same effect in any other of the Directors—with great esteem and regard I am—Dr Sir Yr Obedt friend and Affecte Servt

                                        Go: Washington

ALS, owned (1992) by Mr. Ralph G. Newman, Chicago, Illinois.

1. GW may have been referring to his letter to Tench Tilghman in Baltimore of 17 July in which he enclosed a letter to Michael Hillegas of that date, which in turn covered a letter of 14 July with enclosures to Thomas Smith.

2. See the editorial note in Thomas Smith to GW, 9 Feb. 1785, for GW's suit of ejectment brought against the people living on his Millers Run property.

From Richard Henry Lee

Dear Sir,   New York July the 23d–31] 1785

I lately had the honor of forwarding a packet for you by Post that came enclosed to me from France, by the author of a Dramatic piece on the former situation of Capt. Asgil. The subject is not a bad one, but the Author of this work seems not to have made the most of it.[1]

On the 1st of May Mr Du Mas writes us, that the parties still continue to negotiate the peace *in a very threatening manner*—In truth, this whole affair is involved in much mystery, and perhaps the truth is only known in the interior cabinets of the greatest powers.[2] The Marquiss de la Fayette, in a late letter seems to think that the collected combustibles may be put in flame by various accidents. The Emperor he says is restless, the Empress of Russia ambitious, the King of Prussia old, with other combining causes renders the peace of Europe precarious—The Marquiss proposes to visit this summer the Manœuvering Troops of Austria & Prussia in the North of Europe.[3] We have lately receivd a letter from his most Ch[ristia]n Majesty, in answer to one from Congress to him recommending the Marquiss, in which his Majesty is pleased to express himself in such a manner of the Marquis as promises well for the future promotion of that Nobleman[4]—Mr Adams writes that he has been received in due form at the Court of London, has had his audience, and deliverd his Credentials to that Sovereign—No treaty when he wrote had been commenced, but we expect soon to hear of the commencement & progress of that business.[5] Mr Jay is commissioned by Congress to open negotiations with Mr Gardoque the Spanish Plenepo[tentiary] here, concerning the navigation of Mississippi, Boundary, Commerce &c. The Spanish Minister appears to be well disposed towards us. It gives me singular pleasure to hear that the plan for opening the navigation of Potomac goes on successfully, as it promises such capital benefits to our country. It is sometime since I wrote to Colo. Fitgereland desiring that he would put me down for a share.[6]

Is it possible that a plan can be formed for issuing a large sum of paper money by the next Assembly? I do verily believe that the greatest foes we have in the world could not devise a more effectual plan for ruining Virginia. I should suppose that every friend to his country, every honest and sober Man would join heartily to reprobate so nefarious a plan of speculation.[7] Be pleased Sir to present my best respects to your Lady and be assured that I am, with sentiments of the greatest respect, esteem, & regard, dear Sir Your most affectionate and obedient servant

Richard Henry Lee.

P.S. Altho I began this letter on the 23d my ill state of health and much business have prevented me from finishing it until this day the 31st of July[8]—I thank God that my health is now much better than it has been. R.H.L.

ALS, DLC:GW.

1. For the "Dramatic piece" based on the Asgill affair, see Lebarbier to GW, 4 Mar. 1785, and the source note of that document. See also GW to Lee, 22 August. Lee's most recent letter to GW, dated 18 April 1785 from New York, was by mistake not printed in volume 2 of *Papers, Confederation Series*; it appears in *Memoir of Richard Henry Lee*, 2:63–64.

2. The letter from Dumas has not been found in DNA:PCC. Dumas wrote to GW on 28 May 1785.

3. After his return to Paris in late January, Lafayette wrote to a number of

Americans in the spring about the political situation in Europe, but none of those printed or listed in Idzerda, *Lafayette Papers*, volume 5, fit the description that Lee gives here. On 16 Mar. Lafayette wrote Lee: "matters are now taking a pacific turn"; and as early as 8 Feb. he wrote to John Jay from Versailles: "Upon the whole, I strongly am of opinion No War will take place, at least for this Year" (ibid., 306–7, 293–95).

4. The letter from Congress to Louis XVI is dated 11 Dec. 1784 (*JCC*, 27:682–83); the king's response is dated 10 May 1785 (DNA:PCC, item 120).

5. A packet from England arrived in New York on 24 July bringing John Adams's letter of 1 June to Secretary John Jay reporting that he had presented his credentials and had been received by the king on that day. Not until 26 Aug. did Lee and the Continental Congress receive a decoded copy of Adams's famous letter to Jay of 2 June in which Adams gives a full account of his conversation with George III at their meeting on 1 June (Jay to the president of Congress, 22 July, 26 Aug., DNA:PCC, item 80; *JCC*, 29:662–63).

6. This is John Fitzgerald of Alexandria, one of the directors of the Potomac River Company.

7. Reporting on the recently completed session of the Virginia legislature, James Madison wrote Thomas Jefferson on 22 Jan. 1786: "A considerable itch for paper money discovered itself, though no overt attempt was made" (Rutland and Rachal, *Madison Papers*, 8:472–82).

8. Lee was absent from Congress from the middle of August until the end of September when he went to visit springs near Philadelphia for his health. See Lee to GW, 11 Oct. 1785.

Letter not found: from Edward Newenham, 23 July. GW wrote Newenham on 25 Nov.: "I have been favored with your letters of the 3d of March, 25th of May, & 23d of July."

Letter not found: to Edmund Randolph, 23 July. On 29 July Randolph wrote GW: "Your favor of the 23d instant came duly to hand."

To George Weedon

Dr Sir,   Mt Vernon 23d July 1785.

It is some time since I received the enclosed Bill, under cover from the Drawer: among a multiplicity of other letters it got buried & forgot; until a line from Mr de Marbois the other day, forwarding the third bill of same tenor & date, reminded me of it.[1]

As I do not know who the Treasurer of the Society of the Cincinnati of this State is, I take the liberty of committing the Bill to your care, with a request that you would be so obliging as to ask him personally if he is near you, or by letter if he is at a distance for a receipt for it, that I may transmit the same to Colo. De Corney, with an apology for my long silence.[2] If I knew who the state Treasurer is, I would not give you any trouble in this business; but as I really do not, I hope it will be received as an excuse for having done it. I am &c.

G: Washington

LB, DLC:GW.

1. GW is referring to the bill drawn by Ethis de Corny on Jeremiah Wadsworth to pay for Corny's admission to the Virginia Society of the Cincinnati. See Barbé-Marbois to GW, 12 June.

2. See Weedon to GW, 10 August.

From William Fitzhugh

Dear General   Millmont July 25th 1785

I had the Honor of Your favr of the 14th Currt—it came to hand Yesterday—I return'd on Saturday last from Annapolis, where I placed for You a Letter in the Post Office to which, as I have no doubt of its safe Passage I beg leave to refer[1]—Your Excellencys Letters of the 21st of may & the 14th Inst. so clearly Ascertain The Building materials that I shall be at no loss to select those which are desirable—nor do I believe it will be difficult to find a Good Passage for them to Alexandria, from whence to Baltimore is a Weekly Packet—And as I intend to visit my son near Baltimore, by Water next Month, I will take the Goods up with me, & send them in the Packet, to the care of Our friend Colo. Fitzgerrald. with respect to Payment, I beg you will give Yourself no trouble, or concern—I must go to Virga to attend a Sale of Lands the 20th of September, & shall have the pleasure to Visit Mount Vernon, Either going or returning.[2]

I am Glad You will have a tryal of the Guinea Grass & Shou'd it succeed, Shall be thankful for a Little of the seed next Season. Mrs Fitzhugh, & my son William who is now here, Join with Me in respectful Complts and best wishes to You Your Lady & Family. I have the Honor to be with perfect Esteem & respect, Your Excellencys Affect. & Oblig'd H. Sert

Willm Fitzhugh

ALS, DLC:GW. Millmont is in Maryland.

1. Fitzhugh's letter is dated 16 July.

2. William Fitzhugh, his son William, and Dr. Thomas Marshall spent the night of 13 Sept. at Mount Vernon. At that time, GW paid Fitzhugh £46.17. 9½ for the building material with which Fitzhugh had supplied him. See *Diaries*, 4:193, and Ledger B, 204. GW began corresponding with Fitzhugh about this material to be used in his New Room at Mount Vernon after Fitzhugh told him on 2 May that he could let GW have a large number of items that he had purchased but did not need.

From William Grayson

Dear Sir   New York July 25th 1785.

The inclosed letters were handed to me the other day by young Mr Adams, son of Mr John Adams, who has arrived in the last packett, and no private opportunity offering, I do myself the honor of transmitting them by Post.[1]

Congress are informed by a letter from Mr Adams, that he has been introduced to the King of G.B. in due form, and recieved, as a public Minister from the U.S. of America.[2]

They have also recieved from the Commrs for forming commercial treaties projects of two treaties; the one with the King of Prussia, the other with the Grand Duke of Tuscany; the former it is expected is signed before this by the American Ministers.

Don Diego de Gardoqui (who has plenipotentiary powers) has been recieved and Congress have passed a commission to Mr Jay Secretary for foreign affairs to negotiate with him.

Congress have lately paid great attention to the proposed alteration of the 9th article of the Confederation, and it has been debated several times. I did myself the honor of inclosing this paper some time ago; there seems to be three opinions; some are for the alteration as reported provided Eleven & not nine States have the exercise of the powers, others are for forming a navigation act, & submitting the same to the States, a third opinion is against any change whatever.

I expect after the subject has been thoroughly investigated, it will by consent be put off till the members have had an opportunity of consulting the legislatures.[3]

The requisition for the current year is nearly finished; By this the states are called upon to pay three Millions of dollars, i.e. one Million in specie, and two Millions in Interest on liquidated certificates—The whole containing a provision as well for the purposes of Government as for the Interest on the foreign & domestic debt.

I beg leave to inclose propositions respecting the coinage of Gold Silver & Copper, which are at present before Congress.[4] I have the honor to be with the highest respect Yr Affect. h[umbl]e & Most Obed. servt

Willm Grayson

ALS, DLC:GW.

1. Included in these letters for GW brought from Paris by John Quincy Adams were those from Lafayette of 11 and 13 May and, probably, David Humphreys' letter of 10 May.

2. See Richard Henry Lee to GW, 23 July, n.5.

3. For the request to alter the Articles of Confederation to give Congress the power to regulate trade, see Grayson to GW, 4 May, n.4.

4. One hundred copies of "Propositions Respecting the Coinage of Gold, Silver, and Copper" were run off on 2 June by John Dunlap (*JCC*, 29:922). See 13 May 1785, ibid., 28:354–58.

To David Humphreys

My dear Humphreys   Mount Vernon July 25th 1785.

Since my last to you I have received your letters of the 15th of Jany and (I believe) that of the 11th of Novr; & thank you for them both[1]—It always gives me pleasure to hear from you; and I should think, if amusements would spare you, business could not so much absorb your time as to prevent your writing to me more frequently; especially as there is a regular & safe conveyance once a month, by the Packett.

As the complexion of European politics seem now (from the letters I have received from the Marquisses de la Fayette & Chastellux—the Chevr de la Luzerne, &ca) to have a tendency to Peace, I will say nothing of War, nor make any animadversions upon the contending Powers—otherwise I might possibly have added, that the retreat from it seemed impossible, after the explicit declarations of the Parties.

My first wish is, to see this plague to Mankind banished from the Earth; & the Sons & daughters of this World employed in

more pleasing & innocent amusements than in preparing implements, & exercising them for the destruction of the human race.
Rather than quarrel abt territory, let the poor, the needy, & oppressed of the Earth; and those who want Land, resort to the
fertile plains of our Western Country, to the second Land of
promise, & there dwell in peace, fulfilling the first & great Commandment.

In a former letter I informed you, My dear Humphreys, that
if I had talents for it, I have not leizure to devote my time &
thoughts to commentaries. I am conscious of a defective education, & want of capacity to fit me for such an undertaking. What
with Company, letters, & other Matters, many of them extra-
neous, I have not yet been able to arrange my own private concerns so as to rescue them from that disordered state into which
they have been thrown, by the War; and to do which, is become
indispensibly necessary for my support, whilst I remain on this
stage of human action.

The sentiment of your last letter on this subject gave me great
pleasure. I should indeed be pleased to see you undertake this
business. Your abilities as a writer—Your discernment respecting the principles which lead to the decision by Arms—Your personal knowledge of many facts as they occurred, in the progress
of the War—Your disposition to justice, candour & impartiallity,
and your diligence in investigating truth, combining, fits you, in
the vigor of life, for this task. and I should with great pleasure
not only give you the perusal of all my Papers, but any oral information of circumstances which cannot be obtained from the
latter, that my memory will furnish. And I can with great truth
add, that my House would not only be at your Service during
the period of your preparing this work, but (and without an
unmeaning compliment I say it) I shoud be exceedingly happy
if you would make it your home. You might have an Apartment
to yourself in which you could command your own time. You
would be considered, & treated as one of the family. And would
meet with that cordial reception & entertainment, which are
characteristic of the sincerest friendship.[2]

To reverberate European News would be idle; and we have
little of a domestic kind worthy of attention. We have held treaties indeed with the Indians, but they were so unseasonably delayed that these people from our last accts from the Westward

are in a discontented mood—supposed by many to be instigated thereto by our late enemy—now, to be sure, good & fast friends; who, from anything I can learn, under the indefinite expression of the treaty, hold, & seem resolved to retain, possession of our Western Posts. Congress have also—after long & tedeous deliberation—passed an Ordinance for laying of the Western territory into States, & for disposing of the Land; but in a manner, and on terms, which few people (in the Southern States) conceive can be accomplished. Both sides are sure, & the event is appealed to—time must decide. It is to be regretted however, that local politics, & self interested views, obtrude themselves into every measure of public utility. But on such characters, be the obloquy—My attention is more immediately engaged in a project which I think is big with great political, as well as Commercial consequences to these States, especially the middle ones. It is, by removing the obstructions—and extending the inland Navigations of our Rivers, to bring the States on the Atlantic in close connection with those forming to the Westward, by a short & easy Land transportation. Without this is effected, I can readily conceive that the Western Settlers will have different views—seperate interests—and other connections.

I may be singular in my ideas, but they are these, that to open the front door to, & make easy the way for those Settlers to the Westward (which ought to progress regularly & compactly) before we make any stir about the Navigation of the Mississipi, and before our settlements are far advanced towards that River would be our true line of policy. It can I think be demonstrated, that the produce of the Western territory (if the Navigations which are now in hand succeed, and of which I have no doubt) as low down the Ohio as the Great Kanhawa (I believe to the Falls) and between the parts above, & the Lakes, may be brought to the highest shipping Port either on this, or James River, at a less expence, with more ease (including the return) and in a much shorter time than it can be carried to New Orleans, if the Spaniards, instead of restrictions were to throw open their ports, & envite our trade—But if the commerce of that Country shd embrace this channel, and connections be formed, experience has taught us (and there is a very recent one in proof, with Great Britain) how next to impracticable it is to divert it—and if that shd be the case, the Atlantic States (especially as those to the

Westward will, in a great degree, fill with foreigners) except to excite—perhaps with too much cause—our fears that the Country of California, which is still more to the Westward, & belonging to another Power. Mrs Washington presents her compliments to you, and with every wish for your happiness I am—My dear Humphreys Yr sincere friend and Affectionate Hble Servt

Go: Washington

ALS, Poland: Jagiellońska University; LB, DLC:GW. GW marked his ALS "Duplicate."

1. GW shortly was to receive Humphreys' letter of 10 May, and Humphreys had already written still another letter on 17 July. GW last wrote to Humphreys on 25 Nov. 1784.

2. For Humphreys' suggestion that he undertake a biography of GW, see Humphreys to GW, 15 Jan. 1785.

To Lafayette

My Dear Marquis,   Mount Vernon 25th July 1785.

I have to acknowledge & thank you for your several favors of the 9th of February—19th of March & 16th of April, with their enclosures; all of which (the last only yesterday) have been received since I had the honor to address you in February.

I stand before you as a Culprit; but to *repent* & *be forgiven* are the precepts of Heaven: I do the former—do you practise the latter, & it will be participating of a divine attribute. Yet I am not barren of excuses for this seeming inattention; frequent absences from home—a round of company when at it, & the pressure of many matters, might be urged as apologies for my long silence; but I disclaim all of them, & trust to the forbearance of friendship & your wonted indulgence: indeed so few things occur, in the line on which I now move, worthy of attention—that this also might be added to the catalogue of my excuses; especially when I further add, that one of my letters, if it is to be estimated according to its length, would make three of yours.[1]

I now congratulate you, & my heart does it more effectually than my pen, on your safe arrival at Paris, from your voyage to this Country, & on the happy meeting with Madame la Fayette & your family in good health—May the blessing of this long continue to them—& may every day add increase of happiness to yourself. As the clouds which overspread your hemisphere are dispersing, & peace with all its concomitants is dawning upon your Land, I will banish the sound of War from my letter: I wish to see the sons & daughters of the world in Peace & busily employed in the more agreeable amusement, of fulfilling the first and great commandment—*Increase & Multiply*: as an encouragement to which we have opened the fertile plains of the Ohio to the poor, the needy & the oppressed of the Earth; any one therefore who is heavy laden, or who wants land to cultivate, may repair thither & abound, as in the Land of promise, with milk & honey: the ways are preparing, & the roads will be made easy, thro' the channels of Potomac & James river.

Speaking of these navigations, I have the pleasure to inform you that the subscriptions, (especially for the first) at the surrender of the books, agreeably to the Act which I enclosed you in my last, exceeded my most sanguine expectation: for the latter, that is James river, no comparison of them has yet been made.

Of the £50,000 Sterlg required for the Potomac navigation, upwards of £40,000, was subscribed before the middle of May, & encreasing fast. A President & four Directors, consisting of your hble Servant, Govrs Johnson & Lee of Maryland, & Colo. Fitzgerald & Gilpin of this State, were chosen to conduct the undertaking. The first dividend of the money was paid in on the 15th of this month; & the work is to be begun the first of next, in those parts which require least skill: leaving the more difficult 'till an Engineer of abilities & practical knowledge can be obtained;[2] which reminds me of the question which I propounded to you in my last, on this subject, & on which I should be glad to learn your sentiments. This project, if it succeeds & of which I have no doubt, will bring the Atlantic States & the Western Territory into close connexion, & be productive of very extensive commercial & political consequences; the last of which gave the spur to my exertions, as I could foresee many, & great mischiefs which would naturally result from a separation—& that a separation would inevitably take place, if the obstructions between the two Countries remained, & the navigation of the Mississippi should be made free.

Great Britain, in her commercial policy is acting the same unwise part, with respect to herself, which seems to have influenced all her Councils; & thereby is defeatg her own ends: the restriction of our trade, & her heavy imposts on the staple commodities of this Country, will I conceive, immediately produce powers in Congress to regulate the Trade of the Union; which, more than probably would not have been obtained without in half a century. The mercantile interests of the *whole* Union are endeavouring to effect this, & will no doubt succeed; they see the necessity of a controuling power, & the futility, indeed the absurdity, of each State's enacting Laws for this purpose independant of one another. This will be the case also, after a while, in all matters of common concern. It is to be regretted, I confess, that Democratical States must always *feel* before they can *see*: it is this that makes their Governments slow—but the people will be right at last.

Congress after long deliberation, have at length agreed upon a mode for disposing of the Lands of the United States in the Western territory—it may be a good one, but it does not comport with my ideas. The ordinance is long, & I have none of them by me, or I would send one for your perusal. They seem in this instance, as in almost every other, to be surrendering the little power they have, to the States individually which gave it to them. Many think the price which they have fixed upon the Lands too high; and all to the Southward I believe, that disposing of them in Townships, & by square miles alternately, will be a great let to the sale: but experience, to which there is an appeal, must decide.[3]

Soon after I had written to you in Feby, Mr Jefferson, & after him Mr Carmichael informed me that in consequence of an application from Mr Harrison for permission to export a Jack for me from Spain, his Catholic Majesty had ordered *two* of the first race in his Kingdom (lest an accident might happen to *one*) to be purchased and presented to me as a mark of his esteem. Such an instance of condescension & attention from a crowned head is very flattering, and lays me under great obligation to the King; but neither of them is yet arrived: these I presume are the two mentioned in your favor of the 16th of April; one as having been shipped from Cadiz—the other as expected from the Isle of Malta, which you would forward. As they have been purchased since December last, I began to be apprehensive of accidents; which I wish may not be the case with respect to the one from Cadiz, if he was actually shipped at the time of your account: should the other pass thro' your hands you cannot oblige me more, than by requiring the greatest care, & most particular attention to be paid to him. I have long endeavoured to procure one of a good size & breed, but had little expectation of receiving two as a royal gift.[4]

I am much obliged to you My dear Marquis, for your attention to the Hounds, & not less sorry that you should have met the smallest difficulty, or experienced the least trouble in obtaining them: I was no way anxious about these, consequently should have felt no regret, or sustained no loss if you had not succeeded in your application.[5] I have commissioned three or four persons (among whom Colo. Marshall is one) to procure for me in Kentucke, for the use of the Kings Garden's at Versailles or elsewhere, the seeds mentioned in the list you sent me from New York, & such others as are curious, & will forward them as soon as they come to my hands; whch cannot be 'till after the growing Crop has given its seeds.[6]

My best wishes will accompany you to Potsdam, & into the Austrian Dominions whenever you set out upon that tour. As an unobserved spectator, I should like to take a peep at the troops of those Monarch's at their manœuverings upon a grand field day; but as it is among the unattainable things, my philosophy shall supply the place of curiosity, & set my mind at ease.

In your favor of the 19th of March you speak of letters which were sent by a Mr Williams; but none such have come to hand. The present for the little folks did not arrive by Mr Ridouts Ship as you expected; to what cause owing I know not.[7] Mrs Washington has but indifferent health; & the late loss of her Mother, & only brother Mr Barthw Dandridge (one of the Judges of our supreme Court) has rather added to her indisposition. My mother & friends enjoy good health—George has returned after his peregrination thro' the West Indies, to Burmuda, the Bahama Islands, & Charlestown; at the last place he spent the winter. He is in better health than when he set out, but not quite recovered: He is now on a journey to the Sweet Springs, to procure a stock sufficient to fit him for a matrimonial voyage in the Frigate F. Bassett, on board which he means to embark at his return in October: how far his case is desperate, I leave you to judge—if it is so, the remedy however pleasing at first, will certainly be violent.

The latter end of April I had the pleasure to receive in good order, by a Ship from London, the picture of your self, Madame la Fayette & the children, which I consider as an invaluable present, & shall give it the best place in my House.[8] Mrs Washington joins me in respectful compliments, & in every good wish for Madame de la Fayette, yourself & family; all the others who have come under your kind notice present their compliments to you. For myself, I can only repeat the sincere attachment, & unbounded affection of My Dr Marqs &c. &c. &c.

G: Washington

LB, DLC:GW.

1. GW wrote Lafayette on 15 Feb. and again, briefly, on 12 April. He was to receive in August Lafayette's letters of 11 and 13 May.

2. For the first meeting of the Potomac River Company, in which elections were held, see GW to Thomas Johnson and Thomas Sim Lee, 18 May 1785, n.1.

3. For the passage of the Land Ordinance of 1785, see William Grayson to GW, 27 May 1785, n.1.

4. GW reveals here that he is unaware that Lafayette as well as the king of Spain is proposing to give him a pair of jacks. See William Carmichael to GW, 3 Dec. 1784, n.1, and especially, Lafayette to GW, 16 April 1785, n.4.

5. The hounds, brought to New York by John Quincy Adams, arrived at Mount Vernon on 24 August. See GW to Lafayette, 1 September.

6. GW wrote Thomas Marshall about this on 3 May. See Thomas Marshall to GW, 12 May.

7. In his letter of 19 Mar. 1785, Lafayette alludes to letters from his children to GW's grandchildren, "By Mr Williams," and on 16 April he writes of toys sent for the grandchildren. The toys did not arrive until 1786 (see the marquise de Lafayette to GW, 15 April 1785, n.2).

8. A visitor to Mount Vernon reported in November 1785 that there was "a fine family picture in the Drawing room of the Marquis de La Fayette, his lady and three children" (John Hunter [Robert Hunter, Jr.], "An Account of a Visit Made to Washington at Mount Vernon, by an English Gentleman, in 1785," *Pennsylvania Magazine of History and Biography*, 17 [1893], 76–82).

From Alexander White

Sir   Woodville 26 July 1785

I had the honour of your Excellencys letter 16th instant enclosing Mr Frauncis's which I have answered by this Post[1]—As your Excellency has no knowledge of Mr Frauncis's demand it would be impertement in me to trouble you with my opinion of it—I can only say, that I am anxious to discharge every just debt, and that your Excellencys Countenance afforded to Mr Frauncis will induce me to pay particular attention to his Claim—I spent a Month last Winter adjusting the Affairs of General Lees Estate with Congress and Mr Morris, and put things in such a train that, I hoped, as soon as our dispatches should arrive in England to be enabled to draw mony sufficient to discharge all his debts but his debters' cavil at the Powers sent, and refuse payment—Other Writings have been drawn there, and transmitted to Mr Morris for him and me to execute, he writes me they are arrived, and that he is waiting an opportunity to send them to me, and that if one does not soon offer he will send an Express[.] I hope on their return Matters in England will be agreeably adjusted though Miss Lee in a Letter of 23d March seems of a different opinion, and thinks nothing will be paid till it is recovered by Law—I have wrote her most pressingly, if that should be the Case to advance £600 Sterg to enable me to pay the many small debts which remain unpaid to the disgrace of the Generals memory. I hope she will comply—I am really anxious to discharge all his debts.[2] as soon as it is in my Power I shall give notice to his Crediters in general, and particularly to your Excellency, and am with Sentiments of the highest Respect Your Excellencys Most Obt Servt

Alexr White

ALS, DLC:GW.

    1. The letter-book copy of GW's letter to White is dated 14 July.

    2. For White's role in the settling of Gen. Charles Lee's estate, see Sidney Lee to GW, 23 May 1784, n.3. For other references to complications on the English side in the settlement of Lee's estate, see Sidney Lee to GW, 5 April 1785.

Letter not found: to Otho Holland Williams, 26 July. On 15 Aug. Williams wrote to GW and referred to "Your Letter dated Mount Vernon July 26th."

To Clement Biddle

Dear Sir: Mount Vernon, July 27, 1785.

    Your letter of the 5th. came duly to hand, and should have been acknowledged sooner, if it had been in my power, conveniently.[1] I thank you for your attention to the Certificates which

I committed to your care; and will obtain an order from Gilbert Simpson, by which the Interest may be received. This money is all I am likely to get for a Mill which he ran me to the Expence of £1200 hard money to build, near Yohiogany, now tumbling down, and for which I can not get a farthing, rent. If Mr. Stelle has the cover, in which the Certificates were wrapped, I should be glad to have it returned to me, or, if there is any thing within, useful to him, a Copy of the memn. on the back of it. It is the only minutes I took of the different Interests in the Certificates, it enclosed.[2]

Since your last conference with Messrs Dunlap & Claypool, their Advertiser has come to hand regularly. I am content therefore to have it continued.[3]

As you think my small Commissions will not give you more trouble than they are worth, I shall, when I find occasion, continue them with pleasure.

We expect to begin our operations on the Potomack Navigation about the 6th of next Month, under the Management of a Mr James Rumsey. If the Miners therefore, who have been accustomed to the blowing of Rocks under Water, are desirous of employment in this way, and are not extravagant in their demands, I am persuaded he would hire them, were they to apply to him, either at the Seneca falls, or the Falls of Shannondoah; neither of which are far from Frederick Town in Maryland, or, if they think the distance too great to come on an uncertainty if through you, they will communicate to me their lowest terms, I will see that an answer to them is obtained. Mrs. Washington joins me in compliments to, and best wishes for you, Mrs. Biddle and the family and I am, etc.

Printed in Fitzpatrick, *Writings of Washington*, 28:211–12, with the note: "This text is from that printed in a sales catalogue in 1924."

1. Letter not found.

2. For a summary of Biddle's handling of Gilbert Simpson's certificates for GW, see GW to Biddle, 1 Feb. 1785, n.8.

3. See GW to Biddle, 1 Feb. 1785, n.3.

From Thomas Freeman

Redstone [Pa.]

May it Please your Excellency   July 27th 1785

In my last to you I informed you of my Necessity of Advertising for the Rebuilding and repairing the Mill, the meeting of the Undertakers to be the first Ult. I had the Mortification to find myself disappointed by none, at least none to undertake meet me, so that the Mill is not doing any good at all I have some Inclination to try a Second Advertisement on the same Acct but shall wait for your Approbation as this will come Imediately into your Hands by the Bearer Mr Jackson.[1]

I met Mr Smith at Union Town last Term & took his Advice in regard to the Arrearages from the Tenants in the Bottome and am Prosecuting his directions therein,[2] I likewise have seen Coll Stephenson & enquired of him what he knew relative to your Claims in Washington County but he nor his Brother, knows nothing of certainty in regard to it. Mr Charles Morgan seems to be the Principal evidence that is to be met with in this Country of which I informed Mr Smith, who had already got Intellegence of him.[3]

Mr Simpson has Informed me fully of his determination to leave the Place he Occupies this fall, I have not yet got any Person to take Possessions nor do I know wether I shall be Justifiable in so doing untill further Order from you. I believe I can get some part of it sown down this Season & have made some Advances thereto—Mr Simpson offers putting in the Corn Ground and finding Seed at fifteen Shillings Per Acre I have Offered Ten and I will give no more, however if you would wish to have any thing done concerning that Place I hope you will communicate it to me by some speedy Oppertunity.[4]

As to Applications for the Lands on the Ohio & Kanhawa I have had none since I wrote to you, nor shall have any I imagine, the Indians seems to be much unsettld and untoward. I have the Honour to be your Excellencys most Obedient Humble Servant

Thomas Freeman

ALS, DLC:GW.

1. See Freeman's "last," dated 9 June. For GW's despairing view about his mill's future, see his letter to Clement Biddle of this date.

2. The "Bottom" is Washington's Bottom in Fayette County, Pa., a 1,644-acre tract owned by GW and until September 1784 managed by Gilbert Simpson, Jr.

3. In his letter of 11 April, GW instructed Freeman to assist GW's attorney, Thomas Smith, in preparing his case against the settlers on GW's Millers Run property. Freeman was to seek information from his neighbors and from William Crawford's half brothers, Col. John and Marcus Stephenson. Charles Morgan, who was a witness for GW in his Millers Run ejectment suits, may be the man of that name who went down the Ohio from Fort Pitt on 20 Oct. 1770 with GW, William Crawford, and others (see Thomas Smith to GW, 9 Feb. 1785, n.15). In 1794 Morgan became collector of GW's rents in Pennsylvania (Morgan to GW, 26 Nov. 1794).

4. See Freeman to GW, 9 June, n.6.

To Battaile Muse

Sir,   Mount Vernon 28th July 1785.

A few days ago by a Mr Hickman, who either is, or wants to be a tenant of mine in Frederick County—I sent you a dozen blank Leases. The tract on which he says he is fixed, is part of two Lots which I purchased at the sale of Colo. George Mercer's Estate, in the year 1774; a plat of which I send you, that the whole may be arranged into four tenements—as conveniently disposed as water &c. will admit.[1]

In September last, whilst I was at my brothers in Berkeley, many persons applied for this Land; but from causes which then existed I came to no positive agreement with any; refering them to Mr Snickers, who was so kind as to promise that he would fix matters for me (as I was in a hurry & could not go upon the Land myself) on the terms which, if I recollect right, I gave him in a letter. Some time after, two men of the name of Winzer & Beaven, with the letter enclosed from Mr Snickers, came here, & were told that I would comply with whatever agreement was made with them by him. Among other things they said Mr Snickers had promised them Leases for fourteen years; this I observed could not, in my opinion, be the case, because I had expressly named ten years (the term for which Mr Burwell let his Lands adjoining)—but notwithstanding if the case was so, & Mr Snickers would declare it, the Leases should be filled up accordingly: this I repeat—& as far as the matter respects Winzer, for it seems Beaven has changed his mind, the other conditions endorsed on the back of Mr Snickers's letter to me, are to be granted him; he paying all the taxes wch may be laid on the Land he holds. However, as filling up one Lease may be a guide with respect to the others, I enclose one in the name of Winzer, with the blanks as completely filled as I can do it under my uncertainty with respect to the term of years for which he is to have it, and which is to be determined by Mr Snickers; & for want of the quantity of acres in, & a description of the Lot which he is to have.

There are already three Tenants on this tract, to whom you may fill up Leases on the same terms which I have done for Winzer; & whenever they will bring evidences to prove them, I will sign them. As Beaven has declined taking the Lot which he agreed for first with Mr Snickers & afterwards with me, you may let it to any good tenant who offers, upon the terms on which the others are held. The three now engaged will have rents to pay thereon the first of next January.[2] It will be necessary to take an Assignment of Mr Whitings Lease, before one can be made to Mr Airess; or some instrument of writing by which it will be cancelled, in order to render the new one valid; and I hope payment of the money due on the replevy Bonds of the former, will not be delayed longer than the time mentioned in your last letter—viz.—September.[3]

Having got a Gentleman to assist me in my business, I hope shortly to have my Accots so arranged as to be able to send you a rental of what is due to me in Loudoun, Fauquier & Berkeley Counties.[4] I have a Lot in the town & common of Winchester, of which, when you have occasion to go thither, I beg you to enquire into the state & condition, & give me information of what can be made of them: the one in the Town, I believe a Doctr McKay has something to do with.[5]

I would be obliged to you for enquiring of Mr Wormley's manager, if he has any good red clover seed for sale—what quantity & the price thereof—& let me know the result by the first conveyance to Alexandria.[6] I am &c.

G: Washington

LB, DLC:GW. The ALS was listed for sale by Parke-Bernet in its catalog, in part one of the John Gribbel collection, item 775, 30–31 Oct. and 1 Nov. 1940.
    1. For GW's involvement in the sale of George Mercer's Frederick County

land in 1774, see GW to John Tayloe, 30 Nov. 1774, n.2, and GW to Francis Lightfoot Lee and Ralph Wormeley, Jr., 20 June 1784, particularly the source note and the references therein. See also note 1 in Edward Snickers to GW, 17 May 1784. At the end of the Mercer sale in November 1774, GW bought two of the lots in the 6,500-acre Mercer tract lying along the Shenandoah River in Frederick County. The two lots, which GW wished to rent out in four parcels, totaled about 560 acres. GW indicates in this letter that there were already three tenants living on this tract in Frederick County. He names two of them, Joseph Windsor (Wenzor) and a Mr. Beaven, both of whom held leases from Edward Snickers (see note 2). The third may have been Joseph Hickman. In any case, GW confirmed Snickers's lease with Windsor for 172 acres at an annual rent of £17.4 for fourteen years from 1 Jan. 1785, and in December 1785 he signed agreements with William Kercheval (Kerchevell), whose lease for 172 acres at £17.6 per annum ran for thirteen years from 1 Jan. 1786, and with Joseph Hickman and John Williams, both of whose leases ran for fourteen years from 1 Jan. 1785. Hickman rented 116 acres for an annual rent of £11.12, and Williams rented 100 acres for £10. On behalf of GW, Muse sued all four tenants—Kercheval, Windsor, Hickman, and Williams—for back rent (J. Milton's receipt, 28 Feb. 1790, NcD: Battaile Muse Papers). For the record of Muse's dealings with the four tenants from 1786 to 1790, see Muse's Rental Rolls for GW, 1788–90 (ViMtV) and Muse's accounts as rental agent, 1 July, 3 Mar. 1786, 8 May, 28 Nov. 1788, 5 Mar., 17 April, 29 May, 30 June, 23 July 1789, 20 June 1790 (Battaile Muse's Accounts as Rental Agent, 1785–90, NjMoNP: Smith Collection).

2. On 4 Sept. 1784 GW accepted the offer made by Edward Snickers to secure tenants for his 570 acres of the tract. Snickers lived near the Mercer tract on the Shenandoah and after the sale in 1774 had bought a number of lots in the tract (see Snickers to GW, 17 May 1784, and notes). A week later, on 12 Sept. 1784, Muse wrote GW offering to collect rents for him in Berkeley, Frederick, and Fauquier counties, and on 3 Nov. 1784 GW accepted Muse's offer, with a promise to supply Muse with a "Rental of the Sums . . . which are due." Up until this time, GW seems only to have entrusted Muse with handling the collection of the rent due from Henry Whiting (see note 3 in GW to Muse, 3 Nov. 1784), and it was not until 18 Sept. 1785 that GW was able to supply Muse with a tentative list of tenants and of rents due. By November Muse was actively collecting rents for GW in Berkeley, Frederick, Fauquier, and Loudoun, the counties above Fairfax where GW owned land (Muse's Accounts as Rental Agent, 1785–1790, NjMoNP: Smith Collection and Muse's Rental Rolls for GW, 1788–90, ViMtV).

3. For the rental by John Ariss of the 600-acre tract of GW's Bullskin land in Berkeley County which Francis Whiting had been renting, see Ariss to GW, 5 Aug. 1784, nn.1 and 2.

4. See GW to Muse, 18 Sept., n.2.

5. Muse wrote to GW in some detail on 6 and 14 Sept. about Dr. Robert Mackey's rental of GW's two lots, one in and one near Winchester.

6. For Muse's response with regard to Ralph Wormeley, Jr.'s clover seed,

see Muse to GW, 16 August. See also GW to Muse, 22 Aug., and Muse to GW, 6 September. The two had further correspondence about the clover seed in early 1786 (GW to Muse, 5 Jan., 4 Feb. 1786, Muse to GW, 17 Jan. 1786).

From Edmund Randolph

Dear sir   Richmond July 29. 1785.

Your favor of the 23d instant came duly to hand. But I am sorry to be unable to execute the request contained in it. The council-books are destroyed.

The general restriction of settlement on the western waters does, I acknowledge, extend to military rights, as well others. But it continues only, until the King's further pleasure should be known. The patent in your hands is abundant evidence, in my judgment, of his further pleasure having removed the restriction from military rights. For would a governor oppose a proclamation, without special instructions? How could an individual procure a copy of any instruction without his permission, and who can tell, that the governor has ever deposited that instruction in any of the public archives? So that to require a copy of the instruction, which wiped away the effects of the proclamation, might amount to the requiring of an impossibility.[1]

It will not be amiss to obtain the certificate you mention; supported by the seal of the state. But I cannot any where procure it. Should you be able to obtain it, Mr A. Blair, the clerk of the council, will immediately authenticate it.[2] I mention him, that you may not be disappointed by writing to me on the subject as to morrow I leave Richmond for the neighbourhood of Winchester.[3] If I can be of any farther use to you in this matter, I pray you, my dear sir, to command me freely; as I feel the most unfeigned satisfaction in subscribing myself yr affectionate friend & servt

Edm: Randolph

ALS, NhD.

1. GW's letter of 23 July has not been found, but his letter of 13 Aug. makes clear that he was seeking to establish from the journals of the Virginia council the date it first permitted "Warrants to issue on military Rights" for land barred from settlement by the Proclamation of 1763. Although unable to confirm it by reference to the council's journals, Randolph simply argues that the fact the governor issued GW a patent for the Millers Run land was sufficient

proof that he had been given authority to lift the ban in the case of military claims and that such authority had been given him before the date of the warrant. As a matter of fact, the copy of the journals of the Virginia council deposited in the Public Record Office in London reveals that on 11 Oct. 1773 Lord Botetourt, governor of Virginia, conveyed to the Virginia council the king's order in council, dated 7 April 1773, making exceptions in the ban on patents for western lands of the "Officers and Soldiers who are intitled to grants of Land in Virtue of his Majesty's Royal Proclamation of the 7th of October 1763" (*Exec. Journals of Virginia Council*, 6:541–42); but questions were raised about whether this applied to provincials (see GW to Thomas Lewis, 17 Feb. 1774).

2. GW apparently had asked for certification "that the recognition of military rights was previous to October 1773" (GW to Randolph, 13 Aug. 1785). See note 1. The clerk of the council was Archibald Blair (c.1753–1824).

3. See Randolph to GW, 8 August.

Letter not found: from Thomas Brereton, 30 July 1785. On 12 April 1786 Brereton wrote GW: "I had the Honor to Address your Excelency the 30th of July last."

To Edmund Randolph

Dear Sir,   Mount Vernon July 30th 1785.

Altho' it is not my intention to derive any pecuniary advantage from the generous vote of the Assembly of this State, consequent of its gratuitous gift of fifty shares in each of the navigations of the rivers Potomac and James; yet, as I consider these undertakings as of vast political & commercial importance to the States on the Atlantic, especially to those nearest the centre of the Union, & adjoining the Western Territory, I can let no act of mine impede the progress of the work: I have therefore come to the determination to hold the shares which the Treasurer was directed to subscribe on my account, in trust for the use & benefit of the public; unless I shall be able to discover, before the meeting of the Assembly, that it would be agreeable to it to have the product of the Tolls arising from these shares, applied as a fund on which to establish two Charity schools, one on each river, for the Education & support of the Children of the poor & indigent of this Country who cannot afford to give it; particularly the children of those men of this description, who have fallen in defence of the rights & liberties of it. If the plans succeed, of which I have no doubt, I am sure it will be a very productive & encreasing fund, & the monies thus applied will be a beneficial institu[tio]n.

I am aware that my non-acceptance of these shares will have various motives ascribed to it, among which an ostentatious display of disinterestedness—perhaps the charge of disrespect or slight of the favors of my Country, may lead the van: but under a consciousness that my conduct herein is not influenced by considerations of this nature—& that I shall act more agreeably to my own feelings, & more consistent with my early declarations, by declining to accept them; I shall not only hope for indulgence, but a favorable interpretation of my conduct: my friends, I persuade myself, will acquit me, the World I hope will judge charitably.[1]

Perceiving by the Advertisement of Messrs Cabell, Buchanan and Southall that half the sum required by the Act, for opening & extending the navigation of James river, is subscribed; & the 20th of next month appointed for the subscribers to meet at Richmond, I take the liberty, of giving a power to act for me on that occasion.[2] I would (having the accomplishment of these navigations much at heart) have attended in person; but, the President and Directors of the Potomac Company by their own appointment, are to commence the survey of this river in the early part of next month; for which purpose I shall leave home tomorrow.[3] Besides which, if the Ejectments which I have been obliged to bring for my Land in Pennsylva. are to be tried at the September Term, as Mr Smith, my Lawyer, conceived they would, & is to inform me—I shall find it necessary I fear, to attend the trial;[4] an intermediate journey therefore, in addition, to Richmond would be impracticable for me to accomplish. I am Sir &c. &c.

G: Washington

LB, DLC:GW.

1. For a discussion of GW's response to the gift by the state of 50 shares in the Potomac River Company and 100 shares in the James River Company, see Benjamin Harrison to GW, 6 Jan., n.1.

2. The James River Company was established by Virginia at the same time Maryland and Virginia were establishing the Potomac River Company. See James Madison to GW, 9 Jan. 1785, n.3. The following advertisement, dated 14 July, appeared in the *Virginia Gazette, or the American Advertiser* (Richmond), 16 July: "WHEREAS more than one half of the Capital has been subscribed for clearing and improving the navigation of James River; the Subscribers are

therefore desired to meet at the Public Buildings, in the City of Richmond, on the 20th of August next, in order to elect a President and Directors, as the law requires WILLIAM CABELL, TURNER SOUTHALL, JAMES BUCHANAN, Managers." GW was elected president of the company (see Edmund Randolph to GW, 2 Sept., n.1).

3. See GW to James Rumsey, 8 Aug., n.1.

4. See editorial note, Thomas Smith to GW, 9 February.

To Noah Webster

Sir,   Mount Vernon July 30th 1785.
I received your letter of the 19th Instt.[1]

Being convinced from the respectable characters whose names are prefixed to your Gramatical Institute, as well as from the cursory examination I have had it in my power to bestow on the Books, of the judicious execution, and usefulness of the Work; it would give me pleasure if I could be instrumental, in any degree, towards the introduction of it to public notice. But I am a little at a loss, from the purport of your letter, to decide, whether it is your desire that my name should appear amongst those who have already subscribed to the utility of the Work; or, by introducing its Author to some of the first characters in the Southern States (under the favourable impression he has made upon me) to act more remotely. If the first is meant, I wish to decline it; because I have not leizure to examine the Institute with that attention which ought, always, to precede a certificate—and because I do not think myself a competent judge, if I had. But if the other is your object, I shall have great pleasure in giving you Letters of recommendation to some of the first Gentlemen of my Acquaintance in Charleston, or elsewhere—being Sir Yr Most Obedt Hble Ser⟨vt⟩

                                                    Go: Washington

ALS, NN: Washington Collection; LB, DLC:GW.

1. Webster's letter is dated 18 July, but GW docketed it "19th July 1785."

From James McHenry

Dr Sir.   New York 1st Augt 1785.

Whilst the Marquiss de la Fayette was on his late visit to this country he suggested to me that if I could recollect the train of his military proceedings and commit them to paper, that you would send them to Doctor Gordon who is engaged in writing a history of the revolution; at least so I understood him on this occasion, for the subject being delicate I did not seek explanation. My desire that the military and patriotic proceedings of the Marquiss may be truely stated by the Doctor has been a further inducement with me to execute his wish notwithstanding it interferd with my other avocations. I have therefore comprehended in the inclosed sketch every material feature of that noblemans history, so far as the same is connected with our revolution, which I hope you will introduce to Doctor Gordon in such a manner as may render it of utility to his undertaking. It is incumbent upon history to render her aid in paying a debt to those characters which America cannot pay.[1]

The Marquiss writes by every packet such information as he thinks may be of service to the union, and frequently tells congress what they do not hear from any other quarter, and does them acts of Kindness which no other person could do them. The court of France (through his mediation I imagine) has ordered their charge des affairs to withdraw the demand made some time since for the surrendrg of Lonchamp, which relieves Congress from much serious embarrassment. Yet one can see that the French court is not pleased, and hence, that we are not likely very soon to have a French minister—unless Congress do something more than what has been done to satisfy the insult.[2]

Since I have entered upon Congressional politics I must take the liberty to detain you a little Longer. Congress have had it under consideration to recommend to the several States to vest them with the power of regulating the trade of the States as well with each other as with foriegn nations. This power to constitute a part of the confederation and to be exercised by nine states in Congress assembled. Its object to enable Congress to lay as heavy duties and restrictions upon the trade of foreign nations, as foreign nations lay upon the trade of the United States. I apprehend that both the genius and interest of the Southern States will be found to be opposed to granting this power. I believe the Eastern States New York & Pennsylvania are exceedingly anxious for it; but I do not wonder at their anxiety to obtain a monopoly of the carrying trade of the union. What would be the consequence to the Southern States in particular were foreign vessels to be prevented from exporting their products. They would for example having only American vessels to carry off their commodities of export, have fewer purchasers for them, hence their prices would be unavoidably lowered. They would also have less foreign goods imported, which would oblige the consumers to pay dearer for what they must buy. It would seem therefore to be good policy in the Southern States to encourage the number of buyers for what they have to sell, and the number of importers of those articles they must buy, till they become as well peopled as the Eastern States, when a naval defence will be easily established, or come of itself without the aid of restrictions. In the mean while however it may be said, that we ought to lay the foundation for a marine, and therefore ought to begin by discouraging foriegn shipping and encouraging our own, for that the riches arising from buying what we want cheap and selling what we raise dear will avail us nothing without a navy to protect them. But is it true that a navy is at present necessary, and if necessary is it true that our people could go to the expence of supporting it? Would it be right to add to our present burthens; can we pay our present debts? Are we in a situation to enter into a war of imposts and prohibitions to force Great Britain or France to open to our shipping their west Indian possessions? Have we shipping enough to carry on our exports and imports? When Great Britain passed the navigation act she had in her harbours more than a sufficient number of vessels for her own trade. Great Britain too, was well peopled at that period and the capital of her traders equal to the exportation and purchase of her products. But our situation is different in both respects, and yet it is said we ought to force a navy—that we ought to prohibit British ships from exporting our products.

Perhaps the point of true policy lays between forcing the growth of our shipping and doing nothing that may forward their increase. Perhaps the Southern States should give up something, and the other States should not ask every thing.

Were Congress under the latter idea to frame a navigation act, the operation of which would gradually and slowly tend to augment the seamen and shipping of the States without sensibly wounding in its progress the interests of any State, and recommend the same to their adoption, is it not highly probable in such a case that the good sense of the States would readily induce them to come into the measure. Upon this plan they would see what they were to give—that it could not hurt them—and that it might work a general benefit. They could repeal it too, if it was found to hurt them, which alone would be a great inducement with some states to pass it.[3]

You will excuse me for being thus particular: but the subject is among the most interesting and that lead me to it, well knowing that although you have withdrawn yourself from all public employments, yet that there is nothing so near your heart as the public welfare. With respectful compliments to Mrs Washington and ardent wishes for your health I am Dr Sir very sincerely Your ob. St

James McHenry

ALS, DLC:GW; ADfS, DLC: McHenry Papers.

Dr. James McHenry (1753–1816) became GW's secretary in 1778 and served until August 1780, when he joined Lafayette's staff. He at this time was a member of Congress from Maryland.

1. GW transmitted to William Gordon on 31 Aug. McHenry's sketch of Lafayette's military career, with a strong endorsement of the contents. For Gordon's negative reaction to McHenry's appraisal of Lafayette's role, see Gordon to GW, 26 Sept.; for GW's rebuttal, see GW to Gordon, 6 December. See also Gordon to GW, 16 Feb. 1786.

2. For the Longchamps affair, see Jacob Read to GW, 29 June 1784, n.3.

3. For GW's strong statement opposing McHenry's views on the regulation of trade as expressed here, see GW to McHenry, 22 August. For the movement to give Congress the power to regulate trade, see William Grayson to GW, c.4–8 May 1785, n.4.

From Gouverneur Morris

Dr Genl   Philadelphia 1 Augt 1785

I write this Letter as a Companion for some Shoes of Miss Bassett and if it is addressed to you rather than to her you must for that Trouble as well as many others accuse that Celebrity which you had no little Trouble in acquiring. But you must tell the Lady that I am far from thinking that she ought not be as much celebrated as any General among you. Indeed between ourselves I think she will probably be entitled to the civic Crown as soon as the Modes and Forms of the World will permit a free Use of the Means. Not perhaps like a roman Soldier for a Citizen saved but like a good American Wife for a Citizen born. That this Praise may be speedily and frequently carried and long enjoyed is my sincere Wish and I know not of any better Epithalamium tho I have read some more pleasant.[1]

Since I arrived at this Place I have heard of a Person who it was thought would suit you and I desired to see him and his Letters recommendatory &ca since which I have heard nothing more of him.[2] Adieu[.] Present me in all proper Respect to Mrs Washington and beleive me ever yours

Gouvr Morris

ALS, DLC:GW.

1. Gouverneur Morris (1752–1816), who left Mount Vernon on 7 July, addressed this letter to "His Excellency Genl Washington at his Seat Mount Vernon Virginia with a Bow for Miss Bassett." See GW to Tench Tilghman, 6 July 1785, n.1. Frances Bassett and George Augustine Washington were married at Mount Vernon on 15 October.

2. Morris probably is referring to GW's search for a secretary. The day after Morris left Mount Vernon GW agreed to William Shaw's terms, and Shaw began work as GW's secretary before the end of the month.

To William Bailey

Sir,   George town [Md.] 2d Augt 1785

By a letter which I lately received from Mr Stoddert, I am informed that you had agreed to supply my Nephews George & Lawrence Washington with such articles from your Store as their necessities might require.[1] For which I thank you, & I have no doubt of your doing it upon good terms: the amount of which I hope will always be ready when called for. But I have to beg Sir, that they may not be endulged in any extravagance, or with any thing improper—school boys of their size, & growing, should have decent, but not expensive things; their inclinations too often prompt them to the latter, which grows upon them in proportion as they are indulged: nor should they have pocket money given them, unless the necessity is apparent & the application approved of.

Any Advance for Dancing, French &a which may be directed by their Tutor Mr Balch, will be chearfully repaid. I am Sir &c.

G: Washington

LB, DLC:GW.

1. See Benjamin Stoddert to GW, 21 June, and GW to Stephen Bloomer Balch, 26 June, 22 November.

From John Lowry

May it please your Excellency   Back River 2d Augt 1785

I once had the Honour of an Acquaintance with your Excellency which emboldens me at this Time to crave your Attention & Advice—Mr Tarte & myself have Land Warrents to a considerable Amount, am informed that on the Dismal Swamp there remains a large Tract not as yet taken up[.] as your Excellency is the first of that Company that has large Possessions there beg the favour of You to inform me by Mr Tarte the Bearer of this—whether there is any Land not located and if we claim in Time under our Warrents the Right & Title would stand good—we wish not to injure or disturb the Right of any Person, but if any vacant Land[,] we wish with your Excellency's Approbation to make our Survey there[.][1] if You would condescend to honour me with a Line should esteem it a great Obligation—my Compliments to your good Lady & remain Your Excellencys mo. obedt & Hble Servt

John Lowry

ALS, DLC:GW.

1. GW wrote in his diary on 30 Sept.: "In the Evening a Mr. Tarte—introduced by letter from a John Lowry of Back river came in to request my Sentiments respecting some Entrys they, in Partnership, had made in the Great Dismal Swamp, which I gave unreservedly, that they had no right to" (*Diaries*, 4:199). Back River runs into the Chesapeake Bay in Elizabeth City County across from Norfolk, Virginia. Mr. Tarte could be any one of several men named Tart (Tarte, Tartt) living in Norfolk County at this time.

From Hugh Holmes

Sir,   Dublin 4th August 178[5]

At a time when surrounding Nations justly applaud & admire that unremitting Valour and those great abilities which have contributed in so eminent a degree to the emancipation of your Country, And in which the Liberty of so many others seem eventually concern'd; Permit me Sir, a private Citizen of the Capital of a Nation so singularly thereby interested as the Kingdom of Ireland now is, to join in feeble Congratulation on your successfull efforts; To take the liberty of informing you, that during the Period while Victory yet stood Suspended, I then had the honor of annexing your name with mine to my Only Child; And (in Testimony of that respectfull gratitude excited by your extraordinary exertions) *now* to offer, A piece of our Staple Linnen Manufacture; of wch I earnestly entreat your acceptance, thro' the hands of my Nephew & name Sake.[1]

Permit me further Sir, to express my wish, that you may live to see the Empire in whose Glorious Superstructure you are prov'd the great Architect, arrive at that Conspicuous Eminence, fully to gratify your most sanguine Hopes; And that you may thereto long continue an usefull Ornament—evincing thro' your Brave Fellow Citizens an animating fervor in imitation of your Virtues; And when you discharge the great Debt of Nature, that you may Continue their boast & the Admiration of future Generations. I have the honor to be with great deference & respect Sincerely Sir Your most obedt very Humble Servant

Hu: Holmes

ALS, DLC:GW.

1. GW acknowledged Holmes's letter on 10 Mar. 1786: "Sir, For the honor you have done me in calling your only child by my name, & that too, you add, when the issue of the american struggle stood suspended—I pray you to accept my best acknowledgments.

"My thanks are also due for your politeness in sending me a peice of Linen of your staple manufacture: and I am particularly indebted to you for the favorable wishes & flattering expressions of your letter to me of the 4th of August last.

"Your Country has my best wishes for the fullest fruition of every thing which is interesting to the rights of mankind—& you, Sir, that you may be a principal sharer of them, being, Your most Obt &c. Go: Washington" (LB, DLC:GW).

From Solms

Sir   de la Fortresse de Konigstein en Saxe 4 Augt 1785
     I owe you this Satisfaction the more Complete, that I have tried it for a long time My General, & My Heroe I have Just Received your Picture, & I am entirely taken up to give it a Sufficient embellishment by Placing it between the King of Prussia, & his Illustrious Brother Henry. You See, that this is a Trio very Harmonical, I would willingly have thank'd you for your great Complaisance, but I dare not, as I Could not have express'd myself in Writing in Proportion to the thanks that is due. It must be that the Picture resembles, for I regard it, as the greatest Ornament of my Fortress. I Shew it to all the Strangers, amongst whome Some are French & Some are English, many have had the Happiness of Being acquainted with you.[1] I am with the Greatest Respect Your Excellency's Most Obedt Servt
                              Le Comte de Solme

I must yet inform you, that for to Complete my Happiness the Picture of your Excellency arrived in Saxe upon my Birth Day.

Translation, DLC:GW; LS, in French, DLC:GW. A copy of the original letter is in CD-ROM:GW.
     1. The portrait of GW that Solms hung on the wall of his castle was done for him by Joseph Wright. See GW to Solms, 3 Jan. 1784, nn.1 and 3.

From John Harvie

Dr Sr   Land Office [Richmond] Augt 5th 1785
     The Attorney General directed the mode of Entering your Caveat against the Heirs and Devises of Michael Cresup decd on their Survey upon your tract of Land call'd the Round Bottom.[1] and I now Inclose you a Summons from the Clk of the General Court which you will be pleas'd to forward to the Sherif of the County where any of the Divisees reside[2]—& if they live out of the State, I should think that the Sherif of the County where the Land Lyes will be the proper Officer to make the Return of their not being Inhabitants, upon which Return the process will be by proclamation publish'd in the papers—The names' of the Divisees I believe are Luther Martin & Mary his wife, Elizabeth Cresap & Sarah Cresap which had titles be In-

clos'd on the Back of the Summmons for the Information of the Sherif.[3] I have the Honour to be Sir Yr most obt H. servt

Jno. Harvie

Note[:] I am told it is ⟨*illegible*⟩ of the General Court to Dismiss Summon's upon caveat unless this Summons is Return'd to their Clks office by the 6th Day of the terms—yet if the Summons come dureing their Sitting the Cause will be Reinstated.[4] Since Writeing this Letter I have seen the clk of the General Court & have got him to Insert the names of Divisees in the Summons.[5] J.H.

ALS, DLC:GW.

1. GW sent his caveat to Harvie, 31 May 1785, which see.

2. GW wrote to the sheriff of Hampshire County (James Crane) from Mount Vernon on 15 Aug.: "Sir, The enclosed came under cover to me; I send it to you, & beg it may be executed & returned in time.

"Captn Jacobs married the widow of Captn Michael Cresap; which, if it was a fact unknown to you before, is given as a clue by which you may come at the parties, & serve the summons" (LB, DLC:GW). The enclosed summons from the clerk of the Virginia General Court has not been found. Michael Cresap, who died in 1775 at the age of 33, was married to Mary Whitehead of Philadelphia. Mrs. Cresap had married John Jeremiah Jacobs, who was a first lieutenant in the 6th Maryland Regiment.

3. Luther Martin (c.1748–1826) on Christmas Day 1783 married Maria (Mary) Cresap, the oldest daughter of Michael Cresap. In 1785 Martin, who practiced law in Baltimore, was a delegate to Congress. Elizabeth and Sarah were Michael Cresap's younger daughters.

4. The procedure for entering caveats of this sort are set down in "An act for establishing a Land Office and ascertaining the terms and manner of granting waste and unappropriated lands" (10 Hening 50–65).

5. See note 2.

Letter not found: from Clement Biddle, 8 August. GW wrote Biddle on 17 Aug.: "Your letter of the 8th came safely by last Post."

From Edmund Randolph

Dear sir   The rocks August 8. 1785.

Being so near you, as I understand myself to be, I should certainly have endeavoured to pay my respects to you today in person, were it not for the fatigue, which I have lately undergone in travelling hither.[1]

A business, similar to that, in which you are now engaged, will oblige me to return to Richmond by the 20th instant. The subscribers to the opening of James river are then to meet. I was desired by several of them to learn, if possible, whether you would have any objection to be our president. It is not expected, that you should undertake any troublesome part; but we wish to be considered, as having your particular patronage.[2]

I hope that before this you are well prepared against your adversaries at Fort Pitt. If I can do anything farther on my return, I beg you to command me.[3] I am Dear sir with the sincerest regard yr obliged friend & serv:

Edmd Randolph

ALS, DLC:GW.

1. The Rocks was a hunting lodge built on the Shenandoah River at the mouth of Long Marsh Run. On 8 Aug. GW and his party were at Harpers Ferry at the confluence of the Potomac and Shenandoah rivers. Ralph Wormeley, Sr., Randolph's host at The Rocks, was among the "Many Gentlemen of the Neighbourhood" who visited GW on this day (*Diaries*, 4:179).

2. For GW's election to the presidency of the James River Company and his reaction, see Randolph to GW, 2 Sept., n.2.

3. See Randolph to GW, 4 June, and the references in note 1 of that document.

To James Rumsey

Sir: Shanadoah Falls 8th Augt 1785.

As you have attended the President & Directors in their View and Examination of the River from the upper Part of the Seneca Falls to the Great Falls and from the flat water above to the flat water below the Shanadoah Falls, you are possessed not only of their Opinion of the Course in general to be improved and their idea of the manner of effecting ⟨the work, but also of their sentiments on many particular⟩ Spots[1]—The President and Directors have no doubt could they personally attend the Work in its progress and see the River at those places in its different Situations they might in many Instances depart from their present Opinions—The Nature of the Work and our Situations make it therefore necessary to leave it in your discretion to vary from what you may have concieved our Opinion to be as to the Tract or manner of executing the Work. And we do it the more chearfully as you seem to be equally impressed as Ourselves with the Importance of a straight Navigation and the Advantages of avoiding as far as well may be cross currents.[2] The Opportunity you will have to watch the Water at different Heights and your Industry in examining more minutely the different obstructions, will enable you to exercise the discretionary Power left with you to your own Credit and our Satisfaction.

You are already apprised of our Change of Resolution as to the place of working the upper Party and the Reasons which induced that Change, and as effecting the Navigation through the Shenadoah and Seneca Falls will be immediately advantageous to a great Extent of Country you are not to consider yourself restricted to the Number of fifty Hands for each Party, but you are to employ as many as you have an Opportunity to engage and you can work to advantage so that the work may be expedited; but you must immediately, on exceeding one hundred in the whole give information to the President least any Disappointment should happen in the ready Payment of the Company's Debts, which by all means is to be avoided[3]—for the President & Directors, G. Washington

LB, DNA: RG 79, Records of the Potomac Co. and the Chesapeake and Ohio Canal Co., item 159. This copy of the letter is taken from the minutes of the meeting on 8 Aug. of the president and directors of the Potomac River Company "at the Shanadoah Falls" (Harpers Ferry), with GW and the directors George Gilpin, John Fitzgerald, and Thomas Johnson present. The letter is preceded in the minutes by the following paragraphs: "The President and all the Directors having Yesterday viewed and examined the Shanadoah Falls from the flat Water above to that below were unanimously of Opinion that the Navigation may be carried through the falls without a Lock and that the purposes of the Incorporation would be best promoted by the spediest removal of the Obstructions within the above described Space.

"It is therefore ordered, that the Party directed by the former Order to be employed above the Shanadoah Falls be immediately employed in clearing and improving the River for Navigation from Payne's upwards through the Shanadoah Falls.

"The following Letter of Instruction was wrote to Mr Rumsey the principal Conductor."

1. The Potomac River Company held its second meeting in Georgetown, Md., at noon on 1 Aug. "when the President [GW] & directors of the Company made a report of their transactions since their appointment" at the first company meeting on 17 May 1785 (*Diaries*, 4:170). For the first meeting of the Potomac River Company, see GW to Thomas Johnson and Thomas Sim Lee, 18 May 1785, n.1; for the "transactions" of the company's directors, see GW

to James Rumsey, 5 June, n.4, and 2 July, n.3. After the company's meeting at noon on 1 Aug., according to GW: "The Board of Directors then sat, and after coming to some resolutions respecting rations to be allowed the Workmen— the mode of payment—manner of keeping an acct. of their work &ca. &ca. and to a determination of proceeding first to the Senneca Falls and next to those at the Mouth of Shannondoah for the purpose of investigation & to direct the operations thereat adjourned Sine Die" (ibid., 170). The minutes of the directors' meeting on 1 Aug. show that they examined eight accounts presented against the Potomac River Company and ordered a total of £182.7.4 to be paid. They also ordered £50 Virginia currency to be given to James Rumsey to be expended "for the use of the Company" (DNA: RG 79, Records of the Potomac Co. and the Chesapeake and Ohio Canal Co., item 159). Finally the directors issued the following instructions which perhaps reflect the president's experience with military procedure: "Ordered, That each Overseer keep a Book in which the Name of every Person employed under his Direction must be enrolled and with Columns properly ruled to keep an exact Account of the Days on which each Hand is employed and also of the Time he shall not be engaged in the Service which Account once in every Fortnight is to be rendered to the Assistant Manager, who if he approves the same shall give a certificate thereof, and shall afterwards be examined by ⟨the⟩ principal Manager and if approved also by him to be a⟨n⟩ Authority to the Treasurer to furnish such Sums of Money as will be sufficient to discharge the same—And it is the Order of this Board that twenty six working Days are to be accounted as a Month" (DNA: RG 79, Records of the Potomac Co. and the Chesapeake and Ohio Canal Co., item 159).

On 2 Aug. GW "Left George Town about 10 Oclock, in Company with all the Directors except Govr. Lee" and with others to go up the Potomac. Rumsey and his assistant manager, Richardson Stewart, joined GW's party on 3 Aug. in canoes "to examine the falls . . . beginning at the head of them . . . through the whole by water, and continued from the foot of them to the Great fall" (ibid., 170–71). The party then walked back on the Maryland side of the river from the Great Falls to Seneca falls (or rapids), a distance of about five miles. Before the meeting on 8 Aug. at Harpers Ferry, GW, the directors, and the supervisors of the work examined the river up to Shenandoah falls and observed Rumsey's workmen as the clearing of the river got under way (see source note). GW's diary for the first ten days of August provides a detailed account of his movements and observations in his inspection of the upper Potomac (ibid., 169–81).

2. After their examination of the river from the Seneca to the Great Falls on 3 Aug., GW wrote in his diary: "The Water through these Falls is of sufficient depth for good Navigation. . . . The principal difficulties lye in rocks which occasion a crooked passage. These once removed, renders the passage safe without the aid of Locks. . . . It appearing to me, and was so, unanimously determined by the Board of Directors, that a channel through the bed of the river in a strait direction . . . would be preferable" (ibid., 172).

3. For new decisions reached by the directors of the Potomac River Com-

pany regarding a labor force for Rumsey, see GW to Thomas Johnson and Thomas Sim Lee, 10 Sept., n.1.

From John Sedwick

Sir   August the 8th 1785

My Father Benjamin Sedwick Deceased Purchased at the Sale of Mr Mercers Land one of the Lots and gave his Bond with Capt. Brady his Surety to yourself and the other Trustees for the Purchase Money taking a Bond for the Conveyance.[1]

Afterwards my Father in 1776 Sold the Land to Edward Snickers who by Agreement was to pay of the bond as a part of the Price. Mr Snickers in 1779 or 1780, Paid of the Bond in your Absence to Mr Lun Washington and obtained the Bond, and though he has had the Land in possession ever Since 1776, he has now brought A Suit in your Name, I dare say without your knowledge, on my Fathers Bond against his Executors and Security—Mr Jones the Attorney for the Executors of whom I am one, has advised me to request A Certificate from you that you did not order the Suit, and Says on its being obtained there will be and end of it, otherwise that we shall be oblige to go into a troublesome and Expensive Chancery Suit,[2] to avoid which Sr I Trouble you with my earnest request that you will be Pleased to give me Something from under your hand to the effect of what Mr Jones recommended which will very much oblige Your Most Obedt Hble Servt

John Sedwick

ALS, DLC:GW.

1. Sedwick's "Capt. Brady" and George Gilpin's "Capt. Bready" (Gilpin to GW, 10 July 1785) may be the same man, and he may be William Brady who was a captain in the Berkeley County militia at the time of the sale of George Mercer's land in the county in November 1774.

2. For the Mercer land that Edward Snickers acquired in 1774 and afterwards, and for the dispute over the particular Mercer lot, or tract, that Snickers bought from Benjamin Sedwick, see Snickers to GW, 17 May 1784, and notes. See also GW's words of assurance on this day, 8 Aug. 1785, to Benjamin Sedwick's son John, and see John Sedwick's letter to GW of 11 April 1786 telling of the failure of Snickers's suit in the General Court. Sedwick's attorney Jones is probably Gabriel Jones.

To John Sedwick

Sir,   Falls of Shannondoah 8th Augt 1785.
In answer to your letter of this date, I think I may venture to assure you that no writ has issued by my order, or under my authority, against the Executors & Security of your deceased Father, for the amount of a Bond passed by him to Colo. Tayloe & myself, as Attornies for Colo. George Mercer & his Mortgagers, in England.

The high Court of Chancery of this Commonwealth decreed (I do not at this moment recollect when) that the Bonds, & other papers which were in my possession relative to this business (as my situation did not admit of my acting, & as I had refused to do so)—should be given up to John Mercer Esqr.—which was accordingly done.[1]

If under this Decree such of the Bonds as were made payable to the Attornies aforesaid have been put in Suit in my name as the surviving Attorney; I *presume* it is a matter of course: but how a Bond which you say has been discharged, & not among the papers which were surrendered, should be under this predicament, I am not able to inform you. I am Sir &c.

G: Washington

LB, DLC:GW.

1. In accordance with an interlocutory decree of the Virginia General Court of 9 Nov. 1782, GW instructed Lund Washington to hand over to John Francis Mercer all of the papers relating to the sale of the Virginia property of his half brother, George Mercer, which was conducted by GW in November 1774. See GW to Francis Lightfoot Lee and Ralph Wormeley, Jr., 20 June 1784, and GW's Statement concerning George Mercer's Estate, 1 Feb. 1789 (printed below).

Letter not found: from John Cochran, 9 August. GW wrote John Cochran on 31 Aug.: "Your favor of the 9th . . . came safely a few days ago."

From George Weedon

Dear Sir   Fredericksburg August 10th 1785
Immediately on receipt of yours, I wrote Col. Heath for the enclosed which only came to hand yesterday.[1] I think Mons.

Cornay has taken a round about way to deposit his money by drawing on Mr Wadsworth in Conn. it would have been as well to have requested Mr De Marbois to have paid this money. The old lady your mother talks of paying you a visit in Septr. I mean doing myself the honor of escorting her. My respects to your Lady & believe me, dear General, with sentiments of esteem, Yr obedt Servt

G. Weedon

Sprague transcript, DLC:GW. The ALS was offered for sale in George D. Smith's catalog, item 845, no date.

1. GW wrote Weedon on 23 July. The "enclosed" from William Heth is quoted in GW to Corny, 5 Dec. 1785, n.2.

To Edmund Randolph

Dear Sir,   Mount Vernon 13th Augt 1785.

At the time your letter from the Rocks was delivered to me, I had neither pen, ink, paper, or a table to write on at command; consequently could only verbally acknowledge the receipt of it, which I did by Mr Wormley: since my return home I have met your other favor of the 29th Ulto.[1]

The great object, for the accomplishment of which I wish to see the inland navigation of the Rivers Potomac & James improved & extended, is to connect the Western Territory with the Atlantic States; all others, with me, are secondary: tho' I am clearly of opinion that it will greatly increase our Commerce, & be an immense saving, in the article of transportation, & draft Cattle, to the Planters & Farmers who are in a situation to have the produce of their labor water borne.

These being my sentiments, I wish to see the undertaking progress *equally* in both rivers; & but for my local situation, & numerous avocations, my attention to each should be alike: what little I do for the advancement of the enterprize in this river, is done, as it were en passant; and because I think the difficulties greater than in the other—& not because I give it the preference—For both in my opinion have their advantages, without much, if any interference with each other. The advantages arising from my patronage of either, is probably more ideal than real; but such as they are, I wish them to be thought equally distributed: my contribtion to the works shall be the same—I have already subscribed five shares to the Potomac navigation; & enclosed I give you a power to put my name down for five shares, to that of James river.[2]

With respect to acting as President to the Board of Directors for that Company, it is a delicate subject for me to speak to: every person who knows how much my time (by company & other matters) is occupied, must also know that it would be impossible for me to discharge the duties of the Office, as they should be: even here, where the business for the most part is, & will continue to be done at Alexandria, or George-town (eight miles further from me), it was so evident to me that I could not perform the duties of President with that diligence and propriety which I thought necessary, that I wished to decline it, but could not get excused: How much more would this be the case with James river, where the journey to it alone would be a work of time & labour: & besides, let it not be forgotten my Dr Sir, that tho' *some* of the Subscribers may wish to see me at the head of the Board of Directors; yet there may be others who would feel disappointed & hurt if they are overlooked, and this might have an influence on their connexions. I mention these things to you with the candour & frankness of a friend, & under the rose; after which your own judgment & those of your friends, must dictate for the best. I am persuaded all of us have the same object in view, & what ever shall be deemed, by the concurrent voice of the subscribers, the best means to effect it, shall meet my hearty approbation.[3]

My last letter was written to you in such haste, that I apprehend I was not sufficiently explicit to be understood.[4] It was not my intention to apply for a copy of the Governor's instructions releasing him from the restriction of the Kings Proclamation; but for the Order of Council consequent thereof, directing or permitting Warrants to issue on military rights, agreeably thereto: because if the date of this order had been found to be antecedent to the occupancy of my Adversaries; it would remove them from their grand Fort—for on *possession*, before I took any *legal* steps—I know they mean to place their *sole* defence. The Patent, & thousands of Warrants are evidences that the restriction respecting military settlers was taken off; but they do not ascertain *the time*. My Patent, if I recollect right, was dated in

July 1774; but the Occupants, according to their own accounts, possessed the Land in the Octobr preceeding; if therefore I could have obtained a Certificate of the loss of the Council Books; & any circumstance could have been recollected by which it should appear (as unquestionably the fact is) that the recognition of military rights was previous to October 1773, & so intimated in the Certificate aforesaid;[5] it would have been useful: *Without* this indeed, the matter is so clear, in my judgment, as not to admit of dispute before an *impartial* Jury; but an *impartial* Jury I do not expect—& much less since I have heard that the high Sheriff of the County (lately chosen) is of the fraternity of my competitors, & interested in the decision, so far at least as similar circumstances, & the suffrages of these people in his election, can bias him. Indeed I have lately been told that the decision of this case will be interesting to numbers whose rights are disputed on similar grounds. I am &c. &c.

G: Washington

LB, DLC:GW.

1. Randolph's letter is dated 8 August. On that day, GW and three of the four directors were encamped at the foot of the Shenandoah Falls on the Potomac.

2. Written below GW's letter in his letter book is the following statement: "I hereby empower Edmd Randolph Esqr. to subscribe in my name, & for my use & benefit, five shares in the Navigation of James river; & this shall be his Authority. Given under my hand this 13th of Augt 1785. G: Washington."

3. For GW's election to the presidency of the James River Company, see Randolph to GW, 2 Sept. 1785, n.2.

4. GW's letter is missing, but see Randolph to GW, 29 July.

5. See Randolph to GW, 29 July, n.1.

From Richard Thomas

Hond Sir   Charleston So. Carolina 13th Augst 1785

Having received the enclosed Letter this day from England, have taken the first opportunity of transmitting it to your Excellency.[1]

As the affair has lain dormant so long, it may be some time before it can be properly adjusted; but it appears by this as well as other letters I have received, that this Edmund Richards (of the County of Cornwall) is the right Heir to the Estate of Richd

Richards Esqr. who died in Virginia eighteen years ago. A Copy of the Will I find has been sent by Lawyer Hains to Lawyer Britton of Cullumpton in Devonshire, but he has been dead many years, & the copy cannot be found, so the matter must be left entirely to your Excellency's directions.

I shall esteem it an unbounded favor to have a copy of the Will, together with other particulars for the information of Mr Richards, who has appointed me to act the same as he could do, was he present.[2]

The situation of my Affairs in this City will not permit me to wait immediately on your Excellency in Person, but if the *least matter* will remain unsettled thro' my non attendance, Your Goodness will be pleased to inform me, & I will repair to Virginia with all speed.

I hope your Excellency will be kind enough to interest yourself in this important affair, & whatever directions may be necessary for Mr Richards, by transmitting them to me at Doctor Neufville's No. 108 Broad Street will be conveyed to him with all possible dispatch. I have the Honor to be with profound respect Hond Sir Your Excellency's Obedt Humble Servt

Richd Thomas

ALS, DLC:GW.

1. The enclosed letter, marked "(A True Copy)," from Edmund Richards to GW, 1 Feb. 1785, is in fact not a copy of the letter of that date which was sent to GW and is printed above; it rather is a version of that letter, quite differently worded but conveying the same meaning.

2. For references to GW's exchanges of letters with Thomas and Richards in which GW makes it entirely clear that he has never heard of Richard Richards or his will, see note 1 in Edmund Richards's letter of 1 Feb. 1785. GW answered this letter of 13 Aug. on 5 Dec., saying that he had just received it. Before getting GW's response, Thomas wrote again, for which he apologized on 25 July 1786.

From Otho Holland Williams

Dear Sir.   Bath 15th August 1785

Your Letter dated Mount Vernon July 26th,[1] is the only one that I have had the pleasure to receive from you since the return of peace.

I could not imagine why the Diploma's were not returned,

and, having written to you once or twice on the subject, concluded that it would be more respectful to wait until you should please to send them to me than to give any unnecessary trouble by sending for them.

When I discovered that they had got into the hands of improper persons I made very diligent search after them—found only three, and wrote you a circumstantial account of all I could discover respecting them, which was, indeed, very little.[2] A Fellow detected and committed to Baltimore Goal for a theft had two taken from him by a justice of peace, who finding your name to them enquired of me what they were—I examined the goal and found one more—The fellow (who had many marks of the knave about him) told me that he had found them in a part of the town to which I immediately went & I think I never saw a more abandoned set of Mortals of both Sexes collected together; after an hours fruitless search I went from thence to the Stage office for I conjectured that they had been sent by that conveyance, But could not find any Letter, receipt for the delivery which is common, nor entry in the office books—All these matters were reported in a letter which I had the honor of addressing to you last april and which went by a Gentleman to George Town.

If Colonel Fitzgerald or any other person can prove the delivery I can recover the cost of the Diplomas, which is still due to the Gentleman who advanced money to Major Turner[3] on that account, But I do not think it possible ever to recover the parchments, nor do I think it probable that any attempts have been, or will be, made to apply them to any purposes of imposition. Those I found were very much abused—dirty—rumpled, and bore no marks of forgery, and from the situation in which a wretched old Woman shewed me the others had been, it is impossible that they could be fit for the uses intended. With the most Sincere and respectful Esteem & regard I am, Dear Sir, Your most obedient Humble Servant

O. H. Williams

ALS, DLC:GW; ADfS, MdHi.
1. Letter not found.
2. For the correspondence regarding the loss of the Society of the Cincinnati diplomas, see Williams to GW, 20 April, n.1.
3. At the general meeting of the Society of the Cincinnati in May 1784,

George Turner, secretary of the South Carolina Society of the Cincinnati, and Abraham George Claypoole of Pennsylvania were given the responsibility of having the society's certificates, or diplomas, engraved.

From Battaile Muse

Honorable Sir,   Berkely C[ount]y Augt 16th 1785

Your Favour dated the 28th of Last month I receiv'd the 10th of this month—I shall be Very Attentive to your Requisitions—I shall Visit your Frederick Lands the Last of this week and will make my self acquainted with Every thing necessary—and will do what may be needfull as fare as is in my Power—I shall Call on Mr Whiteing for a writing to Cancel His Lease. I expect to be In Winchester the Last of this Month—then will Inquire after your Possessions their. Mr James Crane Sheriff of this County has Promised to Pay the money due by Mr Whiteing Next Month—should he Fail I shall Execute Mr Whiteing and will Endeavour to recover the Money as speedily as Possable after september Berkeley Court the Time apointed for Mr Crane To raise the money—after the Money falls into my hands it shall be at Mount Vernon within Ten days.[1]

The day after I receiv'd your Letter I sent to Mr Wormleys Manager In consequence of the Clover Seed—and as I Found that many People had applyed for seed and but four bushels to spare I have Engaged that Quantity at £4 P. bushel—the single bushel at £5—should you have Ocation for any—you may have the Hole or any Part. should you not want it I can dispose of it. the seed appears to be good[2]—I shall have about 2,000 bushels of good wheat for sale this next fall and winter—should you Purchase for your Mill I shall be oblige to you to inform me the price you give—My Crops of Wheat are Generally of the first Quality and Command the Highest price.[3]

I shall Visit Colo. Fairfaxes Estate at Belvoir in October —should you be at Home I shall Call on you for your Commands.[4] Please write to me by the first Post adviseing respecting the Clover seed—the Post receives letters for me at the Printing Office. I am sir your Obedient Humble Servant.

Battaile Muse

ALS, DLC:GW. Muse wrote on the cover: "Mr Heartshorn will please forward this Letter as Quick as Possable and Oblige His Hble servant B. Muse augt 16th 1785." William Hartshorne acted as Muse's commercial agent in Alexandria.

1. For Muse's dealings with GW's former tenant Henry Whiting, see GW to Muse, 3 Nov. 1784, n.3.

2. See GW to Muse, 28 July, n.6.

3. GW in his letter to Muse of 22 Aug. spells out in great detail the terms upon which he will buy wheat. This is at the time that GW has embarked upon the manufacture and sale of flour on a large scale. On 27 Oct. GW entered an agreement with Muse to buy one thousand bushels of wheat at six shillings a bushel, to be paid in March 1786 (*Diaries*, 4:215).

4. Muse served as a land agent for George William Fairfax as well as for GW. See GW to Muse, 3 Nov. 1784, n.1. Muse was at Mount Vernon on 27 October.

Letter not found: from Battaile Muse, 16 Aug. GW wrote Muse on 22 Aug.: "Both your letters of the 16th have come safe."

To Clement Biddle

Dear Sir,   Mount Vernon 17th Augt 1785

Your letter of the 8th came safely by last Post[1]—I will, the first time I go to Alexandria, get an order from Colo. Hooe, Mr Hartshorne, or some other who has dealings in Philadelphia (for I have none, & know of no direct and safe opportunity of sending Money) to the amount of the Sum which you have lately paid on my Acct to Mr Boudinot.[2]

The inclosed is to Edward (I do not know his Surname) who formerly lived with Mr R. Morris, but now, I am informed, keeps the City Tavern, to see if he can be instrumental in procuring me a House keeper. I beg you to be so obliging as to direct, deliver, and consult him on the contents of the letter, which is left open for your perusal, & return me an answr as soon as possible.[3]

The Man who at present lives with me in the capacity of a Housekeeper (and is a very good one) is bound for the port of Matrimony, and will, after 4 or 5 Weeks which he has agreed to stay, leave me in a very disagreeable Situation if I cannot get supplied in the meanwhile—I give him £25 this Curry pr Ann. & a suit of Clothes which cannt be less than Seven pounds more—these, with the difference of Exchange, will be equal to abt

£40 pensa Cury. This Sum I am willing to give to Man, or Woman (the former I would prefer) of good character, & really knowing and competent to my purposes.[4]

I have seen an Advertisement in some of the Philadelphia Papers of an Office for this kind of business, but however good it may be as a *channel* for *enquiry* I would not depend upon it, without other testimonials respecting the character & abilites of an applicant for the final adoption. Mrs Washington joins me in best wishes for yourself, and Mrs Biddle & family. I am Dr Sir Yr Most Obedt Hble Ser⟨vt⟩

Go: Washington

P.S. Since writing the foregoing, I have met with, and now inclose you, a bank note for 30 dollars; which please to receive, and carry to my credit. Yr &c. G.W.

ALS, PHi: Washington-Biddle Correspondence.

1. Letter not found.

2. See postscript.

3. Edward Moyston formerly was steward in Robert Morris's Office of Finance, and from 1779 to 1787 he kept the New Tavern (City Tavern or Smith's Tavern) on Second Street in Philadelphia. See GW to Samuel Fraunces, 7 Sept. 1785, and Moyston to GW, 4 April 1787. GW's enclosed letter to Moyston has not been found.

4. In the spring of 1783, Mrs. Washington hired to become in May the housekeeper at Mount Vernon "a very Modest well behaved man" named Richard Burnet, who at the time was living with Benjamin Tasker Dulany and his wife Elizabeth Dulany, probably at Shuter's Hill outside Alexandria (Lund Washington to GW, 12 Mar. 1783). Burnet proved to be a good cook and manager, and all went well for two years until he decided to marry, probably Ann Alton, daughter of GW's old servant, John Alton (d. 1785; see Lund Washington to GW, 1 Oct. 1783, and GW's account with Lund Washington, 1783–85, in Ledger B, 172–89). Burnet seems to have left GW's employ after receiving his wages on 6 Sept. 1785 (Ledger B, 189; see also GW to Samuel Fraunces, 7 Sept.). Thomas McCarty began work as housekeeper at Mount Vernon on 26 Sept. in place of Burnet (*Diaries*, 4:198). On 29 May 1786, however, GW recorded in his diary: "Found, when I was at Dogue Run that Richard Burnet and wife had been living in the House formerly [William] Barrys, since Wednesdy. last"; and on 12 Aug. he wrote: "Richard Burnet took his place on the wages of Thirty Pounds pr. ann." (ibid., 337, 5:26). At the same time, August 1786, GW begins his account with "Richd B[urnet] Walker (Butler)" to serve as "House Steward & Butler @ £30 pr annm," under which name Burnet continued at Mount Vernon until February 1789, shortly before GW left to assume the presidency (Ledger B, 234, 252).

Two days before writing this letter, GW sent an advertisement to the printer:

"The Subscriber wants a HOUSE-KEEPER, or, HOUSEHOLD STEWARD, who is competent to the charge of a large family, and attending on a good deal of company.—One who has been in the practice of these, and can produce testimonials of his (for a man would be preferred) or her abilities, sobriety, honesty and industry, will receive good wages and find a comfortable birth.— Without such testimonials it will be useless to apply. G. WASHINGTON" (*Virginia Journal and Alexandria Advertiser*, 18 Aug.).

To Benjamin Ogle

Sir,   Mt Vernon 17th Augt 1785.

The enclosed from Mr Dulaney did not come to my hands (being from home) until sunday last. I thank you for your obliging offer of two or three Fawns; but presuming the season is now too far advanced either to catch or gentle them, I will not send before I hear further from you on this subject.[1]

If it is too late to obtain them this year, I would thank you for the like number next Spring; by which time I shall have a proper inclosure for them, & for the Deer of this Country, of which I am also endeavouring to procure a stock to breed from.[2] With compliments to Mrs Ogle, I have the honor to be &c.

G: Washington

LB, DLC:GW.

1. The enclosure from Benjamin Tasker Dulany has not been identified, but there is in DLC:GW a letter, docketed by GW, from Ogle to Dulany, dated 12 July. It reads: "I recd yr favr by Cracroft & do assure you Genl Washington (to whom present my Complts) is exceedingly wellcome to two or three fauns, Mr [Richard] Sprigg spoke without Book when he said I was unwilling to part with them, the truth is its very difficult to catch them & I wish the General may not be disappointed, but if he will send a careful hand I will give all the assistance in my power."

2. See Ogle to GW, 20 August.

To Tench Tilghman

Dear Sir,   Mount Vernon 17th Augt 1785

The Baltimore Advertiser of the 12th Instt announces the arrival of a Ship at that Port, immediately from China—and by an advertisement in the same Paper, I perceive that the Cargo is to be sold by public vendue, on the first of Octr next.[1]

At what prices the enumerated Articles will sell—or the terms proposed—can only be known from the experiment; but if the quantity at Market is great, and they should sell as goods have sold by vendue, bargains may be expected. I therefore take the liberty of requesting the favor of you, in that case, to purchase the several things contained in the inclosed list.[2]

You will readily perceive, My dear Sir my purchasing, or not, depends entirely upon the prices. If *great bargains* are to be had, I would supply myself agreeably to the list. If the prices do not fall *below* a cheap *retail* Sale, I would decline them altogether, or take such articles only (if cheaper than common) as are marked in the Margin of the Invoice.

Before October, if none of these Goods are previously sold, and if they are the matter will be ascertained thereby, you will be able to form a judgment of the prices they will command by vendue. Upon information of which, I will deposit the money in your hands to comply with the terms of the Sale.

Since I began this letter, I have been informed that good India Nankeens are selling (at Dumfries not far from me) at 7/6 a ps. this Curry—But if my memory has not failed me, I used to import them before the war for about 5/ Sterlg. If so, though 50 prCt is a small advance upon India Goods, through a British Channel, (with the duties & accumulated charges thereon) yet, quære, would not 7/6 be a high price for Nankeens brought immediately from India, exempted from *such* duties & Charges? If this is a conjecture founded in fairness, it will give my ideas of the prices of other Articles from that Country; & be a government for your conduct therein, at, or before the day appointed for the public vendue.[3] with the highest esteem and regard I am—Dr Sir Yr Affecte friend and Obedt Hble Servt

Go: Washington

ALS, PHi: Dreer Collection; LB, DLC:GW.

1. The Baltimore paper reported on 12 Aug. the arrival on 9 Aug. directly from China of the ship *Pallas*, Captain O'Donnell, with "an extensive variety of teas, china, silks, satins, nankeens, &c. &c." (*Virginia Journal and Alexandria Advertiser*, 18 Aug.).

2. The enclosed list reads: "Invoice of Goods to be purchased, by Tench Tilghman Esqr. on Acct of George Washington, agreeably to the letter accompanying this, of equal date.

　A Sett of the best Nankin Table China

　Ditto—best Evening China Cups & Saucers

*A Set of *large* blue & White China
  Dishes—say half a dozn—more or less
*1 Dozn *small* bowls—blue & White.
*6 Wash hand Guglets & Basons
  6 large Mugs—or 3 Mugs & 3 Jugs.
  A Quartr Chest, *best* Hyson Tea.
  A Leagure [Leaguer] of Battavia Arrack if a Leagure is not large
*About 13 yds of good bla: Paduasoy
*A ps. of fine Muslin—plain
*1 ps. of Silk Handkerchiefs
  12 ps. of the best Nankeens.
  18 ps. of the Second quality—or
    coursest kind—for Servants. Go: Washington."
In the margin opposite the first six entries listing items of china, GW wrote
"with the badge of the Society of the Cincinnati—if to be had." For his later
purchase of a set of china with the badge of the society, see Henry Lee, Jr., to
GW, 3 July 1786.

   3. In the end, Tilghman bought nothing for GW. See Tilghman to GW, 25
Aug., 13 Oct., GW to Tilghman, 29 Aug., 14 Sept. 1785.

From John Marsden Pintard

Sir   Madeira 19th August 1785.
   Your Excellency will be Pleased to Pardon the liberty I now
take in beging your acceptance of the only rarity the Island at
present affords. altho I have not the Honor of being Personaly
known to your Excellency nevertheless Some of my family have
been So fortunate as to meet with your approbation, I mean
my father Lewis Pintard Who was agent for our Unfortunate
Prisoners in New york during Part of the war. I at that time
was with him as an assistant and Scince the peace Have been
appointed Commercial agent for the United States at the Islands
of Madeira & Porto Santo to Manage the occasional concerns of
Congress to assist the American Traders with my advice and to
Solicit their dependencies with the Portugese Government I am
truly Sensible of the Honour of this Appointment and shall ever
study to merit the confidence of my countrymen if your excellency is desirous of Having any Slips of grape vines or young fig
trees it would make me peculiarly happy to be Honored with
your commands and I wd be carefull in putting up different
qualities. That you may for a Series of years to come enjoy evry
Possible degree of health and happiness is the Sincere wish and

constant Prayr of Sir your Excellency's Most obedient and very Humble Servant

John Marsden Pintard

ALS, DLC:GW.

The father of John Marsden Pintard (d. 1811), Lewis Pintard, was a New York merchant engaged in the Madeira wine trade. In October 1783 the Congress made John Pintard its commercial agent on the island of Madeira, where he was acting for his father. See the identification of John Marsden Pintard in Pintard to GW, 16 July 1789. GW wrote John Pintard on 18 Nov. to thank him for "a box of Citrons, Lemons & Onions" and to ask him to send vines of the "best eating Grape; and a young fig tree or two." Pintard sent grapevines and two fig trees in January 1786 (Pintard to GW, 24 Jan. 1786), and GW wrote Pintard on 2 Aug. 1786 that the plants had arrived, all dead except for some of the vines, which showed some "signs of feeble life."

To George Gilpin

Dear Sir,   Mount Vernon 20th Augt 1785

If nothing unforeseen happens, I can be at the Great Falls at any hour you & Colo. Fitzgerald will name, on Thursday next; ready to proceed from thence to the little Falls, if a vessel should be in readiness at the former.[1] I am Dr Sir Yr Most Obt Servt

Go: Washington

ALS, PHi: Gilpin Papers.

1. Four days later, on Wednesday, 24 Aug., GW again wrote Gilpin: "On Saturday I informed you that I could be ready to attend at the Great Falls at any hour to-morrow (Thursday) that you & Col Fitzgerald would name & having heard nothing from you since, I am at a loss how to govern myself.

"It was my intention then and is so still, if the meeting is to take place to go to Mr Fairfax's tonight so that being convenient I can be at the Falls at any hour that be named tomorrow" (typescript, ViMtV). GW did not go to the falls and next met with Gilpin and John Fitzgerald in Alexandria on 9 September.

From Lamar, Hill, Bisset, & Co.

Sir,   Madeira 20th August 1785.

Since we had the honor of writing you under the 22d last June, no oppr. has offered for Alexandria 'till the Bearer of this Captain Moon of the Brig Industry, & having requested the favor of him to take on b[oar]d a Pipe of Wine for you, he told us he could not possibly do it, as only 5 Pipes in all offered on Freight, which he would not venture to carry, because they would subject him to make an entry in the Customhouse, which is attended with additional Expences. We hope same oppr. will soon cast up to our satisfaction, but for fear one should not, request your sentiments on the plan mentioned in our last,[1] and not having at present to add, take the liberty to subscribe ourselves Sir Your most obedient humble Servants

Lamar Hill Bisset & Co.

LS, DLC:GW.

1. GW wrote on 1 Sept. 1785 to Lamar, Hill, Bisset, & Co. in response to their inquiry of 22 June 1785 about filling his order of November 1783 for "a Pipe of fine old Wine." Before receiving GW's instructions to the contrary, the wine merchants sent the pipe of wine for GW to Dr. James Taylor in Norfolk (Lamar, Hill, Bisset, & Co. to GW, 6 Dec. 1785; James Taylor to GW, 4 Feb., 13 Mar. 1786). GW enclosed a letter to the merchants in a letter to Henry Hill of Philadelphia, 3 Aug. 1786, acknowledging receipt of the wine and remitting to Hill "a draft for £43.12.4 on Wakelin Welch."

To Secondat de Montesquieu

Sir,   Mount Vernon 20th Augt 1785.

By a brig belonging to Mr Ridout of Bourdeaux, I had the honor to receive your letter of the 2d of May, & the Wine which accompanied it; which you were so obliging as to send me at the request of your worthy son—it came in very good order. For this instance of his kind remembrance; & your polite attention, I pray you to accept my warmest acknowledgments: my thanks are due also in a particular manner to you, Sir, for the Walnuts you sent me, which are very fine; and I shall endeavour to propagate them in the manner directed by you.

I pray you to forward, when you shall find a convenient opportunity, the enclosed letter for the Baron de Montesquieu, with assurances of my sincere regard and friendship for him.[1] I have the honor to be &c.

G: Washington

LB, DLC:GW.

1. The text of the enclosed letter to the younger Montesquieu is printed in Montesquieu to GW, 25 April 1785, n.4.

From Benjamin Ogle

Sir   Bellair [Md.] Aug. 20 1785

In a day or two after I understood you expresd a Wish for a few Fauns, (which I do assure you will give me particular pleasure to supply) I came to this place & immediately endeavour'd to get, but found them too forward[1]—They begin to drop about the 15h June & unless they are caught within ten days its as difficult as to catch the old ones, but Sir if you will please to send a carefull Servant the 20th you may be certain of not being disappointed,[2] the younger they are taken, the easyer raised— should they drop sooner I will give timely notice—I am with compts to yr Lady Honrd Sir yr Most obedient Humb. Servt

                                        Ben. Ogle

ALS, DLC:GW.

1. See GW to Ogle, 17 Aug., n.1.

2. Ogle is referring to 20 June of the next year, 1786. GW wrote George William Fairfax on 25 June 1786: "Mr Ogle of Maryland has been so obliging as to present me Six fawns from his Park of English Deer at Bell-Air." See also Ogle to GW, 12 July 1786.

Letter not found: from John Rawlins, 20 August. On 29 Aug. GW wrote Rawlins: "Your letter of the 20th of this month, only came to my hands by the last Post."

To Thomas Ridout

Sir,   Mount Vernon 20th Augt 1785.

By the return of the Brig I was favored with your letter of the 1st of May, with several Cases of wine, & a box of sundries which came to hand in good order, & I presume are of good quality; as the wine which you sent to others, is, I am informed, much esteemed—my own I have not tasted. I am obliged to you for sending these things—the amount shall be paid to Colo. Geo: Fitzgerald in a short time.[1]

For your care of the enclosed letters, I will thank you: the one under a blank cover I shall be obliged to you for giving the proper address of the Father of Baron de Montesquieu; from whom I received a letter—but under such a signature as leaves me at a loss how to direct my answer to him. If my letter to the Baron is like to subserve the purpose for which it was intended, it will give me pleasure.[2]

The small packages which the Marqs de la Fayette intended to send by your Brig, must, I presume, have miscarried between Paris and Bourdeaux, as his letters to me speak positively as to their being sent from the former place.[3] I am &c. &c.

G: Washington

LB, DLC:GW.

1. On 9 Feb. 1786 GW paid John Fitzgerald £21.13.8 (Ledger B, 211).

2. GW's letters to the Montesquieus, father and son, are dated 20 August.

3. Ridout wrote GW on 31 Aug. about this package from Lafayette. For the toys being sent to the Custis children, see the marquise de Lafayette to GW, 15 April 1785, and note 2 of that document.

To William Grayson

Dear Sir,   Mount Vernon 22d Augt 1785.

During my tour up this River with the Directors, to examine & form a ⟨plan⟩ for opening and extending the Navigation of it agreeably to the Acts of the Virginia & Maryland Assemblies; your favor of the 25th Ulto came here; with the letters brought by young Mr Adam's from France. for your care of which I thank you. Apropos, did you hear him say any thing of *Hounds* which, (the Marquis de la Fayette has written to me) were committed to his care? If he really brought them (and if he did not, I am unable to account for the information) it would have been civil in him to have dropped me a line respecting them; especially as War is declared against the Canine species in New York; and they, being strangers, without Alliances for selfdefence; distressed, & friendless; may not only have been exposed thereto, but to pestilence & famine also. If you can say any thing on this Subject pray do it.[1]

I thank you for the several articles of intelligence contained in your letter, and for the propositions respecting a Coinage of Gold, Silver, & Copper—a measure which, in my judgment, is become indispensably necessary. Mr Jeffersons ideas upon this subject are plain and simple, well adapted I think to the nature of the case, as he has exemplified by the plan. Without a Coinage, or some stop can be put to the cutting & clipping of money, our Dollars, Pistoreens &ca will all be converted (as Teague Says) into five quarters; and a Man must travel with a pair of money scales in his pocket, or run the risque of receiving gold at one fourth more by Count, than weight.[2]

I have ever been a friend to adequate Congressional powers; consequently wish to see the 9th Art. of the Confederaton amended and extended. Without these powers we cannot support a National character; and must appear contemptable in the eyes of Europe. But to you, My dear Sir, I will candidly confess, that, in my opinion, it is of little avail to give these to Congress. The Members seem so much affraid of exerting those which they already have, that no opportunity is slipped of *surrendering*, or *referring* the exercise of them to the states individually. Witness your late Ordinance respecting the dispersal of the Western Lands, in which no state with the smallest propriety, could have obtruded an interference.[3]

No doubt the information of Congress from the back Country, on the operation of these ordinances, is better than mine; but I have understood from some sensible people therefrom, that besides going they do not know where to purchase, the Lands are of so versatile a nature, that to the end of time, they will not, by those who are acquainted with this circumstance, be bought either in Townships, or square miles. This, if I recollect right, was the sentiment I delivered to you on the first reading of the report; but past experience you said was brought in support of the measure, and appealed to for the issue—I submitted to its decision, without changing my opinion.[4]

We have got the Potomack Navigation in hand—Workmen are employed, and the best Manager and assistants we could obtain, at the Falls of Shannondoah and Seneca; and I am happy to inform you, that upon a critical examination of them by the Directors, the Manager, & myself, we are unanimoustly of opinion that the difficulties at these two places does not exceed the expectations we had formed of them—and that the Navigation through them, may be effected without the Aid of Locks. How far we may have been deceived with respect to the first (as the water, though low, may yet fall) I shall not decide; but we are not mistaken I think in our conjectures of the other.[5] With very great esteem & regard I am—Dear Sir Yr Affecte Friend and Obedt Hble Servt

Go: Washington

ALS, NjP: deCoppet Collection; LB, DLC:GW.

1. Two days after this letter was written, the seven hounds sent to GW by Lafayette arrived at Mount Vernon (*Diaries*, 4:186). See GW to John Cochran, 31 Aug., and Grayson to GW, 5 September. See also Lafayette to GW, 15 April, 13 May 1785.

2. GW is referring to Thomas Jefferson's "Propositions Respecting the Coinage of Gold, Silver, and Copper," of 13 May 1785. See "Jefferson's Notes on Coinage" in Boyd, *Jefferson Papers*, 7:150–203.

3. For GW's views on the proposal to give Congress the power to regulate trade, see GW to James McHenry, this date.

4. For GW's fullest expression of misgivings about the Land Ordinance of 1785, see his letter to Grayson of 25 April 1785.

5. For the inspection trip up the Potomac, see especially, GW to James Rumsey, 8 Aug., n.1. A document headed "List of Labourers Employed at the Seneca Falls under Richardson Stewart to the 19th Augst inclusive 1785" gives the names of forty-three workmen (and one overseer) who individually had worked as many as fifteen days or as few as two days. The charges for the labor, £28.16.3 Virginia currency, were approved by GW and the trustees at their meeting on 26 September. The document in 1989 was owned by Mr. Jerry L. Williams of Tampa, Florida.

To Richard Henry Lee

Dear Sir, Mount Vernon 22d Augt 1785.

In my absence with the Directors of the Potomack Navigation, to examine the river and fix a plan of operations, your favor begun on the 23d and ended the 31st of July, came to this place. I am sorry to hear of your late indisposition, but congratulate you on your recovery; hoping that the reestablishment of your health will be of long continuance.

The packett which you were so obliging as to send me, came safely; and I thank you for your care of it. but for want of knowledge of the language, I can form no opinion of my own of the Dramatic performance of Monsr Servitieur la Barbier.

The currt of my information from France is, that the dispute between the Emperor & Holland will be accomodated without bloodshed: but after the explicit declarations which have been made on both sides, I do not see how either (especially the first) can recede from his claims. To save appearances, & to let the contending parties down *handsomely,* say some of my letters, is now the greatest difficulty. but all agree that, a spark may set the whole in flames. indeed Bavaria it is expected will yet do that.

It is to be hoped that our Minister at the Court of London will bring that Government to an explanation respecting the Western Posts, which it still retains on the American side of the line, contrary to the spirit, if not to the letter, of the Treaty. My opinion from the first, and so I declared it, was that these Posts would be detained from us as long as they could be held under any pretence whatsoever. I have not changed it, though I wish for cause to do so, as it may ultimately become a serious matter. However singular the opinion may be, I cannot divest myself of it, that the Navigation of the Mississipi, at *this time*, ought to be no object with us; on the contrary, till we have a little time allowed to open & make easy the ways between the Atlantic States & the Western territory, the obstructions had better remain.

There is nothing which binds one Country, or one State to another, but interest. without this cement, the Western inhabitants (which more than probably will be composed in a great degree of Foreigners) can have no predeliction for us; and a commercial connection is the only tie we can have upon them—It is clear to me that the Trade of the Lakes, and of the river Ohio as low as the Great Kanhawa, (if not to the Falls) *may* be brought to the Ports on the Atlantic easier, and cheaper (taking the *whole* voyage together) than it can be carried to New Orleans. but once open the door to the latter before the obstructions are removed from the former, let commercial connections (which lead to others) be formed, and the habit of that trade be well established, and it will be found no easy matter to divert it. and vice versa —When the Settlements are stronger & more extended to the Westward, the navigation of the river Mississipi will be an object of importance; and we shall be able then (reserving our claim) to speak a more efficacious language than policy, I think, should dictate at present.

I never have, and I hope never shall hear, any serious mention of a paper emission in this State—yet such a thing may be in agitation—Ignorance & design are productive of much mischief—the first, is the Tool of the latter, and are often set to work as suddenly as unexpectedly—those with whom I have conversed on this subject, in this part of the state, reprobate the idea exceedingly.

We have lately had the pleasure of Miss Lees, and Miss Hannahs Companies at this place.[1] They were both well five days ago. Mrs Washington prays you to accept her complimts, and with Sentimts of great respect, esteem & regard, I am—Dear Sir Yr Most Obedt and Affecte Hble Servt

Go: Washington

P.S. Your name, I well remember, stands amongst those of the Subscribers for a share in the Potomack Company. G.W.

ALS, PPAmP: Correspondence of Richard Henry Lee and Arthur Lee; LB, DLC:GW.

1. On 27 July Richard Henry Lee's eldest daughter (b. 1764), Mary Lee, visited Mount Vernon; Hannah Lee (1766–c.1801), Richard Henry Lee's second daughter, came on 12 August.

To James McHenry

Dear Sir,   Mount Vernon 22d Augt 1785.

Your letter of the 1st Instt came to this place whilst I was absent on a tour up the Potomack, or an earlier acknowledgement of it would have been given. The inclosure shall, either by this, or the next Post, be sent to Doctr Gordon for his information, and that justice may be done to a character so deserving of American gratitude, & the pen of a Historiographer as that of the Marquis de la Fayette's.[1]

I am very glad to hear that Congress is relieved from the embarrassment which originated with Longchamp; had the demand of him been persisted in, it might have involved very serious consequences. It is better that the Court of France should be a little miffed than for it to have persevered in their demand of him.

As I have ever been a friend to adequate powers in Congress, without wch it is evident to me we never shall establish a National character, or be considered on a respectable footing by the powers of Europe, I am sorry I cannot agree with you in sentiment not to enlarge them for the regulation of Commerce. I have neither time nor abilities to enter upon a full discussion of this subject; but it should seem to me, that, your arguments against it—principally—that some States may be more benefitted than others by a Commercial regulation, applies to every matter of general utility; for where is the case in which this argument may not be used, in a greater, or less degree. We are either a United people under one head, & for Fœderal purposes, or, we are thirteen independent Sovereignties, eternally counteracting each other. If the former, whatever such a Majority of the States, as the Constitution requires, conceives to be for the benefit of the whole, should, in my humble opinion, be submitted to by the Minority. Let the Southern States always be represented. Let them Act more in unison—Let them declare freely, & boldly what is for the interest, & what is prejudicial to their Constituents, and there will—there must be, an accomodating spirit. In the establishment of an Act for Navigation, this, in a particular manner ought, & will, doubtless, be attended to; and if the assent of nine (or as some propose, of Eleven) States is necessary to give validity to a Commercial system, it insures this measure, or the Act cannot be obtained—Wherein then lyes the danger? but if your fears are in danger of being reallized, cannot certain provisos in the Law guard against the evil? I see no difficulty in this if the Southern Delegates would give their attendance in Congress, and follow the example, if such an one should beset them, of hanging together to counteract combinations.

I confess to you candidly that I can foresee no evil greater, than disunion—than those unreasonable jealousies (I say *unreasonable*, because I would have a proper jealousy always awake, and the United States always upon the watch, to prevent individual States from infracting the Constitution, with impunity) which are continually poisoning our minds, and filling them with imaginary evils, to the prevention of real ones. As you have asked the question, I answer, I do not know that we can enter a War of Imposts with G. Britain, or any other foreign Power, but we are certain that this War has been waged against us by the former, *professedly*, upon a belief that we never could unite in opposition to it. and I believe there is no way of putting an end to—at least of stopping the increase of it, but to convince them of the contrary. Our Trade in all points of view is as essential to G.B., as hers is to us—and she will exchange it upon reciprocal & liberal terms, if an advantage is not to be obtained. It can hardly be supposed, I think, that the carrying business will devolve wholly on the States you have named; or remain long with them if it should—for either G.B. will depart from her present selfish system, or the policy of the Southern States in forming a general Act of Navigation, or by Laws individually passed by their respective Legislatures, will devise ways & means to encourage seamen for the transportation of their own produce—or for the encouragement of Manufactures; but admitting the contrary, if the Union is considered as permanent, and on this I presume all superstructures are built, had we not better encourage Seamen among ourselves with less imports, than divide it with foreigners & by encreasing them, ruin our Merchants; & greatly injure the mass of our Citizens?

To sum up the whole, I foresee, or think I do it, many advantages which will result from giving powers of this kind to Congress (if a sufficient number of States are required to exercise them) without any evil save those which may proceed from inattention or want of wisdom in the formation of the Act. whilst without them, we stand, I conceive, in a ridiculous point of view in the eyes of the Nations of the Earth; with whom we are attempting to enter into Commercial Treaties without means of carrying them into effect and who must see, & feel, that the Union, or the States individually, are Sovereigns, as it best suits their purposes. In a word that we are one Nation today, & thirteen tomorrow—Who will treat with us on such terms? But perhaps I have gone too far, & therefore shall only add that, with great esteem & regard I am—Dear Sir Yr Most Obedt & Affecte Hble Servt

Go: Washington

P.S. Mrs Washington offers her Compliments & best wishes for you. Go: W.

ALS, CSmH; LB, DLC:GW.
1. See GW to William Gordon, 31 August.

To Joseph Mandrillon

Sir, Mount Vernon 22d Augt 1785.
Thro' the hands of Mr Van-Berkel, I had the honor to receive your letter of the first of March.[1] It rests with a General Meeting

of the Society of the Cincinnati to admit foreigners as honorary
members; tho' it has been done by many of the State Societies,
where the subject proposed was a resident. The general Meeting
is triennial, and will not assemble again before May 1787; but if
my memory serves me, there were some particular reasons
given at the last, which induced a resolution to suspend the further appointment of honorary members, as well Citizens as foreigners: but if I should be mistaken in this, I shall have great
pleasure in proposing you as a member of that body, which have
associated for the purpose, amongst others, of commemorating
the great events to which, under providence, they owe the deliverance of their Country from systematic tyranny.[2] With a grateful sense of the flattering expression of your letter, & with much
esteem & regard I have the honor to be &c.

                                                    G: Washington

LB, DLC:GW.
   1. Mandrillon's letter of 1 Mar. 1785 has not been found, but on this day,
22 Aug., GW wrote Pieter Johan Van Berckel (1725–1800): "Sir, The letter
which your Excellency did me the honor to write to me on the 5th of last
month, came to this place whilst I was from home—or I should have paid my
respects to you at an earlier period.
   "I thank your Excelly for your care of Mr Mandrillons letter, & take the
liberty of troubleing you with the enclosed answer to it; and of congratulating
you on the safe arrival of Miss Van Berkel who I hope enjoys good health. I
have the honor to be with sentiments of esteem respect & consideration Yr
Excel'ys &c. &c. G: Washington" (LB, DLC:GW).
   2. For the identity of Mandrillon and a description of GW's correspondence
with him, see Mandrillon to GW, 11 June 1784, and source note.

To Battaile Muse

Sir,   Mount Vernon Augt 22d 1785
   Both your letters of the 16th have come safe[1]—As you have
engaged the Clover Seed of Mr Wormeleys Manager I will take
one Bushel of it, though I had no idea of giving tha[t] price, as
I could have got the same quantity from Philadelphia (I suppose
equally) good for half the sum if I had applied in time—If you
send it to the care of Mr Hartshorne in Alexandria, it will come
safe, and the sooner it is done, the better—Pay for it out of the
first money you receive for my use.

I am willing to take your wheat if the quality is good, and well cleaned; and free from the fly; provided it is delivered at my Mill, to which the road (by being less used) is better than that either to Alexandria or Dumfries—My prices are always governed by the Alexandria *Cash* Market—for I neither give more, nor expect it for less. The price current there, at present (according to Richards's Gazette) is five shillings; but the state of our trade at this time is so uncertain, that it is almost impossible to determine whether it will be more, or less. If the present restriction of our Commerce continues, the manufacturing of wheat must be broke up altogether; as the West India Markets which affords the greatest demand for our Flour, are shut against our vessels. If you chuse to take the certainty of five shillings for your Wheat, it may be a bargain at that, provided you determine immediately. Or, if you prefer to abide by the rise or fall of the Alexandria market, I am willing to agree to this also, provided there is a period at which you shall determine to accept the price, which is *then* existing. By this I mean, and it is necessary to declare it in order to avoid misunderstandings, that if you should, for instance, be from the first of October until the first of April delivering your Crop, I shall not think myself under an obligation to allow the highest price that is given within that period—because the price *may* rise to Six Shillings, and then *fall* to four, according to the demand arising from circumstances. It would be as unreasonable therefore for you to expect that I should give the highest price at which wheat had sold, within that period, as for me to suppose that, you ought to take the lowest. However to be more clearly understood, (if the price is to be regulated by the Alexandria *cash* market, for I shall not be governed by what the Merchants offer in Goods.) it must be the price of the day on which you determine to take it—that is, if wheat should start from 5/ and keep rising until the first of December it had reached 6/ and on that day you inform me personally, or by letter that you will take the price then given, I shall think myself bound to allow six shillings for your Crop. On the other hand, if you should expect that the price would get higher and wait for its doing so until it should fall to 4/ I will pay no more than four shillings.

I have been thus explicit because I dislike disputes, and wish to avoid them; which makes it necessary for me to mention an-

other thing that sometimes happens; and that is, that what a few
Bushels of wheat may sell for, or what a merchant, when he has
got a Vessel just loaded may give, rather than detain her at high
charges, is not to be considered as the Market price; You, from
your distant situation and long Land transportation, are not in
a situation to take advantage of the case last mentioned, and a
few Bushels of particular wheat, or wheat for a particular use,
can have no influence upon the general price; which is always
very well established in such a place of Trade as Alexandria.
After all, I confess it would be more agreeable to me to fix, between ourselves, a price. but I cannot at this time exceed 5/ as
that is the price now cur[ren]t.[2]

When you come down in October I shall be glad to see you
here, by that time I expect to have the accts against my Tenants
brought into some kind of order. If you could engage me about
250 lbs. of good Fall butter from such farmers as you can depend upon for the quality, and their punctuality, I should be
obliged to you[3]—If you let me have your wheat it may come
down occasionally with that. I am Sir Yr Very Hble Servt

Go: Washington

ALS, owned (1983) by Mr. Joseph Rubinfine, West Palm Beach, Fla.; LB,
DLC:GW.

1. Only one letter from Muse dated 16 Aug. has been found.

2. GW and Muse agreed on Muse's price of six shillings a bushel on 27
October. See Muse to GW, 16 Aug., n.3. See also Muse to GW, 6 September.

3. Muse wrote GW on 6 Sept. that he could provide GW with 100 pounds
of his own butter and would try to secure another 150 pounds for him. Muse
wrote again on 10 Dec. that he was sending down two cases of salt butter and
one of fresh butter weighing a total of 211 ct. and costing £10.11. Because of
bad weather the butter did not arrive at Mount Vernon until over a month
later. See also GW to Muse, 5 Jan. 1786, and Muse to GW, 12, 17 Jan. 1786.

From Levi Hollingsworth

Honourd Sir　　　　　　　　　　Philad[elphi]a 24 August 1785

Mr Samuel Jackson of your Neighbourhood, mentioning to
Mr Arthur Donaldson of this City, the desire your Excelency had
of raising manure from the mud in the bed of the River Pato-
mack for the purpose of manuring Land,[1] Mr Donalson shewed
Mr Jackson his new invented Machine for Cleansing our Docks,

which with a horse & three hands will raise 60 a 80 tons ℔ day. Mr Donalson the Ingenious Inventor, is so obliging as to offer your Excelency any information that may be wanting for the Constructing the machine, by a model or other wise, and begs me, while he is shewing Mr Jackson the Construction, to write you[.] Mr Donalsons mechanical abilities in the raising the Chevaux de frize from the bed of our river, together with this Contrivance, which he calls a Hippopotamos, places him amongst men of the first abilities in point of invention, and as I have seen his Hippopotamos often at work I can assure your Excelency of its great facility in raising mud or Sand from any depth of water.[2] I am with great regard Your Excelencies most obedient Humble Svt

Levi Hollingsworth

I take the liberty to present my Compliments to Colo. Jno. Augustus Washington, your Brother, & to give him our price Current for Produce,[3] viz. Fine Flour 43/6 ℔ Bbl of 1.3.0 Ntt wheat 7/6 @ 8/ Corn 3/10 @ 4/—Hemp 5½ ℔ Lb. Tobacco Jas River 55/ best Patowmack 45 @ 50/ Bills of Exchange 75 @ 80 ℔ £. L.H.

ALS, DLC:GW.

Levi Hollingsworth was a Philadelphia merchant and speculator in Virginia land. He, like GW, was a member of the agriculture society in Philadelphia.

1. GW did not get this letter until 17 Sept. because Hollingsworth sent it to Samuel Jackson at Red Stone Old Fort, near Washington's Bottom in Pennsylvania. Jackson probably had met with GW when GW visited Pennsylvania in September 1784. See GW to Hollingsworth, 20 Sept. 1785.

2. For Arthur Donaldson's full description of his "Hippopotamos," the precursor of the modern clamshell dredge, see his letter to GW of 1 October. Chevaux-de-frise were placed in the Delaware River during the Revolution for the defense of Philadelphia (see, for instance, Philippe C. du Coudray's memoir enclosed in his letter to GW of 30 Aug. 1777 and printed in *Pennsylvania Magazine*, 18 [1894], 330–33).

3. John Augustine Washington arrived with his family at Mount Vernon for a visit on 19 October.

From John Jay

Office for foreign Affairs [New York]
Dr Sir   25th August 1785
  In pursuance of an Act of Congress of the 19th Instant, of
which a Copy is herewith enclosed, I have desired Mr Taylor,
one of the Clerks of this Office, to wait upon your Excellency,
and agreeable to your Letter of the 5th April last to Mr Thomson, to take Copies of the papers mentioned in it, and in the
enclosed Act of Congress.[1] With the best and most sincere
Wishes for your Health and Happiness, & with the highest Esteem & Regard I am Dr Sir Your most obt & very hble Servt
                                                John Jay

LS, DLC:GW; LB, DNA: RG 59, Domestic Letters.
  1. Jay was sending his clerk George Taylor to Mount Vernon to make a copy
of the rolls listing the blacks who sailed from New York in 1783 when the
British evacuation of the city was being negotiated. See Jacob Read to GW, 9
Mar., and notes; GW to Charles Thomson, 5 April; and Thomson to GW, 22
April. Jay enclosed an extract of a letter from Thomson suggesting that Jay
send a clerk to Mount Vernon rather than require GW to give up his copy of
the rolls; a letter from Jay to Richard Henry Lee, president of Congress, en-
dorsing Thomson's suggestion; and a copy of the resolution of Congress of 19
Aug. instructing Jay "to employ some Person" to obtain from GW a list of the
people carried off from New York by the British.

From Tench Tilghman

Dear Sir   Baltimore 25th Augt 1785.
  I am honored with your favor of the 17th. Altho' the greater
part of the Cargo of the Ship Pallas is advertised for public Sale
on the 1st of October next, it is not a matter of certainty that it
will be disposed of in that manner—at least the whole of it. At
any rate—I expect it will fall in a great degree under my Management, as Mr O'Donnell the Owner, who is a perfect Stranger
in this Country, finds himself obliged to seek the assistance of a
person acquainted with Characters here, and with our modes of
Business. Before he left India he was recommended to Mr Morris, and it is thro' my Connection with him that I have to do in
the matter.[1] A large Parcel of the Teas on Board were the property of Major Shaw and Capt. Randall who went out Super Car-

goes of the Empress of China—Those Teas have all gone to Philada.[2]

Whether these Goods are sold at public or private sale, your Commission shall be punctually attended to. If at public—the several Articles shall not be purchased for you except they go at such Rates as are much below the usual Retail prices—the few marked thus in your letter * excepted—which shall be bought if they are as cheap as goods usually sell for Cash—if a private Sale should be determined on, you shall be made acquainted with the lowest prices, and then you may judge for yourself—I beg you, my Dear Sir, not to think of lodging Money with me previously—A Leagure of Arrack is a large Butt. I am told it is rather new—and therefore not very desirable either on Account of Quantity or Quality.

Mr O'Donnell has a curiosity which pervades all Strangers, that of seeing Genl Washington before he leaves America. If he carries his present intentions into Execution, I shall take the freedom of giving him a letter of introduction. He is a Gentleman of large fortune—polished Manners, and from 16 years residence in the different parts of India very capable of giving satisfactory accounts of that Country.

The Crew of this Ship are all Natives of India—most of them from the Coasts of Malabar and Coromandel, and are much of the Countenance and Complexion of your old Groom Wormely —There are four Chinese on Board, who are exactly the Indians of North America, in Colour, Feature—Hair and every external Mark.

Be good eno' to make Mrs Tilghmans Compliments with mine to Mrs Washington, and assure her that every care shall be taken to have such Goods as may be purchased, the most fashionable and perfect of their kinds—With true Respect and Esteem I am Dear Sir Yours most sincerely

Tench Tilghman

P.S. I have heard that your packet for Mr Smith of Carlisle was delivered into his own Hands.

A ps. of fine Muslin is mentioned. If Mrs Washington will be pleased to mention the use for which she intends it a better judgment can be formed of the kind which will suit.

ALS, DLC:GW.

1. See note 3 in Tilghman's letter of 17 August. John O'Donnell (died c.1805), an Irishman who had been employed by the East India Company, settled in Baltimore and was the master and owner of the merchant ship *Pallas* which was the first to convey goods directly from Canton to Baltimore.

2. Samuel Shaw and Thomas Randall, who had served together during the war in two Continental artillery regiments, were sent out from New York as supercargoes in the *Empress of China* in February 1784 for Daniel Parker, the agent of the merchants shipping to China a cargo of ginseng. The arrival of the *Empress of China* at Macao six months later signaled the opening of the China trade to American merchants and vessels.

From John Woddrop

Sir,

Bridge-Street of Glasgow, the 25th of August, 1785.

I have this day sent off this letter for your Excellency to the Ambassador from the States of North America at the Court of London.

And which is chiefly to advise you, Sir, that I do now know, for certain, of one hundred heads of familys, and who, with their Wives and Children &ca will make a Number of five hundred & fifty, or Six hundred persons, And all natives of Scotland, who propose for to Emigrate to settle in the territories belonging to the Thirteen, free, and Independant United States of north America. They are all of them brought up to the fishing trade and line of bussiness, in the Shetland Islands, on the Coast of Scotland—and as I apprehend, such a body of good, hardy fisher Men & Seamen may of consequence be of some use to the States of America. I have Communicated this news to the American Ambassador, & to your friend William Lee, Esquire, late of Westmoreland County in the State of Virginia, this I did on the 17th of this Current Month, and sent the letter to Mr Lee, under Cover to the American Ambassador in London. I presume these people may be got to Embark sometime the next year. Now any approbation this Measure may be found to deserve the Attention of from your Excellency &ca I will like to be informed of, and as soon as possible. The Ling, the Tusk, the Cod Fish taken on the Coast of Shetland is selling for Export this year at 19/6 d. Sterling, prCt or 100 lb. of Ling, 17/6 d. for Tusk, & 15/6 d. for Cod. These are the real prices at the Shetland Islands this very year, & just at this very time, for CtWt—or for every 100 lib. Weight of the above kind of Fish.

I have thought proper to notice as much to you, Sir, by this your friends in America may be able to form some idea what the British fish will bring at the different Markets in the Commercial nations in Europe.

I referr you to my Letter, last Spring, by Capt. William Chisholm of the Ship, Janet, bound from Glasgow to the towns of Dumfries & Alexandria on Potomack River in Virginia.[1] With the most justly deserving Estimation, and sincer & perfect Respect. I have the honour to be, Sir, your most Obedient Humble Servant

John Woddrop

ALS, DLC:GW. The many meaningless commalike marks in the manuscript have not been retained.

1. See Woddrop to GW, 16 Sept. 1784, and notes.

Letter not found: from Richard Varick, 28 August. GW wrote Varick on 26 Sept.: "Mr Taylor brought me your favor of the 28th Ulto."

To John Rawlins

Sir,   Mount Vernon 29th Augt 1785.

Your letter of the 20th of this month, only came to my hands by the last Post, or I would have replied to it sooner.[1]

I have a room 32 by 24 feet, & 16 feet pitch, which I want to finish in stucco: it is my intention to do it in a plain neat style; which, independantly of its being the present taste, (as I am inform'd) is my choice. The Chimney is in the centre of the longest side, for which I have a very elegant marble piece; directly opposite thereto is a Venetian window, of equal breadth & pitch of the room; on each side of the Chimney is a door, leading into other rooms; & on each of the short sides is a door & window.

I mention these things that you may be apprized of the sort of work; the time it may take you to execute it, and that you may inform me upon what terms; and also, if you are inclined to undertake it, that you may have leisure to think of a design. The season being so far advanced, I had given up the idea of doing anything to the room this year; but if I could enter upon the work with well founded assurances of accomplishing it soon, I am ready & willing to go on with it immediately; having by me stucco, & seasoned plank for the floor & other parts (if necessary)—and good Joiners of my own to execute what may be wanting in their way.

You will please to let me hear from you without delay on this subject, & I pray you to be explicit; because, as I would undertake it at once, or not at all this year, I should like to know your terms & sentiments precisely, that I may govern myself accordingly. I am Sir &c.

G: Washington

LB, DLC:GW.

John Rawlins, an English stucco worker living in Maryland, completed GW's New Room in 1786. See Rawlins to GW, 15 Nov. 1785, n.1.

1. Letter not found. GW sent this letter to Tench Tilghman on this date for delivery to Rawlins. Tilghman speaks highly of Rawlins in his letter to GW of 31 August.

To Tench Tilghman

Dear Sir,   Mount Vernon 29th Augt 1785

Your favor of the 25th in answer to mine of the preceeding week, came safely. At the time I wrote that letter, I was uninformed of the circumstances which you have since made me acquainted with. However, you will be at no loss from the contents of it, to discern that it was *Bargains* I had in contemplation; and which, from the quantity of Goods at Market—Scarcity of Cash, according to Newspaper Accts—distress of the Trade—& the mode of selling, I thought might probably be obtained; but if I am mistaken therein, I shall content myself with the few marked articles, or such of them as can be had cheap. Fine Jaccanet Muslin (apron width) is what Mrs Washington wants, and abt 5 ⟨à⟩ 7 Yards would be sufficient. As the Arrack is in large Casks & New, I decline taking any.

If Mr O'Donnell should feel an inclination to make this part of Virginia a visit, I shall be happy in seeing him—and if, instead of giving him a *letter* of introduction, you should change the mode and introduce him in your own Propriæ Personæ it would add much to the pleasure of it. Before your letter was received, from my reading, or rather from an imperfect recollection of what I had read I had conceived an idea that the Chinese though droll in shape & appearance, were yet white.

I am glad to hear that my Packet to Mr Smith had got safely to hand as there were papers of consequence transmitted. I expect some other documents for my Law Suit in the course of a few days from our Attorney Genl (Edmd Randolph Esqr.) which I shall take the liberty of enclosing to you to be forwarded to Mr Smith—And as I seem to be in the habit of giving you trouble, I beg the favor of you to cause the inclosed letter to be delivered to Mr Rawlins—I leave it open for your perusal—My reason for it is, that thereby seeing my wants, you would be so obliging as to give me your opinion of Mr Rawlins with respect to his abilites and diligence as a workman—whether he is reckoned moderate or high, in his charges—and whether there is much call, at this time, for a man of his profession at Baltimore—for on this, I presume, his high or moderate terms will greatly depend.[1]

Mrs Washington joins me in best respects to Mrs Tilghman and yourself and thanks you for the obliging assurance of chusing the articles wanted, perfect of their kind. With great esteem & regard I am—Dear Sir Yr Affecte friend & Obedt Hble Servt

Go: Washington

P.S. Since writing the foregoing, Mrs Washington has requested me to add that if any fine thin Handkerchiefs with striped or worked borders are to be had, she would be glad to get Six of them. G.W.

ALS, NN: Lee Kohns Collection; LB, DLC:GW.

1. GW sent a letter of 10 Sept. addressed to his attorney Thomas Smith, with enclosures, to Tilghman on 14 Sept. for him to forward to Pennsylvania. GW's letter to John Rawlins is dated 29 August.

Letter not found: from Thomas Johnson and Thomas Sim Lee, 30 Aug. 1785. On 10 Sept. GW wrote Johnson and Lee: "Your favor of the 30th ulto did not reach me until the 8th instant."

To John Cochran

Dear Sir,   Mount Vernon 31st Augt 1785

Your favor of the 9th by Captn Packard, accompanying the Hounds sent by the Marqs de la Fayette to your care for me, came safely a few days ago. For the trouble you have had with the latter, I offer you my thanks; and if any expences have been incurred previous to their re-embarkation at New York, I will pay them on the first notice.[1]

I persuade myself you are too well convinced, my dear Doctor, of my friendship, and of my inclination to promote your interest, or wishes, to doubt my ready compliance with the request of your letter (respecting the Office of Continental treasurer) were it compatible with that line of conduct I had prescribed for my government. But from my knowledge of the Composition of Congress—The State politics of its Members—And their endeavors to fill every civil Office with a Citizen from their own State, (if not altogether, at least by compromise), that I early took up a determination not to hazard the mortificaton of a refusal, or of the passing by, my application, by not asking *any thing* from it. And to this resolution I was further prompted, by the numberless applications with which it was impracticable, and in many instances would have been improper for me, to have complied. Except in a single one, and that not pointed directly to any Office, I have never gone beyond the general recommendation which accompanied my resignation; nor do I believe I ever shall.[2]

Mrs Washington who does not enjoy good health, presents her compliments to, and offers best wishes for, Mrs Cochran[3] & yourself; to whom please to add, and accept, those of Dear Sir Yr Most Obedt & Affecte Hble Servt

                              Go: Washington

ALS, CaQMM; LB, DLC:GW.

Dr. John Cochran (1730–1807) was surgeon general of the Continental army in 1777 and director general of hospitals in 1781. He became commissioner of loans in New York in 1786. See Cochran to GW, 1 May 1789, and notes.

1. Letter not found. For the arrival of the French hounds sent by Lafayette, see GW to William Grayson, 22 Aug., n.1.

2. See GW's recommendation of David Humphreys to Thomas Mifflin, 14 Jan. 1784.

3. Cochran was married to Gertrude Van Rensselaer, the sister of Philip Schuyler's wife and the aunt of Alexander Hamilton's wife.

To William Gordon

Dr Sir,   Mount Vernon 31st Augt 1785.

In my absence from home on a tour up this river, to view the nature of it & to direct the improvements agreeably the Acts of Assemblies of Virginia & Maryland; the enclosed memoirs arrived here, covered by a letter, of which the following is an extract, from a member of Congress.[1]

As I am fully persuaded it is your wish to transmit to posterity a true history of the revolution, & of course you desire to receive every information which will enable you to do justice to the principal Actors therein; it cannot be unpleasing to you to receive a narrative of unadorned facts which serve to bring forward, circumstances which, in some measure, may be unknown to you: I therefore make no apology for transmitting the enclosed; nor shall I do more than hint to you, the propriety of keeping the Marquis's wishes in this business, behind the Curtain; your own good sense must dictate the measure, & furnish the reason for it.

The noble, conspicuous, & disinterested part which this Nobleman has acted on the American theatre deserves all the gratitude which this Country can render him, & all the eloge which the pen of a faithful historian can bestow, with its appearing to be the object of his wishes.

The family is as well as usual; Mrs Stuart has been sick, but is now getting better. Mrs Washington does not enjoy good health, but joins me in best respects to Mrs Gordon. I am Dr Sir &c.

G: Washington

LB, DLC:GW.

1. There is an asterisk here which refers to the statement at the bottom of the letter: "See Mr [James] McHenry's Letter to me dated 1st Augt 1785." See note 1 of that document.

From Thomas Ridout

Sir   Bordeaux 31. August 1785.

I had the honor of writing to you the first of May last, by the Fanny Captain Smith bound to Alexandria by whom I sent you a few Cases of Wine. I had a day or two before that Vessel's sailing, received a letter from the marquis de la Fayette informing me that he had sent to my Care a package for Your Excellency & which was to have been shipped in the Fanny; but by a mistake in the Carrier's direction who had got some other name for mine—I could not find it out till near two months after the vessel had sailed; & since that time, there has been no opportunity for Baltimore from hence, which has not a little vext me.[1]

I have now shipped it on board the Peggy Capt. Cunyngham, a Brig I have chartered for Baltimore that will sail in two or three days, but is to touch at Charles Town on her way.[2] I shall address it to the Care of Col. Tilghman, who will forward it by the first opportunity—I have the honor to be with the greatest respect. Your Excellency's most obedient servant

                                              Thos Ridout

ALS, DLC:GW; copy, DLC:GW. After his signature, Ridout wrote: "The Marquis [de Lafayette] is at Berlin." Ridout wrote the copy of this letter on the back of his letter of 7 September.

1. See GW to Ridout, 20 Aug., n.3.

2. Ridout is probably referring to Charleston, the port on the Northeast River in Cecil County, Md., rather than Charlestown in Charles County, Md., usually called Port Tobacco.

To Arthur St. Clair

Dr Sir,   Mount Vernon 31st Augt 1785.

Your favor of the 21st ulto inclosing a letter written in behalf of the Society of the Cincinnati in the State of Pennsylvania on the 9th of July in the preceding year, came to this place in my absence on a tour up the river potomac with the Directors, to examine the obstructions & to point out a mode for the improvement and extension of its navigation.

I am perfectly convinced that if the first institution of this Society had not been parted with, 'ere this we should have had the Country in an uproar, & a line of separation drawn between this society & their fellow Citizens. The alterations which took place at the last general Meeting have quieted the clamours which in many of the States were rising to a great height; but I have not heard yet of the incorporation of any Society by the State to which it belongs—wch is an evidence in my mind, that the jealousies of the people are rather asleep than removed on this occasion.

I am always made happy, when I hear that any of my fellow labourers have received appointments that may in some measure compensate them for their past services & losses in the late revolution: I feel it in two respects, first, as it benefits the individual—& next, as it is a testimony of public gratitude; be assured then my Dr Sir, that your appointment to the office which you now hold gave me much pleasure, as I am told the emoluments of it are handsome. My best wishes will ever attend you: with sincere esteem & regard, I am Dr Sir, &c. &c.

G: Washington

LB, DLC:GW.

From Tench Tilghman

Dear Sir　　　　　　　　　　　　Baltimore 31st Augt 1785.

I have recd yours of the 29th with a letter for Mr Rawlings inclosed. I have delivered it to him. He has Business as far as Annapolis, and as he thinks he can judge better of the cost of finishing your Room after he has conversed with you upon the subject, he purposes to extend his ride as far as Mount Vernon; where he will be in the course of a few days.[1] He is a Man of reputation in his Business, and esteemed a masterly Workman. There are many Specimens of his Abilities at Annapolis. He is the only one of his profession, and therefore I imagine makes his own terms—tho' I cannot find he has been reckoned exorbitant—He has a great deal of Work in the plain way, that is finishing Cornices &ca.

I wish it were in my power to recommend a good Housekeeper to you, either Man or Woman—but I beleive there is little chance of procuring one here.[2]

I shall attend to your orders for India Goods—If Mr O'Donnell adheres to his intention of selling at public sale, you cannot come in there, because the Lots will be larger than your Wants: I do not think a public sale will answer his purpose—and so he begins to think now. When his Goods are assorted and priced, I can easily let you know how he holds them, and then you may purchase or not at your pleasure—I do not find any Muslin Handkfs among the Cargo.

The Chinese of the Northern provinces are fairer than those of the south, but none of them are of the European Complexion.

When your other packet for Mr Smith of Carlisle comes to hand, I will endeavour to find a safe Conveyance for it.

I beg you, my dear Sir, never to think any of your commands can be a trouble to me. There is only one I regret that I have it not in my power to comply with, and that is, the pleasure of making you a Visit after your repeated and kind Invitations. My Business ties me down to the Circle of Baltimore—I have the honor to be with sincere Respect and Esteem Yr obliged and obt Servt

Tench Tilghman

ALS, DLC:GW.

1. GW writes to Tilghman on 14 Sept. of John Rawlins's visit to Mount Vernon to prepare an estimate of what he would charge to complete the New Room.

2. GW enclosed this note in his letter to Tilghman, of 29 Aug.: "Could you recommend a good Housekeeper (a man would be preferred) who is competent to the charge of a large family and providing handsomely for a Table? One who has been in the practice, & could come well recommended, would meet with good wages from G. Washington" (ALS [photocopy], owned (1991) by the Gallery of History, Las Vegas, Nev.). See GW to Clement Biddle, 17 Aug., n.4, for an account of GW's successful efforts to secure a housekeeper.

To David Humphreys

My Dr Humphreys,   Mount Vernon 1st Septr 1785.

In the latter part of July I wrote to you very fully,[1] since which I have received your favor of May. As nothing has occurred since that period worthy of observation, except that the Indians, supposed to be instigated thereto by the B—— are getting more & more our of humour, this letter will be shorter than I usually write to you.

I find by your last that your time has been more occupied by your official duty than I had conceived; for, to be frank, I supposed that amusements more than business had been the occasion of the brevity of your letters to me.

The times are full with us—the Assemblies are in their recess; & the Merchants are preparing Petitions to them respectively to enlarge the powers of Congress for Commercial purposes. In Congress I understand diversity of opinion prevails respecting the extent of these powers. They are also deliberating on the establishment of a Mint for the Coinage of Gold, Silver & copper; but nothing final is yet resolved on respecting either. Our Winter has been severe, but different (in the middle States) from the one you last saw in America; it was long, wet & disagreeable. We are just emerging from a drougth which it was supposed eight days ago, would have annihilated the Indian Corn in the lower parts of this, & the neighbouring States; & tho' it has been raining incessantly for several days past, I am of opinion that a great deal of this Corn is irrecoverably lost for want of the farina (the tassel being dry) to impregnate the young shoots· The calamity which you apprehended from the drougth which had followed the hard Winter in France, has yielded I hope, to more pleasing prospects.

I thank you for your attention to the Medal which was voted for me by Congress; I expected it was to have remained on the Journals of that hon[orabl]e Body as a dead letter; & never having hinted—so I never intended to hint my knowledge of such a Vote; or my apprehension of the effect of it, to any one in Power or in Office. You may believe me sincere when I assure you that I am Yrs &c. &c. &c.

G: Washington

LB, DLC:GW.
   1. GW's letter is dated 25 July.

To Lafayette

My Dr Marqs,   Mount Vernon 1st Septr 1785.

Since my last to you, I have been favored with your letters of the 11th & 13th of May by young Mr Adams, who brought them to New York, from whence they came safely to this place by the

Post: the first is in *Cypher*; & for the communications therein contained I thank you: My best wishes will always accompany your undertakings; but remember my dear friend it is a part of the military art to reconnoitre & *feel* your way, before you engage too deeply—More is oftentimes effected by regular approaches, than by an open assault; from the first too, you may make a good retreat—from the latter (in case of repulse) it rarely happens.[1]

It is to be hoped that Mr Adams will bring the British Ministry to some explanation respecting the Western Posts. Nothing else can, I conceive, disturb the tranquillity of these States; but if I am mistaken in this conjecture, you know my sentiments of, & friendship for you too well to doubt my inclination to serve *you* to the utmost of your wishes, & my powers.

It gives me very singular pleasure to find the Court of France relaxing in their demand of Longchamps; to have persisted in it would have been a very embarrassing measure to this Country under the Laws & Constitution of the Fœderal Government, & those of the several parts which compose it.

The Hounds which you were so obliging as to send me arrived safe, & are of promising appearance: to Monsieur le Compte Doilliamson; (if I miscall him, your hand writing is to blame, & in honor you are bound to rectify the error), & in an *especial* manner to his fair Competesse, my thanks are due for this favor: the enclosed letter which I give you the trouble of forwarding contains my acknowledgement of their obliging attention to me on this occasion.[2]

If I recollect right, the letter which was written by the Marquis de St Simon was on the business of the Cincinnati, and was laid before the general Meeting at Philada in May 1784; consequently, the answer must have proceeded from the Society either specially to him, or generally, thro' the Counts de Estaing & Rochambeau, who were written to as the heads of the Naval & military members of that Society in France; but as all the papers relative to the business of the Society were deposited in the care of the Secretary General, Knox—or the Assistant Secretary, Williams—I have them not to refer to; but will make enquiry & inform you or the Marqs de St Simon more particularly of the result.[3]

Your constant attention, and unwearied endeavors to serve

the interests of these United States, cannot fail to keep alive in them a grateful sensibility of it; & the affectionate regard of all their Citizens for you. The footing on which you have established a Market for whale Oil must be equally pleasing & advantageous to the States which are more immediately engaged in that Commerce.

Having heard nothing further of the Jacks which were to be sent to me from Spain, & which by Mr Carmichael's letter (enclosing one from the Count de Florida Blanca) of the 3d Decr were actually purchased for me at that date, I am at a loss to account for the delay, & am apprehensive of some accident. Be this as it may, if you could my Dr Marquis, thro' the medium of Admiral Suffrein, or by any other means that would not be troublesome, procure me a Male & female, or *one* of the former & *two* of the latter, upon the terms mentioned in your letter of the 3d of May, I should think it a very fortunate event & shou'd feel myself greatly indebted to your friendship. The Mules which proceed from the mixture of these Animals with the horse, are so much more valuable under the care which is usually bestowed on draught cattle by our Negroes, that I am daily more anxious to obtain the means for propagating them.[1]

When George returns from the Springs & gets a little fixed, I will set him about copying your letters to me, which will be better than to hazard the originals at Sea, where an accident might occasion the loss of them to both of us.[5] In my last I informed you of his intended marriage, which I suppose will take place in the early part of next month.

I should have given an earlier acknowledgment of your letters of the 11th & 13th of May aforementioned, had I been at home when they came to this place; but at that time I was on a tour up this river with the Directors (Johnson, Lee, Fitzgerald & Gilpin) to examine the obstructions, & to fix upon a plan of operation; which having done, we commenced our labours on the 5th of last month, under a full persuasion that the work will not prove more arduous than we had conceived before the difficulties were explored. The James river Company, by my last Accounts from Richmond, is formed; a meeting of the members was summoned to be held on the 20th of last month, but what the determinations of it were, I have not yet heard; Nor (so barren are the times) have I a tittle of news to communicate to you;

the several assemblies are in their recesses but will be addressed I presume at their Autumnal meetings by the Commercial interests of the United States to vest Powers in Congress to regulate the Trad[e] of the Union which they see clearly must be directed by one head in order to obtain consistency & respectability at home & abroad. I am My Dr Marqs &c. &c.

G: Washington

LB, DLC:GW.

1. GW last wrote Lafayette on 25 July. He is here referring to Lafayette's letter of 11 May.

2. See Lafayette to GW, 13 May, n.3. The text of the enclosed letter to the comte Doilliamson (d'Oilliamson) of this day reads: "I have just received seven very fine Hounds, for which, the Marqs de la Fayette informs me, I am indebted to your goodness. I know not in what terms to acknowledge my gratitude for the obligation, but pray you to be assured that I have a due sense of the honor; & feel in a particular manner the force of the goodness of Madame la Comptesse, to whom the Marqs adds, I am beholden for a *favorite* hound. I pray you to offer my best respects, & to make my acknowledgement of this favor, acceptable to her; at the same time I beg you to assure her that her favorite shall not suffer under my care, but become the object of my particular attention" (LB, DLC:GW).

3. No mention of Saint-Simon's letter appears in Winthrop Sargent's journal of the General Meeting of the Society of the Cincinnati in May 1784 (*Papers, Confederation Series*, 1:332–54). See Lafayette to GW, 13 May 1785, 6 Feb. 1786, and GW to Lafayette, and to Saint-Simon-Montbléru, both 10 May 1786.

4. On 25 or 26 Oct. GW received word that the surviving jackass of the pair sent to him on behalf of the king of Spain had arrived in Gloucester, Mass., with a Spanish caretaker. See Thomas Cushing to GW, 7 Oct., and GW to Cushing, 26 October. Lafayette had written GW on 16 April that he was sending GW a jack from Cadiz and would send another from Malta, but GW misunderstood and assumed that Lafayette was referring to the jacks that the king of Spain had promised. See also Lafayette to GW, 6 Feb. 1786.

5. GW sent to Lafayette on 10 May 1786 the copies of Lafayette's letters made by George Augustine Washington. See GW to Lafayette, 8 Nov. 1785, n.4.

To Lamar, Hill, Bisset, & Co.

Gentn   Mount Vernon 1st Septr 1785.

I am honored with your favor of the 22d of June. As I have been very unlucky hitherto, in the transportation of Wine (in the common Craft of the Country) from one port, or one from one river to another; I had rather the old Madeira ordered by

Mr Hill for my use should remain with you (as I am not in im-
medate want) until a conveyance may offer directly to Alexandria. But if this is not likely to happen soon, & you should think
it safe to Ship it to the address of Doctr Taylor of Norfolk; I
should be glad in that case, to have it well secured against adul-
teration; for I had rather lose the whole, than to have part taken
out & the deficiency supplied with water—which is too common
a practice with the river Skippers. Or if neither of these is done,
I would next pray that Doctr Taylor may be requested to detain
the Wine in his cellar until a conveyance; on which he can rely,
may offer to Alexandria, or to my house which is nine miles
below on the bank of the River.[1] I am Gentlemen Your most
Obt Servt

G. Washington

LB, DLC:GW.

1. For the correspondence regarding the shipment of this wine, see Lamar,
Hill, Bisset, & Co. to GW, 20 Aug., n.1.

From Jonathan Trumbull, Jr.

Dear Sir   Lebanon [Conn.] 1st of Septemr 1785
A painfull task is fallen to my Lot—I depend on your goodness to form for me an excuse, should I, by indulging the relation of a melancholly Tale, be the means of producing to your
mind a saddening tho't of grief, or wetting your Cheek with a
sympathizing Tear of momentary distress: for be assured Sir! I
wish you nothing but the uninterrupted enjoyment of perpetual & unceasing felicity.

I have to inform you, That my Father—my Mind scarcely real-
izes the Tale, while my pen is writing it—My Father—the aged
parent—the venerable patriot—the benevolent friend to his
Country & to Mankind, is now no more—that heart which was
once warmed with sentiments of high regard for your person, &
deep veneration for your character, has ceased to beat—and his
earthy remains, secluded from the World, are now resting
in gloomy silence, waiting the solemnities of a future all important & eventful Day.

The 17th of last Month produced this melancholly Event. The
4th he was siezed with a violent fever, of the putrid kind, which

continuing to rage with unabating fury for 13 Days, terminated the unequal Contest—For some time before I had been able to observe a gradual decline of vigor & activity, altho an unusual Share of both, as well as of his mental faculties, had been indulged him, considering his advanced Age. Highly favored as he had been, through a long Life, in point of bodily pains & distress, the common Lot of humanity having never been exercised with any hard sickness—he was equally so in his last illness—Altho parched with a fever, he experienced at this closing period, scarcely any pain or distress whatever—but an unusual Weakness & Lassitude seized him at the first Attack & continued: so that he breathed his last in seeming Ease & quiet, like one gently yielding to the Influence of a sweet & pleasant sleep—Thus has this venerable patriot paid the Debt which he owed to Nature, and exchanged a Life of Care, of labour & Toil for, I trust, a State of greater Ease & peace, with more durable felicity than this could afford. Our Consolation is, that few Men could have left the World, with happier reflections, or more glorious prospects.

I am no preacher my Dear General! but solemn reflections & useful Admontions, arising in your own Mind on this Occasion, will be the result of this serious Event.

You will pardon me Sir! while I indulge the pleasing tho't, that your regard to our dear deceased parent will lead you to mingle a sympathizing Tear with our solemn Grief—Be assured that I feel the Want of this Consolation—for however expected this Event ought to have been ⟨*mutilated*⟩ yet the Stroke which severs forever, that intima⟨*mutilated*⟩ connects near & dear relations, is sen[s]iblly ⟨*mutilated*⟩tandg all the Aids I can derive from reas⟨on⟩ & religion.

My tenderest respects & Regard await Mrs Washington—which I beg Your Excelly to be so good as to present for me—while I beg you to believe that I am, with every sentiment of respectful Attachment Dear Sir Your faithfull friend & Most Obedient Servant

Jona. Trumbull

ALS, DLC:GW; ADf, advertised in Stan V. Henkel's catalog no. 778, 1897.

Jonathan Trumbull, Jr. (1740–1809), was GW's secretary from 1781 until the end of the war. Trumbull's father, who was governor of Connecticut from 1769 to 1784, died at the age of 74.

From Edmund Randolph

Dear sir   Richmond Sepr 2. 1785.

I accomplished my purpose of being present at the meeting of the subscribers to the James river company. Those books alone, which were opened here, were laid before us. By them it appeared, that the whole number of shares was nearly compleated; but it was thought adviseable to postpone the admission of other subscribers, until the success of the upper books should be known. This step was very fortunate; as one of the managers above the falls came to town soon after we rose, and gave us an account of subscriptions, which will probably overrun the capital sum.

The president and directors are instructed to obtain a definition of these terms in the law, "the highest point practicable." They are first to attempt to prevail on the assembly to give the company a power to fix this point by their own vote. This, if impracticable, is to be followed by a petition to the legislature to fix it.

They are also instructed to prepare and report to the next meeting, such amendments as the law seems to require.

I endeavoured to deliver you from the appointment to the office of president. But the universal suffrage called you to the post; without an expectation, however, that you should undergo more of the business, than your own convenience may reconcile to you. Messrs John Harvie, David Ross, and William Cabell and myself are directors.[1]

Will you do me the favor of directing a copy of the Potomack proceedings to be forwarded to me, if not too lengthy or secret in their nature? I am induced to make this request from an earnest desire to fulfil the work, assigned to us, and to lose no opportunity of procuring of every possible light—Any hint, which you may think proper to suggest, will be very grateful to us.[2]

I have proposed a meeting of the directors at Richmond on the 26th day of this month.

As to the order of council, which you mention in your favor of the 13th Ulto, it cannot be procured. I am sorry for the loss of the records; but I cannot help thinking, that the title, which you can shew, is sufficient to evidence the fact, which you wished to prove by that order.[3] I am Dear sir yr much obliged and affectionate friend

Edm: Randolph

ALS, DLC:GW.

1. Randolph wrote on 8 Aug. suggesting the likelihood that GW would be elected president of the James River Company at its first meeting on 20 August. GW replied on 13 Aug. that it would not be possible for him to serve as president of the company. After receiving this notification of his election, GW wrote Randolph on 16 Sept., expressing his regret that he would not be able "to discharge the duties of the office of President" of the company. See also Randolph to GW, 3 Dec. 1785. Randolph in his letter to GW of 2 Mar. 1786 enclosed the Proceedings of the James River Company between 20 Aug. and 22 Dec. 1785.

2. See GW to Randolph, 16 Sept., and note 1 of that document.

3. For the "lost" order of the Virginia council, see note 1 in Randolph to GW, 29 July.

From James Warren

Sir,   Milton (near Boston) Septr 2d 1785

When I review the Scenes I pass'd through in the Course of a Revolution which will always distinguish the present Age, I reflect with great Pleasure, on those, which took Place when I was honour'd with your particular Friendship and Confidence. No Man has proferr'd a more Uniform Esteem and Respect for You, than I have, and if it is my Fault that a Correspondence once begun was not continued, it was more my Misfortune, and the same Cause which produc'd both Apologizes for the First, & in my Mind has alleviated the Last, I did fear giving You Trouble, & Interruption, when I knew You was engag'd in Matters of great Magnitude, Importance, and Difficulty, my Ambition then gave Place to the Feelings of Regard and Friendship. Mrs Washington's Letter to Mrs Warren gives me the Pleasure of thinking I still possess your Recollection, and encourages me to write to You at a Time when you have more Leisure.

The War has ended with great Glory, and Advantage, to our Country, and while I congratulate You and America on this Event, I am sorry to have so many Reasons to deplore that Want of Justice, Publick Spirit, and good Policy which are necessary to make a proper Improvement of them; Our Finances are in a wretched Situation, and Publick Credit of Course on a bad Footing, and these may finally have a fatal Effect on the Union, upon which every Thing depends. I am fully convinc'd that the Abilities of this Country properly exerted are quite equal to the Discharge of their present Debt, and the Provision for their future Security; & I wish exceedingly to see some General Measures adopted for those Purposes, for my own Part I could be willing to live in a Country, so amply provided with the Necessaries and Conveniences of Life as this is, with little or no Foreign Trade, but Commerce has become so necessary to the Power, Greatness, & Reputation of every Country, that it seems to claim our particular Attention, at least in a Degree subordinate to that of Agriculture. and I do not see how it can be conducted without being subject to some general Direction, nor in that Case can I conceive it can be cultivated to Advantage loaded & fetter'd with those Illiberal Duties and Restrictions, calculated to raise a Revenue, which now in various Degrees employ the several Legislatures and distract the whole System. It is Notwithstanding some Consolation, that however the Politicks of America are conducted (if not bad in the Extreme) the Nature of Things, and the prevailing Disposition for Improvements, will make Us a Great and probably happy People. Your great Plan for opening a Large and Extensive Internal Navigation in Virginia will be to future Generations a standing Monument of the Spirit and Enterprize of the present Age. And while they enjoy the Blessings and Advantages derived from it, they must recollect with Gratitude those who contrived and executed it. After all Agriculture is the great Basis upon which the whole Fabrick of Greatness, and Happiness, however constructed and put together, must stand. and it affords no small Pleasure to see such a Spirit of Enquiry on that Subject prevailing. A Laudable Example is seen in Philadelphia.[1] Some such Measures are thought of here, and although I hear nothing of that particular Kind from Virginia I presume Mount Vernon can exhibit many Instances of Improvement beneficial to the Country.

I have always flatter'd Myself with Hopes of seeing You in the Massachusetts after the Return of Peace. may I still expect that Pleasure? Mrs Warren joins Me in Respects & Compliments to

Your Lady & Yourself. I am, Sir with the greatest Esteem Yr most Obediet Hume Servt

Jas Warren

LS, DLC:GW.

James Warren (1726–1808), who became president of the Massachusetts Provincial Congress on 19 June 1775 and speaker of the new Massachusetts house of representatives one month later, was made postmaster general of the Continental army on 27 July 1775, a post he held until April 1776, during GW's siege of Boston. Warren's wife, Mercy Otis Warren (1728–1814), the pamphleteer and historian, wrote to Abigail Adams on 17 April 1776 of visiting Martha Washington, whose "Manners . . . affability, Candor and Gentleness" she found admirable (Butterfield, *Adams Family Correspondence*, 1:385–86). GW wrote James Warren from his headquarters on 31 Mar. 1779 thanking him for his "obliging favour of the 16th of Decr" (which is missing) and complaining of the "Speculation—peculation—engrossing—forestalling" that were hampering the war effort. On 7 Oct. 1785 GW thanks Warren for writing "after a silence of more than six years."

1. For reference to the Philadelphia Society for Promoting Agriculture, of which GW was an honorary member, see Samuel Powel to GW, 5 July 1785 (second letter), n.1.

From Lafayette

My dear General   Vienna September the 3d 1785

This letter Has been Requested of me as an Introduction for Mr André Michaux whom for Many Reasons I am Very Happy to present—in the first place I Know you will Be Glad to Know a Man whose Genius Has Raised Him Among the Scientifick people, and who, as a Botanist, Has at His own Expense travelled through Countries very little Known—He Now is Sent By the King to America, in order to Know the trees, the Seeds, and Every Kind of Natural production Whose growth May be either Curious, or Useful, and for them the King Will set up a Nursery at a Country Seat of His which He is Very fond of—I am the More pleased with the plan as it oppens a New channel of intercourse and Mutual farming good offices Between the two Nations—I Beg, My dear general, You will patronize this Gentlemen, and I much Want it to Be Said in france that He Has Been Satisfied with His Reception in America.[1]

I Have Been Visiting the prussian army, and Now am in the Austrian Capital—I Had But an Hour ago a long Conversation with the emperor about the United states and American trade, in which I took Care properly to Answer His Questions—Where ever I go I Enjoy the Unspeackable pleasure to Hear My Beloved General Spoken of with that Respect He So well deserves.[2] Adieu, My dear General, My Best Respects Wait on Mrs Washington, Remember me to the Young ones. Most Respectfully and affectionately Your

Lafayette

ALS, PEL.

1. GW wrote in his diary on 19 June 1786: "A Monsr. Andri Michaux—a Botanest sent by the Court of France to America (after having been only 6 Weeks returned from India) came in a little before dinner with letters of Introduction & recommendation from the Duke de Lauzen, & Marqs. de la Fayette to me. He dined and returned afterwards to Alexandria on his way to New York, from whence he had come; and where he was about to establish a Botanical garden" (*Diaries*, 4:350). André Michaux (1746–1802), accompanied by his young son François-André (1770–1855), arrived in New York on 14 Nov. and in the following spring established his garden, or nursery, in Bergen Neck, New Jersey. In September 1786 he embarked for South Carolina and made his famous garden 10 miles from Charleston. He remained in America until 1795. Lauzun's introduction of 25 Aug. reads: "I beg leave to introduce to your Excellency Mr Michau Gentleman of a distinguished caracter by his knowledge and his zeal For every kind of improvement—Mr Michau is presently appointed by the king to a grand tour ⟨thru⟩ the whole wordle making the most compleat collection in his power of trees, seeds and vegetals unknown in France, wich collection will be destined for the king's private garden at Rambouille and afterwards, propagated in his whole kingdom. the protection of your Excellency will be of the greatest Service to Mr Michau, and he will deserve by his good disposition and behaviour" (DLC:GW). GW acknowledged Lauzun's letter on 31 July 1786. See also Michaux to GW, 20 June 1786.

2. Later on this day Lafayette talked about American trade with the Austrian chancellor Prince Kaunitz (Wenzel Anton, Prince von Kaunitz-Reitberg; 1711–1794). On 4 Sept. Lafayette wrote Thomas Jefferson in Paris at some length about his discussion of American affairs earlier with Frederick II of Prussia and on this day with Emperor Joseph II and Prince Kaunitz (Idzerda, *Lafayette Papers*, 5:345–47).

To Thomas Newton, Jr.

Sir,   Mount Vernon 3d Sept. 1785.

I am now about to inform you of the reason why I have suffered your letter of the 27th of April, with its enclosures, to remain so long unacknowledged.

In an absence of almost nine years from home, my private concerns had got so much deranged, and my accounts & papers, by the frequent hasty removal of the latter to get them out of the reach of the enemy when their shipping appeared, had got into such a jumble & confusion that it was next to impossibility for me, without spending much time, to adjust the former: I still hoped however that after a while I should have been able to accomplish it, & that long 'ere this I should have sent you a statement of the account as it stands between us. But reckoning without my host, I have been obliged to hire a Clerk to settle all my accounts, & to take this business off my hands; as from a variety of circumstances I found it impracticable for me to attend to it myself.[1]

Inclosed is his statement of the account between you & me, made out from my books & your return of Sales. The balance from his accot differs widely from yours; arising first, from the charge of Jacob Williams's payment of £178.9.8. to James Hill; whereas £50—only of that sum, according to Lund Washington's accot (who superintended my business) was received from Williams. Secondly, from £123.7.4½ charged me, as paid by Mr Wm Holt, of which I have no account. Thirdly, between £174, charged me as paid to Colo. Lewis, & my credit of £170 *only* which was received from him; & lastly, from the Debts yet due; amounting pr your List to £175.16.2. The three first of these you will please to enquire into; & the last, to use the most speedy, and which to you may seem the most effectual means of obtaining them.[2]

The sum which is in your hands, I could wish to have remitted, or an order given me on some Gentleman in Alexandria: Or, which *in part* would answer my purpose equally, I wou'd take one hundred pair of large, strong & well made Negro Shoes, provided I could have them at a reasonable price & by the 20th of October; formerly I know these were to be had at Norfolk readily; & it is essential for me to know immediately, whether, I may depend upon you for them or not.[3]

The Drought has been so severe in these parts, that my Mill was entirely stopped: the rain which has fallen within these ten days, has done no more than to enable her to grind for my own consumption—when I begin to manufacture I will consign you a parcel of superfine flour, as well to try the Norfolk Market, as to prove a new Miller whom I have lately got, & who comes well recommended to me from some of the best Judges in Pennsylvania.

If you should be able at any time to put me in a way of securing the Debt due to me from Balfour & Baraud, it would be rendering me a very acceptable service: without this, or unless some proof could be had (as I believe the fact undoubtedly is) of the partnership of these Gentlemen or connexion in this business with Messrs Hanburys of London, I must loose upwards of £2000 by my sale of Flour to them.[4] With great esteem & regard I am Dr Sir &c.

G: Washington

LB, DLC:GW.

1. Neither Newton's letter of 27 April nor its enclosures have been found, but GW indicates in this letter that one of the enclosures was Newton's account with GW. With the expiration of his agreement with Carlyle & Adams for its purchase of his wheat, GW in early 1773 began milling wheat to make flour on a large scale. Thomas Newton, Jr., a merchant in Norfolk, Va., became agent for GW to sell his flour and herring, usually in Norfolk and the West Indies. See Ledger B, 85, and the correspondence between GW and Newton beginning 11 Jan. 1773 and through 12 April 1775.

2. No copy of the account that GW sent Newton has been found. The ledger entry of £50 paid to GW on behalf of Newton by Jacob Williams is dated 12 Aug. 1778, and the payment of £170 by Fielding Lewis on behalf of Newton is dated 6 Aug. 1774 (Ledger B, 85). At the bottom of the contra side of GW's account with Newton, GW's clerk has written "1789 March 18th—Note, there appears by this Acct to be a considerable balance in favor of Mr Newton but this is erronious for he was credited for the Cash recd from time to time for the sale of flour but not charged with all the flour sent him to sell—And it will appear by his Letters that there is a balance due G.W. for flour sold by him." The "Letters" that GW refers to here have not been identified.

3. GW received two payments in the 1780s on Newton's behalf, one for £60 on 25 Feb. 1786, one for £70 in May 1787 (Ledger B, 85).

4. GW's account with Balfour & Barraud shows charges of £1,748.17 against the firm for 1,000 barrels of flour sold to it in 1775 (Ledger B, 136). The account is carried over to Ledger C, 3, in 1793. On 26 April 1786 GW wrote in his diary: "Meeting with Mr. Thos. Newton of Norfolk, he informed me that Mr. Neil Jameeson late of that place, now a merchant in New York, was Executor of Jno. Shaw (also of Norfolk) who was possessed of the Books of Messrs. Balfour & Barraud & to whom he advised me to apply, thinking it probable that I might obtain, a list of the Ballances due to that House and thereby recover what was due to me therefrom" (*Diaries*, 4:317–18). On 20 May 1786 GW wrote Neil Jamieson, who before the Revolution was a partner in Norfolk of the Glasgow firm of John Glassford & Co., about the money

owed him by Balfour & Barraud, and in the absence of Jamieson from New York, Colt MacGregor responded to GW's inquiries on 29 May 1786, telling him that the books of Balfour & Barraud had passed from hand to hand and were then in the possession of "a Mr John Clapham, lately from England." James Balfour and Daniel Barraud, both of whom were now dead, had been merchants in Norfolk.

To Chastellux

Dr Sir,   Mount Vernon 5th Septr 1785.

I am your debtor for two letters—one of the 12th of Decemr —the other of the 8th of April. Since the receipt of the first, I have paid my respects to you in a line by Majr Swan; but as it was introductory only of him, it requires an apology, rather than entitles me to a credit in our epistolary correspondence.[1]

If I had as good a nack my dear Marquis, as you have at saying handsome things, I would endeavor to pay you in kind for the flattering expressions of your letters, having an ample field to work in; but as I am a clumsy workman in the manufactory of compliments, I must first profess my unworthyness of those which you have bestowed on me, and my inability to meet you on that ground; and therefore will not expose myself in the attempt.

It gives me great pleasure to find by my last letters from France, that the dark clouds which hung over you[r] hemisphere, are vanishing before the all-chearing Sunshine of peace. My first wish is to see the blessings of it diffused through all Countries, & among *all* ranks in every Country; & that we should consider ourselves as the children of a common parent, and be disposed to acts of brotherly kindness towards one another. In that case all restrictions of trade would vanish; we should take your Wines, your fruits & surplusage of other articles: & give you in return our Oils, our Fish, Tobacco, naval stores &ca; and in like manner we should exchange produce with other Countries, to our reciprocal advantage: the Globe is large enough, why then need we wrangle for a small spot of it? If one Country cannot contain us another should open its arms to us. But these halcyon days (if they ever did exist) are now no more; a wise providence, I presume, has ordered it otherwise, &

we must go in the old way disputing—& now & then fighting, until the Globe itself is dissolved.

I rarely go from home; but my friends in & out of Congress sometimes tell me what is on the carpet; to hand it to you afterwards would be a circuitous mode, & altogether idle, as I am persuaded you have Correspondents at New-York who give it to you at first hand, & can relate it with more clearness & perspicuity than I can. I give the chief of my time to rural amusements; but I have lately been active in instituting a plan which, if success attends it & of which I have no doubt, may be productive of great political as well as commercial advantages to the States on the Atlantic, especially the middle ones: it is the extending & improving the inland navigations of the rivers Potomac & James, & communicating them with the Western waters by the shortest & easiest portages & good roads. Acts have passed the Assemblies of Virginia & Maryland authorising private Adventurers to undertake the work; Companies in consequence have been incorporated; & that on this river is begun, but when we come to the difficult parts of it we shall require an Engineer of skill & practical knowledge in this branch of business; & from that country where these kind of improvements have been conducted with the greatest success. With very great esteem & regard I have the honor to be &c.

G: Washington

LB, DLC:GW; copy, ScC: Washington Letters.

1. Neither of Chastellux's letters has been found; the text of GW's letter of 28 Feb. 1785 introducing James Swan is printed in note 1, GW to Henry Knox, 28 Feb. 1785.

From William Grayson

Dear Sir   New York Sepr 5h 1785.

I had the honor of your favor by Post: The hounds you allude to arrived here in the midst of a hot war against their fraternity: they were not however friendless: your Acquaintance Doctr Cochran took very good care of them while they remained at this place & has sent them by Capt. Packard's sloop to Mount Vernon. I make no doubt that they have got there safe.[1]

We have little news from Europe or elsewhere. Mr Otto came over in the last packett as chargé des affaires in the room of Mr Marbois who goes to the West Indies—We are informed the Chevalier de la Luzerne is to be here shortly in quality of Minister—The demand of the body of Longchamp is withdrawn.[2]

For some time past there has been very few States on the floor, of course very little has been done.

I am happy to hear that after inspection, you are of opinion the obstructions on the Potowmac, are not greater than you had supposed them to be. I have the honor to be With the highest respect Yr Affect. fd & Most Obed. servt

Willm Grayson

ALS, DLC:GW.

1. For the French hounds, which arrived at Mount Vernon on 24 Aug., see note 1 in GW to Grayson, 22 August. On 4 Aug. the *New-York, or the Weekly Register* urged calm in the city "at a time when terror is excited, by a variety of reports respecting MAD DOGS, and thereby conjuring up imaginary ills, calculated to disturb the minds of people whose nervous system is not very strong."

2. Louis-Guillaume Otto, comte de Mosloy (1754–1817), arrived in New York on 25 Aug. to replace Barbé-Marbois as the French chargé d'affaires, a post he held until his return to France in 1792.

To David Henley

Sir,   Mount Vernon 5th Septr 1785.

I am sorry the enclosed account should be brought against me in my private character: It is a fact which I thought had been well known to all the public Departments, & to those employed by the public, that expences of the nature of Otis & Henley's Accots (which is for clothing for the servants I was obliged to employ in my public character) were paid from the public funds.

If I mistake not Otis & Henley were Agents for the purpose of supplying clothing (or materials for it) for the Army: to them in this character I apply'd; & never, until the enclosed account was presented, had I any other idea of the matter, than that the amount had been settled for by them in their public accounts. As this is not the case, had it been presented to me whilst I had authority to do so, I should have ordered the paymaster to have discharged it, but as the matter now stands, I can do no more than certify that the Goods were receiv'd on public Account for my use; for I really cannot pay for them out of my private purse.[1] It is to be regretted that the matter has lain over so long. I am Sir &c.

G: Washington

LB, DLC:GW.

1. The enclosed account has not been found, but on 1 Feb. 1785 Samuel Allyne Otis presented a petition to Congress on behalf of Otis & Andrews, Samuel Allyne Otis, and Otis & Henley, agents for purchasing military stores, asking to have their accounts adjusted and settled (DNA:PCC, item 42, 6:109). Congress on 15 April 1785 accepted its committee's recommendations that the accounts be referred for settlement to "the Commissioner for settling the Accounts of the Department of the Cloathier General" (*JCC*, 28:262–63). Otis & Henley's accounts, however, were included on 17 Sept. 1788 in a list of unsettled accounts in the Clothing Department as certified by Joseph Nourse (PCC). The letter-book copy of GW's certificate for Henley is written below the letter. It reads: "I certify that the Goods which are charged within were required on Public Account to clothe the servants who attended me in my public character; & is a proper charge against the United States—not against me as a private person, who derived no other benefit therefrom. G: Washington." Samuel A. Otis and David Henley (1748–1823) were merchants in Boston (see GW to William Gordon, 6 Dec. 1785, n.3).

To La Luzerne

Sir,   Mt Vernon 5th Septr 1785.

I am indebted to you for your several favors of the 20th of Decr introductory of Mr de Chateaufort—of the 15th of Feby & 25th of March, which I should not have suffered to have remained so long unacknowledged, if anything had occurred, the relation of which could have compensated for the trouble of reading my letter.

Long as I have waited for such an event, nothing has yet happen'd of much importance in our political movements, & the Assemblies of the different States being now in their recesses, nothing probably will occur 'till they have met. In the meanwhile the mercantile interest *feeling* the necessity of giving a controuling power to Congress to regulate the trade of this Country, have prepared, & are now preparing Addresses to their respective Assemblies for this purpose. They are now clearly convinced that this power cannot be exercised with propriety unless one system pervades the whole Union, & is made competent to the ends. It has happened in this instance as in the revolution itself, that the means which G: B. pursues to obtain advantages, defeat her own ends; for I am certain, that if she had forborne to tax our trade with those restrictions &, imposts, which are laid on it by Acts of Parliament, or Orders of the King in Council; that half a century would not have produced those powers in Congress, which, more than probably will be given to them in a few Months, & by which equal restrictions & duties may be laid; and in the interim, sorry I am to add, she would have monopolized in a very great degree, the commerce of the United States.[1]

At length Congress have adopted a mode for disposing of the western Lands; but I confess it does not strike me as a very eligible one: however mine is only an opinion, & I wish to be mistaken in it, as the fund wou'd be very productive & afford great relief to the public creditors if the Lands meet with a ready sale.

Treaty has been holden with the Western Indians at Fort McIntosh on the Ohio, (twenty five miles below Pittsburgh) & advantageous terms entered into with those who met, for they ceded without any compensation as large a District, North west of that river, as we have any occasion for at present: but it should seem that others of their respective Tribes are dissatisfied, & keep the settlers of the Western Territory in a state of disquietude. This I am persuaded will be the case whilst the British retain the Posts within the American lines—& when they will be surrendered, is not for me to decide.[2]

Congress have had also under contemplation a Mint for the coinage of Gold, Silver & Copper; a committee has reported in favor of the measure, but I believe no ultimate decision is yet come to on the subject, by that Hon[orabl]e Body.[3]

From the last European accounts we have reason to hope that the clouds which seemed to be gathering in your hemisphere, will yield to a tranquil sky; & Peace, with all its blessings will spread its mantle over the threatened Lands. My first wish is to see the sons & Daughters of the World mixing as one family, enjoying the sweets of social intercourse, & reciprocal advantages: the Earth certainly is sufficient to contain us all, & affords every thing necessary to our wants; if we would be friendly & endeavour to accommodate one another. Why then should we wrangle, & why should we attempt to infringe the rights & properties of our Neighbours? But lest you shou'd suppose that I am about to turn preacher, I will only add that, with the highest esteem & consideration, I have the honor to be &c.

G: Washington

P.S: I had not the pleasure of seeing Mr de Chateaufort: upon the receipt of your letter of the 20th of December, enclosed to me by that Gentleman from Philada; I wrote to him praying that I might be honored with his company on his way to Carolina; but he found it more convenient at that hot season to go thither by Sea in the Packett.[4] G. W———n

LB, DLC:GW.

1. For GW's views on the regulation of trade by Congress, see GW to James McHenry, 22 August. See also William Grayson to GW, c.4–8 May 1785, n.4.

2. "Articles of a treaty concluded at Fort M'Intosh . . . [on 21 Jan. 1785 with] the Wiandot, Delaware, Chippawa and Ottowa Nations . . ." are printed in Kappler, *Indian Treaties*, 2:6–8.

3. See GW to William Grayson, 22 Aug., n.2.

4. See GW to Châteaufort, 15 June 1785.

From John Rumney, Jr.

Sir   W[hi]t[e]haven [England] 5th Septr 1785

I had the Honor to receive your esteemd Favor of the 22d June ⅌ the Cæsar Ct. Atkinson, & agreeable to your request, shall send out in a Ship which will sail for Alexandria the latter End of Decr as much of the White Stone you mention as will floor the Gallery in Front of your House, I have given the Dimensions to the Masons who are now preparing them, & have not a Doubt they will be done in a neat Manner. We shall contrive the cheapest & safest Mode of packing them. I was very happy to hear that the Joiner gives Satisfaction. With the Greatest respect I am Sir Yr most Obt & hble Servt

John Rumney

ALS, DLC:GW.

From Battaile Muse

Honorable Sir,   Sepr 6th 1785

I received your Favour dated 22d of Last month—in answer to which—I shall send to the Care of Mr Heartshorn one bushel clover seed[1]—I will endeavour to secure the Butter for you, but the Quantity of 250 lb. is reather uncertain—I shall make 100 lb. my self—that Quantity you may depend On and that it shall be good—their are but few to be depended on, was I to engage it—it would be uncertain—whether it would be good—if to be had at all; I can only say that I will endeavour to Furnish you with 250 lb. Butter.[2] the Certainty will be Known the Last of October—as I expect to waite on you about that Time—my business at present is too uncertain to mention the day, or week that I shall be down. at Present I expect I shall waite on you between the 20th and the Last of October with the money from Mr Whiteing.[3]

I was in Winchester a few days ago and made inquiry about your Lotts—Doctr McKey has the one in Town Enclosed—apart of which is apart of His Garden. the out Lott is made no use of, the Lott in Town is too much out of the way of business to be of any value to any other Person but the Doctr. The Doctr was at Bath, I Left a Letter to Know of Him what He would give ℔ year for the Lott—and to give me and answer this week.[4] I have been twice to Frederick about your Land their—Capt. Snickers was so unwell He Could do nothing—I have fixed the Time for to Lay off the four Lotts the first week in October and will Endeavour to have it done then—in order to make return to you when I come down. Capt. Snickers sayes your Letter to Him specifies the Leases to be 14 years—some of the Tenants are not able to Pay for a Lott so Large—Please inform me whether you will Allow more Lotts than four—or more than One Tenant on a Lott—your Instructions to me is for four Lotts, and not more than four Tenants, which Instructions I shall attend to.[5]

as I came through Fauquier a few days ago I was inform'd that some of your Tenants by the name of Rectors was about to move to the Back County—I shall be In Fauquier the 26th of this month if you will send me Instructions respecting those Tenants I will then Endeavour to Secure you the rents.[6]

I am much oblige to you for the offer you make for my wheat. I shall hold it up for the price of 6/ ℔ bushel when Ever you think you Can afford to give that price I shall be glad to Hear from you.[7] I am Sir your Obidient Humble Servant

Battaile Muse

ALS, DLC:GW.

1. See GW to Muse, 28 July, n.6.

2. See GW to Muse, 22 Aug., n.3.

3. Muse arrived at Mount Vernon on 27 Oct. when he conducted "some business" with GW "respecting my Tenants" and got GW to agree "to allow him Six pr. Ct. for Collecting" GW's rents. He also got GW's agreement to buy 1,000 bushels of wheat at Muse's price of six shillings per bushel (*Diaries*, 4:215). See also GW to Muse, 22 August.

4. See GW to Muse, 28 July, and Muse to GW, 14 September. Dr. Robert Mackey was a surgeon in the 11th Virginia Regiment who settled in Winchester after the Revolution. When the trustees offered GW's lot in Winchester for sale in 1802, they advertised it as a one-half-acre lot adjoining Dr. Mackey's with a post and rail fence around it.

5. See GW to Muse, 28 July, nn.1 and 2.

6. For Muse's dealings with the Rectors, see particularly Muse to GW, 28 Nov., nn.5 and 6.

7. See Muse to GW, 16 Aug., n.3.

To Clement Biddle

Dear Sir,   Mount Vernon Sepr 7th 1785.

The man who at present lives with me in the capacity of a Housekeeper, or Household Steward, will leave me in a day or two; which (until his place can be supplied) will throw a great additional weight on Mrs Washington. I therefore beg, if you, or Mr Moyston, should have met with a person whom you think would answer my purposes (as described in my former letters) that you would engage him (or her) absolutely, instead of conditionally, and send him on the Stage. In the meanwhile, if one should offer to my liking here, my engagement shall be conditional. No disappontmt therefore can happen to the person engaged by you.[1]

Inclosed is a letter to Mr Frauncis (als black Sam) late of New York, now of some place in the Jerseys. I leave it open for your perusal, to be forwarded, or destroyed, as circumstances may require. If you should have succeeded at Philadelphia, or are in the way of doing so, the latter will take place; if not, the sooner it can be got to his hands, the better. My best respects, in which Mrs Washington joins, are offered to Mrs Biddle. I am—Dr Sir Yr Most Obedt & very Hble Servt

Go: Washington

ALS, PHi: Washington-Biddle Correspondence; LB, DLC:GW.

1. For an account of the resignation and rehiring of Richard Burnet as housekeeper at Mount Vernon, see GW to Clement Biddle, 17 Aug., n.4.

To Samuel Fraunces

Sir,　　　　　　　　　　　　　　Mount Vernon 7th Septr 1785.

As no person can judge better, of the qualifications necessary to constitute a good Housekeeper, or Household steward, than yourself, for a family which has a good deal of company & wishes to entertain them in a plain, but genteel style; I take the liberty of asking you if there is any such an one within your reach, whom you think could be induced to come to me on reasonable wages. I would rather have a man than a woman—but either will do, if they can be recommended for their honesty, sobriety, & knowledge of their profession; which in one word, is to relieve Mrs Washington from the drudgery of ordering & seeing the Table properly covered—& things œconomically used: nothing more therefore need be said to inform you of a character that would suit me, than what is already mentioned.

The wages I now give to a man who is about to leave me in order to get married (under which circumstance he would not suit me) is about one hundred Dollars pr annum; but for one who understands the business perfectly, & stands fair in all other respects, I would go as far as one hundred & twenty five dollars. Sometime ago I wrote to Colo. Biddle, & to Mr Moyston (who keeps the City tavern in Philada) to try if they could procure me such a person as I want; I therefore beg, if you know of one that would suit me, & is to be had upon the terms above, & who can attend properly to a large family (for mine is such, with a good many workmen)—that you would immediately inform Colo. Biddle of it, before any engagement is entered into by you on my behalf, lest one should be provided at Philada & embarrassments arise from the different engagements.[1] I am sorry to give you so much trouble, but I hope you will excuse it in, Sir Yr &c.

　　　　　　　　　　　　　　　　　　　　　G: Washington

LB, DLC:GW. GW sent the letter to Clement Biddle on this day for forwarding to Fraunces.

1. See GW to Biddle, 17 Aug., n.4, and 7 September.

From Thomas Ridout

Sir   Bordeaux. 7. September 1785.

The letter on the other side is Copy of that I had the Honor to write your Excellency the 31 of last Month—by way of L'orient; this goes by the Brig, Peggy Capt. Cunynghame bound to Charles Town So. Carolina & to Baltimore on board of whom I have shipped a bale directed to you from the Marquis de la Fayette, with orders to be delivered to Colo. Tench Tilghman at Baltimore to whom I have written & sent the bill of lading[1]— Wishing you May receive it in good Condition, I have the Honor to be with the greatest respect Your Excellency's Most Obedient servant

· Thos Ridout

ALS, DLC:GW.

1. Ridout writes GW on 4 Nov. that the "bale" referred to here was the package from Lafayette which GW asked about in his letter to Ridout of 20 August. GW on 20 May 1786 acknowledges receipt of the package.

To Rochambeau

My dear Count,   Mount Vernon Sepr 7th 1785

Since I had the honor to address you last, I have been favored with your letters of the 9th of Septr and 24th of Feby. The first enclosing a list of the new promotions, and the additional members of the Society of the Cincinnati as consented by the King; for which I thank you, as it will enable me to give answers to those Gentlemen who, unacquainted I presume, with his Majesty's pleasure, are still offering to me their pretensions to be admitted into this Order.[1]

Every occasion that assures me of your health, encreases my happiness, as I have a sincere respect, and affectionate regard for you. My time now, as the Marquis de la Fayette has informed you, is spent in rural employments, and in contemplation of those friendships which the revolution enabled me to form with so many worthy characters of your Nation, through whose assistance I can now sit down in my calm retreat, and under my own vine, and my own fig tree, enjoy those pleasures which are rarely to be found in the more active pursuits of life, in a larger theatre.

I hope the storms which rumbled about you all the Winter, and wch seemed to portend so much mischief, are dispersed; and that a tranquil sky has succeeded. Although it is against the profession of Arms, I wish to see all the world in Peace. How long this blessing may be dispensed to us, I know not, the British still hold the Posts upon the Lakes, within the Territory of the United States; and discover no inclination (that has come to my knowledge) of giving them up. With respect to the Spaniards, I do not think the Navigation of the Mississipi is an object of great importance at present—when it becomes so—when the Banks of the Ohio are thick settled—and when the fertile plains of that Western Country are covered with people, they will not be deprived of natural advantages.

I am very thankful for the polite attentions of Madame de Rochambeau, to whom I pray you to present my best respects—and to any of our worthy compatriots in the late War. Mrs Washington, sensible of your kind remembrance of her, begs you to accept her Compliments. With sincere friendship and perfect attachment I am—My dear Count Yr Most Obedt and Very Hble Servt

Go: Washington

I take the liberty of putting the enclosed letter under your cover as it contains original papers wch might be a loss to Captn de Pusignan.

ALS, DLC: Rochambeau Papers; LB, DLC:GW.
   1. See note 1 in Rochambeau to GW, 9 Sept. 1784.

To Jean de Neufville

Sir,   Mount Vernon Septr 8th 1785.
I have lately been honored with your favors of the 10th & 15th of March. Until the latter explained the mistake of the former, I was puzzled to get at the meaning of it; because, I did not recollect that I had ever made application to your Son for the loan of any money; but since the subject has been started, I will take the liberty of pursuing it.[1]

I am a member of a company in this State, who associated many years ago for the purpose of reclaiming what is called the

Great dismal Swamp near Norfolk. The War gave considerable interruption, indeed almost put an entire stop to the progress of the business; but in May last the members (for the first time since the war) had a meeting, & resolved to prosecute the work with vigour: for this purpose they are inclined to borrow money on interest; & to import, if they can do it upon advantageous terms, a number of Hollanders, or Germans, as being best acquainted with the nature of the work; which is to drain & bank level, low & wet Land, which would from its situation, & the quality of its soil, be invaluable if accomplished.

Individually, the members possess considerable property—as a company they have little money at command; but would I believe, bind themselves jointly & severally for the repayment of the principal sum borrowed, in a given number of years; & for such interest as may be agreed upon, annually; & as a collateral security they would moreover, I imagine, mortgage the Estate which they are about to improve.

Under this statement of the matter, permit me to ask you frankly, if four or five thousand pounds could be borrowed in Amsterdam; at what interest & for how long a term? And wether it is a matter which could be easily accomplished, to import about three hundred labourers (a few women among them would be no objection)—for what time they might be engaged & upon what wages? And what expence would attend the importation?[2]

Since my last to you I have had the pleasure of your son's company at this place; he appeared at the time to be in good health, and I hope has been able to put your business in this Country on a more favourable footing, than your letter of the 15th of June last year indicated; in a word, I hope it is placed on as good a footing as the nature of the case will admit.[3] I have the honor to be &c.

G: Washington

LB, DLC:GW.

1. Neither letter has been found.

2. Resolutions of the Dismal Swamp Company, dated 2 May 1785, calling for floating a loan, are printed above. For further details of GW's approaching de Neufville on behalf of the Dismal Swamp Company, see GW's letter to John Page, 3 Oct. 1785. See also George Taylor, Jr., to GW, 17 October.

3. Leonard de Neufville, the son of Jean de Neufville (1729–1796) of Am-

sterdam, had dinner with GW at Mount Vernon on 12 June 1785. See *Diaries*, 4:151. GW wrote Jean de Neufville on 6 Jan. 1784. Jean de Neufville's letter of 15 June 1784 has not been found.

From John Page

Rosewell [Gloucester County]

My dear General   Sept. 9th 1785

   A thousand Accidents have happened which prevented my writing to you since I had the Pleasure of seeing you at Richmond—for some Time I comforted myself with the Hope of being able to wait on you: & when I was appointed by the Convention one of their Deputies to the gen'l Convention to be held at Philada I then determined to wait on you in my Way[1]—but the Situation of my Affairs has detained me at Home, & Mrs Page's State of Health, who is advised to accompany me to Philada requires that she should go a great Part of the Way by Water so that I can only now send you this late Apology for a long seeming Neglect[2]—When I saw you I told you how unfortunately I missed seeing you when I went to wait upon you at York, & how totally the public Business in which I had been engaged since your Return from the Army to the Northward, had engrossed my Time & Attention; & as to not writing to you, I thought it was better, that you should suppose for some Time I had neglected you; than that I should be one amongst the thousands who I was certain were troubling you with Letters, so as to be sufficient to make you wish some of them had forgotten you. As I think you may by this Time have a little Leisure to receive my Apology, I beg you will accept this Letter as one; & you may be assured that a sincere Regard for you occasioned my refraining from troubling you with an Address so early as I could have wished—As no Man is more truly sensible of the Obligations our Country is under to you for your great & glorious Exertions in her Support than I am; so I may venture to say, no one was ever more deeply affected with Gratitude & Esteem; or more eager to shew it than I have been—I admired, & highly esteemed you before the late War; you may easily judge then, how much I must admire & venerate you now—Although I know your Delicacy, I could not my dear Sir refrain from saying what I have: I could no longer restrain the Feelings of my Heart; nor need I, for Praise much higher than I can give, is your peculiar due; & Flattery can never be charged on any one who praises you—Mrs Page unites with me in presenting our Compts & best wishes to yourself & Lady—I am my dear Sir with every Sentiment of the most perfect Respect & Esteem yr most obedt hbe Servt

J. Page

P.S. I expect to be at Philada about the 25th inst. & shall be proud to execute your Commands—If you have not yet applied to any one in that City to procure Emigrants or Redemptioners for the Use of the Dismal Compy I will do anything you shall be pleased to recommend respecting that Business—The Managers have not met since I was appointed one of them—I have pressed Mr Jameson & Mr N. Nelson to go down & look into the Affairs of the Co. on the Spot & see what the Carolina Co. will bc willing to do towards opening the Canals & am in Hopes they will go down.[3]

ALS, DLC:GW.

1. GW and John Page (1744–1808) were among the members of the Dismal Swamp Company who met in Richmond on 2 and 3 May. For the meeting, see GW to Thomas Walker, 10 April, n.1. Page had recently been elected the lay delegate from the Virginia diocese to the general convention of the Episcopal church in Philadelphia beginning on 27 September.

2. Page's wife, Frances Burwell Page, daughter of Robert Carter Burwell, bore him twelve children before her death later in this decade.

3. See Resolutions of the Dismal Swamp Company, 2 May 1785, printed above. Nathaniel Nelson, the younger brother of Gen. Thomas Nelson (1738–1789), died suddenly in the spring of 1786.

From William Gordon

My dear Sir   Jamaica-Plain [Mass.] Sepr 10. 1785

Till now I have had nothing of late worth communicating, but the following extract from a Letter dated London June 30. 1785 I think will be pleasing, & have therefore sent it your Excellency.

Mr Temple accompanied Mr Adams to the kings levee; after the levee was over, Mr Adams, according to etiquette, was introduced to the kings closet, where (as is usual for foreign ministers) he made a speech to his majesty, in performing which he was somewhat affected, & when he had finished the king said,

"Sir, The whole of this business is so extraordinary, that the feelings you discover upon the occasion, appear to me to be just & proper. I wish, Sir, to be clearly understood, before I reply to the very obliging sentiments you have expressed in behalf of the United States of America. I am, you may well suppose Sir, the last person in England, that consented to the dismemberment of the empire by the Independence of the new States, & while war was continued, I thought it due to my subjects to prosecute that war to the utmost: but Sir, I have consented to their Independence, & it is ratified by treaty, & I now receive you as their minister plenipotentiary; & every attention, respect & protection granted to other plenipotentiaries, you shall receive at this Court: and, Sir, as I was the last person that consented to the Independence of the said United States, so I will be the last person to disturb or in any measure infringe upon their sovereign independent rights. And I hope & trust, that from blood, religion, manners, habits of intercourse & almost every other consideration, that the two nations will continue for ages in friendship & confidence with eatch other &c. &c." Lord Carmarthen Secry of state (who was the only minister in the closet, when Mr Adams made his speech & received the foregoing answer) repeated it to Mr Temple the ⟨day⟩ after. Mr Adams was afterwards presented to the queen, to whom he made a speech (as is custom.) She politely thanked him for his friendly expressions towards her & her family—& was very happy to see him in England.[1] Wishing your Excellency, Lady, my young friend & the rest of the family the best of blessings I remain My dear Sir Your very humble servant

William Gordon

ALS, DLC:GW.

1. Adams reported to John Jay on 2 June what he and George III had said to one another when the king formally received him as a representative of the United States on 1 June (Adams, *Works of John Adams*, 8:255–59). George Nugent-Temple Grenville (1753–1813), the son of George Grenville (1712–1770), became the second Earl Temple in 1779.

To Patrick Henry

Dear Sir,   Mt Vernon 10th Septr 1785.

The enclosed was put into my hands yesterday; & I take the liberty of forwarding it by the post to day, hoping, if no person is appointed in the place of Mr Massey, that your Excellency for the reason assigned by the Maryland Commrs, & on account of the advanced season, will cause it to be done as soon as convenient.[1] With very great esteem & respect I have the honor to be &c.

G: Washington

LB, DLC:GW.

1. The enclosed was a letter from William Deakins, Jr. (1742–1798), of Georgetown, Md., to Henry, seemingly urging the governor to appoint promptly someone to replace Thomas Massey (Massie) who had resigned as Virginia's commissioner "to open and keep in repair" a road between the Potomac and the Cheat or the Monongahela river (*House of Delegates Journal, 1781–1785*, 101). See Henry to GW, 26 Sept., and note 2 of that document. See also GW to Henry (second letter), 29 October.

To Thomas Johnson and Thomas Sim Lee

Gentn   Mount Vernon 10th Septr 1785.

Your favor of the 30th ulto did not reach me until the 8th instant; I went the next day to Alexandria & laid it before Colos. Fitzgerald and Gilpin, who with myself, acceded fully to the propriety of your proposal of buying servants. Of this, the Secretary was directed to inform you; also of our sentiments respecting the hire of Negroes by the year, & to ask your opinion of the number necessary, & of the terms on which to employ them.[1]

Colo. Gilpin has lately seen Mr Stuart, who informed him that fifty hands were then employed at Seneca, & in his opinion going on very well until the waters were swelled by the late rains. He & I, (if I am not prevented by company which I have some reason to expect about that time) intend to be at Seneca on Wednesday the 21st—& at the Great Fall at Eight o'Clock next morning; where we are to meet Colo. Fitzgerald for the purpose of viewing for our private satisfaction, the place talked of for the Canal; & the water between the Great & little falls. Mr Stuart informed Colo. Gilpin that he had never seen the Butcher from

Fredk town; nor had he received an ounce of provisions from him.[2]

I am sorry to receive so unfavourable a report from Shenandoah as your letter contains; I hope it will mend, or the cause must be removed. If the health of Mr Johnson, and the circumstances of Mr Lee would permit them to visit that place now & then; it would, I am persuaded, have a happy effect: the eye of a Director will be of service to the Conductors. With very great esteem & regard I am Gentn &c. &c.

G: Washington

LB, DLC:GW.

1. The letter of 30 Aug. from the two Maryland directors of the Potomac River Company, Johnson and Lee, has not been found. At the meeting in Alexandria on 9 Sept. GW and the two Virginia directors, John Fitzgerald and George Gilpin, found "that the Hands employed in the work of opening the Navigation of the River are irregular and disorderly in their Behaviour" and voted to buy "sixty Servants" in Baltimore or Philadelphia (DNA: RG 79, Records of the Potomac Co. and the Chesapeake and Ohio Canal Co., item 159). The three met again in Alexandria on 26 Sept. and recorded that Stewart & Plunket of Baltimore and John Maxwell Nesbit of Philadelphia had been written about the purchase of servants for the company and would be written to again. They passed accounts totaling £182.8.3, including £88.11.7 for the wages of the workers hired by the company from 19 Aug. to 17 September. (A list of the laborers employed under Richardson Stewart from 19 Aug. through 26 Sept., giving the number of days each man worked and the total that he earned, is privately owned, and a transcript of it appears in CD-ROM:GW). GW and the directors instructed James Rumsey to rehire the good workers, and they voted that he and Richardson Stewart should be informed of the next meeting of the board of directors of the Potomac River Company scheduled for 17 Oct. (DNA: RG 79, Records of the Potomac Co. and the Chesapeake and Ohio Canal Co., item 159). A full meeting of the board of directors of the company was held at Great Falls on 17–18 Oct. (see *Diaries*, 4:207–8). In the meantime, Thomas Johnson had written GW, on 21 Sept., urging the preferability of hiring slaves to the purchase of indentured servants, "common white Hirelings," and at the full meeting of the board at Great Falls on 18–19 Oct., the directors voted to hire one hundred slaves. For the minutes of the directors' meeting of 8 Aug., see GW to James Rumsey, 8 Aug., source note.

2. GW left home for his inspection of the Potomac between the Great and Little falls on the afternoon of 20 Sept. and returned to Mount Vernon on the morning of 23 September. For his description of his trip, see *Diaries*, 4:195–97.

To Thomas Smith

Sir,   Mount Vernon 10th Septr 1785.

My last letter to you was so full, that I should not have troubled you again at this early period,[1] but to observe as I did before, that upon reading the Proclamation which I then enclosed (and which I had scar[c]e time to run over before it was dispatched), it appeared to me that as it forbid in general terms, the settlement of Lands upon the western waters, it might be necessary for me to adduce the subsequent Act of the Kings Governor; by which the military rights under that proclamation were recognized, & exempted from the restriction thereof. Accordingly, I wrote to our Attorney General Mr Randolph, for a certified copy thereof; under which the warrants for surveying these claims were directed to be issued; but in some measure he misconceived my request. However, his answer and reasoning applies with as much force to the order of Council, as it does to the instruction which gave rise to it; I therefore send his letters, with a Certificate of the Governor & the seal of the Commonwealth to give validity to the Acts wch have been already forwar[d]ed to you from the registers Office, under the direction of Mr Harvie.[2]

My title to the Land in dispute, in my own judgment, is so clear, that I can scarce conceive what my opponents will urge, that can have the least weight with an impartial Court & Jury; but as I apprehend there will be some management in obtaining the latter, it may not be amiss to apprize you, that from my best information (& a gentleman on whom I can depend, told me that he had it from Mr prothonotary Scott, brother to my principal opponant) a majority of the Occupants settled on the Land after my Patent had actually issued, & consequently in his opinion, could not have the shadow of a claim. Putting my military right then, & all the steps which were taken in consequence of it, out of the question; my improvement (admitting there never was more than one) which stands on the Land to this day, & which was acknowledged by themselves to be there when the Defendants first came to it, will entitle me, for settlement & preemption rights, to 1400 acres under our Laws, as you may perceive by the authentic documents already sent you: and these 1400 acres, without the aid of an irregular form & unnatural extension, would comprehend James Scott's farm, & I presume all those which were seated before I obtained my Patent. It appears to me therefore that in one way or other, they must be overthrown.[3]

It has been reported to me (and as *report* only I give it) that the Defendants are preparing to remove off. Whether, if true, the measure proceeds from a conviction of the futility of their claim—or that they mean to be prepared against the worst—or, as it was said whilst I was out, their only design was to gain time, I shall not decide: but be it as it may, as they have withheld the Land from me ten or twelve years after all the admonition I could give, & the favorable offers which have been made them—& finally have put me to the expence & trouble of bringing & supporting Ejectments, it is my wish & desire, whether they leave the land voluntarily, or are compelled to do so by a course of Law, that you will sue them respectively for Trespasses, rents or otherwise as you shall judge best & most proper to obtain justice for me. I should be glad to hear that this & my former letter had got safe to hand. I am Sir &c.

G: Washington

LB, DLC:GW.

1. GW's letter to Smith is dated 14 July. Smith answers both letters on 17 November.

2. See Edmund Randolph to GW, 29 July, and notes.

3. For a discussion of GW's extended controversy with the people who moved onto his Millers Run land, see editorial note, Smith to GW, 9 Feb. 1785.

Letter not found: from Joseph Brown, 12 Sept. 1785. On 30 May 1786 GW wrote Brown: "I have been favored with your letter of 12th September." See note 1 in GW's letter.

From Richard Söderström

Sir   Newyork 12th Sepr 1785.

The personal acquaintance which I had the honour to form with your Excellency some time ago will, I hope be sufficient apology for the liberty I presume to take, in introducing to your Excellency the right Honle Fred. von Walden Esqr. Captain in His Swedish Majesties Navy, who on his Tour to Virginia promises himself the honour of paying your Excellency a Visit.[1] Any attention and Civilities your Excellency shall be pleased to render him will add to the great esteem with which I have the honour to remain your Excellencys most Obedt & most Hle Servant

Richd Söderstrom

ALS, DLC:GW.

Richard Söderström was the new Swedish consul at Boston.

1. GW has this entry in his diary for 30 Sept.: "Mr. Hunter [William Hunter, Jr.], and the right Honble. Fred[erick] von Walden, Captn. in the Swedish Navy—introduced by Mr. Richd. Soderstroin came here to Dinner, and returned to Alexandria afterwards" (*Diaries*, 4:199). Walden had recently presented Congress with a proposal to coin copper (*JCC*, 29:587).

From Barbé-Marbois

Sir, New york Septr 14th 1785.

I have had So many proofs of your Excellency's interest to my concerns that I hope you'll learn with pleasure that the King has appointed me an Intendant for his Colony of hispaniola. This appointement is the more agreeable to me as the connection with america is not entirely broke of for me by my removal, & especially as I Shall have the pleasure to meet there the Count de la luzerne as the commandant of the Colony: to his brother the Chevalier I owe especially this mark of the King's confidence, I wish I may answer it fully, but though I Know all what I want for Duly discharging the trust, it will be neither Zeal nor a desire of doing good.[1]

I hope your former dispositions & friendship will accompany me in this new Station, & I would be truely happy if it could afford me opportunities to Evince my respect & veneration for you[2] & the consideration with Which I have the honour to be, sir, Your excellency's Very humble obedient servant

De Marbois

ALS, DLC:GW.

1. César-Henri, comte de La Luzerne (1737–1799), the elder brother of the French ambassador to the United States from 1779 through 1783, Anne-César, chevalier de La Luzerne, went in 1786 to the West Indies as governor of the Îles sous la Vent and remained only one year. Barbé-Marbois remained the intendant at Santo Domingo until 1790.

2. On 25 Sept. GW congratulated Barbé-Marbois on his appointment in these terms: "Sir, I have had the honor to receive your favor of the 14th Instt from New York.

"At the moment I congratulate you on your late appointment, and on this fresh instance of your Sovereigns attention to your merits, I cannot but express my sorrow that you are so near the eve of your departure from America.

"I shall remember with pleasure, Sir, the friendship you have always expressed for me; and with gratitude shall recollect the many instances of your partiallity, and attention towards me. I shall receive with great satisfaction the account of your safe arrival at Hispaniola, and of every other event which is interesting and pleasing to you; being with much truth, and great esteem & regard Sir Your most Obedt & Very Hble Servt Go: Washington" (ALS, Staatsbibliothek, Berlin: Darmstaedter Autograph Collection; LB, DLC:GW). The dateline reads: "Mount Vernon 25th Sep. 1785."

To William Hartshorne

Sir,   Mount Vernon 14th Septr 1785.
   Colo. Wm Fitzhugh of Maryland has this day requested me, to enter his name for one share of the Potomac navigation; of which I give you this information: he has also deposited in my hands ten pounds for the first & second advances thereon; which I will pay you when I come next to town, or to your order at any time.

   I should take it very kind of you to forward the enclosed letter by the first safe conveyance: it contains a summons of some consequence to me.[1] I am Sir &c.

                                                    G; Washington

LB, DLC:GW.
   1. This may be GW's letter to Thomas Johnson and Thomas Sim Lee of 10 September.

From Battaile Muse

Honorable Sir,   Sepr 14th 1785
   I wrote you Last week Fully respecting your Business—I have now sent to the Care of Mr Hartshorn one bushel Clover seed.[1]

   some Persons has applyed to me Respecting Leaseing Some of your Lands In Fauquier Cy—and I am Told that some of the Tenants are about To remove. I can do nothing respecting that Land as I have no Instructions from you—I shall go to that County about the 25th of this month if its Convenient you will Please to Send me your Instructions Perticularly Respecting

Transferrences and the Conditions for now renting and whether Paying arrears will be sufficient To receive a new Tenant.[2]

Doctr MacKey wishes to rent your Lotts In Winchester on Lease and desires you to say what is your Conditions—the Lotts are so Sittuated that unless the Doctr rents them no one will, as its not Convenient to any Person but Him—I shall be glad to Hear from you next week by Post.[3] I have the Honour to be your Most Obedient Humble Servant

Battaile Muse

ALS, DLC:GW.

1. Presumably Muse is referring to his letter of 6 September.
2. See GW's response of 18 September.
3. See Muse to GW, 6 Sept., n.4. GW does not refer to Dr. Robert Mackey or to his lots in Winchester when he writes to Muse about his tenants on 18 September.

To Tench Tilghman

Dear Sir,　　　　　　　　　Mount Vernon 14th Sepr 1785

Mr Rawlins brought me your letter of the 31st Ulto, and I thank you for sending him. He is to furnish me with a design for my Room, and an estimate of the cost; after which I shall be better able to make an estimate of his conscience.

When Mr O'Donnell has determined on his plan, I shall expect to hear from you.

Enclosed is the Packet mentioned in my last for Mr Smith of Carlisle, wch I pray you to send by a safe, rather than the first opportunity which may offer to that place.[1] With great truth I am—Dear Sir Yr Affecte Hble Servt

Go: Washington

P.S. Since writing the above, Mr W. Fitzhugh of your state, has informed Mrs W. that there is, or was, very fine and pritty Dimety Muslin selling on board the India ship at half a dollar pr yard—If this is yet the case, she desires me to tell you, that she should be much obliged to you for getting her two or three pieces.[2]

ALS, RPJCB; LB, DLC:GW.

1. See GW to Thomas Smith, 10 September.
2. GW's attempts to secure bargains in O'Donnell's sale in Baltimore came to nothing. See Tilghman to GW, 13 October.

To Edmund Randolph

Dear Sir,   Mount Vernon 16th Septr 1785.

It was not in my power to obtain the enclosed in time, to forward them by the last Mail; but they will, I hope, reach you seasonably for your intended meeting on the 26th—by the present mail.[1]

I feel very sensibly, the honor and confidence which has been reposed in me by the James river Company; & regret that it will not be in my power to discharge the duties of the office of President of the Board of Directors, with that punctuallity & attention with the trust requires. Every service however that I can render, compatible with my other avocations, shall be afforded with pleasure; & I am happy in being associated in the business with Gentlemen so competent to the purposes of their appointment—and from what I have heard of the navigation, & seen of the Falls, I think your work may be soon & easily accomplished—& that it will be of great public utility, as well as private emolument to the Subscribers when done: for the advantage of both, tho' I believe the business lies in another line, I would earnestly recommend it to you to press the execution of the Survey between James river & the navigable waters of the Kanhawa, & a proper investigation of the latter. It will be a source of great commerce with the Capitol, & in my opinion will be productive of great political consequences to this Country: the business of a similar nature, as it respects this river, is at an entire stand. Mr Massey, who was first appointed on the part of this State, having declined acting; the Maryland Commissioner knows of no other in his room, & is unable, tho' ready to proceed.[2]

Besides what appears in the minutes which are enclosed, it is in contemplation by the Board of Directors of the Navigation of this river, to endeavor to hire a number of Slaves next year as labourers therein: and as the Great Falls are tremendous, & the navigation thereof, in whatever manner it is attempted, will require much skill & practical knowledge in the execution; we propose, before this is undertaken, to invite a proper person from Europe, who has been employed in works of this kind, as a superintendant of it: With respect to the other parts of the river, tho' what are called the Shanondoah Falls are as difficult in my opinion as the Falls of James river, at Westham, we seem to have confidence enough in ourselves to undertake them; & mean so to do without having recourse to either Canals or Locks. Thro' all the Falls & rapids *above the Great falls*, we mean to attempt nothing more than to open a strait passage to avoid, as much as possible, Currents; giving sufficient depth, & as much smoothness as may be to the surface; and if Rumseys project fails (of which he has not the smallest apprehension) to pull the Boats up by chains floated by buoys; the latter, when Ice begins to form may be slipped & thereby saved; whilst the former riveted to rocks at bottom, may remain during the intemperate season undisturbed & without injury.

Upon an estimate of the expence of these Chains & Buoys, we (that is, the Directors of the Potomac navigation & myself) are of opinion, without having an eye to the probable advantages which are expected to be derived from Rumseys mechanical discovery, that it will be infinitely less than what must arise from cutting canals, building Locks, making track paths &ca, as was the design of Ballendine & others; and will have this advantage over them, that when once done, that is when the passage is opened in a straight direction in the natural bed of the river, it is done as it were forever; whereas Canals & Locks, besides the natural decay of them, are exposed to much injury from Ice, drift-wood, & even the common freshes; in a word, are never safe where there are such sudden inundations & violent torrents, as the rivers in this Country are subject to.

It has so happened that Thursday the 22d inst: is a day of my own appointing to meet the Directors at the Great Falls of this river, for the purpose of examining the place proposed for a Canal; & the river & ground from thence to tide water, on which business I expect to be employed (at least to be from home) four or five days.[3]

Altho' I see no impropriety myself in laying the Proceedings of the Potomac Company before the Board of Directors of the James river navigation, it being my wish that every intelligence which one can give to the other should be mutually afforded; yet it is my desire that the Act may be considered as transmitted for the private information (if it shou'd convey any light) of yourself & the Directors.

We are endeavouring to engage our Miners to bore by the

foot, rather than by the day; but as yet have not agreed with any in this way: they ask a shilling, which we think is too much—to common labourers we pay 40/ per month; and we find paying the workmen every fortnight, rather troublesome—once a month would do better: as they will be frequently moving, we have provided Tents as most convenient & least expensive, for their accommodation.

I find I have been under a mistake with respect to the subscriptions for the James river navigation; I conceived the Books were to lie open 'till the general meeting appointed (as that for this river was) by Law; & if the aggregate amounted to more than the sum required by the act, at such Meeting—they were then to be reduced in the manner therein directed.

The expression of the Law, "the highest point practicable"—is certainly too indifinite; & in the hurry which the Act passed, the import of it was not sufficiently adverted to: but how far it may be politic for the Potomac Company to meddle in the matter, I will not at this moment undertake to decide; as the concurrence of *two* States to effect the alteration, & as one of them it is said by those who are unfriendly to the measure, has been surprized into it.

If it would not be too troublesome for your Secretary, it would be a satisfaction to me to receive a copy of your proceedings. With great esteem & sincere friendship I am Dr Sir &c.

G: Washington

LB, DLC:GW.

1. Randolph on 2 Sept. asked GW for "a copy of the Potomack proceedings." As GW indicates later in this letter, he enclosed for Randolph copies of the minutes of the meetings of the Potomac River Company, held on 17 May and 1 Aug., but not the minutes of the meetings of the company's directors.

2. See Randolph to GW, 2 Sept., n.1.

3. See GW to Thomas Johnson and Thomas Sim Lee, 10 Sept., nn.1 and 2.

From the Mademoiselles Chavexult

Sir   17th Septr 1785.

Two French Ladies, who have always Admired your Virtues, find themselves, by an Unlucky accident, in great Distress, & we take the liberty of Addressing you, as to a feeling, & Compassionate Heart, (with the Same Confidence, that all the World have[)]. Adieu. 3000 Ml. Livres in a Purse, will be of Great Service to us,[1] we have the Honour to be with Respect Sir Your Hble & Obedt servt

Chavexult

My Adress is at Saulieu[2] en Bourgonie, This is the third letter, we had the Honour to write you.[3]

Translation, DLC:GW; ALS, in French, DLC:GW. The translation of the address on the cover of the letter reads: "To Mr Washington General of the Army, of the United States of America, at New England By Nante." A transcription of the ALS is in CD-ROM:GW.

1. The clause in the original after "Heart" ("coeur") reads: "et avec la meme confianse que tou les home en nont a dieu 3000 millione arjan de franse ferai le boneur de notre vie."

2. Saulieu is 23 miles north of Autun on the northeast slopes of the Morvan mountains.

3. What the writer of the letter wrote was: "jai lhoneur de vous ecrire par triplata," meaning that she had written the letter in triplicate. There is in DLC:GW a document dated October 1785 that appears to be a second (partial) translation of the Chavexults' letter.

To Battaile Muse

Sir,   Mount Vernon 18th Sepr 1785.

I have received two or three letters from you of late. The clover Seed which was sent to the care of Mr Hartshorne I have got, and am obliged by the dispatch with which you have sent it.[1]

The great inattention to my Tenants during the nine years that I was absent, and the traffick which they made of my Land (expressly contrary to the Tenor of my Leases) renders it next to impossible for me without being upon the Land, and obtaining oral information, to make out the Accts or to discover in whose possession the Lotts now are precisely—The best sketch I can give, is herewith enclosed; but I do not suppose it to be accurate.[2]

The Man from whom you could have obtained the best information respecting the Tenants—their arrearages of Rents—Transferances, &ca on that Tract of Land which I hold in Ashbys bend (partly in Fauquier & partly in Loudoun counties) was one Lewis Lamart, but he died last spring, after having Collected some of the Rents for me—to Whom to advise you in the next place, I am at a loss. Captn Robert Ashby has a pretty good knowledge of some matters, but either he, or one [of] his Son's, stands I believe among the list of delinquents, which may render his information dubious where his knowledge is most perfect.[3]

Besides the Lotts and Tenants mentioned in the list enclosed, there are, or ought to be, several more of the latter on a Tract I have on Chattins run of Goose Creek, adjoining Captn Robert Ashby; among whom, I presume the Rectors are. But with respect to this Land, I can give less information than on any other. Whether any Leases have ever been given, or not, I am unable to say. What follows, is taken from a Memorandum which I found tied up in the bundle of Leases.[4]

Memm March 16th 1774.

"Agreed with one [   ] Thompson for the Land at the upper end of my Chattins run Tract; That is to give him a lease for it at the rate of £5 pr hundd Acres. He is to have all the Land So. W[es]t of the branch which runs through the Tract, unless there should be enough for two lotts; in which case he is to have but one Lott. Rent to be pd the 25th Decr 1777.[5]

"Also agreed to let Edwd Grymes have the Lott he lives on, extending towards Chattins run & Ashbys mill path for quantity. He also is to have a lease, & to pay at the rate of £5 pr hundd Acres next Christmas.[6]

"Also agreed to Lease Enoch Ashby 150, or 200 Acs. upon the back line, & middle run; he paying at the rate of £5 pr hundd to commence the 25th Decr 1777.[7]

"Also was spoke to for the Lott adjoining this & Edwd Grymes's, by Robt Ashby for one Richard Watts upon the same terms."[8]

The foregoing was taken upon the Land at the time I was there for the purpose of renting it, but what has happened since, as I have observed to you before, I am unable to inform you.[9] I am willing to preserve good faith with every Tenant; and am ready to fulfil all my engagements with them—not only such as are legal & just, but those that are honor⟨able⟩—nay more, such as have no other claim but upon my generosity, where there shall appear a proper conduct on their part—But where you shall find they have taken advantage of me by paying paper Money when Six pence or a Shilling would pay a pound—where they have paid little or no rents at all—and there sole aim seems to have been to make a prey of me, by bartering & selling my Land, solely for their own emolument, I should have no scruple in any of those cases, or any other, which shall appear unjustifiable, to take advantage of the Covenants in the Leases where they have been given; & to refuse them when they have not, set them aside, and re-rent the Land to the highest bidder, & best possible advantage to my Interest.

Enclosed I send you a short power, which may do for the present; & when you come down in October it may be enlarged, & some further light, perhaps, thrown on this business.[10] You will observe that the list inclosed does not include the rents of the present year.

Except in cases where the Tenants are about to remove, and the rents thereby, or by other means are endangered; I would wish you to avoid making distress until you have more precise information, and have had an interview with me in October:[11] for besides the Ballances which appear to be due by the inclosed list, many of my Leases require an alienation Rent for every transference; which, at present, I have not time to look into; but will prepare by October: at which time I will put thc Leases into your hands. In the meanwhile, it would be well for you to examine each Tenant, that I may know by what authority he camc on the Tenemant, how far he has complied with the Covenants of the Lease, what Transferences have taken place—and what Rents (by their receipts, or authentic proofs which no doubt every one of them can shew) has been paid—By doing this some line of conduct may be adopted which will avoid evil & bad consequences either to the tenant or myself. I am Sir Yr Very Hble Servt

Go: Washington

P.S. If you could transmit, previously to your coming down, an account of the information you get, on the above points, the accts may be prepared against you arrive here in October.

ALS, PWacD: Sol Feinstone Collection, on deposit PPAmP; LB, DLC:GW.

1. Muse had written to GW at least twice since GW on 22 Aug. acknowledged the receipt of two letters from Muse written on 16 August. Muse's letters are dated 6 and 14 September.

2. See source note in Lists of Tenants, this date.

3. Lewis Lemart, who leased from GW a 150–acre lot of the Ashby's Bent tract that GW bought in November 1767 from the George Carter estate,

agreed in April 1784 shortly before his death to act as GW's land agent (see Agreement with Lewis Lemart, 10 April 1784, and notes, and Lists of Tenants, 18 Sept. 1785, n.19). Capt. Robert Ashby (1707–1792) lived at Yew Hall in Fauquier County adjoining GW's Chattins Run tract. In the memorandum that he cites in this letter, GW indicates that Enoch Ashby rented land in the Chattins Run tract in 1774.

4. GW acquired his 600–acre Chattins Run tract in Fauquier County from Bryan Fairfax in 1772. See Fairfax to GW, 20 Jan. 1772, and 3 Aug. 1772, n.4. On 28 Nov. 1785 Muse wrote GW giving him a rundown of the people living on the four Chattins Run lots. Only the first man named by GW in this document, John Thompson, was listed as a leaseholder by Muse in November 1785.

5. For a description of John Thompson's tenancy on lot no. 1 of the Chattins Run tract, see Muse to GW, 28 Nov., n.4.

6. This is lot no. 4 of the Chattins Run tract, occupied by three tenants, Edward Graham and James and Peter Rector (see Muse to GW, 28 Nov., n.7).

7. This is lot no. 2 of the Chattins Run tract, occupied by Charles Rector (see Muse to GW, 28 Nov., n.5).

8. This is lot no. 3 of the Chattins Run tract, occupied by William Hansbrough (Handburry) and Jacob and Jesse Rector (see Muse to GW, 28 Nov., n.6).

9. GW was at Lewis Lemart's house on 14 and 15 Mar. 1774, "with my Tenants & making Leases" (*Diaries*, 3:239).

10. The enclosed "Power [of attorney] given to Mr Battaile Muse" reads: "I do hereby authorize, constitute & appoint Mr Battaile Muse to be collector of my rents in the Counties of Berkeley, Frederick, Loudon & Fauquier: and do by these presents empower him to settle with the Tenants, & to make distress for the rents on all cases where it shall be found necessary. I also empower him to rent any of my Lotts which are now vacant; and where he shall find the covenants of the Leases which have already been granted—unattended to by the Tenants—& a disregard of that mutual interest which induced me to dispose of my Lands on the terms therein mentioned, whereby forfeitures are incurred; that he will use every just & proper means to set them aside, & rent them to others on the most advantageous terms for my use, & in my behalf. Given under my hand at Mount Vernon this 20th day of Septemr 1785. Geo: Washington" (LB, DLC:GW).

11. By "making distress," GW means employing a common law remedy to secure the payment of debt by claiming the debtors' personal property.

Lists of Tenants

[Mount Vernon, 18 September 1785]
List of Ballances due His Excelly—Genl Washington by his Tennants in Berkely County, to Date 25th Decr 1784—

[Lot] Nos.	18th Septr 1785	
1	Mr John Reiley[1]	£ 30.
2	Mr Moses Collett[2]	30.
3	Mr Abram Swanger not Entd[3]	
4	Mr Joseph Kersins[4]	36.
5	Mr William Bartless not Entd[5]	
⟨6⟩	Mr Anthony Gholston[6]	26.
7	Mr Saml Scratchfield leas'd David Rankin Examine Scratchfield acct ⟨*illegible*⟩ 26[7]	22.
⟨8⟩	Mr Saml Bailley not Entd[8]	
⟨9⟩	Mr Francis Whiting Esqr.[9]	199. 8

List of Ballances due His Excelly Genl Washington by his Tennants in Fauquier & Loudon, to Date 25th Decr 1784

Lott Nos.	June 18th 1785	
1	Mr Peter Romine[10]	£ 44.
2	Mr Jas Dinson[11]	78.
3	Mr Michael Henry, Leas'd Israel Morris[12]	57.
4	Mr Jas Ballinger[13]	52.
5	Mr Thos Slater, Leas'd Francis Ballinger[14]	52.
6	Mr David Keas, Held by Saml Taylor[15]	25.
7	Mr John Oliphant, Leas'd to William Thomson & Bot of John Dyers[16]	16.⟨*mutilated*⟩
8	Mr Richd Watts, Leas'd to Geo. Russell[17]	2⟨7.*mutilated*⟩
9	Leas'd Mr Edwd Wisely but not Entd[18]	
10	Mr Lewis Lamart, His rect Inclosed[19]	
11 & 12	Mr Thos West, for One Halfe, Leas'd to William Wood	17.⟨*mutilated*⟩
11 & 12	Mr Jos. Milnor, for One Half, Leas'd William Wood, & by West to Do[20]	54.⟨*mutilated*⟩

13 &14	Mr Ezekiel Phillips, Leas'd John Dyers[21]	
16	Mr Ezekiel Phillips, Leas'd Abram Morgan[22]	20.
15	Mr William Donaldson[23]	28.
17	Mr Jas Deermont, Leas'd to Thos Loyd[24]	31.17.7
18	Vacant, or not Leas'd[25]	
19	Mr Deel Clymans[26]	47.18.4
20	Leas'd Mr Isaac Milnor, but not Entd[27]	
16	Mr Abram Morgan, that Leas'd it of John Glascock, owes a Ball.[28]	58.4 ⟨*mutilated*⟩

D, NjMoNP: Smith Collection. William Shaw, who began work as GW's clerk, or secretary, in early August 1785, made the copies printed here of lists of tenants on GW's land in Berkeley County and on his Ashby's Bent tract in Fauquier and Loudoun counties. Shaw copied a third, undated list headed "List of People not Entered," which gives the names of many of those in the two printed lists and also indicates the names of men who had rented lots from the original lessees (see notes below). A fourth, undated but roughly contemporaneous list of the lessees of the nine Berkeley lots and the twenty Fauquier-Loudoun lots is in GW's hand and gives the acreage of each lot and the annual rent charged. At some point, after Battaile Muse as GW's rental agent had supplied the information, Shaw wrote in the margin of GW's list of tenants opposite the lot numbers the name or names of men who had rented that lot from its lessee; the fact that Shaw annotated it indicates that GW's list was retained at Mount Vernon. Reference to Battaile Muse's accounts as GW's rental agent, 1785–90 (NjMoNP: Smith Collection), to miscellaneous memoranda in the Battaile Muse Papers (NcD), and to Muse's correspondence with GW reveals that during the fall and winter of 1785–86 Muse discovered, and made known to GW, payments of rent by the lessees during the Revolution to Samuel Washington, Lund Washington, and Lewis Lemart which were not reflected in the amounts that Shaw set forth in the lists printed here as due. That Shaw heads the list of tenants in Berkeley County with the date 18 Sept. 1785, the date of GW's letter to Muse in which GW says he is enclosing lists of his tenants with the amount of rent due from each, may be only coincidental and not indicate that it is in fact the list that GW enclosed, but there can be little doubt that Shaw copied the lists after his arrival at Mount Vernon in August 1785 and before the end of the year.

Battaile Muse at this time was the agent to collect the rent due on the lots, or tracts of land, that GW held in Frederick, Berkeley, Fauquier, and Loudoun counties, which GW had leased to tenants before the Revolution. Most of the nearly 2,000 acres that GW leased out in Berkeley County was land that he had acquired for himself as a surveyor in the early 1750s on Bullskin Creek and Evitts Run in what was then Frederick County (see George Washington's Professional Surveys, 22 July 1749–25 October 1752, n.24). The twenty lots listed in Fauquier and Loudoun counties, as many as seven that were partly in Fauquier and partly in Loudoun and the rest in Fauquier, are the parcels that GW created in 1769 out of the 2,682–acre tract at Ashby's Bent which he bought from George Carter's estate in 1767 (see Lease to Francis Ballinger, 17 Mar. 1769, and the source note which gives the location in the Fauquier County Deed Book, no. 3, of GW's other leases). Not listed here are the tenants on the 560–acre tract on the Shenandoah River in Frederick County, which GW bought at George Mercer's sale in November 1774, and those on the 600–acre Chattins Run tract in Fauquier County which GW acquired from Bryan Fairfax in 1772. For GW's tenants on the Shenandoah tract, see GW to Muse, 28 July, n.1; for the tenants on the Chattins Run tract, see Muse to GW, 28 Nov. 1785.

There also were two other individual tracts of land in Berkeley County belonging to GW which are not listed here and for which Muse collected rents: the 700–acre Bullskin tract "Near the white House" leased in 1784 by John Ariss for £60 per annum and the tract of 225½ acres "above harewood" leased by Alexander Fryer for £6.15 per annum (Muse's Accounts as Rental Agent, recapitulation of 1790; see also the entries in Muse's other accounts, and Ariss to GW, 5 Aug. 1784, GW to Ariss, 8 Aug. 1784). For the four lots in Frederick County, see GW to Muse, 28 July 1785, n.1.

As the footnotes below indicate, most of the information about GW's tenants and Muse's dealings with them is contained in GW's Ledger B, Battaile Muse's accounts as GW's rental agent, 1785–90 (NjMoNP: Smith Collection), Muse's Rental Rolls for GW, 1788–90 (ViMtV), Robert Lewis's copy, with notations, of Muse's summary of rental accounts (ViMtV), and the Battaile Muse Papers (NcD). Muse's accounts as rental agent are simply a running record of receipts; but when turning over a copy of his accounts to George Augustine Washington in June 1790, Muse included a recapitulation of the tenancy situation for each lot, or tract, in Frederick, Berkeley, Fauquier, and Loudoun counties for which he had collected rent. In ViMtV there is a copy, with additions, of Muse's recapitulation and notations regarding suits against tenants and arrears in their payments, made by GW's clerk Robert Lewis in 1791. Muse's own summary of accounts is cited as recapitulation of 1790, and Lewis's copy as recapitulation of 1791; neither document appears to be extant in its entirety. Muse's Rental Rolls for GW, 1788–90 (ViMtV) are also a running record of debits and credits, but this document arranges the information by lessee and lot number, as in the recapitulation, rather than merely chronologically, as is the case with the NjMoNP ledger.

Between 25 Nov. 1785 and 8 June 1790 Muse records collecting a total of more than £2,200, a good part of it, particularly that from the Fauquier and Loudoun tenants, secured by the order of the county court and through the agency of the county sheriff.

1. On 25 Dec. 1772 John Reiley (Riley) began renting GW's lot no. 1 at the head of Bullskin Run in Berkeley County. The 200–acre tract at the time was

leased to William Peterson, and the lease was transferred to Reiley at £6 per annum "for three lives, viz. his own, and his two Sons Jams & Alexander." Reiley died soon after paying Battaile Muse £18 in back rent on 17 Feb. 1786. The place was taken over by his son George, who paid the annual rent regularly and was the tenant when Muse gave up his position of rent collector for GW in June 1790 (GW to Samuel Washington, 4 Feb. 1773, n.4, Ledger B, 71, 281, Muse's Accounts as Rental Agent, 17 Feb., 6 April 1786, 6 April 1787, 5 April 1788, 2 June, 22 Oct. 1789, 5 May 1790, recapitulation of 1791).

2. In 1773 Moses Collett leased GW's Bullskin lot no. 2, formerly leased to Jacob Fry and containing 200 acres, at an annual rate of £6 for "three lives." After Collett's death, John Steen in 1784 became the tenant. He paid Muse the annual rent regularly until Muse discontinued collecting in 1790 (GW to Samuel Washington, 4 Feb. 1773, n.4, Ledger B, 72, 282, Muse's Accounts as Rental Agent, 6 April 1786, 6 Feb. 1787, 18 Mar. 1788, 9 Feb. 1789, 20 Feb. 1790). For GW's dealings with Collett, see Dolphin Drew to GW, 13 Feb. 1784, nn.2 and 3, and Muse to GW, 15 Nov. 1785, n.3.

3. Lot no. 3 of GW's Bullskin tract, 200 acres at £6 per annum, was leased to Abram Swangar on 22 Mar. 1769 for his life and those of his wife and their son, all three of whom were still alive (see CD-ROM:GW for a transcription of the lease). Col. David Kennedy had at one time rented the lot, but John Dimmitt was now renting the place and still doing so as late as 1790 (Ledger B, 199, 282; Muse's Accounts as Rental Agent, 12, 29 Oct., 5 Nov. 1786, 10 Feb. 1787, 5 Feb. 1788, 14 Jan. 1789, 15 Jan. 1790, recapitulation of 1791; see also GW to Muse, 25 Feb. 1789).

4. On 25 Dec. 1772 Joseph Kerlin leased lot no. 4 "in the Barrens of Bullskin" on Bullskin Run for his life and the lives of his wife Philis and their son Peter. The lot contained 200 acres and rented for £6 per annum. While at his brother Charles's house, Happy Retreat, in September 1784, GW received from Thomas Griggs (Grigg), John Augustine Washington's overseer in Berkeley County, £24 for back rent, and Grigg at this time or later became the tenant on the lot (Ledger B, 101, 199, 283; Muse's Accounts as Rental Agent, 19 Mar. 1786, 5 Feb. 1787, 16 Jan. 1788, 23 Jan. 1789, 4 Jan. 1790, GW to Muse, 8 Mar. 1786). According to Muse's own account with Kerlin, on 30 Sept. 1784, Kerlin was in arrears more than £12 (Battaile Muse Papers, NcD).

5. Before the Revolution lot no. 5 in GW's Bullskin tract containing 125 acres was leased by William Bartlett for £6 per annum. Bartlett died during the Revolution, and the lease passed to his wife, Mary Bartlett. Mrs. Bartlett, who moved to Kentucky, made her final settlement in July 1786 through James Crane, sheriff of Berkeley County. John Bryant who was renting the place took over the lease (Ledger B, 283; undated memorandum and transfer of lease, 5 July 1786, Muse Papers, NcD; Muse's Accounts as Rental Agent, 22 Mar., 5 July 1786, 5 Feb. 1787, 16 Jan. 1788, 26 Jan. 1789, 1 Feb. 1790, recapitulation of 1791). See also Warner Washington to GW, 7 Mar. 1786, and Muse to GW, 11 July 1786.

6. Anthony Gholson took over the rent of GW's Frederick (Berkeley) County lot no. 6 on Evitts Run at the "head of Worthington Marsh" in 1768 from GW's lessee James Bernard. Gholson's lease of the 113 acres at £4 per

annum was for his lifetime and that of his wife Elizabeth and of their son William (Gholson's lease, dated 22 Mar. 1769, is in CD-ROM:GW). Muse has an undated memorandum in his papers stating that Gholson paid the rent in 1775, 1776, and 1777 (see also GW to Muse, 16 Dec. 1787). As early as 1779 David Fulton was occupying the place and paying the rent; GW received payments from Fulton of £10 in September 1784 and £15 in April 1786. Fulton remained the tenant in good standing in 1790 (Ledger A, 266, 305, Ledger B, 199, 284; Muse Papers, NcD; Muse's Accounts as Rental Agent, 10 April 1786, 17 Mar. 1789, 7 Jan. 1790, recapitulation of 1791).

7. David Rankin's lease of lot no. 7 at the "head of Worthington's Marsh" on Evitts Run in Frederick (Berkeley) County, 113 or 114 acres at £4 per annum, dated 22 Mar. 1769, is in CD-ROM:GW. Samuel Scratchfield became the tenant on the lot in 1772. He paid GW £6 in rent at Happy Retreat in September 1784, and he settled his account with Muse in 1786. At that time first James Kircheval (Kirchwell), and then his son Benjamin became tenants on Rankin's leasehold. Benjamin Kircheval was the tenant in 1790 (Account with David Rankin, 17 July 1788, Muse Papers, NcD; Ledger A, 306, Ledger B, 32, 199, 284; Muse's Rental Rolls for GW, 1788–90 [ViMtV], Muse's Accounts as Rental Agent, 27 April, 21 Sept., 3 Nov. 1786, 18 Feb. 1787, 17 Jan. 1788, 11 Feb. 1789, 7 Jan. 1790, recapitulation of 1791).

8. In December 1776 Samuel Bailey leased an unnumbered lot of 183 acres in Berkeley County, described in GW's ledger as "adjoining Wormley." Bailey agreed to pay £10 per annum, and the lease was to run through three lifetimes, his and those of his niece and nephew, Sarah and John Rust. Muse's account with Bailey of 25 Dec. 1785 indicates that Bailey had settled his account, and on 11 July 1786 Muse wrote GW that the Hites were claiming the lot, which GW refuted (see particularly Thornton Washington to GW, 6 June 1786, and GW to Muse, 1 Aug. 1786). Thomas Truman Greenfield was living on the place and paying the rent by 1786. He remained the tenant in 1790 (Muse Papers, NcD; Ledger B, 285; Muse's Accounts as Rental Agent, 28 Jan., 3 July, 9 Oct. 1786, 18 Feb. 1787, 7 Oct. 1788, 9 Feb. 1789, 23 Jan. 1790, recapitulation of 1790, 1791).

9. For Francis Whiting's lease of a 700–acre tract of land in Frederick (Berkeley) County for £50 per annum, see GW to Muse, 3 Nov. 1784, n.3. See also Ledger B, 113, and Ariss's lease, dated 20 April 1786 (ViMtV).

10. Peter Romaine (Romine) leased GW's lot no. 1 in Fauquier County, 120 acres at £4 per annum, in 1773 (Ledger B, 74). Muse wrote GW on 28 Nov. that the lessees of lots 1 and 2 in Fauquier were "Worth nothing." Peter Romaine ran away. Aaron Ruse then rented the land in 1786, but by March 1787 he also had run away. Thereafter William Smith became the "Tenant at Will," but he "was Very Poore & not able to Pay." John Harper "Took a Lease to rent" beginning in 1790 (Ledger B, 287; Muse's Accounts as Rental Agent, 1 Feb., 29 Mar. 1787, 26 Mar., 10 Oct. 1789, recapitulation of 1790).

11. GW opened an account on 25 Dec. 1772 with James Dinson with these words: "the Lott he Lives on—to be Leasd to him⟨,⟩ containg 140 Acres—being Lott No. 2 in Fauquier County—£6." The last entry in the account shows £60 due for the years 1774 to 1784, which was "Settled by my Collector" on

some unspecified date. Living on the lot at this time was a man "not worth anything," named Michael Ruse, who soon ran away. Daniel Harrel began renting the lot as of 25 Dec. 1785 and remained on the land until as late as 1789, when he also "run away." William Collins, who was renting lot no. 4, agreed to rent lot no. 2 as well; his first payment of rent on lot 2 was due 25 Dec. 1791 (Ledger B, 73, 288; Muse to GW, 26 Nov., 28 Nov. 1785; Muse's Accounts as Rental Agent, 1 Feb., 28 Nov. 1787, 20 Sept. 1788, 26 Mar., 5 April 1789, 27 Feb. 1790). In his recapitulation of 1790, Muse indicates that the lot would be leased to James McIntosh instead of to Collins, who was backing out.

12. On 17 Mar. 1769 GW leased his 120–acre lot no. 3 in Fauquier County to Israel Morris for £5 per annum, the lease to run for Morris's lifetime and those of his wife Lettie and son John, all of whom at this time were living in North Carolina. Michael Henry was living on the land in 1772 and remained a tenant through 1784 when Henry Shover (Shoffer) took his place and for the rest of the decade remained behind in his payment of rent (Ledger B, 101, 288; Muse's Accounts as GW's Rental Agent, 1 Mar., 22 May 1786, 2 Sept. 1787, 29 Feb., 25 Mar. 1788, 4, 27 May, 10 Oct. 1789, 27 Feb. 1790, recapitulation of 1790; Muse Papers, NcD, memoranda, 5 Feb., 28 Mar., 26 May 1789; see also Muse to GW, 4 Feb., 15 Oct., 7 Nov. 1787, 7 May 1788, and GW to Muse, 8 Nov. 1787, Lease to Francis Ballinger, 17 Mar. 1769, source note).

13. James Ballinger (Ballenger) was leasing lot no. 4, 120 acres in Fauquier County in 1769. No record of rental payments for this lot before 1788 has been found. In February 1788 there was rent due from one Bates "who run away." William Collins rented the place for £10 per annum in 1788 and 1789 and was offered a ten-year lease which he rejected. James McIntosh rented the lot in 1791 (Lease to Francis Ballinger, 17 Mar. 1769, source note; Ledger B, 71, 289; Muse's Accounts as Rental Agent, 29 Feb. 1788, 26 Mar., 4 May, 10 Oct. 1789, 16 Feb. 1790, recapitulation of 1790, 1791).

14. GW's lot no. 5 in Fauquier County was leased to Francis Ballinger in 1769 and was assigned to the tenant on the place, Thomas Slater, who was to pay the annual rent of £4 beginning on 25 Dec. 1772. The Lease to Francis Ballinger, 17 Mar. 1769, is printed in *Papers, Colonial Series*, 8:171–77. Slater paid the rent for 1772, 1773, and 1774. GW's account with Slater notes that he owed £40 in 1784, which was "Settled by my Collector," no date. William Wood seems to have rented the tract for a while in the 1780s; but John Mc-Donald, whom Muse called "a well disposed Man," secured a lease to the place, on which he lived, to run for ten years from 25 Dec. 1787 (Ledger B, 70; Muse's Accounts as Rental Agent, 27 May 1789, recapitulation of 1790, 1791; Muse's Rental Rolls for GW, 1788–90).

15. A notation on GW's own list of tenants (see source note and Lease to Francis Ballinger, 17 Mar. 1769, source note) indicates that David Keyes (Keas) by January 1779 had paid £18 rent on GW's lot no. 6. The tract of 100 acres rented for £5 per annum. Muse sued and secured a judgment against Keyes in the Fauquier County court on 23 May 1786 for the rent he owed on lots nos. 6 and 7 (see note 16). Keyes on the same day paid £13.10 of what he owed on lot no. 6. He died later in 1786, but by the terms of the lease the lots

passed to his sons Isaac and Jacob (John), who with their mother, Margaret Keyes, continued to rent the two lots. Lot 6, which was initially, in March 1769, leased to James Wood of Fauquier County (Lease to Francis Ballinger, 17 Mar. 1769, source note), was rented after Keyes died by Nathan Cochran who had married the widow Keyes (Ledger B, 290; Muse's Accounts as Rental Agent, 23 May 1786, 29 May, 26 Nov. 1787, 25 Mar. 1788, 7 April, 10 Oct. 1789, 5 Feb. 1790, recapitulation of 1790, 1791; Muse to GW, 4 June, 26 Nov. 1786).

16. William Thompson's lease for three lives of GW's lot no. 7 in Fauquier County was for 115 acres at £4 per annum. John Dyer bought Thompson's lease on 4 Mar. 1775 with the payment of £16, Thompson's four years of unpaid rent. Dyer in turn sold the lease on 25 Dec. 1778 to John Oliphant. Before this date in 1785, Oliphant's account had been settled by GW's "Collector," and David Keyes was renting lot no. 7. Lot 7 remained in the hands of Keyes's widow and sons after his death in 1786. His son Isaac was living on the place in 1790 (Ledger B, 37, 139, 290; Muse's Accounts as Rental Agent, 22 Jan., 1 June, 26 Nov. 1787, 25 Mar. 1788, 7 April 1789, recapitulation of 1790, 1791; Lease to Francis Ballinger, 17 Mar. 1769, source note; see also note 15 and *Diaries*, 3:161). Angle brackets and an em dash are used here and hereafter to indicate mutilated portions of the manuscript.

17. George Russell leased on 17 Mar. 1769 GW's 106–acre lot no. 8, partly in Fauquier County and partly in Loudoun, for £4 per annum. The lease was for Russell's life and those of his wife Ann and daughter Elizabeth, all of whom were alive at this time. Richard Watts was the tenant on the place from the beginning and continued to pay rent during the earlier part of the Revolution. GW's memorandum (of 16 Sept. 1774) quoted in his letter to Muse of this date (18 Sept. 1785) indicates that Watts in 1774 sought to rent a lot in the Chattins Run tract. Abner Griggs (Grigg) had by 1785 been the tenant on lot no. 8 for some time, and after Muse sued and secured a judgment against him, Griggs on 11 April 1786 paid £31.17.10. Muse continued to have trouble with Griggs, and on 19 Feb. 1789 GW instructed Muse to cancel the lease. David Hague, who "went on the Lott in winter 1788 without consent," was renting the place in 1790 (Lease to Francis Ballinger, 17 Mar. 1769, source note; Ledger B, 67, 291; Muse's Accounts as Rental Agent, 11 April 1786, 1 June, 28 Aug. 1787, 13 Oct. 1788, recapitulation of 1790, 1791; Muse's Rental Rolls for GW, 1788–90; see also Muse to GW, 12, 17 Jan. 1786, and ibid., 2:77, 134).

18. GW's lot no. 9, 130 acres of "Very Poore Land" in Fauquier and Loudoun counties, which earlier had been leased to Edward Wisely for £2.10 per annum, had not been "liveed on for many years if Ever" and remained unoccupied in 1790 (Muse to GW, 28 Nov. 1785; Ledger B, 291; GW's List of Tenants [source note]; Muse's Accounts as Rental Agent, recapitulation of 1790, 1791).

19. Lewis Lemart, who had acted as GW's rental agent briefly until his death in the spring of 1785, was a tenant on the land in GW's lot no. 10 which GW had leased to Robert Thompson on 17 Mar. 1769. The lease of the 150 acres in Fauquier and Loudoun counties at a rent of £7 a year was to run through the lives of Thompson, Daniel McPherson (son of Richard McPherson), and Alice Gibson (daughter of Josiah Gibson). Ann Lemart and her sons

continued to rent the property after Lewis Lemart's death. Mrs. Lemart was barely able to pay the current rent for the next three years, but she paid £11.7.6 on 29 Mar. 1787, and on 12 Oct. 1789 she paid £27.4 in arrears (Ledger B, 68, 292; Lease to Francis Ballinger, 17 Mar. 1769, source note; Muse's Accounts as Rental Agent, 18 Jan. 1786, 29 Mar. 1787, 21, 25 Mar., 12 May 1788, 12 Oct. 1789, 6, 18 Feb., 10 May 1790, recapitulation of 1790, 1791; see also Muse to GW, 18 Jan. 1786).

20. On 17 Mar. 1769 William Wood, Jr., obtained a lease on GW's lots 11 and 12 in Fauquier and Loudoun counties. The lease of the two lots totaling 220 acres at a rent of £9 per annum was to run through Wood's life, the life of his brother John and of William Young, the son of John and Margaret Young. Thomas West took possession of the two lots after Wood leased them to him and in 1771 released half the acreage to Joseph Milnor. Milnor paid a total of £24.11.9 in rent between 1774 and 1784 when he settled with GW's "Collector." Between 1784 and 1790 Samuel Oliphant, John Linley, Enoch Furr, James Jones, and Jesse Harris each lived on part of the land in these two lots and paid rent (Ledger B, 67, 108, 292; Lease to Francis Ballinger, 17 Mar. 1769, source note; Muse's Accounts as GW's Rental Agent, 1 Mar., 23 May, 13 June, 16 Oct. 1786, 13 May, 10 Sept., 8 Oct., 13 Nov. 1787, 29 Feb., 21 May, 11 Nov. 1788, 12 Oct. 1789, 5 Feb. 1790, recapitulation of 1790, 1791).

21. Lots 13 and 14 in Fauquier and Loudoun counties contained a total of 227 acres. GW leased them to John Dyer on 17 Mar. 1769 for £10 per annum, to run through the lives of Dyer and his two sons. Dyer assigned one of the lots to Ezekiel Phillips in 1774, who on 24 Mar. 1778 paid £15 for "3 Year's Rent." Phillips is charged in GW's ledger rent for this lot through 1785 and still owed part of it in 1786. On 25 Nov. 1785 Daniel Harris, who by 1783 was renting the other lot, paid £18 and on 1 Feb. 1786, £16.12. James Newland rented the lot where Phillips was living (Ledger A, 328, Ledger B, 37, 139, 293; Lease to Francis Ballinger, 17 Mar. 1769, source note; Muse's Accounts as Rental Agent, 25 Nov. 1785, 23 Jan., 1, 28 Feb. 1786, 14 May, 1 Nov. 1787, 12 May 1788, 7 Jan., 28 Mar., 12 Oct. 1789, 5 Feb. 1790, recapitulation of 1790, 1791; see Muse to GW, 28 Nov. 1785). Muse's memorandum listing receipts before 28 Feb. 1786 for lots 13 and 14 from Phillips and Harris is in the Battaile Muse Papers, NcD.

22. On 17 Mar. 1769 John Glasscock, Jr., secured from GW for his life and the lives of his wife Elizabeth and son Hezekiah a lease of lot no. 16, an 100–acre lot in Fauquier County, at a rental of £5 per annum. He transferred the lease on 25 Dec. 1772 to Abram Morgan, who paid GW £15 in back rent. In 1784 the tenancy was transferred to Ezekiel Phillips, but Robert McWhorter by this time (September 1785) was the tenant. Muse sued McWhorter for rent several times and in 1790 called him "very lazy" (Ledger A, 328, Ledger B, 37, 294; Lease to Francis Ballinger, 17 Mar. 1769, source note; Muse's Accounts as Rental Agent, 8 April 1786, 23 Mar., 29 May, 26 Nov. 1787, 26 May, 24 Nov. 1789, 24 May 1790, recapitulation of 1791). See also Muse to GW, 20 Feb. 1786. GW wrote Muse, 19 Feb. 1789, urging him to collect what McWhorter owed.

23. William Donaldson's lease of 17 Mar. 1769 of lot no. 15 in Fauquier

County, 100 acres at a rent of £4 per annum, ran for his life and the lives of his wife Mary and their son Andrew. Donaldson paid rent through 1783, but as late as March 1787 he owed the rent for 1786. Joseph Parker was now in 1785 the tenant living on the land and remained until late 1789 or early 1790 when he "run away and left a very poor Wife in great distress" (Ledger A, 328, Ledger B, 38, 293; Lease to Francis Ballinger, 17 Mar. 1769, source note; Muse's Accounts as Rental Agent, 8 April 1786, 29 Mar., 30 Aug., 26 Nov. 1787, 26 May 1788, 18 Oct., 24 Nov. 1789, recapitulation of 1791; account of William Donaldson's lease, 25 Dec. 1770–29 Mar. 1787, Muse Papers, NcD).

24. Thomas Loyd's lease of 17 Mar. 1769 of lot no. 17 in Fauquier County provided an annual payment of £5 for 100 acres beginning 25 Dec. 1772. (Muse's records show rent due from 1771.) It was to run for the lives of Loyd, his wife Ann, and of Sarah Sheres, daughter of Thomas Sheres, all of whom were alive at this time. James Dermont (Deermont; Dearman), who was assigned Loyd's lease in 1771, remained a tenant until his death in 1786 shortly after Muse had secured a court order for payment of back rent. William Dermont took over in 1786 and was renting the place in 1790 (Lease to Francis Ballinger, 17 Mar. 1769, source note; Ledger B, 69, 294; Muse's Accounts as Rental Agent, 23 May 1786, 29 May, 26 Nov. 1787, 22 Sept. 1788, recapitulation of 1791; undated memoranda, Muse Papers, NcD). See also Muse to GW, 26 Nov. 1786.

25. Daniel McPherson and John Linley rented lot no. 18 in Fauquier County, 140 acres for £10, before Gerrard McDonald on 25 Dec. 1786 leased it from GW for ten years (Ledger B, 295; Muse's Accounts as Rental Agent, 9 Mar. 1787, 29 Feb. 1788, 28 Mar. 1789, 8 June 1790, recapitulation of 1791; see also Muse to GW, 18 Jan. 1786, and note 4 of that document, and 20 Feb. 1786). McDonald is identified as Israel McDonald in Ledger B.

26. Deel Clymer (Clymant) leased on 17 Mar. 1769 lot no. 19, 160 acres in Fauquier County, for an annual rent of £5, during his and his wife Mary's lives and for the life of his son Philip (Ledger B, 295; Lease to Francis Ballinger, 17 Mar. 1769, source note). Opposite Clymer's name in GW's list (see source note), there is the notation: "1779 Jany 18 £15." Muse took frequent action to force payment from Clymer (Ledger B, 295; Muse's Accounts as Rental Agent, 8 April, 23 May 1786, 29 Mar., 26 Nov. 1787, 26 May, 22 Sept. 1788, 26 Mar., 26 May 1789, 6 Feb. 1790, recapitulation of 1791). For charges that Muse treated Clymer with undue harshness, see Muse to GW, 19 Nov. 1787.

27. On his list, GW indicates that lot no. 20 included 120 acres in Fauquier County and rented for £4 a year. In the "not Entered" list, there is this entry: "Mr Thos Harper, for Isaac Milnor's Lott." See source note. William Wood leased the lot for ten years on 25 Dec. 1787 for a yearly rental of £5 but had run away by 24 Nov. 1789. Muse negotiated a new lease with Job Ward for this "very poor Lott," to run from 25 Dec. 1790. A man named John Raynals (Reynolds) rented the lot for the year 1786, and Joseph Milnor rented it the following year (Ledger B, 296; Muse's Accounts as Rental Agent, 6 Dec. 1787, 29 Feb. 1788, 24 Nov. 1789, recapitulation of 1791). Lewis wrote that Wood's "Obligation of little Acct as he is worth nothing."

28. See note 22.

From William Gordon

My dear Sir   Boston Sepr 19. 1785

Have ⟨just recd⟩ your letter with the Contents written by Mr Mc⟨Henry⟩, & shall attend to your obliging hints, will be more full in my next.[1] Was alarmed at the black seal, & find no particular mention of the occasion.[2] Wish your Lady better health, in which Mrs Gordon would join me & in best respects to yourself, did she know of my writing. Your sincere friend & humble servant

William Gordon

ALS, DLC:GW. The manuscript is mutilated, and the words in angle brackets are conjectures.

1. See GW to Gordon, 31 August. See also Gordon's letter of 26 September.

2. Martha Washington's mother and brother, Frances Jones Dandridge and Bartholomew Dandridge, died in April 1785.

From Benjamin Franklin

Dear Sir   Philad[elphi]a Sept. 20. 1785.

I am just arrived from a Country, where the Reputation of General Washington runs very high,[1] and where every body wishes to see him in Person, but being told that it is not likely he will ever favour them with a Visit, they hope at least for a Sight of his perfect Resemblance by means of their Principal Statuary Mr Houdon, whom Mr Jefferson and my self agreed with to come over for the purpose of taking a Bust, in order to make the intended Statue for the State of Virginia. He is here, but the Materials and Instruments he sent down the Seine from Paris, not being arrived at Havre when we sail'd, he was obliged to leave them, and is now busied in supplying himself here. As soon as that is done, he proposes to wait on you in Virginia, as he understands there is no Prospect of your coming hither, which would indeed make me very happy, as it would give me the Opportunity of congratulating with you personally on the final Success of your long & painful Labours in the Service of our Country, which have laid us all under eternal Obligations.[2] With the greatest and most sincere Esteem & Respect, I am, Dear Sir, Your most obedient & most humble Servant

B. Franklin[3]

ALS, DLC:GW.

1. Franklin arrived in Philadelphia from France on 14 Sept.; GW wrote on 26 Sept. to welcome Franklin home before receiving this letter from Franklin later in the day. See GW to Franklin, 26 September.

2. See GW to Jean Antoine Houdon, 26 September.

3. Below his signature, Franklin wrote: "with Six Letters enclos'd." The letter of this date from Franklin's grandson and secretary, William Temple Franklin (1762–1823), seems to indicate that the younger Franklin enclosed in that letter this letter from his grandfather, Lafayette's letter to GW of 14 July, probably Thomas Jefferson's letters of 10 and 17 July "which were committed to the care of Mr Houdon" (GW to Thomas Jefferson, 26 Sept.), and probably others.

From William Temple Franklin

Sir,   Philad[elphi]a 20th Septr 1785.

Not knowing when I shall have an Opportunity of paying my Respects to your Excellency, an honor which I have long ambitioned, I take the Liberty of forwarding pr Post the Letters committed to my Care.[1] Among these is one from the Marquis de la Fayette, who is well acquainted with my Reverence for your exalted Character and eminent Services, and of which he promised me to acquaint your Exy; but should he have neglected it, I hope you will not be less persuaded of the sincerity thereof, as well as of the Regret I have, in not being at present able to assure you personally of the same. With great Respect, I have the honor to be, Sir, Your Excellency's most obedt & most humble Servant

W.T. Franklin

ALS, DLC:GW.

1. See Benjamin Franklin to GW, this date, n.3.

To Levi Hollingsworth

Sir:—   [Mount Vernon, 20 September 1785]

Your letter of the 24th ult. did not get to my hands until the 17th inst., and then came by Post; for Mr. Jackson is an Inhabitant of Red Stone, 250 miles from me—I am obliged to him however for having taken notice of a wish of mine, which was accidentally expressed before him—More so to you for having facilitated it,—and in a particular manner to Mr. Donaldson, for obligingly offering to carry it into effect.

I have long been convinced, that the bed of the Potomac before my door, contains an inexhaustable fund of manure; and, if I could adopt an easy, simple, and expeditious method of raising, and taking it to the Land, that it may be converted to useful purposes—Mr. Donaldson's Hippopotamus, far exceeds any thing I had conceived with respect to the first; but wether the manner of its working will answer my purposes or not, is the question—By his using a horse, I fear it will not; as I shall have to go from one to eight hundred or 1000 yards from high water mark for the Mud, though I believe any quantity may be had at the lesser distance—The depth of water at the greater, will not exceed eight feet, and not much swell, unless the wind is turbulent, Under this information it would give me great satisfaction to have Mr. Donaldson's opinion of the utility of his Hippopotamus for my purposes; as mud, which is deep and soft, is to be raised at a distance from, and to be brought to the shore, when the tide is up, in vessel that draws but little water, and he would add to the favor (if the Machine is applicable to my wants) to inform me what kind of a Vessel is necessary for its operation—what would be the cost of this Vessel—and of the Machine which is to be employed thereon—wether by a Model the whole could be constructed by good workmen here—or must be done under his own eye, and in that case, what would be the additional expense of bringing them from Philadelphia to this place?[1]

The kind offer of Mr. Donalson, for which I pray you to return him my sincere thanks, to furnish me with a model; or other information,—and your obliging communication thereof, has drawn upon you both this trouble—instead therefor of making an apology for giving it, I will assure you both that I have a grateful sense of the kindness and am his & Yr Most Obed and Obliged Hble Serv't

GEO WASHINGTON

Printed in Thomas Birch's Sons catalog 677, item 1, 15–16 Dec. 1891; LB, DLC:GW.
1. See Arthur Donaldson to GW, 1 October.

From Uzal Ogden

Dear Sir, State of Jersey, Newark 20 Sep. 1785.

Though late, permit me to congratulate you on the Establishment of Peace and Independence to these States, and to mention that I feel Sensations of Gratitude to those, who, under Providence, have been instrumental in obtaining these invaluable Blessings.

May they, by our *Virtue* and *Wisdom*, ever be secured to us, with the Enjoyment of each earthly Good!

I have taken the Liberty to inclose two Pamphlets, which I beg your Acceptance of,[1] and am, with affectionate Regards to Mrs Washington, Dear Sir, Your most obedient and very humble Servant

Uzal Ogden

ALS, DLC:GW.

Uzal Ogden (1744–1822), an Episcopal clergyman from Newark, was a pamphleteer who became a controversial figure in the church after the General Convention in 1799 refused to approve his election as first bishop of New Jersey.

1. The two pamphlets, both of which are in the Boston Athenæum, are entitled: *A Sermon Delivered at Morris-Town, on Monday December 27, 1784, It Being the Festival of St. John the Evangelist, before the Fraternity of Free and Accepted Masons, of Lodge No. 10, in the State of New-Jersey* and *An Address to Those Persons at Elizabeth-Town, and Newark, and in Their Vicinity, in the State of New Jersey, Who Have Lately Been Seriously Impressed with a Desire to Obtain Salvation to Which is Annexed, a Prayer Adapted to a Person in a State of Penitence* (Griffin, *Boston Athenæum Collection*, 154). Both pamphlets were printed in New York in 1785.

From Thomas Johnson

Sir. Fred[eric]k [Md.] 21 Septr 1785.

I received your Letter of the 10th Inst. five days after it's Date and the next Day had an Opportunity of shewing it to Mr Lee he had very lately been to see Mr Rumsay and was Spectator of several successful Blasts—Rumsay had discharged several disorderly Fellows and had but one left that he was any way desirous of getting rid of he had then about twenty Hands. Mr Lee says the Men seemed to work with Spirit and the Difficulties appear less in the progress of the Work than were expected it seems they only want more Strength.

We both think it desirable to hire Negroes as well as purchase Servants but imagine very few can be got in this State perhaps indeed they cannot be removed from hence on the Virginia Side of the Great Falls with propriety[.] we think your supply must be altogether from Virga and we are altogether unacquainted with the common Terms[.] we both must and are willing to submit this Point to yourself and the other Gent. as you are so much better informed than we are[1]—we think their Labour will be more valuable than that of common white Hirelings—As to the Number there's no other check as we see but Employment for them in Winter—your and the other Gents. View of the Great Falls will have enabled you to fall in with my Ideas as to beginning the Cut there or induce you to correct my Guesses[.] if we should go on I imagine we might find Employmt for 100 Hands perhaps more[.] amongst the Servants I think it would be well to have four Smiths some Carpenters and a wheel right or two—As the Season is fast approaching in which we must resolve whether to do any Thing this Winter or not I had determined to meet you at Seneca today and to have gone with you to the Great Falls Tomorrow[2] but last Night I received a pressing Message to go to Annapolis I therefore gave up so much of my Design as to seeing the Great Falls and a very rainy Day prevents my Meeting you at Seneca to remedy it[.] as far as my Situation will allow though I would prefer half an Hours Conversation on the Subject to all I can write aday I have amused myself with writing my Ideas on the Canal and Locks in detail and making Calculations of the Expence which indeed surprizes me for it's smallness in the Amount though I do not see where to add to bring it nearer my former Conjectures—I inclose them to you my Intention must be their Recommendation—I propose to myself the pleasure of seeing you before long.[3]

The Butcher who was to have supplied Mr Stewards party would not enter into the Contract on my Return without being ascertained there should be 50 Rations issued I told him there was a probability of more instead of less and prevailed on him to take a Letter from me to Mr Steward[.] he set off with it but came back without going near Steward or coming to me on his Return[.] I was unwell and knew nothing of his Beh[avio]r for a Week or ten days afterwards[4]—I fear Mr Steward has been equally disappointed about Boats Colo. Clapham has been ill and as has been common with us this Season has had a great proportion of his people sick—he has been obliged to take his own People out of his Crop for he could not hire Hands I dare say he is as much chagrined at the delay as Mr Steward for no Body is more friendly to the Success of the Work than he is.[5] I am Sir Your most obedt Servant

Th: Johnson

ALS, MdHi.

1. See GW to Thomas Johnson and Thomas Sim Lee, 10 Sept., n.1.

2. Because of the heavy rain, GW and his companions did not get to Seneca Falls on the Potomac until late afternoon on this day. They were at the Great Falls the next day (*Diaries*, 4:195–97).

3. Johnson's enclosure has not been identified.

4. In his letter of 10 Sept. to Johnson and Lee, GW notes that the assistant director of the Potomac River project, Richardson Stewart, had complained to George Gilpin that the butcher from Frederick never did show up.

5. On 31 May, at their first meeting, the directors of the Potomac River Company agreed to have Abraham Sheppard and Josias Clapham each build a 35–foot boat for the use of the company. See the minutes of the meeting printed in note 4, GW to James Rumsey, 5 June 1785.

To Thomas Freeman

Sir,   [Mount Vernon] 22d Septr 1785.

If Mr Jonathan Johnson will give one hundred Dollars per ann: for my tract at the Great Meadows, he may have a Lease therefor, for the term of ten years without any other conditions annexed than those of reclaiming the Meadow & putting the whole under a good fence—leaving it to himself to place such buildings on the premises as his own inclination may prompt him to.[1]

Or, if he will build a dwelling House 36 feet by 24; with three rooms below & four above—with two stone chimneys, & fire places in each room—the House to be of hewed Logs or framed work, with glass windows. A Kitchen 16 by 20 feet, of the same kind of work with one stone chimney; And a Stable sufficient to contain twelve horses conveniently—I will allow him two years of the ten, exempt from rent. I am &c.

G: Washington

LB, DLC:GW.

1. See Freeman to GW, 9 June, n.3.

To Darrot

Sir,   Mount Vernon 25th Septr 1785.

Your kind remembrance of me in a letter of the 15th of July from the Island of Tobago, does me much honor; at the same-time that the knowledge of your appointment as Governor of that place, & of your good health, gave me much pleasure. I pray you to be assured that nothing which comes from Colo. D'Arrot can be considered as a trouble; & that to hear, at his moments of leisure, that you are in the enjoyment of perfect health, & the smiles of your Sovereign will always be pleasing; as I recollect with gratitude those instances of attention with which you have honored me, & the circumstances that brought us acquainted.

In the enjoyment of ease & tranquillity, which your sword has contributed to procure, I am now seated under my own Vine & my own Fig-tree in the occupations of rural life, at the Seat which you once honored with your presence; & where I should be happy to meet you again.

At present we have no news that could afford you any enter-tainment: these States are in the full enjoyment of peace; and nothing, it is to be hoped, will disturb the quiet of them. Tho' there is something misterious & not easy to reconcile with the spirit of the treaty, in the British still continuing their Garrisons at the posts of Niagara, Detroit &c.—which are on the American side of the territorial line, notwithstanding a demand has been made of them.

Mrs Washington, who remembers with pleasure your calling here with some Officers of your Legion, thanks you for your attention, & prays you to accept her compliments. With senti-ments of great esteem & regard I have the honor to be Sir, &c.

G: Washington

LB, DLC:GW.

To Lebarbier, the Younger

Sir,   Mount Vernon 25th Septr 1785.

I have been honored with the receipt of your letter dated at Paris the 4th of March; & pray you to accept my thanks for those

copies of your Dramatic performance which you had the goodness to send me; & in which you have made such honorable &
flattering mention of my name.[1]

I lament Sir, that my merits are not equal to your praises—&
regret exceedingly that my deficiency in the knowledge of the
French language does not allow me to become master of the
Drama, & of those sentiments which I am told are beautifully
expressed in it by the author. Upon my gratitude you have a
large claim for those expressions of esteem with which your letter is replete, & which, from a Gentlemen who professes not to
compliment, are the more to be valued. I have the honor to
be &c.

G: Washington

LB, DLC:GW.
    1. See also Richard Henry Lee to GW, 23–31 July 1785, and GW to Lee,
22 August.

To Pusignan

Sir,   Mount Vernon 25th Septr 1785.
    It is not fourteen days since I was honored with your letter of
the 16th of last Octr; to what cause the delay is to be ascribed I
am unable to inform you; but lest this answer with the inclosure
should meet with any accident, I dispatch it under cover to
Count de Rochambeau at Paris.

I am sorry Sir, it is not in my power to comply with your
wishes in regard to the Order of the Cincinnati. The institution
itself points out the different grades of Officers who are to be
admitted into this Society; and at its last General Meeting, the
members thereof in France, of which the Counts de Rochambeau & de Estaing were placed at the head; one in the Military,
the other in the naval Line, were empowered to hold meetings & to decide upon the Claims of Officers belonging to either
department in that Country.

It is there Sir, your pretensions must be offered; & if they are
not precluded by the determination of your Sovereign, will I
doubt not, meet with the liberal & favourable interpretation to
which your merit entitles you. I have the honor to be &c.

G: Washington

LB, DLC:GW.

Letter not found: from Charles Vaughan, 25 Sept. 1785. GW wrote Vaughan on 18 Nov.: "I have had the honor to receive your favor of the 25th of Septr."

To Otho Holland Williams

Dear Sir,   Mount Vernon 25th Sepr 1785.

Your letter of the 15th of Augt from Bath, only got to my hands on Sunday last. The one alluded to, of April, as giving an acct of the miscarriage of the Diplomas, & the best information you could obtain respecting them, nor any other since that which accompanied the Parchments, and wch received an immediate acknowledgement, have reached me at all.[1]

In a word, I never had the least intimation; or knowledge of the accident until Major Jacksons Letter (copy of which I sent you) was delivered to me.[2]

I have since enquired of Colo. Fitzgerald if he could recollect in whose care they were placed—his memory he says does not serve him on this occasion, but he is sure they were entrusted to safe hands, or such as appeared to him at the time to be so—It is a little extraordinary therefore that this person, whoever he may be, should not have given notice of the loss either to him, from whom the parcel was received, or to you, to whom it was intended.

It is to be feared, under these circumstances, that neither the Diploma's, or the money advanced for them, will ever be recovered. however, if you conceive that an Advertisement will effect any valuable purpose—or be satisfactory to the Gentlemen for whose benefit they were designed, you can, as Secretary, recite the event and request information from any who may have it in their power to give it. With great esteem & regard I am—Dear Sir Yr Most Obedt Servt

Go: Washington

ALS, PHi: Dreer Collection; LB, DLC:GW.

1. For references to the correspondence between GW and Williams regarding the loss of the certificates of membership for the officers belonging to the Pennsylvania Society of the Cincinnati, see note 1, Williams to GW, 20 April. Bath was Berkeley Springs.

2. William Jackson's letter is dated 19 July 1785. GW's letter to Williams of 26 July forwarding a copy of Jackson's letter has not been found.

To Benjamin Franklin

Dear Sir,   Mount Vernon 26th Septr 1785.

I had just written, & was about to put into the hands of Mr Taylor, (a Gentleman in the Department of the Secretary for foreign Affairs) the enclosed Letter, when I had the honor to receive by Post your favor of the 20th inst.[1]

I have a grateful sense of the partiality of the French nation towards me; & feel very sensibly the indulgent expression of your letter which does me great honor.

When it suits Mr Houdon to come hither, I will accommodate him in the best manner I am able, & shall endeavour to render his stay as agreeable as I can.[2]

It would give me infinite pleasure to see you: at this place I dare not look for it; tho' to entertain you under my own roof would be doubly gratifying. When, or whether ever I shall have the satisfaction of seeing you at Philada is uncertain; as retirement from the public walks of life has not been so productive of the leisure & ease as might have been expected. With very great esteem & respect, I am Dr Sir, Your most obt &c.

G: Washington

LB, DLC:GW.

1. GW's 25 Sept. letter of welcome to Franklin from Mount Vernon reads: "Dear Sir, Amid the public gratulations on your safe return to America, after a long absence, and the many eminent services you have rendered it—for which as a benefited person I feel the obligation—permit an individual to join the public voice in expressing his sense of them; and to assure you, that as no one entertains more respect for your character, so none can salute you with more sincerity, or with greater pleasure than I do on the occasion. I am—Dear Sir Yr most Obedt and Most Hble Servt Go: Washington" (ALS [facsimile], NN: Emmet Collection; LB, DLC:GW). See also George Taylor, Jr., to GW, 17 October.

2. See GW's letter to Houdon of this date.

To William Temple Franklin

Sir,   Mount Vernon 26th Septr 1785.

The last post gave me the pleasure of receiving your favor of the 20th inst: covering, among others, a letter from the Marquis de la Fayette, who speaks of you to me in very advantageous terms.[1] but your own merit Sir, of which I have heard frequent mention, is alone sufficient to impress me with very favourable sentiments of you; of which I should be happy to give you personal assurances at this place—if inclination, or business should induce you to visit this part of the United States. I am Sir, &c.

G: Washington

LB, DLC:GW; LB, MHi: Adams Papers. For the delivery of this letter, see George Taylor, Jr., to GW, 17 October.

1. See Benjamin Franklin to GW, 20 Sept., n.3. See also Lafayette to GW, 14 July.

From William Gordon

My dear Sir   Jamaica Plain [Mass.] Sepr 26. 1785

I hope your tour has proved satisfactory, & that the obstructions in the river are not invincible, but that the expence of removing them, will be far short of the advantage. The memoirs furnish me with some circumstances, to which I was before a stranger. But in certain places the colouring is too strong.[1] It did not require the bold judgment of a most experienced general to relinquish the Canada expedition, when there were not the means of prosecuting it with any reasonable prospect of success.[2] There was no great manoeuvring in his extricating himself from the critical situation into which he had been brought, perhaps not wholly by the negligence of the militia, but partly by his dropping the night before the hint of his meaning to remain upon the spot till the next morning, & which was forwarded to the British commander. The stupidity of Grant in not going down immediately to & securing the Ford, but passing down a *longer* road to come upon the Marquis, that the Marquis had to pass in order to his gaining the Ford, opened a door for the escape of the latter, which his good sense could not miss of improving. But I should be glad to know from your Excellency, whether Grant had seven thousand men; & whether besides Grays being on the Marquis's left with the light infantry, Generals Howe & Clinton were advancing by the Ridge road with the main body of the British army.[3] I am apprehensive, that Howe had quitted the command before the affair alluded to happened. I have frequently recollected what our friend Genl Knox said to me upon the occasion, "Here we were saved by pure providence without any interposition of our own."

I do not recollect having had the matter represented before as in the Memoirs, on the arrival of the French fleet the Marquis was joined by 3000 French troops, when taking command of the whole, he put in motion all the springs he got ready, Cornwallis was now entangled on every side, while the Marquis took a strong position at Williamsburg. Wish to be informed, whether the French joined the Marquis after landing, & whether he commanded the whole, & whether the French were with him, when he took his strong position at Williamsburg.[4]

As to what follows in the Memoirs "The inducements for attacking the British general, before he had finished his works, had never been so strong as at this moment, but the Marquis still governed by the dictates of that judgment &c. would not sacrifice a sure operation for the uncertain glory of a battle" it might have been spared; for nothing would have been more censurable than an attack at that period, when he was acquainted with the plan of operations concerted against Cornwallis.

Though I cannot place him next to Genl Washington, yet I shall attend to your Excellency's observation, that the Marquis deserves all the gratitude which this country can render, & in speaking to his commendation I shall take heed to do it, in the way you suggest. Information as to the points above mentioned, when leisure will admit of your giving them, will further oblige Your Excellency's sincere friend & humble servant

William Gordon

Mrs Gordon unites in best regards to Self & Lady, for whom I have laid aside some tulips & other flowering roots which I mean to send by the first ship for Alexandria.

ALS, DLC:GW.

1. On 31 Aug. GW forwarded to Gordon the account by James McHenry of Lafayette's role in the American Revolution, which, according to McHenry, he wrote and sent to GW for Gordon at Lafayette's suggestion. See McHenry to GW, 1 August.

2. In January 1778 Congress chose Lafayette to lead an invasion of Canada, labeled by GW "the child of folly" (GW to Thomas Nelson, Jr., 8 Feb. 1778). With Lafayette's support, Congress abandoned in the spring of 1778 plans for

the campaign (see Lafayette to the President of Congress, 11 Mar., and GW to Lafayette, 20 Mar. 1778, in Idzerda, *Lafayette Papers*, 1:344–46, 372–73).

3. Lafayette's "no great manoeuvering" was at Barren Hill, Pa., on 20 May 1778 when he escaped with his men after James Potter's Pennsylvania militia fled from the advancing forces of the British generals James Grant, Charles Grey, William Howe, and Henry Clinton.

4. The French forces under Claude-Henri, marquis de Saint-Simon, were placed under Lafayette's command pending the arrival of GW and Rochambeau at Yorktown.

From Patrick Henry

Dear sir   Richmond Sept. 26th 1785

Your Favor covering Mr Deakins's Letter I received this Morning.[1] As soon as Mr Massey's Resignation was handed to me, the Appointment of Mr Neville was made & sent out to him with a Copy of the Resolution of Assembly. But for Fear they may have miscarry'd I inclose you a Copy, which I must beg you to put in a Way of being forwarded.[2] With the highest Esteem & Regard I am dear Sir Your most obedient Servant

P. Henry

ALS, DLC:GW.

1. See GW to Patrick Henry, 10 September.

2. On 1 Jan. 1785 the Virginia house of delegates: "*Resolved*, That Thomas Massey, Esq., or in case of his death or failing to act through other cause, such person as shall be appointed by the Executive in his stead, be authorised, in conjunction with the person appointed or to be appointed on the part of Maryland, to open and keep in repair a convenient road from such part of the waters of the Potomac, to such part of the river Cheat or of the river Monongalia, as on examination, they shall judge most eligible; and that the sum of 3,333 1–3 dollars arising from the taxes of the year 1784, out of the money subject to votes of the General Assembly, be paid by the treasurer on the joint order of the persons to be appointed as aforesaid, to be by them applied, together with a like sum voted by the State of Maryland, to the purpose aforesaid" (*House of Delegates Journal, 1781–1785*, 101). Thomas Massie (Massey) resigned as major in the 2d Virginia Regiment on 25 June 1779. Presley Neville (1756–1818), who moved from Frederick County, Va., to land on Chartiers Creek in Pennsylvania in 1775, served for a time during the Revolution as a lieutenant colonel in the 8th Virginia Regiment and as one of Lafayette's aides-de-camp.

To Jean Antoine Houdon

Sir,   Mt Vernon 26th Septr 1785.

By a letter which I have lately had the honor to receive from Dr Franklin at Philada, I am informed of your arrival at that place;[1] many letters from very respectable characters in France, as well as the Doctors, inform me of the occasion—for which, tho' the cause is not of my seeking, I feel the most agreeable & grateful sensations. I wish the object of your mission had been more worthy of the masterly strokes of the first Statuary in Europe; for thus you are represented to me.[2]

It will give me pleasure Sir, to welcome you to this seat of my retirement: and whatever I have, or can procure that is necessary to your purposes, or convenient & agreeable to your wishes; you must freely command—as inclination to oblige you, will be among the last things in which I shall be found deficient, either on your arrival, or during your stay. With sentiments of esteem, I am Sir &ca

G: Washington

LB, DLC:GW.
   1. See Benjamin Franklin to GW, 20 September.
   2. For letters introducing Houdon, see Thomas Jefferson to GW, 10 July, and note 1 of that document. Houdon arrived at Mount Vernon on 2 Oct. for a two-week stay.

To Thomas Jefferson

Dear Sir,   Mount Vernon 26th Septr 1785

I have had the honor to receive your favors of the 10th & 17th of July which were committed to the care of Mr Houdon; but I have not yet had the pleasure to see that Gentleman. His Instruments and materials (Doctr Franklin informs me) not being arrived at Havre when they Sailed, he was obliged to leave them; & is now employed in providing others at Philadelphia, with which he will proceed to this place as soon as they are ready.[1] I shall take great pleasure in shewing Mr Houdon every civility, & attention in my power during his stay in this Country, as I feel my self under personal obligations to you & Doctr Franklin (as the State of Virginia have done me the honor to direct a Statue to be erected to my Memory) for havg entrusted the execution of it to so eminent an Artist, & so worthy a character.

I have the pleasure to inform you, that the subscriptions to the inland Navigations of the Rivers Potomack & James require no aid from Foreigners. the product of the first when the Books were exhibited at the General Meeting in May last, amounted to £40,300 Sterling, and is since nearly compleated to the full Sum required by Law. That of the latter, of the General Meeting in August, were superabundant. The work of the former began the first of August, & is progressing very well—the latter I am persuaded will do *more* than keep pace with it, as the difficulties are much less.

I have the further pleasure to inform you (& I should have done it long since, had I not supposed that your information would have been more full & perfect from some of your friends in the Assembly) that a resolution authorizing the Executive to appoint Commissioners to explore & report the best communication between the Waters of Elizabeth River & those of Albemarle passed last Session—That the Commrs have proceeded to the Survey—and have reported in favor of that which will pass through Drummonds pond to the Pasquetank; but what will be the result I am unable to inform you, as I find by some of the principal characters of No. Carolina (Members of Congress) who have called here, that jealousies prevail, & a powerful opposition will be given to any Water Communication between the two States, lest Virginia should derive the benefits arising from their Exports &ca.[2]

I am very happy to find that your sentiments respecting the interest the Assembly was pleased to give me in the two navigations of Potomack & James River, coincide so well with my own. I never, for a moment, entertained an idea of accepting—the difficulty which laboured in my Mind was how to refuse without giving offence. Ultimately I have it in contemplation to apply the profits arising from the Tolls to some public use—In this, if I knew how, I would meet the wishes of the Assembly; but if I am not able to get at these, my own inclination leads me to apply them to the establishment of two charity Schools, one on each river, for the Education & support of poor Children; especially the descendants of those who have fallen in defence of their Country.[3]

I can say nothing decis[iv]ely respecting the Western Settlement of this State. The Inhabitants of Kentucke have held several Conventions, and have resolved to apply for a Seperation. But what may be the final issue of it, is not for me, at this time, to inform you—Opinions, as far as they have come to my knowledge, are diverse. I have uniformly given it as mine, to meet them upon their own ground—draw the best line, & best terms we can of seperation and part good friends. After the next Session of our Assembly more may be discovered, and communicated, and if you should not receive it through a better channel, I will have the honor to inform you.[4]

I am sorry I cannot give you full information respecting Captn Bushnals projects for the destruction of Shipping. No interesting experiment having been made, and my memory being treacherous, I may, in some measure, be mistaken in what I am about to relate.

Bushnel is a Man of great Mechanical powers—fertile of invention—and a master in execution—He came to me in 1776 recommended by Governor Trumbull (now dead) and other respectable characters who were proselites to his plan. Although I wanted faith myself, I furnished him with money, and other aids to carry it into execution. He laboured for sometime ineffectually, & though the advocates for his scheme continued sanguine he never did succeed. One accident or another was always intervening. I then thought, and still think, that it was an effort of genius; but that a combination of too many things were requisite, to expect much Success from the enterprise against an enemy, who are always upon guard. That he had a Machine which was so contrived as to carry a man under water at any depth he chose, and for a considerable time & distance, with an apparatus charged with Powder which he could fasten to a Ships bottom or side & give fire to in any given time (Sufft for him to retire) by means whereof a ship could be blown up, or Sunk, are facts which I believe admit of little doubt—but then, where it was to operate against an enemy, it is no easy matter to get a person hardy enough to encounter the variety of dangers to which he must be exposed. 1[.] from the novelty 2[.] from the difficulty of conducting the Machine, and governing it under Water on Acct of the Currents &ca 3[.] the consequent uncertainty of hitting the object of destination, without rising frequently above water

for fresh observation, wch when near the Vessel, would expose
the Adventurer to a discovery, & almost to certain death—To
these causes I always ascribed the non-performance of his plan,
as he wanted nothing that I could furnish to secure the success
of it. This to the best of my recollection is a true state of the
case—But Humphreys, if I mistake not, being one of the proselites, will be able to give you a more perfect Acct of it than I have
done.[5] With the most perfect esteem & regard I have the honor
to be Dear Sir Yr Most Obedt Servt

Go: Washington

ALS, DLC: Jefferson Papers; LB, DLC:GW.

Jefferson's docket of the letter indicates that it was delivered to him by Houdon on 30 December.

1. See Benjamin Franklin to GW, 20 September.

2. As early as 9 Jan. 1785, James Madison wrote Jefferson of the appointment of commissioners "to survey the ground for a canal between the waters
of Elizabeth river and those of N. Carolina, and . . . to concert a joint plan and
report the same to the next Session of Assembly" (Rutland and Rachal, *Madison Papers*, 8:226). For the report of the commissioners, see Patrick Henry to
GW, 11 Nov., n.2. See also Patrick Henry to GW, 10 June, n.2.

3. For GW's earlier references to the disposition of the stock in the James
River and Potomac River companies given to him by the state, see note 3 in
Jefferson to GW, 10 July. For GW's formal refusal to accept the stock for his
personal profit, see his letters to Madison and Gov. Patrick Henry of 29 October.

4. Although Kentucky formally remained a part of Virginia until 1792, a
Kentucky convention on 28 Oct. submitted a petition to the Virginia legislature calling for the constitutional separation of the Kentucky district from Virginia. A bill to authorize the separation of the Kentucky district from Virginia
was introduced in the Virginia house of delegates in December 1785 and was
passed by the Virginia legislature in early 1786 ("Act Concerning Statehood
for the Kentucky District," 22 Dec. 1785, ibid., 450–53). Madison wrote Jefferson on 27 April of the first of several Kentucky conventions, which he expected
"would be the mother of a separation," a development which would have Madison's support (ibid., 265–72).

5. In his biography of Israel Putnam, David Humphreys gave this description of David Bushnell's submarine in action: "It was the latter end of June,
when the British fleet, which had been at Halifax waiting for reinforcements
from Europe, began to arrive at New-York. To obstruct its passage, some marine preparations had been made. General Putnam, to whom the direction of
the whale-boats, fire-rafts, flat-bottomed boats, and armed vessels, was committed, afforded his patronage to a project for destroying the enemy's shipping by explosion. A *machine*, altogether different from any thing hitherto devised by the art of man, had been invented by Mr. David Bushnell, for *submarine navigation*, which was found to answer the purpose perfectly, of rowing

horizontally at any given depth under water, and of rising or sinking at pleasure. To *this machine*, called the American Turtle, was attached *a magazine of
powder*, which it was intended to be fastened under the bottom of a ship, with
a driving screw, in such sort, that the same stroke which disengaged it from
the machine, should put the internal clock-work in motion. This being done,
the ordinary operation of a gun-lock at the distance of half an hour, an hour,
or any determinate time, would cause the powder to explode, and leave the
effects to the common laws of nature. The simplicity, yet combination discovered in the mechanism of this wonderful machine, were acknowledged by
those skilled in physics, and particularly hydraulics, to be not less ingenious
than novel. The inventor, whose constitution was too feeble to permit him to
perform the labour of rowing the Turtle, had taught his brother to manage it
with perfect dexterity; but unfortunately his brother fell sick of a fever just
before the arrival of the fleet. Recourse was therefore had to a sergeant in
the Connecticut troops; who, having received whatever instructions could be
communicated to him in a short time, went, too late in the night, with all the
apparatus, under the bottom of the Eagle, a sixty-four gun ship, on board of
which the British Admiral, Lord Howe, commanded. In coming up, the screw
that had been calculated to perforate the copper sheathing, unluckily struck
against some iron plates where the rudder is connected with the stern. This
accident, added to the strength of the tide which prevailed, and the want of
adequate skill in the sergeant, occasioned such delay, that the dawn of day
began to appear, whereupon he abandoned the magazine to chance, and after
gaining a proper distance, for the sake of expedition, rowed on the surface
towards the town. General Putnam, who had been on the wharf anxiously
expecting the result, from the first glimmering of light, beheld the machine
near Governor's-Island, and sent a whale-boat to bring it on shore. In about
twenty minutes afterwards the magazine exploded, and blew a vast column of
water to an amazing height in the air" (Humphreys, *Life of Putnam*, 108–12).
See also David Bushnell, "General Principles and Construction of a Submarine Vessel," *Transactions of the American Philosophical Society*, 4 (1799),
303–12.

To Richard Varick

Dear Sir,   Mount Vernon 26th Septr 1785
    Mr Taylor brought me your favor of the 28th Ulto and I have
received your other letter of the 2d of December.[1] for both I
thank you—as also for the proceedings of the Mayors Court in
the case of Rutgars & Waddington, enclosed in the latter. I have
read this with attention, and though I pretend not to be a competent judge of the Law of Nations—or of the Act of your Assembly—nor of the spirit of the Confederation in their niceties,
yet, it should seem to me that the interpretation of them by the

Court is founded in reason & common sense, which is, or ought to be, the foundation of all Law & Government.[2]

I am sorry to hear of your long indispositions, and repeated attacks—It may be well to nurse yourself a little. Disorders, often times, are easier prevented than cured. And while you are in the way to re-establish your health (on which I heartily congratulate you) it is better to use preventatives than alteratives &ca &ca of which the Materiæ Medicæ is replete.

As you are at the source of foreign intelligence, I could only reverberate what you have before heard; and having no domestic News worth communicating, I shall be rather laconic in my pres[en]t address. I enjoy, thank God, very good health; but Mrs Washington is scarce ever well—She joins me in best wishes for you and I am Dear Sir Yr Affecte friend and Obedt Hble Servt

Go: Washington

ALS, NIC; LB, DLC:GW.

1. Letters not found. John Jay's clerk, George Taylor, Jr., left Mount Vernon on 28 Sept., probably with this letter and the letter to Jay of 27 Sept., among others, in hand (*Diaries*, 4:190, 198; see Taylor to GW, 17 Oct., n.1). For GW's association with Richard Varick, see GW to Varick, 1 Jan. 1784, source note.

2. For GW's earlier comments on *Rutgers v. Waddington*, see his letter to James Duane, 10 April 1785.

To John Jay

Dear Sir,   Mount Vernon 27th Sepr 1785

Mr Taylor presented me the honor of your favor of the 25th Ulto—and gave me the pleasure of hearing that Mrs Jay & yourself were well, when he left New York.

Upon your safe return to your native Country, after a long absence, & the important services you have rendered it—in many interesting negotiations—I very sincerely congratulate you, and your Lady.

It gave me great pleasure to hear of your late appointment as Secretary of the United States for the Department of Foreign Affairs—a happier choice, in my opinion, could not have been made—and I shall always rejoice at any circumstance that will contribute either to your honor, Interest, or convenience.

Mr Taylor having accomplished his mission, returns to you with the proceedings and report of the Commissioners, who were sent into New York to inspect the embarkations; which, by the by, was little more than a farce as they inspected no more property than the British chose they should be witness to the embarkation of.[1] It will always give me pleasure to hear from you—Mrs Washington joins me in respectful compliments to, and best wishes for Mrs Jay & Yourself. I am—Dear Sir Yr Most Obedt & Most Hble Servt

Go: Washington

ALS, ViMtV (photocopy); LB, DLC:GW.
   1. See GW to Richard Varick, 26 Sept., n.1. See also George Taylor, Jr., to GW, 17 October.

From Samuel Fraunces

Sir,   New York September 28th 1785
   With the utmost respect I have the Honor to address your Excellency and return my sincerest thanks for your kind inter-position in my business with Mr White[1]—I shall never be able to recompense with my poor services the many obligations your goodness lays me under—for still I am afraid Necessity forces me to be troublesome, I beg your Excellencys patience to hear my numberless misfortunes I am at present in this Cyty but have been obliged to sell my property for very little to pay off a Mort-gage and have bought a small retreat in New Jersey. Notwith-standing I am still unfortunately in debt and cannot receive one penny of or from those that owe me to discharge the same—all the dependence I have is that your Influence being kindly inter-posed will Occasion Mr White to be speedy in assisting me—As my Account is no more than a Book debt I have no further Vouchers (which Mr White requires) than my Books, which have for thirty years past been always proved just; and a Certificate from Gen. Lee which your Excellency is acquainted with, My Son kept my Books and any thing that he can do to satsify Mr White shall be done but I know not whether there be occasion. Your Excellencys goodness emboldens me to tell you I have through necessity been obliged to accept of a small Subscription from a few Gentlemen to relieve my family from Want, could I dare ask such a favour of your hands I would—but I have been too much an imposition on such extreme generosity already, I

have only left to offer up my prayers for your health and happiness and that the latter may exist here and hereafter. I am Sir Your Excellencys Most Obedient and devoted Humble Servant

Samuel Fraunces

ALS, DLC:GW.

1. See Fraunces to GW, 26 June, GW to Alexander White, 14 July, and White to GW, 26 July 1785.

From Arthur Donaldson

Worthy Sir   Philadelphia Octr the 1st 1785

I Esteem my Self highly honourd by your Excelencys faivour to Mr Hollingsworth[1] and Shall Imbrace the Opertunity of Serving you with the greatest freedom Theirfore in the first place hope to remove your doubts of the Hippopomos being Applicable to your purpose by Viewing the Inclosd draught & discription which was publishd in the Pennsylvania Magazine for May 1775[2] but on Account of the War was not put into practice untill this Sumer having the Small Alteration of bringing the hoisting rope Over the horses back & Inverting the Capston. My Maner of useing this Machine is by having Severall large lighters to Carry off the mud &c. to the most Convenient place whilst the Machine is fully Imployd in raiseing it Another Methood may probably be more Convenient for your purpose I would recomend a Vesell about 50 ft long 20 ft broad & about 4 ft deep So as to load the mud in the Same vesell that has the machine in lett hir be Intirely flatt at botom She will lay Stedy on the water & Contain 40 or 50 Cart loads & not Exceed the draught of 3 ft water when loaded She may be dischargd Again by the Griples the Contents thrown in to wagons or on a Shore that is Convenient with A border of a wharf when it may be too Soft to Shovel with Conveniency their it can lay a few days to dry hard enough to move with more ease this will Save a consider expence in equiping & working difrent vesells as well as Shoveling &c. but is not applicable here as Such a Vesell Could not work in many docks whare most wanted & other reasons which may not accur with you In adopting this alteration it will be necessary to Consider the Situation of your ground & Safety of harbour if your Shore is Clear of Stones the botom near levell it will be the better but will require a Safe harbour in rough weather twoo or three men with a horse may load this vesell in a few howers & by take-ing advantage of the tide Come on Shore whare She may Ground safely untill dischargd as above I flatter my Self this mode will be Equell to your Excellencys wish and will not add above one third to the Expence of the within discribed vesell but in Case more dispatch is required then this mode will Admitt of you Can adopt the difrent Vesells in Either Case the Expence of Machinery will be much the Same the whole of which will add about one hundred pound to the price of the vesell & horse to work with.

If After this Information youl think proper to go into the buis-ness by Either method and will honour me with your direc-tions[3] I Shall proceed Accordingly if you wish to have a Good workman Sent to Conduct the building a Sutable vesell Shall endeavour to procure one to whome I Can give particular direc-tions it may be best to gett the Prin[c]iple Ironwork don here by the hand that did mine whoes Experience may be Improv'd and on whome I Can readily Attend & when ready have them Con-veyd round by wa⟨ter⟩ If you wish to hurrey the work (as I Conccive the winter frost us⟨c⟩full to pulverize the manure) I Shall make free to recomend the procureing 1500 or 2000 ft of 2 & ½ Inch Oake plank & the Same Quantity of 2 In. d[itt]o which may probably require time the other Stuff can undoubt-edly be got on Short notice Such as the large Vesell would Cost about £300 in this place but Expect your plenty of timber will greatly reducc the price as to the other methood you Can be better informd the Cost of lighters by your neighbours If you wish to Imploy a Carpenter in your neighbour hood to direct the building I will Send you a Sutable Draught or modell for him to work by if required of Either Sort you Chuse—In Case you proceed I will do my Self the pleasure of an Excurtion into your neighbourhood a few weeks to See the works put together when prepared for beliv⟨e⟩ me Sir it will give me great pleasure to have it in my power to Convay Any usefull Information to mankind More Especially in So usefull an Obiect as the rein-stateing the firtilety of so valuable a part of your first Setlements under the patronage of the first Charactor to whome the united States are Indebted theirfore heartily desire your Exceleny to use the freedom of nameing Any thing I have in my power to

Serve you in without entertaneing the Idea of trouble to me I will not for the present tire your patience with more particulars but to Inquire if you think to Imploy the griples in any thing but Soft Mud as difrent Shapes are necessary for difrent purposes I have twoo pair one without teeth for Soft Mudd and Sand (which I raise for morter) the others have Circular lips with Strong teeth for hard dirt gravell Stones &c. the former supose to be most Sutable for your purpose. I have the honour to be with submition your Excelencys Most Obligd H. Sert

Ar. Donaldson

ALS, DLC:GW.

    1. GW to Levi Hollingsworth, 20 Sept. 1785.

    2. Donaldson enclosed from the May 1775 *Pennsylvania Magazine: or, American Monthly Museum*, the full-page engraving of his dredge (1:206) and the "Description of the Engine" (1:207–8). The artist Pierre-Eugène du Simitière recorded in his notebook in 1775 having made "—a drawing in India ink of a machine for cleansing docks & harbour done for arthur donaldson the Inventor[,] for the Pennsylvania magazine" (William John Potts, "Du Simitiere, Artist, Antiquary, and Naturalist, Projector of the First American Museum, with Some Extracts from His Notebook," *Pennsylvania Magazine of History and Biography*, 13 [1889], 341–75).

    3. See GW to Donaldson, 16 October.

From Louis-Guillaume Otto

Sir.   Newyorck Ober 1st 1785

The Court having thought proper to promote Mr de Marbois to the Intendancy of Hispaniola, has in the same time entrusted me with the place, he had the honor to occupy near the United States of America. It is peculiarly flattering to me in this circumstance to have the adventage of a former aquaintance with Your Excellency and I take hold of the first opportunity to recall myself to your kind remembrance—On my return to France I have been a Witness to the anxiety with which all orders of Citizens expected your arrival there. The Court equally expressed the Warmest desire to receive a man who has excited the admiration of the present and will deserve that of future ages. Many personal friends You would have met with in a Country so closely united with Your own and which seems to be equally indebted to Your exertions for the tranquillity and happiness it now enjoys.

Amongst these the Chevalier de la Luzerne is perhaps the most devoted to your Excellency; he enjoined me particularly to remember him to You and to assure You that on his return to America which will probably take place next Spring he will be extreemely flattered to renew his former intimacy. If in the meanwhile I can be of any use to You at Newyorck or in France I beg You to dispose of my feeble Services and to be persuaded that in affording me such an opportunity You will confer upon me the most flattering favour. With great respect I have the honor to be, Sir, Your Excellency's—Most obedient and very humble Servant.

L.W. Otto.

ALS, DLC:GW.

To Jonathan Trumbull, Jr.

My dear Sir,   Mount Vernon Oct. 1st 1785.

It has so happened, that your letter of the first of last Month did not reach me until Saturdays Post.

You know, too well, the sincere respect & regard I entertained for your venerable fathers public and private character, to require assurances of the concern I felt for his death—or of that sympathy in your feelings for the loss of him, which is prompted by friendship. Under this loss however, great as your pangs may have been at the first shock, you have every thing to console you.

A long, & well spent life in the Service of his Country, placed Govr Trumbull amongst the first of Patriots. In the social duties he yielded to none—and his Lamp, from the common course of Nature, being nearly extinguished—worn down with age & cares, but retaining his mental faculties in perfection, are blessings which rarely attend advanced life. All these combining, have secured to his memory universal respect & love here, and no doubt immeasurable happiness hereafter.

I am sensible that none of these observations can have escaped you—that I can offer nothing which your own reason has not already suggested upon this occasion—& being of Sterne's opinion, that "Before an affliction is digested, consolation comes too soon—and after it is digested—it comes too late: there is but a mark between these two, as fine almost as a hair for a comforter to take aim at." I rarely attempt it, nor shall I add more on this subject to you, as it would only be a renewal of sorrow by recalling afresh to your remembrance things which had better be forgotten.

My principal pursuits are of a rural nature, in which I have great delight, especially as I am blessed with the enjoyment of good health—Mrs Washington on the contrary is hardly ever well, but thankful for your kind remembrance of her, and joins me in every good wish for you, Mrs Trumbull & your family. Be assured that with sentiments of the purest esteem & regard I am, Dear Sir Yr Affecte friend and Obedient Servant

⟨Go: Washington⟩

ALS, ViMtV; LB, DLC:GW; copy (photocopy), DLC:GW. Trumbull endorsed the letter: "Mount Vernon 1 Octo. 1785 from His Exy G. Washington Esqr. —Answer to mine informg of the Gov.'s Death."

From George Mason

Dear Sir   Gunston-Hall [Fairfax County] Octor 2d 1785

I take the Liberty of inclosing You a Memorial and Remonstrance to the General Assembly, confided to me by a particular Freind, whose Name I am not at Liberty to mention; and as the Principles it avows entirely accord with my Sentiments on the Subject (which is a very important one) I have been at the Charge of printing several Copys, to disperse in the different parts of the Country. You will easily perceive that all Manner of Declamation, & Address to the passions, have been avoided, as unfair in themselves, & improper for such a Subject, and altho' the Remonstrance is long, that Brevity has been aimed at; but the Field is extensive.[1]

If upon Consideration, You approve the Arguments, & the principles upon which they are founded, Your Signature will both give the Remonstrance weight, and do it Honour.[2] I wou'd have waited on you personally, upon this Occasion; but have been so shattered by a late violent Fit of the convulsive Cholic, complicated with the Gout in my Stomach, that I am hardly able to walk across the Floor.

The Bearer will deliver you a packet, inclosing another Copy for my Friend Dr Stuart. I am in Hopes He, & his Colleague, will endeavour to forward the Subscriptions in this County. Mrs Mason, & the Family here, present their Compliments to You, Your Lady, & Miss Bassett, with Dear Sir Your affecte & obdt Sert

G. Mason

ALS, DLC:GW.

1. For the text of James Madison's anonymous Memorial and Remonstrance against religious assessment, directed to the Virginia general assembly and dated c.20 June 1785, and for the editors' discussion of the pamphlet, see Rutland and Rachal, *Madison Papers*, 8:295–306.

2. For GW's equivocal response to Mason on this issue, see GW to Mason, 3 October.

From William Grayson

Dear Sir   New York Octob. 3rd 1785

The requisition is at length finished, & which I have now the honor of inclosing; the article of *30,000 dollars* for fœderal buildings at Trenton is expunged; & I think the opposition to that measure is gaining strength. Some of the Southern States begin to view it in a different light.[1]

Congress have passed a resolution authorizing the Post Master general under the direction of the Board of Treasury to contract with the Owners of the Stage coaches for the transportation of the Mail; it is expected the contracts will be formed in the course of the next month: after which there will be three mails a week through the Southern States. A new Ordinance for the Post Office is ready to be reported in which there are clauses for cross posts from Alexandria to Fort Pitt, & from Albany to the limits of Canada, but it is doubtful whether in this present Congress either will take effect.[2]

Mr Payne has a memorial before Congress, to be allowed a sum of money for his services, to which there is a favorable report from a Commee but I am fearful that nothing of consequence will take effect.[3] I have the honor to be with the highest respect Yr Affect. fd & Most Obedt Serv.

Willm Grayson

ALS, DLC:GW.

1. The enclosed broadside, a resolution of Congress dated 27 Sept. 1785 calling upon the states to pay into the common treasury three million dollars

by 1 May 1786, is in DLC:GW. Included in the resolution are the estimates of expenditures for the civil and military departments of the Confederation government, for contingencies, and for interest on both the foreign and the domestic debts, as well as a list of the quotas to be paid by each state. GW's copy of the broadside, signed by Charles Thomson, the secretary of Congress, has this notation: "requisition—1785—200 Copies—received in the office—1st of October—1785—Printed by Mr Dunlop [John Dunlap]."

2. Grayson seconded the resolution that Congress adopted on 7 Sept. to authorize the postmaster general, Ebenezer Hazard, to enter into contracts for carrying the mail from Portsmouth, N.H., to Savannah, Ga., and from New York City to Albany. On 5 Oct. Congress voted to instruct the postmaster general "to establish cross posts, where the same shall thereby be rendered necessary" (*JCC*, 29:684–85, 807–8). On 1 Jan. 1786 mail for the first time was officially transported by stagecoach instead of postrider, but not until the nineteenth century was it carried by coach as far as Savannah. See Oliver Wendell Holmes, "Shall Stagecoaches Carry the Mail?: A Debate of the Confederation Period" (*William and Mary Quarterly*, 3d ser., 20 [1963], 555–73).

3. Congress on 26 Aug. had "*Resolved*, That the early, unsolicited and continued labours of Mr. Thomas Paine, in explaining and enforcing the principles of the late revolution, by ingenious and timely publications upon the nature of liberty and civil government, have been well received by the citizens of these states, and merit the approbation of Congress; and that in consideration of these services, and the benefits produced thereby, Mr. Paine is entitled to a liberal gratification from the United States" (*JCC*, 29:662–63). On this day, 3 Oct., Congress ordered the Board of Treasury to pay Paine "the sum of three thousand dollars, for the considerations mentioned in the resolution of the 26th of August last" (ibid., 796). For GW's earlier attempts to have the state of Virginia reward Paine, see GW to James Madison, 12 June 1784, and Madison to GW, 2 July 1784.

To George Mason

Dr Sir   Mount Vernon 3d Octr 1785.

I have this moment received yours of yesterday's date enclosing a memorial & remonstrance against the assessment Bill, which I will read with attention; at *present* I am unable to do it, on account of company. The Bill itself I do not recollect ever to have read: with *attention* I am certain I never did—but will compare them together.

Altho' no mans sentiments are more opposed to *any kind* of restraint upon religious principles than mine are; yet I must confess, that I am not amongst the number of those who are so much alarmed at the thoughts of making people pay towards the support of that which they profess, if of the denominations of Christians; or declare themselves Jews, Mahomitans or otherwise, & thereby obtain proper relief. As the matter now stands, I wish an assessment had never been agitated—& as it has gone so far, that the Bill could die an easy death; because I think it will be productive of more quiet to the State, than by enacting it into a Law; which, in my opinion, wou'd be impolitic, admitting there is a decided majority for it, to the disgust of a respectable minority. In the first case the matter will soon subside; in the latter it will rankle, & perhaps convulse the State. The Dinner Bell rings, & I must conclude with an expression of my concern for your indisposition. Sincerely & affectionately I am &c. &c.

G: Washington

LB, DLC:GW.

To John Page

My Dr Sir,   Mount Vernon 3d Octr 1785.
The last Post from Richmd gave me the pleasure of your favor of the 9th from Roscwell. Expressions of friendship from good men, & the congratulations of those who are not addicted to unmeaning compliments, cannot fail to be acceptable. In this light I view & thank you for the obliging and endulgent sentiments of your letter, which have affected my mind with gratitude & pleasure.

It will be unnecessary I hope Sir, to assure you of the pleasure I shou'd have felt at seeing you & Mrs Page at Mount Vernon on your way to Philada, if you could have made it convenient & agreeable to have taken this rout—at all times I should be happy to see you here.

Soon after I returned from Richmond in May last, I spoke to a Dutch Merchant in Alexandria on the subject of importing Germans; but not receiving any satisfactory information from him, tho' he was perfectly willing to oblige, I requested him, as he was on the eve of a journey thro' Baltimore to Boston, at both which Dutch Houses are established, & in the last he is concerned, to make every enquiry he could respecting the mode—the terms, & practicability of obtaining the number we want: but meeting with no precise information here neither[1]—

I wrote some little time ago to Mr De Neufville, a Gentleman of very respectable character at Amsterdam, with whom I have long corresponded, for full information; & to know also, if £5000 could be borrowed for the use of the Company on such terms, & upon such securities as it proposed to give. Herein also I have been unlucky; for soon after I had written & had sent my Letter to New York to obtain a passage by the Packet, I received an account of this Gentlemans arrival at Boston.[2] These delays following the enquiries, which I only considered as auxiliary to those of the Managers, to whom I intended to communicate the result, will be unlucky if they have taken no steps in the mean while themselves. Would it not be advisable in case My good Sir, for you as one of them to go fully into the matter whilst you are at Philadelphia, where, it is to be presumed, the best information on this side the Atlantic is to be obtained; & the most likely place to enter into contracts—unless a person in behalf of the Company, should be sent to Holland expressly for this purpose; or a gentleman there, in whom confidence could be placed would undertake it. But unless Mr Anderson should succeed in negotiating the loan he was requested to obtain—or the like sum could be borrowed in Holland, we shall be without funds to carry the Plan into effect, & consequently cannot advance beyond the limits of enquiry—or preliminary agreement.

Mrs Washington joins me in respectful compliments to Mrs Page, who we hope will reap all the benefits which are expected from the change of climate. With very great esteem & regard I am Dr Sir, Yr most Obt &c.

G: Washington

LB, DLC:GW.

1. The "Dutch Merchant in Alexandria" was Huiberts of the firm of Leertouwer, Huiman & Huiberts. See GW to Robert Townsend Hooe, 21 Feb. 1786, n.2.

2. GW's letter to Jean de Neufville is dated 8 September. For the carrier's inability to deliver the letter, see George Taylor, Jr., to GW, 17 October.

To Lucretia Wilhelmina Van Winter

Madame,   Mount Vernon 5th Octr 1785.

To find that the letter which I had the honor of writing to you on the 30th of March last, in acknowledgement of the Poem you had the goodness to send me through the hands of Mr Vogels, has never reached you, gives me pain. I now enclose a copy of it, presuming that the original must have miscarried from my having addressed it to the care of that Gentleman at Philadelphia when, possibly, he might not have been in this Country.[1]

I have now to acknowledge the receipt of your favor of the 10th of April, with the duplicate of the above Poem for which I thank you,[2] and can only repeat to you my wish, that the subject of it was more deserving of your lays. I pray you, Madame, to have the goodness to offer my Compliments to Mr Van Winter, and to be assured of the respect & esteem with which I have the honor to be Your Most obedt & Most Humble Servant

Go: Washington

ALS, Collectie Six, Amsterdam, Holland; LB, DLC:GW. The letter is endorsed 31 Jan. 1786. Lafayette transmitted GW's letter from Paris on 21 Jan. 1786 with a very brief covering letter.

1. The enclosed copy of GW's letter of 30 Mar. 1785 is printed above, under that date.

2. Letter not found. For Van Winter's poem, see Gerard Vogels to GW, 10 Mar. 1784, n.1.

To Armand

My Dr Sir,   Mount Vernon 7th Octr 1785.

Your Letter of the 19th of May was brought to this place by Mr Houdon, who arrived here the 3d of this month. I delay no time to acknowledge the receipt of it, & to thank you for the several communications you have had the goodness to make me.

You are too well acquainted with my wishes for every thing which can promote your interest, honor, or happiness—to suppose that I did not rejoice at the prospect of your being appointed to the command of a Corps; which is agreeable to your own inclination, & which suits your talents: every thing which gratify's the first, & favors the latter, I sincerely wish you may enjoy.

At present every thing in America is tranquil, & I hope will long remain so. It is not our interest to seek new broils—& I hope our neighbours will not commence them. It is not a little misterious however, that the Western Posts, on the American side the territorial line, should still be possessed by British Garrisons: the mistery, it is to be presumed, will *now* soon be explained; as an american Minister has been received at the Court of London.

I never expect to draw my sword again, I can scarcely conceive the cause that would induce me to do it; but if, contrary to all expectation, such an event should take place—I should think it a fortunate circumstance—& myself highly honored, to have it supported by yours. My time is now occupied by rural amusements, in which I have great satisfaction; & my first wish is, altho' it is against the profession of arms & would clip the wings of some of you young soldiers who are soaring after glory, to see the whole world in peace, & the Inhabitants of it as one band of brothers, striving who should contribute most to the happiness of mankind.

Mrs Washington, thankful for your kind remembrance of her, desires me to present her compliments to you. It is unnecessary to assure you of the high esteem & regard with which, I have the honor to be &c.

G: Washington

LB, DLC:GW.

Letter not found: from William Brown, 7 Oct. 1785. GW wrote Brown on 24 Nov.: "I am really ashamed, at this late hour to have the receipt of your favor of the 7th of Octor, to acknowledge."

From Thomas Cushing

Dear Sir   Boston October, 7th 1785

I have the pleasure to Acquaint you of the safe arrival of a very fine Jack Ass, which I have just received from Glocester, a Town in this State, It was Sent to me by Mr David Pea[r]ce a Merchant there, who writes me, it came in a Ship of his from Bilboa & that he was directed to send it to me in order to be forwarded to your Excellency, It was accompanied by a Spaniard, to whose special Care he was Committed untill delivered;[1] All the Intelligence I have directly from Spain relative to this matter is contained in a Letter I have received from Wm Carmichael Esqr. dated Madrid, July 22 1785, Wherein he writes me, that "By the Vessell that conveys this Messrs Gardoqui mean to

Send one of the Jack Asses presented by the King of Spain to our late Commander in Cheif and in Consequence I take the Liberty of repeating my request to you to forward this Animal by the mode you shall judge most expedient to the Southward. Messrs Gardoqui's Correspondent at Beverly will have the Honor of sending you advise of the Arrival of the Vessell and at the same time Inclose you this Letter." Thus far Mr Carmichael —as I received this Letter of Mr Carmichael, not from Messrs Gardoqui's correspondent at Beverly, but by a Vessell that arrived at Glocester, I conclude another of these Animal's has been shiped by a Vessell bound directly to Beverly & whose arrival may be hourly expected.[2] I have taken care that the Spaniard and The Jack Ass should be well provided for, he is a fine Creature, just fifty Eight Inches high, & the largest that I beleive ever came into this Country,[3] As he has been something Bruised upon the Passage by the frequent tossing of the Vessell, although no ways essentially hurt, I shall suspend sending him forward untill he is recruited or perhaps untill the arrival of the other and in the mean Time I should be glad to be favoured with your directions whether to Send them by Land or water, The sooner I have them the better, as it is said Cold Weather does not agree with these animals; It will naturally occur to you, Sir, that it will be very expensive to Send them by Land as I understand the Spaniards (who have the Care of them) are to Accompany them untill delivered to Your Excellency, and as they cannot Speak English must be furnished with an Interpreter and Guide, on the other hand it must be Considered that sending them by water, although it will be less expensive, yet it be attended with a greater Risque; Which ever way you please to have them sent I shall comply with your directions and you may depend, Sir, I shall in this Instance, as well at all other times, with great pleasure execute your Commands and cheerfully contribute all in my Power either to your Pleasure or Emolument.[4] Mrs Cushing my Son & Daughter join with me in tendring their best regards to yourself & your Lady.[5] I remain with great Esteem and respect Your Most Obedt humble servt

Thomas Cushing

ALS, DLC:GW.

Thomas Cushing (1725–1788) represented Boston in the Massachusetts General Court from 1761 and was speaker from 1766 until the colony's charter was revoked in 1774. After the adoption of the Massachusetts constitution of 1780, Cushing was elected lieutenant governor, an office that he held until his death.

1. GW had been anxiously awaiting word of the safe arrival of two jackasses since receiving William Carmichael's letter of 3 Dec. 1784 from Madrid saying that the king of Spain was giving the hero of the American Revolution a pair of the animals. For a general description of the negotiations for the two jacks and of the safe passage of one of the two to Massachusetts and overland from there to Mount Vernon, see note 1 in Carmichael's letter of 3 Dec. 1784. For the details of the shipment of the surviving jackass from Bilbao, Spain, to Gloucester, Mass., see David Pearce to GW, 6 Nov., n.1. The Gloucester merchant was named David Pearce, not Peace, and the Spaniard was Pedro Tellez.

2. As Cushing suspected, Carmichael's letter to him referred to the second jack, the one, as Cushing was soon to learn, that had died at sea. This notice appeared in the *Salem Gazette* (Mass.) on 25 Oct.: "Capt. Ashton, who arrived at Beverly, a few days ago, from Bilboa, brought out one of the four [two] Jack-Asses sent as a present from the King of Spain to General Washington; but the animal, notwithstanding the extraordinary precautions which were taken for insuring his health & safety, died on the passage." In a letter of 3 Aug. 1785 John Gardoqui at Bilbao informed John and Andrew Cabot that he had "shipt on Board the Bearer hereof Capt. John Ashton of the Brigg Remmitance by directions from our very worthy freind Wm Carmichael Esqr. of Madrid a Jackass for Breed, which is to be presented in the name of H.C.M. to Generall Washington therefore as the Brig is bound to your port; we have to request the favour of your forwarding on receipt hereof the within leters to the Honble Thos Cushing Esqr. of Boston who will provide the method of the animals being conveyd to the Generall" (MHi: Nathan Dane Papers).

3. The bill of lading, dated 8 Aug. 1785, referred to in note 1 of William Hartshorne & Co. to GW, 26 Nov., describes the animal being sent to David Pearce as "a he Jack ass fourty four Spanish Inches high." On the back of the manifest, or bill of lading, Lund Washington wrote: "Captn Sullivan informs me 12 of our Inches make 13 Spanish—at same time says in some parts of the Country 12 of our Inches are equal to 14 Spanish—L. Washington."

4. See GW to Cushing, 26 October.

5. Cushing was married to Deborah Fletcher Cushing (d. 1790). His son was Thomas Cushing, Jr. Cushing may have been referring to his unmarried daughter Margaret.

To James Warren

Dear Sir,   Mount Vernon Octr 7th 1785.

The assurances of your friendship, after a silence of more than six years, is extremely pleasing to me.[1] Friendships formed under the circumstances that ours commenced are not easily eradicated, and I can assure you that mine has undergone no diminution. Every occasion therefore of renewing it, will give me pleasure; and I shall be happy, at all times, to hear of yr welfare.

The War, as you have very justly observed, has terminated most advantageously for America—and a large & glorious field is presented to our view. But I confess to you, my dear Sir, that I do not think we possess wisdom, or justice enough to cultivate it properly. Illiberality, Jealousy, & local policy mix too much in all our public Councils for the good government of the Union. In a word, the Confederation appears to me to be little more than an empty sound, and Congress a nugatory body; the ordinances of it being very little attended to.

To me, it is a solecism in politics, indeed it is one of the most extraordinary things in nature, that we should Confederate for National purposes, and yet be affraid to give the rulers thereof who are the Creatures of our own making—appointed for a limited and short duration—who are amenable for every action— recallable at any moment—and subject to all the evils they may be instrumental in producing, sufficient powers to order & direct the affairs of that Nation.

By such policy as this the wheels of government are clogged; & our brightest prospects, and that high expectation which was entertained of us by the wondering world, is turned into astonishment. and from the high ground on which we stood we are descending into the Valleys of confusion & darkness. That we have it in our power to be one of the most respectable Nations upon Earth, admits not, in my humble opinion, of a doubt, if we would pursue a wise, Just, & liberal policy towards one another—and would keep good faith with the rest of the World. That our resources are ample, & encreasing, none can deny; But whilst they are grudgingly applied, or not applied at all, we give the vital stab to public credit, and must sink into contempt in the eyes of Europe.

It has long been a speculative question amongst Philosophers and wise men, whether foreign Commerce is of advantage to any Country—that is, whether the luxury, effeminacy, & corruption which are introduced by it, are counterballanced by the conveniencies and wealth of which it is productive. But the right decision of this question is of very little importance to us. We have abundant reason to be convinced, that the spirit of Trade which pervades these States is not to be restrained. it behoves us therefore to establish it upon just principles; and this, any more than other matters of national concern cannot be done by thirteen heads, differently constructed; The necessity therefore of a controuling power is obvious, and why it should be with-held is beyond comprehension.

The Agricultural Society—lately established in Philadelphia—promises extensive usefulness, if it is prosecuted with spirit—I wish most sincerely that every State in the Union would institute similar ones; and that these Societies would corrispond fully, & freely with each other; & communicate all useful discoveries founded on practice, with a due attention ⟨to⟩ climate, Soil, and Seasons, to the public.

The great Works of improving and extending the inland navigations of the two large Rivers Potomack & James, which interlock with the Western Waters, are already begun; and I have little doubt of their success. The consequences to the Union, in my judgment, are immense—& more so in a political, than in a Commercial point; for unless we can connect the New States, which are rising to our view in the Regions back of us, with those on the Atlantic by interest, the only cement that will bind, and in this case no otherways to be effected than by opening such communications as will make it easier & cheaper for them to bring the product of their labour to our Markets, instead of carrying them to the Spaniards Southwardly, or the British Northwardly, they will be quite a distinct People, and ultimately may be very troublesome neighbours to us. In themselves, considered merely as a hardy race, this may happen; how much more so if linked with either of those Powers in Politics, & Commerce?

It would afford me great pleasure to go over (with a mind more at ease) those grounds in your State which I travelled in the years 1775 and Six; and to congratulate, on the happy change, with those characters who participated of the anxious cares with which those moments were filled; and for whom I entertain a sincere regard; but I do not know whether to flatter myself with the enjoyment of it. The deranged state of my affairs from an absence, and total neglect of them for almost nine years, & a pressure of other matters, allow me little leizure for gratifications of this sort. Mrs Washington offers compliments &

best wishes to Mrs Warren, to which be so good as to present those of Dear Sir Yr Most Obedt Hble Servt

Go: Washington

ALS, MHi: Warren-Adams Correspondence; LB, DLC:GW.

1. Warren wrote GW on 2 September.

To Thomas Blackburn

Monday 10th Octor 1785

Genl & Mrs Washington present their compliments to Colo. & Mrs Blackburne; are much obliged to them for their kind invitation to the Wedding on Thursday. They would attend with pleasure, but for the indisposition of the latter; & the particular engagements of the former which confine him at home this week, & oblige him to attend the Board of Directors at George town, the Great Falls &c. the beginning of next.

The Genl & Mrs Washington will always be happy to see the young couple at Mount Vernon.[1]

LB, DLC:GW.

1. Julia Ann (Nancy) Blackburn, daughter of Col. Thomas Blackburn (d. 1807) and Christian Scott Blackburn, was married to GW's nephew Bushrod Washington, at Rippon Lodge near Dumfries on 13 October. GW posed for Houdon all this week, and on Saturday, 15 Oct., there was a wedding at Mount Vernon when GW's nephew George Augustine Washington married Martha Washington's niece Frances (Fanny) Bassett.

From Lawrence Kortright

Good Sir   New York 10th Octor 1785

Give me leave to address myself to your Excellency, in order to put in my power to get settled my Acct against the United States, in regard to my Sloop Hester, wch Capt Randall, at perticular request of your Excellency, had in the Service for an Arm'd Vessell, wch was taken into pay the 8th April 1776 & discharg'd the 23d August, wch has been Valued And apprais'd by the Wardens of this port wch will undoubtedly be paid. on my Sloop Hester being discharg'd, it was thought proper to dispose of her, w[it]h her warlike stores, for fear of her falling into the hands of the British. Accordingly She was apprais'd for Twenty Eight

Hundred pounds, wch Mr Isaac Sears took at the ap-
praisement, & says he gave Col. Moiland his obligation for the
Same; payable to your Excellency, Col. Moiland Says, if so, it
must have been lost w[it]h the papers he sent to Brunswick. The
Wardens of this port have valued my Sloop w[it]h [t]he Tackel,
at Eleven Hundred & Eighty one pounds, so that a Ballance of
Sixteen Hundred & Nineteen pounds is in Favor of the States,
w[it]h Interest. I shall esteem it a particular kindness done me;
if your Excellency will be kind enough to order, in w[ha]t way I
shall get payment for my Vessell. Your Goodness in this, will
much Oblige your Excellency's Very Humble Sert

Lawrence Kortright

ALS, DLC:GW.

Lawrence Kortright (d. 1794), a merchant in New York whose daughter
Elizabeth within a few weeks, on 16 Feb. 1786, was to marry James Monroe,
made his fortune in privateering during the French and Indian War but, according to Monroe, was now "injur'd in his fortunes by the late war" (Monroe
to Thomas Jefferson, 11 May 1786, in Boyd, *Jefferson Papers*, 9:510–12). Kortright was a large landowner, and in 1790 he was conducting his business at 90
Broadway in New York City.

1. In the spring and summer of 1776, until as late as 27 July, Lt. Col. Benjamin Tupper patrolled the Jersey shore from Amboy to Sandy Hook in the
sloop *Hester*. On 3 Aug. as captain of the *Washington* he was in command of the
galleys that engaged the *Phoenix* in the Hudson River off Tarrytown (Tupper
to GW, 27 July, 3 Aug. 1776, in Morgan, *Naval Documents*, 5:1244–45, 6:37–38).
Capt. Thomas Randall, who was a privateer and New York merchant, managed the privateers commissioned by the state of New York operating out of
Elizabethtown, now known as Elizabeth, New Jersey. Isaac Sears (1730–1786)
in 1776 was acting in Long Island under the directions of Gen. Charles Lee.
Stephen Moylan (1737–1811), a Philadelphia merchant, was GW's aide before
being promoted in 1776 to quartermaster general with the rank of colonel.
No record of Kortright's making a claim on the United States for the loss of the
Hester has been found in the papers of the Continental Congress. For Tupper's
activities in 1785, see Benjamin Tupper to GW, 26 Oct. 1785, n.1.

From Samuel Powel

Dear Sir   Philadelphia 10 October 1785

As I am confident that every Thing, that appears likely to be
of use to our Country, will be readily promoted by you, I have
taken the Liberty of sending you a small Quantity of Wheat imported from the Cape of Good Hope. It is thought to be of a

superior Quality & as such may be worth planting for the Sake of procuring Seed. I have planted nearly as much as I have now sent you, in Clumps of Six Inches square, which gives nine Grains to a Clump, thus [   ],[1] with an Interval of Six or Eight Inches between each Clump in order that the Ground between each Clump may be stirred in the Spring. This is Mr Bordeleys Method, who thinks it is attended with many Advantages over the broad-Cast or drill Sowing.[2]

Mrs Powel begs Leave to join her best Comps & Wishes for yourself & Mrs Washington to those of Dear Sir Your most obedt humble Servt

Samuel Powel

ALS, DLC:GW. "Favored by the revd Mr Griffith" is written on the cover. David Griffith may have delivered the letter on 15 Oct. when he was at Mount Vernon in attendance at the wedding of George Augustine Washington and Fanny Bassett.

1. The diagram inserted here is a square made of three lines of three dots.
2. See GW to Powel, 2 November.

From Richard Henry Lee

Dear Sir,   New York October the 11th 1785

I make no doubt but that you have seen in the public papers that my ill state of health had compelled me to quit this City and Congress to seek relief from leisure and the Chalybiate springs near Philadelphia[1]—It is that circumstance that has prevented me from the pleasure of replying sooner to your favor of August the 22d, which I now do with many thanks for its obliging contents. The advantage that I received to my health from relaxation and the medical power of the springs I visited, has been very flattering, and will I hope furnish me with a stock of health sufficient to finish my Presidential year with some degree of comfort. I hear with singular pleasure that the very important business of opening the navigation of Potomac goes on so well. I well know how much the community will be obliged for success in this useful work to your exertions. By a letter lately received from the hon. Colo. Monroe, who is at Pittsburg and intends to be at the Indian Treaty this month at the mouth of Great Miami; we learn that the temper of the Indian Nations *as nations*, is not unfriendly to the U. States, and promising success, as well to the coming Treaty, as to the execution of the plan for surveying and disposing of territory beyond the Ohio for payment of the public debt. Colo. Monroe represents the Intruding Settlers N.W. of Ohio to be very few in number and they disposed to obey quickly the orders of Congress.[2] The negotiations with Mr Gardoque proceeds so slowly, and as yet so ineffectually, that I fancy the free navigation of Mississippi is a point that we may take it for granted will not hastily be concluded upon. So that mischiefs from that source are probably postponed to a distant day. In G. Britain, they have been so engrossed with Irish affairs, that as yet Mr Adams has done nothing at that Court. He represents the Ministry, or a majority of them, as seemingly well disposed to us; but fearing to do any thing decisive because of the discontent and irritability of the National mind, which he thinks only wants money to recommence the War with us—On which account he recommends careful, steady, & moderate conduct on our part. The dispute between the Emperor & Holland is not yet settled that we know of—But a formidable league of Prussia, Tuscany, & Hanover; with some other powers, is actually signed to preserve inviolate the present State of the Empire against the intrigues of the Emperor who is stated as being much alarmed at this League.

My brother A. Lee, who will have the honor of delivering you this letter will also supply any defect of intelligence that may have happened on my part.[3]

I pray you Sir to present my respectful compliments to your Lady with my wishes for her health. I have the honor to be, with the most perfect esteem, respect, and regard; dear Sir your most affectionate and obedient Servant

Richard Henry Lee

ALS, DLC:GW.

1. Chalybeate springs are mineral springs flavored or impregnated with iron.

2. James Monroe had gone in August to join the commissioners who were to hold a treaty with the western Indians to fix a new boundary. The treaty at Fort McIntosh was not completed until January 1786.

3. GW's response to this letter has not been found, and he makes no mention in his diary of a visit by Arthur Lee until 15 April 1786, but Richard Henry Lee himself with his son Ludwell Lee was a visitor at Mount Vernon on 15 Nov. 1785.

From Richard Graham

Sir,   Dumfries October 12, 1785

I received your packet by last post directed to Mr Henderson enclosing the Surveys of the Great Kanhawa Lands—& the courses of the Lands on the Little Kanhawa for which your Excellency will please accept our thanks. I have taken a Copy of the Surveys & now return them.[1] I must make out a plott of the Little Kanhawa Lands including these Surveys that we may See what Land is left out on the dividing Ridge where Col. Crawford has entered between 40 & 50,000 Acres for Mr Henderson & myself—& we are likely to meet with some difficulty in finding them out—We have the first fifty seven enterys that were made on Mr Maddisons Books Surveyor at that time, of Monongalia 'County—I have taken the liberty to Send you a sketch of the Enterys—As you probably may be able, from your knowledge of that Country to give us Some usefull hints[2]—I have the honor to be with the highest esteem Your Excellencys Most Obedient Servant

Richd Graham

ALS, DLC:GW.

1. The copy of the surveys of his Great Kanawha lands (see GW to Lewis, 1 Feb. 1784, and notes) that GW "directed" to Alexander Henderson (d. 1815) has not been identified. Henderson, a merchant in Colchester, and Richard Graham (d. 1796), who was a merchant in nearby Dumfries, were both heavily involved in speculation in western lands.

2. The "sketch of the Enterys" that Graham enclosed is in DLC:GW. Graham wrote in the margin of his listing: "We are informed that the Lands on the Dividing Ridge are very fine—." "Mr. Maddison" may be William Strothers Madison.

From Tench Tilghman

Dear Sir   Baltimore 13th Octobr 1785

You will wonder at my long silence; but you will excuse me when I inform you, that your letter of the 14th of Sept. found me confined to my Bed by a most Severe nervous Fever, which kept me there near four Weeks. I am now far from being recovered, but as I can mount my Horse, I take daily Exercise, and find my Health and Strength returning by slow degrees.

The packet for Mr Smith, contained in your last, was forwarded, immediately to Carlisle, by a Gentleman in whom I could place intire dependance.

Mr O'Donnells sale, or rather no sale, is over. He held his Goods so extravagantly high, that you might have bought them cheaper out of any Store in Town. He has an Idea they will be in great demand in the Spring, and therefore holds them up.

Be pleased to make my Compliments to Mrs Washington, and inform her, there was no truth in the report she heard of fine dimity Muslin selling at 3/9 ℔ yd on board the ship. I have the honor to be with the highest Respect & Esteem Dear Sir Yr Sincere & Affect: Hble Servt

Tench Tilghman

ALS, DLC:GW.

From Patrick Henry

Dear sir.   Richmond October 14th 1785

I beg Leave to introduce to your Acquaintance the Bearer Capt. Lewis Littlepage who wishes for the Honor of being known to you. I have no Doubt but the Merits of this young Gentleman will render him agreable to you. I have spent some little Time in his Company very happily, & feel myself interested in his future Welfare.[1]

As soon as the Report concerning the intended Water communication with Carolina is made, I shall certainly communicate it to you.[2] I expect it now daily. With the highest Regard & Esteem I am dear sir your very obedient Servant

P. Henry

ALS, DLC:GW.

1. Lewis Littlepage (1762–1802), of Hanover County, did not arrive at Mount Vernon with this letter until 8 November. He carried with him a draft of £300 on the state of Virginia for Houdon in Paris in partial payment for Houdon's statue of GW and was en route to Poland where he was to enter the service of King Stanislas II. Upon leaving Mount Vernon on 9 Nov. he wrote his stepfather, Maj. Lewis Holladay (1751–1820) of Spotsylvania County, from Alexandria: "I have just arrived here from General Washington's, and shall set out in Tomorrow's stage. I was highly pleased with my visit at Mount Vernon, and the General has been kind enough to furnish me with letters of introduction, one to the Governor of Pensylvania in case I should be detained in

Philadelphia, and some others of the same nature for other parts. In other respects I found General Washington much less reserved in conversation than I had been taaught to expect, and was peculiarly happy in having an opportunity of informing myself of many interesting circumstances of the american war, which no person but the General can properly attest" (Holladay Papers, ViHi). For the controversy with John Jay in which Littlepage became embroiled after his arrival in New York, see Lafayette to GW, 6 Feb. 1786, n.10, and Jay to GW, 2, 16 Mar. 1786.

2. Governor Henry enclosed the commissioners' report on the Elizabeth River Canal, dated 15 Oct., in his letter to GW of 11 November. See note 2 of that document.

To Arthur Donaldson

Sir:—   [Mount Vernon, 16 October 1785]

Your letter of the first inst. did not reach my hands until last night, or I would have replied to it sooner.

I am much obliged to you for the Model of your Hippopotamus, and the information which accompanied it,—I have a high expectation of its answering very valuable purposes, if the mud, in the beds of our Rivers, is of that fertilizing nature which the appearance indicate; of which I mean to make a full experiment upon a small scale this fall, having the command of a flat bottom Boat, a scow, with which I can get out as much as will try the effect of different quantities upon small squares of exhausted Land, in all points similar[1]—If the quantity of mud which shall be found necessary from this essay to dress land properly, when added to the expense of the Machine for raising it—bringing it to the Land,—cartage, &c &c does not come too high, I should certainly adopt the measure next year, and will then avail myself of the kind offer you have made me,[2]—In the mean while, I pray you to accept my thanks for your politeness in this instance. I am Sir Yr Most Obed Hble Servt

GEO WASHINGTON

Printed in Thomas Birch Sons catalog no. 677, item 2, 15–16 Dec. 1891.

1. GW borrowed George Gilpin's scow in early November to take mud from the Potomac which he placed on a plot at his River farm. See GW to Gilpin, 29 Oct., n.1.

2. Although GW continued from time to time to experiment at Mount Vernon with the use of mud from the river as fertilizer, no further correspondence with Donaldson regarding his dredge has been found.

To Thomas Freeman

Sir,　　　　　　　　　　　　　　　Mt Vernon 16th Octr 1785.

It is sometime since I wrote in very great haste an answer, or rather an acknowledgement of your letter of the 9th of June. I will now by Mr Craig, endeavour to be more explicit than I was, or could be at that time.[1]

With regard to my Lands on the Ohio & Great Kanhawa, I am not yet inclined to relax from the terms of my printed Advertisement, with a copy of which I furnished you: When I see cause to do it, you shall be duly advertised of the change: in the mean time, if you could discover the *most* advantageous terms which could be obtained, & would advise me thereof, I should be obliged to you.[2] As to the Great Meadow tract, you may rent it on the best terms you can, not exceeding ten years from the first day of January next.[3] My sentiments with respect to the Mill were so fully given to you in my last (by Dr Knight) that it is unnecessary to add aught on that score now. It has cost me too much already (without any return) to undergo a repetition of the like expence. If you cannot rent or sell her as there directed, let her return to dust—the first loss may be best.[4]

I informed you in my last,[5] & I presume you were well convinced of it before, that I made no agreement with the Tenants on the tract near you, which could exonerate them from paying the rents which were *then* due; consequently they must be *made* to pay them; otherwise the most deserving of favor (by having paid) are on a worse footing, than the least deserving who ought to have paid before I went into the Country & explained the terms on which I had directed them to be let.[6]

With respect to Mr Simpsons quitting the Tenement—I observed to you in my last; that when I *make* a bargain I consider it, to all intents & purposes, as binding on me; consequently that it is so on the person with whom it is made. He may well remember, that upon his expressing an idea that he would try the place one year on the rent it now goes at, I told him *explicitly* he must take it for the period on which it was offered, or not at all; as I did not intend to go thro' the same trouble every year by making an annual bargain for it; & that he acquiesced thereto. It behooves him therefore, & the Tenant likewise, to consider what they are about—as one or the other will be liable to me for the rent, agreeably to the tenure of the Lease. I informed you in my last what had been done with the Accounts which were put into my hands by him & Mr John Jones, & requested him to assign the Certificate which I then enclosed, & to return it to me; but have heard nothing from him since on the subject—which is a little surprizing.

I hope the Hay, Corn & other articles have been sold 'ere this, & that you have received the Cash for them, or good security for the payment of the amount of them.

If Mr Simpson, contrary to his agreement and good faith, should have moved off my Land; I am at a loss to decide what had best be done with my Negroes. It was in consideration of his taking the Plantation, that I agreed to let him have the negroes so cheap: If he is gone, or going from it, he shall hold them no longer on the same terms he has them this year—but my wish would be that you could send them to me at this place, if the measure can be reconciled to them. Simon's countrymen, & Nancy's relations are all here, & would be glad to see them; I would make a Carpenter of Simon, to work along with his shipmate Jambo. At any rate I will not suffer them to go down the river, or to any distance where you can not have an eye over them.[7]

What Capt: Crawford did upon my Land on Shirtee in order to save it, must, undoubtedly be well known to those who were most intimately connected with him & his movements at that period. Mr Chas Morgan is as likely to possess this knowledge as any other; but certainly there must be more, & it may be essential to find them out & to call upon them as evidences in the cause.[8]

In a former Letter I informed you that I had obtained a Patent for the round Bottom; & that it might be rented on the same terms with my other Lands on the Ohio & Great Kanhawa; & I repeat it in this, lest a miscarriage should have happened.[9]

When I was out last fall, I left all my Baggage at Mr Simpson's —viz.—Tents—Bed—Bedding & many other things; of which I hope proper care has & will be taken, if he has, or is about to leave the place. Among other Articles there were two, eight gallon Kegs of West India rum—one of them of the first quality. As this is a commodity which is subject to a variety of accidents &

misfortunes, I request it may be sold: I will take my chance to procure more when I may come into that Country; which, at present, is uncertain. If the Tents & bedding should get wet, & are not dryed, they will be ruined; I therefore pray that particular attention may be paid to them, my Canteens, travelling Trunk &c. &c.

If you have received & paid anything on my account since I was out; it may be well to render a statement of it by Mr Craig, who will offer a safe & good opportunity to remit what Cash may be in your hands consequent of the sales of last fall or by other means, after you have deducted your commissions. If the Bonds which were taken at that time are not paid agreeably to the terms of them—delay no time to recover the money as soon as you can; as I am not inclined to be put off with unmeaning promises, & obliged to sue at last.

If my Negros are to come down, the sooner it could happen the better for the young ones: & a careful person should be hired to take care of them. In this case I would wish to have my Baggage (except the Liquor) sent to me at the same time—one trouble & expence would serve both purposes. I am &c.

G: Washington

LB, DLC:GW.

1. GW wrote a brief letter to Freeman on 22 September. Freeman had written to GW on 27 July as well as on 9 June.

2. GW's Advertisement: Ohio Lands, [c.10] Mar. 1784, is printed above as an enclosure in GW to John Witherspoon, 10 Mar. 1784. GW made Freeman his land agent in Pennsylvania in September 1784 (GW to Freeman, 23 Sept. 1784).

3. See Freeman to GW, 9 June 1785, n.3, and GW to Freeman, 22 Sept. 1785.

4. GW's "last (by Dr [William] Knight)" was clearly not that of 22 Sept., in which he does not mention the mill; perhaps he is referring to the missing letter of 11 May. For references to the mill at Washington's Bottom, see Freeman to GW, 9 June 1785, n.4.

5. See note 4.

6. GW is referring to the tenants on the lots at Washington's Bottom.

7. See GW to Clement Biddle, 1 Feb. 1785, n.8, and Freeman to GW, 9 June 1785, n.6.

8. For the case involving settlers on GW's Chartiers Creek tract, see the editorial note in Thomas Smith to GW, 9 Feb. 1785.

9. See GW to Freeman, 11 April 1785, and note 2 of that document.

To George Gilpin

Dear Sir, Mount Vernon Octr 16th 85.

I think your proposition is a very good one—If any question should come before the Board on wch you have not already given your opinion, it may as well be decided at the Falls as elsewhere; your going thither therefore, in the first instance, will certainly expedite the business which occasions (at least in part) the meeting. Indeed it wd seem now (for I do not recollect the cause which induced it) that the meeting at George Town, first, as we are to proceed to the Great Falls afterwards and the Maryland Gentlemen are, in a manner, to pass by them, and then to return to them, is altogether nugatory; for the business of the meeting might as well have been done wholly at that place as partly at both.[1] I am Dear Sir Yr Most Obedt Servt

Go: Washington

ALS, PHi: Gilpin Correspondence.

1. As had been agreed upon, the directors of the Potomac River Company met the next day at Georgetown, Md., "Where, having all assembled, we proceeded towards the Great Falls. . . . Colo. Gilpin—I should have said before—had proceeded on to prepare the way for levelling &ca. at that place, in the morning" (*Diaries*, 4:207).

From George Taylor, Jr.

Sir, New York 17th October 1785

From a desire to give some information respecting my Success in Executing the Commands I had the Honor of receiving from, I have 'till now delayed writing to Your Excellency, nor can I at present give any satisfactory account with respect to a conveyance for the Apples; not a Vessel at present, that I can find, being advertised to Sail for Virginia: But as your Excellency may wish to be informed of the manner in which I have disposed of the Letters committed to my Care, I have the Honor to give you the following account, Vizt.

On my arrival in Philadelphia I waited on the Honorable Doctor Franklin, to whom I delivered the Letter addressed to him —The one enclosed for his Grandson, he requested I would bring on with me, he having left Philadelphia for this Place a few days before, which I accordingly did, and delivered it to Mr

Franklin at the Office. The Letter for Mr Jay I also delivered on my arrival here, I enquired of him, agreeably to your Excellency's desire, whether the Postage of Letters, by the Packet for Europe, was paid here, and was informed that it was not paid until their arrival in Europe. Your Excellency's Letters for Paris will be forwarded with Mr Jay's dispatches by the Packet, which I am told will Sail in three or four Days from this.[1]

When in Philadelphia I made inquiry for Mr De Neufville and was told that he had come on to this Place; but on my repeating it here, I found that he had returned. I therefore took the Liberty of Lodging your Excellency's Letter for that Gentleman with the Dutch Embassador, supposing, that it would have a much more direct and safe conveyance from him, than I could possibly give it.[2]

I did myself the Honor to call on His Excellency the Governor and make your Excellency's and Mrs Washington's compliments to Mrs Clinton and himself—the former was then indisposed and has since been blessed with a Daughter.

Agreeable to your Excellency's desire, I made the Governor acquainted with your Reason for not writing him by me—His Excelly told me that Business had prevented him from writing your Excellency the long Letter he promised on his return from the northward.

I shall delay the purchase of the Apples until I find a Conveyance, which I am informed is very uncertain at this Season—Your Excellency may rely, however, on their being sent, should a seasonable one offer.[3]

Mr Hardy, late a Delegate in Congress from Virginia, died this Morning—He has not been confined to his bed, but I am informed he has long been in a weakly state of Health.[4]

I do myself the Honor to enclose herewith, for your Excelly's perusal, some late News Papers which contain all the News we have here. Permit me to present my most respectful compliments to Mrs Washington. I have the Honor to be, with every Sentiment of Respect, Your Excellency's, Most obedient and Very humble servant,

Geo: Taylor, Junr

ALS, DLC:GW.

1. On 28 Sept., having completed making a copy of the slave embarkation lists (see Jay to GW, 25 Aug., n.1), Taylor left Mount Vernon for Alexandria to

take the stage to New York. GW wrote to Benjamin Franklin on 25 and 26 Sept., to William Franklin on 26 Sept., and to John Jay on 27 September. The "Letters for Paris" undoubtedly included those to Houdon and to Thomas Jefferson, both dated 26 September.

2. See GW to Jean de Neuville, 8 September. See also John Page to GW, 9 Sept., and GW to Page, 3 October.

3. Taylor did not send the apples until spring. See Taylor to GW, 21 Feb. 1786.

4. Samuel Hardy (born c.1758) of Isle of Wight County was elected to Congress in 1783 and 1784, but his illness prevented his attendance after 24 Dec. 1784 (Burnett, *Letters*, 7:lxxvi).

From Grouchet

My General   Paris 20th Octr 1785
Desirous of that which leads to Glory, & the Protection of those, who Commands, I aspire to that of your Excellency, in Demanding to be admitted into the Military Order of Cincinnatus, the Marechall de Richelieu whose Lieutenant I am, & who will be Answerable for me, as he has been a Witness of my first Campaigne at Port Mahon, in the Electorate of Hanover; The Orders of My King, having Oblig'd me to America, whc. I have done my Endeavours to Shew you, by the Writing & Ccrficate; that I have now the Honour to Inclose you. If Mr Suffren, whose Relation I am, had been at Paris, he would have Join'd his Supplication to mine, having told me the last year, to ask this favour of your Excy, Emulous of your Esteem my General, Certain of your Justice, I Conjure you beforehand, the Profound Respect, for your Goodness, & the Gratitude, that a Heart like mine owes to the Kindnesses, of a Great Soul like yours, whc. does So much honour, to Humanity I am with the most Profound Respect My General your Excys most Obed. H. S.
                                                         Grouchet

to Mr le Cte de Grouchet lieut. of the Marechl of France at Dept of St Germain en Paye ches le Marechall de Richelieu in his Hotel at Paris.[1]

Translation, DLC:GW; ALS, in French, DLC:GW. There is a copy of the translation in DLC:GW misdated 20 Oct. 1786.

1. GW responded from Mount Vernon on 19 June 1786 in these terms: "Sir, I have had the honor to receive your letter of the 20th of Octr 1785. together with the certificate of the Duke de Richelieu, Marechall of France.

"The high estimation in which I hold the French nation in general, & the particular respect which I have for those Gentlemen who served in America in the late war, would lead me to grant to a person of your merit every request which I could consistently comply with; but at the last general meeting of the Cincinnati (which is holden but once in three years) those Gentlemen in France who are of that order, were empowered to examine the claims of those of their countrymen who should apply for admission into it, & judge of their qualifications.

"I have not the least doubt Sir, but that upon an application to those gentlemen, (at the head of whom are the Counts d'Estaing & rochambeau) you will meet with every attention you could wish. I am Sir &c. G: Washington" (LB, DLC:GW).

Letter not found: from James Madison, 20 Oct. 1785. On 29 Oct. GW wrote Madison: "Receive my thanks for your obliging favor of the 20th."

To James Madison

Dear Sir   Mount Vernon Oct 22nd 1785

I thank you for the perusal of the enclosed reports—Mr Jay seems to have *laboured the point* respecting the Convention.[1]

If any thing should occur that is interesting, & your leizure will permit it, I should be glad to hear from you on the subject;

Printed in Henkels catalog no. 694, item 30, 6–7 Dec. 1892; copy, MH: Sparks transcripts.

1. The editors of the *Madison Papers* (8:380–81) speculate that Madison either left the "reports" at Mount Vernon on 14 Oct. or forwarded them in a lost letter of c.16 October. The enclosures, which have not been found, undoubtedly were two of John Jay's reports to Congress, one of 4 July 1785 "respecting french and american Consuls" and the other of 19 Sept. 1785 "respecting the number of Consuls necessary to be appointed and for what foreign Ports" (*JCC*, 29:500–515, 722–24). GW's letter to Madison of 29 Oct. supports this supposition. Both of Jay's reports had been printed in New York.

From Caleb Gibbs

My Dear General   Boston Octobr 24th 1785.

The uneaqual distribution of this worlds goods amongst mankind make it necessary for those in a dependent Line to look seriously about them for the mere comforts and necessaries of life, and more particularly when necessity spurs on the subject.

Weavering fortune some times smiles on those (perhaps) lest deserving, in consequence of which makes them happy in this life, with a competency sufficient, to set themselves down in the lap of ease and Independence, while others is carried away with the current of shagreen and disappointment.

This is the case with many of my worthy Brother Officers who have left service, and I will candidly confess, I feel the force of the argument myself, for when thinking to retire from the Feild of Glory after having been instrumental in the establishment, of the Liberties, and Independence of my Country, to be obliged to part with *my notes at two shillings in the pound* (which is the current price they sell for here & which I have received from the public as silver and Gold) makes my blood thrill thro my veins.

This necessity obliges me to live œconomical in every instance, and to part with no more of my securities than my wants immediately call for, yet trusting, if possible to survive a few years longer, that this Country cannot but make good *the money paid to their Army*

Since the dissolution of the Regiment Commanded by Genl Jackson (in which I had the honor to be arranged) I have been floating about from Philadelphia to New Hampshire, negociating a little business partly on Commission, and have never determined to fix muself till within these few months. The unsettled state in which I have lived has occasioned my being totally seperated from my baggage, and since I have collected it, in perusing my papers I find a ballance due me from the United States of 1603 continental dollars, which I borrowed, and lent principally in the month of Octobr 1780, for the use of the Commander in Chiefs family. This your Excellency will easily find by stating the foot of the Account of Expences at the time I left your family, with the monies drawn and received by me; No monies could be obtained from the Pay Master General in all the month of Octobr and in fact none from the public, except of Colo. Pickering of whom on the 15th of Novembr I received 1,000 dollars which was the last sum I received from the public.[1] On the 28th of Novr we went into winter quarters, On the 15th of Decr I went on furlough and returned to Head Quarters, On the 21st of April following and Joined my Regiment the 23d of the same month the day which I gave your Excellency the Books and papers.

Those papers alluded too I have never seen from the time I Joined my regiment till with these few months past, and altho the ballance is intrinsickly small, yet it will be of great service to me, and if any person who has been a Creditor of the United States and can call on them for any ballance no one can do it with more propriety than the American Officers and Soldiers.

If your Excellency agrees with me as I am fully persuaded you will, I will thank you to transmit me a Certificate by an early conveyance, that it may be presented the board of Treasury for payment after they have liquidated the sum agreable to the scale of depreciation between the 4th and 28th of Octobr 1780. If your Excellency directs to me at this place your Letter will find me here, as I shall not leave this Capital but for a few days this winter.

My Love and regard for you and Mrs Washington has several times prompt me the last season to undertake a visit to Mount Vernon but on reconnoitreing my finances I have found it impossible to attempt the march. Therefore I could only offer you to heaven for the best of protections in this life, and the full enjoyment and fruition of Happiness in that which is to come.

Continental as well as State bodies too soon forget their esteem for those they expressed freindship for when in hour of danger, particularly this State, not one Officer since the dissolution of the American Army has been appointed to any post of profit and I beleive with propriety I may venture to assert will not be till they totally eradicate the Idea of his ever being a Continental Officer.

Congress in like manner soon forgot their promise to your Excellency at the time you took leave of them when they told you that those Gentlemen who had been nigh your person thro' the principal dangers of the War should be remembered on some future day (or in words to this effect) that day is far distant for some I fear and which is honesty to confess is somewhat mortifying more especially when we see those who were only Soldiers of a day filling posts of honor and profit.

I beg your Excellency to offer me in most respectful terms to Mrs Washington and family, and all those who ever ask after me.

I have the honor to be With the most profound respect And Esteem Your Excellency's Most Obedient and most humble Servant

C. Gibbs

ALS, DLC:GW.

Caleb Gibbs (c.1750–1818) of Marblehead, Mass., became captain of GW's guards on 12 Mar. 1776. Until 1780, he supervised GW's military household and, from June 1776, kept his household accounts. For a full identification of Gibbs, see GW to the New York Committee of Safety, 6 May 1776, n.2.

1. For Gibbs's record of expenditures for the household between 1 Oct. and 21 Nov. 1780, see Majr Gibbs's Rect Book, 1776–80, DLC:GW, 5th ser., vol. 27; see also vol. 28. No reply to Gibbs's letter has been found.

From William Jackson

Dear General,   Philadelphia October 24th 1785.

In obedience to an order of the Pennsylvania State Society of the Cincinnati, I do myself the honor to transmit Two hundred and fifty diplomas for your Excellency's signature.

Availing ourselves of General Knox's presence in Philadelphia—we presumed to request that he would countersign the diplomas before they were sent to you—and, in order to secure the safe transmission of them, Captain Fullerton, the Assistant Secretary, does himself the honor to wait upon your Excellency in person.[1]

The enclosed address is intended as the prefatory introduction to a pamphlet, containing the general Institution and proceedings of our State-Society, which is now in the press—and which, when completed, I will do myself the honor of transmitting to your Excellency.[2]

We have good reason to conclude, from the present temper of our fellow-citizens, that the Assembly, which meets tomorrow, will grant a charter of incorporation to the Society. With the most respectful sentiments of esteem and affection, I am My dear General, Your obedient humble Servant

W. Jackson

ALS, DLC:GW.

1. For the loss of the Society of the Cincinnati diplomas of the Pennsylvania members sent earlier to GW and signed by him, see Otho Holland Williams to GW, 20 April, and note 1 of that document. Richard Fullerton (d. 1792), who

was brevetted captain in the 1st Pennsylvania Regiment in 1783 and was at this time the assistant secretary of the Pennsylvania Society of the Cincinnati, came to Mount Vernon on 31 Oct., at which time GW signed the new diplomas.

2. The enclosed pamphlet, printed by John Steele in Philadelphia in 1785, is entitled: *Proceedings of the Pennsylvania Society of the Cincinnati. To Which Is Prefixed, the General Institution of the Order, as Originally Framed, and Afterwards Altered at the General Meeting, in May, 1784.*

From Arthur St. Clair

Dear Sir   Philad[elphi]a Octr 25th 1785

This will be handed to you by Capt. Fullerton who waits upon you to obtain your Signature to a number of Diplomas for the Society of the Cincinnati—The Circumstance of their being previously countersigned by General Knox Major Jackson has I hope explained[1]—which, with the Wish the gentlemen of this State have to see their Title compleated, with the Accident that formerly happened will excuse that Irregularity. The Jealousys that have subsisted with Respect to the Institution are, certainly, as you observe, rather asleep than subsided, that is in every part of the Country—I believe they are subsided here, and I trust it will not be long before we shall obtain a Charter—all Ranks of People appearing to be satisfied with the Alterations in the original Constitution, and that Charity and Benevolence are now the only Pillars on which the Institution rests.

I should have done myself the honor to acknowledge the receipt of your very obliging Letter earlier[2] but that this Journey of Captain Fullerton has been some time in Contemplation, and I do not like to obtrude myself tho I have very much Pleasure in every Opportunity of testifying my regard and Affection, and if I had had your Letter by me at present I might perhaps have replied more particularly but Sir I feel and ever shall feel the whole force of the very delicate Compliment you were pleased to pay me upon the Appointment to the Office I now hold— It was certainly very convenient to me tho far from being so lucrative as is generally supposed—but its worth to me arose from the Motive you have suggested. I beg you will present my Compliments to Mrs Washington and believe me to be ever Dear Sir your very sincere and affectionate humble Servant

Ar. St Clair

ALS, DLC:GW.
1. See William Jackson to GW, 24 October.
2. GW wrote St. Clair on 31 Aug. 1785.

To Thomas Cushing

Dear Sir,   Mount Vernon 26th Octor 1785.

The last Post gave me the honor of your favor of the 7th inst: for which & your care of the Jack and his Keeper, I pray you to accept my grateful thanks.

As the Jack is now safely landed, & as I am unwilling to hazard him again at Sea, I have sent a man in whom I can confide, to conduct him & the Spaniard to this place by Land. The person I send has not the smallest knowledge of the Spanish language, consequently there can be little communication between him & the Spaniard on the road; but if there is a convention established by means of an Interpreter at Boston, & essentials well understood by the parties before they commence their journey; there will not be such an occasion for an Interpreter on the road, as to be a counterpoize for the expence, as Mr Fairfax whom I send will be both guide & paymaster, leaving nothing for the Spaniard to do but to be attentive to the animal. The hour for starting in the morning & putting up in the evening, and feeding in the meantime being fixed: the halting days, & kind of food for the Jack & manner of treating the Spaniard settled & clearly understood; will remove all difficulties of consequence on the road—at least 'till they get to New York, where by means of the Spanish Minister's attendants an explanation of them, if any there be, may enable the parties to pursue the rest of their journey with more ease.[1]

As I expect two Jacks it would give me great pleasure if the second should have arrived; that one trouble & expence might serve both.[2] Mr Fairfax, the bearer of this, goes from hence to Boston in the Stage, & will have to buy a horse to return home upon. I prefered this method on account of the dispatch with which he would reach Boston; & because the whole journey might be too much for one horse taken from hence, to perform in a short time. If the Jack is led, two horses will be wanted—& if two Jacks are arrived—three may be necessary. These uncertainties, and the danger of trusting a large sum in specie to a man who has not been much accustom'd to the care of it, tho' perfectly honest, have induced me to request the favor of you to obtain from any of the Merchants in Boston who have dealings in, & who may want to make remittances to Alexandria, as much money as will make these purchases, & defray the expences of the Men & Horses back to me; the Bill, for the amount of which, shall be paid at sight; as also the charges which Mr Pea[r]ce may have against me—the cost of getting him from Gloucester to you,[3] & such other expences as may have arisen during their stay in Boston—in short the whole. Mr Fairfax has directions with respect to the kind of horses I want, & will take your advice how to procure them on the best terms, as well as in all other matters—for the favor of which I shall be much obliged to you. Mrs Washington joins me in respectful compliments to Mrs Cushing, your son & daughter; & with great esteem & regard, I have the honor to be &c.

G: Washington

LB, DLC:GW.

1. See GW's instructions to John Fairfax, this date.

2. For the loss of one of the jackasses, see Cushing to GW, 7 Oct., n.2.

3. For David Pearce's charges, see William Hartshorne & Co. to GW, 26 Nov., n.1.

To John Fairfax

Mount Vernon 26th Octr 1785.

You will proceed in the Stage from Alexandria to Boston, without losing a day that can possibly be avoided; & when arrived at the latter place, deliver the Letter herewith given you to the Hone Thos Cushing, Lieut: Governor of the State of Massachusetts, who resides in the town of Boston, & whose directions you are to follow.[1]

The intention of your going thither is, to bring one—perhaps two Jack asses, which have been imported for me from Spain: a

Spaniard is arrived with, & attends the first; & probably if the
second is arrived, there will be one with him also: one, or both
of these men, according to the instructions they may have received in Spain, or agreeably to the directions you may receive
from the Lieut: Governor, are to come on with you & the Jacks.

As you will have to ride back, & as this will be the case also
with the Spaniards, (if there are more than one) Horses, if it is
thought improper to ride on the Jacks, will be to be bought—&
as females will answer my purposes best, I desire you to buy
Mares: let them be young, sound & of good size, as I propose to
put them to the Jacks in the season for covering: Lieut: Govr
Cushing will furnish you with money, and aid you with his advice in this purchase; as also to defray your expences in returning.

You know too well the high value I set upon these Jacks, to
neglect them on the road in any instance whatsoever; but if the
one which is now at Boston, & the other if it arrives in time,
should come on under their proper keepers, your business will
then be to see that every thing necessary is provided—leaving
the management of them to the Spaniard or Spaniards who will
attend them, & who best know how to travel & feed them. See
however (if their keepers are drunken & neglectful) that due
attention & care are bestowed on these animals.

As I do not mean to be at the expence of hiring & bringing
on an Interpreter (altho' neither of the Spaniards should speak
English) you would do well before you leave Boston, where by
means of one you can communicate your sentiments to each
other, to settle all the necessary points for your journey: that is,
your hour for setting out in the morning, which let be early;
taking up in the evening—number of feeds in the day, & of what
kind of food—also the kind & quantity of Liquor that is to be
given to the Spaniards in a day. In this govern yourself by the
advice of the Lieut: Governor—I would not debar them of what
is proper; any more than I would indulge them in what is not
so. Be attentive to the conduct of these men, as from their good
or bad dispositions I shall be enabled to judge whether to keep
one of them or not; if either shou'd incline to stay in the Country
with the Jacks. Having settled the principal points with them
before you leave Boston, you will easily understand each other
in smaller matters by signs, 'till you return to New York; where,

by means of the Spanish minister's attendants, you may if necessary, settle a fresh plan.

Not expecting that you will travel back faster than the Jacks can walk, it is possible you may reach New York before you take a halting day, which, if not *too* far, would be best, as here probably the Spaniards will require it, on account of meeting their Countrymen in the family of Mr Gardoqui, the Spanish Minister: however, if they think a halt sooner is necessary, you must be governed by their opinions—as the Jacks must not be hurt by travelling them too fast, or improperly.

Let the Jacks be put separate & with no other Creatures, lest they should get kicked, & hurt themselves or hurt others; & if it is necessary they should be cloathed, (which you must know before you leave Boston) provide Blankets or such other cloathing as their keepers think best, at that place.

Keep an exact account of your expences from the time you leave home until you return to it again; remembering that Dollars in the States of Maryland, Delaware, Pennsylvania & part of New Jersey, pass at 7/6; bordering on New York, & in that State for 8/—and in all the New England Governments at 6/ as in Virginia—all other silver, & gold, in that proportion.

Altho' I do not think there is any probability of the Jack, or Jacks having left Boston before you will arrive there; yet at, & after you leave the City of New York, it may be well to enquire now & then along the road whether this may not have taken place; the circumstance of which will be very notorious if it has happened. For this reason, if there is a Stage which passes thro' Hartford in Connecticut, & so along the post road to Boston; it will be better to pursue this rout than to go by the Stage-boat from New York to Providence.

As soon as the Stage gets to its Quarters at night, immediately engage your passage for the next day—lest you may be too late & thereby detained a day or two for its return. Make use of the Stage *Waggons*—the Stage Coaches are too expensive.

As soon as you get to Boston, write to me, or get somebody to do it, by the Post—informing me whether there are one, or two Jacks; in what condition they are, with other particulars—& when you expect to commence your journey back.

G: Washington

LB, DLC:GW.

John Fairfax (d. 1843), the son of William Fairfax, of Maryland, and Elizabeth Buckner Fairfax, a native of Virginia, became an overseer at Mount Vernon in 1784 or 1785 as a very young man. He remained in GW's employ until 1790 when he moved to Monongalia County. There he became a successful planter and represented the county in the Virginia house of delegates in 1809–10 and 1814–15 (Cartmell, *Shenandoah Valley Pioneers*, 247–48).

1. See GW to Thomas Cushing, this date.

From Benjamin Tupper

Dear General,   Pittsburgh Octr 26th 1785.

We have just returned to this place from an unsucessful attempt to Survey the Western Territory, Coll Parker who will deliver this will be able to inform your Excellency the reasons of our not succeeding agreeable to our wishes—I am greatly charmed with the Country, it exceeds any I ever saw, and I know of nothing that will prevent me Commenceing one of the first adventurers in that delightfull Country—I intend on my return to Consult with General Putnam and no doubt we shall fall upon some plan to engage a number of our friends to join in a scheme so interesting as that of settling in that Garden of America—One thing which will induce me to settle in that Country is, that your Excellency promise to honour us with a visit which I shall set more by than the Interest I possess in Massetchusetts.[1]

I hope these will find your Excellency in possession of all the happiness human nature is capable of—Coll Sherman, Capt. Martin and the Surveyors with us desire their most dutiful regards to your Excellency, please to present mine to your Lady, to Mr Lun Washington and his Lady.[2]

Dear General, some of your friends may exceed me in expressions of regards &c. but believe me when I assure your Excellency that no one can exceed in affection that of Your Excellencies most dutiful humble Servant

Benj. Tupper

ALS, DLC:GW.

1. At the urging of his friend Rufus Putnam, Benjamin Tupper (1738–1792) was named by Congress to serve in Putnam's place as the Massachusetts surveyor in the expedition of September 1785 to begin the survey of the seven ranges under the Land Ordinance of 1785. Tupper in the company of surveyors from other states left Pittsburgh for the Ohio country in mid-September.

Because of threats of violence from the Indians north of the Ohio, Thomas Hutchins (1730–1789), who as Geographer of the United States headed the mission, decided on 15 Oct. to discontinue the survey, and the surveyors arrived back in Pittsburgh on 23 October. Putnam and Tupper were organizers of the Ohio Company in 1787 and leaders of the settlement at Marietta on the Muskingum beginning in 1788. See Thomas Hutchins to President of Congress, 15 Sept., 24 Nov. 1785, Rufus Putnam to Congress, 11 June 1785, and Motion of Massachusetts Delegates, 18 July 1785, DNA:PCC, items 60, 56, 36. See also Putnam to GW, 5 April 1784, and notes. Alexander Parker, an officer in the 2d Virginia Regiment from 1775 until the end of the war, was the surveyor for Virginia on the expedition.

2. Isaac Sherman served in the 2d, 5th, and 8th Connecticut regiments during the Revolution, reaching the rank of lieutenant colonel, and Absalom Martin served throughout the war as an officer in the 1st or 4th New Jersey regiments. Sherman was the surveyor on the expedition for Connecticut, and Martin, for New Jersey.

Letter not found: to Battaile Muse, 27 Oct. 1785. In the Thomas Birch's Sons catalog no. 683, April 5–6, 1892, this letter is described as "Acknowledging the purchase of 1000 bushels of wheat from Battaile Muse, for which he agrees to pay 6 shillings per bushel."

To George Gilpin

Dear Sir,   Mount Vernon Octr 29th 1785.

As you were so obliging sometime ago as to offer me the use of your Scow to enable me to get mud from the bed of the River to try the efficacy of it as a manure; I would thank you, if it is convenient, for the lent of it next Week, & will send up for it on Monday, if you will let me know to what place, and of whom it is to be had.[1]

I will avail myself also of your kind offer of getting me a Water level & staff made, in the best manner. I have joiners that could execute the Wooden Work as well as it can be done any where, but my Smith is too great a bungler to entrust anything to him that requires skill, or exactness; for which reason, if you conceive, by furnishing me with the Iron part of the level, I could not get the Wood well put to it here, I would thank you for the whole, compleat, & will pay the Workmen who do the seperate parts, with pleasure. Conceiving that the length of the level contributes to the truth of it, I beg, if the whole is made with you, that mine may not be less than four feet. With great esteem & regard I am—Dr Sir—Yr Obedt Sert

Go: Washington

ALS, ViMtV.

1. See GW to Arthur Donaldson, 16 Oct., regarding GW's plans to experiment with using mud from the Potomac as fertilizer. Monday was 31 Oct., and Gilpin was not able to send his scow until later in the week (see GW to Gilpin, 1 Nov.). GW's entry for 3 Nov. in his diary includes: "Borrowed a Scow from Colo. Gilpin, with which to raise Mud from the Bed of the river or Creek, to try the efficacy of it as a Manure, and sent it to the river Plantation for that purpose. Went over there myself to mark off a piece of ground to spread it on, after it should get mellowed by the frosts of the Winter" (*Diaries*, 4:217–18). GW does not again refer in his diary to this particular mud.

To Patrick Henry

Dear Sir,   Mount Vernon Octr 29th 1785

Inclosed I give your Excellency the trouble of receiving an official letter from me, which I beg the favor of you to lay before the General Assembly.[1]

Your letter of [   ] enclosing the appointment of Colo. Neville, in the room of Majr Massey, came duly to hand; & the latter was forwarded by a safe convey[anc]e.[2]

I have never yet seen the report of the Commissioners for examining the best course for a cut between Elizabeth River & the Waters of No. Carolina—Your Excellency was so good as to offer me a copy of it, but the matter has either slipped your memory, or the letter which contained it has miscarried.[3] With respectful compliments, in which Mrs Washington joins me, to Mrs Henry—& with very great esteem & regard. I have the honr to be—Dear Sir Your Most Obedt Hble Servt

Go: Washington

ALS, PHi: Dreer Collection; LB, DLC:GW.

1. See GW's letter to Henry of this date, printed below.

2. Henry's letter is dated 26 Sept., which see.

3. Henry sent the commissioners' report on the Elizabeth River Canal on 11 November. See note 2 in Henry's letter to GW of that date.

To Patrick Henry

Sir   Mount Vernon Octr 29th 1785

Your Excellency having been pleased to transmit me a copy of the Act appropriating to my benefit certain shares in the Companies for opening the navigation of James and Potomack Rivers, I take the liberty of returning to the General Assembly through your hands, the profound & grateful acknowledgments inspired by so signal a mark of their benificent intentions towards me. I beg you, Sir, to assure them, that I am filled on this occasion with every sentiment which can flow from a heart warm with love for my Country—sensible to every token of its approbation and affection—and sollicitous to testify in every instance, a respectful submission to its wishes.

With these sentiments in my bosom, I need not dwell on the anxiety I feel in being obliged, in this instance, to decline a favor which is rendered no less flattering by the manner in which it is conveyed, than it is affectionate in itself.

In explaining this obligation, I pass over a comparison of my endeavours in the public Service with the many honorable testimonies of approbation which have already so far overrated, and overpaid them; reciting one consideration only which supercedes the necessity of recurring to every other.

When I was first called to the station with which I was honored during the late conflict for our liberties, to the diffidence which I had so many reasons to feel in accepting it, I thought it my duty to join a firm resolution to shut my hand against every pecuniary recompence. To this resolution I have invariably adhered. From this resolution (if I had the inclination) I do not consider my self at liberty, to depart.

Whilst I repeat therefore my fervent acknowledgments to the Legislature for their very kind sentiments and intentions in my favor—and at the sametime beg them to be persuaded that a remembrance of this singular proof of their goodness towards me, will never cease to cherish returns of the warmest affection and gratitude, I must pray that their Act, so far as it has for its object my personal emolument, may not have its effect. But if it should please the General Assembly to permit me to turn the destination of the fund vested in me from my private emoluments, to objects of a public nature, it will be my study in selecting these, to prove the sincerity of my gratitude for the honor conferred on me, by preferring such as may appear most subservient to the enlightened, and patriotic views of the Legislature.[1] With great respect & considn I have the honor to be Yr Excellencys Most Obedt Hble Servt

Go: Washington

ALS, InU; LB, DLC:GW.

1. This letter was read in the house of delegates on 11 Nov. and referred to a committee of thirteen. On 15 Nov. the committee recommended the passage of an act "for changing the destination of the shares in the Potomac and James River Companies," and it was agreed that the committee should bring in such a bill. The house passed the committee's bill on 18 Nov.; the senate followed suit the next day. In his letter of 21 Nov. Archibald Cary, the president of the senate, indicated that the general assembly had complied with GW's request in this matter, and on 7 Dec. Benjamin Harrison, speaker of the house of delegates, sent GW a copy of "An act to amend the act intitled An act for vesting in George Washington, esq. a certain interest in the companies established for opening and extending the navigation of James and Potowmack rivers" (DLC:GW). The amending act quoted in part both the original act and this letter from GW and then provided: "That the said shares with the tolls and profits hereafter accruing therefrom, shall stand appropriated to such objects of a public nature, in such manner, and under such distributions, as the said George Washington . . . shall direct and appoint" (12 Hening 42–44).

To James Madison

My Dr Sir,   Mount Vernon 29th Octor 1785.

Receive my thanks for your obliging favor of the 20th—with its enclosure—of the latter I now avail myself in a letter to the Governor, for the General Assembly. Your delicate sensibility deserves my particular acknowledgements: both your requests are complied with—the first, by congeniality of sentiment; the second because I would fulfil your desire.

Conceiving it would be better to suggest a wish, than to propose an absolute condition of acceptance; I have so expressed myself to the Assembly—and shall be obliged to you, not only for information of the result—but (if there is an acquiescence on the part of the Country) for your sentiments respecting the appropriations—from what may be said upon the occasion, you will learn what would be most pleasing, & of the greatest utility to the public.[1]

By Colo. Henry Lee I sent you the reports of the Secretary for foreign affairs on the Consular Department. I hope you have received them.[2] With every sentiment of esteem & regard I am Dr Sir &c. &c.

Geo: Washington

LB, DLC:GW.

1. In his letter of 20 Oct., which has not been found, Madison gave GW suggestions about how GW might best indicate to the Virginia general assembly his unwillingness to hold for his personal profit the shares in the Potomac River and James River companies given to him by the legislature. For GW's formal request to the assembly for permission "to turn the destination of the fund vested in me from my private emoluments, to objects of a public nature," see his second letter to Gov. Patrick Henry of 29 Oct., and note.

2. See GW to Madison, 22 Oct., n.1.

Letter not found: to Charles Washington, 29 Oct. 1785. On 23 Nov. Charles Washington wrote GW: "Your Letter of the 29 of Octr, I recd by Mr Muse."

To David Humphreys

My dear Humphreys.   Mount Vernon Octr 30th 1785.

Since my last of the 1st of September I have received your favor of the 17th of July, which was brought to this Country by Mr Houdon; to whom, tho I had no Agency in the matter, I feel great obligation for quitting France, & the pressing calls of the Great Ones to make a Bust of me, from the life. I am not less indebted to the favourable opinion of those who you say are anxious to perpetuate my name, and to be acquainted with the Memoirs of my life. So far as these are connected with the history of the revolution, and other public documents, they may easily be got at—all beyond these is, I conceive very unimportant. My letter of the 25th of July which I presume you have received long 'ere this (but for fear of a miscarriage, having a rough copy by me, I send you a duplicate) will have conveyed my sentiments so fully that I shall add nothing further on the subject at this time, than to assure you that I was then, and am still, perfectly sincere in the proposal it contained.

I am very much obliged to you for the Poem you sent me, I

have read it with pleasure, and it is much admired by all those to whom I have shewed it.[1]

Nothing new has happened since my last; nor is it probable anything interesting will happen until the different Assemblies convene—Congress as usual, are proceeding very slowly in their business—and, shameful as it is, are often at a stand for want of a sufficient representation. The States have been addressed by them on the subject, but what will be the effect I know not. To me there appears such lassitude in our public Councils as is truly shocking; & must clog the Wheels of Government; which, under such circumstances, will either stop altogether, or will be moved by ignorance, or a few designing Men. With every sentiment of esteem and regard I am your sincere friend and affecte Servant

Go: Washington

ALS, MiDbGr; LB, DLC:GW.

1. See Humphreys to GW, 17 July 1785, n.4.

From Charles McKiernan

Sir.   Philadelphia October 30th 1785.

The inclosed letter from Sir. Edward Newingham with the small package that accompanies this, I hoped to have the honor of delivering to your Excellency in person, but I find that my deceased fathers affairs require my immediate attention in this quarter.

I regret Sir. that no opportunity has offered to forward them to you before.[1]

Somtime before I return to Europe I intend myself the honor to wait on your Excellency in person, to receive your commands, should you be pleased to favour me with any, for that part of the world—I am respectfully your Excellencys most Humble and verry Obedient servant

Charles McKiernan

ALS, DLC:GW.

1. GW wrote Sir Edward Newenham on 25 Nov. to thank him for "Magazines, Gazettes &ca" and for three letters, one of 3 Mar. by Captain Bayles, one of 25 May, and one of 23 July, none of which have been found. McKiernan enclosed one of these letters here with the package from Newenham, and he

then sent the third under this cover: "Sir I wrote your Excellency, the 31st Ultimo, and sent a package with a letter enclosed in mine, from Sir Edwd Newingham, Pr Doctor Eustace, on looking over my Apparel, I find another Address'd to Your Excellency, which I was not Apprized of." McKiernan dates this covering letter "October 8th 1785," and GW notes that he did not receive it until 25 Nov., the day that he wrote Newenham thanking him for the package and three letters. The contents of McKiernan's covering letter and the fact that on 10 Dec. GW acknowledges McKiernan's letters of 30 Oct. and 8 Nov. strongly suggest that McKiernan's letter should be dated 8 Nov. and not 8 October. The "packet" that McKiernan sent on 8 Nov. was in fact intended for Thomas Bibby (GW to Bibby, 10 Dec.).

From L. Cuisnier

My Lord (Copy)   Baltimore 31st Octr 1785
   I am a Frenchman, Arrived in the Continent the 14th June 1782. I was One of the Passengers of the Briga[ntine] Betsey, Obliged to Save ourselves at Lewis Town, at the Entrance of the Delaware, that Briga[ntine] having been Captured by Two of the Ennemy's Frigates; Monsr Le Chevlr de La Luzern, Gave me Charge of the Affairs of his House, of his Cash, of his Correspondence, & of his Private Bussiness, I found it Dissagreeable in his House, as the Ennemy's I had in France followed me. I Complain'd of it, in a Letter I had the Honour to write Monsr Luzerne, then at his Country House, he wrote me for Answer I had nothing to fear from my Ennemy's in Continuing to do my duty, & I Stayed with him till the time of his Departure. I have tried for this Some time, to have myself Instructed in the language of this Country, for which reason, I wish'd to place myself with an American in his Counting House, not having Succeeded, I put up Different Bills in Philadelphia, that I would work in a Counting House, or with any other Person, in another line of Bussiness, Should it be in the Town or in the Country, without demanding a Farthing of Wages. I was at that time in a Condition to make that Sacrifice, Monsr Luzerne having given me at Parting 1000 Tournois of Gratuity, & 500 for my Passage, when I would Return home, with a Certificate of his Satisfaction & not having Succeeded there, I Came to Baltimore. Monsr Danmeurs has received me in Quality of his Secretary the 27th June last, I have Suspected that Some Persons here, or Some of my Phila. Ennemy's have endeavoured to Dissaffect the

Peop⟨le⟩ that Interest themselves in my favor, against me, I Can Attest My Lord, that I have never Said any thing, to the Prejudice of any Person, in France, or upon the Continent, nor have I wrote any thing either Directly or Indirectly, (but what my Superiors made me write) I know my Ennemys Seek to hurt me, with all their Power, which is very unlucky for me, but Nevertheless, I hope My Lord, that you will permitt me, to lessen my Trouble, in taking my Part, for that Slander is always Dangerous for a Person, that has not any Protection in a Country, If there was any Proof to the Contrary of that, I now have the Honour to write you, my Lord, I merit your Indignation & Punishment having Spent the Money I had for my Passage to France & not havng any thing for my Present Employ, If I Could be of any Service to you My Lord in Managing any Part of your Affairs, I Should think myself much Oblig'd to you in obtaining that favor, I have it in my Power to be of Some Service, Should it be in writing & to take Care of your Possessions, as also in Agriculture. I am &c.

L: Cuisnier

I know not My Lord, to Speak the English Language, but I Can write it tolerable, or pretty well, but as I write with greater ease the French language, I use it to write this Letter.

Translation, DLC:GW; ALS, in French, DLC:GW.

From Timothy Dwight

May it please your Excellency,   [October 1785]

This letter accompanies the Conquest of Canaan to your Excellency.[1] In the year 1778, an application, under the countenance of General Parsons, was made to your Excellency, for permission to inscribe to you this poem, then intended for an earlier publication. A permission was politely & condescendingly granted. Since that time, the public appearance of the book has been unavoidably delayed by a variety of intervening obstacles.

In The book marked No. 1. the Errors of the press are, in general, truly but awkwardly corrected.

The fear lest the work should not possess such a degree of

merit, as to occasion no pain in a considerate & delicate mind, upon seeing it inscribed to your Excellency, creates in the writer very humiliating sensations. Should this unfortunate circumstance prove real, the only reflection which could alleviate his mortification, is that he has very faithfully endeavoured to prevent it.[2] With the most fervent wishes, & prayers for your Excellency's present & future happiness, I am with the most entire respect, your Excellency's very obedient, & very humble Servant

Timothy Dwight

ALS, DLC:GW. For the dating of this letter, see note 2.

1. In a letter of 7 Mar. 1778 from West Point, Brig. Gen. Samuel Holden Parsons (1737–1789) commended his chaplain of brigades, Timothy Dwight (1752–1817), to GW and endorsed Dwight's letter of 8 Mar. 1778 asking for GW's permission to dedicate to him "a poem in the *Conquest* of *Canaan* by *Joshua*," on which he had been working "for several years." GW's letter giving his permission is dated 18 Mar. 1778. *The Conquest of Canaan*, printed by Elisha Babcock in Hartford, Conn., in 1785, is listed in the inventory of GW's library taken after his death (Griffin, *Boston Athenæum Collection*, 483). The epic poem, made up of eleven "books" and running to 304 pages, has this dedication following the title page: "To his Excellency, George Washington, Esquire, Commander in chief of the American Armies, The Saviour of his Country, The Supporter of Freedom, And the Benefactor of Mankind; This Poem is inscribed, with the highest respect for his character, the most ardent wishes for his happiness, and the most grateful sense of the blessings, secured, by his generous efforts, to the United States of North America, by his most humble, and most obedient servant, Timothy Dwight. Greenfield, in Connecticut, March 1, 1785." The printer added a page of errata keyed into line numbers in the different "books."

2. Acknowledging receipt of the poem from "Mount Vernon 1st April 1786," GW wrote: "Sir, I have been favored with a letter from you (without place or date) accompanying the conquest of Canaan; for both I pray you to accept my grateful thanks, & the acknowledgment of the honor you have done me by the dedication.

"Your fears with respect to the merits of the Poem, I hope are removed, for it is a pleasing performance, and meets the approbation of all who have read it. I have never had an opportunity of subscribing to the work, or I should have done it with pleasure. With very great esteem & respect I am &c. G: Washington" (LB, DLC:GW). Someone has added a dateline "Nov. 1785," to Dwight's letter, but GW endorses it: "From Timothy Dwight without date recd 29th Novr 1785." Dwight wrote GW on 5 July 1786 to apologize for the omission and said the letter "was written from New York, the last of October."

To George Gilpin

Dear Sir,   Mount Vernon Novr 1st 1785.

After I had written to you on Saturday, I saw Lund Washington, who informed me that he had seen you the day before, & understood from you, that it would not be convenient for you to spare your Scow until next Week—as your letter to me says it may be had tomorrow I fear, in order to accomodate me, you have been induced to put your self to an inconvenience. To prevent which, I give you the trouble of this letter, as it would give me real concern if this were to be the case. The difference to me is very trifling whether I get it this Week or next; I therefore beg that you would make the time perfectly suitable to your own business, & let me know it, to which I will conform thankfully.[1]

I am much obliged by the assurance of procuring me a level, and shall depend upon it. and am very much so, for your kind offer to come down & put me in the best mode of getting up Mud, which may facilitate my experiments greatly[2]—With great esteem & regard I am—Dear Sir Yr Most Obedt Servt

                                                  Go: Washington

ALS, RPB.
  1. See GW to Gilpin, 29 Oct., n.1.
  2. See GW to Arthur Donaldson, 16 October.

From David Humphreys

My dear General   Paris Novr 1st 1785

Being uncertain whether this letter will arrive at Bourdeaux in time to be carried to America by the vessel which brought me your favour of the 25th of July, I will content myself with assuring you how deeply I am penetrated by those expressions of confidence & friendship with which it is replete. Whether I should, or should not be at liberty to accept the liberal offer you make I cannot at this moment decide. I shall not however lose sight of the object—& so much I am able to assert, the execution of the task in contemplation would be a very favourite pursuit, because with your oral assistance alone it could be completed in a satisfactory & useful manner.

I had the honour of writing to you on the 10th of May &

17 of July, since which no remarkable events have taken place in Europe.

The public tranquility seems not likely to be soon interrupted—& on the subject of peace let me observe, that there never was since the creation of the world a moment in which so little hostility existed on the earth as at present—indeed I know of none except the depredations committed by the African Pirates on some of the christian nations—it is scandalous & humiliating beyond expression to see the powerful maritime kingdoms of Europe tributary to such a contemptible Banditti—This sinister policy will force us in some degree to the same measure—You have doubtless heard of their having taken several American vessels—the number has been exaggerated by English lies—The Emperor of Morocco has given up the prisoners with the only vessel captured by his cruizers & seems disposed to make peace with us—The Algerines have lately taken two vessels (one from Boston, the other from Phi[l]a.) this is the most potent of the Barbary States & will probably be the most insolent & intractable—The American Ministers in Europe who have been authorized to enter into negotiation with them are at this moment sending Mr Barclay (Consul Genl in France) to Morocco & a Mr Lamb of Connecticut to Algiers as Agents to negotiate Treaties under their Instructions.[1]

The Marquis la Fayette has just returned from Prussia highly pleased with the reviews—he concurs with our general information that the English Papers have inculcated almost universally reports very much to the prejudice of the American character & politicks. it rests for us by honour & honesty to give those reports the lye—Adieu my dear Genl, be pleasd to present me respectfully to Mrs Washington & believe ever your sincere friend, & most Hle Servt

D. Humphreys

ALS, DLC:GW.

1. John Lamb in September brought from Congress to the American delegation in Paris authorization to appoint persons to treat with the marauding Barbary States. Lamb was one of the agents appointed, and he left Paris for Algiers shortly after 4 Nov. (see Thomas Jefferson to John Adams, 19 Sept. 1785, and Jefferson to William Carmichael, 4 Nov. 1785, in Boyd, *Jefferson Papers*, 8:526–27, 9:13–17). The other agent chosen, Thomas Barclay (1728–1793), the United States consul general in France, had to delay his departure for Morocco until mid-January 1786 (see Jefferson to Humphries, 5 Jan. 1786,

ibid., 9:152–53). Jefferson found Lamb's "manner and appearance" to be "not promising." When Lamb was rebuffed by the dey Mohammed, he retreated to Spain and in mid-1786 resigned his commission. On 18 July 1787 Congress ratified the treaty that Barclay had negotiated with the emperor of Morocco.

From William le Washington

Sir   Philadelphia 1st Novr 1785

I have the Honour to Inclose your Excellency a Lr which Charles Anderson Pelham Eqr. Member of Parliamt in England gave me, w'erein he inform's me he has acquainted your Excellency who I am & my Intent of making a Tower of America.[1]

Having Deposited fifteen hundread Pounds Stirling in the Hands of Messrs Saml Smith & Son, Bankrs—London, of which they, give me an acknowledgment in their Lrs of Credit to me dated the 7th, & 9th July 1785—to be disposed of in Bills of Exchange as I may find it Necessary—Upon which Lrs I have received One Hundread pounds Stirling of Nath. Tracy Esqr. Boston, but Some Merchts in this City not knowing Messrs Saml Smith & Son, Sign[at]ur[e] made difficultys in taking my Drafts.

Mr Pelham likwise informes me he has a Short time ago had the Honour of Introducg a gent. to your Excellency so that his Sign[at]ur[e] I make no dought but is known to your Excellency.

As I find a Difficulty in disposing of my drafts as afore mentioned, I take the Liberty of forwarding the Inclosed Letter of Introduction from Mr Pelham to your Excellency requesting that if your Excellency find the Inclos'd Lr to your Sattisfaction that you'll do me the Honour of a Letter by the Earliest Oppertunity which may give Sattisfaction to the Merchts of this City in regard to my person & Cercumstances.

As Soon as I have Setteled my Affairs in this City I Shall have the honour to pay my respects in person to your Excellency as I pass for South Carolina—and I most Sincearly wish that my personally Acquaintance may procure me an Oppertunaty in having it in my power to return the great Obligation which your Excellency will lie me under by applying with my request. I have the Honour to ratify myself with the Highest respect & Esteem Your Excellencys most Obedt & most Hble Servant

Willm le Washington

ALS, PHi: Gratz Collection. On the cover Washington gives his address in Philadelphia as "at Mrs Hous's Fifth Street Cornr Mkt St."

1. The letter ostensibly written by Charles Anderson Pelham on 7 July 1785 from Arlington Street in London reads: "Sabo William le Washington Kt of the Grand Sword of Asia—Son of Sir Charles Lee Washington Kt F.R.S. informs Me he intends makeing a tower of America & not haveing any Letters for your Excellency I take the Liberty as a Member of the British Parliment to Introduce him to You so far as to inform your Excellency that Sabo William, is a Man of Independant Fortune & is Travelling entirely for his Amusement.

"If it Should ever be my good Fortune to have it in my power to serve any of your Excellency's Freinds how happy will it make Me. I have the honour to be with the highest respect & Esteem Yr Excellencys Most Obedient & Most hble Sert C.A. Pelham" (MH: Sparks Papers). Charles Anderson Pelham (1749–1823), who had added Pelham to his name in 1763, owned large estates in Lincolnshire and was a member of Parliament from 1768 to 1794, sitting for Lincolnshire from 1774.

From William Fitzhugh

My Dear Sir   Chatham, Novr 2n[d] 1785

I beg Leave to return you my Thanks for the Loan of Peter—and I am happy that I have it in my Power to send him Home unhurt. Tarquin has recover'd the Laurells he lost at Alexandria—His Opponents were, old Cumberland, and Herod, the Property of Doctr Ross; both which he beat with great Ease.[1]

I have a fine 2 year-old Doe, perfectly tame, which I beg your Acceptance of. She shall be sent with the Orchard Grass Seed, as soon as I can get a small Cart or waggon that can carry her without Injury.[2] I am with respectfull Compliments to your Lady & Family, in which I am join'd by Mrs Fitzhugh, Dear Sir your Aff. & most Ob. Ser.

                                   W. Fitzhugh

ALS, DLC:GW.

1. Tarquin, a roan gelding owned by William Fitzhugh (1741–1809) of Chatham, won one of the Fredericksburg Jockey Club purses on 5 Oct., and on Friday, 21 Oct., he came in second in both heats in the four-mile race at Alexandria. The races at Falmouth, across the river from Fredericksburg, began on 30 October. A slave named Peter, an expert horse handler belonging to David Stuart, was in GW's employ (see GW to Stuart, 12 Feb. 1787). Dr. David Ross lived in Bladensburgh, Maryland.

2. GW recorded in his diary for 20 April: "Sowed a Bushel of Orchard Grass seed (given to me by Wm. Fitzhugh Esqr. of Chatham) in my last years Turnip patch at the home house" (ibid., 315). For further correspondence about Fitzhugh's gift of does to GW, see Fitzhugh to GW, 17 Jan. 1786, and Benjamin Grymes to GW, 24 April 1786.

From Jean Le Mayeur

sir   Richmond 2 9bre [November] 1785
    the letters of introduction your Excellency was pleased to honor me for frederiskBurg and Richmond have all been delivered, in consequance of them i have received Great civility from Mr Fitzhugh, General Spotswood, the attornay General, Mr harrison spiker of the house of delegates, Mr Carry, speker of the Senate, and Mr George weeb;[1] i have dine or Engage'd to dine with Every one of this gentlemen. i Lodge in the same house with Col. Carry and we dine togedeur whan he is in town.
    Gouvneur henry to whom i Gave the first letter offerd me his services.
    i am short of Expretion to make proper thinks for your Excellencys fevors as well by these letters of introduction as by your other kindness. also to make to honorable Mrs Washington sufficient ackenoledgments for the Extreme obligation i am under to her—i have the honor to be with a Great Respect of your Excellency the most obeissain and humble serviteur
                                        doct. Le Mayeur

The races have bigen this day and the flage of trus bilong to Mr Good wene, also at petesburg.[2]

ALS, DLC:GW.
    1. Jean-Pierre Le Mayeur, the French dentist who worked on GW's teeth in 1783 and again at Mount Vernon in the summer of 1784, visited Mount Vernon in September 1785 when GW wrote for him the missing letters of introduction to William Fitzhugh of Chatham, who was a member of the state senate, to Gen. Alexander Spotswood (1751–1818), to Attorney General Edmund Randolph, to Speaker of the House Benjamin Harrison (d. 1791), to President of the Senate Archibald Cary, and to George Webb (b. 1723) of New Kent County, former state treasurer. Le Mayeur ran a notice dated 18 Oct. for two months in the *Virginia Gazette, or the American Advertiser* "to inform the LADIES and GENTLEMEN that he has arrived in the City of Richmond, where he intends to stay a few weeks, and will perform any operations on the teeth, hitherto performed in Europe, such as transplanting, &c. &c. &c. Besides, he puts natu-

ral teeth instead of false, to people who cannot have naturalties" (29 Oct. 1785). In November Le Mayeur advertised "Any Person that will dispose of their FRONT TEETH (slaves excepted) may receive TWO GUINEAS for each" (*Virginia Gazette, or the American Advertiser*, 26 Nov.).

2. Le Mayeur was saying: "The races have begun this day and Flag of Truce belonging to Mr Goode won." Colonel Goode's Flag of Truce also won, on 4 Oct., the second race of the Fredericksburg Jockey Club Purse (*Virginia Gazette, or the American Advertiser*, 22 Oct.). Flag of Truce, reportedly the winner of ten out of the eleven purses that he ran during his career in Virginia, was acquired as a colt by Col. Robert Goode of Whitby of Chesterfield County.

To Samuel Powel

Dear Sir,   Mount Vernon 2d Novr 1785.

I have had the honor to receive your favor of the 10th ulto together with the wheat from the Cape of Good Hope; which you were so obliging as to send me by the revd Mr Griffith; for both I thank you. The latter shall have a fair trial in the same inclosure with some presented to me by Colo. Spaight, (a Delegate in Congress from No. Carolina) which had been planted, & had obtained a vigorous growth before yours came to hand. This also was from the Cape, & brought probably by the same Vessel.[1] I sowed it in Drills two feet apart, & five inches asunder in the rows, to make the most I could of it by cultivation in the Spring: this method will in my opinion be more productive than Mr Bordeley's. It ought to be so indeed, as the expence of ground is much greater, & the workings will probably be oftener.[2]

I pray you to present my best wishes & most respectful compliments to Mrs Powel—to which please to add, & to accept yourself those of Mrs Washington. I have the honor to be &c.

G: Washington

LB, DLC:GW.

1. GW on 27 Aug. sowed the wheat that Richard Dobbs Spaight (1758–1802) had given him on 1 July. It was probably on his visit of 15 Oct. that David Griffith (1742–1789), the rector of Fairfax Parish, brought GW the wheat that Powel had sent. See *Diaries*, 4:158, 187, 206. GW recorded in his diary on this date, 2 Nov.: "Perceived the Wheat from the Cape, which had been sent to me by Mr. Powell of Philada., & which I sowed on the 19th. of last Month had come up very well" (ibid., 217).

2. See Powel to GW, 5 July (second letter), n.2, for reference to John Beale

Bordley's recent publication on the raising of crops. Perhaps the copyist changed to "expence of ground" GW's "expanse of ground."

To Tench Tilghman

Dear Sir,   Mount Vernon 2d Novr 1785.

I had heard—with great concern—before your favor of the 13th Ulto came to hand, of your indisposition; and congratulate you very sincerely on your recovery.

I shall be much obliged to you for causing the enclosed letter to be safely delivered to Mr Rawlins—who, when here, promised to furnish me in *nine* days, with a plan and estimate for my new Room; since which (near, or quite as many weeks) I have not heard a tittle from, or of him.[1]

It is the third time I have been served in this manner by workmen who have partly engaged to finish this room.[2] All I now ask of Mr Rawlins is, to put me upon a certainty; as I am determined, in case he disappoints me, to write to Ireland for a man, in his way, to compleat it. I am with great esteem & regard—Dr Sir Yr Most Obedt & Affecte Servt

Go: Washington

ALS, RPJCB.
1. GW's letter has not been found, but see GW to Tilghman, 14 Sept., and Tilghman to GW, 11 November.
2. Going Lanphier completed the exterior of GW's New Room at the north end of the house at Mount Vernon during the Revolution. Earlier this year GW had negotiated with Edward Vidler, a contractor in Annapolis, to finish the interior, and in May 1785 he contracted with Richard Boulton of Charles County, Md., to do the work, but Boulton backed out of the agreement (GW to William Fitzhugh, 21 May 1785, n.1).

Letter not found: to Patrick Henry, 3 Nov. 1785. The ALS was advertised by Charles Hamilton, sale no. 98, item 298, 29 July 1976.

From Thomas Johnson

Sir.   Fred[eric]k [Md.] 4 Novemr 1785.

The little Time we had at our last Meeting just allowed an Opportunity to mention several Things which were left very imperfect though we seemed much in the same Opinion; amongst them Applications to the Assembly's to release the Company from a part of the depth of the Canals: as the four feet draft of Water, in our Circumst[ance]s, is so far from necessary that it is in some degree injurious I wish to see it in the Road of Correction and I flatter myself that an Application cannot fail—the Friends of the Company being such on the principle of public Utility, they must be inimical to a wasteful Expendit. of even private Money—the Enemies to the project being such on the principle of Economy in the public Money they must be desirous of saving as much of the 5,000£ public Money as they possibly can so that we may fairly count on all the Votes for the Correction if the new proposition will not render the navigation less useful. To lay a proper Foundation I have gone into the inclosed Calculation No. 1. I may have erred in my principles or Deductions, for I do not set up for Accuracy, and therefore wish it revised and set to rights if wrong. No. 2. is the Draft of a petition and No. 3 the Draft of a Bill; as I had only my own Ideas to guide me I make no doubt but that they may be much improved in the Matter and am confident they may in the Language the Time is too short for much Intercourse on the Subject and if they are thought sufficient for a Groundwork the only Favor I request for them or myself is that you would treat them with intire Freedom by altering as you may think best for I feel nothing of favouritism to any part my views will be intirely answered in obtaining a Release from the useless part of the Burthen.

Since my Return Home my Thoughts have run a good deal on the Situation of the Great Falls for Locks and the Manner of constructing them and their Gates. I was puzzled about the latteral pressure of Water for the Situation seems to point out Locks of great depth but unless we can come at some Rule to know the Force of a given Body of Water we do not know the Quantity of Force or degree of St[r]ength necessary to oppose to it or whether we have it in our power to oppose it with Success or not—I have no Books of my own nor am I in a favourable place to borrow Books on the Subject however I obtained one and have extracted No. 4. which I thought applicable—My Attempt No. 5. on this Foundation may probably be so far from accurate as to be intirely wrong for I have no Learning in this Way the only Merit or rather the Excuse I can claim is the Intention—Yet I cannot but be struck with the Hints started at the

Falls and hope that we may accomplish a resisting Force superior to the Action of the Water let us raise it in the Locks to what height we please and I candidly confess I feel a kind of Pride in the originality or at least uncommonness of the Gates proposed—if by a Deviation from the usual Manner we can combine Strength Dispatch and Ease in a superior degree and at a less Expence than the Europeans my Ambition will be highly gratified and I flatter myself the Occasion offers.[1] I should either forbear giving you this Trouble or apologize for it if I did not think your desire to pick out some thing useful from the crudest Thoughts and my unreserve will make this prolixity acceptable for I much more wish to add than to take from the few of your leisure Moments. I am Sr Your most obedt & most hble Servt

Th. Johnson

ALS, MnHi.

1. None of Johnson's enclosures found at the Minnesota Historical Society appear to be numbered, but Johnson's computation regarding the pressure of water at various depths against the sides of locks would appear to be his enclosure no. 1; his draft to the Virginia and Maryland legislatures that the depth required of canals to be built by the Potomac River Company at the falls of the river be reduced from four to two feet is his no. 2; the draft of the proposed hill (his no. 3) is missing; his excerpt from John Rowning's *A Compendious System of Natural Philosophy, pt.* 2 (London, 1744), 26–27, presenting a theory for measuring the pressure of water against its banks is Johnson's no. 4; and his enclosure no. 5 is his proposal for making lock gates which would be raised and lowered by counterweight rather than having them hinged. Transcripts of the enclosures are in CD-ROM:GW. GW was not able to send copies of the petition, signed by him as president of the Potomac River Company and enclosing copies of the proposed bill, to the Virginia and Maryland legislatures until 3 December. The two legislatures promptly passed the proposed bill amending the "Act for Opening and Extending the Navigation of the Potowmack River" that both had passed at GW's behest the year before (12 Hening 68–69). See GW to Samuel Chase, 3 Dec., and notes, GW to Charles Simms and David Stuart, 3 Dec., and GW to Thomas Johnson, 20 December.

From Thomas Ridout

Sir— Bordeaux 4th Novemr 1785.

I had the honour to receive a few days ago Your Excellency's letter of the 20 August, inclosing others for the Marquis de la Fayette, Mr Humphreys & the Baron de Secondat the two first I forwarded immediately—the other I directed & delivered.[1] I have not yet had the pleasure to see the Baron de Montesquieu. As he passed thro' this place not many days ago, on his way to a Seat in the Neighbourhood of it—he was so obliging as to call on me, but unfortunately I was not at home; he will spend the winter here.

I wrote your Excellency the 7th of September by the Brig Peggy Capt. Cunnyngham, bound to Baltimore by whom I sent the Package mentioned in your letter—& which by mistake, had not been delivered me in due time—I addressed it to the Care of Colo. Tilghman, who has I hope by this time received it—I have the honor to be with the greatest respect Your Excellency's Most Obedient & very Humble Servant

Thos Ridout

ALS, DLC:GW.

1. GW wrote both to David Humphreys and to Lafayette on 1 September. His letter to the baron de Secondat de Montesquieu is dated the same as that to Ridout, 20 August.

To Edmund Randolph

Dr Sir,   Mount Vernon 5th Novr 1785.

Pursuant to the request of your last letter (dated about the middle of Septr) I had an attested copy of the proceedings of the Potomac Company—& those of the Directors, taken from their Books and sent it to you by Post, in time for the Meeting which was proposed to be held by the Directors of the James river navigation on the 26th of that month in Richmond; and requested, if it should be agreeable, to have a copy of your proceedings sent me in return.[1] Having heard nothing from you since, & having experienced many instances of inattention & neglect in the Post Offices; I now take the liberty of enquiring whether my letter written as above, has reached you—If it has not, I will send another copy, tho' it will not come so seasonably as the first. My best respects to your Lady, & with very great esteem & regard I am Dr Sir &c.

G: Washington

LB, DLC:GW.

1. Randolph's letter is dated 2 September. GW sent to Randolph the Potomac River Company material on 16 Sept., which he "duly received," but Randolph did not get this letter of 5 Nov. until 2 Dec. (Randolph to GW, 3 Dec.).

From Thomas Cushing

Sir   Boston Novr 6th 1785

I had the Honor this day of receiving your Favor of the 26th of Octr last, by Mr Fairfax, in Answer to a Letter I wrote you the 7th of the same month relative to the Jack I received from Spain on Your Account, he has gained flesh since he came on shore and is in much better order than when I receivd him, I shall send him on, as soon as I can purchase a good mare, with Mr Fairfax & the spaniard—who will proceed to Virginia to take care of this animal. only *one* mare will be wanted as the spaniard says he must walk & lead the Jack. Mr Fairfax desires me to inform you that he was detained at Newyork three days as there was neither a Stage nor Packett to convey him or he should have arrived at this place sooner; I am sorry to be obliged to Inform you that the other Jack Ass that was shiped on your Account from Bilboa by a Vessell bound to Beverly in this state, was lost at sea in a great Storm.[1] I have the Honor to be dear Sir Your Most Obedient humble Sert

Thomas Cushing

P.S. I have taken such measures that there may be an understanding between Mr Fairfax & the spaniard on the Road, as will render it needless to be at the Expence of an Interpreter, Mr Fairfax will be near 50 days on his Journey as the spaniard says the Jack must not travell more than 15 miles ⅌ day & there must be here & there a resting day.[2]

ALS, DLC:GW.

1. See note 2 in Cushing to GW, 7 October.

2. John Fairfax and Pedro Tellez left Boston with the jackass on 10 Nov. (see Cushing to GW, 16 Nov.) and arrived at Mount Vernon on the evening of 5 Dec., a journey of only twenty-five or twenty-six days.

From David Pearce

Exclent Sur   Glocestur [Mass.] 6 Novmr 1785

have it once mor to hand your oner my Respeckts ass it has So hapend I had a Ship at bilboa onbord Sd Ship Mnsur Gardequa Pleased to Ship a jackass for your oner & Sd anemal Saf has arived & from my Regards have goot him on ther & Nursed him

Stroong & by gardequa Dereckton have Sent him on to boston to Letent governr how after he had him was Desears to have me Carey him by warter ass I had a wesell bound to your Place I allso aquanted him that I would cary him but after wating a most a weeck heard nothing from him the wind f[a]ir was obligd to Send Sd wesell on I have Persented by the hands off mr Harts horn the bil of Ladn & charg of Paseg & wilst at cap ann wish if free from arror Pleeas to Pay ℔ gentelman.[1] Reman your Very Humbel St

David Pearce

ALS, DLC:GW.
    1. For Pearce's bill of lading, or shipping manifest, dated 8 Aug. 1785, and for a copy of Pearce's account ("Charg of Paseg"), see William Hartshorne & Co. to GW, 26 Nov., n.1.

Letter not found: from William Gordon, 7 Nov. 1785. GW wrote Gordon on 6 Dec.: "I come now, my good Doctor, to acknowledge . . . the receipt of your obliging favor of the 7th ulto."

Letter not found: from ——, 7 Nov. 1785. On 30 Nov. GW writes: "I have had the honor to receive your favor of the 7th."

Letter not found: from William Brown, 8 Nov. 1785. In his letter to Brown of 24 Nov. GW refers to "your second favor of the 8th inst."

To Lafayette

My Dr Marqs   Mount Vernon 8th Novr 1785.
    Having written fully to you about the first of Septr; & nothing having occurred since worth reciting, I should not have given you the trouble of receiving a letter from me at this time, were it not for the good opportunity afforded me by Captn Littlepage, & my desire not to suffer any of your letters to remain long by me unacknowledged.[1]
    I have now to thank you for your favors of the 9th & 14th of July; the first by Mr Houdon, who stayed no more than a fortnight with me; & to whom, for his trouble & risk of crossing the Seas (altho' I had no agency in the business) I feel myself under personal obligations. The second giving an account of your intended tour, which, if compleated in the time you propose, will

exhibit a fresh instance of the celerity of your movements. My good wishes have attended you thro' the whole of it; and this letter I hope will find you arrived at Paris in good health.

Doctr Franklin has met with a grateful reception in Pennsylvania. He has again embarked on a troubled Ocean; I am persuaded with the best designs, but I wish his purposes may be answered—which, undoubtedly are to reconcile the jarring interests of the State. He permitted himself to be nominated for the City of Philadelphia as a Counsellor—a step to the chair, wch no doubt he will fill; but whether to the satisfaction of both parties is a question of some magnitude, & of real importance to himself—at least to his quiet. His Grandson shall meet with every civility & attention I can shew him when occasions offer.[2]

One of my Jacks is, by advices, arrived at Boston; but I still adhere to the request contained in my last, if you can have it complied with without much difficulty.[3]

Your old aid George has taken to himself the wife of his choice: the *honey Moon* is not yet passed; when that is over, I will set him about copying your Letters.[4] I add no more at present but the sincere & affectionate regard which I bear to you, & in which Mrs Washington & all here join—as we do in respectful compliments & best wishes for Madame de la Fayette & your little flock. It is unnecessary to tell you how much I am, My Dr Marquis Yrs &c. &c.

Geo: Washington

LB, DLC:GW.

   1. Lewis Littlepage en route to Europe to enter the service of Stanislaus II Augustus, king of Poland, spent the night of 8 Nov. at Mount Vernon. GW refers to the young man as "an extraordinary character" (*Diaries*, 4:220–21). See Lafayette to GW, 6 Feb. 1786, n.10.

   2. Shortly after his return to Philadelphia from France on 14 Sept., Benjamin Franklin, aged 79, was elected to the Supreme Executive Council of Pennsylvania and, as GW predicts, was chosen president. He served for three years and, contrary to GW's expectations, succeeded in remaining above the fray.

   3. See Thomas Cushing to GW, 7 October.

   4. On 11 May Lafayette asked that the letters that he had written to GW be returned so that copies could be made of them. On 1 Sept. GW wrote Lafayette that he would have George Augustine Washington make copies and would send them to Lafayette, and he wrote him on 10 May 1786 that he was sending "herewith the copies of your private Letters to me, promised in my last, & which have been since copied by your old aid."

From Thomas Cushing

Sir   Boston November 9th 1785

This will be handed you by Mr Fairfax, to whom I have delivered the Jack, & sincerely wish you may receive him in safety, & in good order—I have directed Mr Fairfax in general to observe the directions received from Spain, with respect to managing & feeding this animal. I have delivered him also a good Mare which I have purchased on your account, for one hundred spanish dollars. I did not purchase another as it was unnecessary—the spaniard declined to ride, he said it was necessary for him to walk in order to lead the Jack—I understood upon his first arrival that he was to accompany this animal in order to take the care of him until he was delivered to you, but now he says, it was left with him to do as he pleased, either to go forward to Virginia, or to return to Spain from this State—I suppose his being something out of health & a little home sick, discourages him from proceeding on so long a journey—however I have prevailed upon him to proceed as far as NewYork, where I hope the Spanish Minister will either persuade him to proceed on to Virginia or permit one of his servants, who may understand the management of these creatures, to proceed with & take the care of the Jack—I have furnished Mr Fairfax with thirty dollars to defray their charges upon the road, I offered him as much more as he should judge necessary to carry him thrô the Journey, but he said, as he had some money left that you gave him, he did not chuse to take any more, for fear of being robbed on the road, more espescially as he could readily procure more at NewYork, Philadelphia, or Baltimore, if he found he had occasion for it[1]— he has bought a saddle & bridle to return with for which he gave three pounds, Nine shillings Lawfull Money. I remain with great respect Your Most obedient, humble Servt

Thomas Cushing

LS, DLC:GW; copy, DLC:GW. Cushing enclosed the copy of this letter in his letter to GW of 16 November.

1. John Fairfax got 10 dollars from Robert Morris in Philadelphia on 29 November. See Morris to GW, 28 Jan. 1786, n.1.

From George Mason

Dear Sir   Gunston-Hall Novemr 9th 1785.

The Bearer waits on you with a Side of Venison (the first we have killed this Season) which I beg Your Acceptance of.

I have heard nothing from the Assembly, except vague Reports of their being resolved to issue a Paper Currency: upon what Principles, or Funds, I know not; perhaps upon the old thread-bare Security, of pledging solemnly the Public Credit.[1] I believe such an Experiment wou'd prove simular to the old vulgar Adage, of carrying a Horse to the Water. They may pass a Law to issue it, but twenty Laws will not make People receive it.

I intended to go down to Richmond about the 15th of this month, to have reported the Compact with the Maryland Commissioners;[2] but I have lately had so severe a Fit of the convulsive cholic, or the Gout in my Stomach, that I dare not venture far from Home: it held me from Sunday Evening 'til Tuesday Morning, & has left me so weak, that I am hardly able to walk across the Floor.

We hope to hear that you, your Lady, & Family are well; to whom Mrs Mason & the Family here present their best Compliments, with those of Dear Sir Your affecte & obdt Sert

G. Mason

ALS, DLC:GW.

1. James Madison reported to Jefferson on 22 Jan. 1786 that "no overt attempt" was made in the session of the Virginia legislature just completed to reintroduce paper money (Rutland and Rachal, *Madison Papers*, 8:477).

2. Both the Virginia and Maryland legislatures in their current sessions ratified the compact relating to the navigation of the Potomac that commissioners from the two states had entered into on 28 Mar. 1785 at the conference at Mount Vernon. The text of the compact is printed in Rutland, *Mason Papers*, 2:816–22; for the act of the Virginia legislature ratifying the compact, see 12 Hening 50–55.

Letter not found: from Samuel Vaughan, 9 Nov. 1785. On 30 Nov. GW wrote Vaughan that he had received his "favor of the 9th."

To George William Fairfax

My Dear Sir,   Mount Vernon 10th Novr 1785.

Inclosed you have a copy of my last;[1] since which nothing has occurred worthy of observation, except that in this part of the Country our Crops—particularly of Indian Corn, have suffered exceedingly by a drought in July & august, and a storm in September.

As I am in the habit of giving you trouble, I will add a little more to what my last, I fear, may have occasioned.

The two youngest children of Mr Custis—the oldest a girl of six years—the other a boy a little turned of four, live with me. They are both promising children; but the latter is a remarkable fine one—& my intention is to give him a liberal education; the rudiments of which shall, if I live, be in my own family. Having promised this, let me next my good Sir, ask if it is in your power conveniently, to engage a proper preceptor for him? At present, & for a year or two to come, much confinement would be improper for him; but this being the period in which I should derive more aid from a man of Letters & an accomptant than at any other, to assist me in my numerous correspondences, & to extricate the latter from the disordered state into which they have been thrown by the war, I could usefully employ him in this manner until attention should be more immediately required for his pupil.

Fifty or Sixty pounds Sterling pr ann:, with board, lodging, washing & mending, *in the family*, is the most my numerous expenditures will allow me to give; but how far it may command the services of a person well qualified to answer the purposes I have mentioned, is not for me to decide. To answer *my* purposes, the Gentleman must be a master of composition, & a good Accomptant: to answer his pupil's, he must be a classical scholar, & capable of teaching the French language grammatically: the more universal his knowledge is, the better.

It sometimes happens that very worthy men of the *Cloth* come under this description; men who are advanced in years, & not very comfortable in their circumstances: such an one, if unencumbered with a family, would be more agreeable to me than a young man just from college—but I except none of good moral character, answering my description, if he can be well recommended.

To you my Dr Sir, I have offered this my first address; but if you should think my purposes cannot be subserved in your circle, upon the terms here mentioned; I beg, in that case, that you will be so obliging as to forward the enclosed letter as it is directed. This gentleman has written to me upon another subject, & favored me with his lucubrations upon Education, wch mark him a man of abilities, at the sametime that he is highly spoken of as a teacher & a person of good character. In Scotland we all know that education is cheap, & wages not so high as in England: but I would prefer, on accot of the dialect, an Englishman to a Scotchman, for all the purposes I want.[2]

We have commenced our operations on the navigation of this river; & I am happy to inform you, that the difficulties rather vanish than increase as we proceed. James river is under similar circumstances; & a Cut between the waters of Albemarle in No. Carolina, & Elizabeth river in this State, is also in contemplation—and if the whole is effected—& I see nothing to prevent it, it will give the greatest & most advantageous inland Navigation to this Country of any in the Union—or I believe, in the world: for as the Shannondoah, the South branch, Monocasy & Conogocheague are equally capable of great improvement, they will no doubt be immediately attempted; & more than probable a communication by good roads will be opened with the waters to the Westward of us; by means of the No. Branch of Potomac, which interlocks with the Cheat river & Yohoghaney (branches of the Monongahela) that empty into the Ohio at Fort Pitt—The same is equally practicable between James river & the Green briar a branch of the Great Kanhawa, which empties into the same river 300 miles below that place; by means whereof the whole trade of that Territory which is now unfolding to our view, may be drawn into this State—equally productive of political as commercial advantages.

As I never ride to my plantations without seeing something which makes me regret having [continued] so long in the ruinous mode of farming, which we are in; I beg leave, tho' I am persuaded it will give you trouble, to recall your attention to the requests of my former letter, the duplicate of which you now have.[3] Miscarriages, & where this is not the case, delays of letters must be my apology for reiterating the matter, that there may be time for decision, before the intervention of another year.

The marriage mentioned in my last is celebrated, but a fit of the gout prevented Colo. Bassett from being at it—consequently I am to lay a little longer out of your kind present.[4] Mrs Washington who has very indifferent health, joins me in the sincerest and best wishes for every blessing which can be bestowed on Mrs Fairfax & yourself. With great esteem & regard, I am &c. &c.

G: Washington

P.S. Since writing the above & foregoing I have seen Mr Battaile Muse who looks after your Estate; & upon enquiry of him, am authorized to inform you that your negroes, & every thing under his care are tolerably well, & your prospect of a crop midling, which is saying a good deal *this year*.

I have the pleasure also to inform you that your Brother & his family were very well a few days ago when I was there, attending the business of the Potomac company at the Great Falls. Your Sister and family are likewise well. I saw her three oldest daughters last week—the elder of them, Milly, is on the eve of matrimony with a Mr Ogden Throckmorton—a match not very agreeable, it is said, to *her* friends, & kept off by Mrs Bushrod 'till her death which happened some three or four months ago—by now is yielded to by her Parents.[5]

G: Washington

LB, DLC:GW.

1. GW wrote to Fairfax on 30 June.

2. The enclosed letter to George Chapman, to whom GW wrote on 15 Dec. 1784 thanking him for a copy of his *Treatise on Education*, was also dated 10 Nov. and was never delivered. On 11 Nov. GW wrote the following letter to Fairfax: "My Dr Sir, I was at the point of sealing the dispatches herewith enclosed, when I recd a visit from a Gentleman of New England—& happening to mention my want of a person for the purposes recited in my letter to you of yesterday's date—he seemed to think that such a character as I have there described, might be had from their Colleges upon very moderate terms—& promised to make enquiry, & to advise me of the result in a little time after his return.

"The intention therefore of this letter is to request that the enclosure for Mr Chapman may be detained in your hands until you hear further from me on this subject. But I would wish, notwithstanding, that *you* would do me the favor to extend *your* enquiries, & revolve characters in your own mind, against

I shall hear from my New England correspondent that in case of a disappointment *there*, & I am not sanguine in my expectations from that quarter, I may be advanced in this business on your side the Atlantic" (LB, DLC:GW). Shortly after hiring Tobias Lear as secretary and tutor to Eleanor Parke Custis and George Washington Parke Custis, GW wrote Fairfax on 25 June 1786 to burn "the letter which I put under your cover for Mr Chapman." GW's letter-book ·copy of his letter to Chapman reads: "Sir, I rely more upon your goodness than on any just claim I can have for your excuse, for the liberty I am about to take with you.

"I have a little boy something turned of four, & a Girl of six years old living with me, for whom I want a Tutor. They are both promising children—the latter is a very fine one—and altho' they are of an age when close confinement may be improper; yet a man of letters, master of composition, and a good accomptant, would in other respects be essentially useful to *me* for a year or two to come. May I ask you therefore Sir, if it is in your power, conveniently, to engage a person of this description for me?

"Having already informed you what my wants are, it is needless to add what those of the children must be; your own judgement, when I inform you that I mean to fit the boy, in my own family, for a University, will point these out. The greater the knowledge of his preceptor is, the better he would suit—To teach French grammatically is essential, as it is now becoming a part of the education of youth in this Country.

"I could not afford to give more than £50 Sterlg pr ann:—but this sum, except in the article of Cloathing, wou'd be clear—as the Gentleman would eat at my table; & have his lodging and washing found him—& his Linen & stockings mended by the Servants of my Family. It may happen that an Episcopal clergyman with a small living, & unencumbered by a family may be had to answer this description—such an one would be preferred: but I except none who is competent to my purposes, if his character is unimpeached.

"I will make no apology to you Sir, for this liberty—you will oblige me if you can serve me; but I do not mean to put you to much trouble to do it. At any rate let me entreat an acknowledgement of this letter, with your sentiments upon it; as I shall remain in a state of suspence until I hear from you" (DLC:GW).

3. This is GW's letter of 30 June.

4. For the Robert Edge Pine prints that Fairfax sent nearly two years before, see Fairfax to GW, 10 June 1784, n.1.

5. On 17 Oct. GW and Thomas Johnson spent the night with Bryan Fairfax en route from Georgetown to the Great Falls of the Potomac during the meeting of the directors of the Potomac River Company. Fairfax's sister was Hannah Fairfax Washington, wife of Warner Washington. Their oldest daughter Mildred (c.1766–1804) married Albion Throckmorton (1731–c.1795) of Frederick County in December. Mildred Washington Bushrod was the bride's aunt.

From Tench Tilghman

Dear Sir   Baltimore 10th Novemr 1785.

I have had the honor of your letter of the 2d with one for Mr Rawlins inclosed, which I delivered myself. He confesses his delinquency, but pleads sickness—business at Annapolis and other matters, by way of Excuse—he however has promised to have your Designs compleated by saturday Night—If he keeps his word, I will forward them by the Monday's Stage under cover to Fitzgerald.[1] Mrs Tilghman desires to be joined in Compliments to Mrs Washington and yourself with Dear Sir Yr most Affect: Hble Servt

Tench Tilghman

ALS, DLC:GW.

1. See Rawlins to GW, 15 Nov., and Tilghman to GW, 18 November.

To William Fitzhugh

My Dr Sir   Mount Vernon 11th Novr 1785.

I pray you to accept my thanks for your favor of the second, & for the present which it announced—than which nothing could be more acceptable, as I am desireous of getting into a stock of Deer with as much expedition as the nature of the case will admit. But if the Doe you offer me is not inconvenient to yourself; I shou'd be glad if she could remain at Chatham until a small paddock which I intend to enclose this Winter for the reception of these animals, is railed in—when I will fall upon some method, least liable to accidents, to bring her up.

I congratulate you on your success on the Falmouth turf. Our old acquaintance Saml Gallaway retired from the Alexa races, & from the pomps & vanities of this World almost in the same instant—having taken his departure for the impervious shades of death as soon as he got home.[1] My respectful compliments, in which Mrs Washington [joins], are offered to Mrs Fitzhugh. I am Dr Sir &c.

Go: Washington

LB, DLC:GW.

1. Samuel Galloway, a Quaker merchant of Tulip Hill south of Annapolis, a great lover of horseflesh, had been an occasional visitor at Mount Vernon before the Revolution.

From Patrick Henry

Dear sir.   Richmond novr 11th 1785

The post Yesterday brought me your Favors. That which was official I have just sent down to the Assembly.[1] The Result shall go to you as soon as I get it—The Report concerning the intended Canal I could not send you 'til now, having obtained a Copy of it only two Days ago. Mr Andrews tells me the Comrs could not take a very particular View of the Ground, having gone to it shortly after the great Storm which happen'd in Sepr. But it seems universally agreed that the Cut ought to go from Pasquotank thro' the Dismal as reported. I understand Opposition will be made to this usefull Undertaking by some people in Carolina, & that it will be usher'd forth under the Guise of public Spirit, taking Alarm at a Measure which will place the Trade of that Country in a Situation of Dependance upon the Will & Pleasure of this—To obviate such Cavils I have recommended to some Friends of the Scheme to preface the Act proposed to be passed on the Subject with a Declaration, in the clearest Terms, that the Benefits resulting shall be reciprocal to both States, & that a Conference be offer'd to hear & refute Objections—I am apprehensive that the Measure may not be brot forth into Discussion with the Advantages that could be wished, & the Nature of it requires: The Men of Business in the House being generally unacquainted, & in some Measure inattentive to it. I think a Line from you on the Subject, if the Report has yr approbation, would have a good Effect—If Success can be given to this Navigation, & at the same Time to that of Potowmack & James River, great Things must result. And indeed, nothing more is necessary in this Canal Business, than giving a proper Direction to the Efforts which seem ready for Exertion.[2]

Mr Andrews further tells me he thinks one Lock necessary for the southern, & another for the northern End of the Canal, for letting out & in the Vessels, &c. & that the Waters of the Lake will be sufficient for a constant Supply to the Canal. I wish the Report had been more particular, but such as it is I inclose it to you, & will be much obliged by yr Observations on the Subject. Mrs Henrys Compliments with mine are respectfully presented to your self & your Lady & with the most sincere Attachment I remain dear sir your most humble Servant

P. Henry

ALS, DLC:GW.

1. GW sent Governor Henry two letters dated 29 Oct., the one enclosing the other giving GW's official decision to the Virginia legislature regarding its gift to him of shares in both the Potomac and James River companies.

2. On 1 Jan. 1785 the Virginia house of delegates adopted a resolution calling for the governor to appoint three commissioners to "fix on the most convenient course for a canal" from the Elizabeth River "to those passing through the State of North Carolina" and report to the general assembly. The commissioners' report of 15 Oct. 1785 to Benjamin Harrison, speaker of the house of delegates, a copy of which James Madison also enclosed in a letter to GW of this date, was the basis for a bill being prepared and debated in the October 1785 session of the house. On 19 Jan. 1786 the delegates voted to suspend further consideration of the bill and to authorize the governor to approach the governor of North Carolina for the purpose of arranging for commissioners from each state to meet and prepare a bill providing for opening and operating a mutually advantageous Elizabeth River (or Dismal Swamp) canal (*House of Delegates Journal, 1781–1785*). The report to Harrison of 15 Oct. 1785, from Portsmouth, Va., reads: "Sir, According to the Commission given to us by His Excellency—the Governor and the Honorable the Council we have viewed the Country which lies between the Waters of Elizabeth River and those of the State of North Carolina, and have informed ourselves of the Courses & Navigation of these Waters. It appears to us that the most convenient Course for a Canal between these Waters is from the Head of either Deep Creek or new mill Creek, Branches of the Southern Branch of Elizabeth River to the head of Pasquotank River in the State of North Carolina, the Communication with the upper Country by this Route being much shorter than that by the North River, which empties into Currituck Sound, and free from the great Dangers & Difficulties which attend the Currituck Navigation. We are farther induced to prefer this Route on account of its immediate Communication with a very fertile and extensive Country, and as it seems to be the only one approved of by the Citizens of North Carolina, or which they think will be of much Advantage to them. The Length of a Canal this Way will be about 18 Miles, and we are of Opinion that the Expence of cutting it will not exceed twenty four thousand pounds. The State of North Carolina not having appointed Commissioners we had no Opportunity of holding any public Conference on this Business but we have reason to believe that Carolina will readily concur in it provided its Trade through the Canal be secured from Imposts for the Benefit of the State of Virginia. We have the Honor to be &c.

Robert Andrews[,] David Meade" (DLC:GW). See GW to Henry, 30 November. Not until 1 Dec. 1787 did the Virginia assembly pass "An Act for cutting a navigable Canal from the waters of Elizabeth river, in this State, to the waters of Pasquotank river, in the State of North Carolina." It was not to go into effect until "the passing of a like act by the general assembly of North Carolina," which North Carolina did not do until 1790 (12 Hening 479–94). See also Henry to GW, 10 June 1785, and notes.

From James Madison

Dear Sir   Richmond Novr 11. 1785

I recd your favor of the 29th ulto on thursday. That by Col. Lee had been previously delivered.[1] Your letter for the Assembly was laid before them yesterday. I have reason to believe that it was received with every sentiment which would correspond with yours. Nothing passed from which any conjecture could be formed as to the objects which would be most pleasing for the appropriation of the fund. The disposition is I am persuaded much stronger to acquiesce in your choice whatever it may be than to lead or anticipate it: and I see no inconveniency in your taking time for a choice that will please yourself. The letter was referred to a Committee which will no doubt make such report as will give effect to your wishes.[2]

Our Session commenced very inauspiciously with a contest for the Chair which was followed by a rigid scrutiny into Mr Harrison's election in his County. He gained the Chair by a majority of 6 votes and retained his Seat by a majority of still fewer. His residence was the point on which the latter question turned. Doctr Lee's election was questioned on a similar point and was also established; but it was held to be vitiated by his acceptance of a lucrative post under the United States.[3] The House have engaged with some alacrity in the consideration of the Revised Code proposed by Mr Jefferson Mr Pendleton & Mr Wythe. The present temper promises an adoption of it in substance. The greatest danger arises from its length compared with the patience of the members. If it is persisted in it must exclude several matters which are of moment, but I hope only for the present Assembly.[4] The pulse of the H. of D. was felt on thursday with regard to a general manumission by a petition presented on that subject. It was rejected without dissent but not without an avowed patronage of its principle by sundry respectable members. A motion was made to throw it under the table, which was treated with as much indignation on one side, as the petition itself was on the other. There are several petitions before the House against any Step towards freeing the slaves, and even praying for a repeal of the law which licences particular manumissions.[5] The Merchants of several of our Towns have made representations on the distresses of our commerce, which have raised the question whether relief shall be attempted by a reference to Cong[res]s or by measures within our own Compass. On a pretty full discussion it was determined by a Large majority that the power over trade ought to be vested in Congress, under certain qualifications. If the qualifications suggested & no others should be annexed, I think they will not be subversive of the principle tho' they will no doubt lessen its utility. The Speaker Mr M. Smith & Mr Braxton are the champions against Congress. Mr Thruston & Mr White have since come in, and I fancy I may set down both as auxiliaries. They are however not a little puzzled by the difficulty of substituting any practicable regulations within ourselves. Mr Braxton proposed two that did not much aid his side of the question; the 1 was that all British vessels from the W. Indies should be excluded from our ports—the 2. that no Merchant should carry on trade here untill he sd have been a resident —— years. Unless some plan freer from objection can be devised for this State, its patrons will be reduced clearly to the dilemma of acceding to a general one, or leaving our trade under all its present embarrassments. There has been some little skirmishing on the ground of public faith, which leads me to hope that its friends have less to fear than was surmised.[6] The Assize & Port Bills have not yet been awakened. The Senate will make a House today for the first time. With the greatest respect & regard I have the honor to be Dr Sir, Yr Obedt & very humble Servt

J. Madison Jr

P.S. Inclosed herewith are two reports from the Commsrs for examining the head of James River &c. and the ground between the waters of Elizabeth River & N. Carolina—also a sensible pamphlet said to be written by St George Tucker of this State.[7]

ALS, DLC:GW; LB, DLC: Madison Papers.

1. See GW's letter of 22 October.

2. See GW to Patrick Henry, 29 Oct. (second letter), n.1. Madison wrote Thomas Jefferson on 22 Jan.: "The donation presented to Genl. W. embarrass[ed] him much. On one side he disliked the appearance of slighting the bounty of his Country and of an ostentatious disinterestedness. On the other an acceptance of reward in any shape was irreconcileable with the law he had imposed on himself. His answer to the Assembly declined in the most affectionate terms the emolument allotted to himself, but intimated his willingness to accept it so far as to dedicate it to some public and patriotic use. This Act recites the original act & his answer, and appropriates the future revenue from the shares to such public objects as he shall appoint. *He has been pleased* to *ask my* ideas with regard to the *most proper objects. I suggest in* general only, *a part*[i]*tion of the fund* between some *institution* which would *please the* [phil]*osophical world* and some other which may be of [a] *popular cast.* If your knowledge of the *several institutions, in France* or *else where*, should suggest *models, or hints, I could wish for your ideas* on the *case which is* no less *concerns the good of the common* wealth than *the character of its most illustrious citizen*" (Rutland and Rachal, *Madison Papers*, 8:472–82).

3. Arthur Lee's election from Prince William County was challenged on the points of residency and of holding a paying position from Congress. On 31 Oct. he was declared ineligible to serve in the house on the second count (*House of Delegates Journal, 1781–1785*).

4. For the revisal of the Virginia code, see the editorial note in "The Revisal of the Laws, 1776–1786" in Boyd, *Jefferson Papers*, 2:305–665. See also Madison's report of 22 Jan. 1786 to Jefferson on the progress made in this session on the revision and "Bills for a Revised State Code of Laws" (Rutland and Rachal, *Madison Papers*, 8:472–82, 391–99).

5. A petition for the emancipation of the slaves drawn up and circulated in the summer and fall of 1785 under the guidance of the Methodist leaders Francis Asbury and Thomas Coke was read in the house on 8 Nov. and rejected 10 Nov. without dissent. The legislative history of the unsuccessful attempt in the Virginia house of delegates during this session to amend or repeal the act permitting the manumission of slaves is given in note 4 of this letter from Madison to GW as printed, Rutland and Rachal, *Madison Papers*, 8:403–5. See also Madison to Thomas Jefferson, 22 Jan. 1786, ibid., 472–82.

6. Joseph Prentis introduced in the house of delegates four resolutions for vesting in Congress the power to regulate trade, but after much controversy the house took no action until the last day of the session when it passed a resolution "proposing a general meeting of Commssrs from the States to consider and recommend a fœderal plan for regulating Commerce" and appointing seven commissioners from Virginia (Madison to Thomas Jefferson, 22 Jan. 1786, ibid., 472–82; see also "Resolution Authorizing a Commission to Examine Trade Regulations," ibid., 470–71, and Madison to GW, 9 Dec. 1785, n.1). Madison identifies Benjamin Harrison, Meriwether Smith, and Carter Braxton as the leading opponents of empowering Congress to regulate trade.

7. For the report on the Elizabeth River Canal, see Henry to GW, 11 Nov.,

n.2. St. George Tucker has been identified as the author of a pamphlet published in Richmond entitled *Reflections on the Policy and Necessity of Encouraging the Commerce of the Citizens of the United States of America, and of Granting Them Exclusive Privileges of Trade*.

From Battaile Muse

Honourable Sir,   Berkeley County Novr 15th 1785
    as I returned from Alexandria I directed the Overseers on Doctr Seldens Estate to get out their Wheat as Fast as Possable and Send it down, which I expect they will do. I have ready here 200 bushels but I cannot get waggons to Hall it untill next month—when the weather Permits I Shall Send down as fast as I can get waggones to hall it. what butter I have which may be about 140 lb. I shall Lodge at Mr Andrew Wales, about the 10th of next month.[1]
    I shall be much oblige to you to give me Perticular Instructions how I am to settle with the Tenants where they have paid Paper money—as its' a Matter of Consequence to you as well the Tenants, a Final Settlement cannot Take place until that is fixed—and where the Tenant In possession has Purchased He is desirous to have the Matter setled before He Pays for His write of the Lease, the Former Tenant will not Make good the depreciation and forbids the Tenant in Possession to do so—therefore if the Law is in your Favour they will not Pay nor settle only agreeable to the receipts given them unless they are distressed—which must be the Case Should the Law Intitle you to a settlement by the secale. I am not Fully acquainted with the Law but in my opinion that the words of the Law are that where their has not been a Final Settlement of accts that then the depretiation is To Take Place—but where accts have been fully Settled they are to remain so.[2] I See by a receipt of Mr Lunn Washington given Collet for £36 in 1779 when their was only thirty pounds due this Looks Like their might have been something said on the Subject when Mr Washington received the money. I shall be much Oblige to you to Instruct me Perticularly on this business[3]—as I wish to sattisfy the Tenant⟨s⟩ and to make a Proper statement in a Renttal that it may be Known from Time to Time the ballances due. I Suppose Colo. Samuel Washingtons receipts given the Tenants are good and that I need not Take

up any receipts of His or others. I have the Honour to be your Obedient Humble Servant

B. Muse

P.S. I have not received any money, I Visit your Fauquier Tenants next week—I a⟨s be⟩fore. B.M.

ALS, DLC:GW.

1. Dr. Wilson Selden owned land on Goose Creek in Loudoun County (12 Hening 404). The longtime brewer in Alexandria, Andrew Watts Wales (c.1737–1799), acted as Muse's business agent in the town.

2. "An act directing the mode of adjusting and settling the payment of certain debts and contracts, and for other purposes" (10 Hening 471–74), enacted in the November 1781 session of the Virginia general assembly, provided the scale of payment of debts or contracts entered into between 1 Jan. 1777 and 1 Jan. 1782, a period when paper currency became greatly inflated.

3. For GW's prior dealings with Moses and Isaac Collett, see Dolphin Drew to GW, 13 Feb. 1784, n.1, and Isaac Collett to GW, 22 Feb. 1784.

From John Rawlins

Honner'd Sir   Baltimore Novr 15th 1785

I am exceedingly sorry I have Dissopinted you so Long, of the Drawing and Estemate for your Room—its bein sickness and other Circumstances in my family that's prevented it—to Ornaments in Ceiling, Cove, Cornice, & moulding at top of cove, with pannels on the walls plaine—my Lowest termes I can posibley, finish it for his £168 pounds this Currency, you finding my people and paying Travleing Charges[1]—and remaine Honner'd Sir Yr Most Obdt Hble Svt,

John Rawlins

N.B. the Ornaments to Ceiling as pr Drawing you saw.

ALS, NjMoNP.

1. GW wrote the stucco worker John Rawlins on 29 Aug. giving him a description of his New Room at Mount Vernon and inviting Rawlins to give an estimate of what he would charge to complete it. Rawlins came to Mount Vernon in mid-September to view the room. Although GW objected to Rawlins's estimate of the costs, he accepted his terms and entered an agreement with him on 25 Feb. 1786. See GW to Rawlins, 30 Nov. 1785, GW to Tench Tilghman, 29 Aug., 14 Sept., 30 Nov. 1785, 7 Jan., 22 Feb., 10 Mar. 1786, Tench Tilghman to GW, 31 Aug., 10, 18 Nov., 13 Dec. 1785, 16 Jan., 1 Mar. 1786, and *Diaries*, 4:291–92.

From Antoine-Félix Wuibert

General   Hispaniola Cap-français 15. of November 1785

Pray, give me the Leave to remember to your Excellency my most Respectfull duty, & Enquire about the present State of your Health, for Which Every good Citizen must pray, Since you are our Common father & the Protector of those Who Have Endured the Calamities of this Last Great War.

Altho' I came over here on account of the Benefit of the air for the Recovery of my Health; & Shelter myself under the Hospitable Roof of few Charitable friends of mine against the Want I Was, in While in Philadelphia; & the disagreable Consequences of the Horrid poverty in a Country Where I Had no Credit, nor friend, nor any Kind of Support to relieve & Keep myself With; I am, However, no Less resolved & it is my only & Last Wish to Return to the Liberty-Land again & Die in a Country Which I Have always Considered as my own native one, Ever Since June 1776.

Therefore, General, I do Humbly Entreat you Would be So good as for tell me, in the most Certain Way, When & in What time the Congress Will pay the interets of our Certificates, mine is a *Continental* one, Also my Little proportion in the Lands to be divided among the officers & Soldiers of the Late Continental Army: I do Sincerely Wish to Have Some good Information about that, for I do much dislike to be at the Other's Expence & troubles; Indeed, I do not Live but in the most piercing Anguish of mind! Here is, then, the Sad Consequences Which fall upon us, But much more peculiarly on mySelf, Who Have amazingly Suffered or in England or on Board of the British Squadrons for mostly all the War. Since the close of the Hostilities, I Was Confined in my Bed By many Infirmities for near 9 months: Doctr Chovet one of the Phisicians I Had Called for, Governor Dickinson, Colo. Shee & many other good & Credible gentlemen Dare Say & assert that I Was on the point to Lose my Left Leg. In that fatal Illness during 9 months, I Was twice in Less than 4 in a Dying State, Walking afterwards on my Hands & Knees for 6 Weecks; & upon Crutches for 3 months: I do only thank to Doctr Chovet's Sagacity & tender Cares; &, Since, the Change of the air in Hispaniola Which has been of great benefit to me, Since my Both Legs are Entirely Cured & Safe: Nevertheless I am not Less reduced, as now, to the grievous & Shamefull Condition to ask to Some & Beg to Other for my But too Well deserved Bread.

Pardon me, Worthy & Memorable Commander, for this Sudden Start from my part! I do Really Know But too Well all What you Have Said & Done in the Behalf of Every Individual of your Army: all America, But What I Say! all the World Rightly proclaims your Eminent Virtus & Hallow your Blessed Name! When, then, Shall We Cease to be tormented By the Horros of su⟨ch⟩ Distress; & Complain for the Congress's undeserved forgetfulness? it is What I dont ⟨see⟩.

Suppose the Congress Would not Soon pay the interets of the Continental Certificates, *So is mine*, neither deliver up our allowance of Land; I shall Humbly Beg Your Excellency's goodness & recommandation, for Some new appointment of Engineer in the Congress or any of the States Service; then I Shall Dccm mySelf much Honored & too Happy to find Some opportunity to Shew My faithfull attachment to the Public Service: at Least, General, at Least, I ⟨would⟩ Honestly keep my Life![1]

I Do quietly Live on a retired Place, the Marquis De Gallifet's plantation, 6 miles from the City of Cap-français, administered By one Mo. Odelucq Senior, an old friend of mine, Who, With much ado & Cares, has, at last Restored me to the former State of Health Which I had Lost for this 2 years past. the Said plantation, Sugar Work, is the Very Rural delights Seat for Somebody Who don't Like the noise of the World, on account of Mo. Odelucq⟨'s⟩ peacefull, meek & Studious temper, &, above all, His aversion for all Who We may Rightly Deem Hurtfull in the Least to the Body, Estate & the dignity of the Man. Not Any Body, General, But men of Credit & Wisdom, Comes Here, unless invited By my friend: I dare Say that Gentleman is one of the most devoted, among the french, to the Continental Soldiers, & the Best Wishes for the good & the Wellfare of the American Liberty; for He took always Very friendly much part in our distresses as Well as in our Prosperity; In a Word he is true Republican & Born to be free. He Would Esteeme Himself But too Happy in Entertaining the Protector of the Rights of Mankind Rather than many Idle & Vain Glorious Generals in the World, By Some of Whom he is Sometimes diverted from, When they Land Here; this is his Dearest Wish & Greatest piece of Consolation, about What We talk together most all Long Day. There is about one thousand of Slaves upon that plantation, all Well & tenderly Keept & managed accordingly to the principles of Humanity & Charity of that Honest Superintendant 12 years ago There is one fine Kitchin garden Wherein Roots, Vegetables of Every Kind may be Seen. the Waters abundantly Runs all the year, in the Spite of the Hotest Summer's Days, through the plantation, So that the people may Commodiously Wash & Bath any Where they Walk about the place. the game is But Very Little; But as for the fish, there is in plenty. Saddle & chair-horses are in great number. We Have one Very good & able Phisician With a Very Large & Compleat apothecary's Stock. In fine that Place is Generally provided With all the Conveniencies of the Life; profit With pleasure may, at Will; be found & Joined in this Beautifull & Solitary Country-Seat. I have the Honor to Be With the most profound Respect General your Excellency's The Most Humble & the most obedient Servant

Colonel Wuibert, Cinctus
of the Late Continental Corps of Engineers

P.S. Being one among the members of the Society of the Cincinnati, I do now Stand in Need of the Engraved Patent or Diplome & the Silver medal of our Order, for Such pieces Cannot be dispensed With: the french are much Cavilling upon that Head. I do Belong to the Committee of the State of Pennsylvania. Pardon, General, Pardon, if I take upon mySelf to be So free & Give you So many Troubles. ⟨A.⟩ Wbt

ALS, DLC:GW. GW received and endorsed two other copies of this letter in Wuibert's hand and signed by him, dated 15 and 25 December. The latter of these was enclosed in George William Fairfax to GW, 23 Jan. 1786.

Antoine-Félix Wuibert (Weibert, Viebert) de Mézières, a French volunteer, served as an engineer in New York under GW until taken prisoner at the fall of Fort Washington on 11 Nov. 1776. Held a prisoner in England until exchanged in December 1778, Wuibert volunteered to serve with John Paul Jones and was aboard the *Bonhomme Richard* when she engaged the *Serapis* in September 1779. He was captured at sea twice in 1780 while trying to return to America, but he succeeded in rejoining the army in 1781 and served in America until November 1783.

1. See GW's response of 31 July 1786.

From Thomas Cushing

Sir   Boston November 16th 1785

The foregoing is a copy of mine of the 9th instant by Mr Fairfax, who set out on his journey together with the Spaniard & the Jack on the 10th instant—I have not as yet been able to procure from Mr Peirce of Gloucester, nor from Mr Cabot of Beverly their respective Accounts for the passages of the Jack Asses, & therefore cannot as yet send your account of expenditures relative to the Jacks,[1] but have at present taken the liberty to draw a Sett of bills of exchange dates November 16th 1785 for the sum of three hundred dollars in favour of Messrs Isaac & William Smith merchants of this Town on their order, payable at ⟨*mutilated*⟩ sight, which I doubt not you will honour,[2] ⟨as soon⟩ as I can procure the accts above referrd to, I shall send forward your account. In the mean time, I remain With great respect & esteem Your most humble Servant

Thomas Cushing

ALS, DLC:GW.

1. For David Pearce's charges for transporting the jackass from Bilbao to Gloucester, see William Hartshorne & Co. to GW, 26 Nov., n.1. Cushing paid on GW's behalf the charges for the passage of the jackass that died at sea (see William Hartshorne to GW, 25 Mar. 1786).

2. GW paid Cushing's draft on Isaac & William Smith "the moment it was presented" (GW to Cushing, 5 April 1786).

From David Stuart

Dear Sir,   Novr 16th [17]85 Richmond

It was my misfortune soon after my arrival here, to be confined for several days by sickness; occasioned by lodging in a house newly built, whose walls were perfectly damp—I mention this circumstance by way of accounting, for my not having written to you as yet, and given you some account of our proceedings—Tho' indeed so little is yet done, that I can now only inform you of what is proposed to be done, rather than what is done—Much time at the beginning, was spent in examining the legality of the Speaker's, and Mr Lee's elections. I have only to observe on this matter, that from the manner in which it was conducted, it appears to have originated more from a spirit of faction, than any regard to an infringment of the Constitution[1]—An attempt is making, which I fear will prove too successful, to postpone the payment of the present taxes—Indeed, some state the inability of the people to be such, as to require an entire remission—This, considering the pressing demands of Congress, and the necessity of a punctual compliance with our own domestic engagements, is certainly strange policy—I think for my part, it may be attended with very fatal consequences; since the people, from being unaccustomed to a regular payment of taxes, may at length refuse to pay any. I have heard so many express favorable sentiments of the Port bill, that I am induced to hope, it will take place; and with the amendment, of striking out some of the places now nominated[2]—Soon after the news of the declaration of war by the Algerines, against us, arrived; information was given to the Executive, that there had three of that nation just come to Norfolk—As it was concieved they were spies, they have been sent for—On examination, however, it seems they are Moors, and subjects of the Emperor of Morocco—Tho' not confined, yet I understand they are watched. The inhabitants of Kentuck, have sent in their petition by their Delegates, praying a separation—It is so sensible, respectful, and moderate, that it seems to produce conviction on every mind, of the propriety of the measure—The members nominated to Congress, in lieu of Mercer and Hardy, are Coll Lee, and Coll Carrington—There were several other Candidates for these places, who were not ashamed openly to sollicit votes. Indeed, I am very sorry to observe, that Richmond abounds with people watching for place⟨s⟩ and who omit no opportunity of paying court to the *very honourable* Members—Mr Braxton has been chosen into the Council—The embarrassed state of his affairs, ought to perhaps to have been an objection to putting him in a place, which may be considered in some measure as an asylum[3]—Your letter to the Governor has been read in the House; and a bill is brought in, repealing the former law according to your petition; and giving you full power, to appropriate to any purposes you may think fit, the donations of the Assembly—It will I suppose be transmitted to you by order of the House, as soon as it has passed. I have heard much approbation and satisfaction expressed at your declining those donations[4]—I inclose to you a bill, now under the consideration of the House, giving powers to Congress to regulate our trade—its fate will not be decided till friday week. If therefore any amendment occurs to you, I shall receive it with pleasure[5]—I believe I have now unloaded my budget—I therefore conclude with desiring my Compliments to Mrs Washington, and the family at Mount Vernon—I am Dr Sir with sincere regard Your Obt Servt

David Stuart

ALS, DLC:GW.

1. For Madison's more detailed report on the disputed elections of Benjamin Harrison and Arthur Lee, see James Madison to GW, 11 November.

2. See Madison's report on the tax bill and the Kentucky petition in Madison to GW, 9 December.

3. By joint ballot of the house and senate, the general assembly on 15 Nov. elected to Congress Richard Henry Lee, William Grayson, James Monroe, Edward Carrington, and Henry Lee, Jr., and elected Carter Braxton to the Council of State in the place of William Nelson, Jr., who had resigned (*House of Delegates Journal, 1781–1785*). Samuel Hardy died in New York on 17 Oct.; John Francis Mercer, who was reelected to Congress in June 1784, had not attended in 1785.

4. See GW to James Madison, 11 Nov., n.2.

5. See Madison to GW, 11 Nov., n.6, and 9 December.

From Thomas Smith

Sir,   Carlisle [Pa.] 17th[–26] November 1785

When the Letter which you did me the honour to write to me on the 14th of July last, was brought to Carlisle, I was in Philadelphia, & did not receive it till my return in August—I could not answer it before my return from the western Courts, because I had left your Papers at Bedford, (where I leave all the Papers respecting my business in the Western Courts, which are not necessary to be brought to this Place)—they were locked up in a Private drawer of mine, and, as I was obliged to go up so soon, I did not think it proper to trust any person to bring them down.

On my return from those Courts, I was honoured with your Letter of the 10th of September, and, if I could have devoted one hour to the examination of all the Papers, I would certainly have done myself the pleasure to have written to you, before I went to Westmoreland, with the Judges of the Supreme Court; But as soon as the business of the County Court at this Place, was finished, I was obliged to follow them, & could not overtake them, till they arrived at Westmoreland: indeed the Chief Justice had been so obliging as, at my request, to postpone holding that Court, from the 24th to the 31st of October. Had I been favoured with your first letter two weeks sooner, I should have requested the Judges to have holden a Court of Nisi Prius in Washington County this season, & it is probable I might have prevailed; but it was afterwards too late, as they had made their arrangements as to the other Counties. Some Ejectments have been Tried in Westmoreland; in which the Title of the Defendants was their Improvement, made before the Plantiffs had obtained their office right, notwithstanding which, the Plaintiffs recovered—there was only one case so circumstanced in which the Jury gave a Verdict for the Defendant, which the Judges immediately declared, was contrary to Law, & that they would grant a new Trial, if applied for in Philadelphia, which will be done: In their charge to the Jury, they laid down the Law respecting improvements in opposition to office rights, so pointedly & decidedly in favour of the latter, that I believe their decision must very materially operate in your favour, so far as the Defendants claim by settlements made under the Jurisdiction of Pennyslvania—In the last Ejectment which was Tried, I had this point brought fully before the Court (having an eye to your Ejectments)—the Defendants claimed by an Improvement only—I objected to its being given in Evidence—the Court ruled that it should not, & the Plaintiff producing an order & Survey, had a Verdict the jury not going from the Bar—hea[r]ing no Evidence on the part of the Defendant—this decision will produce very important effects on the Property of that County and will, I think shake the confidence of your opponents in the goodness of their Title—I assure you, it has made me more sanguine that I was before, and will warrant me in directing my attention chiefly to your Legal Title, on the Trial, although I think it necessary to keep the other in view. permit me to make a few remarks on that Title.[1]

The Date of Capt. Posey's Warrant does not appear, by the Patent, or by any Paper in my Possession, that I at present recollect.

I hope you will not think that I put you to unnecessary trouble in proving the Execution of Capt. Posey's Bond; because although the recital of it in the Patent is evidence against Virginia, by which the Patent was granted, yet it is no evidence against any other, & your opponents claim under Pennsylvania.[2]

I know little more of the mode of obtaining titles to Land in Virginia than what I have learned from your Papers, & therefore some observations which I have made and may make to you, may be unnecessary. I have understood & I think I mentioned to you that the Time of the entry of the Warrant with Mr Lewis the County Surveyor, is material as it is Located & fixed to the spot from that Time only; if it be, is a certified Copy from him, proof of the Time, by the Laws of Virginia? I understand that the Defendants have informed themselves, what Time it was entered with him & are much encouraged thereby; but this is only surmised to me.

I will write to Mrs Crawford respecting his Commission; but if she cannot produce it (& it should be necessary) a Certificate of it may, I Suppose, be obtained from William & Mary College—if you can readily obtain such Certificate & without trouble, it may be of some use; but I am some what inclined to believe it is not necessary, because he was known to be an officer de facto, & that act recognized by the Colony.[3]

I am pleased with Mr Randolph's arguments; but if the Proclamation exists, which takes off the restrictions in that of 1763 & extending the benefits of it to the Western Waters, I think it might obviate a specious objection, if you could obtain an authenticated Copy of it.[4]

The Chief Justice told me that he believes a Court of Nisi Prius will be held in Washington County in the latter end of May or beginning of June next—I asked him whether I might give you this information? he said I might—I told him that as several points of Law would arise in your Ejectments I wished to try them before him—the judges will in january make their arrangements for the Spring circuit, & Mr McKean says that if Mr Rush will cross the Mountains, he will come with him—(the difficulty is occasioned by some coolness, about rank, which subsists between the two other Judges)—at any rate, he has been so obliging, as to assure me that he will inform me, as soon as it is fixed who goes to the westward—as soon as I gain this information, I will again have the honour of writing to you by the first Conveyance—I am going up to the western County Courts in the mean Time, & if I can discover any thing new, or if any thing should occur to me, I shall beg leave to mention it. I took down the names of several Witnesses from Col. Shephard & Mr McCormick; but they could not tell me with precision what they could testify; but as the decision of the Supreme Court is so materially variant from those in the County Courts of late, respecting improvements, I do not think that your Title to those Lands will so very much depend upon their Testimony, as I once supposed—however it may still be of importance.[5]

In the last Letter, which you did me the honour to write to me, you signified your desire that I would bring actions of Trespass for mesne Profit against all the Defendants respectively—this may produce a good effect by convincing them that you are sensible of the injury they have done you, & determined to have every satisfaction which the Law can give you—or it may produce a bad effect, in the minds of the jury who are to try the Ejectments—their modes of thinking may lead them to believe the Defendants rather unfortunate, then blameable, and that as these double actions will well nigh ruin most of them; will not the jury be willing to lay hold of every point however trifling which may make against your title or in favour of the Defendants.

Pardon this liberty Sir, believe me these sentiments are dictated by the most pure & ardent desire to promote whatever may be for your interest. I was lately taken in at the Trial of such an action brought *after a recovery* in Ejectment in Westmoreland and the Jury, thinking that the Improvements which the Defendants had made were of more value to the Plaintiff then all his expenses & loss; found a verdict for the Defendant—the counsel on both sides agreed that they must find *some* Damages, as it was *after* a recovery in Ejectment—& the Court at the instance of both sides, sent them out again—they returned, & still found for the Defendant—his Counsel then agreed to confess Judgement for 1 d. Damages to save the eventual expense of a Writ of Error. Had this action been brought *before* the recovery in Ejectment, the Defendant might have gone into the Trial of the Title again, & the Plaintiff might have been obliged to pay the Costs.

However, I will act agreeably to your orders, unless you should countermand them before the next Court at Washington County; to which I must go, in less than 4 weeks.[6]

I shall endeavour to order matters respecting the appointment of the Jury in such a manner, as to be as free from objections or influence as possible—we have a new law, respecting Juries—they are drawn by Lot, out of four times the number, returned by the Sheriff, so that neither party can certainly know one of the Men who may try his cause. I will endeavour to inform myself how the Sheriff stands affected, & if I shall have the least reason to suspect that he will not be impartial I will attempt to have a special jury named by the Court, & struck by me, with the assistance of your friends. I have the Honour to be with the utmost respect Sir your most obedient humble Servant

Thomas Smith

P.S. 26 Nov. 1785 I have waited since the 17 for a Conveyance to Baltimore, & have been disappointed. I therefore send this to Philadelphia, by a gentleman in whom I can confide, who has promised to put it into the Post Office, as soon as he reaches the City.

ALS, DLC:GW; copy, NhD.

1. Thomas Smith's handling of the suits brought by him on GW's behalf in Washington County, Pa., to eject the settlers on GW's Millers Run land in Pennsylvania is recounted in the editorial note, Smith to GW, 9 Feb. 1785. Although in the present letter Smith is responding to GW's letters of both 14 July and 10 Sept. 1785, for the most part it deals with points GW raised in the letter of 14 July.

2. See GW to Smith, 14 July, and note 2 of that document.

3. William Crawford first surveyed the Millers Run tract for GW in 1771, and because of some question of his right to survey any but the soldiers' land under the proclamation, he surveyed it again in 1774 as deputy to the surveyor of Augusta, Thomas Lewis, who subsequently issued a patent to GW for the tract. See Crawford to GW, 8 May 1774.

4. See Edmund Randolph to GW, 29 July 1785.

5. Smith tried the ejectment suits before Chief Justice Thomas McKean in Washington County, Pa., in October 1786. See the editorial note, Smith to GW, 9 Feb. 1785, and references.

6. See GW to Smith, 10 Sept. and 7 December.

To Lamar, Hill, Bisset, & Company

Gentn   Mount Vernon 18th Novr 1785.

Inclosed you have a copy of my last—Since which I have been honored with your favor of the 22d of Augt—This Letter will be

conveyed to you by —— in the ——, which will return immediately to this river & afford a safe & good conveyance for the
Wine ordered by Mr Hill—the cost of wch as soon as I am advised of it shall be paid by a Bill on London.[1] I am Gentn &c.

G: Washington

LB, DLC:GW.
    1. For the correspondence regarding a pipe of Madeira for GW from the
vintners, see Lamar, Hill, Bisset, & Co., 20 (not 22) Aug. 1785, n.1.

To John Marsden Pintard

Sir,   Mount Vernon 18th Novr 1785.

I have had the honor to receive your favor of the 19th of August from Madeira, accompanied by a box of Citron, Lemons &
Onions;[1] for which I pray you to accept my grateful thanks. If a
favourable opportunity should offer directly to this river, at a
proper season of the year, you would encrease the obligation
you have already laid me under, by sending me a few slips of
the vines of your best eating Grape; and a young fig tree or two.[2]

From my esteem for your father, & the good opinion I have
always heard expressed of you, it gives me pleasure to learn that
you are appointed by Congress Commercial Agent for the
United States at the island of Madeira & Porto Santo, & I wish
you may long continue in the Office to the mutual satisfaction
of yourself & employers. I am Sir, Yr mo: Obt hble Servt

Geo: Washington

LB, DLC:GW.
    1. Perhaps the copyist mistook the word "orange" for "Onions."
    2. See Pintard to GW, 24 Jan. 1786.

To John Rumney, Jr.

Sir,   Mount Vernon 18th Novr 1785.

Since my last,[1] I have been favored with your Letter of the 3d
of July, accompanied by patterns of the Irish flag; but as the
prices were not annexed, I could form no judgment, nor make
any choice from a comparison thereof with those of the former:
nor indeed is it now essential, as the one I had fixed upon in my

last, is cheaper I presume than either of the present samples wou'd be, & will answer my purposes equally well. I hope too the former are in forwardness, & that I may expect them soon—at any rate before the season for laying them shall advance upon me.

Inclosed I send you a Bill on London for fifty pounds sterling, towards payment for those Flags; & will follow it with another to the full amount as soon as I am informed of the Cost of them.[2]

I acquainted you in my last that the House Joiner whom you sent me, answered my expectations fully. He is a good workman & a sober well behaved man. I am thankful to you for making so advantageous a choice; but as there seems to be a difficulty in obtaining a Brick layer, & indeed a risk attending it which I was not acquainted with at the time I applied to you to procure these artizans for me—I now wish you to decline all further enquiries after one.

I pray you to present (when opportunity offers) my respects to your father; and to be assured yourself of the esteem & regard with which I am, Sir, &c.

G. Washington

LB, DLC:GW.
    1. GW's letter is dated 22 June.
    2. GW drew the bill on Wakelin Welch (Ledger B, 234). See Robinson, Sanderson, & Rumney to GW, 28 Jan. 1786, Rumney to GW, 16 April 1786, and GW to Rumney, 15 May 1786.

From Tench Tilghman

Dear Sir   Baltimore 18th Novr 1785
    I have, by dint of dunning, obtained the plans in Stucco from Mr Rawlins, sooner than I expected—I forward them under cover to Fitzgerald, with a desire that he will send them to Mount Vernon as quickly as he conveniently can.[1]

We are told by the prints that his Catholic Majesty has presented you with four Jacks, and that one or two of them have actually arrived. If this be so, and they all come safe, I should suppose you would not keep them all about you, but divide them in such a manner as to make them extensively useful, and at the same time prevent their interfering with each other in covering—In such case, I have been strongly sollicited by a number of Gentlemen upon the Eastern Shore of this State to write to you, and request if you have not already made other arrangements, that you would be good eno' to let one of these useful Animals go to that part of the Country—My Brother James lives at Talbot Court House, the Central spot of the Eastern Shore Counties, and convenient to the State of Delaware also—If you should incline to send one of the Jacks there, he would engage not only to take charge of him, but to be accountable for the Monies you may set upon him for covering—I do not mean to press this matter upon you. I will only say that by complying with the request I have made, you will confer the greatest of obligations upon a number of your fellow Citizens, who from the peculiar situation of their Country, have occasion for draught Cattle less expensive in the Articles of Forage than Horses[2]—I am with Sincere Respect & Esteem Dear Sir Yr most obt & very hble Servt

Tench Tilghman

ALS, DLC:GW.
    1. See John Rawlins to GW, 15 Nov., n.1.
    2. See GW's description of the status of the jacks in his response to Tilghman of 30 November.

To Charles Vaughan

Sir,   Mount Vernon Novr 18th 1785.
    I have had the honor to receive your favor of the 25th of Septr by Mr Corbett.[1]
    I am at a loss to express my sense of the great attention of Mr Vaughan (your good father) to me, or of the obliging manner in which you have executed his request. The Puncheon of rum is safe arrived. & I pray you to receive my acknowledgments of, and to present my thanks for it, to your generous Parent. I wish I had something more agreeable to offer.[2]
    Permit me to ask your acceptance of a dozn barrls of the Superfine Flour which I make at my Mill. The quality of it is generally esteemed, & I hope what I now send will not discredit the Brand.
    It is to be regretted that Countries which could mutually as-

sist & benefit each other, & which have dispositions to do so, should be prevented by an interposing power. but this being the case, I despair of seeing any change in the political system, until G:B. shall be convinced, by experience, that the contracted & illiberal policy she is now pursuing, has recoiled upon herself. In the meantime, it is to be lamented, that, any of her distant dependencies should suffer from the effect of such ill-judged regulations.

Being now fixed under my own Vine & my own Fig tree, it would give me great pleasure to entertain you in the shade of them. There to assure you of the esteem & regard with which I have the honor to be, Sir, Yr Most Obedt and obliged Hble Servt

Go: Washington

The Flour intended for your use, is branded on the head of the Cask, G. Washington Burr Superfine and marked & numbered on the side SV—No 1. a 12.

There was a misapprehension wch occasioned the S. instead of C.[3]

ALS (photocopy), MHi: photostat collection; LB, DLC:GW.
1. Letter not found.
2. See GW to Samuel Vaughan, 30 November.
3. GW endorsed a letter written by the Alexandria merchant Robert Hooe on 5 Dec. to Vaughan: "Dr Sir, I have enclosed one of the Bills lading with the Genls Letter—The others I send you in case the Genl should choose to enclose one by another vessel" (DLC:GW). The enclosed bill of lading signed by Benjamin Bowers shows Hooe & Harrison, by order of GW, shipping in the schooner *Eagle*, Captain Benjamin Bowers, 12 barrcls "Superfine Flour" at the risk of Samuel Vaughan, to Charles Vaughan of Jamaica.

Letter not found: from William Bailey, 19 November. On 22 Nov. GW wrote Bailey: "I have received your favor of the 19th."

To Lund Washington

Dear Lund,   Mount Vernon 20th Novr 1785.
I know as little of G:W.s plans or wishes as you do, never having exchanged a word with him upon the subject in my life. By his Advertisemt—& from what has frequently dropped from Fanny, he is desireous of getting a place in this Country to live at.[1] Before their marriage he & Fanny were both told that it

would be very agreeable to Mrs W. & myself, that they should make this House their home 'till the squalling & trouble of Children might become disagreeable. I have not repeated the matter since, because it was unnecessary—an offer once made is sufficient. It is hardly to be expected that two people as young as they are, with their nearest connexions at extreme points, would like confinement: & without it, he could not answer my purposes as a Manager or Superintendant, unless I had more leisure to attend to my own business, which by the by I shall aim at, let the consequences, in other respects, be as they may.[2]

These however are no reasons for detaining you a moment longer in my employ than suits your interest, or is agreeable to your inclination, & family concerns. But as the proposition is new, & hath never been revolved in my mind, it will take some time to digest my own thoughts upon the occasion before it is hinted to another. In the mean while if I can do with the aids you offer, & for which I sincerely thank you, I will ask your constant attention no longer than this year—at any rate not longer than the next. The inexplicitness of this answer cannot, I presume, put you to much if any inconvenience as yet; because retirement from, & not a change of business, is professedly your object.

However unlucky I may have been in Crops &c. of late years, I shall always retain a grateful sense of your endeavours to serve me; for as I have repeatedly intimated to you in my Letters from Camp, nothing but that entire confidence which I reposed, could have made me easy under an absence of almost nine years from my family & Estate; or could have enabled me, consequently, to have given not only my time, but my whole attention to the public concerns of this Country for that space.[3] I am your sincere friend &ca

Geo: Washington

LB, DLC:GW.

1. The following advertisement, dated 9 Nov., appeared in the *Virginia Journal and Alexandria Advertiser*, on 10 Nov. 1785: "THE Subscriber has for sale in the town of Fredericksburg, THREE LOTS (lately enclosed) on which there are a good house with four rooms on a floor, a kitchen, meat-house, and large stable.—They are agreeably situated for a private family: For business none more so, as they have a great command of the back trade.—They are so situated as to admit of divisions, and will be disposed of as it may be most convenient.—He has also a small TRACT of LAND, about three miles from the said

town, containing between 160 and 200 acres, which he will dispose of like-wise.—Its situation renders it valuable to a resident in the town, being well watered and wooded, and adapted for farming.—Twelve months credit will be allowed without interest, if the money is punctually paid when it becomes due, if not, it is to bear interest from the date.—A mortgage of the premises, with bond and approved security, will be required.—The price will be made known by the Subscriber at Mount-Vernon.—An exchange for land in the County of Fairfax will be prefered. GEORGE WASHINGTON."

George Augustine Washington and his bride left Mount Vernon on 14 Dec. to visit her parents at Eltham (*Diaries*, 4:250), and on 3 Feb. 1786 he wrote GW: "I had no propositions made for my Lot's on my way through Fredericks-burg—one of the Letters You forwarded was asking information and propos-ing a mode of payment." Charles Washington wrote his son George Augustine on 23 Nov.: "I observed in the papers your Property at Fredericksg Advertised in the name of the General, by which I thought you and him had been making an Exchange for Other property" (ViMtV).

2. George Augustine Washington's family lived in Berkeley County at the upper end of the colony and his bride's family, the Bassetts, lived in New Kent County in Tidewater. Within a month GW asked George Augustine Washing-ton about his intentions and learned that he and his wife wished to remain at Mount Vernon. With this assurance and himself newly determined "to attend to the business of my plantations," GW on 20 Dec. gave Lund Washington his release as manager of Mount Vernon.

3. Most of what were undoubtedly hundreds of letters passing between GW and Lund Washington between June 1776 and December 1783 have been lost, but from those that have survived one is left with the impression that Lund Washington bore with remarkable patience a fairly steady flow of criticism about his handling of one thing or another.

From Archibald Cary

My Dear Sir,   Senate Chamber [Richmond] No. 21st 1785

I have to Acknowledge the rect of two of your letters one by Doctor Lamair, an agreable and skilfull Gentleman in his Profes-sion, the other by Mr Webster which I only recd on Thursday last.[1]

It will always Give me pleasure to Shew every Mark of Civility to Any Gentleman who is Honord with your notice. the latter Gentleman has Solicited and obtained an Act *for Secureing to the Authors of Litterary Works an Exclusive Property therein for a limitted Time*, which I think just.[2]

We have had but little business of Consequence before the Senate as Yet, one of the most Consiquence was for appointing

Delegates to Congress. Hardys Death and Doctor Lee's Appointment Occasined two Vacance's which are Fill'd with Edwd Carrington and Henry Lee Junr We have placed Braxton in the Council in the Place of Wm Nelson resign'd and Confirm'd Tazwell on the Genl Court bench.[3]

The House of Delegates have been and are busy on the New Code of Laws, I Expect from them Several of the Bills this day or to Morrow. at this Moment they are debateing a Bill for Takeing off the half Tax which is now Collecting, a very impolitick Step and which if it should pass as it is now on its Passage, I judge will be rejected in the Senate.

I omitted to Mention a Bill which has passd both Houses founded on Your letter respecting James & Potomack Rivers. in which your request is Fully Comply'd with.[4]

I Am realy Fearful we Shall not rise before March. I Am Sure if they go through the new Code of Laws it will Imploy them near that time. Nothing determined yet as to the Assessment but judge it will be rejected. A Petition for a General Emancipation has met justly that Fate. on recollection I mention a Bill Passd both Houses for Naturalisation of the Marquis De La Fayette. and one for Fixing the value of Gold pr Penny waight. all of which Except German is to Pass at 5/4 the latter at 4/⟨10⟩ the Penny Waight.[5]

A Warm Contest took place for the Chair of the Delegates You must have heard our Friend Succeeded, after which a Strong push was made to. Vacate his Seat in the House Many who Assisted in placeing him in the Chair, were of opinion he was not elligible and many who was agst his Takeing the chair were of opinion his Seat was Legal and he Carry both by near the Same Majoraty Say 6. or 7.[6]

When does my Friend Intend Sending for his Bull and his Ladys Cow Calf, they are Fine, and shall be taken good Care of. but I design You shall pay by the Perticular Exertions of Your Jack Ass this Spring on a Jenny of Mine, I had two but by far the Finest died from the bite of a Mad Dog this Summer.

do you never Intend to Spend a little time with Your old J[ame]s River Friends, and altho all are truly so Yet Few of your old ones are left, but Neither on this river or Any other is there one More Sincerely so than Your Most Obt & Hble Servt

Archibald Cary

Present my Complyments to your Lady. the Grass Seed I Gave You is the Guania Grass I saved about 6 Qts of Seed it is an Annual Plant.[7] A.C.

ALS, DLC:GW.

1. GW wrote a letter of introduction to Cary for the dentist Jean Le Mayeur in September and for Noah Webster on 6 November. See Le Mayeur to GW, 2 Nov., and Webster to GW, 16 Dec., n.1.

2. For the text of the act, see 12 Hening 30–31.

3. See David Stuart to GW, 16 Nov., n.3.

4. He is referring to GW's letter to Patrick Henry of 29 Oct. concerning the gift of shares in the two companies.

5. 12 Hening 115–16.

6. See Madison to GW, 11 November.

7. GW sowed the seed in April 1786 (*Diaries*, 4:308, 311).

To William Bailey

Sir,   Mount Vernon 22d Novr 1785.

I have received your favor of the 19th.[1] The expensive manner in which my Nephews are proceeding at George Town, added to some other considerations, have determined me to remove them from the Academy at that place, to Alexandria.

I have already for about fourteen months residence, paid to Mr Stoddart & yourself £125.11.0 on their Accot; & it appears from your letter of the above date, that for near half that time, they are yet owing for Board—& have an Accot besides for cloathing; & these too almost independent of their schooling.[2] I am Sir Yr Obt hble Servt

G: Washington

LB, DLC:GW.

1. Letter not found. GW's nephew Lawrence Augustine Washington brought the letter from the merchant William Bailey in Georgetown on 20 Nov. (*Diaries*, 4:235).

2. For the arrangements that GW had made to have his nephews George Steptoe Washington and Lawrence Augustine Washington obtain schooling in Georgetown, see Benjamin Stoddert to GW, 21 June, and GW to Stephen Bloomer Balch, 26 June 1785.

To Stephen Bloomer Balch

revd Sir,   Mount Vernon 22d Novr 1785.

The expence attending the residence of my Nephews at Georgetown so far exceeds the idea I was led to entertain when they went there, that, in behalf of their Guardian, I am compelled to remove them.

When they were sent to the Academy under your management, I was informed by Colo. Fitzhugh, that the charge for schooling & Board (if I am not mistaken) was £31 each—Cloathing if judiciously applied & properly attended to, I knew could not be a very great expence, for boys of their standing. But to my surprize, I have already paid Mr Stoddert £67.18.6—Mr Bayly £55.5.2—& yesterday in a letter from the latter, I am informed that there is half a years board due to him for each—& an accot of cloathing besides, yet to be exhibited.

The leading motive Sir, which influenced me to send them to Georgetown was, their boarding with you; & I expected from what had passed between us, after the intervention which had occasioned the suspension of it, they would have returned to you: but now Mr Bayly writes me that he also declines boarding them after the 24th inst: & points out a third person.

These several circumstances combining, added to a conviction founded in experience, that I cannot restrain the profuse & improper advances of Goods for them at a distance, have induced me to bring them to Alexandria, where I shall be a witness to their wants, and can supply their necessities upon more advantageous terms, than they have been hitherto.[1] I am revd Sir &c.

G: Washington

LB, DLC:GW.

1. GW wrote in his diary for 23 Nov.: "Sent Mr. [William] Shaw through Alexandria, to agree for the Schooling & Board of my Nephews George & Lawrence Washington now at the Academy at George Town & thence to the latter place to conduct them to the former for the purpose of going to School at the Alexandria Academy." Two days later he wrote: "Mr. Shaw returned, having removed George & Lawe. Washington to the Alexandria Academy & fixed them at the Widow Dades [probably Parthenia Alexander Massey Dade]" (*Diaries*, 4:236, 241). See GW to William Bailey, this date.

From Henry Knox

My dear sir   New York 22 Novr 1785

I have often been on the point of acknowledging your Kind favor of the 18th of June, and have as often deferred it, from the hope of having the pleasure of visiting you at Mount Vernon, on my way to James River, at which place there is a quantity of public Stores. Having been hitherto disapointed I shall no longer trust to the chapter of accidents, but embrace the opportunity which presents itself by Major Farlie.[1]

I render you my sincere thanks for your kind opinion of the disposition of the troops on the western frontier. We have been able to recruit six companies only, out of the ten, directed by Congress—three of them are now on their march for Forts Mc-Intosh, and Pitt, where we shall be under the necessity of posting them for the winter. One Company has gone with the commissioners who are to hold the treaty at the great Miami; and two companies have taken post at the mouth of the Muskingham—The remaining four companies will I hope be raised and march early in the Spring.

The indians generally have discovered a restlessness and discontent with the treaties they made at Forts Schuyler and McIntosh the last year. They were then told that Great Britain had ceded to the united States the posts now in the occupancy of the british troops, and that all of them would soon be delivered up to us. But they experience the Contrary and the british and refugee emissaries are continualy embittering their minds against us by urging that we deceived them at the treaties, and as a proof of the deception, that the british still retain the Forts.

The indians may in a degree be guided by the treaty now holding with them at the great Miami but they will not be perfectly so, untill the british government shall deliver to us, the posts on the lakes. of this event there is not at present any prospect, on the contrary it is asserted under credible circumstances, that Sir Guy Carleton is coming out with troops to Canada, the next Spring, in the capacity of Vice Roy. This event might compell us to take those steps upon which our safety and dignity as a nation may depend.

Major Farlie will give you a detail of the proceedings of the new York society of the Cincinnati with respect to the reception

of the new institution proposed by the General Meeting on the
12th of May 1784. I flatter myself that the society of this State
will receive the alterations notwithstanding any appearances to
the contrary I am uninformed how many of the States have
adopted it, but New Hampshire has rejected it as it respects the
funds, and it is said Connecticut have also declined adopting
it—I am apprehensive that it may be as difficult to get it universally adopted as it is to obtain an universal assent of the respective legislative assemblies to any recommendation of Congress.

I am mortified and chagrined beyond bearance, that the person who I directed and to whom I have written five times on the
Subject has neglected to send you lime stone from St Georges to
Boston, although I directed him to do it at my expence—I had
made an arrangement with a gentleman at Boston to forward it
to Alexandria. I have such repeated proofs of his inattention to
my requests that I am unable to place any further dependence
on him.[2]

Mrs Knox unites with me in paying our affectionate compliments to Mrs Washington with our sincere wishes for your mutual health and happiness I am my dear Sir with perfect respect
and warm affection Your obliged humble Servant

H. Knox

ALS, DLC:GW; ADfS, MHi: Knox Papers.

1. James Fairlie (d. 1830), aide-de-camp to Steuben during the Revolution,
arrived at Mount Vernon in the afternoon of 8 December. Alexander Hamilton wrote GW on 25 Nov. about the New York Society of the Cincinnati. Presumably Fairlie delivered both Knox's and Hamilton's letters.

2. For Knox's failed attempts to secure lime for GW, see GW to Knox, 5 Jan.
1785, n.6.

From William Drayton

Sir,   Charleston S.C. 23. Nov. 1785

As Chairman of the Committee of the South Carolina Society
for promoting & improving Agriculture & other rural Concerns,
I am directed to inform your Excellency, that you are unanimously elected the first honorary member of that Society.

This mark of their Respect the Society thought ⟨wa⟩s with peculiar Propriety due to the man, who by ⟨his⟩ gallantry & Conduct, as a Soldier, contributed so ⟨em⟩inently to stamp a Value

on the Labours of every ⟨A⟩merican Farmer; and who by his Skill and Industry ⟨in⟩ the Cultivation of his own Fields, has likewise distinguish'd himself as a Farmer.[1]

It adds to the Satisfaction, which I feel in conveying to you these Sentiments of the Society, that it affords me at the same Time an opportunity of expressing the high Esteem & Regard, with which I have the Honour to be, Sir, Your most obedient & most humble Servant

Wm Drayton, C.J.

ALS, PP; Sprague transcript, DLC:GW.

William Drayton (1732–1790), former chief justice of the colony of South Carolina and at this time a judge of the state's vice-admiralty courts, was one of the founders of the recently established Agricultural Society of South Carolina.

1. See GW's response of 25 Mar. 1786.

To Elizabeth French Dulany

Friday—past 2 'Oclock [c.23 November 1785]

General Washington presents his best respects to Mrs Dulany with the horse blueskin; which he wishes was better worth her acceptance.[1]

Marks of antiquity have supplied the place of those beauties with which this horse abounded—in his better days. Nothing but the recollection of which, & of his having been the favourite of Mr Dulany in the days of his Court ship, can reconcile her to the meagre appearance he now makes.

Mrs Washington presents her Compliments and thanks to Mrs Dulany for the Roots of Scarcity.[2]

AL (photocopy), MdHi.

Benjamin Tasker Dulany (c.1752–1816) of Maryland, John Parke Custis's fellow student under the tutelage of the Rev. Jonathan Boucher in Annapolis, was a frequent visitor at Mount Vernon in 1772 and 1773 when he was courting Elizabeth French, who became his wife in 1773. Mrs. Dulany's mother, Penelope French, at this time was continuing to refuse to surrender her life right in the French-Dulany tract on the neck at Mount Vernon to which GW was seeking to gain title (see *Diaries*, 4:84).

1. Blueskin was one of the horses GW rode throughout the Revolution.

2. Roots of scarcity are usually identified as mangel-wurzel (*Beta vulgaris macrorhiza*), a kind of coarse beet used in Europe to feed cattle, which seems an unlikely gift for Mrs. Dulany to send to Mrs. Washington.

From Charles Washington

Dear Brother   Happy Retreat Novr 23d 1785
    Your Letter of the 29 of Octr, I recd by Mr Muse,[1] and am
Sorry to find the two Little boys are at a place where they are
gaining so little Improvement at so high an Expence, perhaps
they might do better at Alexandria, Mr McCray tils me there
is a well Established School at that place, and supposees there
Expence would not amount to nere what it is at present,[2] or if
you think it more advisable for them to go to a prvet School,
there is a high learnt Man a Minester in about two miles of me to
whom my Little Son gose to, will take them, and there Brother
Thornton Washington will Board them I shall be happy to have
your Advice on the Accation.[3]
    I have Muster'd up for the present £26:2:6 which I send you
by Mr McCray, and am in hopes it will not be long before it will
be in my power to send more.[4] the Family join in Love to you
Mrs Washington and new Married Couple and am Dear Sir with
Esteem your Loving Brother
                                        Chas Washington

ALS, NjMoNP.
    1. Letter not found. Battaile Muse had dinner at Mount Vernon on 27 Oct.
and then "went up to Alexandria" (*Diaries*, 4:215).
    2. See GW to William Bailey and to Stephen Bloomer Balch, both 22 No-
vember. Robert McCrea (c.1765–c.1840), a Scot, was a merchant in Alexandria.
    3. The minister was the Rev. Robert Stubbs. See Charles Washington to GW,
30 December.
    4. At the bottom of the page Charles Washington wrote:

74 Dollars	£22. 4.0
Double Guinea	2.16.0
Pistole	1. 2.6
	£26. 2.6

To William Brown

Sir,   Mount Vernon 24th Novr 1785.
    I am really ashamed, at this late hour to have the receipt of
your favor of the 7th of Octor, to acknowledge: but the truth is
it was handed to me among many other Letters, got buried, &

was forgot until your second favor of the 8th inst: brough[t] it to remembrance.[1]

Since the receipt of the latter, my time has been much occupied with several matters—some of which were pressing: these, with the expectation of a personal interview (for I have been twice since in Alexandria without seeing you) must plead my excuse for a seeming, tho' far from an intentional disrespect.

As nothing is of more importance than the education of youth, so consequently nothing can be more laudably beneficial than the association which is formed in Alexandria to effect this desireable purpose. I therefore not only highly approve the institution, but am thankful for the honor done me by enrolling my name among the Managers of it; & as far as it is in my power will give it support.[2]

There is a matter which I will take some other opportunity of bringing before the Trustees for their consideration; that, if it can be made to comport with the present establishmt of the Alexandria Academy, & engrafted therewith—it may become part of the institution. At an hour of more leisure I will communicate it.[3] In the mean while, I am Sir &c.

G: Washington

LB, DLC:GW.

Dr. William Brown (c.1752–c.1792), who was trained at the University of Edinburgh, began practicing medicine in Alexandria before the Revolution.

1. Neither letter has been found.

2. Construction of the building for the Alexandria Academy was begun in early fall and was scheduled for completion in January 1786 (*Virginia Journal and Alexandria Advertiser*, 15 Sept., 17 Nov. 1785). See also GW to Stephen Bloomer Balch, 22 Nov., n.1.

3. For GW's proposal to endow Alexandria Academy, see his letter to the trustees of the academy, 17 December.

From Alexander Hamilton

Dr Sir   November 25. 1785

Major Fairly is just setting out on a visit to You I believe on some business relating to the Cincinnati—The society of this state met some short time since and took into consideration the proposed alterations in the original frame of the Institution—Some were strenuous for adhering to the old constitution a few for adopting the new and many for a middle line—This disagreement of opinion and the consideration that the different state societies pursuing different courses—some adopting the alterations entire others rejecting them in the same way—others adopting in part and rejecting in part might beget confusion and defeat good purposes—induced a proposal which was unanimously agreed to, that a Committee should be appointed to prepare and lay before the society a circular letter expressive of the sense of the society on the different alterations proposed & recommending the giving powers to a General meeting of the Cincinnati to make such alterations as might be thought adviseable to obviate objections and promote the Interests of the society—I believe there will be no difficulty in agreeing to change the present mode of continuing the society; but it appears to be the wish of our members that some other mode may be defined and substituted & that it might not be left to the uncertainty of Legislative provision—We object too to putting the funds under legislative direction. Indeed it appears to us the Legislatures will not at present be inclined to give us any sanction.

I am of the Committee and I cannot but flatter myself that when the object is better digested & more fully explained it will meet your approbation.[1]

The Poor *Baron* is still soliciting Congress, and has every prospect of Indigence before him—He has his imprudencies; but upon the whole he has rendered valuable services; and his merits and the reputation of the Country alike demand that he should not be left to suffer want—If there could be any mode by which Your influence could be employed in his favour; by writing to Your friends in Congress or otherwise—The Baron and his friends would be under great obligations to you. I have the honor to be with sincere esteem Sir Your Obedt & humb. servant[2]

Alex. Hamilton

ALS, DLC:GW.

1. See Henry Knox to GW, 22 November. For the debates over changes in the Institution of the Society of the Cincinnati and for the changes adopted, including the renunciation of the hereditary membership, see Winthrop

Sargent's Journal and notes, printed above as Appendix II in General Meeting of the Society of the Cincinnati, 4–18 May 1784.

2. For the correspondence regarding the Baron von Steuben's public accounts, see GW to Thomas Jefferson, 15 Mar. 1784, and notes.

To John Paul Jones

Sir,   Mount Vernon Novr 25th 1785

I have been honoured with your letter of the 18th of July from Paris enclosing certificates in favor of Captns Stack & Macarthy.

I pray you to be assured that I should have pleasure in doing justice to the merits of these Officers, and obliging you if the power of deciding lay with me. But, though I am in sentiment with the Gentlemen who have declared in favor of the pretensions of Captns Stack & Maccarthy's right to become members of the Cincinnati, yet, in matters of opinion I have no authority to pronounce them such.

As French Officers, having borne Continental Commissions, my opinion is that their best mode *would* have been, to have got themselves admitted as members of State Society before the Kings edict, or order in Council took effect, for if I mistake not all Officers in the Service of France whose names are not particularly enumerated in that order are excluded thereby.[1] This however is a matter of which they, or you, can be better ascertained of than I. At any rate nothing can be done in this Country until the next *General* Meeting; and that cannot happen in less than Eighteen months, and may be much longer delayed. I have the honor to be Sir Yr Most Obedt Hble Servt

Go: Washington

ALS, NNPM; LB, DLC:GW.
1. See Rochambeau to GW, 1 Mar. 1784.

To Lawrence Kortright

Sir,   Mount Vernon 25th Novr 1785.

If it was in my power to give you the information, & the satisfaction which is required in your letter of the 10th of October; I would do it with pleasure: but not recollecting enough of the particular circumstances attending the Sloop Hester—the whole of the business respecting this & other vessels, being entirely within the Department of the Quarter Mr General, I can offer nothing which will facilitate your settlement with the public.

I do remember very well that the service, in the Spring of 1776, required an impress, & purchase of Vessels; that orders issued to the Quarter Master General for that purpose; & I have some recollection that the Sloop Hester was one of those Vessels which were taken into the service of the public, & that she was afterwards sold to Colo. Sears: but upon what terms; what became of her after that; how the Accots respecting her stand—or how the matter is to be finally settled, I know not. I am Sir &c.

G: Washington

LB, DLC:GW.

To Edward Newenham

Dear Sir,　　　　　　　　　Mount Vernon 25th Novr 1785

Since I had the honor of writing to you on the 20th of March, which was done in haste (having but little notice of Capt: Boyle's intended departure, before the time appointed for his sailing—& then to send my dispatches to Richmond 125 miles)—I have been favored with your letters of the 3d of March, 25th of May, & 23d of July.[1] The first was forwarded to me by Captn Bibby, whom I have not yet had the pleasure of seeing; tho' he gives me assurances of it, & to whom I shall have pleasure in rendering any services in my power consistently—if it should be found necessary.

The opposition which the virtuous characters of Ireland have given to the attemps of a British Administration's interfering with its manufactures, fettering its commerce, restraining the liberties of its subjects by their plan of reform &[c]a &ca, will hand their names to posterity with that veneration & respect to which their amor patriae entitles them.

Precedents, as you justly observe, are dangerous things—they form the arm which first arrests the liberties & happiness of a Country. In the first approaches they may indeed assume the garb of plausibility & moderation, & are generally spoken of by the movers as a *chip in porrage* (to avoid giving alarm)—but soon are made to speak a language equally decisive and irresistible; which shews the necessity of opposition in the first attempts to establish them, let them appear under what guise or Courtly form they may; & proves too that vigilance & watchfulness can scarcely be carried to an excess in guarding against the insiduous arts of a Government founded in corruption.

I do not think there is as much wisdom & sound policy displayed in the different Legislatures of these States as might be; yet I hope every thing will come right *at last*. In republican Governments it too often happens that the people (not always seeing) must *feel* before they act: this is productive of errors & temporary evils—but generally these evils are of a nature to work their own cure.

The situation of affairs in Ireland, whilst the propositions were pending in the Parliament of it, would, I concluded, be a means of postponing your voyage to this Country; but as those seem to have met their quietus, I hope nothing else will intervene to prevent your fulfilling your expectation of coming in the Spring; the season will then be favourable for crossing the Atlantic.

Had I been present & apprized of your intention of making an aerial voyage with Monsr Potain, I should have joined my entreaties to those of Lady Newenham to have prevented it. As yet, I see no object to warrant a gentleman of fortune (happy in himself—happy in a family wch might be rendered miserable by a disaster, against which no human foresight can guard) running such a risk. It may do for young men of science & spirit to explore the upper regions: the observations there made may serve to ascertain the utility of the first discovery, & how far it may be applied to valuable purposes. To such *alone* I think these voyages ought at present to be consigned—& to them handsome public encouragements should be offer'd for the risk they run in ascertaining its usefulness, or the inutility of the pursuit.[2]

I have neither seen, nor heard of Mr Tharpe the s[t]ucco worker mentioned in your letter of the 23d of July. A *good man* acquainted with that business would have come very opportunely to me, as I had, & now have a large room which I am about to finish in this way. I have at length engaged a person to do it; who from having no rival, imposes his own terms, which

I think are exorbitant—good workmen of any profession, would meet encouragement in these States.[3]

For the many marks of attention which you have been pleased to bestow on me—I feel myself your Debtor: could my picture which is placed in a groupe with Dr Franklin, the Marqs de la Fayette & others in your library, speak the sentiments of the original, it would salute you every morning with its acknowledgements. I have never seen more than one picture of Genl Green, & that a mezzotinto print, sent to me a few days ago only, by the publisher a Mr Brown at No. 10 George Yard, Lombard street, London; taken it is said from a painting done at Philada.[4]

The Magazines, Gazettes &ca which you had the goodness to forward to me, came safe: & I pray you to accept my thanks for them.[5] My best respects, in which Mrs Washington joins, are presented to Lady Newenham & yourself. With sentiments of great esteem & regard, I am Dr Sir Yrs &c.

G: Washington

LB, DLC:GW.

1. None of these letters has been found.

2. Shortly after this, on 8 Dec., the *Virginia Journal and Alexandria Advertiser* printed this news item: "RICHMOND, December 3. On Saturday last, between four and five o'clock in the afternoon, Mr. Busselot, a French gentleman, raised a Balloon from the capitol square on Shockoe-Hill, in this city, which ascended to a great height. The wind setting North-east, it took that course, and descended before night ten miles distant from the city, on the plantation of Captain John Austin, in Hanover." See GW's earlier marveling at the flight of balloons in Paris in his letter to Duportail, 4 April 1784.

3. In April 1786 when he came to Mount Vernon to complete GW's New Room, John Rawlins brought with him the plasterer Richard Tharp (Thorpe) who did most of the ornamental plasterwork (see *Diaries*, 4:314; GW to Newenham, 10 June 1786).

4. See GW to Joseph Brown, 30 May 1786.

5. See Charles McKiernan to GW, 30 Oct., n.1.

Farm Reports

Editorial Note

In the fall of 1785 Lund Washington indicated to GW his wish to give up the management of the Mount Vernon plantation, a task he had performed for the past twenty-one years including the nearly nine years that GW was away during the war (GW to Lund Washington, 20 Nov. 1785). GW decided to ask his nephew George Augustine Washington, who was living at Mount Vernon with his bride, Fannie Bassett Washington, to assume Lund Washington's position, which the young major agreed to do before departing in December to spend the winter with the Bassetts at Eltham in New Kent County. In the meantime GW himself had taken over the day-to-day general supervision of his five Mount Vernon farms, Muddy Hole, Dogue Run, River, Ferry, and Home House. The first three of these had overseers who were slaves, and the half brothers Hezekiah and John Fairfax were the overseers of the Ferry and Home House farms respectively. Upon his return to Mount Vernon at the end of March 1786, George Augustine Washington was able to relieve GW of some of the tasks relating to the management of the plantation. The arrival three weeks later of the English farmer James Bloxham, whom GW had hired with the help of George William Fairfax, also meant that in the future GW would have additional expert aid in his efforts to improve agricultural practices at Mount Vernon. But GW remained, as before, intimately involved in all the details of plantation life. See GW to Lund Washington, 20 Dec. 1785, George William Fairfax to GW, 23 Jan. 1786, George Augustine Washington to GW, 3 Feb. 1786, and *Diaries*, 4:302, 315.

Five days before writing to Lund Washington consenting to his departure from Mount Vernon, GW began, on 15 Nov. 1785, to take an inventory of the horses, cattle, tools, and implements on each farm at Mount Vernon. In February 1786 he made a detailed census of the 216 slaves on the five farms, classifying each according to age, sex, and skill, function, or condition. Both of these inventories he included in his diaries, in which he customarily recorded when at Mount Vernon the main decisions made and actions taken each day regarding the operation of the farms. He also began on 10 Jan. 1785 to enter in a separate notebook what he called "Notes and Observations" on his farming operations. These notes and observations form a running record of the sowing, planting, cultivating, and harvesting of crops in the fields and gardens at Mount Vernon. The contents of the notebook, which runs until the end of 1786, and also includes GW's general discussion of individual crops raised and harvested during the year, have been transcribed for CD-ROM:GW, but because GW incorporated in his diaries nearly all of the material contained in the notebook, this particular manuscript is not being printed in the *Papers*. Similar notes or observations on his farming which GW made at other times have been printed as part of his diaries.

When he assumed direct control of his farms in November 1785, GW began keeping still another running record of his farming operations, the one printed here. He assembled these farm reports himself through the week of 15 April, when he turned the task over to George Augustine Washington. For the rest of his life GW demanded from his estate manager these weekly farm reports, as they were called. They are simply reports on what work had been undertaken and accomplished on the Mount Vernon farms during the preceding week. Many sets of the farm reports, some covering only a brief time and others running for many months, have been located. Only a few will be printed in the volumes of the *Papers*; all eventually will be included in the CD-ROM:GW edition.

The initial farm reports prepared by GW himself and printed here set the pattern for those that followed. Every Saturday, aided by reports from the overseers of River, Dogue Run, Muddy Hole, Ferry, and Home House farms, GW compiled a report of what tasks had been assigned each day to the agricultural workers on the plantation and also recorded births and deaths in his livestock during the week. According to his slave census of February 1786, these agricultural workers included 86 field hands (38 male, including the overseers, and 48 female), 4 carpenters, 3 coopers, 3 drivers and stablers, 2 blacksmiths, 2 stock keepers, 1 wagoner, 1 miller, 1 carter, and 1 gardener. In recording how each of these was employed during the week, GW often identifies the worker by name. The names of more than thirty of them appear in the reports at least once, many of them several times. The farm reports printed here are essentially GW's record of how he sought to manage his labor force during the winter and spring of 1786.

[Mount Vernon, 26 Nov. 1785–16 April 1786]
1785—Morris's People—26th Novr[1]

Monday—Sowing Seed—the Women—Men getting Corn. Tuesday all hands treading & getting out Wheat—Wednesday taking an Acct of Stock & cleaning Wheat. Thursday cleaning the above Wheat & getting Corn. men making drains in the meadow. Friday treading a Bed of Wheat—Men getting Corn.

Saturday cleaning up the Wheat which was tread yesterday—& making a bridge over Dogue run.

Muddy-hole 26th Novr

The People at this Plantation gathering drawing in, and husking Corn at the Neck.

Dogue Run—26th Novr

Gathering & Husking Corn—Grubbing—One of the old Cows in the Meadow dead.

Davy—26th Novr[2]

Gathering Corn 4 Days—2 days thrashing Wheat. Cart with one hand helped Carrying Hoop poles to the Mill.

Dogue Run—3d Decr

Finished Gathering husking & Lifting of Corn. In all, besides what the Hogs had Eaten, amounting to [   ] Barrels. Tread out a Bed of Wheat yesterday & cleaning it up to day—People not employed in this Work grubbing the Swamps. Stock all well.

Muddy hole—3d Decr

Gathering husking measuring & Lifting of Corn—112 Barrels—Hogs have eat 28 and is laid by for them 28 Barrls—one day beating out Corn. Stock all well except an old sheep dead—2 Lambs since acct taken.[3]

Ferry Plantation 3d Decr

Gathering Corn & Getting Wheat & Carrying it to the Mill. the Stock all Well. Recd on Accot of Ferriages £3.14.9

River Plantation—3d Decr

From Timber Landing all the Corn has been brought in and lifted. 153 in all. The Remainder of the Week getting in Corn breaking Oxen—and Carting rails to make the Fence round the fodder stock high. the Cut next the Gate, left hand side is got to the Corn House and husked.

Dogue Run. 10th Decr

Treading a bed of Wheat Tuesday—Wednesday cleaned it up— Thursday put down another bed—but cd not clean it up on accot of the Rain yesterday: Making up the Fence round the Wheat yard—Men cutting & mauling—grubbed a little. Stock all well—one Cow has calved. The Beef killed on monday came from this Plantation.

Muddy-hole 10th Decr

Monday beat out all the old Corn—viz.—two loads one for the Home Ho[use] the other for themselves. Made a Pen to winter the Colts at the farm pen—All the People thrashing until last Night—cleaning Wheat to day—Stock all well. 19 young Lambs 2 killed by Eagles

River Plantatn 10th Decr

Gathering and Measuring Corn all the Week—the whole of the hands—Stock all well—except an old ewe which is dead.

Ferry Plantation 10th Decr

Finished getting out wheat & carrying it to Mill—Gathering & huskg of Corn—stock all well.

Muddy hole—17th Decr

Monday Catching & bringing the fatting Hogs to the Home House. the rest of the day grubbing—3 days & an half grubbing—the other days thrashing Wheat & moving Day into the Neck.

Ferry Plantation 17th Decr

People employed in Killing & cleaning Hogs—and in Gathering, bringing in, & husking of Corn.

River Plantation—24th Decr

3 days gathering Measuring and lofting of Corn—Thursday the women cleaning up Wheat to carry to Mill—the Men cutting & mauling of Rails—Friday put in half a stack of Wheat into the Barn. Men mauling &ca Rails—Saturday Thrashing of Wheat.

Dogue Run—24th Decr

Women all grubbing until Friday—3 of the Men at home House cutting wood for Christmas—the rest getting Posts for fencing except two who were plowing—Friday women raking up the old Dung of the last years Pens—Men still getting Posts. Saturday grubbing when not raining—Men cutting posts—Stock all well. One Lamb.

Muddy hole—24th Decr

4 days grubbing with all hands except the Carter who was Carting wood at the House, & Mink Will[4] who was two days & half Plowing—Friday about the Wheat Field Fence—and getting in wood. Saturday threshing Wheat all day.

Ferry Plantation—24th

All hands employed on Monday in gathering & measuring of Corn—Tuesday, wednesday & thursday in Carting & lifting it. Friday in sevl kinds of Jobbs—& Saturday getting w[oo]d for Christmas.

Carpenters—24th

Isaac all the Week at the Mill—James repairing Barn & Stables at Muddy hole and Tom & Sambo[5]—pointing 1073 Pallisado's.

Dogue Run Qr Decr 31st

Stock all well. had one young Calve and one Lamb this Week. Men cutting—& women grubbing thursday Friday & this day— Plowed a little when the ground was not too hard froze or too wet.

River Plantn 31st Decr

Thursday getting Posts for fencing and other Timber for Rails— and cutting down Corn stalks with the Women. 4 Plows at work in the afternoon after the ground had thawed. Friday afternoon 4 Plows at Work. Men cutting & mauling Rails Posts, & Forks— and women threshing & putting up Farm pen. Saturday same.

Ferry Plantn 31st Decr

Men employed since the Hollidays making Horse pen's— Women cutting down Corn Stalk. Saturday covering the Horse Pen.

Muddy hole Plantn 31st Decr

Thursday & Friday Grubbing—Saturday beating out Corn & sending it to Mill & filling farm Pen with leaves. Plough at work when the weather would permit. Jupiter[6] getting Rails.

Carpenters—31st Decr

Pointing 876 Rails, for Parke Fencing getting a Stock for arms of Mercht Mill Wheel.

Dogue Run—Jany 7th 1786

Stock all well. 3 Lambs fallen this week and then calved. Men cutting and women scrubbing all the Week—today (Saturday) putting Straw in the Farm pen—Old Man Bonny dead[7]—and one old ewe dead.

Ferry Plantation Jan. 7th

Preparing with one hand, Shelter for the Horses &ca—the rest grubbing & cutting in front of the House. Stock all well and no alteration.

River Plantation Jan. 7th

Monday all hands threshing—Tuesday Women filling gullies, Men cutting—Wednesday thursday friday & Saturday ⟨some⟩ of men cutting the rest & the women making farm Pen for cattle which was compleated and littered this day.

Muddy hole. 7th Jany

Will Ploughing when the ground would admit & he & Jupiter Cutting & Mauling of Rails when it wd not—all hands threshing a day and half and the remainder of the Week grubbing in front of the House. Stock all well—no deaths nor increase.

Carpenters—7th Jany 1786

700 Rails pointed—One stock sawed 17 feet long 14 Inches broad 3 pieces 4¾ Inches thick 4 Oars 20 feet long of Pine— Monday Raining & working in the Shop.

Dogue Run—14th Jany

Men Cutting and Mauling Rails as usual—Monday Women Grubbing—Tuesday and ever since adding a fence to enlarge the upper meadow clearing all within and repairing the fence round it. Stock All well—fallen 15 lambs this week two of which (dble ones) dead. No Calves this Week—Ewes & Lambs turned into the Wheat field.

River Plantation—14th Jan.

Men Cutting & Mauling all the Week except the day it Snowed—when they were (half the day) cutting mortices, & hewing Posts for Post & Rail fencing—Waggon & Cart Carting Rails ensuing fencing of the Corn fields—Monday Women putting up a cross fence. Tuesday & Wednesday filling up gullies— Thursday & friday littering farm pen with leaves—today filling up gullies.

Muddy hole. 14th Jany

41 Old Sheep—16 Lambs—2 Men Cutting & Mauling (except one day Will was sick) women Grubbing all the week.

Carpenters—14 Jany

Pieces for a Ladder for the Ice house[8]—10 feet long 5 by 3 when sawed. A Stock for the framing of a door: 26 Posts Morticed 8 pieces tenanted at each end. 1000 Rails pointed—James & Sambo Sawing 2 days. Made 2 Hoops for gravel Sieves. Sawed a stock into 16 ps. 20 ft long—4 by 3.

Ferry Plantation 14 Jany

Grubbing all the Week except a few odd Jobbs No alteration in the Stock.

Dogue Run—21st

Fencing all the Week with the women—Men Cutting and Mauling as usual and morticing some of the Posts. 3 Lambs came this Week—one old Ewe dead—one calve this week—4 in all—and

21 Lambs. all the Horses well except the Dray & Caleb Stones Mares[9]

River Plantation 21st Jany

Monday & Tuesday the Women were filling up Gullies in the large field. Overseer Will[10] & the Women two days making Fence—two days Women *only* threshing Wheat—Men for a days Cutting & Mauling of Rails—two days the Men Hewing and Morticing of Posts—5 Days Cart & Waggon drawing Rails—one Sheep dead one Lamb yeaned—Horses & Cattle well.

Ferry Plantation 21st Jan.

The People cutting and grubbing till Thursday when the weather set in—after that employed in Jobs. An Increase of 1 Calf and 1 Ewe Lamb.

Muddy hole—21st 1786

4 days grubbing & clearing and two days threshing—One Ewe killed by Dogs—all the Horses & other Stock as usual.

Carpenters—21st

An axle tree for the Cart over the Creek with skeens in it. 5/—1 pr of Boxes put in the wheels for a Cart 5/. Sides of A new Waggon body framed—Rough hewed the timber for a harrow plow—A Rack made for the Cow Ho. 12 feet long 22 yds in it. 300 rails hewed from end to end for the Paddock—600 d[itt]o pointed. One Tongue for the New Roller.

River Plantation 28th Jany

Monday threshing Wheat with the women. Tuesday Cleaning Wheat with half the Women—the other half making fence— The other 4 days the Women all making fences—Six days the men cutting & mauling Rails. 2 Carts & Waggon Carting Rails the whole week except carrying Wheat & Corn to Mill. 2 young Calves—one of the yearlings in the field dead.

Muddy hole Plantn 28th Jan.

41 Sheep—16 Lambs—32 Cattle—22 Horses—Monday women threshing in the Barn—the other 5 days grubbing— little Will[11] 6 days cutting Rail Timber and Posts. Jupiter 3 days Mauling—& 3 days sick.

Carpenters—Jany 28th

30 feet of R⟨ac⟩ks with 60 sticks in it—Waggon gates framed & planked—sides planked. 58 White Oak saplins got & split for Sheep fold. 300 Sticks got for it. 335 Rails hewed & pointed for

Park fencing. 15 forks & 8 large Poles cut for the removal of the Garden Houses.[12] p⟨ieces tie⟩d up for a harrow plow.

Ferry Plantn—28 Jany

Women Grubbing all the Week. Men cutting & mauling rails all the Week. One old mare dead—1 Ewe killed by Dogs. The rest as usual.

Dogue run—28th Jan.

Finished the fence from the Mill Meadow to the other Meadow—& began the cross fences by the wood. Men cutting & Mauling—old Mary getting better[13]—3 young Lambs this Week 24 in all—2 young Calves this Week.

River Plantation Feb 4th

Monday, Women Threshing—Men (except Essex[14] who was making Baskets for home house) Morticing posts. Tuesday, Women making fence round Timberlanding field; Men cutting and Mauling—Wednesday—Ditto—D[itt]o—Thursday the same—Friday same. Saturday Women Toating leaves into the Farm pen—Then, assisting in removing Houses at Mt Vernon. & then making a pen to feed Jocky hogs the year round—One old Cow dead—& one Calf came. 10 lambs—Carts getting rails to fence—2 days Plowing with 4 plows.

Dogue Run. 4th Feby

Men Cutting & Mauling as usual. Women making new fence along the Wood to the Corner by the old gate, & from thence to the present Wheat field fence with old rails—lodging all the New ground in order to Hoe,[15] all—also did part of the fence from the New fence towards the Meadow fence by the House. plowed a little yesterday and today within the enclosure of the upper meadow—2 lambs Yeaned this week & one died—25 in all—6 Calves in all—an old Oxe Pompey dead.[16] The old mares mending.

Carpenters—4th Feby

42 White Oak Saplins for sheep fold—125 bars rived for D[itt]o 2 trees cut down & 4 cuts taken of one for Do—11 forks for removing the Garden Houses—12 Stocks 10 feet long 12½ Inches Square—2 of which sawed.

Ferry Plantation 4th Feby

Women Grubbing except Flora,[17] who was sick—2 Men getting rails for the Plantation—2 Lambs and 1 Calf this Week—all the rest of the Stock as usual. Ferry men (when not in the Boat) cutting where the women are Grubbing.

Muddy hole Plantn 4th Feb.

41 Sheep—17 Lambs (one yeaned this Week) 32 Cattle—22 Horses—Women grubbing all the week with the overseer. little Will plowed half a day Monday, tuesday, Wednesday & thursday, & all friday. & part of this day after going from M. Vernon. Charles & Jupiter[18] Mauling, Will cutting Rails &ca when not plowing—Cart drawing Rails round fence yesterday, & part of this day.

Dogue Run Plantn 11th Feb.

Finished Staking & ridering all the new fences—Hoed up a good deal of the fresh land lying in this fence and in the Swamps. Three plows at work all the week—Men cutting & clearing in the swamps—2 more lambs this week—27 in all. ⟨*illegible*⟩ Calf this week—the old dray Mare declining again—the other

Ferry Plantn 11th Feby

1 hand plowing & laying of Corn ground—1 Mauling & getting of Rails 1 D[itt]o carting—Women Grubbing—Ferry men all have turns cutting—increase one calf—and one Lamb—all the rest of the stock as it were.

River Plantation—11th Feb.

6 days 6 plows at Work—5 days filling up gullies with the women—4 days 3 Men cutting & Mauling—5 days 2 Carts hauling Rails—1 day making fences with the women—25 Lambs this Week—one cart went to the mill today. 2 Calves this Week—1 Cow (old) died this week.

Muddy-hole—11th Feby

Overseer sick and no acct from thence.

Carpenters—11th Feb.

Sawing Posts and Rails for yards for the Jack & Magnolia— amountg to 506 ft—getting 5 Stocks 9½ feet long 12 inchs sqr. Making two Plows 5/ each—4 Posts for an Ox Sling for shoeing—9 feet long 10 Inchs sqr. and getting 2 ox yokes.

Dogue Run—18th Feby

Monday hoed up ground with the Women. Men cleaning up the swamps—cleared up the ground where the Hog pen was & continued the cross fence toward the Ho. House meadow as far as the logs would go. cleaning & burning up the swamps—Men during the bad weather hueing Posts. One Lamb this week (28 in all)—Black Mare in the lift all the rest of the stock well.

River Plantation 18th Feb.

Monday filling up Gullies with the Women—5 days threshing with D[itt]o—Monday 7 plows running. 4 Men cutting & mauling in the Woods—Tuesday Men morticing Posts; & 4 days cutting & mauling in the woods. 2 Carts hauling Rails 4 days & the Waggon two days—8 Lambs this Week—1 Calf.

Carpenters—18th Feby

66 Mortices dug two Inches wide & 6 Inches deep 80 Tenants made 1 Inch thick—300 laths rived of pine—2 Corner posts got today & sawed for the inclosures for the stud horses—Isaac lame all this week and last.

Ferry Platn 18th Feby

1 Fellow plowing & cutting straw all the Week. 1 D[itt]o Mauling and loading the Waggon with Hay 1 Do employed Carting— Sam & London[19] when not at the ferry employed Cutting—and all the Woman grubbing this Week—Stock all well, & as usual— 1 Lamb this Week.

Dogue Run—Plann Feb. 25th

Men cutting & mauling all the week in the swamp—women cleaning up D[itt]o—Old black Mair dead—the other two old Mares better. 3 Lambs dead—one of which just Yeaned

Ferry Plantn 25th Feby

Monday 2 hands cutting straw. 2 days plowing—3 days mauling—2 Women plowing 1 day all the rest except Betty[20] (who was sick) grubbing—Cupid Cutting[21]—Cart hauling rails Straw &ca—Stock all as usual—One of the fatting Beeves brought from thence a few night ago.

River Plantation—[Feb.] 25th

Women threshing & cleaning Wheat all the Week—Men cutting & Mauling all but one day when they were Hueing & morticing Posts except some that were threshing 1 plow laying off rows Tuesday—Waggon 2 days carrying Wheat to the mill—2 Carts drawing rails for fencing & old rails to fill up gullies—7 Lambs this Week & 1 Calf.

Muddy hole—[Feb.] 25th

Overseer sick no Acct given in.

Carpenters—[Feb.] 25th

147 rails tenanted for the deer paddock 20 for the pen for the stud horses. 8 Posts headed: 850 laths rived for the New Room.

River Plantation—Mar. 4th

Monday women cutting down Corn stalks half the day. the other part taking into the Barn a stack of Wheat. Tuesday & Wednesday employed in making a fence with them—thursdays, threshing & cleaning wheat with them—Men 4 days cutting & Mauling Rails—Two other days cutting & morticing Posts—4 days 2 Carts & the Waggon Carting Rails—stock as usual—No calves nor no lambs this Week.

Ferry Plantation Mar. 4th

Monday 3 plows at Work—1 hand Carting—1 Mauling—Sam & London cutting Wood when not at the Ferry & the Women Grubbing. The same kind of employment through the Week when the Weather would permit the people to be out & the Plows to run.

Carpenters—4th March

160 Tenants in the rails for the Paddock—2 Stock 18 feet long & 1 Sixteen feet got, and the two first sawed into scantlings 4 by 5—1 stock of Poplar sawed 10 feet long 18 inches deep—7 plank 2 Inches thick—3 Boxes put into New Wheels & the Mortices cut—One axle got for the ferry Cart—20 feet of Hurdle done in the bad Weather.

Dogue Run—4th March

No account from thence.

Muddy-hole—4th March

No acct from thence neither.

Muddy hole—11th March

40 Sheep (one old ewe dead since last acct rendered)—22 Lambs. (5 since last acct). 32 head Cattle. 1 young Calf since last acct—22 horses—Women all except Peg[22] & Nanny grubbing all the Week. Nanny sick 5 days & Peg one day. 3 Men Morticing Posts monday & part Tuesday. little Will plowing 3 days—and Morticing Posts 3 days.

Dogue run—11th Mar.

Monday so wet could neither hoe ground nor clean up the Swamps Men Morticing Posts—Tuesday Men & women both logging[23] up ground. Wednesday Thursday & friday cleaning up the Swamps & preparing the ground for the Plows. Friday one plow laying off Corn rows, one D[itt]o doing the same to day, & 2 braking up ground. The Bull & 1 Cow dead since last. only 16 Lambs—12 have died out of 28—11 Calves in all 4 Since last acct. Ox Cart & 2 hands at the home House all the Wk—29 Posts for fencing Morticed in all.

River Plantatn—11th Mar.

Three days with one Man & 4 Women cleaning wheat—the other 3 days making fences all the rest of the women abt farms. The Men cutting & mauling—Nat & Doll[24] 2 half days plowing—8 plows at work today in the ground intended for oats—2 half days (Mornings) cutting down Corn stalks—1 Calf this week (9 in all)—2 Cows dead.

Ferry Plantation—11th Mar.

Monday—men cutting & mauling—women grubbing. Tuesday—the same. Wednesday Caesar plowing[25]—the other men cutting & mauling & women Grubbing—Thursday 3 plows at Work—2 hands ½ a day getting Beef to Ho[me] Ho[use]—Men cuttg & mauling women Grubbg—Friday 3 plows at Wk other people employed as yesterday & loadg waggon with hay—Saturday 3 plows at Work rest employed as yesterday—Doll 4 days sick.[26]

Carpenters—11th Mar.

A poplar stock Hewed 17 Inches deep and sawed into 7 pieces 14 feet long. 1 six inches thick—1[,] 3½ inches thick split into 3 pieces, 5½ by 3½—the rest of 7 pieces were 2 Inches thick— One Oak Stock 14 feet long 12 Inches square split into two pieces—2 Axle trees made—1 for Morris & 1 for Muddy hole 5/ each—221 Rails Tenanted—2070 laths.

Dogue Run—18th Mar. 1786

Monday & Tuesday Men & Women Hoeing—Wednesday raining—Men did something to the Posts—Thursday completed the cross fence & removed all stumps and other rubbish along the Wood side & cross fence. Yesterday (friday) cleaning before the plows again. 3 plows at work—2 laying off the flush plowing & breaking in a young mare. 11 Posts Morticed this Week. 21 Lambs (5 this Week) No calves this week—stock all well.

River Plantation 18th Mar.

Monday 2 plows laying off the grd for Corn &c., 7 plows crossing the ground for oats. Women filling gullies—2 Men grubbing—1 sick—on Tuesday the same except that one plow was added to the 7 abt the oat ground & taken from laying off. Wednesday 1 plow laying off, & 8 cross plowing oat ground half the day the other half the day men morticing posts & women threshing in the Barn. Friday 1 plow laying off, and 8 plows crossing Oat ground 2 Men removing stumps 1 sick—and women threshing. Saturday 6 plows crossing oat ground till twelve oclock—Then went to listing in timber landing field 2 others laying off—& 1 plowing in the first plow—3 Men removing stumps & women making fence anew round Wheat field— Waggon Carting rails thursday—One cart carrying stuff to fill up gullies two days—2 days and an half carting rails—the other half carting Provender & litter for the stock. 7 Lambs this Week & two Calves.

Muddy hole—18th Mar.

40 Sheep 22 Lambs 32 Cattle & 1 young Calf—the same as last week. 22 horses—Monday 3 plows crossing—2 Men Cutting Rails & Mauling—Women grubbing except Peg who was sick— Tuesday 3 plows crossing—2 Men cutting & Mauling—same women grubbing—Wednesday plows stopped by rain 3 Men Cutting & mauling—women all on the New ground—Thursday—the same as yesterday—Friday—2 plows laying off 2 Men Cutting & mauling—women all into the new grd Saturday—1 Man cuttg—1 went to Alexandria in the Boat—1 Sick—Women all in the new grd.

Carpenters—18th Mar.

Stable-partition 26 feet in length 6 feet high—2 gates one to each division—a Rack and Manger in one end. 2 Axle trees got & made—one for the river & the other for the Plantations— 30 feet of hurdles—1 new lay gum—9 boxes for setting turkeys—Poplar stock 14 feet long 17 Inches deep—Sawed into 2 planks 2 Inch thick—1 ditto 3½ Inch thick & split into 2 pieces 8½—Tom makes 3 days repairing fish Boat

Ferry Plantn 18th Mar.

Monday 3 days plowing—1 loading Waggon with Hay for the Ho. House & mauling between while—Cupid Mauling—London & the Women grubbing—The Cart hauling straw to the farm pen—Tuesday and Wednesday all hands employed as on Monday. Thursday & friday Cæsar cutting straw for horse feed Sam mauling London, Cupid & the women grubbing—Saturday 3 people plowing Sam cutting & Mauling London cupid and the women grubbing. Tuesday Wednesday thursday friday Cart employed at the Ho. House, & Saturday in Carting straw to the farm Pens.

Dogue run Plantn 25th March

Monday Hoeing until it rained—Tuesday hoeing all day— Wednesday hoeing till the afternoon and then repairing Piney run dam. Thursday till dinner time repairing leaks and breaches in the Mill race—afterwards Hoeing. Friday Hoeing all day. Sowing & harrowing Oats till the afternoon—then plowing them—Saturday—making up pasture (or outward) fencing— Plows at Work all the Week—one laying off—the others listing till yesterday afternoon & this day when they were plowing in Oats—8 Posts morticed this Week by Brunswick[27] one lamb this week (making 22 in all). 1 calf this Week. 1 cow & Calf brot to home house this Week—1 fatted weather ditto.

Muddy hole—25th Mar. 1786

40 Sheep. 22 Lambs. 32 Cows & a calf as last week 22 horses— Monday Charles mauling—little Will & Jupiter sick. first of the day 3 women plowing the rest in the new ground—the latter part threshing Wheat. Tuesday Mauling Rails with Charles Will & Jupiter Sick—Women all in the New ground Wednesday—Charles went to Town Will & Jupiter sick—3 plows at Work (with women) rest of the women in New ground—Thursday Will & Jupiter sick 3 plows at Work, all the rest of the people repairing fencing for Corn ground. Friday Jupiter & Will yet sick—3 Women plowing all the rest repairing fencing—Saturday: Will and two Women plowing all the rest (including Jupiter) repairing fencing. Monday Gabriel[28] & the Cart at Ho. House till it began to rain—Tuesday & Wednesday Carting rails to the new ground—Thursday, Friday & Saturday (except bringing Meal from the mill) stopped and Gabriel assisting about the fencing.

River Plantn 25th Mar.

Monday—nine plows running till the rain began Tuesday Nine plows running all day—the same Wednesday, thursday, friday & Saturday. part of friday afternoon, & all Saturday, 8 of them were plowing the Oat ground—Women taking in a part of a stack of Wheat & threshing on Monday. Men threshing, morticing posts, & carrying a roller &ca from Ho. House—Tuesday, Wednesday, Thursday & friday: 3 Men digging stumps. The rest of the Men (not at the Plan[tation]) & the Women making fence round the orchard—Tuesday, Wednesday, & thursday cutting down corn stalks—friday filling up gullies & making fences— Saturday turning dung. Adam with the Oxen,[29] 3 days harrowing ground for oats—3 Men carried 52½ bushels of wheat to the mill in the large Boat. 3 Calves this week 3 Lambs ditto stock (the rest) as usual.

Carpenters—25th Mar.

1 Stock for rafters 12 inches square, 24 feet long sawed into 12 rafters 4 by 3—1 ditto 18 feet long 12 by 15 square, sawed into 15 rafters—1 ditto 18 feet long 12 inches square—sawed into 12 rafters. 1 ditto 12 feet long 10 by 12 not sawed—1 Sill for the Gt House 22 feet long 9½ by 12 Inches. 44 feet of Sill for the ferry fish house put in 6 inches by 8—22 rafters put up at the said House. 163 boards sawed, dubbed, and nailed up. 1 pannel of the Sheep hurdle made & 2 or 3 pieces dressed for more— Thom. Noaks 3 days repairing fish Boat.

Ferry Plantatn 25th [Mar.]

Monday—Cæsar cutting straw for horse feed—the rest grubbing & cutting, till it set into raining—after which London & Cupid went about Baskets, and the Women to shelling Corn. Tuesday, Wednesday, thursday, friday & Saturday Cæsar and two women plowing (except one day Cæsar was stopped by the breaking of his plow) Sam Kit cutting and Mauling all the Week. and London Cupid and the Women grubbing. The Cart employed all the Week in taking out dung—except when it went to Mill for Meal & Bran & carried home Oats—Increase one young colt—the rest of the stock as usual.

Muddy-hole. April 1st

40 Sheep. 2 lambs. 32 Cows & a Calf. 22 horses. Monday & Tuesday. Charles & Gabriel about a drain—Ov[ersee]r Jupiter and the Women about Corn field fence. Little Will Nan & Nancy[30] cross plowing. Wednesday Thursday & friday little Will laying of Rows in the plowed ground—the other two plows listing & harrowing after him—Cart assisting on thursday to carry Corn to the Mill—the rest of the hands about the Corn Stalks—Cart Carting dung all day friday. Saturday threshing & cleaning.

River Plantation—Apl 1st

Monday All the Plows were at Work—viz.—one laying off. 7 Plowing in Oats—& one Team harrowing ditto—Breechy Ben & Bath[31] digging stumps—Women til ten oclock heaping dung—afterwards cutting Corn stalks in the Crk field—Tuesday—the same—2 Carts carrying out dung—Wednesday the same—excepting that the Plows havg finished Plowing in Oats went to listing in Timberlanding field till abt 1 Oclock & then to plowing a piece of ground in front of the Overseers Ho. for grass seeds. Thursday—the same as yesterday—Friday, plows went again (having plowed & cross plowed the ground for grass) to listing in Timberlanding field and the harrow to harrowing the grass ground—women making fence. Saturday—Women threshing—men that were not threshing were employed in Morticing Posts—One Cow had a Calf pulled from her yesterday & is very bad to day—another in the same condition today. An old Cow—& a yearling on the lift—all the rest as usual.

Dogue run Plantn Apl 1

Monday hoeing & cleaning up ground in the Swamp with the women & part of the men—the rest at the Plow—Tuesday Plows at Work—the rest cutting down stalks—Wednesday & part of thursday the same—the remainder of thursday pounding of Clods in the Oat field—Friday till 12 Oclock breaking clods again and then went to hoeing ground for Mellon patch—Men abt Posts—Brunswick did 10 this Week—Stock all well—1 Calf this Week.

Carpenters Apl 1

22 rafters put up at the fish Ho. at the ferry 22 Studs put up. ⟨A plate⟩ 6 inches square and 22 feet long got & put in the main body of the Ho. 5⟨02⟩ boards nailed up. 2 doors 4½ feet square made for the same Ho. 53 rails mauled & pointed & 4 Posts for the Paddock fencing—1 length of sheep hurdle. Sambo sick 3 days.

Ferry Plantn Apl 1st

Monday 3 hands plowing—the Cart hauling straw the rest of the people cutting Corn stalks. Tuesday 3 hands plowing—Cart hauling Corn stalks the rest of the people picking them up. Wednesday 3 hands plowing, Cart hauling & the rest cutting Stalks—Thursday 3 hands plowing Cart carrying Corn to the Mill to be spread in the loft. the rest cutting stalks the forepart of the day the latter part getting ground in order for Spring Wheat. Friday 3 hands plowing—Cart hauling dung, & straw for the Stock—the rest pulling Corn Stalks—Saturday—Caesar cutting straw—men making baskets—women shelling corn. Increase of 4 calves this Week—the rest of the stock as usual.

Muddy-hole Apl 8th

40 Sheep. 22 lambs—32 Cattle besides a young calf 22 Horses. Monday Charles & the women cleaning Wheat in the Barn little Will Jupiter and Gabriel Hewing & Morticing Posts—Tuesday the same except that Charles went to the fishing landing—Wednesday and thursday all hands about Fencing (except Charles). Friday little Will and one woman plowing—a little while fixing & trying my drill plow but chiefly laying off ground for Corn—Women cutting & burning Corn Stalks—Saturday the same as yesterday except that the Cart made one trip to the Mill. & that little Will was employed drilling in Oats & Nanny harrowing.

River Plantn 8th Apl

Monday 2 Men & all the women threshing Wheat—the rest of the men cutting & mauling in the Woods. Tuesday & Wednesday the same except some of the Men being employed in Morticing Posts Wednesday—Thursday & friday 5 Women were cleaning wheat in the Barn—the rest making fencing—Breechy & Bath came to the fishing landing on thursday—the rest of the men taking up straw. Friday the plows, which had been stopped all the preceding days of the week began to work again. Saturday—Spread the manure plowed twice & harrowed the Oats in the ground intended for the experiment—after which the Plows returned to listing again—& the Women to cutting stalks. Monday & Tuesday the Waggon carried Wheat to Mill Thursday Carting rails—Monday Tuesday thursday friday & Saturday two Carts carrying out Dung. 2 Calves this Week 3 lambs D[itt]o—2 Cows & 1 calf dead—& 1 cow & a working steer upon the lift.

Dogue run—8th April

Monday carrying logs over the Swamp & began to make the fence up to the Meadow—Tuesday & Wednesday raining & nothing done Thursday about the fence again wch was finished to day—stopping gullies—laying off to day—the 3 young calves dead 2 oxen upon the lift—One small Sorrel work mare dead—the rest of the horses & sheep well. One Cow & Calf sent to the Mill for the use of the Miller.

Carpenters—8th Aprl

800 boards got—304 nailed up—13 short studs to support the rafters all for the Fish house at the ferry. 1 poplar stock sawed into 5 pieces 5 by 3 Inches—40 feet of sheep hurdles—James two days Sick—Tom Nokes with the Sein Haulers.

Ferry Plantn 8th Apl

Monday, Cæsar cutting straw & carrying Mare to Jack. The Rest of the hands fencing Corn field—Tuesday the same, in the first part the day latter part the men making baskets—the women shelling Corn (being raining)—Wednesday the same (was then still raining)—Thursday all hands fencing—Friday 3 hands listing Corn ground the rest fencing—Saturday the same. Cart employed in hauling Rails, dung, & Meal from the Mill—The Ferrymen hauling Sein when they were not transporting travellers across One Lamb yeaned—and one lost, supposed to be stolen.

River Plantation 15th Apl

Sunday 9 plows at Work—3 days 12 women cutting corn stalks. 3 days 2 men & 3 Women planting grass seeds. 2 days 2 men cutting stumps 6 days 2 Carts carrying dung—2 Cows dead.

Muddy hole—Plantn 15th Apl

Monday & Tuesday 8 people picking Corn Stalks & cutting them down. Wednesday 8 ditto sowing Carrots. Thursday 8 d[itt]o grubbing. friday & saturday doing the same. 6 days plowing & harrowing with 3 teams. 6 days Carting dung. 1 Ewe dead—the rest of the stock as usual—2 colts which were in the wheat field brought to the home house pasture.

Dogue run—15th

Monday, Tuesday & Wednesday tredding & cleaning wheat. with the women—Men that were not at plow & Cart, cleaning up Swamp & logging it—1 Jack constantly at the fishing landing[32]—Thursday & friday Hoeing Saturday Spreading dung on ground intended for Carrots—Monday & Tuesday horses treading wheat the rest of the days plowing—Oxen carrying Wheat to Mill, Dragging the Roller, and Carting Dung 1 Mare (Hunter) dead—1 Ox very low—3 young Calves.

Ferry Plantn 15th Apl

Monday, Tuesday, & Wednesday getting grd in order & Sowing Spring wheat—the rest of the People employed in Spreading dung these 3 days. Thursday 3 plows at work listing, Cupid & the women picking up Corn Stalks; Friday 3 plows listing till dinner time, then breaking up ground for Potatoes, & drilled Corn—Cupid & the Women fencing meadow. Saturday the same—Sam & London fishing—carting dung 3 days. Stock all well.

Carpenters 15th Apl

535 Boards nailed on at the Fish House at the ferry landing, 2 doors hung there one with a lock—A stock for Posts got 16 feet long, 9 Inches sqr.—2 Stocks 11 feet long 16 inches sqr. for outer gate 80 feet of sheep hurdles putting in 4 boxes to new Charriot Wheels.

AD, DLC:GW. Beginning on 22 April, George Augustine Washington writes the reports. These Farms Reports, running from 26 Nov. 1785 through 30 Dec. 1786, have been transcribed as a single document for CD-ROM:GW.

1. GW wrote 1786 and changed it to 1785. Morris, a dower slave about GW's age who was brought to Mount Vernon in 1759, had been overseer at Dogue Run farm since 1766. The overseer at Muddy Hole farm was a mulatto named Davy, a dower slave, who also had been an overseer since before the Revolution. When John Alton, the overseer of River farm, died in December 1785, GW made Davy the overseer of that farm in his place and sent a slave named Will, who was probably the son of the dower slave Doll of River farm, from the Home House farm to Muddy Hole farm to replace Davy as overseer (*Diaries*, 4:252).

2. See the editorial note.

3. The inventory at Muddy Hole was taken on 16 November. See the editorial note.

4. The only carter that GW lists in his slave census of February 1786 is Simms at the Home House farm. Mink Will was a farmhand at Muddy Hole farm, as distinguished from Doll's Will who was the overseer of the same farm. Both Wills were dower slaves.

5. In his slave census of February 1786 GW lists Isaac, James, Sambo, and Tom Nokes as his four carpenters, all at Home House farm. Tom Nokes is the only one of the four whom GW labels a dower slave in February 1786. An Isaac, age 28, in 1759 was a dower slave, but the name does not appear on GW's list of tithables until 1773 (*Papers, Colonial Series*, 6:282; 9:238). Among GW's tithables at Muddy Hole farm in 1760 and 1761 is a slave named James, but the name does not reappear as a tithable until 1773 when a James is listed as a tradesman, or artisan (ibid., 428; 7:45, 139; 9:238).

6. Jupiter, a dower slave who had been a farmhand on the Custis's Ship

Landing plantation in York County, was listed as a tithable at Muddy Hole farm as early as 1762 (ibid., 6:218, 229, 312, 7:139). GW refers to him in 1787 as "my old Negro fellow Jupiter" (*Diaries*, 5:145). The Jupiter whom GW names here and frequently hereafter in the reports seems to have worked closely with the Muddy Hole overseer, Will, and may be another younger Jupiter.

7. "Old Man Bonny" was a "very old" bay horse (ibid., 4:228).

8. GW corresponded at length with Robert Morris in 1785 about the building of an icehouse at Mount Vernon, and he records his progress in constructing it in his *Diaries*. He began putting ice into it on 16 Jan. 1786 (ibid., 264).

9. The Arabian horse Magnolio, which had belonged to John Parke Custis, was at this time standing at Dogue Run where he served as a stud for mares brought to Mount Vernon (ibid., 232, 234). GW hired Caleb Stone in 1773 to oversee his slave carpenters (see Cash Accounts, October 1773, n.5).

10. Davy was the overseer of River farm. See note 1. Will was one of the three or four dower slaves named Will.

11. GW lists only two adult Wills at Muddy Hole farm. See note 1 and *Diaries*, 4:282.

12. For the moving of the garden houses on 4 Feb. 1786, see ibid., 271.

13. GW does not record the death of Mary, but he does not list her at Dogue Run on 18 Feb. (ibid., 282).

14. A slave named Essex is first listed in GW's List of Tithables, c.9 June 1762, on Muddy Hole farm, and on Dogue Run farm c.10 June 1763 (*Papers, Colonial Series*, 7:139, 228, 313, 376, 443, 515).

15. By "lodging" he means beating down old crops.

16. In his inventory of livestock at Dogue Run farm in November 1785, GW lists seven working oxen (*Diaries*, 4:229).

17. Flora was on the River farm at Mount Vernon as early as 1762 (*Papers, Colonial Series*, 7:139).

18. Charles, whom GW mentions a number of times in these farm reports, was one of only five male farm laborers, including the overseer, working at Muddy Hole farm. GW lists a Charles as early as 1760, and in 1762 he bought another Charles, a one-handed man from Samuel Washington (ibid., 6:220, 428; 7:45, 109). He lists only one Charles, at Muddy Hole, in his census of February 1786.

19. Sam Kit was a dower slave at Claiborne's plantation who was brought up to Mount Vernon in 1770 (ibid., 6:311). In 1786 there was also a Sam working at the Home House farm. London's name first appears on GW's list of tithables as a blacksmith in 1760 and as a laborer on Dogue Run farm in 1763 (ibid., 6:428, 7:228). GW mentions London's working on his millrace in August 1772 (*Diaries*, 3:128). At this time in 1786 London was serving as a ferryman, but GW on four other occasions in the farm reports refers to his doing farmwork.

20. Betty, one of several slaves at Mount Vernon of that name, was a dower slave and was probably either the Betty on Muddy Hole farm or the one on Dogue Run farm first listed as tithables in 1760 (*Papers, Colonial Series*, 6:428).

21. Cupid was a dower slave. For his possible identity, see Joseph Valentine to GW, 21–23 Nov. 1770, n.2.

22. There was at this time on River farm a woman named Peg who may have been the Peg listed as one of the tithables on River farm in the 1760s. There was a dower slave named Peg (Pegg) in 1759, and GW lists a dower slave named Peg at Dogue Run farm in his census of February 1786. As late as 1774 only one Peg appears in the list of tithables (ibid., 6:218, 7:139, 228, 313, 377, 443, 516).

23. See note 15. In DLC:GW there is a document headed "Memorandum of things delivered to the different Plantations from the 12th of Apl 1786." It records after George Augustine Washington takes over until 31 Aug. 1786 the number of bushels, and occasionally pecks, of corn, oats, barley, bran, peas, potatoes, clover seed, salt, and limes delivered to the farms. George Augustine Washington's farm reports to the end of 1786 are recorded in the same notebook that GW entered his to this date.

24. Nat, an expert plowman, was listed as a tithable on River farm as early as 1762. Doll, a dower slave, was first listed as a tithable on River farm in 1761 (*Papers, Colonial Series*, 7:139, 45). She was probably the mother of Will, the overseer of Muddy Hole farm (see notes 1 and 26).

25. Caesar was a dower slave and a skilled cradler. He was brought up from York County, probably in 1770 (see Joseph Valentine to GW, 21–23 Nov. 1770, n.2).

26. There were at this time four adult dower slaves named Doll or Dolly at Mount Vernon, two at Home House farm, one at River farm (see note 23), and this one at the Ferry farm.

27. Brunswick, whom GW listed as "Ruptured" in his census of 18 Feb. 1786, was a dower slave. Joseph Valentine wrote to GW on 16 Sept. 1766: "at yorke [Ships Landing plantation] Brumswick one of the Best hands all most in the estate has gave out this two years and never will do any more." This older Brunswick who "gave out" was married to a woman named Moll whose name appears on the Dogue Run farm list in GW's census in February 1786 (*Diaries*, 4:280). In 1759 Moll is listed as having a child named Brunswick, who is probably the Brunswick named here (*Papers, Colonial Series*, 6:229). To list is to prepare the land for a crop of corn.

28. No Gabriel appears in the pre-Revolutionary lists of tithables.

29. Adam, whom GW lists as a tithable in 1766, died in June 1786 (*Papers, Colonial Series*, 7:443; *Diaries*, 4:339). This may be the slave Adam whom GW inherited from Augustine Washington and who was on GW's Bullskin plantation in Frederick County in the 1750s.

30. Nancy was 15 or 16 years old. See *Diaries*, 5:381.

31. Ben, a dower slave, worked on the Custis's Bridge Quarter in York County. The first Ben listed as a tithable at Mount Vernon was a hand on the Home House farm in 1761, but by 1767 there were three Bens, one at Home House, one at Dogue Run, and one at River farm (*Papers, Colonial Series*, 6:217, 7:45, 515–16). Breechy, who GW indicates in his 1786 census was a dower slave, may be the house servant from New Kent County who was 24 years old in 1759. He began serving in the house at Mount Vernon in 1760 and still was

a house servant in 1774. No other dower slave named Breechy has been found. A slave named Bath at River farm was listed as a tithable in Fairfax Parish in 1774.

32. Jack may be the slave named Jack who ran away from Dogue Run farm in 1761 and subsequently worked at Home House farm (ibid., 7:45, 139, 313, 376, 443, 515, but GW probably is referring to a jackass.

To John Fitzgerald

Dear Sir,   Mount Vernon Novr 26th 85

If the necessary alterations are made in the petition and Bills which were drawn by Mr Johnson—and fair copies of them taken the sooner they are forwarded to the respective assemblies the better.[1]—Time is gliding away—at the latter part of a session the members get impatient and but too often reject matters, because they will not spare time to attend to them.—I am—Dear Sir Yr Obed. Servt G. Washington

P.S. I am to dine with Col. Lyles on Monday[2]—If there is anything before the Board, and you will let me know the hour of attendance; and will give Colo. Silpit [Gilpin] notice of it, I will be there—not expecting, nor indeed will it be convenient for me, to be up again in a short time. G.W.

Typescript, ViMtV.

1. For the petition and draft of a bill regarding the depth of the proposed Potomac River Company's locks and canals which Thomas Johnson prepared for presentation to the Virginia and Maryland legislatures, see Thomas Johnson to GW, 4 Nov., n.1.

2. William Lyles, formerly of Charles County, Md., had a distillery and dry goods store in Alexandria. GW dined with Colonel Lyles on Monday, 28 Nov., at his rented house on Prince Street, but there does not seem to have been a meeting of the trustees of the Potomac River Company (*Diaries*, 4:241).

From William Hartshorne & Co.

Sir   Alexandria Novr 26. 1785

The Enclosed Letter and Account we recd under cover from our Friend Mr David Pearce of Gloucester New-England with an order on you for the Amount say £63.5.6—as the account is not very plain & you may not be acquainted with the hand writing I have sent a Copy of it[1]—I am Respectfully Yours

Wm Hartshorne & Co.

LS, DLC:GW.

1. In his letter of 6 Nov. enclosing his account with GW, David Pearce indicated that he was also enclosing a bill of lading, but Hartshorne's letter of 10 Feb. 1786 seems to indicate that the document was received later. There is in DLC:GW a filled-out printed form, dated 8 Aug. 1785, which records that John Gardoqui was shipping a jackass, 44 Spanish inches high, on the *Ranger*, Job Knight master, from the river of Bilbao to be delivered to David Pearce in Gloucester, Massachusetts. The bill of lading was signed by Knight. On the obverse side of the form, someone listed such things supplied for the jack as feed and horseshoes. Hartshorne's clerk made the following copy of Pearce's charges at the end of the present letter:

Dr His Excellency Genl Washington

To Freight of an Animal called a Jack Ass from Bilboa to Boston	£35. 0.0
Building a House for Him ℔ agreement	7.10.0
Boarding the Spaniard who attended him	1.10.0
Cash pd for Brandy to Bathe the animals joints	.10.0
Wine & Bran for said Animal	1. 4.0
Oates for ditto	. 6.0
Your Stable while at Do hired	1. 0.0
Cash paid Spaniards washing	. 6.0
Cash Expences to Boston and a Man to go wth him 3 days	1.16.0
the hire of a Boat to Land said Animal	. 3.3
Keepers passage omitted	14. 0.0
	£63. 5.6

Sir Please to pay the above a/c to Mr Wm Hartshorne and you will oblige Your obedt Humble Servt David Pearce (Copy).

GW challenged Pearce's account (see David Pearce to GW, 22 Jan. 1786, William Hartshorne to GW, 10 Feb., 6, 25 Mar. 1786, GW to Hartshorne, 20 Feb. 1786, and GW to Thomas Cushing, 5 April 1786).

From Battaile Muse

Honorable Sir,   Fauquier C[ount]y Novr 26th 1785

the bea[rer] Mr Daniel Harrel who Lives in this County is desirous to become a Tenant of yours on Lott No. 2. 140 acres—which Lott is now Inhabited by Michael Ruse a Man not worth anything—I have recommended the bearer to you for your approbation for a Lease on the following Terms—to have a Lease agreeable to the Covenants of your Late Lease for the Term of

Ten years His paying the annual rent of Ten pounds ℔ year—
the small grain that is now soun the said Harrel is to Pay for on
demand at what Ever its Valued at by Capt. John Edmonds—the
Said Harrel is to Produce to you a Sattisfactory recommendation
respecting His Carracter.[1] I am now on the Land and Shall advise you soon of my Proseedings the Back rents of this Lott No.
2 appears to be Lost as well some others by removeal of the
tenants.[2] I am Sir your Humble Servt

Battaile Muse

ALS, DLC:GW. Postscript in GW's hand.
    1. GW wrote at the bottom of the letter: "Agreed to let Danl Harrel have
the aforesaid Lot No. upon the terms mentioned in this letter—and promised
Harrel that I would write to Mr Muse accordingly." Muse leased GW's lot 2 in
Fauquier County to Harrel at £10 per annum for ten years to end 25 Dec.
1795. See Lists of Tenants, 18 Sept., n.11, Muse to GW, 28 Nov., GW to Muse,
4 Dec. 1785, and Ledger B, 288. Harrel remained on the lot only until 1790.
    2. See Lists of Tenants, 18 Sept. 1785, n.11.

Letter not found: from Thomas Smith, 26 Nov. 1785. On 28 July 1786
GW apologized for "not having acknowledged the receipt of your letters of the 26th of Novr. . . ."

From William Gordon

My dear Sir   Jamaica Plain [Mass.] Nov 28. 1785
    My design of publishing is now in such forwardness, that I
expect the proposals for the History of the American Revolution, will be circulated through the United States by the first
week in January. I have given direction, that a few should be
forwarded to your Excellency from New York as soon as printed.
Shall think myself greatly honoured & served by your countenance.[1] I have requested of my friend Mr Roberdeau to receive
subscriptions for me at Alexandria, & promise myself from his
former acts of kindness, that he will oblige me in it; through
the advice of Col. Gibbs have made a like application to Col.
Fitzgerald; Col. Gibbs has supported by a letter. Mrs Gordon
unites in sincere regards to your Excellency, your Lady, & the
rest of the family, the young gentleman especially, with my Dear
Sir, Your sincere friend & very humble servant

William Gordon

ALS, DLC:GW.

1. Gordon's *History of the Rise, Progress, and Establishment of the Independence of the United States* was published in four volumes in 1788 in London. See Griffin, *Boston Athenæum Collection*, 510–11. See also GW to James Mercer, 20 Jan. 1786.

From Battaile Muse

Honourable Sir,   Berkeley County Novr 28th 1785

I returned yesterday from your Lands In Fauquier I received only Eighteen pounds which was paid me by Daniel Harris who informs me that He Lives on Lott No. 11 He beleaves[1]—Least you Should want the money I have enclosed and order on Mr Andrew Wales in Alexandria for £20 being over what I have Received, the Tenants all Promise to Pay after Christmast but I expect it will be next spring before I shall receive money from them. I have advised them to make good Payments if they expected to have indulgence and the Sooner they get clear the better—they in general are so Very Pooer in Fauquier that I expect many will never Pay up the arrears, which will Ocation a Loss to you and an Evil to the Tenant—had the rents been annually Collected they would have been in a Better Sittuation as well your accts, which I am not able to Settle nor Can it be done in my Opinion with any Certainty unless you are on the Spot—they not haveing all their receipts and Two Tenants on one Lease add to this the Conveyances that has hapned and many other circumstances—makes it uncertain for me to State a Final Settlement So as to make my Self Safe therefore could you or Mr Lunn Washington who is Perhaps acquainted with their sittuations attend a True state might be made—after which Should I be Favoured with the business I will Ensure that all things needfull shall be done. I Shall Collect all I Can by next spring and when i can with Certainty state their accts I will endeavour to do So—there is on the Tract Land in Ashbys Bend three Lotts Vacant—I mean that the Persons there are Worth nothing—Lott No. 1. No. 2. No. 9 which Lott No. 9 no one has liveed on for many years if Ever.[2] Please to advise whether I am to advertise the renting them or whether I Shall Let them by private Bargain as Some of them are Under Lease's—the number of years Let them for, & what rents. There is three more Lotts that are in a bad sittuation, I am Told their is good Men Comeing to them which will Pay the Back rents—which if done, I suppose will be Sufficient—as the Land is not Very good—but Very few has Complyed with their Leases—but they promise they will attend to the Covenants now as Quick as Possable—the Widow Lemart is not able to Pay the ballance of her acct She Promises to Pay me rent after Christmast,[3] the others that Can Pay att al, say they will Try To make up half of their arrears by next Spring and Pay the other half out of the next Crop—but their Complying is a Doubt with me, and indeed I am Certain that half of them will not Comply To distress them they Can not give Security and to Sell their all would not Pay off. I shall not distress unless in Cases of Necessity untill they worke of some of their arrears unless you advise It. where only one rent is due I make a Point to distress unless its Paid in a reasonable Time so as To Prevent Two rents To be due at once.

There are Several Tenants on Chattins run Tract—Lott No. 1 John Thompson Lives 196 acres in the Lott He says He only agreed to Pay for one Lott which was not to exceed 130 acres He is a Very Poor Man but of good Carrecter—would it not be best to divide the Lott as He will not be able to Pay more than for 96 acres at £5. Take of that Quantity and Lease out the 100 acres for Ten years and charge Thompson with arrears for 130 acres which is more than He will ever Pay.[4] Lott No. 2— 206 acres has a good Tenant—one Charles Rector who is able to Pay arrears & the annual Rent he sayes He will Pay half next spring and the hole if He can Possably Collect His Money[5]— Lott No. 3. 278 acres has three Persons thereon—William Hanburry, Jacob Rector & Jesse Rector I can say nothing in Favour of those People and as I think they have Trespassed they should be distressed for the arrears of rents.[6]

Lott No. 4—200 acres—Lives three Tenants—Edward Graham who is not able to worke—James Rector who works for the old Man Graham—Peter Rector who is to Pay half of the rents— these People are Poor therefore the arrears will be dificult to Collect.[7]

The foregoing is as full a State of your Tenants as I have yet had in my Power to Communicate—I have been Tedious and Expect to be Troublesome to you untill I am better acquainted with your affairs—as Its' my desire to do all things for the best. indeed I am so Fearfull of doing wrong that it's Possible I Fail some Times in doing what I Aught to do—with your advice I shall do every thing I can untill the spring by that Time things may be better understood—in this Time the Vacant Lands should be Let as the Lotts Improvements may not be Lost—as the Lands are not rich I suppose they might be Let for three Years on the old Terms on Paying up the arrears by such Time— when there is no Probability of geting arrears a Lease for Ten years on Paying agreeable to the present Improvements & Soil, I suppose will be sufficient—as I before observed I wish to be advised whether its Necessary To Advertise Those Places that are Vacateed.

I have 1,000 bushels of wheat ready to send down but I cannot get waggons to engage to go to your mill—the bearer of this takes down a Load and If Possable your mill shall receive a Quantity by Christmass as its necessary that Some instruement of writeing should be produced respecting a Bargain in case of Death—I shall be oblige to you to Send me a line respecting Your Purchase of the thousand Bushels wheat—the Butter I mentiond to you shall be down at Mr A. Wales on or before the 23d day of December unless the roads are not Passable.

Should the rents in Berkeley and Frederick not be discharged by the first day of March it's my Opinion that distresses should Take Place as the Inhabitants here Look for Law before Payment otherwise I do not expect you will recover the rents in the Course of next year as their is so many stages of Law to Pass through[8]—I have the Honour to Be your Obedient Humble Servant

Battaile Muse

ALS, DLC:GW.

1. John Dyer leased from GW in 1769 lots 13 and 14 lying in Fauquier and Loudoun counties, and Daniel Harris was renting the two lots at this time. See Lists of Tenants, 18 Sept. 1785, n.21.

2. See notes 10, 11, and 18 in Lists of Tenants, 18 September.

3. The widow of Lewis Lemart lived on GW's lot no. 10 in Fauquier County. See Lists of Tenants, 18 Sept., n.19.

4. Under the terms of his lease, John Thompson was to pay on 25 Dec. 1777 his first annual rent of £6 for lot no. 1 on Chattins Run. When he left the place in the spring of 1786, he owed about £40. Muse sued him for the back rent in early 1787, and shortly thereafter Thompson, whom Muse consistently described as very poor, fled from Fauquier County. In September 1787 Thompson paid £20, "which," Muse conceded, "was all the Man was able to

Pay." The lot was empty in 1789, but in 1790 a man named Simon Harrell was "Tenant at will" and "a Bad Tenant" at that. By this time Thompson was renting half of lot no. 3 at Chattins Run (see note 6). See GW to Muse, 16 Dec. 1785, 4 Dec. 1786, 19 Feb. 1789, Muse to GW, 26 Nov. 1786, 20 Jan., 4 Feb., 15 Oct. 1787, Muse's Rental Rolls for GW, 1788–90 (ViMtV), and Muse's Accounts as Rental Agent (NjMoNP: Smith Collection), 15 Sept. 1787, 29 April 1789, recapitulation of 1790, 1791 (see source note in Lists of Tenants, 18 Sept. 1785).

5. A year later Muse had quite a different view of Charles Rector as a tenant. On 26 Nov. 1786 he wrote GW: "one Charles Rector that Took the place Let to Enock Ashby [see GW to Muse, 18 Sept. 1785] run away while I was below £83.2.0 in Debt—He has moved To Frederick County." Muse declared him to be "Too Poor to Bear" being sued, but he did bring suit in Frederick County in 1789 and secured a judgment against Rector for "£105 or there abouts." Muse's rental rolls note "One Rowley To Pay" Rector's debt, but Robert Lewis noted in 1791 that Charles Rector was "now in Frederick Prison," owing £113.4.3. Muse gave Benjamin Rust a ten-year lease on Chattins Run lot no. 2, to run until 25 Dec. 1796 at a rent of £12 per annum. See GW to Muse, 4 Dec. 1786, Muse to GW, 26 Nov. 1786, 20 Jan., 4 Feb., 15 Oct. 1787, 21 Mar. 1789, 20 July 1790; Muse's Rental Rolls for GW, 1788–90 (ViMtV); Muse's Accounts as Rental Agent (NjMoNP: Smith Collection), 23, 26 Oct. 1786, 24 May 1788, recapitulation of 1790, 1791, and Ledger B, 297.

6. Muse's efforts to collect the annual rent on the Chattins Run lot no. 3 were directed to Jacob Rector until 1789 and 1790 when he sought payment from Frederick Rector. He sued Jacob Rector in May 1786 for £130, ten years' rent, and secured a judgment against him in the Fauquier County court. He received from the sheriff Jacob Rector's payments of £34.8 on 23 Oct. 1786, £52.13.6 on 26 Mar. 1787, and £15.10.11-½ on 30 Aug. 1787. Thereafter, with the help of the courts, Muse was able to collect for lot no. 3, from Frederick Rector, £8.13 on 18 Mar. 1789 and £10 on 24 May 1790. In his final accounting for this lot, Muse noted that "Frederick Rector who run away—but is Expected to return" was in arrears £5.5 for 1788 and owed in rent and taxes £13.18 for 1789 and for 1790, for which Muse would sue him upon his return. Muse noted in 1790 that he had rented one half of lot no. 3 to "one Singleton" and the other half for two years to John Thompson (see note 4). See Muse's Accounts as Rental Agent (NjMoNP), Muse to GW, 4 June, 11 July, 26 Nov. 1786, 4 Feb. 1787, and Muse's Rental Rolls for GW, 1788–90 (ViMtV). "William Hanburry" is William Hansbrough (see Hansbrough to GW, 20 Nov. 1786).

7. Muse leased for ten years, until 25 Dec. 1796, lot no. 4 of the Chattins Run tract to Daniel Brown for a rent of £12 per annum. Muse resorted in 1787 and 1788 to the Fauquier County court to collect the rent from Brown, but when giving up his post as collector in 1790, Muse indicated that Brown owed only £3.3, and on 27 Nov. 1791 Brown paid £13.18.8 in rent (Muse's Accounts as Rental Agent [NjMoNP: Smith Collection], 25 Mar., 24 Nov. 1789, recapitulation of 1790, 1791; Ledger B, 298).

8. See GW to Muse, 4 December.

To Wakelin Welch

Sir,   Mt Vernon 28th Novr 1785.

I request the favor of you to send me for the use of Mrs Washington, a handsome & fashionable gold watch, with a fashionable chain or string, such as are worn at present by Ladies in genteel life.

These to be paid for, as the other things are, from the fund in the Bank.[1] I am &c.

G. Washington

P.S. Let the hour & minute hands be set with Diamonds. G.W.

LB, DLC:GW.

1. GW is referring to the Bank of England stock belonging to the Custis heirs. See GW to Welch, 27 July 1784, n.2.

Letter not found: from Clement Biddle, 29 Nov. 1785. GW wrote Biddle on 11 Dec.: "I have received your favor of the 29th Ulto."

To Patrick Henry

Dear Sir.   Mount Vernon Novr 30th 1785

I have had the honor to receive your Excellency's favor of the 11th & am much obliged to you for the Commissioners report respecting the cut from the Waters of Elizabeth River to those of Albemarle Sound. And it is with great pleasure I have since heard that that matter is in a prosperous way in our Assembly, & placed on a footing (reasonable & just I think) which is likely to meet the approbation of the Legislature of No. Carolina.

It has always been my opinion since I first investigated the Great dismal Swamp as a member & manager of that Company that the most advantageous Cut would be found to be through Drummonds pond to the head of Pasquotank and I have Surveys & Notes which prove this I think, incontestably[1]—Mr Andrews's conjectures, with respect to Locks, I conceive is justly founded;[2] for if the bed of the lake is above the level of the Water of Elizabeth River & Pasquotank the reflux by means of the Canal being greater than the influx must undoubtedly drain the Pond & render it useless as a reservoir without these Locks— but the places at which it may be proper to establish them must

I should suppose depend upon the level & suitableness of the ground to receive them after the cut is made which should be begun at the extreme ends that the water may run of (and if with any velocity) to contribute to the work.

If this cut is effected, the obstructions in the Roanoke removed (which will most assuredly follow) and the inland Navigation of the Rivers James & Potomack compleated according to Law it will open channels of convenience & wealth to the Citizens of this State that the imagination can hardly extend to and render this the most favoured Country in the Universe. These measures only require a beginning to shew the practicability, ease & advantage with which they may be effected. Rappahanock & Shanondoah (the latter through a long extent of it) will follow the example & I see nothing to prevent the two b⟨ran⟩ches of York River from doing the sam⟨e.⟩ The consequence in the article of draug⟨ht⟩ Cattle alone—and to our Roads will be inconceivably great. The latter with small amendments will always be in good order when the present number of Carriages are no longer taring them to pieces in the most inclement seasons of the year. and the ease to, and saving in the former will be felt most interestingly by the farmer & Planter in their annual operations.

But until these things are accomplished & even admitting they were done, do you not think, my good Sir, that the credit, the saving, and the convenience of this Country all require that our great roads leading from one public place to another should be shortned—straighned—and established by Law—and the power in the County Courts to alter them withdrawn? To me these things seem indispensably necessary, & it is my opinion they will take place in time the longer therefore they are delayed the more people will be injured by the Alterations when they happen—It is equally clear to me, that putting the lowest valuation possible upon the labour of the people who work upon the roads under the existing Law & custom of the present day the repairs of them by way of Contract to be paid by an assessment on certain districts (until the period shall arrive when turnpikes may with propriety be established) would be infinitely less burthensome to the community than the present mode. In this case too the Contracter would meet with no favor—every man in the district wd give information of neglects—whereas negligence under the present system is winked at by the only people who know how, or can inform against the Overseers—for strangers had rather encounter the inconvenience of bad roads than the trouble of an information and go away prejudiced against the Country for the polity of it.[3] With great esteem & respect I have the honor to be Dr Sir Yr Most Obedt Hble Servt

Go: Washington

ALS, Vi; LB, DLC:GW.

1. See source note in Dismal Swamp Land Company Articles of Agreement, 3 Nov. 1763, printed above.

2. GW undoubtedly intended to write "not justly founded." See the last paragraph in Henry's letter of 11 November. GW wrote to an unidentified person on this date, Nov. 30: "Dear Sir. I have had the honor to receive your favor of the 7th & am much obliged to you for the list. My friend Mr [Robert] Andrews seems wrong in his conjectures—Mr Lyons also sent me a list of the Lands I think Govr Henry will arrange matters to the satisfaction of all—With great esteem & respect I have the honor to be Dr Sir Yr Most obed. Hble Ser. Go: Washington" (ALS, NjP: Straus Autograph Collection). In point of fact, both GW and Robert Andrews were far wide of the mark as to the number of locks that would be required for the canal (Brown, *Dismal Swamp Canal*, 35). Mr. Lyons may be Peter Lyons (d. 1801) of Hanover County, whom GW had attempted to visit in May (*Diaries*, 4:132).

3. Under the "Act concerning public roads" of 1785, the county courts continued to divide the county into precincts and appoint surveyors in each precinct to maintain the roads with the labor of "All male labouring persons, of the age of sixteen years or more, except such as are masters of two or more male labouring slaves" as were appointed by the court (12 Hening 174–80). Despite the criticism of GW and others, the principle of personal service for maintaining roads continued until the Civil War.

To James Madison

My dear Sir,   Mount Vernon Novr 30th 1785.

Receive my thanks for your obliging communications of the 11th—I hear with much pleasure that the assembly are engaged, seriously, in the consideration of the revised Laws. A short & simple code, in my opinion, tho' I have the sentiments of some of the Gentlemen of the long robe against me, would be productive of happy consequences, and redound to the honor of this or any Country which shall adopt such.

I hope the resolutions which were published for the consideration of the House, respecting the reference to Congress for the regulation of a Commercial system will have passed. The proposition in my opinion is so self evident that I confess I am at a loss to discover wherein lyes the weight of the objection to the measure. We are either a United people, or we are not. If the former, let us, in all matters of general concern act as a nation, which have national objects to promote, and a National character to support—If we are not, let us no longer act a farce by pretending to it. for whilst we are playing a dble game, or playing a game between the two we never shall be consistent or respectable—but *may* be the dupes of some powers and, most assuredly, the contempt of all. In any case it behoves us to provide good Militia Laws, and look well to the execution of them—but, if we mean by our conduct that the States shall act independently of each other it becomes *indispensably* necessary—for therein will consist our strength and respectabity in the Union.

It is much to be wished that public faith may be held inviolate—Painful is it even in thought that attempts should be made to weaken the bands of it. It is a dangerous experiment—once slacken the reins and the power is lost—and it is questionable with me whether the advocates of the measure foresee all the consequences of it. It is an old adage that honesty is the best policy—this applies to public as well as private life—to States as well as individuals. I hope the Port and assize Bills no longer sleep but are awakened to a happy establishment. The first with some alterations, would in my judgment be productive of great good to this Country—without it, the Trade thereof I conceive will ever labor & languish—with respect to the Second if it institutes a speedier administration of Justice it is equally desirable.

It gives me great pleasure to hear that our assembly were in a way of adopting a mode for establishing the Cut betwn Elizabeth river & Pasquotank which was likely to meet the approbation of the State of No. Carolina—It appears to me that no Country in the Universe is better calculated to derive benefits from inland Navigation than this is—and certain I am, that the conveniences to the Citizens individually, and the sources of wealth to the Country generally, which will be opened thereby will be found to exceed the most sanguine imagination—The Mind can scarcely take in at one view all the benefits which will result therefrom—The saving in draught Cattle, preservation of Roads &ca &ca will be felt most interestingly—This business only wants a beginning—Rappahanock—Shannondoah—Roa-noke—and the branches of York River will soon perceive the advantages which water transportation (in ways hardly thought of at first) have over that of Land and will extend Navigation to almost every Mans door.

From the complexion of the debates in the Pensylvania it should seem as if that Legislature intended their assent to the proposition from the States of Virginia & Maryland (respecting a road to the Yohiogany[)] should be conditional of permission given to open a Communication between the Chesapeak & Delaware by way of the rivers Elk & Christeen—which I am sure will never be obtained if the Baltimore interest can give it effectual opposition.[1]

The Directors of the Potomack Company have sent to the Delegates of this County to be laid before the Assembly a Petition (which sets forth the reasons) for relief in the depth of the Canals which it may be found necessary to open at the great & little Falls of the River—As public œconomy and private interest equally prompt the measure and no possible disadvantage that we can see will attend granting the prayer of it, we flatter ourselves no opposition will be given to it.

To save trouble—to expedite the business, and to secure uniformity without delay, or an intercourse between the Assemblies on so trivial a matter we have taken the liberty of sending the draught of a Bill to Members of both Assemblies which if approved will be found exactly similar.[2] With the highest esteem and regard I am Dr Sir Yr Obedt & Affecte Hble Ser.

Go: Washington

ALS, NjP: deCoppet Collection; LB, DLC:GW.

1. For the proposal of Virginia and Maryland that a road be built in Pennsylvania from the Potomac to a stream flowing into the Ohio, see Madison to GW, 1 Jan. 1785, n.4.

2. See Thomas Johnson to GW, 4 Nov., n.1, and references.

To John Rawlins

Sir,   Mount Vernon 30th Novr 1785.

Your Letter & plan came safe; tho' I do not pretend to be a competent judge of this kind of work, yet from the little experience I have had in it, & from a certain knowledge that most of the mouldings & decorations are with great ease & expedition cast, of a material too which is by no means expensive, I do not scruple to declare that your Estimate exceeded my expectation.

This, & not understanding the plan fully from an unaccustomedness to drawings, together with the indifinite charge of travelling expences, which may be great or little; and a desire of having something finally determined without giving the trouble of coming here again; or of fixing matters by an intercourse of letters which might be tedious & troublesome—& the first of which by no means suiting me, as I must be upon a certainty—having been twice disappointed & put to much inconvenience for want of the room. These reasons I say, have induced me to communicate my ideas to Colo. Tilghman on this business, & to authorize him on the spot to fix matters decidedly with you. Any Agreement therefore which he may make on my behalf, will be as obligatory on me as if I was present to sign & ratify it.[1]

If an Agreement takes place, I wish to know precisely, & as soon as may be, what will be previously necessary for my Joiners & Carpenters to do, or to prepare that there may be no delay after you arrive; for besides the inconvenience I already feel from the want of the new room—you know that to complete this, the communication with another must be opened—& that unless both are finished before the season arrives which requires fire, I shall be much distressed. Whilst the weather is warm, the Common Hall & piazza will do very well, as a substitute for the Drawing room or Parlour; but when the weather becomes cool, we must retire to a fireside.

I think it highly probable that the ceilings of my upper rooms may want plaistering, which would make the job more deserving attention; some of them I am sure do, & if we can agree upon a price I may be inclined to renew the whole. I am &c.

G: Washington

LB, DLC:GW.

1. John Rawlins's letter is dated 15 November. GW enclosed this letter to Rawlins along with Rawlins's plan and estimate for completing the New Room in a letter of this date to Tench Tilghman, authorizing Tilghman to enter into an agreement with Rawlins on GW's behalf.

To David Stuart

Dr Sir,   Mount Vernon 30th Novr 1785.

Your favor of the 16th came duly to hand, & I thank you for its several communications. The resolutions which were published for consideration, vesting Congress with powers to regulate the Commerce of the Union, have I hope been acceded to. If the States individually were to attempt this, an abortion, or a many headed monster would be the issue. If we consider ourselves, or wish to be considered by others as a united people, why not adopt the measures which are characteristic of it, & support the honor & dignity of one? If we are afraid to trust one another under qualified powers there is an end of the Union— why then need we be sollicitous to keep up the farce of it?

It gives me pleasure to hear that there is such an accordance of sentiments between the Eastern & Western parts of this State. My opinion of the separation has always been, to meet them halfway, upon fair & just grounds; & part like friends disposed to acts of brotherly kindness thereafter—I wish you had mention'd the territorial line between us. The Port Bill; the Assize Law (or any substitute for the speedy Administration of Justice) being established; good faith with respect to treaties, preserved by public acts; taxation continued & regularly collected, that justice to one part of the community may keep pace with relief to the other, & our national character for *Justice*, thereby supported; a due attention to the Militia, and encouragements to extend the inland navigation of this Commonwealth where it is useful & practicable, (which will not only be of amazing convenience & advantage to its Citizens, but sources of immense wealth to the Country through some of its channels)—are among the great & important objects which will come before you; & a due attention to them will, I hope, mark the present epocha for having produced able statesmen, sound patriots & liberal minded men.

At a late meeting of the Directors of the Potomac navigation at the great Falls, & from a critical examination of the ground at that place; we unanimously determined to petition the Assemblies of the two States to be relieved from the expence of sinking our Canals four feet deep; as a considerable *expence*, & *no advantage* that we could discover, was likely to attend it. As the petition which is herewith sent under cover to you & Colo. Syme, recites the reasons on which it is founded I shall not repeat them: the public as well as the company's interest calls for an œconomical use of the fund which is subscribed for this undertaking; the enemies therefore (if there are any) to the navigation, are equally bound with its friends, to give it support.[1]

I should be much obliged to you for desiring the public printer to send me the Journals of the present Session from its commencement, & to do it thro' the session as fast as they are printed, by the Post. I pray you to pay him for *them*, & for my Gazette (if Hay is the public printer)—& I will repay you with thanks when you return.[2]

I am very glad to hear you have got so well over your fever. Mrs Stuart has had a bad cold, but is getting better. all here join me in best wishes for you—& I am &c. &c.

G: Washington

LB, DLC:GW.

1. See Thomas Johnson to GW, 4 Nov., n.1.

2. James Hayes, who was the printer of the *Virginia Gazette, or the American Advertiser* (Richmond), was also the printer for the commonwealth of Virginia. On 27 Jan. 1786 GW paid Hayes £1.4.2 for "1 Years Gazettes, & 22 Sheets of Journals of House of Delegates @ 50. ⟨℔⟩ Sheet" (Ledger B, 207).

To Tench Tilghman

Dear Sir,   Mount Vernon 30th Novr 1785

Since my last I have been favoured with your letters of the 10th & 18th Instt. The last covering Mr Rawlins's plan & estimate for my new room—for your exertions to obtain which, I thank you.

The plan is plain, as I requested—but the estimate, I think, is large; however as I pretend not to be a competent judge of work, and know that we are always in the power of workmen, I will not decide absolutely upon the moderation he pretends to have observed; especially as I confess that I do not clearly understand the plan—but as your readiness to oblige me in this business has already involved you in trouble, I will request the favor of you to take a little more, to bring it to an explanation, & close.

For this purpose, I send you herewith Rawlins's plan & estimate; and would beg the favor, as I have understood that Mr Goff of Baltimore has had much work of this kind done by Rawlins, to compare my plan & estimate with his work & prices; and if Mr Goff is a Gentleman of information, & one who scrutinizes into work & prices by a comparison of them, to ask his opinion of these charges. If the result of your enquiries is in favor of Mr Rawlinss moderation I have then to pray that the matter may be fixed with him; and a time (not to exceed if possible the middle of April) agreed on to begin the work with a serious intention to execute it with dispatch. also, that the article of travelling expences may be defined, & reduced to a stipulated sum. or, which would come cheaper to me, that my Waggon (a covered one) should remove his people & Tools hither & back; and an equivalent named in lieu of expences for *himself.* This will leave no ground for discontent on either side; than which nothing being more disagreeable to me—I always endeavour to avoid. I wish to know also whether he or I are to furnish the materials. If on the other hand it shall be found that his terms are too high (for it is not amiss to observe here, that almost the whole of the mouldings & ornaments are cast) I should be obliged to you to know from him whether he will take less; and precisely the sum; to execute the work according to the Plan. and this too without much time for consideration, for having been twice disappointed already, & the work thereby conside[r]ably delayed to my great inconvenience; I am determined if Mr Rawlins will not do it reasonably & begin it seriously in the Spring, to write immediately to Sir Edward Newenham of Dublin, who hath already introduced the subject to me, and has given me assurances of a visit in the spring, to bring me a complete workman when he comes, on yearly wages; but this I would avoid (as you will please to inform Mr Rawlins) if he will do my work at near its value, & in season. If you finally engage with Mr Rawlins, I should like to have a specific agreement drawn, to prevent mistakes, or further delay; for the drawing of wch I would chearfully pay an Attorney.[1]

Inclosed is a letter for Mr Rawlins, open. Had the public prints spoke truth respecting the present from his Catholic Majesty, & the Jacks had arrived, it would have given me great pleasure to have obliged your friends on the Eastern shore, by a compliance with your request. There were only two presented to me by the King of Spain. one of which by the advices I have received from Boston, was lost on its Passage to Beverley, in a storm—the other will scarcely do more (if he gets home safe) than answer my own purposes. but if you, or any friend of yours, has a she Ass that you would wish to put to him, for preservation of the breed, he shall be much at your service, & you shall be welcome to the use of him to her. Mrs Washington joins me in best wishes for Mrs Tilghman & yourself, and with sentiments of sincere esteem & regard I am—Dear Sir Yr Affecte frd & obedt Serv.

Go: Washington

ALS, RPJCB; LB, DLC:GW.

1. For Tilghman's dealings with Harry Dorsey Gough (Goff; c.1745–1808) and his further dealings with John Rawlins on GW's behalf, see Tilghman to GW, 13 Dec., 30 Dec. 1785, 16 Jan., and 1 Mar. 1786. See also GW to Tilghman, 7 Jan. and 22 Feb. 1786. Gough, who lived at Perry Hall in Baltimore County, was a merchant who speculated extensively in land in Baltimore.

To Samuel Vaughan

Dr Sir,   Mount Vernon 30th Novr 1785.

I have been honored with your favor of the 9th[1]—& have received the pamphlet which you were so obliging as to send me, entitled "Considerations on the Order of Cincinnatus, by the Count de Mirabeau." I thank you my good Sir, for this instance of your attention; but wish you had taken time to have perused it first, as I have not yet had leisure to give it a reading.[2] I thought, as most others seem to think, that all the exceptionable parts of that Institution had been done away at the last general Meeting; but with those who are disposed to cavil, or who have the itch of writing strongly upon them, nothing can be made to suit their palates: the best way therefore to disconcert & defeat them, is to take no notice of their publications; all else is but food for declamation. There is not I conceive, an unbiased mind that would refuse the Officers of the late Army the right of associating for the purpose of establishing a fund for the support of the poor & distressed of their fraternity—when many of them it is well known are reduced to their last shifts by the

ungenerous conduct of their Country, in not adopting more vigorous measures to render their Certificates productive. That
charity is all that remains of the original Institution, none who
will be at the trouble of reading it can deny.

I have lately received a letter from Mr Vaughan (your son) of
Jamaica, accompanied by a puncheon of rum, which he informs
me was sent by your order as a present to me.[3] Indeed my Dr
Sir, you overwhelm me with your favors, & lay me under too
many obligations to leave a hope remaining of discharging
them. Hearing of the distress in which that Island, with others
in the Wt Indies is involved by the late hurricane, I have taken
the liberty of requesting Mr Vaughans acceptance, for his own
use, of a few barrels of superfine Flour of my own manufacturing. My best respects, in which Mrs Washington joins, are offered to Mrs Vaughan, yourself & family, & with the highest
esteem and regard, I am, Dear Sir &c.

G: Washington

LB, DLC:GW.
    1. Letter not found.
    2. Mirabeau's pamphlet published in London in 1785 was listed in the in-
ventory of GW's library after his death.
    3. See GW to Charles Vaughan, 18 November.

To Rochambeau

My dear Count,   Mount Vernon Decr 1st 1785.
    Your letter of the 2d of June, which you had the goodness to
write to me at the moment of taking leave of the venerable Doctr
Franklin, now lyes before me; and I read the renewed assurances of your friendship with sentiments of gratitude and pleasure, short of nothing but the satisfaction I should feel at seeing
you; and the recollection of the hours, in which, toiling together,
we formed our friendship—A friendship which will continue, I
hope, as long as we shall continue Actors on the present theatre.
    A Man in the vigor of life could not have borne the fatigues
of a passage across the Atlantic, with more fortitude, and greater
ease than Doctor Franklin did; and since, instead of setting himself down in the lap of ease, which might have been expected
from a person of his advanced age, he has again entered upon

the bustling scenes of public life, and in the chair of State, is endeavouring to reconcile the jarring interests of the Citizens of Pensylvania—If he should succeed, fresh laurels will crown his brow; but it is to be feared that the task is too great for human wisdom to accomplish. I have not yet seen the good old Gentleman, but have had an intercourse by letters with him.[1]

Rumours of War still prevail, between the Emperor and the Dutch; & seem, if News Paper Accounts are to be credited, to be near at hand. If this event should take place, more powers must ingage in it, and perhaps a general flame will be kindled 'ere the first is extinguished. America may think herself happy in having the Atlantic for a barrier, otherways, a spark might set her ablazing. At present we are peaceable; & our Governments are acquiring a better tone. Congress, I am persuaded will soon be vested with greater powers. the Commercial interest throughout the Union are exerting themselves to obtain these, and I have no doubt will effect it. We shall be able then, if a Commercial treaty is not entered into with Great Britain to meet her on the restrictive & contracted ground she has taken; and interdict her Shipping, & trade, in the same manner she has done those of these States. This, and this only, will convince her of the illiberallity of her conduct towards us—or, that her policy has been too refined, & over strained, even for the accomplishment of her own purposes.

Mrs Washington is thankful for your constant remembrance of her & joins me in every good wish for you & Madame de Rochambeau—with sentiments of the warmest attachment, & greatest respect I have the honor to be My dear Count yr Most Obedt and Very Hble Servt

Go: Washington

ALS, DLC: Rochambeau Papers; LB, DLC:GW.
    1. See GW to Benjamin Franklin, 26 September.

To Samuel Chase

Dr Sir,   Mt Vernon 3d Decr 1785.
    Enclosed you have a petition from the Directors of the potomac Company, which we pray you to lay before the Maryland

Assembly, & to use your exertions & influence to carry it into effect.

The measure prayed for is so reasonable, that we do not conceive there can be any other opposition given to it, than what may proceed from delay; for the enemies to this undertaking (if there are any) ought to support the present Bill upon the principle of public œconomy.

Mr Johnson is the drawer of the Bill which accompanies the Petition; exact copies of both are sent to the Assembly of this State. We took the liberty of furnishing the draft, that they may be exactly similar in both States without the trouble of an intercourse between the Assemblies on so trifleing a business.[1] I have the honor to be &c.

Go: Washington

LB, DLC:GW.

1. For the petition and bill to allow the Potomac River Company to reduce from four to two feet the depth of the canals it was to build, see Thomas Johnson to GW, 4 Nov., n.1. On the same day that he wrote Chase, GW wrote in similar vein to Nathaniel Ramsay (Ramsey; 1741–1817), a member of Maryland's lower house for Cecil County, and to two members of the Maryland senate, Charles Carroll of Carrollton and Thomas Stone (1743–1787) of Charles County. The text of his letter to Ramsay is: "Dr Sir, The Directors of the Potomac Company find it necessary to apply to the Assemblies of the States of Maryland & Virginia to be relieved from an unnecessary depth of Canal at the Great & Little Falls of the river; which, upon a strict investigation of the ground at the former & the ideas they entertain of the latter, they find would be attended with a heavy additional expence, without the smallest equivalent in return. The enemies therefore to this navigation (if there be any) must be friends to the petition we now offer, on the principle of public œconomy.

"The Petition is sent to Mr Chase (as a member of the Company) to present to your Honorable House. To save trouble, & an intercourse between the two Assemblies on this trifling business, we have accompanied the petition by a Bill; exact copies of which now go to the Assembly of this State, not doubting its passing into a Law.

"We apprehend no other opposition in either Assembly, than what may proceed from delay; to obviate this, is the reason of my giving you the trouble of this letter, praying your good offices to carry the petition into effect in your Assembly" (LB, DLC:GW).

The text of his letter to Carroll and Stone is: "Dr Sir, The Directors of the potomac Comy upon a strict examination of the ground at the Great Falls of the river, & their ideas of that at the little Falls, find it necessary to apply to the Assemblies of the two States, to be relieved from that depth of canal which the late Acts for improving & extending the navigation of the river require.

"The reasons are set forth at large in the petition which, as president of the Board of Directors I now have the honor to transmit to Mr Chase as a delegate, & member of the company; a similar one having gone to the Assembly of Virginia. But in a word, from our view of the matter, it is sufficient to inform you that to dig four feet at these places will add greatly to the expence, without deriving the smallest advantage: we have therefore prayed for two feet depth, instead of four; & apprehending no other opposition but what may proceed from delay, for friends & foes (if there are any of the latter) to the Undertaking, ought to support the Bill upon the principle of œconomy, is the reason of my giving you the trouble of this Letter, praying your assistance in facilitating the passage of the Bill" (LB, DLC:GW). See also his similar letter of this date to the two members of the house of delegates from Fairfax County, Charles Simms and David Stuart.

From Edmund Randolph

My dear sir   Richmond decr 3. 1785.
    The post-offices have not been in fault in every respect; altho' I did not receive from the one here your favor of the 5th Ulto until last night, notwithstanding my application for letters.

Your inclosures of the proceedings of the Potowmack company were duly received by me: and the business of the general court pressing very urgently upon me, the answer to your favor was undertaken by the other directors. It was prepared, but waited for the proceedings; in a copy of which we were disappointed by the clerk. We shall forward them, as soon as he has finished them. Indeed, sir, we shall be obliged from our imperfect knowledge of the business, to intreat your assistance on many occasions; and shall from this as well as many other considerations be anxious for a frequent and unreserved communication with the Potowmack company.

A lengthy and earnest debate has been held on the propriety of vesting congress with a controul of commerce. But the advocates for the measure will scarcely succeed; so strong are the apprehensions in some minds of an abuse of the power. I am my dear sir with the greatest esteem and respect yr affectionate friend & serv.

                                                Edm: Randolph

ALS, DLC:GW.

To Charles Simms and David Stuart

Gentn   Mount Vernon 3d Decr 1785.

As president of the Board of Directors for the Potomac company, I have the honor to enclose you a Petition which we pray you to present to your honorable House; & to use your best endeavours to have the prayer of it enacted into a Law. The petition is so full, & the request of it so reasonable, that we do not suppose there can be the least opposition to it, otherwise than by delay; because the enemies of it (if there are any) must on the score of public saving, yield assent to it.

We have taken the liberty to accompany the Petition with the draft of a Bill to be enacted into a Law. A Petition & Bill similar to these have been sent to the Maryland Assembly. The reasons for this you will see into at once; they are, to render it unnecessary for the two Assemblies to correspond on so trivial a subject—to prevent trouble to each—to prevent delay, & that both Acts may be exactly similar.[1] I have the honor to be &c.

                                                    G: Washington

LB, DLC:GW.

1. See Thomas Johnson to GW, 4 Nov., n.1, and GW to Samuel Chase, 3 Dec., and note 1. The two delegates to the Virginia assembly from Fairfax, Simms and Stuart, presented the Potomac River Company petition, signed by GW, on 9 December. The draft bill was passed, and the speaker of the house signed the bill amending the Potomac River Act on 16 Jan. 1786.

To Battaile Muse

Sir,   Mount Vernon Decr 4th 1785.

Your letters of the 15th & 26th of last month are both at hand. with respect to the latter, I agree that Daniel Harrel may have the Lott No. 2 on the terms mentioned therein. and you may fill up leases accordingly.

In answer to the first letter, rather than involve my self in uncertain Lawsuits—but certain expence & perplexities, I would allow for paper payments of Rents the same as specie—But as you know what has been the practice, and the consequence thereof in your own case as Collector for Colo. Fairfax; and in that of others under similar circumstances, I should conceive that you could determine the point of conduct proper to be pursued better than I, who have been entirely out of the way of knowing what the Law—custom—or judicial proceedings in the Courts have decided. However, as I have already observed, rather than go into a litigation of the matter (unless there is abundant reason to expect a decision in my favor) I would make the same allowance for Paper, however unjust & rascally it has been imposed, as I would for Specie, taking care to shew no indulgence hereafter to those who had made them.[1]

Receipts for Rents from my Brother will be sufficient for the Tenants; but it will be necessary in your Settlement with them to take an Acct of all these payments, that I may be able to settle with his Estate. This is indispensably necessary—as, from what I can learn, he has been very inattentive himself in making proper Entries of the sums paid him. The date of each receipt is as essential as the name of the person is, to whom given. I am— Sir Yr Very Hble Servt

Go: Washington

ALS, ICHi; LB, DLC:GW.
    1. See Muse to GW, 15 Nov., n.2.

To Dominique-Louis Ethis de Corny

Sir,   Mount Vernon 5th Decr 1785.
I am really ashamed to have been so long in acknowledging the receipt of your letter of the 3d of August last year; but circumstances which would be more tedious in the recital, than important when told, have been the cause of it.[1]

I have now the honor of enclosing you the receipt of the Treasurer of the Society of the Cincinnati of this State, for your Bill on Colo. Wadsworth; & wish it was in my power to have accompanied it with a Diploma: but it has so happened, that except a few which were struck at Philadelphia for the members of that State at their own expence, none have yet been presented to me by the Secretary, for signing.[2] I have the honor to be &c.

Geo: Washington

LB, DLC:GW.
    1. Corny's letter of 3 Aug. 1784 has not been found, but see the letter that Barbé-Marbois wrote to GW in Corny's behalf on 12 June 1785.
    2. The treasurer of the Virginia Society of the Cincinnati, William Heth

(1750–1807), wrote a letter for Corny from "Wales near Petersburg 24th Decr [17]85," which was sent "By Stage": "Sir I have some time Since recd Collo. De Cornys first bill on Jeremiah Wadsworth esqr. for 75 Dlrs—together with your letter to General [George] Weedon on the subject, & advising, that you were in possession of the third bill, of the Same tenor & date—expecting of which, hath hitherto prevented my forwarding the first for paiment, and which, I hope, will plead my apology, for troubling you with this" (DLC:GW).

To Louis Guillaume Otto

Mount Vernon Decr 5th 1785

The letter which you did me the honor to write to me on the 16th of October[1] only came to hand the 28th of last month.

My particular acknowledgments are due to you for your recollection of and attention to me; and I pray you to be assured of the pleasure I felt at hearing that the place lately filled by Mr de Marbois, near the Sovereignty of these States, was so happily supplied—On this instance of his most Christian Majesty's attention to your merits, I offer you my sincere congratulations.

For the favourable Sentiments entertained of me in France & particularly by the Court all my gratitude is due: but to none in a higher degree than to the Chevalier de la Luzerne, for whom I have the highest esteem & regard. For yr obliging offers of Service here ⟨or in⟩ France, I sincerely thank you and at the same time I give you the trouble of forwarding a few letters by the Packet, beg you to believe with much truth I have the honor to be, Sir, Yr Most Obed. Very Hblc Serv.

Go: Washington

ALS, Arch. Aff. Etr.; LB, DLC:GW.

1. The letter from Otto that GW is referring to is dated 1 Oct., not 16 October.

To Richard Thomas

Sir,   Mt Vernon 5th Decr 1785.

Having, a few days ago *only*, received your letter of the 13th of August from Charleston, enclosing the duplicate of one from a Mr Edmund Richards of Plymouth Dock, dated the first of Feby last; I delay not a post to inform you, as I have already done the said Edmd Richards, that he is under a delusion which has not a single reality for a support[1]—that I am astonished at his information, and wish he had been at the trouble of enquiring a little more minutely into matters, before he had determined to make such a pointed application to me, or to have communicated his demands of me to others, for an Estate; First, because such an Estate as he speaks of was never left in trust to me; Secondly, because I never had the *least* acquaintance with his uncle Richard Richards, or ever knew that there was such a man in existence; Thirdly, because I have just as much, & no more knowledge of Lawyer Haines & Lawyer Baitain, than I have of Richd Richards; And fourthly, because I never heard of such an Estate as he claims, or the most trifling circumstance concerning it.

Of all these things Sir, you may, as I shall never write to Edmd richards again, give him the clearest & most unequivocal assurances; & add, that the most incontestible proofs of wch he, or you in his behalf, may find, if either are disposed to examine further into the matter. I am Sir &c.

G: Washington

LB, DLC:GW.

1. See Edmund Richards to GW, 1 Feb., and GW to Richards, 15 June 1785. See also Richard Thomas's letters to GW, 10 Dec. 1785 and 25 July 1786.

To William Gordon

Dr Sir,   Mount Vernon 6th Decr 1785.

Altho' I am so great a delinquent in the epistolary way, I will not again tread over the usual ground for an excuse, but rather silently throw myself upon your philanthropy to obtain one.

In reading the Memoir which passed thro' my hands to you (for I have no copy of it) I do not recollect that I was struck with any exagerations or improprieties in it; nor is it in my power to give you a precise detail of the facts about which you enquire, without unpacking my papers, & entering upon a voluminous research therefor; which might not after all elucidate the points.

Whether Genl Howe commanded in person at the intended surprize & attack of the Marqs de la Fayette at Baron Hill, I am unable positively to say; I would suppose however that he did—

first, because the narrative says so—2dly because he did not relinquish the command until within a few days of the evacuation of Philada—& 3dly, because the British army came out in full force. That the column on the right commanded by Genl Grant was strong, can admit of no doubt; (and report to the best of my recollection made the number 7000) because it was design'd to turn the Marquis's *left* flank, get into his rear, & cut of his retreat by the nearest & most direct roads; whilst he was to have been attacked in front, & on his right (which was next the Schuylkill) by the Commander in chief, & light infantry; by the first in front, by the other on the flank.

The French troops which were landed from on board the fleet, formed a junction with the American Troops before, & were all under the command of the Marquis 'till my arrival. The position at Williamsburgh was taken I believe, with a view to form the junction, being favorable to it; the defile between the College Creek which empties into James river, & Queen's Creek which empties into York river, being very narrow, & behind the former of which the French landed in perfect security.[1]

My excursions up this river (for I have made several) have afforded me much satisfaction, as we find the undertaking to extend & improve the navigation of it, is not only practicable; but that the difficulties which were expected to be met with, rather decrease than multiply upon us.

I come now, my good Doctor, to acknowledge in a particular manner the receipt of your obliging favor of the 7th ulto, & to thank you for your kind & valuable present of Fish which is very fine & had a more successful passage than the last, no Accot of which having ever yet been received.[2] I have too Mrs Washington's particular thanks to offer you for the flower roots & seeds, which she will preserve in the manner directed. I have put into a box with earth, shrubs of the redwood (or red-bud) & Fringe tree, which General Lincoln promised his Vessel should heave to & take for you as she passed by. I was going to send other flowering shrubs, but upon mentioning the names of them, the Genl & Colo. Henley said your Country already abounded with them. I forgot however, to ask them if you have the Magnolio; if you have not, I can send some by another opportunity.[3]

I hope this Letter will find you quite relieved from the feverish complaint you had when you wrote last, & Mrs Gordon in perfect health, to whom & yourself Mrs Washington & the family (who are all well) join me in every good wish. Fanny Bassett & my nephew Geo: A. Washington have fullfilld an engagement of long standing, & are now one bone, and one flesh. With great esteem & regard I am Dr Sir, &c. &c.

G: Washington

LB, DLC:GW.

1. GW is responding to inquiries Gordon made in his letter of 26 Sept. after reading James McHenry's memoir of Lafayette's role in the Revolution, which GW had sent Gordon at McHenry's request.

2. Gordon's letter of 7 Nov. has not been found. Gordon wrote GW about sending him fish on 30 Aug. 1784, which GW reported on 20 Dec. 1784 had not arrived.

3. David Henley (1748–1823) of Boston, at this time a commissioner for settling claims for Virginia's cession of western territory, and Gen. Benjamin Lincoln had dinner at Mount Vernon on Sunday, 27 November. Gordon was planning to leave Roxbury, Mass., soon to return to England, and he wished to take American plants with him. He acknowledged receipt of the plants from GW on 16 Feb. 1786. On 13 July 1786 he wrote from England that he had set out the plants which still showed signs of life.

From Lamar, Hill, Bisset, & Co.

Sir,   Madeira 6th Decr 1785.

We wrote to you under the 22d of last June, requesting to be informed if we might ship your pipe of wine ordered by Mr Henry Hill, by way of Norfolk, as vessels seldom offer from hence to Alexandria. We are not yet however favoured with your answer.

Upon the supposition notwithstanding that from the length of time the above order has been lying by us, you may be in some measure in want of Madeira wine, and anxious not to appear neglectful of so old a correspondent, we have ventured to deviate from your instructions, and of our own accord have shipped your pipe of wine to Norfolk, instead of waiting until an opportunity might cast up for Alexandria.

We have consigned the above pipe of wine to our friend Doctor Taylor there, who, we are convinced will take every necessary Care respecting it, until he receives your directions to forward it to your address.

We have thought it prudent, in order to obviate the danger

of it's being either adulterated or pilfer'd, in it's way from Norfolk to your house, to have it cased. We judged it also adviseable to insure it.[1]

If, Sir under these circumstances, it is agreeable to you to receive this pipe of wine, you will be pleased to accept the enclosed draft for its' cost £42.12.4 stg as noted underneath,[2] and when your leisure suits forward it to Mr H. Hill of Philadelphia. Or if on the other hand you disapprove of what we have done, you will take the trouble of writing a few lines to Dr Taylor, and he on your declining to take the wine, has our directions to dispose of it for our account. We have the honour to subscribe ourselves—Sir your most obedient servts

Lamar, Hill Bisset, & Co.

LS, DLC:GW.

1. For the correspondence regarding the pipe of Madeira, see Lamar, Hill, Bissct, & Co. to GW, 20 Aug., n.1.

2. The account "underneath" because of a mistake in addition shows a total charge of £43.12.4 instead of £42.12.4, and the company sends a second letter on 17 Dec. to correct the error: "We had the pleasure of forwarding you the original of the above by Captain Powel of the Active, who also carried the pipe of wine, therein mention'd.

"We have so soon taken the liberty of again addressing you on account of a mistake we have discovered was committed by us, in the amount of the draft enclosed for the cost of the pipe of wine sent, which ought to have been, as you will please to remark by the account sent, £43.12.4 stg instead of £42.12.4 stg, the sum for which it was.

"We have therefore ventured to enclose you a second bill, wherein the above mistake is rectified, and which (if it is agreeable to you to receive the wine) we are to request you will accept, and forward to Mr Hill, in lieu of the former one.

"We are convinced Sir you will be candid enough to excuse the trouble we are thus giving you, and impute it to one of those little oversights which in the hurry of business, even the most careful, are sometimes liable to" (DLC:GW). The new bill was:

One pipe of fine 3 years old Madeira wine, of the common gauge	£37. 0.0
A case for the above	1.10.0
10 per cent for difference of gauge on £38.10. stg	3.17.0
	42. 7.0
Insurance on £42.7.0 at 3 per cent including commn	1. 5.4
	£43.12.4

Letter not found: to Tench Tilghman, 6 Dec. 1785. Tilghman wrote on 13 Dec.: "I have been honored with both your letters of the 30h and 6h instant."

From Benjamin Harrison

My dear Sir   Richmond Decr 7th 1785.

I have the pleasure to enclose to you a copy of the act of assembly, pass'd in consequence of your letter to the Governor, which I hope will meet your entire approbation.[1] your conduct on this occasion will add new lustre to your character and fully prove, if there was a doubt remaining in the melevolent hearts of any, that all your actions have been dictated by the pure motives of virtue and a love to your country. That you may live to perfect any plan you shall think fit to adopt is the fervent wish of Dear Sir your most affectionate and obedient Humble Servant

Benj. Harrison

ALS, DLC:GW.

1. See GW to Patrick Henry, 29 Oct. (second letter), n.1. A copy of the act is in DLC:GW.

To Thomas Smith

Sir,   Mount Vernon Decr 7th 1785.

Your letter of the 26th Ulto came to my hands by the last Post—and the object of this shall be confined to a single point— taking another opportunity of writing to you more fully.

The meaning of my last letter to you was not well expressed, if it was understood that the Actions of Trespass were to be brought before the issue of the Ejectments were known. I had no idea of this, because if my opponents should succeed in the latter, there would be no ground for the former; and I should incur a certain expence without a chance of profit; and from the statement of the cases which you have mentioned, I now leave it altogether discretionary with you, whether to bring them afterwards, or not.

I never should have thought of this mode of punishment, had I not viewed the defendants as willful and obstinate Sinners—

persevering after timely & repeated admonition, in a design to injure me. but I am not at all tenacious of this matter—& take the chance of this letters going by way of Baltimore, and another by way of Philadelphia, to request that these Actions may be at least delayed, if not altogether laid aside, according to circumstances. With very great esteem I am—Sir yr most Hble Servt

Go: Washington

ALS, NhD; LB, DLC:GW. Beneath the dateline the letter is labeled "Duplicate."

From James Madison

Dear Sir   Richmond Decr 9. 1785

Your favour of the 30 Novr was received a few days ago. This would have followed much earlier the one which yours acknowledges had I not wished it to contain some final information relative to the commercial propositions. The discussion of them has consumed much time, and though the absolute necessity of some such general system prevailed over all the efforts of its adversaries in the first instance, the stratagem of limiting its duration to a short term has ultimately disappointed our hopes. I think it better to trust to further experience and even distress, for an adequate remedy, than to try a temporary measure which may stand in the way of a permanent one, and must confirm that transatlantic policy which is founded on our supposed distrust of Congress and of one another. Those whose opposition in this case did not spring from illiberal animosities towards the Northern States, seem to have been frightened on one side at the idea of a perpetual & irrevocable grant of power, and on the other flattered with a hope that a temporary grant might be renewed from time to time, if its utility should be confirmed by the experiment. But we have already granted perpetual & irrevocable powers of a much more extensive nature than those now proposed and for reasons not stronger than the reasons which urge the latter. And as to the hope of renewal, it is the most visionary one that perhaps ever deluded men of sense. Nothing but the peculiarity of our circumstances could ever have produced those sacrifices of sovereignty on which the fœderal Government now rests. If they had been temporary, and the expiration of the term required a renewal at this crisis, pressing as the crisis is, and recent as is our experience of the value of the confederacy, sure I am that it would be impossible to revive it. What room have we then to hope that the expiration of temporary grants of commercial powers would always find a unanimous disposition in the States to follow their own example. It ought to be remembered too that besides the caprice, jealousy, and diversity of situations, which will be certain obstacles in our way, the policy of foreign nations may hereafter imitate that of the Macedonian Prince who effected his purposes against the Grecian confederacy by gaining over a few of the leading men in the smaller members of it. Add to the whole, that the difficulty now found in obtaining a unanimous concurrence of the States in any measure whatever, must continually increase with every increase of their number and perhaps in a greater ratio, as the Ultramontane States may either have or suppose they have a less similitude of interests to the Atlantic States than these have to one another. The propositions however have not yet received the final vote of the House, having lain on the table for some time as a report from the Com[itt]ee of the whole. The question was suspended in order to consider a proposition which had for its object a Meeting of Politico-Commercial Comissrs from all the States for the purpose of digesting and reporting the requisite augmentation of the power of Congress over trade. What the event will be cannot be foreseen. The friends to the original propositions are I am told rather increasing, but I despair of a majority in any event for a longer term than 25 years for their duration. The other scheme will have fewer enemies and may perhaps be carried. It seems naturally to grow out of the proposed appointment of Commissioners for Virga & Maryd concerted at Mount Vernon for keeping up harmony in the commercial regulations of the two States. Maryd has ratified the Report, but has invited into the plan Delaware & Pena who will naturally pay the same compliment to their neighbors &c. &c. Besides these general propositions on the subject of trade, it has been proposed that some intermediate measures should be taken by ourselves, and a sort of navigation act will I am apprehensive be attempted. It is backed by the mercantile interests of most of our towns except Alexandria which alone seems to have liberality or light on the subject. It has refused even to suspend the measure on the concurrence of Maryd or N. Carolina. This folly however can not one would think, brave the ruin which it threatens to our Merchts as well as people at large, when a final vote comes to be given.[1]

We have got thro' a great part of the Revisal, and might by this time have been at the end of it had the time wasted in disputing whether it could be finished at this Session been spent in forwarding the work. As it is, we must content ourselves with passing a few more of the important bills, leaving the residue for our successors of the next year. As none of the bills passed are to be in force till Jan. 1787, and the residue unpassed will probably be least disputable in their nature, this expedient tho' little eligible, is not inadmissible. Our public credit has had a severe attack and a narrow escape. As a compromise it has been necessary to set forward the half tax till March, and the whole tax of Sepr next till Novr ensuing. The latter postponement was meant to give the planters more time to deal with the Mercht[s] in the sale of their Tobo, and is made a permanent regulation. The Assize bill is now depending. It has many enemies and its fate is precarious. My hopes how[ever] prevail over my apprehensions. The fate of the Port bill is more precarious. The failure of an interview between our commissioners and commissioners on the part of N. Carolina has embarrassed the projected Canal between the Waters of the two States. If N.C. were entirely well disposed the passing an Act suspended on & referred to her legislature would be sufficient, and this course must, I suppose be tried, tho' previous negociation would have promised more certain success.[2] Kentucky has made a formal application for independen[ce]. Her memorial has been considered, and the terms of separation fixed by a Com[mitte]e of the whole. The substance of them is that all *private* rights & interests derived from the laws of Virginia shall be secured that the unlocated lands shall be applied to the objects to which the laws of Va have appropriated them—that nonresidents shall be subjected to no higher taxes than residents—that the Ohio shall be a common high way for Citizens of the U.S. and the jurisdiction of Kentucky & Virga as far as the remaing territory of the latter will lie thereon, be concurrent only with the new States on the opposite Shore—that the proposed State shall take its due share of our State debts—and that the separation shall not take place unless these terms shall be approved by a Convention to be held to decide the question, nor untill Congs shall assent thereto, and fix the terms of their admission into the Union. The limits of the proposed State are to be the same with present limits of the district. The apparent coolness of the Representatives of Kentucky as to a separation since these terms have been defined indicates that they had some views which will not be favored by them. They disliked much to be hung up on the will of Congs.[3] I am Dr Sir, with the highest esteem and unfeigned regard Yr obedt & hble Servt

J. Madison, Jr

ALS, DLC:GW; LB, DLC: Madison Papers.

1. For the maneuvers in the house of delegates in this session with regard to the proposal to give Congress the power to regulate commerce, see notes 1 through 4 for this letter in Rutland and Rachal, *Madison Papers*, 8:438–41; see also Madison to Thomas Jefferson, 22 Jan. 1786, ibid., 472–82. In the end, the Virginia house acted to appoint commissioners to meet with commissioners from other states (see David Stuart to GW, 18 Dec., n.3).

2. North Carolina did not enact a bill to join Virginia in building the Dismal Swamp Canal until 1790. See Patrick Henry to GW, 11 Nov., n.2.

3. See Resolutions on Kentucky Statehood, 12 Dec. 1785, in Rutland and Rachal, *Madison Papers*, 8:441–42.

To Thomas Bibby

Sir,   Mount Vernon Decr 10th 1785

The delay in acknowledging the receipt of your favor of the 4th of May from New York, is to be ascribed more to the expectation I have been under of the pleasure of seeing you in this State, & at this House, than to any other cause. and I take the present occasion of assuring you, that if business or inclination should bring you to the Southward, I shall be happy in the opportunity of testifying my respect to the introduction of Sir Edward Newenham, and of offering you the civilities which are due to a Gentlemen of your merit.

By mistake, a packet whh I herewith send, was forwarded to me by a Mr McKiernan; to whose care with another for myself, it was committed by Sir Edward.[1] I hope it will reach you safe; and that the delay occasioned by the circuitous rout it has taken, will be attended with no inconvenience to you. I have the honor to be Sir yr most Obedt Servt

Go: Washington

ALS (photocopy), ViMtV; LB, DLC:GW.

1. Charles McKiernan wrote from Philadelphia on 8 Nov., forwarding this "packet" from Sir Edward Newenham (McKiernan to GW, 30 Oct., n.1). See also GW's letter to McKiernan of this date.

To Charles McKiernan

Sir,   Mount Vernon 10th Decr 1785

I have been favoured with your letters of the 30th of Octr and 8th of November,[1] I thank you for your care of the packets which were entrusted to you by Sir Edward Newenham. The last sent was for Captain Bibby, altho' the outer cover was addressed to me. I now forward it to that Gentlemen.[2]

If business or inclination should bring you to this state, I shall have pleasure in seeing you at this place. I am Sir &c.

Go: Washington

LB, DLC:GW.

1. McKiernan's letter of 8 Nov. is printed in note 1 of McKiernan's Oct. 30 letter.

2. See the letter of this date to Thomas Bibby.

From Battaile Muse

Honorable Sir   Berkely C[ount]y Decr 10th 1785

I have at Last Sent down to be Lodged at your mill three Cask butter Stated below If you Take only the Fresh butter my Price is ⅓ ⅌ Ct for that, if you Take the whole the price is 1/ ⅌ Ct as I am Told that is the Current price, and the Price I Told you I askt for it. Should you not approve of the Butter I shall be much Obliged if you will direct it to the care of Mr Andrew Wales in Alexandria who will procure me a markett for it. as I charge nothing for casks I wish to have the use of them Next Spring when the Butter may be out of them, and they will be of service to me; and perhaps none to you[1]—I am happy To see your millers Receipt that my wheat weighs 61 ct ⅌ bushels as the general weight here is about 56 ct ℔ bushel owing To the unfavorable Season Last Spring and the Farmers being reather neglectfull. I have the Promise of four Waggons To Load with wheat next week for your Mill. I am sir your Very Hble servant.

Battaile Muse

ALS, DLC:GW.

1. Muse wrote GW on 28 Nov. assuring him that the butter "I mentioned" would be in Alexandria by 23 December. The wagon Muse sent out this day got only as far as Leesburg because of the badness of the roads. GW did not receive the butter until late January or early February. See GW to Muse, 22 Aug. 1785, n.13, 5 Jan., 4 Feb. 1786, and Muse to GW, 12, 17 Jan. 1786. At the bottom of his letter Muse wrote that he was sending:

1 Cask Neit Salt Butter	76 ct
No. 2 Salt Butter	75
No. 3 Fresh Butter	60
Neit Butter	211 ct

211 ct Butter @ 1/ £10.11.0   B.M.

To David Stuart

Dear Sir,   Mount Vernon 10th Decr 1785

Since writing to you by the last Post[1] I have finished the measurement of my Corn, and find that I shall not make half enough to serve me. Permit me to request the favor of you therefore to enquire upon what terms any of the Delegates from the Eastern Shore would contract with you in my behalf for 800 Bushls of clean & good Oats—to be delivered at my landing as soon after Christmas as may be.

If you can engage the Oats at a price not exceeding three shillings pr Bushel, I would than pray you to close a bargain without the delay of advising me—and reduce it to writing with a penalty for Nonperformance on either side—but, if they are not to be had at this price to fix the lowest terms on wch they may be had upon my saying yea by return of the Post after they are communicated to me.

The above for Horses—I am under as pressing a necessity to provide for my People, all the Corn I have made not being more than sufficient to support my Plantations My house people are without, and none in these parts to be had—If there the Plantations below (in New Kent & King William) have any to spare I should be glad to get two hundred Barrels for which I will allow the same they sell at to others—or the same price that Corn bears on that River. This would be doubly convenient to me, for to be plain my Coffers are not overflowing with money—You cannot too soon give me a definite answer on this point—Nor indeed with respect to the Oats, as I must not trust to the Chapter of Accidents for a supply.[2] With great esteem and regard—I am Dr Sir Yr Obedt & Affecte Hble Ser⟨v⟩t

Go: Washington

ALS, PHC: Charles Roberts Autograph Letters Collection; LB, DLC:GW.
    1. GW wrote Stuart on 30 November.
    2. See Stuart to GW, 18 Dec., n.1.

From Richard Thomas

Hond Sir   Charleston [S.C.] 10th December 1785
    Having on the 13th of August last enclosed to your Excellency a Letter from Mr Edmund Richards of Plymouth Dock in the County of Devon in England, who informs me of his being the Heir to an Estate left in the hands of your Excellency by Richd Richards Esqr. who died in Virginia many years ago. But having no answer, am led to suppose the Letter never came to hand, for which reason I have taken the liberty to address your Excellency a second time. And shall acknowledge the obligation to be informed of the truth, & whether recoverable.[1]
    By directing for me at Doctor Neufville's No. 108 Broad Street Charleston So. Carolina, it will come safe to hand. I have the honor to be Your Excellency's Obedt Humble Servt

Richd Thomas

ALS, DLC:GW.
    1. See GW to Thomas, 5 Dec., and particularly note 1 of that document. GW's missing letter of 25 Mar. 1786 was in answer to this (Thomas to GW, 25 July 1786).

To Clement Biddle

Dear Sir,   Mount Vernon 11th Decr 1785
    I have received your favor of the 29th Ulto and thank you for your repeated offer of Services in Philadelphia.[1] By Major Fair-

lie I send you Six pounds Pensylvania Curry and would thank you to pay Mr Cary Printer for his Paper—and to pay Oswald for his—I know not upon what footing he sends them. by no order of mine do they come, and it is only now and then, I get one. yet I do not want to lay under any obligation to him—Claypoole & Dunlaps Papers now come regularly & I could wish they were also paid.

For what can sheet copper be bought in Phila. at this time? I believe I shall have occasion to add to the quantity which was sent me from thence last year, to complete my buildings.[2]

Mrs join me in every good wish for you, Mrs Biddle & family—with great esteem I am Dear Sir: Yr Obedt & Affecte Hble Servt

Go: Washington

ALS, PHi: Washington-Biddle Correspondence.

1. Letter not found.

2. In his letter book (ViMtV), Biddle entered an account and memorandum dated "Philad. Decr 27: 1785":

Acknowledged rect of £6 Cash ℔ Major [James] Fairlie.

Paid Dunlaps Accot for News papers		£5.0.0
Paid Careys d. for d. to July next		2.6.3
		7.6.3

And Inclosed the Accot & rects ℔ post—added—Mr Oswald by a late fray in wch he was wounded is Confined to his house therefore I had no Opportunity to pay him yet but it shall be done.

Price of Copper 22½d.

David C. Claypoole and John Dunlap were printers of the *Pennsylvania Packet*, Mathew Carey of the *Pennsylvania Evening Herald*, and Eleazer Oswald of the *Independent Gazette*, all in Philadelphia. For GW's earlier complaints about the delivery of the *Pennsylvania Packet*, see GW to Biddle, 1 Feb. 1785, notes 3 and 4.

To Alexander Hamilton

Dear Sir   Mount Vernon Decr 11th 1785

I have been favoured with your letter of the 25th of November by Major Farlie.

Sincerely do I wish that the several State Societies had, or would; adopt the alterations that were recommended by the General meeting in May 1784. I then thought, and have had no cause since to change my opinion, that if the Society of the

Cincinnati mean to live in peace with the rest of their fellow Citizens, they must subscribe to the Alterations which were at that time adopted.

That the jealousies of, and prejudices against this Society were carried to an unwarrantable length, I will readily grant. and that *less* than was done, *ought* to have removed the fears which had been imbibed, I am as clear on, as I am that it would not have done it; but it is a matter of little moment whether the alarm which siezed the public mind was the result of foresight—envy & jealousy—or a disordered imagination; the affect of perseverance would have been the same: wherein then would have been found an equivalent for the seperation of Interests, which (from my best information, not from one State only but many) would inevitably have taken place?

The fears of the people are not yet removed, they only sleep, & a very little matter will set them afloat again. Had it not been for the predicament we stood in with respect to the foreign Officers and the charitable part of the Institution I should, on that occasion, as far as my voice would have gone have endeavoured to convince the narrow minded part of our Country men that the Amor Pat[ria]e was much stronger in our breasts than theirs—and that our conduct through the whole of the business was actuated by nobler & more generous sentiments than were apprehended, by abolishing the Society at once, with a declaration of the causes, and the purity of its intention. But the latter may be interesting to many, and the former, is an insuperable bar to such a step.

I am sincerely concerned to find by your letter that the Baron is again in straigh[te]ned circumstances—I am much disinclined to ask favors of Congress, but if I knew what the objects of his wishes are I should have much pleasure in rendering him any services in my power with such members of that body as I now and then corrispond with—I had flattered myself, from what was told me sometime ago, that Congress had made a final settlement with the Baron much to his satisfaction.

My Compliments and best wishes, in which Mrs Washington joins me, are presented to Mrs Hamilton I am—Dear Sir Yr Most Obedt Hble Servt

Go: Washington

P.S. When you see Genl Schuyler and family I pray you to offer my best respects to them.

ALS, DLC: Hamilton Papers; LB, DLC:GW.

To Henry Knox

My dear Sir   Mount Vernon 11th Decr 1785.

Majr Farlie gave me the pleasure of receiving your letter of the 22d Instt, & thereby knowing that you, Mrs Knox & the family were all well.

It has always been my opinion you know, that our Affairs with respect to the Indians would never be in a good train whilst the British Garrisons remained on the American side of the territorial line—& that these Posts would not be evacuated by them, as long as any pretext could be found to with-hold them. They know the importance of these Posts too well to give them up soon, or quietly. their Trade with the Indians in a great measure depend upon the possession of them, knowing full well that all the assertions of our Commrs with respect to the Articles of Peace, & their obligation to surrender them, is no more than chaff before the wind when opposed by the scale of possession.

I am sorry the State Societies should hesitate to comply with the recommendation of the General meeting of the Cincinnati, holden at Phila. in 1784. I then thought, & have no cause since to change my opinion, that no thing short of what was then done would appease the clamours which were raised against this Institution. Some late attacks have been made upon it; amongst which a Pamphlet written by the Count de Mirabeau, a French Gentleman, has just made its appearance. It is come to my hands translated into English, but I have not had time yet to read it.[1]

I am sorry you have undergone any chagreen on acct of the lime Stone. I have got through my Summers work without any disappointment therefrom; having had it in my power at all times, when wanted, to buy Shells. Nor would I wish to have any sent me now, unless by contract not to exceed One shilling and three pence at the Ships side at Alexandria, or opposite to my House; and this I do not expect, as Stone lime is oftener higher at the former place.

It is unnecessary to assure you of the pleasure I should feel at seeing you at this place, whenever business or inclination may bring you to this State. Every good wish, in which Mrs Washington joins me, is offered to you, Mrs Knox and the Children— With every sentiment of friendship & regard, I am—My dear Sir Yr Affecte Hble Servt

Go: Washington

ALS, MHi: Knox Papers.

1. Samuel Vaughan sent GW Mirabeau's pamphlet. See GW to Vaughan, 30 November.

From Robert Pleasants

Honour'd General. Curles 12th mo. 11th 1785

Seeing the Lord has done great things for thee, not only in "covering thy head in the day of Battle," but making thee instrumental in bringing about an extraordiny Revolution (a revolution which has given thee great reputation among men, and Calls for reverent thankfulness to him, who "Rules in the Kingdoms of men," and declared by his Prophet that, "he will not give his Glory to another, or his praise to graven Images,") a strong desire attends my mind, that thou may not in any respect Sully in thy private retirement, the honours thou hast acquired in the Field. Remember the cause for which thou wert call'd to the Command of the American Army, was the cause of Liberty and the Rights of Mankind: How strange then must it appear to impartial thinking men, to be informed, that many who were warm advocates for that noble cause during the War, are now siting down in a state of ease, dissipation and extravigance on the labour of Slaves? And more especially that thou, who could forego all the Sweets of domestic felicity for a number of years, & expose thy Person to the greatest fatigue & dangers in that cause, should now withhold that enestimable blessing from any who are absolutely in thy power, & after the Right of freedom, is acknowledg'd to be the natural & unalienable Right of all mankind.

I cannot suppose from the uncommon generosity of thy conduct in other respects, that this can proceed altogether from interested motives; but rather, that it is the effect of long custom, the prejudices of education towards a black skin, or that some other important concerns may have hitherto diverted thy attention from a Subject so Noble and interesting, as well to thy own Peace & reputation, as the general good of that People, and the community at large. But whatever may have been the Cause, I sincerely wish thou may not longer delay a matter of such importance. It is a Sacrifise which I fully belive the Lord is requiring of this Generation; and should we not submit to it, Is there not reason to fear, he will deal with us as he did with Pharaoh on a similar occasion? For as he is declared to be, "no respecter of persons," how can we expect to do such Violence to human Nature in this enlighten'd age with impunity? We Read, "where much is given, the more will be requird(") and as thou hast acquired much fame, in being the Successful Champion of American Liberty; It seems highly probable to me, that thy example & influence at this time, towards a general emancipation, would be as productive of real happiness to mankind, as thy Sword may have been: I can but wish therefore, that thou may not loose the opertunity of Crowning the great Actions of thy Life, with the sattisfaction of, "doing to Others as thou would (in the like Situation) be done by," and finally transmit to future ages a Character, equally famous for thy Christian Virtues, as thy worldly achievements: For notwithstanding thou art now receiving the tribute of praise from a grateful people, the time is coming when all actions will be weighed in an equal ballance, and undergo an impartial examination; how inconsistant then will it appear to posterity, should it be recorded, that the Great General Washington, without fee or reward, had commanded the united forces of America, and at the expence of much Blood & treasure been instrumental in relieving those States from Tyranny & oppression: Yet after all had so far countinanced those Evils, as to keep a number of People in absolute Slavery, who were by nature equally entitled to freedom as himself. O Remember I beseech thee that "God will not be mocked," and is still requiring from each of us, to, "do justly, love mercy and walk humbly before him."

Perhaps General Washington may think it presumptious in me, who cannot boast a perticular acquaintance, to address him in this manner, but I hope when he considers the Nature of the Subject, and that I can have no selfish views in offering these hints to his serious consideration, than what may arise from the pleasure of hearing he had done those things—which belong to his present, & future happiness, and the good of those over whom Providence hath placed him, he will at least excuse the freedom; & believe that I am with great sincerity & Respect, his Real Friend,

Robert Pleasants

P.S. I herewith send thee a small Pamphlet on the subject of Slavery, said to be wrote by John Dickinson,[1] which if thou hast not before seen, I doubt not will afford pleasure in the perusal and am as above &c. R.P.

ALS, DLC:GW.

John Pleasants, the father of Robert Pleasants (1722–1801), was a Quaker and large slave owner in Henrico County who by his will, dated 12 Aug. 1771, attempted to free all of his slaves. During the Revolution, and after his father's death, Robert Pleasants began setting up his slaves on land of their own, and after 1782 when the law allowed it, he emancipated his eighty slaves. Pleasants promoted the education of slaves and freedmen and became a leader of the abolition movement in Virginia.

1. John Dickinson's "Sentiments on What Is Freedom, and What Is Slavery, by a Farmer" appeared in *Illuminations for Legislators, and for Sentimentalists*, printed by Robert Bell in Philadelphia in 1784.

From Chastellux

Dear general   Paris Decber 12 1785

as long as the Marquis continued in America, I persuaded myself that I had an agent near your excellency who could recall his friend to your memory. now the poor helpless and lonely idea of your Servant is wandering about Mount Vernon, desiring, may be in vain, to find admittance through the crowd of your devoted soldiers and good countrymen. how happy are those who after having followed you in the field of battle, are allowed to participate of your leasure! What satisfaction should it be for me, if I was walking upon your bowlingreen, to look upon the Potomack, and endeavour with the help of a Telescope to distinguish, whether the aproaching vessel wears the american, the french or the brittish colours; to say: *'tis a brittish ⟨illegible⟩ who comes and fetch tabacco*; then continue quietly our walk and go towards the grove to observe the growth of your trees, even of your vineyard, that a french man can, I dare say, examine without jealousy; for, my dear general, you can sow and reap laurels, but grapes and wine are not within the compass of your powers: do not be angry, dear general: foreigners have been always welcome at your house, and black billy is an exceeding good gentleman usher for madeyra, champain, and Burgundy's ⟨travellers⟩—but I reflect, my dear general, that while I indulge my nonsense with your excellency, you may expect some important news from Europe. You receive dayly letters and news papers which are all speaking of war. believe me my dear general, we shall have no war: negotiations we ⟨expect⟩ and the emperor is grown now more and more cautious. no doubt but the brittish wish to see a continental quarrel, and hope to mix in the fray, when we began to be exausted: but it will not be the case. they ought to pay the past taxes, and it is beyond their powers; for they continue to run in debts, and there shall be a deficit of one million st. in the recipts of the present year 1784. Peace and the preservation of all the nations in their present state, is the only aim of our government who has nothing to ⟨care⟩ but the universal equilibrium. I wish america might concur in these wise measures, but she must make at home the first trial of what she is to do abroad. your excellency should never forget that you are the soul of a immense body. Your arms may indulge themselve a dear boughten rest, but your genius must always ⟨wake⟩. such is the ardent wish of a friend to America and of your most humble and obedient servant

The Mqis de chastelleux

I have the pleasure to enjoy the presence of Col. Humphrys, and have the happiness to assist him in a very pleasing Task.

permit me dear general to offer my purest respects to Mrs Washington—

ALS, DLC:GW.

From Tench Tilghman

Dear Sir   Baltimore 13th Decemr 1785.

I do myself the honor to introduce to you Count Castiglioni knight of the Order of St Stephen, an Italian Nobleman, who, in pursuit of Botanical Knowledge, has thought it worth his while to visit this, hitherto, almost unexplored Continent.[1] The recommendations he brings from Europe, not only ascertain his Rank, but, what you will esteem of more consequence, they speak in the most favorable manner of the amiableness of his private Character.

The Count having other introductory letters from your Friends to the Northward, rendered this, in fact, unnecessary. I could not however refuse his request of adding mine to the number.[2] I have the honor to be with perfect Respect & Esteem Dear Sir Yr most obt and humble Servt

Tench Tilghman

ALS, DLC:GW.

1. Count Luigi Castiglioni (1757–1832) of Milan traveled about the United States from May 1785 until 1787, and in 1790 he published in Milan his *Viaggio ne gli Stati Uniti dell' America Settentrionale*.

2. The young New York lawyer Edward Livingston (1764–1836), who had spent the night of 26 May at Mount Vernon, wrote GW from New York on 26 Nov. in these terms: "Sir I have the Honor of introducing to your Acquaintance the Count De Castiglioni an Italian Nobleman who has been well recommended to many Gentlemen in this City and appears to be a Man whose Conversation will justify the liberty I take in bringing him acquainted with your Excellency.

"My Mother and Sisters beg to be remembered to Your Excellency & Mrs Washington. I have the honor to be with the greatest Respect, Your Mo. Obdt Sevt Edward Livingston" (ALS, owned [1971] by Dr. Gilbert C. Norton, Endicott, N.Y.).

Castiglioni arrived at Mount Vernon on 26 Dec. and left three days later with this rather noncommittal letter from GW to Gov. William Moultrie (1730–1805) in Charleston, S.C., dated 27 Dec., in hand: "Dear Sir, The Gentleman who favors me with the delivery of this letter to Your Excellency, is the Count Castiglioni—an Italian Nobleman—well recommended to me—As he is about to make a tour through the United States I use the freedom of giving him this letter of introduction to you. Mrs Washington joins me in every good wish for Mrs Moultrie and yourself, and with great esteem and regard I am—dear Sir Your most Obedt Hble Servant Go: Washington" (ALS, NBLiHi). GW misdated the letter "Jany 27th 1785," instead of 27 December.

From Tench Tilghman

Dear Sir   Baltimore 13th Decembr 1785.

I have been honored with both your letters of the 30h ulto and 6h instant.[1] To the first I sent you a verbal answer by Major

Fairlie, not having time then to write—but lest he may have forgotten what I told him, I will repeat it—I waited upon Mr Gough, who is a Gentleman that inspects very minutely into his own affairs and those in which he is concerned with others—you could not therefore have a better hand to check Mr Rawlins should his prices appear extravagant Mr Gough has just removed to Town for the Winter, and not having his Papers yet brought down, he cannot say with precision at what rates he payed Rawlins—He expects them in a few days, when he will give me every information in his power—with his assistance I hope I shall be able to make a proper and reasonable Contract for you.[2] All the points you mention shall be adjusted and the whole committed to writing—in firm, and as soon as possible.

I have had the good fortune to meet with a perfectly safe Conveyance to Carlisle—your letter will certainly reach Mr Smith by the 16th.[3] I am with great truth Dear Sir Yr obliged and obt hble Servt

Tench Tilghman

ALS, DLC:GW.
1. The letter of 6 Dec. has not been found.
2. See Tilghman to GW, 30 December.
3. See GW to Thomas Smith, 7 December.

Letter not found: from Mary Bristow, 15 Dec. 1785. When writing to Mary Bristow on 2 June 1786 GW refers to "your favr of the 15th of December last."

To Battaile Muse

Sir,   Mount Vernon 16th Decr 1785
Since I wrote you last I have received your letter of the 28th of Novr—Although you could not make out an exact settlement of the Accts, as they stand between the Tenants and me, I wish you had returned me a list of them, and the Lotts on which they live, with the Rent each man pays.

I see no advantage that is to be derived *now*, from my being on the Tenemants. As you have power, and your judgment must direct, your enquiries may be extended as far as mine could, was I on the Spot. Supposing this to be the case—What could I do, more than to see, in the first place, to whom Lot No. 1 (and so on with all the rest) was originally granted; in whose possession it now is; and what transferances have taken place. What Rents the lot has credit for in the Acct I sent you (which is the best that could be made out!)[1] and what receipts can be produced—in case of a difference between my Accts and the Tenants, in proof of his having paid more than he stands credited for. What, more than this, I say, could I do were I on the Land? And is not all this in your Power? The Leases which I gave you (for this purpose) testifies to the first. The tentent on the land solves the Second. and the information of themselves, compared, & corroborated by the testimony of the neighbourhood, if necessary, is the only means I know, of coming at the truth of the third matter—that is—the transferences. With respect to the Rents which are due on any lot, my Accts compared with the Tenants receipts, is the only mode by which this can be ascertained. I readily grant that, my business with respect to these people have been most shamefully neglected—but there is no help for that now—to recover it out of the State of disorder & confusion into which it has run—and to place it on as just a footing both for Landlord & tenant as the nature of the case will admit of, is all that remains to be done; and some of the letters which I have already written to you on this subject, and to which I now refer, gives you my ideas *fully* on the Subject. and wch in one word are these—to deal justly, honourably, and even generously by them; But where it shall appear that the Tenants have disregarded every Covenant in the leases, which were intended to secure a mutual benefit to myself; & their *sole* aim has been to make a Market of the Land for their own private emolument. Or where the tenant in possession has taken advantage of the times, & paid their rents in Paper money when it was of no value—In either of these cases, I would have no scruple to set the Leases aside, if they are clearly, & legally forfeited, provided, the Lots can be let to a better advantage than on the present terms, of the Leases. And all these things must be submitted to your own judgment, after the fullest information of the circumstances, is obtained.

If the Tenants have paid money to any other than Lund Washington or myself, I should have an Acct of it; & when it was done; that I may look for it in some quarter—but where there is no reciept, nor no credit in my acct, I shall pay no regard to bear assertions. I may quit scores at once if these are to be considered as discharges. With respect to their being two tenants on a Lot, unless they have something to shew, which authorizes it, the Lease itself must be your guide & director, without application to me. It is evidence of the agreement between the Landlord & tenant, and must be resorted to every year, to see that the terms are fulfilled on the part of the latter; for it may be laid down as a certainty that there is no obligation on the former that will not be exacted.

Lund Washington's going upon the Land could answer no purpose—he knows no more how matters stand than I do—and much less I believe than yourself, or the business would not be in the confusion it is at present.

It is essentially necessary that yr collection should be as large as possible, because, independant of other considerations, I have not made half bread corn enough this year to serve my People & stock; and shall have to purchase it at a high price, in addition to my other heavy & numerous expenditures.[2] Notwithstanding this, it is not my wish to push matters to the last extreme in order to obtain all the rents which may be due, unless there is, in your opinion, good cause for it. in short, circumstances & your own discretion must direct you.

With respect to the vacant Lots I have in the Tracts committed to your Inspection & management I can give but one general direction for them all—And that is this—let the notice that they are to be let, be as long before hand and as extensive as you can conveniently give of the day you will let them—(to the highest bidder if you shall think it best)—and then let them for as much as you can obtain for a term not exceeding 14 years; ten years I should prefer—If the season is now too far advanced, (and it is highly probable that few Tenants have places to look for at this late Season of the year)—perhaps it might be better to rent them upon any terms for the coming year, and endeavor in time next year to render them as advantageous to me as the Land will procure.

I think it would be best to divide the lot of Chattins Run, occupied by John Thompson, and to put it on the footing wch you have suggested[3]—It also appears that the other Lots on the same tract, had also better be divided—they will rent much higher for it, as there are so many more people of small force wanting land than great—& when they are divided, rent them for as much as you can get. An Advertisement of these vacant Lots in the Alexa. Paper—At Dumfries—Falmouth—and Port Tobacco would, I am persuaded, (if the Season is not too far advanced) bring you tenants in abundance—for many have applied to me, and I told them, as I really thought, that I had not an Acre of Land in those part untenanted.[4]

It may be well to attend a little closely to the line between some person, or persons of the name of Rector, and me on Chattins run—It is now, some years ago, since I was told, his Mill was on my Land; and that he was making some other encroachments, and was endeavoring to support a claim to it, merely because it was convenient for, and his interest to possess it.[5]

Inclosed you have a memo. of the agreement between us respecting the Wheat. I made a bad bargain of it—not more than 5/6 has been given at Alexandria for this article—the market there now dull—and the price expected to fall. What Wheat of yours that has come to my Mill, the Miller says is good & I hope your orders will be fulfilled with respect to the good cleaning of that which is to come.[6] It is all I can expect for the high price given. I am sir yr Very Hble Servt.

Go: Washington

P.S. Williams not coming down, the Counterpart of his Lease is not signed by him. I have directed that it shall be delivered to you.[7]

This letter is written in so great a hurry, that I wish it may be understood. If you can get at my meaning it is all I wish. the opportunity for sending it being sudden and unexpected.

ALS, NjMoNP: Smith Collection.

1. See Lists of Tenants, 18 Sept., and notes.

2. See GW to David Stuart, 10 December.

3. See note 4 in Muse's letter of 28 November.

4. Muse wrote GW on 18 Jan. 1786 that he had advertised the lots, but no such advertisement appears in the surviving issues of the Alexandria newspapers in January or February 1786.

5. This is probably Jacob Rector. See note 6 in Muse's letter of 28 Nov., and references.

6. The memorandum of agreement has not been found. Between 29 Nov. 1785 and 9 Jan. 1786, Muse shipped GW 265 bushels of wheat for which GW paid £79.10 (Ledger B, 211).

7. See GW to Muse, 28 July 1785, n.1.

GEORGE WASHINGTON
by Robert Edge Pine

Oil on canvas, 90.7 × 71.7 cm (35¾ × 28¼ in.)

Collection of the National Portrait Gallery,
Smithsonian Institution

Provenance: Owned by the artist who kept it on public exhibition until his death. Owned by the artist's widow who originally offered it for sale in a public lottery (along with other paintings by her husband and his Philadelphia house) which was scheduled to take place in May 1790. The lottery never took place. This painting along with the rest of the collection and the real estate was offered for sale by public auction in June 1792.

At some time, the portrait was acquired by Dr. Anthony Fothergill (1732–1813), an Englishman who practiced medicine in Philadelphia between 1803 and 1812, when he returned to England. Upon his death in 1813, the portrait was inherited by Dr. John Coakley Lettsom (1744–1815) of London. Upon Dr. Lettsom's death, his collection was sold at auction by Leigh and Sotheby 2–4 May 1816. The picture was acquired by Shaw Armour, a dealer who advertised it for sale in Montreal, Canada, 14 December 1816. It was purchased there by Henry Brevoort of New York and inherited by his son, James Carson Brevoort (1818–1887). The picture was then inherited by Grenville Kane, son of Edith Brevoort Kane and nephew of James Carson Brevoort. It was then inherited by his daughter Edith Kane, wife of George F. Baker. It was inherited by her son, George F. Baker, from whose widow it was acquired by the National Portrait Gallery.

George Washington's sittings to Robert Edge Pine are more fully documented than those for any other portraits of Washington. Pine arrived at Mount Vernon on 28 April 1785 and remained there twenty-two days. His arrival was recorded in Washington's diary on that date, and George Washington mentions his presence on 29 April, 6 May, and 19 May when Pine departed in George Washington's phaeton which was to take him as far as Annapolis on his return trip to Philadelphia. Washington's attitude toward sitting to a painter is explicitly described in a letter he wrote during Pine's stay at Mount Vernon (GW to Francis Hopkinson, 16 May 1785). On 1 July 1787, while in Philadelphia, George Washington notes in his diary: "Set this morning for Mr. Pine who wanted to correct his portrait of me."

George Washington never owned Pine's portrait or any of the replicas or copies of it. Pine's portraits of his adopted grandchildren Eleanor, Elizabeth, and George, and Martha Washington's niece Frances Bassett were owned at Mount Vernon.

From Robert Edge Pine

Sir　　　　　　　　　　　　　　　Annapolis 16 decem. 1785

I should have had the honour of addressing your Excellency before, had I sooner receiv'd the enclosed, by the date of which, I must hope that the Case is all ready arrived at Mount Vernon, and its content free from damage.

That the Pictures may meet with an endulgent reception has been my hope, and my ambittion, that they may be honour'd with some degree of approbation, by your Excelly and Mrs Washington—but, as no one can ensure success in an Art so abounding with difficulties as Painting, I will trust to the candour of my Judges, for making known to me, what Errors are observ'd, that I may take the first opportunity of correcting them[.] I am much disappointed in the execution of the Frames, for which, the price is in proportion, (the largest being four dollars, and the four smaller ones three dollars each.).

I must beg your Excy will honour my congratulations by presenting them to Majr Washington, and his amiable Bride, whose portrait, I take the liberty to request may be presented to Mrs Washington (as intended).[1]

I have been some time at Annapolis, painting the Portraits of Patriots, Legislators, Heroes, and Beauties, in order to adorn my large Pictures and expect to pass a few Weeks at Baltimore employed for the same purpose, I think I shall be able to go there in about a fortnight and from thence to Philadelphia, at either of which places, I should be happy to know of the arrival of the Pictures.[2]

My most respectfull Compts wait on Mrs Washington whom, I am willing to hope is well; as allso the young Gentleman and Ladies, I have the honour to be Sir your Excellency's much oblig'd and obt humble Servt

R.E. Pine

P.S. I may be found at Judge Hanson's Annapolis—Coll Rogers's Baltimore—or at the State House Philadelphia.[3]

ALS, DLC:GW.

1. The enclosure has not been identified. "The Pictures" were those that Pine had worked on at Mount Vernon the preceding May. They included portraits of GW, Mrs. Washington, Frances Bassett (now Frances Washington), and

the four Custis grandchildren. See Francis Hopkinson to GW, 19 April, n.1, and Hopkinson to GW, 16 May 1785.

2. Before going to Mount Vernon at the end of April, Pine had been in Philadelphia painting the "Large Pictures" of the major events of the American Revolution, which he never completed. See note 1 in Hopkinson to GW, 19 April 1785.

3. Alexander Contee Hanson (1749–1806), who had served on GW's staff in 1776, was at this time a judge of the Maryland General Court and lived on Church Street in Annapolis. Nicholas Rogers of Druid Hill, Md., served as aide-de-camp to both Philippe Du Coudray and Baron de Kalb during the Revolution.

From Noah Webster

Sir.   Alexandria Decr 16 1785

I have just returned from Richmond where I was happy enough to succeed in my application to the Legislature. For this success I acknowledge myself indebted, in some measure, to your politeness.[1]

Should the same success attend me in the States of Delaware & New York, my whole plan will be accomplished; & if on my return to the Northern States, I find myself in tolerably easy circumstances, I propose to sit down & devote my attention to literary pursuits. This has long been my plan & to this I direct all my views. Within a few days past, a new idea has struck me & made so great an impression on my mind that I have determind to write to you on the subject.

I have thought, Sir, that it might be possible for me to answer your views in the superintendence of your children's education & at the same time, to pursue my own designs. Could these two points be reconcild, Mount Vernon would furnish an agreeable philosophical retreat. The particular motive which has influencd me to mention this, is, that a part of my plan would probably be a work in the execution of which I should have occasion for Letters & other papers in your possession. At any rate I should want many articles of intelligence which I could not obtain in any way so well as by the assistance of your letters.

If your wishes could be gratified in a person of my character & abilities, I should expect no compensation for any services, but your table & other domestic conveniences.

It is uncertain whether I could adopt such a plan myself; even if it should prove agreeable to you & your family; besides, Sir, I can start objections even on your part. No consideration however could prevail on me to suppress this communication.

If any material objection should at once oppose itself to this idea, a line from you, Sir, will satisfy me. If, on the other hand, the plan should strike your mind favourably, I should wish for a more particular explanation before I proced on my journey; as I must, within five or six days.[2] At any rate, no person can be more ready to render you any services in his power, than Sir your most obliged most obedient & very humbl. Servant

Noah Webster jr

P.S. I have been repeatedly solicited to permit the Sketches of American Policy to be retailed in the public papers. I have hitherto declined, partly on account of some exceptionable passages. If, Sir, some extract from the Pamphlet can have any influence in harmonizing the views of the Citizens of different States, I am willing to see them made & published. But I have no copy, & there is none in this State, but that in your possession. If you will mark such passages as you deem most useful & send the pamphlet to Mr Richards or to me, that I may do it, it shall be returned as soon as convenient.[3] N.W.

ALS, PHi: Gratz Collection.

1. Webster secured the passage in the Virginia assembly of a copyright act for authors (12 Hening 30–31). See Archibald Cary to GW, 21 Nov. 1785. When Webster was at Mount Vernon, GW provided Webster on 6 Nov. with this letter of introduction directed to the governor of Virginia and the presiding officer of each of the two houses of the legislature: "Sir, This Letter will be handed to you by Mr Webster whom I beg leave to introduce to your acquaintance. He is author of a Grammatical Institute of the English language—to which there are very honorable testimonials of its excellence & usefulness. The work must speak for itself, & he, better than I can explain his wishes. I am & c. Geo: Washington" (LB, DLC:GW).

2. The prospect of Webster's becoming the tutor for the two Custis grandchildren at Mount Vernon was short-lived. See the exchange of letters between GW and Webster on 18 December.

3. Webster gave GW a copy of his *Sketches of American Policy*, printed in Hartford in 1785 by Hudson & Goodwin, when he visited Mount Vernon in May. See source note, Webster to GW, 18 December.

To Trustees of the Alexandria Academy

Gentn   17th Decr 1785.

That I may be perspicuous & avoid misconception, the proposition which I wish to lay before you is committed to writing; & is as follows;

It has long been my intention to invest, at my death, one thousand pounds current money of this State, in the hands of Trustees—the interest only of which, to be applied in instituting a school in the Town of Alexandria for the purpose of educating orphan children who have no other resource—or the children of such indigent parents as are unable to give it. The objects to be considered of & determined on by the Trustees for the time being, when applied to by the parents or friends of the children who have pretensions to this provision.

It is not in my power at this time to advance the above sum; but that a measure which may be productive of good may not be delayed—I will until my death, or until it shall be more convenient for my Estate to advance the principal, pay the interest thereof (to wit, Fifty pounds) annually.

Under this state of the matter, I submit to your consideration the practicability & propriety of blending the two institutions together, so as to make one Seminary under the direction of a President, Visitors, or such other establishment as to you shall seem best calculated to promote the objects in view, & for preserving order, regularity & good conduct in the Academy.

My intention, as I have before intimated, is that the principal sum shall *never* be broken in upon—the interest *only* to be applied for the purposes above mentioned. It was also my intention to apply the latter to the sole purpose of education, & of that kind of education which would be most extensively useful to people of the lower class of citizens, viz.—reading, writing & arithmetic, so as to fit them for mechanical purposes. The fund, if confined to this, would comprehend more subjects; but if you shall be of opinion that the proposition I now offer can be made to comport with the institution of the School which is already established; & approve of an incorporation of them in the manner before mentioned, and there after, upon a full consideration of the matter, should conceive that this fund would be more advantageously applied towards cloathing & schooling, than solely to the latter, I will acquiesce in it most chearfully—& shall be ready (as soon as the Trustees are established upon a permanent footing) by Deed or other instrument of writing, to vest the aforesaid sum of One thousand pounds, in them & their successors forever, with powers to direct and manage the same agreeably to these my declared intentions.[1]

G: Washington

LB, DLC:GW.

1. See GW to William Brown, 24 November. GW delivered this letter to the academy's trustees in Alexandria on this day and received at once from the chairman, William Brown, this letter of acceptance, also dated 17 Dec.: "Sir The trustees of the Alexandria Academy having considered your proposal of investing one thousand pounds in their hands, for the purpose of educating orphan and other poor children, the interest thereof (Viz. Fifty pounds pr annum) to be paid in the mean time, & applied to that purpose; are unanimously of opinion that the proposal as set forth in your letter of this date addressed to them, is very consistent with the institution of the Academy as already formed, and are ready to accept the same, engaging on their part to do every thing in their power to comply fully with your benevolent intentions.

"As to the proposition of leaving it hereafter at the option of the trustees to apply part of the aforesaid benefaction to the purpose of cloathing the objects of it; the trustees are of opinion it will be better that the whole be directed to be applied towards schooling only—On behalf of the trustees, I am your most obdt hble Servt W. Brown, Chairman" (DLC:GW).

Letter not found: to Thomas Newton, Jr., 18 Dec. 1785. It was advertised by Parke-Bernet Galleries in its second sale of the contents of John Grebbel's library, 22–24 Jan. 1941, as "about 65 words." The letter, quoted in the Carnegie Book Shop catalog no. 193, reads: "I should be glad if it was paid to Doctr David Stuart, a Delegate in Assembly at Richmond from this County and who I am sure would readily oblige me by bringing it up. . . ."

To Benjamin Harrison

My Dr Sir,   Mount Vernon 18th Decr 1785.

I have had the honor to receive your letter of the 7th inst: enclosing an Act of the General Assembly, which passed at my request.

This new proof of the confidence repos'd in me by my Country, lays me under additional obligations to it; and I am equally sensible of its favors, and the polite & friendly wishes with which you accompanied the act.

If the etiquette of business makes it necessary for me officially to acknowledge the receipt of this Act, let me entreat you my Dr Sir, to offer to the House in my behalf but in your own words, the grateful sense I have of its goodness upon this occasion, with assurances that the confidence reposed in me, shall not intentionally be abused. With great esteem &c. &c: I am

G: Washington

LB, DLC:GW.

Letter not found: from Thomas Stone, 18 Dec. 1785. The Libby catalog, 3 Dec. 1892, quoted this sentence from a letter Stone wrote GW from Annapolis: "The Compact made at Mount Vernon was ratified by our assembly I believe without a dissent in either house. I hope it will meet with as friendly a reception in your Assembly."

From David Stuart

Dear Sir, 18th Decemr—[17]85—Rich[mon]d

I yesterday made the contract you desired me, for oats, with Mr Savage, at two and six-pence the bushel, as you will see by the inclosed, which I send you. This Gentleman was employed by Mr Dandridge, to rescue Mr Custis's estate on the Eastern shore, from Posey's hands; and having befriended it in a particular manner without recompence; I early in the Summer sollicited a continuance of his kindness—As the estate there is all rented out, and the money arising from the rents will be due the first of January, I have desired him to detain the amount of the contract—This was indeed a great inducement to him, to make the contract, and I considered it as agreeable to all parties—Mr Henley falls greatly short of his expectations, both in corn and tobacco—he has not yet informed me how much he will have for sale—I shall know by Christmas, and shall instruct him to reserve for you the quantity you request.[1]

An act has just passed for paying in hard money, the interest due on money put into the Continental loan office—I send you the act, lest you might not attend to it in the papers—If you have any business of this sort to be transacted, I shall be happy to serve you in it—But you will observe the time will be soon elapsed—It did not occur to me before, that you might have money in the Office, or I should have given you earlier notice of it.[2]

You will have seen from the journals, that nothing is yet done on the subject of trade. I doubt much if any thing effectual will be done—If there is, it may be ascribed to a letter from the legislature of Maryland, requesting an appointment of Commissioners by each State to fix on a similarity of restrictions.[3]

The consideration of British debts is now before us, and from the opposition made by Mr Smith to leave, to bring in a bill on that subject, I have my fears about the success of it.[4] I expect to get the bill you transmitted, passed the ensuing week; as it is reported reasonable by the Committee, to whom it was referred[5]—The situation of the roads in our part of the Country, has induced my Colleague and myself, to sollicit leave, to bring in a bill for putting and keeping them in better order, in future—As one expedient, we have fixed on a moderate toll on all carriages, at the two great entrances to the town—It is in other respects, similar to the bill passed in the ⟨yr⟩ seventy two[6]—I am Dear sir very respectfully and sincerely Your Obnt Servant

David Stuart

ALS, DLC:GW.

1. See GW to David Stuart, 10 December. George Savage was a planter in Northampton County on Virginia's Eastern Shore. The enclosure was a memorandum of agreement between Savage and Stuart, dated 16 Dec., in which Savage agreed to deliver 800 bushels of oats at GW's wharf at Mount Vernon, which was done in early February (GW to Stuart, 5 Feb., and GW to George Savage, 8 Feb. 1786). Bartholomew Dandridge, Martha Washington's brother, had been in charge of the late John Parke Custis's estate until his own death in April 1785, when Stuart, who had married Custis's widow, Eleanor Calvert Custis, took over. John Price Posey, the son of GW's old friend and neighbor, John Posey, and manager of Custis's plantations, seems to have had control of Custis's business affairs as things went from bad to worse before Custis's death in late 1781. Leonard Henley, the husband of Martha Washington's sister Elizabeth, managed the Custis plantations in King William and neighboring counties. He was able to provide GW with 200 barrels of corn from "the lower Plantation in King-William county belonging to the Esta. of the late Mr Custis" (Henley to GW, 27 Feb. 1786). See also Henley to GW, 14 April.

2. For the provision regarding the payment of interest due on Continental loan office certificates in specie, see Article 2 of "An act to amend the act, intit-

uled An act to amend and reduce the several acts for appropriating the public revenue, into one act" (12 Hening 55–60). GW sent his certificates to Stuart on 24 December. In his Cash Accounts he records receiving £171.6.10 on 12 Jan. from "the Treasury of Virginia, by the hands of Doctr Stwart, in Excha. for Int. on Certificates whc. had been Recd for Loans, to this State" (Ledger B, 207).

3. After considerable controversy in this session of the Virginia legislature over the proposal to cede to Congress the power to regulate commerce, the house of delegates at the end of the session, on 21 Jan. 1786, chose eight delegates as commissioners to meet with commissioners from other states "to take into Consideration the Trade of the United States to examine the relative situations and trade of the said States, to consider how far an uniform System in their Commercial regulations may be necessary to their common Interest and their permanent Harmony" ("Resolution Authorizing a Commission to Examine Trade Regulations" in Rutland and Rachal, *Madison Papers*, 8:470–71). Commissioners from the convening states set their meeting at Annapolis on the first Monday in September.

4. Meriwether Smith of Essex County opposed the trade bill (see note 3) as well as the bill regarding the payment of just British debts. Madison reported to Jefferson on 22 Jan.: "A Bill was brought in for paying British debts but was rendered so inadequate to its object by alterations inserted by a Committee of the whole that the patrons of it thought it best to let it sleep" (ibid., 472–82).

5. This is the bill dealing with the depth of the canals to be built by the Potomac River Company. See GW to Charles Simms and David Stuart, 3 December.

6. Provisions for keeping in repair roads leading to Alexandria was enacted in 1772. See Article 7 of "An Act for clearing a road from the Warm Springs in Augusta, and for other purposes therein mentioned" (8 Hening 546–51). Stuart in this session secured the passage of "An act for regulating the streets in and adjoining to the town of Alexandria" (12 Hening 205–6).

From William Washington

Sir   Sandy-Hill [S.C.] Decembr 18th 1785

In complyance with the request contain'd in your Letter of June 30th it gives me much pleasure to forward to Mr Wm Hammond in Baltimore two Boxes, one containing Acorns & the other, Plants of the Live-Oak-Tree, which I have requested him to send you by the first opportunity. You will observe a difference in the Form of the Acorns, those of an oval Figure are from the Live-Oak Tree, an ever-green much esteemed for Ship-building & the delightful Shade it affords: those which are nearly round are from a Tree called the Water-Oak, which altho'

not an ever-green, is tall & majestick in appearance. I don't recollect having observ'd any of the same species to the Northward
of this State. I have not sent you so many of the Live-Oak Acorns
as I cou'd have wish'd, there were near a Peck collected, but I
had the mortification to find that most of them were destroy'd
by the Rats. In order however to repair the loss in some measure
I have sent you a box containing twenty odd of the Plants which
have been growing in it ever since they were placed there by the
hands of Major Washington.[1] In the ⟨closed⟩-Box you will find a
paper containing some seeds of the Laurel-Tree which are all
that I could procure; the Birds are so fond of them that it is a
difficult matter to get them fully ripe. The Laurel-Tree is an
evergreen, grows very tall & bears a large Beautiful Flower very
fragrant in its smell.[2] In the Box containing the Live-Oak Plants
I have inserted upwards of twenty of the sweet-scented Shrub,
which bears an odoriferous Flower.[3] It will allways give me pleasure to execute any commands you may have in this country.
Mrs Washington joins me in best respects to yourself & Lady I
am Dr Sir With much esteem & respect yr Very obedt Servt
W. Washington

ALS, NNMM: William A. Smith Collection.

1. The deciduous water oak (*Quercus nigra*) and the evergreen live oak
(*Quercus virginiana*) both grow as far north as parts of Virginia. For the collecting of seed and plants for Mount Vernon by George Augustine Washington
during his stay with William Washington in South Carolina, see GW to George
Augustine Washington, 6 Jan. 1785, n.3. See also GW to William Washington,
10 April 1786.

2. GW wrote in his diary for Tuesday, 2 May: "Planted 140 Seed sent me by
Colo. Wm. Washington and said by him to be the Seed of the large Magnolio
or Laurel of Carolina" (*Diaries*, 4:321). GW was assuming that those were the
seed of the *Magnolia grandiflora*, but it may be that by "Laurel-Tree" William
Washington meant the sweet bay tree (*Magnolia virginiana* or *glauca*), which is
sometimes called a swamp laurel.

3. On 1 May GW "Planted or rather transplanted from the Box sent me by
Colo. Wm. Washington of So. Carolina 6 of the Sweet scented, or aromatic
shrub in my Shrubberies, on each side the Serpentine walks on this (or East)
side of the Garden gate" (*Diaries*, 4:321). The sweet-shrub, or Carolina allspice
(*Calycanthus floridus*), has dark reddish blossoms which are particularly fragrant
when crushed.

To Noah Webster

Sir,   Mount Vernon 18th Decr 1785

Your letter of the 16th, with others, were put into my hands yesterday in Alexandria; but being engaged at the time I did not open them until I returned home in the evening; or, I would have sought an opportunity of conversing with you on the subject of it, whilst I was in Town.

On the footing you have placed your offer, though I feel myself obliged by it, I am unable, from the indecision of it, to return a satisfactory answer. It would by no means suit me to await the determinations of the Assemblies of those States (which are mentioned in your letter) on the applications you are about to make to them; and *afterwards*, a consultation of your circumstances & convenience, before you could resolve on what plan to fix. Nor indeed, does your offer go to more than *one* point, whilst I have *three* objects in view—namely—the education of the Children—aiding me in my corrispondencies—and keeping my Accounts—The last of which, I beleive might be dispensed with—or, at any rate when they are once digested, and brought into order (which is the present employment of Mr Shaw) they will require very little attention—but the other two are essential to my purposes.

I send you the sketches of American policy, and conceive that the publication of extracts therefrom will be pleasing, and may be beneficial. All possible lights ought, in my opinion, to be thrown on subjects of this importance; for it should seem that, ignorance, or design, have too great a share in the government of public measures.[1] I am with esteem Sir yr most Obedt Servt

Go: Washington

ALS, NN: Washington Collection; LB, DLC:GW. Webster docketed the letter: "Recd At Alexandria, 10 miles from his Seat." He later added a series of unconnected notations: "This Letter answers one in which I had suggested that I might be willing to accept the place of an Instructor & Secretary in the Genls Family—On the whole I Concluded not to do it & Mr Lear was recommended by Genl [Benjamin] Lincoln—N. Webster."

"See Gen. Washingtons Letter of Aprl 17. 1786."

"The Sketches of Amn Policy I put into Genl Washingtons hands in May preceding. N.W."

1. See Webster to GW, 16 Dec., n.3.

From Noah Webster

Sir.   Alexandria Decr 18th 1785

Yours of this date, with the Pamphlet, is just handed me, by which I acknowledge myself obliged.

The determinations of the States, to which my application will be made, will be known next month. These are however not essential to my present plans. My own resolutions on the subject can be formed as soon as I can visit New England; probably before you can recieve an answer from Europe, or furnish yourself with a man from any of the States.

In my last I mentioned one article only, *education*, but I should not have made a proposal which I did not intend should answer your wishes. I meant to be understood as offering what you wanted, if my abilities, in your opinion, should extend so far.

I was not decided, nor did I suppose that you would hazard a decision, without a more perfect knowledge of my domestic character. Certain I am I do not wish it. I supposed, Sir, that my decision on this subject, would be as early as yours, provided no insuperable objection should be immediately started.

The matter is reduceable to a few simple points. If your business requires a man's whole attention & will require it for years, I am not the person. The education of three children would not interfere with my pursuits—On this I can judge. Your correspondences might require all ones time—on this I am incompetent to decide. The other article, you seem to think, may in future demand less attention.

If I understood you, Sir, it is your wish to find a suitable person & employ him for a number of years. I am so far advanced in life & have so far accomplished my wishes, that I have no idea of continuing single for any long period; my circumstances do not require it & my feelings forbid it. You will perhaps smile, Sir, at the expression; but if I am frank, I am certainly not singular. This circumstance may probably be an insuperable objection; it almost prevented my writing to you on the subject. But I considered that it is an objection, if it occurs on your part, that will be against most young gentlemen.

If, Sir, I could do your business & have a small part of my time for other pursuits—if my views of domestic felicity could be in any measure answered, without any accessions of attendants to your family—I should be satisfied with a residence with you, till your purposes are accomplished. My particular view in making the proposal was to obtain from your personal knowledge or from official letters, such articles of intelligence as could not be obtained in any other way: in order to execute a work under your inspection which otherwise I shall not attempt. I would not however undertake the plan, unless I could gratify your utmost wishes in business. Faithfulness & industry are all I can promise—The first, I believe proceeds from principle, the last, both from principle & habit.

I flatter myself that my circumstances will be tolerably easy without making business a drudgery; but it will always be a pleasure. I wish to be settled in life—I wish not for solitude, but to have it in my power to be retired. I wish to enjoy life, but books & business will ever be my principal pleasure. I must write—it is a happiness I cannot sacrifice; & were I upon the throne of the Grand Seign⟨eu⟩r, I feel as tho' I could take pleasure in the education of youth.

Thus, Sir, I have been explicit—tho' I have little expectations that the plan can be reconciled to your views. I have the honour to be with the highest respect Sir your most obedient humble servant

N. Webster

ALS, DLC:GW.

To William Carmichael

sir,   Mount Vernon 19th Decr 1785.

One of the Jacks with which his Catholic Majesty was pleased to present me, has arrived safe; & the enclos'd to his Minister is a testimony of my gratitude for this singular mark of his royal notice—I pray you Sir, to do me the honor of presenting it. I hesitated a while, whether to express my sense of this obligation at first, or second hand; but considering the value of it, I determined on the former—& at the same time that I would enclose you a copy of what I had written.[1]

The Spaniard, Seignior Pedro Tellez who accompanied the Jack which arrived safe, has expressed a wish to obtain a line of approbation from me; by means of which he thinks he could obtain some low office in the King's Customs: but it was a liberty I could not take, further than to express in the Certificate I have given him, my sense of his care of the animal which was entrusted to him.[2] But if a word my good Sir, could occasionally drop from you to this effect, it might do an essential service to the poor fellow, (who it seems has a wife & children) & would be considered as an additional favor conferred on, Sir Yrs &c.

G: Washington

LB, DLC:GW.

1. The text of GW's letter of 19 Dec. to Floridablanca is: "Sir My homage is due to his Catholic Majesty for the honor of his present. The value of it is intrinsically great, but is rendered inestimable by the manner, and from the hand it is derived.

"Let me entreat you therefore, Sir, to lay before the King my thanks for the Jack Asses with which he has been graciously pleased to compliment me; and to assure his Majesty of my unbounded gratitude for so condescending a mark of his royal notice & favor.

"That long life, perfect health, and unfading glory may attend his Majesty's reign, is my fervent wish. With great respect and consideration I have the honor to be Sir yr Excellencys Most Obedt & most oblig'd Hble Servt Go: Washington" (ALS, Archivo Histórica Nacional Estado; LB, DLC:GW).

2. The text of GW's certificate for Pedro Tellez is quoted in note 2, GW to Francisco Rendón, this date.

From William Gordon

Dear Sir   Jamaica Plain [Mass.] Decr 19. 1785

I find in my minutes the following story to have been reported, the truth or error of which I wish to have ascertained, & therefore make my application to You as the proper person to establish or contradict it, viz., "When Genl Washington was at Morris Town in 1777 with the fewest men, a British officer was taken in a skirmish, who was permitted to go about upon his parole; within a few days he forfeited his honour & went off. Genl Washington being told it, cried out, *then I am ruined*; but sent for a counter-spy, who went off for Cornwallis; on coming to his quarters, Cornwallis with other officers were in consultation. The spy insisted upon seeing Cornwallis, & sent in his name, on which he was ordered into the room, when he delivered a return to Cornwallis, according to which Genl Washngton had one regiment at Bound Brook, another at this place, a third at that & soon, making his whole force between three & 4,000 men—upon reading of which Cornwallis cursed & said Did I not tell you so? What a pretty scrape we should have been brought into, had we attended to our information! It does not signify, I never will trust to the information of a man that will break his parole—And so nothing was attempted."[1] I am now full as busy as a hen with one chick. Your Excellency will therefore excuse my enlarging, which may possibly be equally adapted to your numerous engagements. Mrs Gordon unites in most sincere regards to Self Lady & friends, the young one particularly, with your Excellys affectionate friend & humble servant

William Gordon

ALS, DLC:GW.

1. GW's response to this inquiry has not been found, but it is evident that GW had responded before Gordon wrote again on 16 Feb. 1786. Gordon does not repeat the story in volume 2 of his *History*, published in London, 1788.

To Francisco Rendón

Sir,   Mount Vernon 19th Decr 1785.

This letter will be handed to you by Mr Peter Tellez, who attended the Jack Ass, which arrived safe, to this place:[1] for want of an Interpreter I have not been able to understand him perfectly; but as far as his wishes have been explained to me, they are, that he may be permitted to return to Spain as soon as possible; that it is proper he should go by the way of New York to see his Excellency Don Gardoqui; that as he was employed by his Catholic Majesty, & in the Kings pay until he return'd (his wife receiving part of it from Mr Gardoqui at Bilboa) he would take none from me.

Under these circumstances I have forwarded him to Nw York, after prevailing on him to take a trifle as an acknowledgment of the obligation I am under to him, for his care of the animal on which I set the highest value.[2] He has some expectation ⟨in⟩deed, that at his return his Majesty may bestow some humble appointment on him, in the Collection of his Customs; & therein he has my wishes, but I could not ask it for him, or even hint it to the Minister.

Not having the honor of an acquaintance with his Excely Mr Gardoqui, I have taken the liberty of making these communications to you; & to pray, if there is anything improper in my sending Mr Tellez to Nw York, or in my conduct towards him, that it may be ascribed to misconception, & misunderstanding his wants by bad interpretation. Altho' unknown, I pray you to make a tender of my respectful compliments to Mr Gardoqui, & to accompany them with the strongest assurances of the pleasure I should feel in seeing him at this Seat of my retirement, if inclination should ever induce him to visit the States to the southward of Nw York. It is unnecessary to offer you the same assurances, because I have repeatedly done it before, & you must have been convinced of my sincerity. With very great esteem & regard, I have the honor to be &c.

G: Washington

P.S. Mr Tellez is charged with a Letter from me to Mr Carmichael, enclosing one to His Exy the Count de Florida Blanca, praying that my homage & gratitude may be presented to his Catholic Majesty for the favor he has conferred on me & for the honor of his royal notice. G. W——n

LB, DLC:GW.

Francisco Rendón was secretary in 1785 and 1786 to Diego de Gardoqui when in 1785 he became Spain's first official representative to the United States. Rendón had come from Cuba in 1779 to serve as secretary to Spain's unofficial representative to Congress, Don Juan de Miralles, and in 1780 had succeeded Miralles. Rendón left New York for Spain in 1786, but he returned to America in 1793 as Spain's intendant in Florida and Louisiana. In 1781 Rendón gave up the house in which he was living in Philadelphia so that GW could live in it for the winter (Robert Morris's diary in Ferguson, *Morris Papers*, 3:303).

1. See the references in note 1 of Thomas Cushing's letter to GW dated 7 Oct. 1785.

2. GW noted in his Cash Accounts on 20 Dec. giving £21 to "Pedro Tellez, Spaniard who brot the Jack" (Ledger B, 205). GW also provided Tellez with a pass and a certificate, both dated 19 Dec.: "Pass for Pedro Tellez The Bearer of this Pedro Tellez, is the Spaniard who was sent from Bilboa in Spain, with one of the Jack Asses which was presented to me by His Catholic Majesty—& is on his journey to New York, to the Minister of Spain, with a view of returning to his own Country from thence.

"Not being able to speak any other language than that of his native tongue, it is requested as a favor of the good people on the road to assist & direct him properly—which will be considered as an obligation conferred on, G: Washington" (LB, DLC:GW).

"Certificate to Peter Tellez I certify that Mr Peter Tellez the bearer of this, has delivered to me in good order one of the Jack asses which was presented to me by his Catholic Majesty; and that I feel myself under very great obligation to the said Peter Tellez for his care of, & attention to this valuable animal, than which nothing could have been more acceptable to me. Given under my hand & Seal at Mount Vernon, in the State of Virga this 19th day of December 1785. G: Washington" (LB, DLC:GW).

To Thomas Johnson

Dr Sir,   Mount Vernon 20th Decr 1785.

It so happened that your letter of the 4th ulto with its enclosures, did not meet a quick passage to me; & that some delays afterwards, more the effect of accident than neglect, prevented the petition & Bill, (which you were so obliging as to draw) from getting to the Assemblies of the two States, so soon as were to be wished; however they are now before them; & from that of Maryland, I am inform'd by a gentleman to whom I had written on the occasion, that the business could meet with no opposition there; & from that of this State that it was reported reasonable. Acts, it is to be hoped, will therefore pass, conformably to our desires.[1]

I feel myself much obliged by the calculations you have been at the trouble to make & to transmit to me; & at all times shall be happy in a full & unreserved communication of your sentiments on this, or any other business. This, in particular, is a new work—stands in need of all the information we can obtain, & is much indebted to you for many estimates, & ideas which have been very useful.

It is to be apprehended, notwithstanding the great encouragements which have been offered by the Directors of the Company for the hire of negroes, that we shall not succeed in obtaining them. An idea is entertained by the proprietors of them, that the nature of the work will expose them to dangers which are not compensated by the terms. Servants I hope are purchased 'ere this; Colo. Fitzgerald was to have gone yesterday to George town for this purpose. If the appearance of the people is at all favorable, the price at which Colo. Deakens offers them will be no obstacle.[2]

This letter, handed to the care of Colo. Deakens, will be accompanied by a small bag of Spanish Chesnutts—half of which you will please to accept, & the other contrive to Mr Lee—they were sent to the Alexandria races in October to be given to him, but the delivery was neglected.[3] It might be well perhaps to put them in sand to prevent an over drying, to the injury of vegetation—With very great esteem & regard I am Dr Sir &c.

G: Washington

LB, DLC:GW.

1. GW is referring to the petition and bill, drafted by Johnson, regarding the depth of canals to be built by the Potomac River Company. See note 1 in Johnson's letter of 4 Nov. and GW to Samuel Chase, 3 Dec., n.1.

2. For further correspondence regarding the purchase of indentured servants from the Georgetown merchant William Deakins, see GW to John Fitzgerald, 5 June 1786. The trustees of the Potomac River Company voted at their meeting of 18–19 Oct. to hire slaves (see note 1 in GW to Thomas Johnson and Thomas Sim Lee, 10 Sept. 1785).

3. GW in October had packed 200 Spanish chestnuts (*Castanea dentata*) in sand for spring planting (*Diaries*, 4:206; see also pages 297 and 340).

From Henry Lee, Jr.

Dear Genl   [20 December 1785]

I had provided for you all the forest trees we possess except the cypress worthy of transplantation, & joined to them some chosen fruit trees.[1]

I directed a label or some designation to be affixed to the fruit trees to shew their kind.[2]

Two oppertunitys having offered to send them up to you. I thought it better to leave them, where they were, than to send them to popes creek[3]—A Captain Hungerford promised certainly to receive them & deliver them at Mount Vernon—if he should deceive, a few negroes of Mr Kendals were to come up by water, by which conveyance the trees would surely be sent.[4] There is also a box with the gloucester nut & the horse-chesnut which is filled with sand agreable to your directions.

Mrs Lee brought up with her all the gloucester nuts we found at home, which she begs your acceptance of—they are only a taste, but will shew the value of the tree—If I can serve you in my absence, your commands will be received with the highest pleasure and executed in the best mode in my power.[5] I sincerely pray for the continuation of your health, & have the honor to be with the most perfect regard your unceasing friend and h: ser.

Henry Lee Jun.

I could not find any person ⟨capa⟩ble of transplanting the ⟨cyp⟩ress; Mr McCarty has sent up some seed for you, I beleive the honey locust. I will send them to Mount Vernon.

ALS, DLC:GW.

1. For an earlier presentation of plants and cuttings for Mount Vernon by Lee, see Lee to GW, 12 Mar. 1785.

2. On Christmas Day Lee wrote that one package of plants had arrived at Alexandria from Stratford and gave the names of the apple, pear, and cherry trees that were sent. When setting out plants in his "fruit garden" at Mount Vernon on 27 Feb. 1786, however, GW noted that "the other 3 trees are from Stratford, given to me by Colo. Henry Lee 1 of which he calls the Medlar Russitan—another the Chantilly pear—and the 3d. the Carnation cherry but this being a mistake, the others are not to be depended upon" (*Diaries*, 4:286).

3. Lee is probably referring to the port at Pope's Creek in Charles County, Maryland.

4. This may have been Woffendell Kendall (c.1740–c.1795) of Westmoreland County who had close ties with the Lees of Stratford Hall.

5. Lee was en route from Stratford Hall to New York City with his wife Matilda Lee Lee to attend Congress as a new member from Virginia. On 30 May 1790 Thomas Jefferson writes to Thomas Mann Randolph about the "Gloucester and European walnuts" at Monticello (Betts, *Jefferson's Garden Book*, 150).

To John Francis Mercer

Dr Sir,   Mount Vernon 20th Decr 1785.

From the assurances you gave me I had flattered myself that I should 'ere this have received a payment from you; & I had no doubt of it after Colo. Fitzgerald informed me, five months ago that £200 had passed thro' his hands from Mr White to you; which was the fund, if I understood you rightly, which you had appropriated for this purpose.[1]

I beg you to be assured that the disclosure I made to you of my circumstances was candid; & that it cannot be more disagreeable to you to hear, than it is to me to repeat that my wants are pressing—some debts which I am really ashamed to owe, are unpaid; & I have been, for want of money, unable to do more with my manufacturing Mill, (which is expensive to me without) than to grind up my own Crops; for wheat is not to be bought on credit, & I have not cash to pay for it. But this is not the worst—I have not made half grain enough to support my people & stock this year—the deficiency must be bought at a high price, and (for there is no question of the Articles bearing it) for ready money. I must therefore get it at an advanced price, if to be had at all, on credit; or I must sell something at a low price to enable me to pay ready money. This is truly my situation. I am &c.

G: Washington

LB, DLC:GW.

1. GW wrote John Francis Mercer on 27 Mar. pressing him for payment on the indebtedness of the John Mercer estate. No "assurances" from Mercer have been found, but Mercer did spend the night of 13 June at Mount Vernon. See also GW to Mercer, 8 July 1784, n.1, and 30 Jan., 12 Aug. 1786. Mercer made a payment on 23 Mar. 1786 of £200 (Ledger B, 221).

To Lund Washington

Dr Lund,   Mount Vernon 20th Decr 1785.

Having come to a fixed determination (whatever else may be left undone) to attend to the business of my plantations; and having enquired of Geo: Washington how far it would be agreeable to him & his wife to make this place a permanent residence, (for before it was only considered as their temporary abode, until some plan could be settled for them) & finding it to comport with their inclinations, I now inform you that it will be in my power to comply with your wishes with less inconvenience than appeared when you first proposed to leave my employment.[1]

The business of the Mill is what both of us, will be most at a loss about at first; & as the people wanting flour are in the habit of applying to you for it, it would be rendering me a service to give your attention to this matter, until he can become a little acquainted with the mode of managing it; & your advice to him afterwards in this & other affairs may be useful.

The mode of paying the taxes, the times of collection, & in what kind of property it is most advantageous to discharge them, & the amount of them, is another business in which he will be to seek; & I have not sufficient knowledge of the practice to instruct him.

Nothing else occurs to me at this time in which it is essential to give you any trouble after the present year; for if I should not be able to visit the plantations as often as I could wish, (owing to company or other engagements) I am resolved that an account of the stock, & every occurrence that happens in the course of the week shall be minutely detailed to me every saturday.[2] Matters cannot go much out of sorts in that time without a seasonable remedy. For both our interests, the wheat remaing in the straw should be an object of your care. I am your sincere friend &c.

G: Washington

LB, DLC:GW. The final portion of an ALS was advertised in the American Art Association catalog sale 3927, item 128, 1931.

1. See GW to Lund Washington, 20 November.
2. See editorial note in Farm Reports, 26 Nov. 1785–15 April 1786.

To David Stuart

Dr Sir,   Mount Vernon 24th Decr 1785.

I have received your favor of the 18th, & am exceedingly obliged to you for the Contract you have entered into on my behalf, with Mr Savage, for 800 bushels of Oats. If you can extend the quantity to be had from him, to 1200 bushels in the whole, upon the same terms, it would add greatly to the favor— as my crop of Corn is much worse than I had conceived it to be when I wrote to you last (not having received the tallies) which together do not amount to one third of what I made last year; which is insufficient to feed my Negroes, much more to afford support for my Horses. This evinces the necessity also of my knowing speedily & precisely, if I may depend upon any from the Estate below—& the quantity.

The Eastern shore oats generally speaking, are light & indifferent; & what is worse, are often mixed with the wild onions: as I mean to sow oats next Spring to help me along, it would be obliging in Mr Savage, if he could send me such as are free from this troublesome, & injurious plant to our fields.

I thank you too for the information respecting the interest of the loans to the Continent in this State: I send what Certificates I possess, to you; but fear that those who live at a distance from the Theatre, have little chance of being benefited by the Act of the Legislature; although they may get their Certificates to the Treasury on or before the time limitted. but if I should be mistaken in this, you would serve me essentially by bringing Cash in exchange for those which are enclosed, agreeably to the list which accompanies them. With great esteem & regard I am Dr Sir &c.

G: Washington

LB, DLC:GW.

Letter not found: to George Augustine Washington, 24 Dec. 1785. On 3 Feb. 1786 George Augustine Washington acknowledged receipt of "Your favor of the 24th Decr."

From Joseph-Armand Duché

Sir   New-york december 25th 1785

the politeness and hospitality wich I expereienced when I had the honor of paying you my respects at your Seat and the goodeness you manifested towards me in the letter wich you gave me to the Marquis de la fayette emboldens me to communicate to you an event very interesting to me, and for what I place your excellency among the number of those to whom I am indebted.[1]

I have just received a Letter from the Marquis de Castries notifying to me my appointement as vice-consul to reside at portsmouth in new-hampshire, and wich he is so obliging as to declare it only introductory to Something of greater importance.

I shall Shortly Set out for *that* station, but previous to doing it I could not refuse myself the pleasure of making you my acknowledgements for the interest you were So obliging as to take in my affairs.

if my new situation Should furnish me with any opportunities of giving your excellency proofs of my attachement, gratitude and veneration I could not be made happier than by Being honored with your commands. I have the honor to be with the highest respect and esteem your excellency's Sir the most obedeint and obliged humble Servant

Duche

ALS, DLC:GW.
    1. See GW to Lafayette, 12 April 1785.

From Henry Lee, Jr.

My dear General   [25 December 1785]
    The shallop I ordered your nuts and trees by, has arrived here and brought up one package—there will be another by another vessel. The apple is the Medley russitan, the pear is known among us by the Name of the Chantilly pear, and the cherry is coronation—all excellent in quality and merit good ground and proper exposure to the south.[1]
    I hope Mrs Lee will be able to set out on thursday. We trust you will certainly favor us with your Commands, should any occur while we are in Newyork. With united wishes for the health and happiness of Mount Vernon I remain your devoted friend and ob. sert

Henry Lee Jun.

P.S. I should have received your box from the shallop but he promised me certainly to deliver it at your landing on his return.

ALS, DLC:GW.
    1. See Lee to GW, 20 Dec., n.2. Lee seems to have been in Alexandria when he wrote both letters.

To Samuel Powel

Dear Sir,   Mount Vernon Decr 27th 1785.
    In looking over the list of premiums proposed by the Agricultural Society of Philadelphia I perceive that those which are offered for the 2d 3d & 4th articles were to have been produced (according to the requisitions) by the 20th instt. Each of these

being interesting to a farmer you would oblige me much by giving me the result of the communications, on these heads to the Society if any discoveries worth notice have been handed to it.[1]

Mrs Washington joins me in presenting the Compliments of the Season to Mrs Powell & yourself, and in best wishes that you may see many returns of it—With great esteem—I am Dr Sir yr Most Obedt Servt

Go: Washington

ALS, ViMtV; LB, DLC:GW.
 1. See Powel to GW, 16 Jan. 1786, and notes.

From Tench Tilghman

Dear Sir   Baltimore 30th Decembr 1785

Since I last had the honor of writing to you, I have had several interviews with Mr Gough, who seems of opinion that Mr Rawlins charge of £160 for finishing your Room is full as reasonable if not more so than what he charged him for Work of the same kind[1]—Upon this I have come to the following heads of agreement with him, which will be committed to firm after I have heard from you.

The Work to be began at Mount Vernon by the 1st or middle of April next—at farthest.

Mr Rawlins to have £13.10/ Maryland Curry for all his travelling Expences.

Mr Rawlins as well as his Workmen to be maintained while at Mt Vernon.

The Charge of transporting the Workmen & their Tools to and from Mt Vernon to be at the Expence of Genl Washington—who is to do it in any manner most convenient & agreeable to himself—The transportation of the moulded Work done at Baltimore (which must be by Water to prevent Breakage) to be also at the Expence of Genl Washington.

The materials to be furnished by you—but it is understood that if you will send round an equal weight of Plaister of Paris with what Rawlins works up here, he is to take it, and set one against the other—N.B. I enquired particularly of Mr Gough in respect to the finding the Materials.

Mr Rawlins to have £168 Maryland Currency, exclusive of the

pregoing, for finishing the room agreeable to the plan he communicated.

There is one more Article to which I could not agree without consulting you—Mr Rawlins will want an advance of about £50 in the course of the Winter. If it be agreeable to you I will make it, as he wants it.

You will be pleased to signify your approbation or disapprobation of the foregoing as soon as you conveniently can. If you approve, the Work, so far as it can be done here, will be immediately put in hand.[2] I am with true Respect & Esteem Dear Sir yr most obt & hble Servt

Tench Tilghman

ALS, DLC:GW.
1. See Tilghman to GW, 13 Dec. (second letter).
2. The agreement that Tilghman concluded with John Rawlins on behalf of GW along the lines set out here is dated 25 Feb. and was enclosed in Tilghman's letter to GW of 1 March.

From Charles Washington

Dear Brother   Happy Retreat Decr 30th 1785

I receiv'd yours by Mr B. Muse and am happy to hear that our Nephews are fix'd in Alexandria being more convenient to you, as they are under your direction, when I mentioned their coming to Berkeley in order to be under the direction of Mr Stubbs, it was with a view of lessening the Expence, however as the continuence of Mr Stubbs is uncertain, hope the matter is better Plan'd—think the Charges you Mention for the board & c. of our Nephews are extravagant[1]—you Mention the Sum recd in consiquence of discharging the above Charges is £85.12—which is £55.12—by Mr Robt Carter & £30, by my Brother John tho' I sent by Mr Robt McCray £24.6—at the time of writing you by Mr McCray—Mr Carter who Manages the Estate of George & Lawrence had sold, a part of the produce to a Certain Merchant for Cash in order to add to the assistance of defraying the above Mention'd Expences, but this Merchant failing in paying Cash we were oblige to take a part in goods which is intended for the purpose of Cloathing for our Nephews George & Lawrence which will be Sent to Alexandria by the first opportunity & Conclude with Mrs Washington joing in Compliments to you & my Sister and am Dr Brother Yours affectionately

Chas Washington

ALS, PHi: Gratz Collection. On the cover Charles Washington wrote "Hond by Mr Robt McCray."

1. GW's letter to Charles Washington in response to his brother's letter of 23 Nov. has not been found, but see GW to William Bailey and to Stephen Bloomer Balch, both 22 November.

From Francisco Rendón

Sir   [New York, c.31 Dec. 1785]

With particular pleasure I have received by Mr Telles the Letter your did me the honour to write by him date the 19th Inst.

Happy I am to hear the safe arrival at mount vernon the Jackass on which you set such highest value, convinced of the great general good it will arise to this Country, and I wish most sincerely that your expectation shall be Compleately answer'd.

I regret very much that Mr Telles for want of Language was not able of making himself understood to you, and I fear that he neither has giving to your people the proper direction which I think necessary to the menagement of the animal, in order that he may become useful to the design purpose. As Mr Telles Commision being at End when deliver'd the animal to you I realy think just his demand to return to his Country, as perfectly proper in you to gave him leave, and is forwarded him to this City, according to his wish. the Minister will with pleasure send him at home by the first good opportunity. and I doubt not, but he will be rewarded there with some thing or other to make his poverty situasion more agreable than it was before.

I did myself the honour of presenting to Mr de Gardoqui your Kind Compliments, adding your sincere wish to see him at your seat of retirement. this Gentleman in return desires me to assure you that your flater assurances of friendly disposeition toward him has impressed in his heart the most deepest sentiments of gratitud, and wish for an opportunity of shewing you his reciprocal Correspondence.

As to your kind expression of assuring me the Continuation

of that friendship with which you was pleased to grant me as a General, I only have to request Mr Washington to accept my most humble acknowledgement for such remarcable favour, & to permit me to love him as a Citizen as I have revered as the father of his Country and the Insurer of domestic happiness to a millions. I have the honour to be, with the greatest respect & Esteem, Sir your most obedt & most humble servt

Francisco Rendon

P.S. Inclose is a Letter from the Minister to you.[1]

ALS, DLC:GW. See source note, Gardoqui to GW, 1 Jan. 1786.
   1. See Gardoqui to GW, 1 Jan. 1786.

From Thomas Ridout

[1785]

I have already had the honor to inform you by my first letter from Havre, that I had sent to Bourdeaux the letter with which you charged me for the Chevalier Secondat Montesquieu, and that I had particularly recommended it to the constituted authority.[1]

I found my father very well. He lives in the country, & there leads the very busy life of a husbandman. He received with gratitude the honorable testimonies of your remembrance of him and of the services which he rendered to the U. States, the expression of which you confided to me, and he charges me to tell you how much he will always be interested for the success of his companion in arms. I am &c.

AL, DLC:GW.
   1. Ridout may be referring to GW's letter to Montesquieu of 20 Aug. 1785, but he is probably referring to that of 23 Dec. 1784. See Charles-Louis de Montesquieu to GW, 25 April 1785, and Ridout to GW, 4 Nov. 1784.

From St. John's Masonic Lodge, Newport, R.I.

[c.1785]

The Petition and Request of the master wardens and members of Lodge St Johns in the City of Newport Sheweth that said Lodge was Constituted in the year 1753 by Francis Axnard Esqr.

then Presideing Grand master of north america[1] and that sd Lodge flourished from that time to the breaking out of the late warr, haveing Increas'd to a very Respectable number of the first Characters and Stood equal in reputation to any Lodge upon the Continent when the beauty & harmony of their happy Connnection was Disturbed & finally entirely broken up by the Enemy takeing possession of this Port, which Occasiond such a Distribution of the Officers and members as to render it impractacable for them to Call a Sufficient number together to form a lodge and that the Said lodge from its Respectability had Sufficient Influence to Obtain a Charter from the General Assembly of this State by which they were Incorporated a Body Politick. So Special and uncommon an Indulgence being worthy our Serious attention we Cannot but feel the most anxious desire that the sd lodge of St Johns may be reinstated to its former Powers & Consequence as some woud Suppose the Charter to be Obsolete from its laying So long dormant. his Excellency is hereby informd that the Lodge has lately been revived by the late master Samel Brenton and his former Wardens &c.—but that a doubt shoud not remain on their minds in respect to the Validity of their proceedings in their endeavours to Increase the lodge & for the promotion of love and harmony among its members it is therefore most Sincerely wishd that your Excellency woud Interfere in our behalfs and from your well known Goodness render that assistance to your petitioners as their Case requires. it is wish'd that your Excellency woud Confirm the present master— with Power of Constitutg Lodges within the State⟨s⟩ as was the Power of the former master Robert Jenkins[2] and your Petitioner as in Duty bound will ever pray &c.

| Jeremiah Clark S. | Wardens | Samel Brenton master |
| H. J. Dayton | | John Handy Secretary[3] |

DS, DLC:GW. Dots are scattered throughout the document; only those that logically serve as periods have been retained.

This petition has been identified as the one enclosed in Samuel Brenton's letter to GW of 21 Jan. 1785, printed above in *Papers, Confederation Series,* 2:276–77. The St. John's Masonic Lodge of Newport, R.I., was organized in 1750 and reorganized in 1753 after its first master acted in a manner "unbecoming a Mason" (Tatsch, *Freemasonry in the Thirteen Colonies,* 168–69). The lodge was inactive during the Revolution, and on 7 June 1780 a second lodge, King David's Lodge, was organized in Newport. According to Tatsch, some of the Newport Freemasons sought aid from GW when he was in Newport in March 1781 (ibid., 174–75). A revived St. John's Lodge had merged with King David's Lodge before GW visited Newport in 1790 and on 17 Aug. received an address from the Freemasons of King David's Lodge.

1. Thomas Oxnard (1703–1754), born in England and made a Freemason in Boston in the 1730s, became Grand Master of the Freemasons in North America in September 1743.

2. Robert Jenkins (c.1700–1773) was a Newport merchant.

3. Jeremiah Clarke (Clark; 1734–1815) of Newport reached the rank of lieutenant during the Revolution. Henry Dayton (1751–1792) was recruiting officer for Newport during the Revolution and captain of the Light Corps (Bartlett, *R.I. Records*, 7:555–56, 8:299, 9:121, 186). John Handy (1756–1828), who read the Declaration of Independence on the Newport courthouse steps in July 1776 and again on 4 July 1826, reached the rank of brigade major during the Revolution and after the war became auditor of accounts for Rhode Island (ibid., 8:268, 512, 10:33; Mason, *Reminiscences of Newport*, 22).

To David Humphreys

Editorial Note

A letter written by George Washington on 7 Feb. 1785, and printed in John C. Fitzpatrick's standard edition of Washington's writings, was overlooked by the editor of the second volume in the Confederation Series of this edition of Washington's *Papers*. It is printed here, at the end of 1785.

My dear Humphreys: Mount Vernon, February 7, 1785.

In my last, by the Marquis de la Fayette, I gave you reason to believe that when I was more at leizure, you should receive a long letter from me; however agreeable this might be to my wishes, the period it is to be feared, will never arrive.[1] I can with truth assure you, that at no period of the war have I been obliged to write half as much as I now do, from necessity. I have been enquiring for sometime past, for a person in the character of Secretary or clerk to live with me; but hitherto unsuccessfully. What with letters (often of an unmeaning nature) from foreigners. Enquiries after Dick, Tom, and Harry who *may have been* in some part, or at *sometime*, in the Continental service. Letters, or certificates of service for those who want to go out of their own State. Introductions; applications for copies of Papers; references of a thousand old matters with which I *ought* not to be troubled, more than the Great Mogul, but which must receive an answer of some kind, deprive me of my usual exercise; and without relief, may be injurious to me as I already begin to feel the weight, and oppression of it in my head, and am assured by the *faculty*, if I do not change my course, I shall certainly sink under it.

After this preamble, which is not founded in fiction, you cannot expect much from me; nor indeed have I ought to relate that should claim much attention. All our assemblies have had long sessions, but I have not heard of any *very* important acts; none indeed more pregnant of political consequences, or commercial advantages, than two which have passed the Legislatures of Virginia and Maryland, for improving and extending the navigations of Potomack and James River as far as is practicable; and communicating them by short and easy roads with the Navigable waters to the Westward. I have sent Mr. Jefferson a copy of the act respecting the river Potomack, but can neither inform him, nor you, of the issue, as it depends wholly upon the subscription of what we have very little of, money.[2]

If we are to credit newspaper accounts, the flames of war in Europe are again kindling: how far they may spread, neither the Statesman or soldier can determine; as the great governor of the Universe causes contingencies which baffle the wisdom of the first, and the foresight and valor of the Second.

All I pray for, is, that you may keep them among yourselves. If a single spark should light among the inflameable matter in these States, it may set them in a combustion, altho' they may not be able to assign a good reason for it.

I have received but two short letters from you since your arrival in France. The first at your place of debarkation.[3] The second from Paris. Your third, altho' (in the beginning of this letter I assured you, and endeavoured to give reasons for it, which in the conclusion you see are invalidated) I am not able to write long ones to you, will not be altogether so laconic. a short transcript of your diary (for I have no doubt of your keeping one) would be amusing to me, although I can give you nothing in return for it. but your own feelings, I am sure, have told you long ere this that there is more pleasure in confering, than receiving obligations.

Mrs. Washington enjoys but indifferent health. My nephew

Geo. A. Washington has been buffetting the seas from clime to clime, in pursuit of health, but, poor fellow! I believe in vain. At present, if alive, I expect he is at Charleston. All the rest of my family are perfectly well, and join me in best wishes for you, with My dear Humphreys yr. etc.

P.S. Whilst I was in the act of enclosing this, yr. letters of the 30th. of Sept. and 11th. of Nov. were put into my hands; judge ye then, if I have leizure to write commentaries.

Fitzpatrick, *Writings of Washington*, 28:65–67.
    1. GW last wrote Humphreys on 25 Nov. 1784.
    2. It was in a letter to Thomas Jefferson dated 25 Feb. 1785 that GW enclosed copies of the acts adopted in January by the Virginia and Maryland legislatures for extending the navigation of the Potomac River. See James Madison to GW, 9 Jan. 1785, and its enclosures.
    3. Humphreys' letters are dated 12 and 18 Aug. 1784.

From Gardoqui

Sir   New york 1st Jany 1786.

There is I beleive few foreigners who can boast of being your sincere admirers at so early a period as mysell, haveing by a variety of circumstances of my private life been well inform'd of the transactions on this Continent. Beleive me Sir that the more I hear'd, the best I wish'd you, but as the world has done due justice to your great meritt & I Know that I am not capable of saying enough on such a deserving Subjectt, I must leave this happy work to better pens, assuring you that your confering me your esteem & freindship will give me the highest satisfaction.

Your obliging Invitation by Mr Rendon's letter in case I shou'd visitt the Southern States, is a Kindness that I shall never forgett & I own candly that shou'd my circumstances permitt me to make such a escurssion it will be principaly for the honour of waiting upon you & that of haveing your personal acquaintance, but in the mean time I must beg the favour of your correspondence & of your advise in whatever may tend to the wellfare & happyness of this Country & that of the King my Master, being the sole view of my hearty wishes.

Tellez arriv'd safe here & I have already provided a passage for him. I am glad that he had the luck to carry the animal safe & that his beheaviour in his line was proper.

Your letter to my freind Mr Carmiachael shall be carefully forwarded,[1] & permitt me to add before I conclude that your real great character & the advise of many of your freinds has induced me to avoid all treatment & to address myself in this freindly stile which hope will be agreable, persuaded of the unfeigned respectt & affection with which I have the honour to subscrive Sir your most obedt humble Servt

James Gardoqui

ALS, DLC:GW; ALS, DLC:GW. GW received and endorsed both copies of this letter. The second has Gardoqui's notation below his signature: "(Duplicate) The original was forwarded on this datte by Mr Rendon's answer." Francisco Rendón's undated reply to GW's letter of 19 Dec. has been given the date of 31 Dec. 1785. Diego Maria de Gardoqui had been in Philadelphia since June 1785 as Spanish chargé d'affaires.

1. GW's letter to William Carmichael is dated 19 December.

From Thomas Jefferson

Sir   Paris Jan. 4. 178[6]

I have been honoured with your letter of Sep. 26 which was delivered me by Mr Houdon, who is safely returned. he has brought with him the mould of the face only, having left the other parts of his work, with his workmen to come by some other conveiance. Doctor Franklin, who was joined with me in the superintendance of this just monument, having left us before what is called the costume of the statue was decided on, I canot so well satisfy myself, and I am persuaded I should not so well satisfy the world, as by consulting your own wish or inclination as to this article. permit me therefore to ask you whether there is any particular dress, or any particular attitude which you would rather wish to be adopted. I shall take singular pleasure in having your own idea executed if you will be so good as to make it known to me. I thank you for the trouble you have taken in answering my enquiries on the subject of Bushnel's machine. Colo. Humphreys could only give me a general idea of it from the effects proposed, rather than the means contrived to produce them.

I sincerely rejoice that three such works as the opening the Patowmac, James river, & a canal from the Dismal are like to be carried through. there is still a fourth however, which I had the honour I beleive of mentioning to you in a letter of Mar. 15 1784 from Annapolis. It is the cutting a canal which shall unite the heads of Cayahoga & Beaver creek. The utility of this, & even the necessity of it, if we mean to aim at the trade of the lakes will be palpable to you. the only question is it's practicability. the best information I could get as to this was from General Hand, who described the country as champain, and these waters as Leading in lagoons which would be easily united. Maryland and Pennsylvania are both interested to concur with us in this work.

The institutions you propose to establish by the shares in the Patowmac & James river companies given you by the assembly, and the particular objects of those institutions are most worthy. It occurs to me however that if the bill 'for the more general diffusion of knowlege' which is in the revisal, should be passed, it would supersede the use, & obscure the existence of the charity schools you have thought of. I suppose in fact that that bill, or some other like it, will be passed. I never saw one received with more enthusiasm than that was by the house of delegates in the year 1778 and ordered to be printed, and it seemed afterwards that nothing but the extreme distress of our resources prevented it's being carried into execution even during the war. it is an axiom in my mind that our liberty can never be safe but in the hands of the people themselves, & that too of the people with a certain degree of instruction. this it is the business of the state to effect, and on a general plan. should you see a probability of this however, you can never be at a loss for worthy objects of this donation. even the remitting that proportion of the toll on all articles transported would present itself under many favorable considerations, and it would in effect be to make the state do in a certain proportion what they ought to have done wholly; for I think they should clear all the rivers and lay them open & free to all. however you are infinitely the best judge how the most good may be effected with these shares.

All is quiet here. there are indeed two specks in the horizon, the exchange of Bavaria, & the demarcation between the Emperor & Turks. we may add as a third the interference by the king of Prussia in the domestic disputes of the Dutch. Great Britain, it is said, begins to look towards us with a little more good humour. but how true this may be I cannot say with certainty. we are trying to render her commerce as little necessary to us as possible by finding other markets for our produce. a most favourable reduction of duties on whale oil has taken place here, which will give us a vent for that article paying a duty of a guinea & a half a ton only. I have the honor to be with the highest esteem & respect Dear Sir your most obedient and most humble servant,

Thomas Jefferson

ALS, DLC:GW. The letter was sent "viâ London by Mr [William] Bingham" (Boyd, *Jefferson Papers*, 9:152).

From Benjamin Lincoln

Boston Jany 4h 1786

I have since my return, My Dear General, been looking agreeably to your request, among my young friends to see whether I could find among them one who would answer your purpose as a private Secy &c. &c.—I have at last found a Mr Lear who supports the character of a Gentleman & a schollar—He was educated at Cambridge in this State—Since he left College he has been in Europe & in different parts of this continent—It is said that he is a good master of language, He reads French, and writes an exceeding good letter—That his abilities are surpassed by few and his integrity by none—From the best information I can obtain I am induced to believe that you will find him the man you described.

For a more particular acct of Character and abilities I beg leave to refer you to the inclosed letter from my son to me—he has an intimate knowledge of Mr Lear—If you should now be in want of his services he will by the first opportunity join your Excellencys family.[1]

The Council of the American Academy have had a meeting here this day. Among other communications we had a very interesting one from the Reverend Mr West of Dartmouth a Gentleman of great Abilities and extensive information He wrote on the subject of extracting by a simple machine without the use of fire fresh water from salt—He informed the Academy that he was admitted into the secret by the original inventor of the operation and that they were now attempting some improvements upon it—However thus far they had reduced the matter to a certainty that three gallons of good fresh water could be extracted from a certain quantity of Sea water (I think a barrel) in seventy or eighty minutes He hoped by some little amendments they were attempting that double that quantity would be produced in the same time—should they never improve upon the present discovery it must be considered as a very important one.[2] With great esteem & regard I have the honor to be My Dear Sir Your Excellencys most Obedent Servant

B. Lincoln

ALS, DLC:GW.

1. Lincoln, who had business connections in Alexandria, last dined at Mount Vernon on 27 Nov. 1785 (*Diaries*, 4:160, 164, 169, 236, 241). GW pursued Lincoln's suggestion regarding the hiring of Tobias Lear (1762–1816) as his secretary and tutor for the two Custis grandchildren (GW to Lincoln, 6 Feb., 10 April, 7 June 1786, and Lincoln to GW, 15 Mar., 3 May, 9 May 1786). Lear wrote GW on 7 May agreeing to accept the position at a salary of $200 per annum. He arrived at Mount Vernon on 29 May to begin a long and fruitful relationship with GW (ibid., 337–38). Benjamin Lincoln, Jr.'s letter to his father, dated 2 Jan., reads: "Mr Lear whose character you wish, I have been some time acquainted with. He is a young man of sobriety, good sense and learning, possesses an honest heart, a generous, elevated spirit and is such a youth as General Washington will esteem and be happy to patronize. He is been unfortunate in the loss of a very handsome patrimony. But his misfortunes while they drained his purse have enriched his understanding and given him a style of thinking which in my opinion at his time of life is preferable to wealth" (DLC:GW).

2. The Rev. Samuel West (1731–1807), pastor of the church in Dartmouth, Mass., is best known for his deciphering for GW a letter from Dr. Benjamin Church to the British in 1775 and for his *Essays on Liberty and Necessity* (1793) in which he argues against Jonathan Edwards's Calvinist theology. The paper on the desalinization of seawater was delivered to the American Academy of Arts and Sciences, founded in Boston in 1780. Lincoln wrote GW on 15 Mar.: "It is *now* said little may be expected from, the supposed invention, of extracting fresh from salt water."

To Battaile Muse

Sir   Mount Vernon Jany 5th 1786

A few days ago a Mr Isaac Jenny of Loudon County was with me respecting a Piece of land which he supposing was Vacant, has been endeavouring to obtain but which upon investigation, he finds belongs to me, & in part of my Chattins Run tract adjoining Robt Ashbys, though claimed by Mr Robt Scott who has Placed a Tenant thereon One Jesse Hit whose first Years Rent is now due. As far as I can understand the Matter the following is a true State of the case.

Both Scott & I bind upon Burgess's Patent & call for ⟨his⟩ Lines One of which it Should seem runs a Certain Course & Distance & Calls for a Red Oak, but in Place of a Red Oak, there is a White Oak, which Mr Jenny says all the Neighbours know to be Burgess's Corner, & he is informed that the Surveyor of the County has established it as such. From hence I Run Two or Three Short Courses with Burgess's lines to a Red Oak—And from there a line with Scotts—But Scott wants, & it Should Seem from Mr Jenny's Account actually got Ashby when he was laying my Land off into Lotts, to leave out those Short courses abovementioned by which a line of Blazed Trees, which were then, or at Some other time made to Subserve the Purpose. I am cut out of 170 or 180 Acres of Land, which are within the lines of my Patent & now Tenanted by Scott to Hit. Inclosed I Send you a copy of the Courses & Boundaries of my Land, taken from the Original Patent & pray the first time you go into the Neighbourhood, that you would have the matter enquired into. I have no objection to Hits having the Land & would give him the Preference but Shall not by any means If the Land is mine think myself bound to fulfill Scott's agreement with him. He must except in the Preference above stand upon the Same footing with me as another Man.[1]

Some time ago Mr Landon Carter informed me that a Patent of which he is Possessed takes away part of my Tract in Ashbys Bent. I reply'd that I wanted no Land but my own, nor to go into a litigation of the right If it is realy his—But that his Right must be clearly ascertained before I Shall Surrender the land: which I mention that if upon enquiry you find he has taken possession of any part of what I hold by Purchase there & which I laid out into lots, I may be informed thereof & prevent his doing it, If it remains to be done.[2]

Be so good as to inform me by the first conveyance, whether clover Seed is to be bought in your Neighbourhood, & if so the quantity & Price of it. On your answer will depend my Purchase with you or at Philadelphia. I have great reason to fear that that which you bought for me last year was good for nothing. If so, & the Man of whome you got it was apprized thereof, I Shall view him in a light infinitely worse than a pick pocket, because the latter only takes your Money whilst the former does this also runs you to a useless cost of Putting land in fine Tilth, for the Seed & occasions the loss of a Year in one's Projects.[3]

I have heard nothing more of the Butter which you were to have lodg'd at Mr Wayles by the 23d of last Month. I hope no dissappointment will take Place, more especially as I Could after I had engaged this of you, have Purchassed any quantity of very fine Butter in Alexandria at 9d. ℔ lb. having obtained 200 lbs. at that Price. I am Sir Your Very Hble Servt

Go: Washington

LS, DLC:GW; LB, DLC:GW. GW's secretary, William Shaw, originally dated this 1785 and then changed 5 to 6.

1. GW included in his diary entry for 28 Dec. 1785: "A Mr. Israel Jenny [Janney; died c.1823] of Loudoun County came here in the Afternoon, respecting some Land which he has been endeavouring to obtain under an idea of its being waste, but which he finds to be within the lines of my Chattin run tract in Fauquier County, though claimed by Mr. Robert Scott who has put a Tenant upon it of the name of Jesse Hitt, who has now been upon it three years and thereafter to pay Rent" (*Diaries*, 4:256). For the lots and tenants of GW's Chattins Run tract on the eastern slope of the Blue Ridge, see GW to Muse, 18 Sept. 1785, and Muse to GW, 28 Nov. 1785, and notes. GW and Muse continued to correspond about Scott's claims and when Muse left GW's employ in 1790, the matter remained unresolved (see GW to Muse, 4 Feb. 1786, Muse to GW, 7 Feb., 21 Mar. 1789, 22 Aug. 1791).

2. GW's "Tract in Ashbys Bent" was the land that he bought in 1767 from George Carter's estate, lying mostly in Fauquier County but partly in Loudoun. The Landon Carter with whom GW had this dispute may have been any one of several men; no other reference to the matter has been found.

3. GW records receiving on 9 Jan. 1786 another shipment of clover seed, a barrel valued at £5, about which Muse writes on 17 Jan. (Ledger B, 211). See Muse to GW, 17 Jan., 11 July 1786, and GW to Muse, 4 Feb., 1 Aug. 1786. For GW's earlier correspondence with Muse about clover seed, see GW to Muse, 28 July 1785, n.6.

From Thomas Evans

Sir,   Monongalia—Morgins Town January 6th 1786
I am informed that you have the principal direction of the cutting of a Road from the nearest Navigation on the Waters of

Potomack to those of the Western Waters, now Sir if you think that I can be of service in the accomplishing this very advantageous business I shall be glad to be imployed in it. I have the Honour to be Sir Yr Mo: obdt Servt

Thomas Evans

ALS, DLC:GW.

From Thomas Jefferson

Dear Sir   Paris Jan. 7. 178[6]

A conversation with the Count de Rochambeau yesterday obliges me to write a supplementary letter to that of the 4th instant. he informs me that he has had applications for paiment from the person who furnished the badges for the Cincinnati, as well the Americans as French. that this person informed him they were not paid for, that he had furnished them indeed on the application of major L'Enfant, but that he did not do it in reliance on his credit, for that he should not have trusted so much to Major l'Enfant of whose means of paiment he knew nothing, but that he considered himself as working for a society who had delivered their orders thro' Major l'Enfant, and always expected the Society would see him paid. Count Rochambeau has written to Major l'Enfant, and the answer is that he has never received the whole, nor expects to be able to collect it, & that being without resources he is obliged, as fast as he collects it, to apply it to his own sustenance. Count Rochambeau told the workman he would pay for the badges delivered him for the French officers (I think he said about 40 in number) but that for the others he must apply to the Marquis de la fayette and Count d'Estaing. as L'Enfant's letter gives room to suppose a misapplication of these monies, and in the mean time the honour of the American officers stands committed, and in danger of being spoken of publicly, I thought it my duty to apprise you of this, that you might take such measures herein as you think best.[1] I have the honour to be with sentiments of the most perfect esteem Dear Sir your most obedient and most humble servt

Th: Jefferson

ALS, DLC:GW; copy, DSoCi. The copy has been endorsed: "Copy recd for Genl Washington from Paris 7th Jany 1786."

1. When L'Enfant left for France in the fall of 1783, he took with him authorization from GW to have a medal designed for the Society of the Cincinnati and orders from individual members of the society, including GW, to have a total of about forty of them made. L'Enfant took it upon himself to have medals made for presentation to French officers on behalf of the American society, and he also had about one hundred extra medals made in expectation of selling them to American officers. L'Enfant returned to America in April 1784 shortly before the society's General Meeting in Philadelphia in May with the medals made of gold in the shape of an eagle. He succeeded in getting the delegates to the General Meeting to approve the purchase of medals for the Frenchmen, but he had less luck in disposing of the extra medals. After GW received Jefferson's complaint about L'Enfant, he sent, on 1 June, a copy of Jefferson's letter to Henry Knox with a request that Knox provide him with information and advice. Knox's reply of 13 June is a full and sympathetic account of L'Enfant's actions regarding the Cincinnati medals, and GW replied to Jefferson on 1 August. L'Enfant wrote GW on 6 Dec. 1786, enclosing a long memorial justifying his actions with regard to the golden eagles. The Cincinnati's General Meeting held in May 1787 at the same time as the Constitutional Convention voted to provide L'Enfant with the money to pay what he owed for the golden eagles, but he still had not received the money a year later. In addition to GW's letter to Knox of 1 June 1786, Knox's to GW of 13 June 1786, and L'Enfant's to GW of 6 Dec. 1786, see Lafayette to GW, 10 Jan. 1784, n.3, L'Enfant to GW, 29 April 1784, 15 April 1786, General Meeting of the Society of the Cincinnati, 4–18 May 1784, GW to Jefferson, 1 Aug. 1786, and GW to L'Enfant, 1 Jan. 1787, 28 April 1788.

To Tench Tilghman

Dear Sir,   Mount Vernon Jany 7th 1786

Your favor of the 30th Ulto did not reach me until last night. Except it is by chance, letters by the Stage never get to my hands so quickly as they do by the Post; nor so safely, because I send regularly every post day to the Office in Alexandria, whilst those by the Stage getting into private hands await accidental conveyances from that place. I mention this circumstance as a reply might have been expected from me sooner.

As it is convenient and indeed essential to me to have the use of my unfinished room as soon as may be, I agree to Mr Rawlins's terms (as stated in your letter) in all their parts; not but that I am convinced from what I know of the business (being once part owner of as accomplished a workman as ever came to this Country, in that way, and the manner of its execution)[1] that Mr Rawlins has imposed upon Mr Gough and now avails himself of the scarcity of Artisans in his profession, to extort high terms from me. Most of this work is cast, and is as quickly done as lead is run into a mould. But rather than encounter further delay—perhaps a disappointment—or ask the favor of a stranger to engage an undertaker to cross the Atlantic, who might be troublesome to me thereafter, I submit to this imposition as the lesser evil.

As Mr Rawlins is a stranger to me, and one, of whose character I have not the smallest knowledge; and as I have had some reason to remember an old adage—that one of the bad paymasters is him that pays beforehand—I persuade myself that you will be satisfied I shall run no risk in advancing him money to the amount of £50 in the course of the Winter, 'ere it is done. And as you are so obliging as to offer to do this, your drafts on me for such advances as you make him, shall be punctually paid.

When the agreement is specifically entered into, and bound, be so good as to request Mr Rawlins to point out the preparative steps for me, that no delays may follow his arrival. I shall rely more upon your friendship & goodness, than upon any apology I could make, for an excuse for the trouble this business has already given you, and is likely to give, before its final accomplishment; and can only assure you that with unfeigned esteem & affection I am Dear Sir Yr most obedt Hble Servt

Go: Washington

P.S. I send this letter to Alexaa to take the chance of a private conveyance, but it is probable the Post will offer the first. G.W.

ALS, PHi: Gratz Collection; LB, DLC:GW.
    1. It is not certain to whom GW is referring here.

From Arthur Young

Bradfield Hall near Bury Suffolk
Sir   Jan: 7. 1786
I scarcely know what apology to make for a letter so out of common forms as the present; but the spectacle of a great commander retiring in the manner you have done from the head of a victorious army to the amusements of agriculture, calls all the

feelings of my bosom into play & gives me the strongest inclination, I fear an impotent one, to endeavour in the smallest degree to contribute to the success of so laudable a pleasure. I should not however have been so abrupt, had I not received an application to assist in procuring you a bailiff well skilled in English husbandry, for wch purpose I had made enquiries, & doubt not should have succeeded, but I hear fro. Mr Rack of Bath that he has met with one likely to suit you: In this little negotiation Mr Fairfax gave something of a sanction to the liberty I at present take in addressing you.[1]

I have sent you by Mr Athawes of London the first four volumes of the Annals of Agriculture a work I am at present publishing Will you do me the honour of accepting them, as a very small mark of my veneration for the character of a man whose private virtues rendered a cause successful and illustrious, which I have been solicitous as an englishman to condemn. Permit me also to send by the same conveyance the rest of the Volumes as they are published.[2]

But Sir—as my love of agriculture is even stronger than that I feel for any species of military glory, you must permit me to speak to you as a brother farmer; & to beg, that if you want men, cattle, tools, seeds, or any thing else that may add to yr rural amusement, favour me with your commands, & beleive me I shall take a very sincere pleasure in executing them.

I find by the extract from your letter sent me[3] that you have discontinued Tobacco & maiz & wish a well regulated farm in the english culture: your expression concerning manure being the ⟨f⟩irst transmutation towards gold, is good, and shews that you may be as great a farmer as a general. The culture of those plants that support cattle you will probably find the true means of improvement, & amongst those, turneps, cabbages and potatoes all very important. Permit me to remain With the greatest Respect, Sir, Your most obedt & Devoted Servt

Arthur Young

ALS, DLC:GW; copy, PPRF. The letter in DLC:GW is docketed by GW; the PPRF may be Young's retained copy.

This letter marks the opening of GW's correspondence with Arthur Young (1741–1820), the great English agriculturalist and prolific writer. Young published *Letters from His Excellency General Washington, to Arthur Young, Esq., F.R.S.*, in London in 1801.

1. See George William Fairfax to GW, 23 Jan. 1786, and enclosures.

2. Young continued to send GW for the rest of GW's life bound volumes of his monthly *Annals of Agriculture, and Other Useful Arts*, to which he was the main contributor. There were thirty-one volumes of the *Annals* in GW's library at the time of his death as well as a number of other works of Young. GW extracted from the volumes of the *Annals* passages of particular interest which are in notebooks that are preserved in DLC:GW. For the arrival of the first four volumes of the *Annals*, see Thomas Fairfax to GW, 30 June 1786.

3. See GW to George William Fairfax, 30 June 1785.

From Bryan Fairfax

Dear Sir   Towlston January the 9th 1786.

I have sent the Bearer for a few Slips of the weeping willow You were so kind as to offer me, as well as to ask your Advice, in case I should not have an opportunity hereafter, where an Execution should be sent vs Dr Savage's Estate. I have brot up with me a copy of the decree whereby we are at Liberty to proceed at Law upon the Judgement obtained. I must apply to the Clerk's office for a scire facias in order to have an execution, as well as to bring on a Judgement upon the subsequent annuities; and in case I should not be able to do myself the pleasure of Going to Mt Vernon before that time, I beg to know Yr opinion into which county it would be adviseable to send an Execution— for No Execution can be had in Carolina without commencing a fresh suit there. The Doctor had Lands in Culpeper & prince William as well as in this county: perhaps an Execution mt be sent into each, of which I shall know more when I hear from Mr Cl: Moore to whom I applyed to prosecute the Business in the county court.[1]

I should not have troubled You with this but I thot this matter of the Execution a material point.

I shall hope to have the Favor of Yr Company when You come into these parts—By what I learn I imagine the managers will have hard work to controul those that they have lately brot up.[2] Our Compliments to Mrs Washington & Family—& I remain Dr Sir Yr obliged & affect. humble Servt

                                                    Bryan Fairfax

ALS, DLC:GW.

Fairfax's house, Towlston Grange, was in Fairfax County.

1. The legal involvement of GW and Bryan Fairfax with the late Dr. William Savage on behalf of his wife Margaret Savage, dating back to the 1760s, returned to plague GW soon after he arrived at Mount Vernon following the war. See Edmund Randolph to GW, 19 Feb. 1784, n.3. For a renewed inquiry about Mrs. Savage's estate and GW's response, see Thomas Brereton to GW, 12 April, and GW to Brereton, 20 April 1786.

2. He is referring to the Potomac River Company workers.

To Bryan Fairfax

Dear Sir,   Mount Vernon 10th Jany 1786

I have ordered my Gardr to furnish your Servant with Six of the weeping Willows that have roots; and as many cuttings as he pleases to take. If he does not bring enough for your purposes— or if these should not succeed, you may have a fresh supply at any time.

I wish it was in my power to offer you any advice that would be availing in the case of Savage: but the truth is, I do not know where his property lyes—and 'till the receipt of your letter knew not, or did not recollect that, he died possessed of a foot of Land in this, or Loudoun County. If the Law will justify us in it, my opinion would be, that the Execution should be laid, or obtained ready to lay, in as much property as will unquestionably answer the demand—when that is satisfied, we want no more, the residue (if any) being untouched, cannot be injured; especially if it consists of Land. I should prefer beginning the Sale in this County—because least troublesome.

By your not mentioning the hound puppies, it is probable you may have altered your mind respecting them; but if the case is otherwise, I am unable to supply you at present, having lost all but one, and the chance of his living not much in his favor.[1]

I shall always have great pleasure in seeing you at this place, and shall be equally happy in paying my respects to you at Towlston. I am sorry to hear that my fears of, are likely to be reallized by, the Servants which were bought for the use of Potomack Compa. To avoid this evil—as much as possible—was the inducement with the Directors to offer such (as we thought) encouraging terms for the hire of Negros, ineffectually it should seem, as I believe we have got none yet. Mrs Washington joins me in Compliments, and best wishes for yourself, Mrs Fairfax & family, and with very great esteem & regard I am Dr Sir Yr Most Obedt & Affecte Hble Servt

G. Washington

ALS, Collections of Lord Fairfax of Cameron, Gays House, Holyport, Maidenhead, England.

1. Perhaps GW was referring to the puppies of "One Doilliamson of the Hound Bitches" sent to him from France by Doilliamson, which gave birth to fifteen puppies on 30 Sept. 1785, seven of which GW had drowned (*Diaries*, 4:199; see GW to Lafayette, 1 Sept. 1785).

To Catharine Sawbridge Macaulay Graham

Madam,　　　　　　　　　　　　Mount Vernon Jany 10th 1786

I wish my expression would do justice to my feelings, that I might convey to you adequate ideas of my gratitude for those favourable sentiments with which the letter you did me the honour to write to me from New York, is replete. The plaudits of a Lady, so celebrated as Mrs Macauly Graham, could not fail of making a deep impression on my sensibility; and my pride was more than a little flattered, by your approbation of my conduct through an arduous and painful contest.[1]

During the time in which we supposed you to have been on your journey to New York, we participated the distresses which we were sure you must have experienced, on acct of the intemperature of the Air, which exceeded the heats common in this Country at the most inclement season; and though your letter was expressive of the great fatigue you had undergone, still we rejoiced that the journey was attended with no worse consequences.

I hope, and most sincerely wish, that this letter may find you happily restored to your friends in England, whose anxiety for your return must, I am persuaded have been great—and that you will have experienced no inconvenience from your voyage to America.

Mrs Washington who has a grateful sense of your favourable mention of her—and Fanny Bassett, & Major Washington who, since we had the honor of your Company, have joined their hands & fortunes, unite with me in respectful compliments to you—and in every good wish that can render you & Mr Graham happy. The little folks enjoy perfect health. The boy, whom you would readily have perceived was the pet of the family, affords promising hopes from maturer age. With sentiments of great respect & esteem I have the honor to be Madam Yr Most Obedt & Very Hbe Servt

Go: Washington

ALS, Leicester City Museum and Art Gallery, New Walk, Leicester, England; LB, DLC:GW.

1. Mrs. Graham wrote GW from New York on 13 July 1785 after completing her visit to Mount Vernon on 14 June.

Letter not found: from James Mercer, 10 Jan. 1786. On 20 Jan. GW wrote to Mercer: "I have been favored with your letter of the 10th inst."

From Samuel Hanson

Sir   Alexandria Jany 12th 1786

When I had last the pleasure of seeing you at Mount-Vernon, you expressed an inclination to peruse the Pamphlets of the Revd Messrs Wharton & Carroll, upon the subject of their religious Controversy. Immediately on my return I wrote to Baltimore for them, but without being able to obtain Mr Carroll's reply. I have hope of procuring it at Annapolis. In the meantime, lest you should suppose me inattentive to your Commands, I forward the Pieces of Mr Wharton, not doubting that Mr Carroll's reply may be had at Annapolis, where it was printed.[1] I beg my Compliments to your lady and remain, with great respect, Sir Your most obedient Servant

S. Hanson of Saml

ALS, DLC:GW.

1. While chaplain to the Roman Catholics at Worcester in England, Charles Henry Wharton (1749–1833), a native of St. Mary's County, Md., left the communion of the Roman Catholic church and in 1783 returned to Maryland. In 1784 he published *A Letter to the Roman Catholics of the City of Worcester . . . Stating the Motives Which Induced Him to Relinquish Their Communion, and Become a Member of the Protestant Church* (Philadelphia). In response, the Rev. John Carroll (1735–1815) published *An Address to the Roman Catholics of the United States of*

America (Annapolis, 1784), which evoked in turn Wharton's *A Reply to an Address to the Roman Catholics of the United States of America* (Philadelphia, 1785). Wharton became a distinguished Episcopal clergyman, and Carroll became archbishop in the Roman Catholic church. Samuel Hanson of Samuel was at this time a merchant in Alexandria.

From Battaile Muse

Honourable Sir,   Berkeley County January 12th 1786

I received your Favours dated December the 4th and 16th and I shall Endeavour to Comply with the Contents. Your Tenants in Fauquir has behaved Very Ill Since I wrote you, Several has run away altho I was with them and Told them To be Industrious and that you would give them a reasonable Time to Pay their arrears of rents. about Christmas two run away—one a Poor Man, the other was able—which was Abner grigg that owed £30—I followed Him four days and Took him with and officer—with a writ as He secrited His Effect after I Took Him by writ He agreed To Give a replevey Bond in which I have got good Security—in consequence of his Leaving the Lott I advertised it To rerent but allowed him Ten days to go and see whether you would allow Him To return To his Place, since which he has return'd and sayes he defies you or my self to dispossess Him This fellow is a great Villain from His Conduct I Judge Him; I wish you Could make and Example of Him—which business may rest untill I See you in april. Abner Griggs Lott No. 8. Should this man Come to you you'll Know him, I shall Shew him no Favour as He has behaved So Ill.[1]

The Vacant Lotts I advertised To rent for the present year, or on Lease for Ten Years. I do not Expect To rent them this year—if I can I will, or rent them on Lease if I can get a Tenant that will give the Value than can be depended on. In consequence of the Tenants running away I have Issued a warrant to Distress those that are able To bear it, what is done I cannot say as I came away before the officer Could go to do the business and I was in pursuit of Grigg whome I was happy To Ketch for Example To others. I do not Expect to collect but a small Propotion of the rents by april—but I certainly Shall do every thing in my Power To reason the Tenants to their duty—I have already given notice to Every Man To Provide Payment by the First day of February and it's my opinion that unless they Pay in a reasonable Time that they ought To be distressed I have from Experience Found it To be necessary—Nevertheless I shall not do it in Berkeley and Frederick untill I See or hear From you unless in Cases of Necessity—your business is New To me—Time will make and amendment—in April I shall make a return of Every Tenemant—and its Sittuation as Far as I can do it—and will use my Endeavours To bring Every Tenant To a Sence of his duty— Please To inform me Whether Mr Ariss is to Pay the Taxes of the Land or reather in what manner I am to Fill up a Lease, He says He is To have the place during His & His Wifes Life on the same Terms Mr F. Whiteing has his Lease, on Paying £60 in-Stead of £50 this business He wants done next spring To have his Lease.[2] you will observe by the Inclosed that I had started a waggone the 10th of D⟨ecr⟩ In order to have your Butter down by Ch⟨rist⟩mas, but the bad roads stopt the waggone about Leesburg, and it has not been in my Power To set His off again untill Now. if you do not approve of the butter I shall be much oblige To you To contrive it To Mr Wales, that I may call for it their. I am Sorry any Man should Loose by a Contract made with me, I hope that the goodness of my wheat will Save you in the price, I have the Quantity out but the roads are not Passable I beg Sir you will Excuse any Imperfectness In my writeing as I am Hurried by the waggoner & write by Candle Light—as Soon as I hear From the Fauquier Sheriff I shall Inform you—I am Honourable Sir Your Obedient Humble Servant.

Battaile Muse

ALS, DLC:GW.

1. Muse wrote GW in similar terms about Abner Griggs on 17 Jan. after Griggs had returned to his farm, lot no. 8 in Fauquier and Loudoun counties, where he remained an unsatisfactory tenant until 1789. See Lists of Tenants, 18 Sept. 1785, n.17. See also GW to Muse, 4 Feb. 1786.

2. In 1784 John Ariss began renting from GW a 700-acre tract on Bullskin Run in Berkeley County formerly rented by Francis Whiting. See Ariss to GW, 5 Aug. 1784, and notes, and GW to Ariss, 8 Aug. 1784. See also GW's response to Muse, 4 Feb. 1786. Ariss obtained a lease, dated 20 April 1786 (ViMtV), a transcript of which is in CD-ROM:GW.

From Samuel Powel

Dear Sir   Philadelphia January 16. 1786

It would have afforded me great Pleasure could I, at this Time, have answered your Queries as fully & satisfactorily as I wish to do; but tho' it is not in my Power to do this now, yet, as the definitive Judgement of the Society respecting the Claims 2 & 3, is to be given on the first Tuesday in February, I shall, when that is pronounced, procure a Copy of the respective Essays & forward them to you. They are, from the Nature of the Subject, rather long, especially No. 2, which, from it's being so essentially fundamental to all good Husbandry, requires to be treated in Detail.

For No. 3 no Claim has been offered—I hope, however, that the Præmium for an Essay on that Subject will be continued for the ensuing Year. At the next Meeting a new List of Præmiums will be offered, in which many of the Subjects of the present List will, doubtless, be continued. Should any Subject, interesting to Agriculture, occur to you⟨,⟩ the Society will be much obliged to you to communicate it.[1]

The Result of actual Experiments, being so much preferable to the most specious & well supported theories, has induced the Society to turn its Thoughts towards the Establishment of an experimental Farm, & the sending to England for a Farmer thoroughly versed in the most approved Mode of english Farming, to execute the Plan. A Committee is appointed to examine into the State of the Society's funds, & to report how far their Ability to execute this Scheme, extends. Should it be found practicable, the present Intention is to rent a worn out Farm, & by a Sett of actual Experiments, to endeavor to ascertain the best Methods of recovering, what is called a worn out Soil. Should an easy Method of doing this, & within the reach of every Farmer be found out, the Discovery will be usefull indeed.[2]

Mrs Powel begs Leave to join me in Thanks to Mrs Washington & yourself for your obliging Compliments of the Season, which we most sincerely return. I am, with great Esteem, Dear Sir Your most obedt humble Servt

Samuel Powel

ALS, DLC:GW.

1. GW's inquiry about the papers submitted to the Philadelphia Agricultural Society is dated 27 Dec. 1785. The minutes of the Philadelphia Agricultural Society for 5 Dec. 1785 have this entry: "The President and Mr. G[eorge] Clymer presented two communications; one, marked No. I., 'An Essay on a Farm-Yard System;' being a claim for the Premium no. 2.—The other, marked No. II., describing a method for counteracting the effects of frost in heaving or spewing up ground, and thereby exposing the roots of plants to injury or destruction; being a claim for premium no. 3." On Feb. 7 the essay on a farm-yard system was read and unanimously voted to receive a gold medal. It was then revealed that the author was Col. George Morgan, along with John Beale Bordley the most frequent contributor of communications to the society and apparently the only recipient of the society's medal before it suspended operations for a decade in 1793 (*Minutes of the Philadelphia Society for the Promotion of Agriculture, from Its Institution in February, 1785, to March, 1810* [Philadelphia, 1854]). On 10 May Powel sent GW a transcription of Morgan's essay.

2. In January 1787 the Philadelphia Agricultural Society adopted a motion that it rent a tract of land and import an English farmer to manage an experimental farm, but no action was taken at the time (ibid., 17; see also Gambrill, "John Beale Bordley," 432).

From Tench Tilghman

Dear Sir   Baltimore 16th January 1786

In consequence of yours of the 7th I have set Rawlins to work—it is more than probable that he, knowing he has no immediate Competitor, may be extravagant in his prices—The only consolation you therefore have, is knowing you are served as cheap as your Neighbours.

Inclosed you have a plan or pattern in paper of the Joiner's Work necessary to be done about the Cornice previous to beginning upon the Stucco Work—This, Rawlins says, your Carpenters will understand—He also desires that the *Grounds* round the Windows—Doors and SurBase[1] may be put up previous to his going down in the Spring—The only materials you will have to prepare will be Laths—Nails—Hair & Lime—The Agreement is drawing and when compleated and executed shall be sent to you—I beleive you will be perfectly safe in making the required advance of £50—Rawlins has a family here, has property and is in good and *profitable* Business as you may reasonably suppose.

I must insist upon your making no Apologies for the Agency

you have given me in this Business. I shall think myself amply repaid if I can at any time find leisure to see in what manner the Work is executed—I shall always have the inclination. I am with sincere Respect & Esteem Dear Sir Yr most obt & humble Servt

Tench Tilghman

ALS, DLC:GW.
   1. The surbase is the molding above the base of the wainscoting.

From William Fitzhugh

Dear Sir   Chatham, January 17. 1786
   I have lately recover'd two fine Does which had stray'd from the Eagles Nest and were lost for several Months. I imagine you have not yet made up the Number you intend to keep, & have therefore desired my Nephew Mr Grymes to have them put on board some Vessell, in a large Box or Cage, with directions to the Skipper to land them at your House.[1] The one I have here is in fine Order, but in continual dread of a Pack of Neighbouring Hounds, who are frequently passing through my Fields, & obliging her to take Shelter in our Kitchen. As soon as you inform me that your Paddock is compleated, I will send her up. I am with respectful Compliments to your Lady & Family, Dear Sir Your Aff. & Ob. Ser.

W. Fitzhugh

ALS, DLC:GW.
   William Fitzhugh, of Chatham in Stafford County, grew up at Eagle's Nest in the Chotank section of King George County, where his nephew, Benjamin Fitzhugh Grymes (died c.1803), now lived.
   1. Benjamin Grymes sent GW from Eagle's Nest on 24 April "the two Does from this place, and a third which I received to day from Chatham." For further correspondence regarding the does, see William Fitzhugh to GW, 2 Nov. 1785, n.2.

From Battaile Muse

Honourable Sir,   January 17th 1786
   your Favour dated the 5th Instant came To my hands Last night, It's uncertain whether I shall be in Fauquier before march[.] the first Time I go down I shall inquire into the Land

that Mr Scott holds. I wish you To direct the County Surveyor To run the Lines as I Know Scott so well that I am Certain He will not give it up—Scott has dispossed Hitt and is about Puting in a nother Tenant as I am now Told.[1] I have distressed Sundrie Tenants of yours in that County as I discovered that they were doing Contrary To Justice and your Interest. One Abner Grigg has behaved Very Ill—should He Ever appear I wish you To remember him—He run away I Followed him four or five days—after I Took Him—He since has gone back To the Lott and Sayes He will stay in defiance To you or any One Else. This Fellow Should be made and Example off To deter others.[2] Several of the Tenants got of[f] but as they were worth nothing I thought it useless To Pursue them I have Taken every Step Consistant with my Knowledge For your Interest as well as the Tenants—matters will be better Known when I come down in april—The Butter I Send down I have directed my waggoner To Take To Mr Wales, I am happy you are Supplyed as I was unneasey Least you should have suffered for that article and a Promise I always hold sacred the disapointment hapned by the waggone Failing to go the Trip and Lodged the butter on the road so that it was out of my Power to Convey it down Sooner. At the Time you wrote me Last Fall in consequence of Cloverseed I was so Fearfull of your being disapointed that I Purchased four bushels of Mr Roper—Mannager for Mr Wormley for which I Paid him £16 Cash—you had one bushel @ £5. The rest Falls on my hands but I expect To sell it next month—if you will Take the whole you shall have it at the price it Cost me—if a Less Quantity the price is £5 ℔ bushel—as To it's not being good I am unable To determin I have bought great Quantities from Mr Roper and I never heard any Complaints before. I always give from £4 To £5 ℔ bushel their is none in this Country but what I have—in my opinion their is a greater risk in Purchaseing Imported seed[3]—I shall be glad To hear from you soon Least I should Loose a Markett for what I have. I am Honourable Sir your Obedient Humble Servant

Battaile Muse

ALS, DLC:GW.
1. See note 1 in GW's letter of 5 January.
2. See Muse to GW, 12 Jan., n.1.
3. See GW to Muse, 5 Jan., n.3.

From Patrick Henry

Dear sir.   Richmond Jan. 18th 1786

Mr Oliver Pollock will have the Honor of delivering you this; & as he begs to be gratify'd in once seeing you, I take the Liberty of introducing him to you.[1]

Mr Wm Ronald who is a Delegate of considerable Weight in the House, & who was one of the Veiwers of the Ground most proper for the Canal from Eliza. River to Albemarle Sound, was fully impressed with the Utility & Importance of the Scheme— And in order to save him & the other Friends of it some Trouble, a Bill for establishing it was drawn & put into his Hands. He introduced it, & it had two Readings & was committed early in the Session. The Wife of that Gentleman dying at the Time, he was absent for near two Months; during which the Business has been totally neglected, notwithstanding repeated Intimations of its high Importance. Mr Ronald is now just returned, but I fear too late to do any thing effectual; & probably the Appointment of a Commissioner to communicate with one from Carolina on the Subject, will be the utmost that can now be done.[2]

More than one hundred Laws have been enacted at this Session, few of which can lay Claim to the public Regard so properly, as an Act on the Subject I allude to. What Pity that the three great Objects you mention, of internal Improvement, could not go on Hand in Hand to Completion! I beg Leave to assure you of the High Regard & Veneration with which I ever am dear sir your obedient humble Servant

P. Henry

ALS, DLC:GW.

1. Oliver Pollock (c.1737–1823), a native of northern Ireland who became a successful trader in New Orleans before the Revolution, arrived at Mount Vernon on Saturday, 28 January.

2. For the legislative action taken on the proposal to build the Elizabeth River Canal through the Great Dismal Swamp, see Henry to GW, 11 Nov. 1785, n.2.

From Battaile Muse

Honourable Sir,   Berkeley County Jay 18th 1786

Some Time ago you wrote me you had a desire To Know who was in Possession of your Lands I here inclose a state of your Tenaments in the Counties of Fauquier & Loudoun Fulley—the State of the Berkeley Tenants I Left with you in October Last[1]— I expect that I shall do Every thing To the utmost of my Abilities for you untill april Next at which Time I expect I shall be able To Convince you that I have discharged the Trust you have Put into my hands—many things I am not able To do under Certain Circumstances altho you have Pointed out a method. its Very True your method is write, but still I am To Consider that I may have and acct To settle with your Executors or you with mine, when accts so Complicated as mine may appear under settlement so Circumstanced as your accts are. My small Estate as well Family may be Involved with Troubles and Loss and after all the accts not appear Properly authenticated—nevertheless I shall Take care To do all I can—and will not Neglect or omitt any thing that I can do in safety To my Self—I have done much business but none To Equal yours[2]—Mr Lemarts accts appear strange To me and Cannot be Settled with any Certainty—⟨I⟩ Find by His accts that He has paid a Considerable Sum for Taxes and has no receipts—I have Congectured that it may be, that you have Taken up the Sheriffs receipts Prior to His Settlement, if so, it Will be Necessary for me To have a Coppy of those receipts To Prevent the Sheriff from Imposing on you, as I Know they make many Erours in their Favour. I have Taken a Coppy of Mr Lemarts accts of the money He received From the Tenants in order To detect Forged Receipts should any be offered.[3] it's a Misfortune that His acct has no dates—and the number of Transfers that has Taken Place may Ocation wrong Credits where receipts are given without Paying any regard to the Lotts on which Such receipts should Specifie—you will Find in some part of my Informations herein you are abused by your Tenants and with such it's my Humble opinion that they should be Called To acct but in april you may be more Perticularly Informed.

The bearer Mr Daniel McPherson Informs me that you received from Him the Sum of £27.12.0 which He meant Should go To the Credit of Lott No. 18—which Lott He Purchased and Expects To have a Lease for the Same on the Terms of three Lives—He applys To me in consequence of a Lease and Produces your receipt—which receipt Specifies that, that Sum is to go to the Credit of Lemart—and not To the Credit of Lott No. 18 It's difficult for me To determine what To do the Lott has never been Legally Leased and now Claimed by Mr Danl McPherson I do not Know what is the annual rent therefore I cannot Tell what is due on the Lott—He sayes He will Pay all the ba⟨ck⟩ rents if He can get a Lease on a reasonable cost for three Lives which is His business down. Please To advise me on the Subject as I wish the Lott not To Lay Idle[4]—I shall Visit those Lands the first of next month to see what can be done for the present year—I have advertised the Vacant Lotts—as I write in a hurry and in Confused Company I have Confidence your goodness will Look over any Imperfectness and Take me To be your Faithfull Obedient Humble Servant

Battaile Muse

ALS, DLC:GW.

1. Muse's statement regarding GW's tenants has not been found.

2. For Muse's role as collector of GW's rents, see GW to Muse, 18 Sept. 1785, and notes.

3. See GW to Muse, 18 Sept. 1785, n.3.

4. Daniel McPherson was at Mount Vernon on 5 January. He rented lot 18 in Fauquier for only one year. See Lists of Tenants, 18 Sept. 1785, n.25.

From Armand

Dear General   la Rouerie 20th January 1786

Since I can not be of any service to your exellency, I look upon the circumstances which apologize for the liberty I take to remind me to you, as thoses happy events in life which make it dear to us; a line from you would be a blessing for the heart of armand, I may Say, of your armand, for he feel more than ever that he is yours.

I am married & that is the event from which I draw the liberty of writing to your Exellency; I have married a good, agreeable & very amiable girl, of what they call in this country a very good house; she brings me a state mixt with my own which is at least equal to mine,[1] thus I find myself at the head of a state of fifty thousend livre's incomb, but the capers of my youth & my Expences in america have loaded a little that handsome state with debts; however they are far from being an obstruction to a very good living & even to our reasonable pleasures; but it is not in our power to be *à la mode* in respect to all the *french* Capricio, who being established on a nonsensical basis, Bring nothing else for interest but nonsensical diversion; in one word, we are a very easy americain's couple & if ever the choice of humane's beings, our great washington, was to honour our abode with his presence, our hearts warmed with a divine fire would make of us the first people of france.

there is not a week but some one or others are asking me, with the most important periphrases why your Exellency does not Come to france; I never answer the first question, but on the recidivation of the Examiner, I answer allways by a Sentence of mine, viz., *perfect great men love to be among wise people* and then I turn about, not without Scratching a little my head, as a token of my Sorrow to have not the privilege of perfect great men— we are allways Expecting the promotion, at which time I will be myself at the head of a handsome regiment of chasseurs half horses, half infantery, but, dear general, who shall be at the head of the whole of us; good god, Sir, when this thought come in to my head, I regret some of our handsome french women had not some ten year ago a private conference with your Exellency; the fruits of such conference might have been a good general now; but as things are going this way, our embition must confine itself to have children who can well carry the fire-lock and kill as fast as they can.

there is no mention of war at present, in this country but that perpetual one which rich people make to the poors; the former have more Succe's than ever, & I who insist allways on knowing the why of things, I have found out that having added to their natural power the art of steeling, which they are at hand to do with much more perfection than the poors to whom the right of robbery seem naturally more allowed, they Squeeze the very soul of thoses last, who after having dropt all her bloud in their pockets drop down herself & never move again.

I have Just wrote to Congress for the payement of the interest of the sums due to us—last year it has been payed with punctuality; but this year, far from punctuality, it is not payed at all; I hope that my lettre to Congress will have at least that effect of reminding them their engagement with us; & I have that great Confidence in them, to believe that nothing else is Nécéssary to bring in activity their princples of honour as representatives of the first republique of the world and zealous lovers of the repu- tation & interest of their Country—if with Conveniency to you, your Exellency Could mention the matter to that hoble Body, I do not doubt but it would have a very favorable effect.[2] permit, me dear general, to request here Madame washington to accept the homage of my best respect—I have the honor to be with the highest degree of that sentiment your Exellency's Most obedt hble servant

Armand Mqs de la Rouerie

ALS, DLC:GW.

1. On 22 Dec. 1785, in the chateau of Saint-Brice-en-Cogles, Armand (Charles Armand-Tuffin, marquis de La Rouërie) was married "avec très haute et très puissante demoiselle Louise-Caroline Guérin, dame-marquise de Saint-Brice de Champinel, baronne des baronnies de Sens et de lu Châtière, châte-laine des châtellenies de Saint-Etienne, la Fontaine-la-Chaise, Parigné, de Sol-lier, le Rocher-Portail, et autres lieux" (Lasseray, *Sous les treize étoiles*, 1:151).

2. In his letter to the president of Congress, dated 18 Jan. 1786, requesting payment of what was owed to him and the other officers of Armand's Legion, Armand also wrote: "The Gentlemen who desire me to write on the Subject of this lettre to the hoble the Congress, request me alsso to mention their rights to the lands promised to them in proportion of their several ranks—although my fortune does not want an addition of that nature, it is too flattering for my heart to have a property in a Country for Ever dear to him, for me not to claim here my share" (DNA:PCC, item 164). GW's response is dated 10 Aug. 1786.

To Gardoqui

Sir,   Mount Vernon 20th Jany 1786.

The letter which your Excellency did me the favor to write to me on the first of this month does me great honor: the senti- ments which you have been pleased to entertain of my conduct are very flattering; and the friendly manner in which they are expressed is highly pleasing. To meet the approbation of a gen- tleman whose good wishes were early engaged in the American cause, & who has attended to its progress thro' the various stages of the revolution, must be considered as a happy circumstance for me; & I shall seek occasionally to testify my sense of it.

With much truth, I repeat the assurances offered to your Excellency thro' Mr renden, of the pleasure I should have in seeing you at my Seat in this State, that I might express personally to you, how sensibly I feel for the proposed honor of your correspondence, & pray you to offer in such terms as you know would be most acceptable & proper, my gratitude to His Catholic Majesty, for his royal present to me—than which nothing could have been more flattering or valuable. With much esteem, respect & consideration I have the honor to be &c.

G: Washington

LB, DLC:GW.

To James Mercer

Dr Sir,   Mt Vernon 20th Jany 1786.

I have been favored with your letter of the 10th inst: with its inclosures the last are returned signed.[1] I also send you a copy of the courses of the Lotts purchased by yourself & me at the sale of your brother's Land, & shall thank you for the conveyances which are necessary to secure the legal right to those which I hold.[2]

I am sorry to hear that you still continue indisposed—you have my best wishes for a speedy & perfect recovery of your health, & with sentimts of sincere esteem & regard, I am Dr Sir &c.

G: Washington

P.S. A few days ago I receeived under cover, several copies of the inclosed proposals from the Author; one of which has obtained a good many subscribers in Alexa. I use the freedom of sending a copy to you, that in case yourself & friends in & about Fredericksburgh should incline to become subscribers to the work, an opportunity may be furnished. As the Doctr, it is to be presumed, will look to me for a return of the number committed to my charge, I shall be glad to receive the enclosed when you shall find it convenient & proper, so as to be ready for his call. I have only to pray that the conditions may be complied with respecting the advance, as I would not incline to have any thing more to do in the business, after the subscription papers are returned.[3]

G: W——n

LB, DLC:GW.

1. Letter not found, and its enclosures have not been identified.

2. For the sale conducted by GW in 1774 of George Mercer's American property and for GW's purchase of two of the lots in Mercer's tract on the Shenandoah River in Frederick County, see GW to John Tayloe, 30 Nov. 1774, to Edward Snickers, 4 Sept. 1784, and to Battaile Muse, 28 July 1785, n.1.

3. William Gordon wrote GW on 28 Nov. 1785 that he expected "the proposals for the History of the American Revolution, will be circulated through the United States by the first week in January." Gordon's printed "Proposals for printing by Subscription" his *History*, dated 1 Dec. 1786, begins: "The writer, in the beginning of 1776, made known his intention to his Excellency the late Commander in Chief of the American Army, and, meeting with desired encouragement, applied himself to collecting materials for the history" (DNA:PCC, item 78). Gordon's letter covering the copies of the prospectus that he sent to GW has not been found, but GW wrote Gordon on 20 April reporting on what success he had had in securing subscriptions to Gordon's proposed history and forwarded him £42. See also Gordon to GW, 4 February.

Letter not found: from Thomas Newton, 20 Jan. 1786. On 9 April GW wrote Newton: "I have been favored with your letter of the 20th of Jany."

From David Pearce

Sir   Gloucester [Mass.] January 22d 1786

I am very sorry that I should so mis the freight of the Jackass—I made enquiry & was told that the freight of an horse from London was equal to a Cabin passinger but may it please your Excellency to settle that part as you please; with respect to the house the Captain says that he did pay twenty five & an half Dollars for the building of it which he has charged me & the Groom is charged as a sterige passinger. I am sorry that I happened to err in the above or any way else, as I take a peculiar pleasure to due my best services and ever shall when ever your Excellency shall please to put it in my power. you will please to settle it with our friend Mr Hartshorne to your own liking and I assure you that it will be to mine.[1] I remain your most obedient & humble Servant

David Pearce

ALS, DLC:GW.
1. For the account that Pearce presented to GW through William Hartshorne & Co., and for references to GW's objections to the account, see note
1 in Hartshorne & Co. to GW, 26 Nov. 1785.

From George William Fairfax

My Dear Sir   Bath 23d Jany 1786.

Being but just now informed that a Vessell is to Sail in a very few days from Bristol for Baltimore Town, I have only time to say, that I have received your favor dated the 30th of June last, and that I immediately applyed to Mr Rack, the Secretary to the Bath Agriculture Society (who corresponds with most of the Societys in this Kingdom) for his friendly assistance in makeing the enquiry for such Farmers as you describe, upon which he was so good as to write to several Gentn upon the subject, particularly to Arthur Young Esqr. who lives in that part of the Island, where it's agreed that Agriculture is brought to the greatest profection, to which you'l receive that Gentns answer.[1] And that I in the mean time have lost no opportunity in prosecuting the same enquiry, and have had some offers, not altogether answering your description, or my approbation. But the bearer James Bloxham (being determined at all Events to go with his Wife and family to America to try their fortune) tho not Competent to all you want, yet he is so strongly recommended by one of our best Gentn Farmers, with whom he has lived 15 years, that I have taken the liberty to direct Bloxham to wait upon you in the first instance, that you may talk to him upon the subject, and be at Liberty to agree or not as you may then think proper. Mr Peacey thinks he will answer any Persons purpose, as a hard working Servant, capable of Ploughing, Sowing, Hedging, Ditching, Shearing, Mulling and Brewing for a family, particularly attentive to Stock, and not inferior to any Man he knows in Thatching of Houses and Barns. in a word, he is in his degree the best I have heard of. insomuch (and in hopes he may be a usefull Member of the community) that I have wrote to Mr Muse to let him have any vacant Lot of mine in Case he should not be employed by you, untill he can look about him, for it seems by his Industry & Care, he has saved upwards of three hundred pounds Sterling, part of which must go for their Passage and the remainder will be lodged in Mr Peaceys hand, to answer his drafts.[2] We shall be still dilligent in our enquiries, and shall from time to time communicate our success, or not, that you may determine how to direct. I have applyed and wrote to several Gentn to make enquiry for a skilful Engineer of practical knowledge in inland Navigation. I have also spared no pains to procure You a Male and Female Deer of the best kind, and have the promise of such from two places, not so convenient for Shiping as I could wish. the surest way of conveying them would be from Bristol, directed to the Care of my friend Mr Benj. Pollard at Norfolk, but I should prefer the Potomack Planter, or any Ship from London going to Alexandria or George Town and not improbable, but Mr T: Fairfax may return in the same, who I dare say would pay some attention to them, and I will endeavour to Plan accordingly.[3]

Mrs Fairfax joins me in most Affectionate regards and every good wish for you and good Mrs Washington, and am with much truth My Dear Sir, Your most Obedt and Obliged humble Servant

Go: Wm: Fairfax

Pray let me know by the very first Opportunitys the utmost Wages you are willing to give for a ski[ll]ful Farmer, and to find him Bed & Board, for We know that its impossible for such a one to supply himself in our Country as they can here.

Having this Evening allowed me, I cannot let this Letter go without saying how much I am vexed, that I should have wrote so unintelligibly in regard to Tom Corbin, nothing being further from my intention than imposing any of that Family upon you. As I did not explain my meaning, give me leave, my Dear Sir, to say that Mr Athawes and the Sollicitor that was employed in the Corbin Cause, before whom all the prooffs came, assured me that Dick had vexed his Brother in the cruelest and most unjust manner, and that Toms character was very unjustly aspersed in those transactions. Mr Athawes, my particular Friend urged, and even insisted that I should write to you upon the subject, least it should get to your Ear, supposing it would be a great point gained if you was informed of matters of fact, and would only say a word in defence of the greatly opprest, and misrepresented, if the subject should be broached in your presence. In vain did I refuse troubling you upon that affair. Athawes & Corbin came from London to my House to obtain that Letter. nor would they take a denial, or quit me without it. three days I possitively refused, but being convinced of the truth of what I wrote, I was prevailed upon, and beg Pardon for taking the liberty. You must blame yourself, for having made your Character so conspicuously great and good. you can hardly suppose how many inconveniences, having the honor of being known to you, draw me into by applications for Letters of introduction. my refusal has already given great offence to the Parties and their friends. One would actually suppose that a Letter to You was to make the Fortune of all that go to any part of America by their importuning.[4]

At present there Exists the most extraordinary Contest upon the above point. The Son of a very worthy Gentn of this City is shortly to be sent by the Commissioners for distributing the Money given by Parliament for the Refugees, to enquire into the legality of their very Exorbitant Claims. One of the Commissioners, Captain Robert Mackenzie who you must remember, applyed to me in behalf of the young Gentn (who by the way bears an excellent Character) for a Letter to you.[5] I possitively refused, tho' assured that He had Letters from Mr Adams our Ambassador at this Court, to Congress, Dr Franklin &ca. The young Gentn came the next day, his Father and at length his amiable Mother to intreat my Wife, but I was steady, feeling myself quite Sore upon the subject of introduction. Could you believe, that after all, they sent Colo. Hunter, our old Friend & acquaintance, who has been our very obliging Neighbour ever since we lived here, and He made it such a Point of friendship, that I could not be off without a quarrel, or at least an affront. therefore this is preparative to your receiving a few lines by the hand of Mr Ansty himself, but do assure you I will not repeat it, when it is possible to decline it. Before I quit this head, it may not be amiss to inform, that the Father of Mr Anstey is a Man of Fortune with a numerous family of Children, but more Conspicuous for Science in the Literal Circle. He is a steady friend to the Liberties of Mankind, and always execrated the American War. The old Gentn also assures me, that his Sons business is entirely divested of all Political matter, and only wishes to make himself as agreable to the States as possible in the private capacity. I have my good Sir been thus Elaborate, that it may be clear to your judgment, and you'l treat the Letter I am compeled to give as you think proper.[6] Adieu my Dear Sir. God bless and preserve you in health, with every enjoyment of life. Yours Go: Wm Fx

ALS, DLC:GW.

1. Edmund Rack (c.1735–1787), the son of a Quaker weaver, became a man of letters and in about 1775 settled in Bath where he participated in the founding of both an agricultural and a philosophical society. On 3 Oct. 1785, in Bath, Rack wrote Fairfax: "I am sorry I was not at home when thou didst me the favour of calling on Saturday last; but I that Morning Accompanied the Earl of Winchelsea [George Finch-Holton, 8th earl of Winchilsea] to Dine & spend the day at our Friend Billingsleys. In reply to thy Application on behalf of General Washington I do not at present know of any person that I could safely recommend to fill either of the stations he describes. I have however written this day to Arthur Young, & a Gentleman in Essex on that business; And flatter my Self One of them will be likely to succeed on these Enquiries; as I wish to procure persons from the East rather than the West, as Agriculture is Carried on there in a manner much superior to what it is with us. As soon as I hear from either of them I will inform thee" (ALS, DLC:GW).

Rack wrote to Fairfax again on 16 Oct. enclosing this letter to himself from Arthur Young at Bradfield Hall, dated 12 Oct. 1785: "Dear Sir[,] I should have acknowledgd your favour before but was prevented by the misfortune of the death of a mother I tenderly loved—and at present I am little able to do more than tell yo. I recd it.

"I should think I might find a proper bailiff for General Washington, but without knowing the salary & other circumstances that will be given, it will be very difficult & uncertain[.] You should advise his friend to write for instructions. I conceive that a proper Suffolk one will demand (for going so far) 50 Guineas a year, a house[,] fuel, a garden and a hog & a Cow kept, if he has no board but if he has board & washing found 35 Guineas.

"It will be the generals best way to have a bailiff Simply, & then by degrees make him a steward[.] If hired for a steward at first then an idea of being at his table he will ask exorbitantly, & soon prove good for nothing. I am very glad to find the General is a farmer—a pro pos, will you favour me with the direction to some proper person to whom I can send a parcel for General Washington as I will desire his acceptance of a set of my Annals.

"I will certainly Send you a memoir for the next Vol. Being with great Truth & esteem Yr obedt & Devoted St A. Young

"Unavoidable business postponed my Tour till another summer" (DLC:GW).

A third letter from Rack to Fairfax, dated 27 Dec. 1785, covered this letter of 24 Dec. to Rack from William Peacey (Peacy) at Northleach recommending James Bloxham: "The bearer is James Bloxham whome I recomend to Sarve Genal Washington. he is come for his recomendation from The Honbl. G. Fairfax Esqr. Plase to read Genrl Washington Letter to him, he can plow and

Sow rape and Mow Make Ricks and Thatch both Ricks and Bildings. make Malt, hedg & Ditch. Plant hedges. he is an Exceeding good Judge in bying and Seling of Cattle. he is a good Judg in the maniageing of all kinds of Stock from thair Breeding up to the Slaughter. I cannot Say to much of his abilaties in the above Bisness. I never yet knew one to Equal him, he have Sarvd me fiveteene years Faithfolly. he is a Indostrioues man & have Aquiered the Sum of £400 by his Indostry" (ALS, DLC:GW).

All of these letters were enclosed in Fairfax's letter to GW, all are now in DLC:GW, and all appear in CD-ROM:GW.

2. James Bloxham arrived at Mount Vernon from England on 21 April 1786 to become GW's "Farmer and Manager" at a salary of fifty guineas a year (*Diaries*, 4:315; Articles of Agreement with James Bloxham, 31 May 1786). Fairfax's letter to Battaile Muse of this date about Bloxham is in ViHi. See also GW to Fairfax, 20 June 1785.

3. For GW's inquiries about securing an English engineer for the Potomac River Company and English deer for Mount Vernon, see his letter to Fairfax of 27 Feb. 1785. Thomas Fairfax (1762–1846), Bryan Fairfax's oldest son, wrote to GW on 30 June 1786 after his return from England, and he spent the night of 21 July at Mount Vernon.

4. For the affair of the Corbin brothers, see Fairfax to GW, 19 Mar. 1785, and GW to Fairfax, 30 June 1785, 25 June 1786.

5. GW and Robert McKenzie, who served as a captain in GW's Virginia Regiment during the French and Indian War, had an interesting exchange of letters when McKenzie was an officer in the British forces occupying Boston in 1774 (McKenzie to GW, 13 Sept. 1774, GW to McKenzie, 9 Oct. 1774).

6. Fairfax's letter introducing John Anstey is dated 25 January. Colonel Hunter is probably Col. John Hunter with whom GW and Fairfax had particular dealings when GW was colonel of the Virginia Regiment in the 1750s (see George Mann to GW, 21 Aug. 1755, n.1). Literal as opposed to numerical "Science" is the performing of mathematical notation and computation by means of letters rather than numbers, i.e., algebra.

From John Marsden Pintard

Sir   Madeira 24th January[–5 February] 1786.

A few days ago I was honoured with your Excellency's favour of the 18th November Acknoledging receipt of mine of 19th August last. The Esteem Your Excellency is Pleased of Express for my father and the very Polite Manner of Conveying your Congratulations to me on my Appointment with your Wishes for my Success are highly flattering to me. More Particularly So as Coming from So Great a Charecter ⟨as⟩ the One to whome (Under the direction of Providence) ⟨my⟩ Country is Indebted for the Blessings of her Independency.

We have been Pestered by four Moorish Corsairs off here two of which have Actualy Anchored in the road of funchall. but from the Precautions I took in having Boats off to give Intelligence of them—three Americans Vessels got In safe and Escaped these Pirates. They have however now left us, I hope never to return; If some method is not Pursued to satisfy these Pests of mankind I am affraid our Commerce will greatly suffer.

Agreeable to your excellencys request I now send the vine slips and the young fig as Pr enclosed list.[1] The vessell they go in Touches at the Cape de Verd, but as there are So Seldom direct opportunities and this being the Proper Season for Sending them I have taken that liberty Especialy as the Capt. has Promissed to take the Greatest care[.] Should they miscarry or any Accident befall them on your Excellency's Informing me they shall be Imediately replaced. In mean time should any direct opportunity offer I will send So⟨me⟩ others which I have ready Put up in earth. It will Allways give me Pleeasure (exclusive of the Honour Confered on Me by it) to execute Your Excellency's Commands and should you wish a Supply of wine from this you may depend on my Greatest Care in the choice of its quality. It gives me Pleasure to find that the House of my Relations Messrs John Searle & Co. of this Place have formerly been honoured with your orders for that Comodity. they as well as myselfe will be happy for the Continuation of that Honour and endeavour to give the greatest satisfaction I cannot but observe that I should be hurt at Seeing Your Excellency Supply'd with wine by any other House on the Island being the only American here and Surrounded by those who are far from well wishers to America. It wd be a satisfaction to me to be taken notice of by my Country men.[2] Wishing your Excellency evry ⟨degry⟩ of health and happiness I have the Honour to Subscribe myselfe Your Excellency's Most obedient Humble Servant

John Marsden Pintard

ALS, DLC:GW; ALS, duplicate, DLC:GW. The letters in angle brackets are taken from the duplicate copy; both are endorsed by GW.

1. The enclosures include the receipt of Capt. James Gibson, dated at Funchal on 24 Jan. 1786, followed by Pintard's list. The receipt reads: "Received of Mr J. M. Pintard on board the Brig Industry myselfe master two Barrells and two half Barrells containing Some Slips of grape vines and fig tree which

are to be delivered to his Excellency General Washington at Mount Vernon State of Virginia."

The list reads:

"No. 1. Fine malmsey Grape

No. 2. Fine verdelha and Muscatell do

No. 3. a delicious white fig—

No. 4. a Black fig."

The Verdelho grape is a warm-climate white variety, sometimes known as Vidonia.

2. GW had ordered the Madeira wine from John Searle & Co. most recently in 1783, but he first dealt with John Searle in 1763 as agent in Madeira of the wine merchants Mayne, Burn, & Mayne. See John Searle & Co. to GW, 3 April, 15 July 1783, GW to John Searle & Co., 21 May 1783, and GW to John and James Searle, 30 April 1763. At the bottom of the copy of this letter, Pintard wrote: "The preceeding is copy of what I had the Honour of writing you on the 24th Ultimo per the Industry Capt. James Gibson by Whome I forwarded the vine Slips &c. a list of which with their Qualities you have at bottom[.] I was Sorry that the vessell they went by did not go direct but as they were carefully put Up I hope they will arrive in good order. nothing material occuring at present. I have the Honour to Subscribe myself Sir your Excellencys most obedient and very Humble Servant John Marsden Pintard." He headed this "Madeira 5th February 1786." Pintard also lists the items that he sent (see note 1).

From George William Fairfax

My Dear Sir   Bath 25th January 1786.

This will I hope be presented to you by John Anstey Esqr. in his Tour through America. He goes upon particular business with the *approbation* of our Ambassador Mr Adams from whom he has Letters to Congress, Doctor Franklin &c.

Mr Ansteys Father is a very worthy Gentleman of Fortune in this City, no Person more respected, and what must be allowed to be a recommendation *to Us*, he always Execrated the American War. It is with pleasure, I assure you that the young Gentn bears an excellent Character, and is much esteemed by all that know his worth, it is his wish to make himself agreable in America, and as his good Father assures me, his only object is *ascertaining* the Claims of the Refugees. I may with Propriety request that He may meet with the favorable reception. I belive he merits as a private Gentn from You, and every respectable

Person in Virginia.[1] I am with great regard, Dear Sir Your Affect: and most Obedient Humble Servant

Go: Wm Fairfax

ALS, DLC:GW. In the dateline Fairfax wrote what appears to be 25d, and GW dockets it 25, not 23, January.

John Anstey (d. 1819), son of Christopher Anstey (1724–1815) of Bath, visited Mount Vernon on 11–12 Dec. 1786 en route to Charleston, S.C., in his capacity as a member of the Commission for Enquiry into the Losses, Services, and Claims of the American Loyalists (*Diaries*, 5:77).

1. John Jay wrote GW from New York on 20 Oct. 1786 introducing Anstey: "Travellers who have judgment to direct their curiosity will in passing thro' the United States, naturally prefer the Road which leads by Mont Vernon. Mr. Anstey purposes, in his way to Carolina, to pay you his respects; and I introduce him, without appologizing for that liberty, from a Persuasion that it will give pleasure to both. Handsome things are said of him, in his own country & in this and as far as my observations extends, his conduct & manners join with me in recommending him to your friendly attention" (Batchelder catalog, no. 11, item 73).

Letter not found: to Battaile Muse, 27 Jan. 1786. Muse wrote GW on 20 Feb.: "Your Favour by Daniel McPherson dated January The 27th Last I received."

From Robert Morris

Dear Sir   Philad[elphi]a Jany 28th 1786

I did intend to save you the trouble of sending up the ten Dollars advanced to Jno. Fairfax on your Account & for that purpose took his draft on you for that Sum & remitted it to Messrs Josiah Watson & Co. from whom I have received it back at my own request & herein transmit the same with a receipt on it.[1]

Whatever belongs to, or is connected with you, will ever meet attention from me. Mrs Morris joins me in thanks to Mrs Washington & yourself with assurances of the Warmest reciprocal good wishes for hers & your Health & happiness. I am with sincere attachmt Dear Sir Your most obedt Servt

Robt Morris

ALS, DLC:GW.

1. The enclosed receipt from John Fairfax (DLC:GW) is dated 29 Nov. 1785, when Fairfax passed through Philadelphia en route from Massachusetts to Mount Vernon with the Spanish jackass.

From Robinson, Sanderson, & Rumney

Sir   W[hit]ehaven [England] Jany 28th 1786.

By the Ship Esther Captn Ledger you will receive your Flags, which we hope may Arrive safe and Answer the intended purpose, There are 1400 Flags which the Mason thinks sufficient to lay the Floor, They are packd with Straw & have not a doubt they will go safe from Breakage, as every care was taken to have them well pack'd.[1] We should be glad to hear they answer your Expectation, and are on all Occasions Sir Your most obt Hble Servts

Robinson, Sanderson & Rumney

LS, DLC:GW.

1. An enclosed bill indicates charges of £43.15 for the tiles at 7½ pence per tile, with other charges including the packing bringing the total cost to £46.13. For GW's dealings with John Rumney, Jr., to obtain flagstones from abroad for his gallery, or piazza, at Mount Vernon, see GW to John Rumney, Jr., 3 July 1784, and the references in note 1 of that document.

To Clement Biddle

Dear Sir,   Mount Vernon Jany 30th 1786

I embrace the good & safe oppertunity afforded me by Colo. Grayson to send you Ten half Johan[ne]s—the application of which shall be the subject of a Letter by the Post, when I have more leizure to write—not being able to mention the purposes for which they are intended at this time[1]—With much truth I am Dr Sir Yr Obedt Hble Servt

Go: Washington

ALS, PHi: Washington-Biddle Correspondence. The letter was "Hon[ore]d by Colo. [William] Grayson."

1. GW sent Biddle his order for goods on 10 February. Biddle wrote an account on the cover sheet of GW's letter showing an expenditure of £37.12.6 for GW between August 1785 and 19 Mar. 1786 as opposed to payments from GW of £47.5, leaving him owing GW £9.17.6. In Ledger B, 207, for 28 Jan.

1786 there is the entry: "By Colo. Biddle, Sent by Colo. Grierson [Grayson], 10 H[alf] Jo[hanne]s—[£]24."

To John Francis Mercer

Dr Sir,   Mount Vernon 30th Jany 1786

The letter which you dropped for me at Alexandria I have received. If you can make it convenient to lodge the money in the hands of any person at that place, it would oblige me. I lie quite out of the line of opportunities to Annapolis—and to send there on purpose, would cost me 2½, or perhaps 5 prCt to fetch it.[1]

If Mr Pine, the Portrait Painter, should still be at Annapolis (which is scarcely to be expected) you would oblige me by paying him Twenty Guineas, and Sixteen dollars; and his receipt, for these sums, will be equal to that much of the £200 promised me. If he should have left Annapolis, I will remit the money to him myself.[2]

Mrs Washington joins me in compliments to Mrs Mercer— We shall always be glad to see you both at this place on your rout to or from Annapolis. My best respects attend Mr Spriggs family I am—Dr Sir Yr Obedt Hble Servt

Go: Washington

ALS, PHi: Dreer Collection; LB, DLC:GW.

1. Mercer's letter has not been found. See GW to Mercer, 20 Dec. 1785, n.1.

2. For Robert Edge Pine's painting of the portraits of GW and his family at Mount Vernon, see Francis Hopkinson to GW, 19 April 1785, and GW to Hopkinson, 16 May 1785, and notes. In his cash accounts, GW has this entry on 27 Jan. 1786: "By R: Pyne, Pd him the 19th May 1785 Omitted to be charg'd £28.0.0" (Ledger B, 207). Pine himself left Mount Vernon on 19 May, but his portraits of Martha Washington's niece, Fanny Bassett Washington, and of the four Custis grandchildren were not delivered to Mount Vernon until 31 Dec. 1785 (*Diaries*, 4:129–31, 258). Not having a response from Mercer, GW on 26 Feb. wrote to Pine acknowledging the receipt of the pictures and enclosing "Twenty guineas & sixteen Dollars; the first for balance due on the pictures— the latter for their frames." This he sent by William Hunter (GW to Hunter, 27 Feb. 1786).

To James Rumsey

Sir,   Mount Vernon 31st Jan: 1786.

If you have no cause to change your opinion respecting your mechanical Boat, & reasons unknown to me do not exist to delay the exhibition of it, I would advise you to give it to the public as soon as it can be prepared, conveniently. The postponement creates distrust in the public mind; it gives time also for the imagination to work, and this is assisted by a little dropping from one, & something from another, to whom you have disclosed the secret: should therefore a mechanical genius hit upon your plan, or something similar to it—I need not add that it would place you in an awkward situation, & perhaps disconcert all your prospects concerning this useful discovery; for you are not, with your experience in life, now to learn that the shoulders of the public are too broad to feel the weight of the complaints of an individual—or to regard promises, if they find it convenient, & have the shadow of plausibility on their side, to retract them. I will inform you further, that many people in guessing at your plan, have come very near the mark; & that one, who had something of a similar nature to offer to the public, wanted a Certificate from me that it was different from yours. I told him, that as I was not at liberty to declare what your plan was, so I did not think it proper to say what it was not.[1]

Whatever may be your determination after this hint, I have only to request that my sentiments on the subject may be ascribed to friendly motives, & taken in good part.

I should be glad to know the exact state in which my houses at Bath are. I have fifty pounds ready, for which you may draw on me at any time; & I will settle for the whole as soon as possible.

Herewith you will receive a Magazine containing the estimates of the expence of the Canal in Scotland. It belongs to Mr Johnson who requested me to forward it to you after I had read it— to him you will be pleased to return the book when you are done with it.[2] With esteem & regard I am Sir &c.

G: Washington

LB, DLC:GW.

1. For GW's earlier dealings with Rumsey regarding his mechanical boat, see Certificate for James Rumsey, 7 Sept. 1784, Rumsey to GW, 10 Mar. 1785,

and GW to Rumsey, 5 June 1785. GW is referring to John Fitch (1743–1796) who made such an inquiry when he stopped at Mount Vernon en route to Richmond to promote his scheme for a steam-driven vessel (*Diaries*, 4:218–19).

2. The magazine, which undoubtedly belonged to Thomas Johnson, has not been identified.

From Rochambeau

My Dear Général   Paris January the [   ]
I but receive now the letter Which you honoured me With on September the 7th ultimo. I Send at once to Captain Pusignan your answer, and I hope you Will be henceforth got clear from all those troublesome askings.

I am Enchanted of the continuation of your good health, of the calm that you are enjoing in the bosom of your family, and under the Shadow of your Laurels.

The Storms Which threatened us on the account of holland are Entirely dissipated, and the france as yet played, in this occasion, the fine part of moderatrix—The troubles for the succession of Bavaria Shall yet threaten us at the death of the Elector of Bavaria, or at that of the King of Prussia of Whom the health is old and reeling—he is at the head of a formidable confederation to hinder the Exchange to Which the Emperor has not renounced When the circumstances will permit it to him.

our Neighbours the English retrieve their finances, the young Pitt gets every day a great majority, and a great confidence in his nation by a good and Wise administration and oeconomy—the against part has lost one of its chief members by the nommination of M. Eden in the Station of commissary to make a treaty of commerce With the france, and they believe that the settlement of ireland will be consolidated this Winter.

I have seen Cornwallis last summer at Calais, he Was Sent by the King of England to Wait on the Duc of york, his son, to the instructive camps of the King of prussia. I gave him a supper in little committee: he Was Very polite, but, as you may believe, I could not drink With him your health in ⟨turn.⟩ The English treat us very politely but I think in the bosome of their hearts they do not love us more than they do they americans. I have many invitations from them to go to London, but I am not hurry to profit of it, and I lake better to See them on my hearths than to go and See them on theirs own. they pretend, by their public papers, that they Wait only for the Construction of Some new forts upon their Limits to deliver up to you those Which they have on yours. it is a pretence that you Can better than any body judge of the value.

I am very glad that the respectable and old Docteur franklin has received in his Country the honour that they owe to his Services.

I beg of you, my Dear Général, to present my respects and give my best Compliments to Mad. Washington and to all your family, and be Well persuaded of my Eternal attachment and of the respect With Which I have the honour to be My Dear Général Your most obedient and Very humble servent,

le comte de Rochambeau

LS, DLC:GW. GW dockets the letter January 1786, and its contents confirm it was written in 1786.

From La Luzerne

Sir   Paris 3rd Feby, 1786

Mr Houdon Delivered me the Letter, That Your Excy Honoured me with of the 5th Novr[1] And I have learnd with very great Satisfaction, that you have Enjoyed very good Health, & that you Promise to your Aquaintances a long Life, that has been Glorious, & Usefull to Your Country.

I return Your Excy my Most Sincere thanks for the Accurate Account, you have given me of the Affairs of the United States, & They are of the Same Opinion at Versailles that you are ⟨as to⟩ The Powers, that the Different States, Ought to Grant to Congress, for to enable them, to Regulate Commerce in General; And that Wise, & Prudent Measure Could not assuredly, Do any detriment to their liberty, & the Americans have Spirritt, & to good a knowledge, for not to be Sensible that the Foreign Powers, who are Interested in Commerce with them, could not Possibly Treat with the Thirteen States, Separately, who also having, all different Interests, could not agree, But for the Congress to adopt the General Measures, which alone could enable them, to Conduct it, for the Good of the Republick; I hope that the first News we Receive from America, will Inform us that the Different Assembly's have put the finishing Stroke to this Grand affair.

We are likewise very desirous, that Something decisively could be done upon the Article of Finances. for the Payment of the Publick Debt, or at least for the Int. of that Debt, In the event of the Ground Ceded by Treaty, some of whc. was not Inhabited before the War, They Should find it Insufficient to Satisfy the Creditors; I hope that the Legislators will be of the Same mind, & that they will Seriously think of means, to Clear themselves of it; We agree here to give to the American Trade, all the Assistance, that would be Cappable of Admitting, agreeing with the Interests of Both Nations.

All the Publick News Assure us, that the Forts Situated upon the Lakes & the River St Lawrence will not be given up to the Americans, & That the English, have made it a kind of Compensation for the Pretended Infraction of the Treaty of Peace; I have too good an Opinion of Mr Pitt, for to Believe, that If he had it in his Power, to Decide that dispute, that it would not be in favor of America, But the Minister has found a Party very Powerfull in the Opposition, that he is So much affraid of, that he Cannot follow the Measures, that he Believes reasonable to Propose, Some People Believe that there will be Soon a Change of the British Ministry; The Cabinett of London is full of Dissentions; All Europe is very Tranquille, & the Change of the Barrier whc. has made Such a noise, makes War appear more Distant than ever, It is Probable that the line of Germany (whc. has been the Fruits of Jealousies, that this Bartering was the cause of it) will Produce the Repose of Europe for a long time, The Interior Dissentions of Holland which was the cause of a great Noise in Europe, has not been of very Troublesome Consequences, that State has been at its ease, Since the Treaty with the Emperor, & its alliance Deffensive with France, although the Republican Party & the Stadtholder, appeared very much incensed, it is nevertheless Probable, that they will be reconciled for the good of the Republick.

I hope that Your Excy will in these moments remember, that you have in France, a Servant very much Attached, & who desires very Sincerely to Give Some Dissinterested Proofs, Of the

Perfect Consideration, & of the Respect with which he is Your Excelly Very Hble & Obedt servt

Le Du de le Luzerne

Will Madame Washington, do him the Honour to accept of his Respects.

Translation, DLC:GW; LS, in French, DLC:GW. A transcription of the LS is in CD-ROM:GW.

1. In La Luzerne's letter, this is "le 5 de 7bre"; GW's letter is dated 5 Sept., not November.

From George Augustine Washington

Hond Uncle   Eltham February 3d 1786
    A Letter from You always meets a most joyful reception— Your favor of the 24th of Decr, tho' it had not a speedy convey- ance gave us the latest information, and the most pleasing as it acquainted us that all were well at Mount Vernon[1]—Not having been from this place since the receipt of Your Letter have had but little opportunity of making inquiry relative to its contents— I cannot ascertain that any person in this part of the Country is possess'ed of a She-Ass, the Secretary and General Nelson, are I am informed the most probable persons if they can I doubt not will most readily furnish You, and on terms that will be agre- able—should I succeed in my commission I will with pleasure take it up with me[2]—The Box which was in the hands of Mr Bracken Mr Bassett conceived hazardous to commit to the Stage, as the direction signified that great care was necessary He theirfore brought it to this place, hoping that a safer conveyance might offer—The Box is 2½ feet by 2¼ but I hope to devise some mode of bringing it safe to You[3]—I have not yet finished Copying the Letters, owing to my not having arrived here so soon as I expected and interuptions of Company, but shall be- fore I set out which will be about the end of the month, the weather pe[r]mitting, for I really most anxiously wish to see Mount Vernon again, the affection I have experienced from You and Mrs Washington has render'd it by much the most de- sireable place to me—The friendly invitation I received from You was a most pleasing mark of Your affection and I hoped a

signification of my conduct being approved by You, which will ever be of the first consideration to me and I most ardently hope that my efforts to deserve it, may equal my wishes—my experience in business but illy qu[a]lifys me for embarking in it, but under Your direction and from Your example I flatter myself I shall derive insight, and I must hope that my attention and integrity, will in some degree make amends for my deficiencies[4]— On my arrival at Richmond I found that an act had been past in favor of the discharge of interest Certificates, on all Loan Office Warrants issued by this State, concieving it a mater of consequence supposing that You might be posses'ed of some, wrote You immediately hoping that I should give You timely information as I put the Letter in the hands of Doctr Lamoy, who was setting out for Fredericksburgh, and who promised to give it a speedy conveyance from that place[5]—he also took charge of 4 pr Shoes which I hope got safe—I had no propositions made for my Lot's on my way through Fredericksburg—one of the Letters You forwarded was asking information and proposing a mode of payment which I fear cannot be made agreeable if He should accede to my terms[6]—I am not yet acquainted with Colo. Bassett's intentions, and I hope my conduct will not discover a disposition to be made so it will be my study to make myself agreeable to Him—Fanny joins me in most affectionate love to You Mrs Washington and the dear Children and Compliments to all inquiring friends—Colo. Bassett and the Young Gentlemen also desire to be rememberd[.] with the most refined sentiments I am Hond Uncle Your truely affectionate Nephew

Geo: A. Washington

ALS, ViMtV.

1. Letter not found.

2. For GW's efforts at this time to import from abroad a female ass, see John Fitzgerald to GW, 7 Feb., and notes. No indication has been found that either Secretary Thomas Nelson (1715–1787) or his nephew Gen. Thomas Nelson (1738–1789) supplied a mate for GW's Royal Gift.

3. John Bracken, rector of Bruton Parish Church in Williamsburg, brought back from England in 1784 for GW from George William Fairfax two framed prints in a box, which had not yet been delivered to Mount Vernon. See Fairfax to GW, 10 June 1784, n.1, and 23 Aug. 1784.

4. Before leaving Mount Vernon in December 1785 for his visit to Eltham, George Augustine Washington had accepted GW's offer to become estate man-

ager at Mount Vernon in place of Lund Washington. See the editorial note in Farm Reports, 26 Nov. 1785–15 April 1786.

5. GW had already received payment for his loan certificates in January. See David Stuart to GW, 18 Dec. 1785, n.2. The letter from George Augustine Washington has not been found.

6. See GW to Lund Washington, 20 Nov. 1785, n.1. The forwarded letter may be that of Robert B. Chew to George Augustine Washington, written from Fredericksburg and dated 11 Dec. 1785, in which Chew refers to the advertisement of "your Lotts in Town & Land adjacient for Sale" and asks for the price and terms (ViMtV). For the Fredericksburg lots, see GW to Lund Washington, 20 Nov. 1785, n.1.

From William Gordon

My Dear Sir   Jamaica Plain [Mass.] Feby 4. 1786
The last week I had the pleasure of seeing Genl Lincoln, from whom I learnt, that You had been so obliging as to send me trees by his vessel, put into a tub or tubs with earth, to preserve them, till the season admits of their being planted. Your Excellency will be pleased to receive my most hearty thanks for this fresh proof of friendship. Believe I shall make an offer of them to Genl Lincoln, as I am about returning to my native country, should an opportunity offer the ensuing April, & my affairs be so far settled as to admit of my going so soon. I should plant them about my present dwelling, did I see any prospect of a successor's being settled with the people; the want of which is no small affliction to me.[1] When at London I design going to the press so as to allow of the History's being finished & received by the subscribers the next May twelvemonth at farthest, indeed by the first spring ships of 87. I shall do myself the honour of writing to you, after I am safely arrived with my family, should it please God so to favour us.[2] As I may possibly have something at one time or other to communicate, which I would wish to conceal from every one but yourself, I propose sending you a Cypher the next week, & if you approve of it let Cornwallis be the key, which keep secret in your own breast.[3] Mrs Gordon joins in best regards to your Excellency, your Lady, my young friend, Mr & Mrs L. Washington & others, with Dear Sir Your sincere friend & very humble servant

William Gordon

May I request your presenting my respects to my good friend
Mr Roberbeau & family, & acquainting him with my intention
of sailing for Europe shortly, that he may double his kindness
by forwarding the subscriptions to the utmost.[4] Mean to write to
him, time enough to admit of my receiving an answer on this
side the Atlantic.

ALS, DLC:GW.
　　1. Gordon wrote GW on 16 Feb. that the plants had arrived and, on 13
July, that they had survived the voyage to England.
　　2. See note 4.
　　3. Gordon enclosed the cipher in his letter of 16 February.
　　4. For GW's involvement in securing subscriptions to Gordon's *History*, see
GW to James Mercer, 20 Jan. 1786, n.3, and GW to Gordon, 20 April 1786.

To Battaile Muse

Sir   Mt Vernon Feby 4th 1786
　　My last by Mr Danl McPherson, would inform you, why I did
not write more fully by that opportunity.[1] and my attendance
since on the Business of the Potomack Company at the Great
Falls, is the reason of the delay, in doing it untill now.
　　Your letters of the 10th Decr & of the 12th 17th & 18th of last
Month are before me, & Such parts of them, as have not been
answered, & appear to require it, Shall be the Subjects of this
letter, taking them in the order of their dates.
　　The Butter is at length arrived, & as I had depended upon it,
I Shall keep the whole, though the price is at least 2d. ℔ lb. more
than I was Supplied with very good for, in Alexandria, in the
Fall; Where there is an evidence of exertion, in the Tenants to
pay Rent & Arrearages, I think you act very Properly, by giving
them encouraging words, & Assurances of indulgence—distress
to them, & little advantage to me, would accrue from a Contrary
Conduct: but where it Shall appear, that there is no such intention[,] that to Postpone payment is the Sole aim, & where the
condition of the leases have been unattended to, by them, &
their only object has been to carry the land, & not the produce
of it to market—here—no favour is due.
　　Abner Grigg has never appeared here. If he comes, I Shall
not forget your information respecting him—In the mean while
let me observe, that it is the compliance, or non-compliance with

the lease, that is to determine his right to return. If he is war-
ranted by the tenor of the lease to do so, I Shall not dispute the
point with him, but watch his ways well in future, without granting him any indulgences. If he is not, then take the Speediest, &
most effectual mode to get rid of him—For your exertions in
the following & catching him, I feel myself obligéd to you, as I
also do for your endeavours to Rent the Vacant lotts although
they Should not be crowned with Success. I hope you will be
more fortunate in your Collection than your letter of the 12th
seems to indicate, as it is on this I much depend for the Payment
of your Wheat. It was unquestionably my intention that Mr
Airess Should pay the Taxes of the Tenement he holds[2]—as an
evidence of it, every lott let at, & Since that time, have been So
expressed in the leases, but whether it was declared in explicit
terms, or even by implication to him at the time, my memory
does not now Serve me, & therefore I will not insist upon any
thing I am not clear in. The term for which he is to hold it, I
recollect well is for his own, & his Wife's life. I[t] must be So
filled.

As I have only Mr Jenny's Accot of the interference of lines, &
as Surveyors Fees (as established by law) are high, perhaps it
might be as well in the first instance, to get the line between Mr
Scott, & me Run by any accurate Man you can hire, as the Surveyor of the County, & hear what he (Mr Scott) has to Say upon
the Subject—I want nothing but Justice, & that, if to be obtained
I will have. But if upon the whole, you find the Business cannot
be so well done by any other, as the Surveyor of the County, I
consent very readily, to your employing him.[3]

Having every reason to believe that the Clover Seed which
you Sent me last fall was bad, I can by no means think of taking
more of it; If my fears of it's not vegitating Should be realized,
I would rather have given £50 for a Bushl of good Seed, than
encounter the dissappointment, & loss of Time, which will be
consequent of it. I will not absolutely Pronounce it bad, till the
Spring vegitation comes on; but I have all the reason imaginable
to dread it. The Seed had from Phila. is not imported, but
the Growth of the Country & cheaper than Mr Ropers; but
cheapness was not the point I aimed at, certainty was my
mark, & if I have missed I have lost my labour, & a Season.[4]
Your letter of the 18th was accompanied with a Statement of the

Tenements, & Rents of my land in Fauquier &c. for whc. I am oblig'd to you.[5] That you will have Trouble in reducing these matters to order, I have not, nor never had any doubt of; but they will be Plain & easy after this year; which will make amends, as I am determined to continue the Collection in the hands of an Agent, who by close attention, will see that I have Justice done, not only in the Punctual Paymt of the Rents, but that the covenants thereof are duely attended to, & complied with. What reply to make to that Part of your letter, wherein you Speak of difficulties whc. may arise in case of the death of either of us, in the Settlement of Accts—I know not: You have powers to act, & Instructions how to act—& I here declare, that if neither of these will comprehend all the cases whc. may arise in the Prosecution of this Bussiness, my desire is that you would act for me, as you would do for yourself. There can be no difficulty then, that I Can foresee, in the case. for these powers, these instructions—& this declaration will always Justify a Conduct, that is not evidently fraudulent; of which there is not the Smallest Suspicion in the present case. but when time will admit of it, State the cases fully, wherein directions are wanted, & my Sentiments therein Shall be handed to you. This will be a further Justification of your conduct.

Inclosed you have Copies of the Accts handed in by Lewis Lemart, & his Widow together with Copies of the Sheriffs receipts which conveys every Information that is in my Power to give you respecting his Collection.[6] I am Sir Yr Very Hble Servt

Go: Washington

LS, PWacD: Sol Feinstone Collection, on deposit PPAmP; LB, DLC:GW.

1. Daniel McPherson was at Mount Vernon on 5 Jan., the date of GW's most recent letter to Muse; but on 20 Feb. Muse identifies the letter brought by McPherson as dated 27 January. It has not been found.

2. See Muse to GW, 12 Jan., n.2.

3. See GW to Muse, 5 Jan., n.1.

4. See GW to Muse, 5 Jan., n.3.

5. Muse's "Statement of the Tenements" has not been found.

6. GW's enclosures have not been found.

From James Taylor

Sir   Norfolk 4th Febry 1786.

The enclosed letter accompanied with a pipe of wine came to my hands a few days ago—I was requested by the Gentlemen in Madeira to receive the wine & store it, & to inform you of the arrival of it.[1] As you had directed the wine to be shipt to Alexandria, they were in doubt if it would be agreeable to you to receive it here, & in that case I was to dispose it on their acctt & they should embrace another oppoy of sending your wine to Potomack. I have paid the freight & Duty thereof & have it safely stored, & wait your orders respecting it.[2] I have the Honor to be Sir Your most obed. Servt

Jas Taylor

ALS, DLC:GW.

1. See Lamar, Hill, Bisset, & Co. to GW, 20 Aug., 6 Dec. 1785.
2. GW's response of 22 Feb. is missing, but see Taylor to GW, 13 March.

Letter not found: from John Marsden Pintard, 5 Feb. 1786. GW wrote Pintard on 20 May: "Your favors of the 24th of January & 5th Feby are at hand."

To David Stuart

Dear Sir,   Mount Vernon Feby 5th 1786

The Vessel which brought the inclosed, has delivered the 800 Bushels of Oats for which you contracted with Mr Savage—Besides these, I have taken 100 more; for which I am to pay Flour. L. Washington has taken anothr & the remaining 200 hundred are taken to Alexandria for you.

I have engaged this Man to bring the Corn from York River—He expects to stay no longer than Monday (to morrow) at Alexandria; if you propose therefore to send Wheat fans by him to the Plantations below you have no time to loose in getting them on board.[1]

I hope Mrs Stuart, to whom & yourself I offer congratulations on the encrease of your family, is quite recovered—With great esteem & regard I am—Dr Sir Yr Obedt & Affecte Servt

Go: Washington

Mrs Washington presents her love to Mrs Stuart and wishes to know how she is.

ALS, DLC:GW.
    1. See Stuart to GW, 18 Dec. 1785, n.1, GW to George Savage, 8 Feb., 17 Mar. 1786, and Savage to GW, 18 Feb. 1786. See also *Diaries*, 4:270–71.

From Patrick Henry

Gentlemen   Council Chamber [Richmond] feby 6th 1786
    There are six men in the public Goal who are pardoned for capital Crimes on Condition of laboring for Years more or less. I beg to know whether the Company over which you preside will accept of these people to labor in accomplishing the purposes of your Institution. It will be expected that their Labor shall be considered as a Compensation for all the Expences of supporting them in the Condition of Laborers & of providing the necessary Means of preventing Escapes.
    I beg to hear from you on this Subject soon as possible[1] & am Gentlemen Your most obedient Servant

                                                            P. Henry

ALS, DLC:GW. Henry's letter was directed to "President & Directors of the Patowmack &c.," and it was endorsed by GW.
    1. GW wrote from Mount Vernon on 5 Mar.: "Sir, Your Excellency's favor of the 6th ulto came duly to hand, but I had no opportunity before the 2d instt of laying it before the Directors of the Potomack Company. By the board, I am desired to inform your Excelly, that they decline taking the Six felons in the public goal, at the sametime that they feel themselves obliged by the offer. I have the honr to be Sir Yr Most Obedt Hble Ser. Go: Washington" (ALS, NbO; LB, DLC:GW).

From Lafayette

My dear General   Paris february the 6th 1786
    Your letters September the 1st and November the 8th Have Safely Come to Hand for which I offer you thanks the Warmer and More affectionate as nothing, while we are separated, Can so much Rejoice Your friend's Heart as the unspeakable Blessing to Hear from His Beloved General—a long time Has elapsed since which my letters Have Been unfrequent, Unin-

stering, and Uncertain in point of Conveyance—My summer has been devoted to princes, soldiers and post Horses—and while I Have Been Rambling through Cassel, Brunswick, Berlin, Breslaw, Vienna, prague dresden, potsdam Again and Berlin, no opportunity offered that I could trust, nor even any that I could Hear of—since I am returned Home, no Packet Has Sailed, and this day for the first time, I can Safely write By a Packet Boat, and put My Letter into Mr Barret's Hands, a Boston Gentleman Who is On His Return to America.[1]

Altho' my former letters Have Given You an Account of My journey, I must repeat to you, my dear General, that at Cassel I saw our Hessian friends, old Knip Among them,[2] I told them they were very fine Fellows—they Returned thanks and Compliments—Ancient foes ever meet with pleasure, which However, I should think must be greater on the side that fought a successfull cause—at Brunswick I got Acquainted With the duke, formerly the Renowned Hereditary Prince, who is Now Arrived at the Height of Military Knowledge, and of the Confidence of the Prussian Army, in which, altho' a Sovereign, He acts as a General[3]—no officer at Berlin seemed to me so worthy of Attention as General Möllendorf whose Name you no doubt Have Heard[4]—to potsdam I went to Make my Bow to the King, and notwisdanding what I Had Heard of Him, could not Help Being struck By that dress and Appearance of an old, Broken, dirty Corporal, coverd all over with Spanish snuff, with His Head almost leaning on one shoulder, and fingers quite distorted By the Gout. But what surprised me much more is the fire and some times the softeness of the most Beautifull Eyes I ever saw, which give as charming an expression to His phisiognomy as He Can take a Rough and threatening one at the Head of His troops—I went to Silesia where He Reviewed an army of 31 Bataillons, and 75 squadrons, Making in all thirty thousand men, seven thousand five hundred of whom were on Horse Back—for eight days I made dinners of three Hours with Him, when the Conversation was pretty much Confined at first to the duke of York the King and myself, and then to two or three more—which gave me the opportunity to Hear Him throughout, and to admire the Vivacity of His wit, the endearing charms of His adress and politness, so far that I did Conceive people could forget what a tyrannic, Hard Hearted, and selfish Man He is—lord Cornwallis being there, He took Care to invite Him at table to a seat By me, Having the British King's son on the other side, and to Make thousand questions on American affairs— Among others I Remember He Asked the duke of York if it was trüe you intended taking an House in London.[5] from Silesia I Hastened to Vienna where I only stayed a few days, Had a very long Conference with the Emperor, saw the Generals Laudon and Lasey, And my Uncle the Ambassador with prince Kaunitz, and after those objects were fulfilled,[6] I posted off through prague and dresden, to potsdam, where the troops were to Make sham fights and every kind of Warlike Maneuvres—Had I stayed in prussia, I might Have gone often to the old king's who Has Been Most peculiarly Kind to me—But the very day I arrived at potsdam, He fell sick and was Near dying—the Maneuvers went on However—and there I Had new opportunities to Know the Hereditary prince of prussia, who is a good officer, an Honest Man, a Man of plain good sense, But does not come up to the Abilities of His two Uncles—this second Uncle prince Henry I Have Kept for the last, because it is By far the Best Acquaintance I Have Made[7]—I don't Examine who is the Greater General His Brother or He, a Question that divides the Military World—But to Abilities of the first Rate, Both as a soldier and a politician—to a perfect litterary knowledge, and all the Endowments of the Mind—He joins an Honest Heart, philantropic feelings, and rational ideas on the Rights of Mankind—I Have spent a fortnight with Him in His Country seat and We Keep up an epistolary Correspondance—as the king Was still Confined and Could not Bear Being seen in that situation, I determined neither to ask for leave of a visit, nor to wait untill He was up, and our Adieus Having taken place By letters, I Returned Home through Magdebourg where the duke of Brunswick Commanded Maneuvers similar to those of potsdam.

it is with the Highest satisfaction that I saw the Prussian Army—Nothing Can Be Compared to the Beauty of the troops, the discipline that is diffused throughout, the simplicity of their Motions, the Uniformity of their Regiments—it is a plain Regular Machine that Has Been set these forty years, and Undergoes no alteration But what Can Make it simpler and lighter—Every supposition in war, and every Motion deriving from it, Has Been from a Constant use so much inculcated into their Heads, that it became almost a Mechanic for them—were the Ressources of France, the Alertness of Her men, the intelligence of Her officers, and National Ambition and Moral delicacy Applied to such a Constant system, we Could Be as Superior to the prussians as our Army is now inferior to theirs—and that is saying great deal—I Have also seen the Austrians—But not together—their general system of Œconomy is more to be admired than the Maneuvres of their troops—their Machine is not plain—our Regiments are Better than theirs—and what advantage they might Have in a line over us, we Can surpass with a little use—indeed, I think there is more instruction of detail in some of our Best Regiments than those of the prussians—But their line Maneuvres infinitely Better than ours—the Austrian Army is much more numerous than either, and Costs much less than the french.

On my journey I Have Examined several fields of Battle, and the whole tour Has Been very useful to my Military instruction—it Has Been also made very agreable By the good Reception, and the flattering testimonies I Have met from those Crowns, staffs, and other great personages—there was at those Camps a croud of English officers—among whom Lord Cornwallis, Clels England, Abercrombie, Musgrave—on our side were Colonel Smith, general portail, and Gouvion—and often did Smith and Myself Make this observation that, Had we Been Unfortunate in the Contest, we would Have cut there a poor figure.[8]

Where Ever I went, my dear General, I Had the pleasure to Hear Your Name pronounced with that Respect and enthusiasm which altho' it is a matter of course, and I am so used to it, never fails to Make My Heart glow with Unspeakable Happiness—With Your Eulogium Began Every Conversation on American Affairs—And to Be Your friend, Your disciple, and Your Adoptive son Was, as it ever Has Been, and Will Be for ever, the pride of my Heart, and the Most pleasing of my thoughts—I wish the other Sentiments I Have Had occasion to discover with Respect to America were Equally satisfactory with those that are personal to you—I need not saying that the spirit, the firmness with which the Revolution Was Carried Has Excited Universal Admiration—that Every one who Cares Any thing about the Rights of Mankind is an Enthusiast for the principles on which the

Constitutions are Built—But I Have often had the Mortification to Hear that the want of powers in Congress, of Union Between the States, of Energy in their Government should Make the Consideration very insignificant—The fact is that those people, Generally Speacking, know very little of the Advantages of democratical governements, of the Ressources to Be found in a free Nation, and the parties which are essentially deriving from the Constitution—But they Cannot Help Being more forcibly struck with all the Blemishes which we Have so often lamented together—it is Conveyed to them through Every Newspaper, and Great pains are taken By the British Ambassadors to Confirm the Reports which they themselves Have Raised—Numberless of these Notions I Have set to Right—the King of prussia, the Emperor, the Great Men in Both Countries I found either ill informed, or informed By people who Had led them the wrong path—By their Conduct in the Revolution, the Citizens of America Have commanded the Respect of the World—But it grieves me to think they will in a Measure loose it, unless they strengthen the Confederation, give Congress powers to Regulate the trade, pay off their debt or at least the interest of it, establish a well Regulated Militia, in a word Compleat all these Measures which You Have Recommended to them—I give very frankly My opinion to Congress on this subject, and will write on the Same tune to all my friends on that Side of the Atlantik.

There are, I am told, Some Better Hopes of a Commercial treaty with Great Britain—their Rancour is Boundless—But I flatter Myself their Mercantile interest will get the Better—I long for the surrender of the Posts, and wish the plenipotentiaries Had Given themselves time to Make France guarantee for the treaty—this Blunder of theirs Has occasioned Great Mischief—My Endeavours are to convince France it is their interest to obtain a Measure that gives them a large share in the indian trade—But in Case Matters were Brought to decided Measures Against Great Britain, Upon You, my dear General, I depend to Know it in time, and to indulge My Wishes to Render further Services to the United States.

Houdon is Arrived in Paris—But Has not Yet Brought Your Bust which He Expects By Water from London—I wait impatiently for it, and am very Sanguine in My Hopes of its likeness with you—On Hearing of the King of Spain's Compliment, I

Had suspended my Negotiation for Asses—what Now Happens is to me a further proof that Kings are Good for Nothing But to Spoil the Sport, Even When they Mean Right—let your Royal Business Go on as it May, I Have Requested Admiral Suffrein to get for me a jack Ass and two females, and Before the Summer is over they will Be Rolling on the Banks of the Pottowmack, and I wish to god I May do the Same—Your letter to M. doillamson Has Been forwarded, with Your Compliments to the lady— I Have also spoken to Marquis de St Simon, But Wish You May write to Him, Because He Has His share of Vanity, and will Be glad if you pay affectionate Compliments to Him, and show a Regard for M. de Menonville His Adjudant General, disclaiming the right to make Cincinnati, and leaving it with Your Best wishes with the Society in Europe[9]—Captain littlepage delivered to me some letters for Holland which I Have sent—His quarrell with M. jay seems to me very indecent, and I Can't Conceive that jay, for so small a debt, Could Condescend to enter the lists with a young man.[10]

it Has Been a Great Satisfaction to me, My dear General, to Hear of My friend George's Matrimonial Happiness—as I write to Him on the Subject I will not trouble you with my Compliments to the Young Couple. I Give You joy on the success of Your pottowmack plans—there is no doubt But what a good Engeneer May Be found in this Country to Conduct the Work— France in this point Exceeds England—and will Have, I think, Every Advantage But that of the language which is something, altho' it may Be Replaced By the Help of interpreters—an application from M. jefferson and Myself to the Ministry, and More particularly an intimation that You set a value By that Measure, will insure to us the Choice of a good Engeneer—they are different from the Military ones, and are Called *ingenieurs des ponts et chaussées*; I think five Hundred guineas a year while the Business lasts, and an Assurance Not to loose His Rank in france will Be sufficient to provide you with the Gentleman You Want.

I Cannot finish this long letter, My dear General, without telling You a Word of European politicks—the System of france is Quite pacific—the Nation Feels a partiality for prussia—Austrian interest, Betwen us, is much supported By the Queen— Count de Vergennes is not inclined this Way, But acts with Caution—from that it Results that We Will patch up as much as We

Can—that the Ambitious views of the Emperor will not Be so decidedly opposed as we might do it—The plans of prussia will Be Cramped By us—But should matters Come to an Extremity, and the Emperor set out on a Wild Scheme Against prussia, we will then be forced to a War Against Him, as the opinion of the people, and that of the Ministry, Most of them at least, is Opposed to imperial Encroachements—With Respect to England, we are Rivalizing Each other, But pretty friendly for the present, and pay Great Regard to our Respective Nations—a treaty of Commerce is upon the Carpet, and I think our politicks on the Continent draw pretty much the Same Way, that of avoiding a War, which However England Wishes to Engage us in, provided she is dispensed with taking a part in it—our Alliance with Holland Has made them very Angry, and I think it very Advantageous to us. We are very Busy about Making a Harbour at cherbourg which is a Wonderfull Undertaking, as it is Made with piles of stones thrown in the High Sea, and will succeed very well—our financeer and Baron de Breteuil are in a oppen dispute, and I don't think the former will last long—But I need not teazing you with the intrigues of Versailles—I thank you most tenderly, my dear General, for the Caution You Give me, which I will improve, and find that Satisfaction in my prudence to think it is dictated By You—I Hope, Betwen us, that in the Course of Next winter the affair of the protestants Will take a Good turn—an other Secret I intrust to you, my dear General, is that I Have purchased for Hundred And twenty five thousand French livres a plantation in the Colony of Cayenne and am going to free my Negroes in order to Make that Experiment which you know is My Hobby Horse.[11]

Great Britain is a little Embarrassed in Her irish Concerns—Some Say their affairs in india are not well—Notwisdanding these Reports, india is to them an immense, amazing source of wealth and power—it seems they are Moderating their Bitter Expressions, their injurious publications Against America, and from what M. Adams writes, I Hope they will, altho' it is slowly, Come into More Rational Measures with Respect to the United States.

The king of prussia is about leaving the stage and Cannot last long—the last accounts from potsdam are very Bad—it will Make But little odds in politicks if His Nephew, as He will no

doubt Be obliged to do, follows the Advices of prince Henry—
the first idea of the Emperor will Certainly Be to do some
thing—But I don't Believe this will produce a War, altho' there
is No Knowing it with a Man of His temper.

While on my tour, I need not Saying that I Have Said in Con-
versations with the Two Monarchs and Every Body all What I
thought could tend to the Advantage of America—in this Country I am endeavouring to oppen as Many Channels as I Can for
American trade—There are far above 25 million french livres
Worth of Articles that the United States Might furnish to
france—those Remittances I Want to Have encouraged By Every possible favour—Upon my applications a Committee has
Been Named Which I am to attend to morrow—the last part of
my Business will not Be an Easy matter—for it tends to No less
than the destruction of the tobacco farm, the greatest Barrier
Against American trade[12]—But I don't Hope my Speeches Can
produce such an effect—M. Barret who takes Care of this letter,
is going to Boston with a six years Contract for whale oil of four
Hundred thousand french livres a year.

Words Cannot Sufficiently Express to You How much I am
pleased with Mr jefferson's public Conduct—He Unites every
Ability that Can Recommend Him With the Ministers, and at
the time possesses Accomplishements of the mind and the Heart
which Cannot But Give Him Many friends. Humphreys is Now
in England—LangBourne is Arrived in Paris these two
weecks—But the same queer fellow you know Him to Be, and
you will Hardly Believe that I could not as yct prevail on Him
to Come and see me.[13]

it is with the utmost Regret, my dear General, that I Heard
the losses Mrs Washington Had the Unfortunate Occasion to lament—I Hope she knows my Heart well Enough to Be Certain
it Has Most Affectionately Simpathised With Hers[14]—I Beg her
to Accept the Homage of my tender Respects—Madame de Lafayette and the little family Beg to Be Respectfully Remembered
to Her, as well as to You, My Beloved General—My Best Compliments Wait on all the inHabitants of Mount Vernon, on all
our friends You Happen to Meet, old Harrison when You write
to Him, My friend tub, and the young ladies—my Best Respects
to Mrs Stuart, to the docter, to Mr Lund and Most affectionately
I Beg to Be Remembered to Your own family, particularly to

Your Respected Mother. I Beg leave to Send under Cover to You a few trifles to Be presented to tub and His Sisters. Adieu, My dear General, You know How affectionately and Respectfully I Have the Honour to Be Your devoted and filial friend

Lafayette

ALS, PEL.

1. Nathaniel Barrett in the fall of 1785 was sent to France by Boston merchants to negotiate contracts for the sale of whale oil.

2. Lt. Gen. Baron Wilhelm von Knyphausen (1717–1800) was the commander of Hessian troops in America during the Revolution.

3. Karl Wilhelm Ferdinand, duke of Brunswick (1735–1806), was a field general in the Prussian army.

4. Wichard Joachim Heinrich von Möllendorf (1724–1816).

5. Frederick, duke of York (1763–1827), was the second son of George III.

6. Freiherr Gideon Ernst von Laudon (1716–1790) and Franz Moritz, Count Lacy (1725–1801), were both Austrian field marshals. Emmanuel-Marie-Louis, marquis de Noailles (1743–1822), was the French ambassador in Vienna.

7. Frederick William II (1744–1797) before the end of the year succeeded his uncle, Frederick II (the Great), as king of Prussia. Frederick the Great's brother was Prince Henry (1726–1802).

8. The British colonels Sir Richard England (1750–1812), Sir Robert Abercromby (1740–1827), and Sir Thomas Musgrave (1737–1812) had all served in the American war. Lt. Col. William Stephens Smith (1755–1816) of the Continental army had served in Lafayette's Light Infantry, and the Frenchmen Duportail and Gouvion had both served in the engineers of the Continental army.

9. For the mix-up about the jackasses, see GW to Lafayette, 1 Sept. 1785. GW's letter to comte Doilliamson is printed in note 2 of GW's letter to Lafayette, 1 Sept. 1785. GW wrote Saint-Simon-Montbléru on 10 May 1786.

10. Not long after his arrival in New York in mid-November, Lewis Littlepage renewed his feud with his old patron, John Jay, now secretary for foreign affairs. He challenged Jay to a duel, and the two engaged in an acrimonious exchange in the New York *Daily Advertiser* for more than a week beginning on 7 Dec. (see Jay to GW, 2 Mar. 1786). At the point of being arrested on 3 Dec. for his large debt to Jay incurred while he was a member of Jay's household in Madrid in the early 1780s, Littlepage surrendered for bail the £300 in Virginia state funds entrusted to him for the payment of Houdon (see Patrick Henry to GW, 14 Oct. 1785, n.1). After Littlepage arrived in Paris, Thomas Jefferson wrote Governor Henry on 24 Jan. 1786: "Mr. Littlepage, to satisfy me, had obtained from the M. de la fayette his engagement to stand bound as Mr. Littlepage's security for the paiment of this money [the £300 intended for Houdon]. . . . if a loss was to be incurred, I knew too well the sentiments of the state of Virginia towards the M. de la Fayette to suppose they would be willing to throw that loss on him. I therefore . . . waited on the Marquis and,

in his presence, cancelled his name from the obligation which had been given me, leaving only that of Mr. Littlepage" (Boyd, *Jefferson Papers*, 9:212–15).

11. See Lafayette to GW, 14 July 1785, n.3. Charles-Alexandre de Calonne (1734–1802) was comptroller general of finances, and Louis-Auguste de Tonnelier, baron de Breteuil (1730–1807), was minister of the king's household.

12. Tax-farmers, or farmers-general, held a royal monopoly on the sale of tobacco in France.

13. William Langborn (1756–1814), a cousin of Martha Washington and a native of King William County, had been an aide-de-camp to Lafayette during the Revolution. At this time he was in the second year of a walking tour of the British Isles and Europe, which ended only in 1796 with his return to King William County (Curtis Carroll Davis, "The Curious Colonel Langborn: Wanderer and Enigma from the Revolutionary Period," *Virginia Magazine of History and Biography*, 64 [October 1956], 402–32).

14. Lafayette is referring to the death of Martha Washington's brother, Bartholomew Dandridge, and her mother, Frances Jones Dandridge, in April 1785. "Old Harrison" presumably is Robert Hanson Harrison of Maryland, who was GW's secretary during the Revolution. "Tub" is young George Washington Parke Custis.

To Benjamin Lincoln

My dear Sir   Mount Vernon 6th Feb: 1786

Your favour of the 4th of Jany never reached me till yesterday, or the receipt of it should have had an earlier acknowledgement.

Let me in the first place thank you for your kind attention to my enquiries. And in the next, pray you to learn, precisely from Mr Lear, upon what terms he would come to me; for I am not inclined to leave matters of this sort to after discussion, or misconception. Whatever agreement is previously made, shall be pointedly fulfilled on my part, wch will prevent every cause of complaint on his.

Mr Lear, or any other who may come into my family in the blended characters of preceptor to the Children, and as a Clerk or private Secretary to me, will sit at my Table—will live as I live—will mix with the Company which resort to the Ho.—and will be treated in every respect with civility, and proper attention. He will have his washing done in the family, and may have his linnen & Stockings mended by the Maids of it.

The duties which will be required of him are, generally, such as appertain to the Offices before-mentioned. The first will be very trifling 'till the Children are a little more advanced—and the latter will be equally so as my corrispondencies decline (which I am endeavouring to effect); and after accts, and other old matters are brought up. To descend more minutely into his avocations I am unable, because occasional matters may require particular Services; nothing how ever derogatory will be asked, or expected.

After this explanation of my wants, I request Mr Lear would mention the annual sum he will expect for these Services; and I will give him a decided answer by the return of the Stages, which now carry the Mail & travel quick—A good hand, as well as proper diction would be a recommendation; on acct of fair entries; and for the benefit of the Children, who will have to copy after it.

The discovery of extracting fresh Water from Salt Water, by a simple process, and without the aid of fire, will be of amazing importance to the Sons of Neptune; if it is not viciated, or rendered nausious by the operation; but can be made to answer all the valuable purposes of other fresh Water, at Sea. Every Maritime power in the world, in this case, ought, in my opinion, to offer some acknowledgment to the Inventor—With sentiments of great regard & friendship I am My dear Sir Yr Affecte Hble Servt

Go: Washington

ALS (photocopy), PU: Armstrong photostats; LB, DLC:GW.

From Bryan Fairfax

Dear Sir   Towlston Febry the 7th 1786.

I received the Favor of Yr Letter from the Great Falls[1]—and was sorry that I did not hear of your being there till after your departure as I should certainly have done myself the pleasure of waiting on You, especially as I had had thoughts from time to time of taking a Ride there. I was the more concerned to hear of your setting off at Night, and was a little afraid that your delicacy in regard to giving trouble at a late hour prevented You from calling at Towlston. But Mr Stewart according to his own Account was to blame, for a man ought not to suffer his own Zeal to oppose entirely the Will of his Patron or best Friend.[2]

With regard to the Wood cut at the Place I purpose to inform Mr Potts, that as I expect and have not doubted but that ample Satisfaction would be made me I am easy with regard to what has been cut, as well as what may be used, which may be settled at a future day.[3] A Man has applied to me for an Acre of ground thereabouts, but I have declined it, not knowing but it might be disagreeable to the Board, and I am since glad that I did, because he might have kept a tipling house and been hurtful—and therefore shall continue to deny till at some future meeting here I may mention the Subject. I am with great Regard, Dr Sir Yr most obliged & obedt Servt

Bryan Fairfax

ALS, DLC:GW.
  1. Letter not found.
  2. GW arrived at Great Falls for the meeting of the trustees of the Potomac River Company on 1 Feb. and returned to Mount Vernon on 3 Feb. (*Diaries*, 4:269–70). Richardson Stewart was the assistant manager of the company.
  3. John Potts, Jr., a merchant in Alexandria, was secretary of the Potomac River Company.

From John Fitzgerald

Dear Sir   [Alexandria, 7 February 1786]
    Upon coming home I immedeatily Conversed with Colo. Lyles on the Subject of the Importation of a She Ass for you & also with the Captain[.] Colo. Lyles is very desirous to effect it & will if it is practicable—The Captain not having any expectation of orders in that way made no enquiry respecting them he says they are plenty & he believes there is no difficulty in obtaining them[.] I think the best way will be for you to Ship 20 or 25 bbls S. fine flour, for which I understand there is room, & in case of disappointmt Colo. Lyles is willing either to be accountable here at the price or run the risque of the Market as you think best[.] the Vessell I believe will be ready to sail by Saturday or Sunday.[1]
    I much want to go up to Berkeley but my Business is such at this time that I believe it will not be in my power for 8 or ten days if then, I will however take care to let you know before I sett out. I am Dear Sir with perfect respect & Esteem yr Obedt Servt

John Fitzgerald

P.S. Mr Rumsey called upon me late the other evening & the only Conclusion we could come upon was that the President & Directors were to hold themselves in readiness to meet by the first of March unless advised previously that the Meeting could be put off without injury to the 15th.

ALS, DLC:GW.

1. William Lyles & Co. of Alexandria immediately wrote GW: "Colo. Fitzgerald has signified to us your wishes of getting an ass imported from the dutch settlement of Surinam, we have a sloop that will sail in three days for that place, and we have made some enquiries from the Captain of the practicability of getting one from thence, who seems not to doubt but it may be done very safely and the season for his return will greatly favor the safety of the creatures passage here.

"The Capt. has no Idea of the probable cost of an ass in Surinam, but supposes 20 or 25 Barrels S. fine flour wou'd be fully adequate to the Cost, we have taken the liberty of giving you this information, and of making a tender of our Services in the execution of this business" (DLC:GW).

GW responded: "Gentn I have received your favor of yesterday & thank you for your ready compliance with my request. As soon as my Boat returns from Alexandria, it shall be dispatched again with 25 Barls of S: flour for your Vessell; for the purpose of procuring (if practicable) a she Ass from Surinam, for my benefit.

"I should be glad to know whether you commit the negotiation of your business to the Captn or consign it to a Merchant of that place, that I may entrust mine to the same person. And as I shall have to write to the Gentleman, would wish, in either case, to know the name & address of the Consignee.

"If I should not succeed in procuring the Ass, I will, if equally agreeable to you, abide the Sale of the flour at Surinam, and receive the amount in Rum, Molasses, or such other articles as come best from that place—advice of which I would thank you for—But, if this should interfere, in the smallest degree, with your freight back, it will be perfectly agreeable to me to have the return in cash. I am Gentn Yr Most Obedt Hble Servt Go: Washington" (ALS, ViMtV: Willard Collection; LB, DLC:GW). Both the Lyles letter and GW's response are dated 8 February.

On Feb. 9 William Lyles & Co. wrote: "We have always before this voyage consigned our vessels to a Mr Saml Branden mercht in Surinam, but as the voyage is generally pretty long we have determin'd to consign the one we now send to the Capt. (Wm Bartlett) as by giving him the Commissions of the Cargoes out and in, we have a very considerable abatement in his wages; Mr Branden is a man of considerable importance in Surinam and perhaps might be usefull on this occation. We can by no means recommend your ordering Rum or Sugar from Surinam, the rum is high proof but badly flavoured and their Sugars extremely dark indeed, Their Molasses and Coffee are superior to any we get from the West Indies—These are their only exports except Cocoa which we make but little use of here.

"You will be so obliging as to order the return of your boat as expeditiously as possible" (DLC:GW). GW records in his cash accounts the payment on 9 Feb. to Fitzgerald of 2s. 6d. for "Drayage of Goods" and £6.3.3 for "Freight of Sundry Goods on Board the Fanny" (Ledger B, 207).

GW's response of 10 Feb. reads: "Gentn As it is my wish to obtain a she Ass of the first kind, & think it is more in the power of a resident at Surinam, than it can be in that of the Captn to procure such an one, I have written the enclosed letter to Mr Branden requesting him to make the purchase accordingly. I hope the Captn will ascribe this preference to no other cause than the one assigned; at the same time that I earnestly request his particular attention to the animal, if one should be shipped on my account.

"In case of the failure in such purchase, I have requested Mr Branden to send the proceeds of the sales of the flour, in Molasses & Coffee. You would oblige me by having the flour inspected—properly marked for Mr Branden, & the bill of lading therefor put under cover with my letter to that Gentn, as it will save time & trouble. I am &c. G. Washington" (LB, DLC:GW).

GW enclosed in his letter of 10 Feb. the following letter to Samuel Branden, also dated 10 Feb.: "Sir, I have lately received from Spain, a Jack Ass of the first race in the Kingdom, & am very desirous of availing myself of his breed. Hearing that she Asses of good appearance are to be had at Surinam, I take the liberty of asking your assistance to procure me one of the best kind, to be sent by the return of Captain Bartlett, who will deliver this letter to you.

"Neither the Captn, or any body else with whom I have had opportunities of conversing, could tell me the cost of one of these animals at Surinam, but have supposed that twenty five barrels of superfine flour, would be adequate to the purchase. This quantity (equal I believe in quality to any made in this Country) I have the honor of shipping to your address: but if it should prove inadequate, the deficiency shall be made up in the way most agreeable to yourself. All I pray is, that I may receive one of the largest & best she Asses that can be obtained in your Country fit to breed from.

"As the Captain is commissioned to purchase a She Ass for his owners, I should be glad, if the Bill of lading for mine (if one is sent to me) may be minutely descriptive of her. I hope every provision will be made for the accomodation & support of her on ship board. but if contrary to my wishes, a disappointment happens, I request in that case that you would be so obliging as to send me in return for the flour, two hogsheads of Molasses, & the remainder in the best Coffee of your Country.

"If, in this request, I have used an unwarrantable freedom, it proceeds from the good character given of you to me, by Messrs Fitzgerald & Lyles of Alexandria, by whose Vessel I write, & who have offered me a passage for the animal. I am Sir, &c. G: Washington" (LB, DLC:GW).

GW wrote Branden again on 20 Nov. 1786 to report that "the Ass arrived safe, & the other Articles agreably to the Bill of Lading." The "other Articles" were molasses and coffee (*Diaries*, 5:40).

From Thomas Smith

Sir   Carlisle [Pa.] 7th February 1786

Major McCormick has this moment called on me in his way through this Place, & informed me that he means to go from Philadelphia by Mount-Vernon on his way home; as his company pursue their Journey in a quarter of an hour, I cannot have the honour of writing more than just to acknowledge the receipt of your Letter of the 7th of December—one Copy of which I received the Day before I went to the Western Courts, & the other was deliverd to me on my journey. until I had the honour of being employed by General Washington, I was vain enough to believe that I had some small claim to the reputation of punctuality & accuracy in my business; but now I am convinced that I ought to blush at my want of both.

Mr McCormick can give you every information that I could add, and more—he will also take your directions—It will be necessary that some *one* Person near the spot should engage to secure such Supœnas as may be thought proper; because when any kind of business is trusted to many it is seldom well done.[1]

I am not yet informed when the Judges go to Washington County, nor which two of them go—as soon as I gain this knowledge, I will again have the honour of assuring you that I am, Sir, with the greatest respect your most obedient humble Servant

Thomas Smith

ALS, DLC:GW.

1. For the details of the ejectment suits handled by Smith for GW involving people living on GW's Millers Run tract in Pennsylvania, see Smith to GW, 9 Feb. 1785, and notes. George McCarmick wrote GW on 31 Oct. 1786 to inform him of the favorable outcome of the suits. GW does not record in his diary a visit from McCarmick.

To George Savage

Sir,   Mount Vernon 8th Feby 1786.

Your skipper, Mr Jno. Whitney, has delivered me eight hundred bushels of oats agreeably to the contract made with Doctr Stuart in my behalf—They are good & clean, for which I thank you.[1]

Mr Whitney informing me that he was authorized to provide

a freight for the Schooner he is in, I have engaged him positively, to bring me eight hundred bushels of Indian corn from the plantations of the deceased Mr Custis on Pamunky river. I hope it is to be had at the lowest plantation (a few miles above West point)—but of this I am not certain—I am to pay him six pence a bushel freight, delivered at my landing.[2]

I expect no delay or disappointment will take place in this contract, as I have had the offer of two other vessels on the same terms, & have rejected them on account of this engagement. I am Sir &c.

G: Washington

LB, DLC:GW.

1. See David Stuart to GW, 18 Dec. 1785, n.1, and 5 Feb. 1786.

2. Savage wrote GW on 18 Feb. that he was sending the schooner to pick up the corn, and GW wrote Savage on 17 Mar. that the schooner had arrived with 1,000 bushels of corn and 6 bushels of peas. See also GW to David Stuart, 5 Feb., and Leonard Henley to GW, 27 Feb., 14 April.

To Clement Biddle

Dear Sir,   Mount Vernon Feb: 10th 1786

A hasty letter which I wrote to you by Colo. Grayson was accompanied with ten half Johans.—the application of which I informed you shd be directed in a subsequent letter.[1]

Let me now request the favour of you to send me the following articles if to be had.

A pair of Boots, and two pair of Shoes, to be made by Mr Star (who has my measure) agreeably to the enclosed Memo.[2]

Young's Six Months tour through England (his tour thro' Ireld I have).

The Gentleman Farmer—by Henry Home.

Tulls Husbandry. All to be neatly bound & lettered.[3]

200 Weight of Clover Seed—to be fresh and good.

12 lbs. of Saint foin seed.⎫
6 lbs. of the field Burnet⎭ If to be had good

A Common Hunting horn of the largest and best sort.

It will readily occur to you, my good Sir, that these Seeds (as they are to be sown this spring) cannot be forwarded too soon. I ought indeed to have wrote for them at an earlier period, but they may yet arrive at a proper Season if they are quickly dispatched. At any rate, inform me if they are to be had, & the prospect there is of forwarding them, for thereon will depend my preparation of the ground.

The Gazettes which were furnished by Mr Dunlap, for my use, during my Military appointment, ought, undoubtedly to be paid for by the public—and I had no doubt but that this had been done, regularly, by the Qr Mr General or his assistt in the State of Pensylvania—If the case is otherwise, I am ready to give my aid towards his obtaining it. My respects to Mrs Biddle. I am—Dear Sir, Yr Most Obedt Hble Servt

Go: Washington

I pray you to be pointed with respt to the goodness of the Seeds: an imposition of bad Seeds is a robbery of the worst kind; for your pocket not only suffers by it but your preparations are lost—& a season passes away unimproved.

ALS, PHi: Washington-Biddle Correspondence; LB, DLC:GW.

1. GW's letter is dated 30 Jan. 1786.

2. The memorandum has not been identified.

3. Arthur Young's *A Six Months Tour through the North of England* was first published in 1770 in London; his *A Tour in Ireland* was published in Dublin in 1779 and in London in 1780. *Horse-hoeing Husbandry* by Jethro Tull was printed in London for the first time in 1733. *The Gentleman Farmer* (Dublin, 1779) by Henry Home (Lord Kames) and Young's *Tour in Ireland* were listed in the inventory of GW's library at his death; the other two works were not. GW wrote Biddle on 18 May that if he had not already done so, Biddle should not buy "Young's Tour Through Great Britain" because GW had just received a letter from Young informing him "of his having dispatched a Compleat Sett of his Works for my acceptance."

From William Hartshorne

Sir   Alexandria February 10th 1786

I have a Letter of the 3d inst. from my Freind Israel Thompson who says he is glad he has it in his power to Supply you with the Buckwheat I wrote for, for your use—The Flaxseed he was doubtfull would be Scarcely got of that which is good, but he would use his utmost endeavors—he had a⟨nother⟩ by him, which should be sent if he could no⟨t do be⟩tter—I have desired him to forward both ki⟨nds as⟩ soon as he could get such as would answer.[1]

As I shall shortly have Occasion to send my account against Capt. David Pearce of New England, shall be glad to know how much I am to charge you for the Freight &c. of the Jack Ass brought in his Ship from Spain. Mr Shaw said he would enquire the Freight of a Horse from London which when known, I believe there will be no difficulty, as the Bill Lading seems to Settle other matters except triffles.[2] I am respectfully Yours

Wm Hartshorne

ALS, DLC:GW. The letters in angle brackets are a speculative reading of a mutilated portion of the manuscript.

1. Israel Thompson (d. 1795) was a Quaker planter in Loudoun County. See GW to Hartshorne, 20 February.

2. For David Pearce's account with GW, see William Hartshorne & Co. to GW, 26 Nov. 1785, n.1. In his reply of 20 Feb. GW refers to the failure of his secretary, William Shaw, and his former estate manager, Lund Washington, to find out what the charges were for shipping a horse from London to Virginia.

From Lafayette

Paris february the 10th [1786]

The inclosed, my dear general, is a vocabulary which the Empress of Russia Has Requested me to Have filled up with indian Names, as she Has ordered an Universal dictionary to be made of all languages—it would greatly oblige Her to collect the words she sends translated into the several idioms of the Nations on the Banks of the Oyho—presley Nevill and Morgan at fort pitt, general Mullemberg in fayette's County and our other friends Could undertake it for us, and be very attentive to Accuracy—I Beg Your pardon, My dear general, for the trouble I give you, But Have Been so particularly Applied to, that I Cannot dispense with paying great attention to the Business.[1]

This goes with so long an epistle of Mine that I shall only present you Here with My Best love and wishes and am my dear general Your respectfull & tenderest friend

lafayette

ALS, DLC:GW; copy, PEL. Both are endorsed by GW.

1. On 20 Aug. GW sent copies of Lafayette's letter to George Morgan and Thomas Hutchins asking for their help. Receiving no encouragement from either, on 27 Nov. he made the same request to Richard Butler, who in August had been made Indian Superintendent for the Northern Department. Butler

assembled the vocabulary and sent it to GW on 30 Nov. 1787. GW forwarded it to Lafayette on 10 Jan. 1788. John Peter Gabriel Muhlenberg (1746–1807) had a distinguished career as a brigadier general in the Continental army during the Revolution, and after the war he had a successful career in Pennsylvania politics.

From David Humphreys

My dear General   London Feby 11th 1786

I wrote to you by the ship which brought me your affectionate favour of the 25th of July; since which I have been honoured by the receipt of your letters of the 1st of Septr & 30th of Octr—they reached me a few days ago in this city, where I have been about two months.

You may naturally expect I should give some little account of *this great wonder of the world* and the reception I have experienced in it. This City is in extent as well as population considerably larger than Paris, the streets are wider & cleaner, and the appearance of some particular squares perhaps more elegant, tho' in general I cannot say I like the style of building here so well as in France. But in Horses & Equipages I must give the preference infinitely to those which I have seen in this Country. The Play-houses, public places, & palaces are by no means equal to the same articles in France. I have frequented the Theatres very often and have found an exquisite pleasure in seeing the famous Mrs Siddons perform who is far superior to any thing I had ever beheld on the stage.[1]

I have been three times at Court, first at the Levee to be presented (by Mr Adams) to the King, then at the Drawing Room to pass thro' the same ceremony to the Queen, and the day before yesterday on the splendid occasion of the Queen's birthday. I was introduced (not as a public character) but as Col. H. from the U.S. of America & was received in the same manner any other foreigner would have been. I forbear to give you a detail of the brilliancy of the birth night ball, as I fear I should make a bad hand of describing that kind of pageantry & I am not certain you would take much pleasure in reading it, supposing the discription to do justice to the exhibition—I will only say in honour of America that Mrs Adams appeared to very good advantage, being an extremely decent Lady, and that Miss Adams in beauty & real tastes in dress was not exceeded by any young Lady in the room.

Now I am on the subject of American Ladies I will venture to add that there have been in Europe some very good specimens of beauty from America since I have been on this side the water, for example, Mrs Platt of Hartford, Mrs Bingham & Miss Hamilton from Philadelphia—Mrs Loyd I have not seen, she is in the Country, her husband I saw one evening quite intoxicated, since which I am told he is in confinement for debt.[2]

With regard to the present temper of this country to America, I can say nothing decisively, until some communication shall come from the part of Administration, in consequence of overtures for a Treaty of Commerce which have been made by us to them—however in my private opinion very little, if any thing will be done—A spirit of infatuation will probably influence their Councels until they shall have diverted our commerce irrevocably into some other channel.

It is an object of the greatest curiosity for an American to be present at the Debates in Parliament. I have heard most of the principal speakers. Mr Pitt is undoubtedly a man of talents as well as elocution. Opposition are not so formidable as they have been, nor does the session promise to be so long or violent as the last. There appears however to be a spirit awakened in India which may bring on some interesting discussions, which may be productive of convulsions, perhaps (one day) of a revolution in that Country.

I have met with few British Gentlemen with whom I had been acquainted in America, such as I have seen, have behaved with civility As have several Members of Parliament, literary, & other respectable characters to whom I have been introduced. George Collier (who commanded the fleet up the North River in 1779) in a large company where Col. Smith & myself were present, having inadvertently mentioned the "Rebel Flag" upon perceiving his mistake came up to us & apologized for it.

I shall set out for Paris in a few days, & possibly for America in the spring; should I not arrive in the month of May I will still hope to receive letters from you, as in that case my residence in Europe may be protracted for some year longer—With the warmest wishes for the health & happiness of Mrs Washington & your immediate connections I have the honour to be, most sincerely your friend & devoted Servt

D. Humphreys

ALS, DLC:GW.

1. During the 1785–86 season at Drury Lane Sarah Siddons (1755–1831) played eight roles including Portia and Ophelia.

2. Ann Willing Bingham went to England in 1783 with her husband William Bingham of Philadelphia. Ann Hamilton was in London with her uncle, William Hamilton of Bush Hill. Mr. Loyd may be Richard Bennett Lloyd (1750–1787), younger brother of Edward Lloyd (1744–1796) of Wye House in Talbot County, Maryland. Richard Lloyd was a captain in the Cold Stream guard when the Revolution broke out, and he resigned his commission. He was married to Amelia Leigh of the Isle of Wight, to whom John Adams referred in his diary in 1778 as his friend Lloyd's "handsome English Lady" (Butterfield, *Adams Diary and Autobiography*, 4:67). Mrs. Platt has not been identified.

From Pierre François Cozette

Monsieur   a l'orient le 15 fevrier 1786.

J'ay eté chargé en 1765 de faire pour l'hotel des Bureaux de la Guerre à Versailles, le Portrait a cheval du feu Roy Louis quinze. l'Esquisse de ce tableau que j'ay fait avec beaucoup de soins m'est resté, et je suis absolument le maitre d'en disposer. je ne me permetteray aucunne reflexion sur ce que cette Esquisse qui a le meritte de la ressemblance est encore entre mes mains et ignoré. je l'y trouve deplacé, et le desir qu'il soit mieux m'a fait penser a l'offrire a quelqu'un qui peut en faire un peu de cas. Cette idée Monsieur, m'a fait naitre celle de vous supplier de me permettre de Vous en faire l'homage. Daignez l'accepter Monsieur, comme un temoignage de la Veneration, et du Respect que m'ont inspiré vos vertus.[1]

Le Major l'Enfant, de qui je suis l'amy depuis qu'il est né poura si vous daignez vous en informer, vous instruire Monsieur de ce que je suis. il me connoit bien. mon mediocre talent ne m'a jamais donné de pretentions indiscrettes, quoy que j'aie fait d'assez bonnes choses, mais je me croiray, de domagé, des desagrements que les circonstances m'ont obligé de supporter si vous daignez Monsieur, ne pas rejetter l'offre que je prends la liberté de Vous faire de cette Esquisse, et l'assurance du profond Respect avec le quel je suis. Monsieur, Votre tres humble et tres obeissant Serviteur.

Cozette,

Professeur de dessein des Cadets Gentils-hommes des colonies

ALS, DLC:GW. No translation of this letter for GW has been found.

1. GW made this reply from Mount Vernon on 19 June: "Sir, The Letter which you did me the honor of writing to me, of the 5th of Feby, I have received. I am highly oblig'd to you for the compliment which you pay me in desiring my acceptance of a portrait of Lewis the fifteenth, on horse back, which done by you & is at your disposal.

"I have not the least doubt Sir, but that the performance does honor to your abilities, & I join with you in wishing that it might be placed in some public & conspicuous situation, where the world could be gratified by seeing the picture of a good King, & where the merit of the performer meet with the applause which is due to it. Upon this principle Sir, (though I feel a grateful sense of the honor which you intended me) I must beg leave to decline the acceptance of it, as it could not here be placed in that conspicuous point of view which would do it justice. I am Sir &c. G: Washington" (LB, DLC:GW).

From William Gordon

My dear Sir   Jamaica Plain [Mass.] Feby 16. 1786

Yesterday I recd from Boston the box with the shrubs. They look as well as I could expect, & am greatly obliged to you for them. How far the severe frosts may have damaged them, must be left to the approaching spring to discover. I have some thoughts of taking a number of them with me to London. Should Providence fix me in that spot or neighbourhood, shall endeavour to furnish your garden & shrubbery, with flowers & plants, that may keep up the remembrance of an absent friend.[1]

Since writing about the Memoir &c. have had an opportunity of satisfying myself as to several particulars. Still I am obliged to you, for what you have written.

The enemy came out in force from Philadelphia to surprize the Marquis; but I have not yet met with *positive* proof of their being commanded by Genl Howe in person. This matter I shall be able to ascertain when in London.[2]

I rejoice most sincerely, that the difficulties respecting the navigation of the Patowmack decrease instead of increasing.

The obliging manner in which your Excellency & your Lady have been pleased to accept the trifling token of my strong gratitude is peculiarly pleasing.

When young people fulfill engagements of long standing, they do themselves honour & prove the genuineness of their affections. May your nephew & niece live long mutual blessings to each other; & a joy & comfort to all around them. I pray to be kindly remembered to them; as also to the Dr & his lady & children at Alexandria; not forgetting Mr & Mrs Lund Washington, & upon no account my young friend.

Have reason for thankfulness, that upon the whole we enjoy good health.

Have drawn out the cypher (which I shall enclose) & given a specimen of the mode of working with it.[3] To you it may have no novelty. I remain with sincerest regards Your Excellency's very humble servant

William Gordon

Col. Henley is likely to be a widower in a short time.[4]

ALS, DLC:GW.
    1. See Gordon to GW, 4 Feb., n.1.
    2. For the correspondence between Gordon and GW regarding a memoir of Lafayette's role in the Revolution written by James McHenry, see McHenry to GW, 1 Aug. 1785, n.1.
    3. The enclosed cipher is in DLC:GW.
    4. GW wrote to David Henley on 5 Sept. 1785.

From Henry Lee, Jr.

My dear General   New York 16th Feby 86

You desired to hear from me now and then, when I left Virginia. I obey your wishes with pleasure, & must assure you, that I continue to feel the same unabating zeal to administer to your happiness, which my public duty formerly commanded from me. I wish that my communications may be always agreable; I apprehend your solicitude for the honor & prosperity of a nation formed under your auspices will illy relish intelligence ominous of its destruction. But so circumstanced is the federal government, that its death cannot be very far distant, unless immediate and adequate exertions are made by the several states.

The period is hurrying on, when no longer delay can be permitted.

The late returns from the continental receivers in the different states prove unanimity in one point among the members of the Union—no money—Congress impressed with the lamentable effects which await the United states from their adherence to temporary and disunited exertions, again have addressed the states. I enclose it[1]—If success attends, we may divert the evils which menace our existence & may still enjoy that happiness which we so arduously contended for. But should the same supineness continue in our councils, jealousy instead of patriotism direct the measures of our governments, consequences most distressing must certainly ensue. Part of the principal of our foreign loans is due next year, & no certain means yet devized to pay even the interest.

Our agents have arrived in Morrocco, and Algiers, & we have some hopes that their negotiations may be successful.

It is very doubtful how our commissioners may succeed with the indians.[2] We have too much reason to fear a war, which among other evils will encrease our finance embarrassments. People here are very inquisitive about the progress of the potomack navigation—the moment that business wears the prospect of certainty, rich emigrants from all the eastern states will flock to our towns. The assembly of this state are in session, & will emit 200,000£ paper. They are violent enemys to the impost, & I fear even the impending and approaching dangers to the existence of the Union will not move them—Please to present my respects to Mrs Washington & accept the best wishes of your friend & h. ser.

H: Lee junr

ALS, DLC:GW.

1. The committee "to whom were referred several Reports and Documents concerning the System of General Revenue, recommended by congress on the 18th of April, 1783" ended their report: "*Resolved*, That whilst Congress are denied the means of satisfying those engagements which they have constitutionally entered into for the common benefit of the Union, they hold it their duty to warn their Constituents that the most fatal evils will inevitably flow from a breach of public faith, pledged by solemn contract, and a violation of

those principles of justice, which are the only solid basis of the honor and prosperity of Nations." Congress adopted the report on 15 Feb. 1786 and voted that "the resolves of Congress of the 18th of April, 1783, recommending a system of general revenue, be again presented to the consideration of the Legislatures of the several States, which have not fully complied with the same" (*JCC*, 30:70, 76, 75). Lee's enclosure has not been found.

2. The commissioners succeeded in late January in having the Shawnee sign a treaty setting the boundary from the forks of the Great Miami to Wildcat Creek and down to the Wabash River (Kappler, *Indian Treaties*, 2:16–18).

Letter not found: from Robert Townsend Hooe, 17 Feb. 1786. On 21 Feb. GW wrote Hooe: "Your letter of the 17th did not get to my hands 'till yesterday."

From George Savage

Sir,   Northampton Feby 18th 1786
Yours by my Skipper Mr Whitney enclosing a Rect for the Oats Contracted for with Doctr Stewart came safe to hand; and in Consequence of the Agreement Mr Whitney entered into with your Excellency, have sent the Schooner Molly & Betsey off to Pamunky for the Corn which I hope will arrive at your Excellency's Landing in good order & in due time—The want of a new Jibb oblig'd me to detain the Schooner 3 or 4 days.[1] I am your Excellency's most Obedt hum. Servt
George Savage

ALS, DLC:GW.
1. See GW to Savage, 8 Feb., and note 2 of that document.

Letter not found: from Clement Biddle, 19 Feb. 1786. GW wrote Biddle on 18 May: "Your favors of the 19th of Feby . . . [is] before me."

Agreement with William Halley

February 20th 1786
I have this Day agree'd to pay for the Use of Genrl Washingtons House and Lott in the Town of Alexandria (lately occupy'd by Doctr Wm Brown) for the Term of one year from this Date Forty Pound Specie, to Fence in the Lott with a Good and sufficient Fence either of Post and Rail or Plank, to cleanse and re-

pair the drain leadg from the Cellar and Glaze the Windows of the said House.

William Halley

I promise to see the above engagement fullfil'd.

Alexandr Smith

DS, DLC:GW. It is in the hand of Lund Washington.

Dr. William Brown, grandson of Dr. Gustavus Brown, came to Virginia in 1770 from the University of Edinburgh, where he received his medical training, and settled in Alexandria. Beginning as early as November 1783, he rented for £40 per annum the house that GW had built in 1769–71 at the corner of Pitt and Cameron streets in Alexandria (Ledger B, 119, 185; see also GW to Brown, 24 Nov. 1785). Brown advertised in the Alexandria newspaper on 6 April 1786 that he had moved his medical practice into his new house between Duke and Prince streets in Alexandria. When Brown left, William Halley rented GW's house for "one Year & 12 days"; he paid the last of the £41.12 in rent that he owed in July 1787 (Ledger B, 239). On 25 Nov. 1788 GW wrote his nephew Bushrod Washington: "If you could accommodate yourself in my small house there (the one in which Doctr Brown formerly lived) you shall be very welcome to the use of the Rent free till you can find a more convenient one." After George Augustine Washington's death in 1793, his widow, Fanny Bassett Washington, moved with their two sons from Mount Vernon into GW's house at Cameron and Pitt streets and lived there until her marriage to Tobias Lear in August 1795. GW left the house and lot to Martha Washington at his death. In Michael Miller's *Pen Portraits of Alexandria, Virginia, 1739–1900* (Bowie, Md.), he mentions (p. 41) this advertisement which appeared on 7 Feb. 1857 in the *Alexandria Gazette*: "It is only a few months since a frame building, on Cameron Street, which was built by Washington and used by him for an office, when he was in town, was torn down."

To William Hartshorne

Sir,   Mot Vernon 20th Feby 1786.

I ought to have acknowledged the receipt of your letter of the 10th sooner, tho' I am at a loss what answer to give it now.

When I sent to Boston for my Jackass, which was previous to the presentation of Captn Pearce's order, tho' subsequent to the date of it,[1] I requested Mr Cushing (the Lieut: Governor) to whose care this animal was addressed, to pay all the charges which had accrued for freight & other accidental expences attending the importation [of] him, and to draw upon me for the amount. In consequence I have answered a Draft, to Mr Taylor of your town, for 300 Dollars; & was informed by Mr Cushing, by letter of equal date with the Draft, that he had not at that time been able to obtain Captn Pearce's Accot—but that it should be transmitted as soon as the matter could be settled with him.[2] In this way the thing has lain ever since; Post after Post I have been looking for some further advice respecting this business, but hitherto in vain. I am ready at any moment to answer Captn Pearce's demand, when it is properly ascertained (if it has not been already paid) but it would be inconvenient for me to advance the money twice; of this, I think both Mr Shaw & L. Washington were requested some time ago to inform you—for if the 300 Dollars has not, in part, been appropriated to the payment of Captn Pearce's demand, I know not for what purpose the order was drawn upon me. All the other charges did not amount to more than one third of that sum.[3]

I depended so much upon others to enquire into the usual freight of a horse from London to this Country, as not, hitherto, to have taken any steps myself, to obtain information; & it is to be feared none has been taken, either by Mr Shaw or L. W——, nor do I know at this moment where to direct my enquiries.[4]

I am thankful for your attention to my request respecting the Buck wheat and Flax seeds, & shall be glad to know when they arrive, as I wish to secure all my Seeds for Spring sowing, in time. I am Sir, Yr most Obt Servant

G: Washington

LB, DLC:GW.

1. GW wrote to Thomas Cushing on 26 Oct. 1785 at the time he sent John Fairfax for the jackass in Boston, and it was not until 6 Nov. 1785 that David Pearce wrote that he was sending to Hartshorne an account of his charges for transporting the jackass from Spain to Boston.

2. See Thomas Cushing to GW, 16 Nov. 1785.

3. Thomas Cushing paid shipping charges for the jackass that died at sea. See Cushing to GW, 7 Oct. 1785, n.2, and William Hartshorne to GW, 25 Mar. 1786. For Cushing's other expenditure on behalf of GW, see Cushing to GW, 9 Nov. 1785.

4. See note 2 in Hartshorne to GW, 10 February.

From Battaile Muse

Honourable Sir, Berkeley C[oun]ty February 20th 1786
Your Favour by Daniel McPherson dated Jany The 27th Last I received,[1] Its out of my power To grant Him a Lease for Lott No. 18 on the first Condition—all the arrears of rents are not Paid up and admiting they were, I See no obligation For Him To have a Lease, the man has been Ignorant in Purchaseing what the Seller Cannot Justify. I repeatedly offered Him the Place on Terms I think Justifiable, but He refuses. I have now To rent it on the best Terms I can for your Interest as well some other Lotts on the Same Tract—the First day of March I have advertised I shall attend To rent the Vacated Lotts, they have been Advertised all the winter but none has apply'd but one, that I would admitt as Tenant. the money that McPherson Paid in my opinion Should go To the Credit of Lott No. 18 and Not To Mrs Lemarts accts as She is not charged with arrears of that Lott, on which acct the money was Paid.

Your Favour dated the 4th Instant I receiv'd by the Last Post—I was very Sorry the butter did not get down in Time, not on acct of the high price, but on acct of my Promise. it lay on the road many weeks as a Quantity of my wheat does at this Time, I had Four waggones Last week returned after reaching as Far as Leesburg owing To the roads & weather being so Severe—the Quantity of wheat I engaged has been ready Some Time, but the roads are not Passable, as their is some on the roads—I cannot say what Quantity has been delivered. I will do all I can To get it down Early. If my overseers in Loudoun do not clean the wheat well I wish your miller would write To them as I Well Know they are Generally Diatily Inclined—the wheat From My House I see well clean'd. I shall Collect all the money I Possable Can From the Tenants before the 20th of april & Shall be down about that Time. I have Collected about £110 Clear of Charges, and I expect To Collect about as much more, but that depends on chance as many of the Tenants are Pooer and Money Very Scarce.

I observe all your Instructions and Friendly Powers given me in the Settlement of the Tenants Accts I Shall attend To all things as Far as my Knowledge Extends—the accts will not be settled this year if so, it will be Late Next Fall—as there are many things

Doubtfull with me—I Find you have given a receipt on John Dyers Lease for rent you Say became due 1774 the Lease Sayes 1770[2]—in Griggs acct He is over charged[3]—Lott No. 16 Ezekiel Phillips is charged with £20. in another place Abraham Morgan is Charged with Lott No. 16 £58.14.0—Some Tenants has not receipts—others do not chews To settle at present as they want Time To avoid distresses—under those Circumstances a Stranger as I am To those accts might Commit and Errour—was my Reason (as Far as I at present recolect) for saying that at a Future day To Explain Every Circumstance Respecting these Accts Put into my hands might be difficult To do—So Clearly as I wish all things To appear From my Transactions—I do not desire any Farther Powers—I Shall Take Care To Close no acct or make Final Settlement (only in desperate cases where distresses are required) unless all things appear Clear To my understanding—To go Farther on this Subject would be Tedious To you as I am sinceble that your are Crouded with Perplexsities the Time Draws nigh when I expect To make ⟨a⟩ Proper report of my Transactions, I should not have ⟨trou⟩bled you on the business so much as I have done only from ⟨pr⟩inciple of wishing To do well. I have seen Mr Scott He sayes Mr Jenny gives a wrong representation of the Lines—when I go down I shall Enquire Farther in the matter—but do not at this Time Intend To make a survey untill the Tenaments on that Tract are Properly Pointed out, so as to do all the Surveying business at once To prevent Trouble as well Expences.[4] I beg Leave To present my Self—To be your Faithfull Obedient and Very Humble Servant

                                                                Battaile Muse

ALS, DLC:GW.

    1. Letter not found, but see GW to Muse, 4 Feb., n.1.

    2. John Dyer's lease of lots 13 and 14 in Fauquier and Loudoun counties is dated 17 Mar. 1769. See Lists of Tenants, 18 Sept. 1785, n.21.

    3. Presumably this is Abner Griggs and not Thomas Grigg. See Lists of Tenants, 18 Sept. 1785, n.17.

    4. For GW's dispute with Robert Scott over a part of GW's Chattins Run tract in Fauquier County, see Muse to GW, 5 Jan. 1786, n.1.

From Jonathan Trumbull, Jr.

Dear Sir Lebanon [Conn.] 20th Febry 1786

I pray you to excuse the Liberty I take in presenting you with a Funeral Sermon preached at the Interment of the late Govr Trumbull.

If it does not appear with all that sentimental Elegance & purity which have distinguished the writings of some Gentlemen, yet I trust it will discover a degree of merit & Ingenuity, which will not discredit the reputation of a *young* preacher, or injure the Character of the deceased; for whose sake I am sure you will not refuse to give yourself the trouble of its perusal.[1]

I rejoice exceedingly Sir that you enjoy a good degree of Health—with satisfaction in your pursuits—I most sincerely wish that Mrs Washington might be a partaker with you in both.

I sometimes meditate a Journey into your State—If this takes place one of the greatest pleasures I promise myself in the Tour, will be the satisfaction I should take in paying my affectionate respects to you & Mrs W. With Sentiments of the most perfect regard & Esteem—I have the Honor to be Dr Sir Your most Obedient & most humble Servant

Jona. Trumbull

ALS, DLC:GW.

1. The sermon, preached by Rev. Zebulon Ely at Jonathan Trumbull's funeral on 19 Aug. 1785, was entitled *The Death of Moses the Servant of the Lord*. The copy sent to GW, which was in his library at Mount Vernon at his death in 1799, was printed in Hartford in 1786 by Elisha Babcock (Griffin, *Boston Athenæum Collection*, 74).

Letter not found: to William Hartshorne, 21 Feb. 1785. On 25 Mar. Hartshorne wrote GW: "Your favor of the 21st inst. came."

To Robert Townsend Hooe

Sir, Mot Vernon 21st Feby 1786.

Your Letter of the 17th did not get to my hands 'till yesterday, or it should have received an earlier acknowledgment.[1]

Mr Hiebert either mistook me, or Messrs Valk, Berger & Schouter have misunderstood him: for acquainting the former that a company of which I am a member was desireous of employing a number of hands to drain the great Dismal Swamp near Norfolk, & that I had been requested by it to enquire upon what terms two or three hundred Palatines or Hollanders could be imported for that purpose, his opinion being asked, he answered that he should see Messrs Valk, Berger & Schouter in a few days, (for he was then on the eve of a journey to Boston) & would know from them, or advised me to apply to them (I do not now recollect which) to obtain knowledge of the practicability & convenience of the measure. All I aimed at was information myself; & if the above gentlemen can give it to me, it would oblige me. The Company would wish to know upon what terms they, or any others, in their opinion would engage to deliver 300 able labourers, Germans or Hollanders, not more than eight women, at Norfolk. Whether these would come under Indenture, & for what term; or upon wages, & what. In a word what they would stand the Company pr poll, in either case, delivered at Norfolk—freight, procuring them, & every accidental expence included, to the moment of such delivery at the Ship's side.[2] I am &c.

G: Washington

LB, DLC:GW.
　1. Letter not found.
　2. In May 1785 at the first meeting of its members after the war, the Dismal Swamp Company voted to investigate the possibility of importing foreign workers to be employed in draining the swamp and putting its land under cultivation (Resolutions of the Dismal Swamp Company, 2 May 1785, printed above). GW wrote Jean de Neufville about this on 8 Sept. 1785. See also GW to John Page, 3 Oct. 1785. The firm of Leertouwer, Huiman, & Huiberts had a store in Alexandria where it sold goods imported from Holland. Mr. Huiberts had dinner at Mount Vernon on 16 Sept. 1785 (*Diaries*, 4:194).

From George Taylor, Jr.

Sir,　　　　　　　　　　　　　　New York 21st February 1786.
　Since the beginning of the Season for gathering Fruit, I have been very particular in my Inquiries for an Opportunity to send the Apples which Your Excellency was pleased to Honor me with a Commission to Purchase, all which have hitherto proved unsuccessful, and had I not met with a disappointment in November last, I should now have been incapable of embracing the

present Conveyance. At that Time I was told by a Gentleman belonging to the House of Messrs Murry & Co., who have also a House at Alexandria, that a Vessel would go from thence to that Place. Upon this, I purchased six Barrels, (Copy of the Bill of which I do myself the Honor to send your Excellency herewith enclosed), and in a few Days after was informed that she was sold. I therefore thought it advisable to keep them 'till a good Opportunity should offer, and of this desired Mr Fairfax, when here, to inform your Excellency, and that should I not be able to send them in Season, I would keep them 'till the Spring, at which Time they would probably be more acceptable.

Not having since heard of any, for Alexandria, till the present Vessel, I have had the six Barrels examined with Attention, and find only five of them in good order, which I have herewith put on board of her. I could have wished they were larger, but believe they were as large as any exposed for Sale the last Season, as the Man of whom I purchased them is said to have one of the best Orchards on Long Island. Indeed their keeping so well is a proof of their being good and gathered with Care.

I am sorry that the Season for Lobsters is past. Permit me, however, the Honor of presenting to Your Excellency a few Pickled and Fried Oysters preserved in Pots—there are Eight of the former and Four of the latter packed in two Boxes, for which, and the five Barrels of Apples, I also do myself the Honor to enclose the Captains Receipt. They are done by a very decent Woman and one who is accustomed to preserve them for the West Indies. I shall be happy if, on their Arrival, they should prove acceptable, and hope that the Pleasure and Satisfaction in using them, may be equal to that which I feel in presenting them.[1]

I shall always esteem myself highly honored in executing any Commands which Your Excellency may be pleased to confide to me.

Permit me to present my most Respectful Compliments to Mrs Washington & Family. I have the Honor to be with the highest Respect, Your Excellency's, Most Obedient, And Very humble servant

Geo. Taylor Junr

I shall do myself the Honor to send a Duplicate of this Letter by the Post.

ALS, DLC:GW.

1. Taylor, whom Jay sent to Mount Vernon in August 1785 to make copies of GW's list of African Americans evacuated from New York in 1783, first wrote GW on 17 Oct. 1785 about sending apples to him. On 18 May 1786 GW acknowledged receipt of both the apples and the pickled and fried oysters. The bill that Taylor enclosed shows that he bought on 10 Nov. 1785 from Jacob Blackwell "6 Barrels New Town Pippins—@ 12/," total charges £3.12. For the firm of Murray, Bowen & Munford of Alexandria and New York, see *Diaries*, 4:325; see also John Murray & Co. to GW, 6 March.

2. On 25 Feb. Taylor wrote: "I do myself the Honor to transmit herewith enclosed, the Duplicate of a Letter which I sent your Excellency by Captain Snow of the Sloop Dove, bound to Alexandria" (DLC:GW).

Letter not found: from Thomas Cushing, 22 Feb. 1786. GW wrote Cushing on 5 April 1786: "I have now the honor to acknowledge the receipt of your several favors of . . . 22d of Feby."

From David Ramsay

Sir   New: York Feby 22d 1786
I beg that you would do me the honor to accept a copy of a book I have lately published & which is herewith transmitted. I only regret that my remote situation precluded me from comprehending the operations of the middle & eastern States in which you were the principal actor.[1] Should the perusal give you a moments pleasure I shall be happy. At all events I beg you would accept it as a token of my gratitude for the important services you have rendered our common country & as an evidence of the particular esteem in which you are held by your Excellencys most obedient & very humble servt

David Ramsay

ALS, DLC:GW.

1. Ramsay's two-volume *The History of the Revolution of South Carolina, from a British Province to an Independent State* (Trenton, 1785) was in GW's library at his death. See GW's acknowledgment, 5 April 1786. Ramsay published his two-volume general history of the Revolution in 1789, for copies of which GW thanked Ramsay on 3 June 1790.

Letter not found: to James Taylor, 22 Feb. 1786. On 13 Mar. Taylor wrote GW: "I had the Honor of yours of 22d febry."

To Tench Tilghman

Dear Sir　　　　　　　　　Mount Vernon 22d Feby 1786

If you have reduced the agreement with Mr Rollins to writing, I should be glad to receive it, and the plan by wch the Work is to be executed, as soon as convenient.[1] At any rate the latter, if I am to depend upon Mr Rollins for the execution; because my Joiners assure me, that if any thing is to be done in their way, to the doors or Windows, it must preceed the Stuccoing—& that the plan must be their guide.

This induces me once more to call upon Mr Rollins for particular directions for them (if any are necessary) that there may be no delay; nor any thing wanting on my part previous to his arrival—If this cannot be done by writing—nor prepared in proper time after he comes by four or five workmen (which I have) I would, if he does not consider it to fall within the spirit of the agreement, rather bear the expence of his journey hither myself, than error, or delay, should result from a want of proper instruction. With great regard, and sincere attachment I am— Dear Sir Your Affecte & Obedt Servt

　　　　　　　　　　　　　　Go: Washington

P.S. If any body within your circle, hath lately imported a horse from London (I suppose any other part of England will be the same) you would oblige me by enquiring what the *freight* of him was. *This*, not comprehending the provision for the voyage, is the freight I am to pay for my Jackass, to Boston.[2]

ALS, RPJCB.

1. Tilghman enclosed the articles of agreement with Rawlins, dated 25 Feb., in his letter to GW of 1 March.

2. See William Hartshorne to GW, 10 Feb., n.2.

Advertisement

　　　　　　　　　　　　　　　　Feb. 23, 1786.

ROYAL GIFT. A JACK ASS of the first race in the kingdom of Spain, will cover mares and jennies (the asses[)] at Mount-Vernon the ensuing spring.—The first for ten, the latter for fifteen pounds the season. Royal Gift is four years old, is between 14 1-2 and 15 hands high, and will grow, it is said, till he is 20 or 25 years of age. He is very bony and stout made, of a dark colour, with light belly and legs. The advantages, which are many, to be derived from the propagation of asses from this animal, (the first of the kind that ever was in North-America) and the usefulness of mules, bred from a Jack of his size, either for the road or team, are well known to those who are acquainted with this mongrel race. For the information of those who are not, it may be enough to add, that their great strength, longevity, hardiness and cheap support, give them a preference of horses that is scarcely to be imagined. As the Jack is young, and the general has many mares of his own to put to him, a limited number only will be received from others, and these entered in the order they are offered. Letters directed to the subscriber, by the post or otherwise, under cover to the general, will be entered on the day they are received, till the number is compleated, of which the writers shall be informed, to prevent trouble or expence to them.

JOHN FAIRFAX, Overseer.

Printed in *Pennsylvania Packet* (Philadelphia), 7 Mar. 1786.

1. John Fairfax, who was the overseer of GW's Home House farm at Mount Vernon, conducted the jackass from Boston, arriving back at Mount Vernon on 5 Dec. 1785. See particularly GW's correspondence with Thomas Cushing in the fall of 1785. The wording of the advertisement is obviously GW's, not Fairfax's.

Letter not found: from Thomas Newton, 24 Feb. 1786. On 9 April GW wrote Newton: "I have been favored with your letters of . . . 24th of Febry."

From William Fitzhugh

My Dear Sir   Chatham February 25. 1786.

I have declined answering your last Favour hitherto,[1] that I might have an Opportunity of seeing the different farming Gentlemen in this Neighbourhood, from whom I might have a Chance of getting you some Oats, & I am sorry now to inform you, that I cannot procure a single Bushell—Page & Spotswood have furnish'd themselves with some valuable Seed of the true black English Oat, and also of the white Poland, from an English Farmer, lately arrived;[2] I have with difficulty obtain'd one Bushell of the black Kind, so that amongst us, next year, I am in Hopes we shall be able to supply you—The Moment the Weather becomes tolerable I shall send off the young Doe—in the mean Time, I am with every good Wish for your Lady & Family, in which Mrs Fitzhugh unites with me, Dear Sir Your Aff: & Obed: Ser.

W. Fitzhugh

ALS, DLC:GW.

1. GW must have responded to Fitzhugh's letter of 17 Jan., but it has not been found.

2. Both John Page and Alexander Spotswood, like GW, were very interested in experimental agriculture.

To Robert Edge Pine

Sir, Mount Vernon 26th Feby 1786.

Your favor of the 16th of Decemr (tho' some what delayed) came safely to hand.

The pictures arrived shortly after in good order, & meet the approbation of Mrs Washington & myself—the first of whom thanks you for the portrait of Fanny Washington, with which you have been so polite to present her—she with the Major are on a visit to her friends in the lower parts of this State, & have been so since the middle of December.

It is some time since I requested a Gentleman of Annapolis (who is owing me money & was to have sent it to me) to pay you Twenty guineas & sixteen Dollars; the first for balance due on the pictures—the latter for their frames; but having heard nothing from him respecting it, I begin to suspect it never has been done, & therefore send these sums by Mr Hunter of Alexandria.[1]

I have lately received a Letter from our old & worthy acquaintance Colo. Fairfax, who again mentions you in terms of great regard.[2] Mrs Washington unites her best wishes to mine for you—on congratulations on the safe arrival of Mrs Pine &c. With great esteem I am Sir Yr most Obedient humble Servant

G: Washington

LB, DLC:GW.

1. See GW to John Francis Mercer, 30 Jan., and to William Hunter, 27 February.

2. GW is referring to George William Fairfax's letter of 23 June 1785, brought to him at Mount Vernon on 5 Dec. 1785 by Dr. William Baynham.

To Josias Hawkins

Sir, Mount Vernon Feby 27th 1786.

At the request of Mr Booth, I give you the trouble of this letter. This request, added to an inclination to do justice, must be my apology, for I have no motive but to rescue his character from the injurious aspersions which he says has been cast it.

My acquaintance with Mr Booth is of more than 30 years standing. I have known him in the characters of Batchelor, husband, & widower; in all of which his conduct has been unexceptionable. In that of husband & father, particularly, it was ever esteemed kind, affectionate, & *remarkable* indulgent. In a word, he has passed through life unimpeached by those who have had the best opportunities of forming a judgment of him; and in every instance, to my best knowledge & belief, has supported the character of a Gentleman.[1] I am Sir Yr Obedt Hble Servt

Go: Washington

ALS (photocopy), ViMtV; LB, DLC:GW.

1. Col. Josias Hawkins (c.1735–1789) of Charles County, Md., was brought by William Booth, formerly of Westmoreland County and now living in Frederick, to dinner at Mount Vernon on 28 July 1785 (*Diaries*, 4:157). Booth married Elizabeth Aylett Booth, daughter of William Aylett (d. 1744) of Nomini plantation in Westmoreland County. Booth left Mount Vernon after a three-day visit on 27 Feb., presumably with GW's letter to Hawkins in hand (ibid., 286).

From Leonard Henley

Sir Newkent Feb: 27th 1786.

Agreeable to your directions I have delivered to Mr John Whitney of the Schoone Betcy & Molly two hundred Barrells of Indian Corn from the lower Plantation in King-william County belonging to the Esta. of the late Mr Custis—The Vessel arrived on Wednesday evening last, & Your letter Came to hand the day after—The badness of the Weather prevented me from puting any Corn on board (except a few Barrells) before Saturday; in consequence of which the Vesel was detaind until today. I am Sorry it has not been in my power to procure for You any of the large gray Pease You wrote for by Mr Dandridge but have Sent Six bushells of the best I cou'd get & hope this may answer[1]—I got from Colo. Bassett's your Case of Pictures & put them on board the Vessel & gave particular directions to the Skipper to take proper Care of them[2]—After conversing with the Skipper, & viewing the Vessel, I was of Opinion that the two Calves from Colo. Cary, Could not be Sent with Safety I therefore thought it best to keep them here until You had a more favourable Oppertunity to get them up—Mrs Henley's love accompany'd with my best wishes are offer'd to your Self Mrs Washington & family. I am with great respect Sir. Your Mo: Obdt humble Sert

L: Henley

ALS, DLC:GW.

1. GW's letter has not been found, but see GW to George Savage, 8 Feb., n.2. See also Henley to GW, 14 April.

2. These are the framed prints that George William Fairfax sent to GW in 1784. See George Augustine Washington to GW, 3 Feb., n.3.

To William Hunter

Sir,   Mount Vernon Feby 27th 1786

Mr Shaw informing me of your intended journey to Philadelphia, I take the freedom of asking you to carry Twenty guineas, and Sixteen Dollars for Mr Pine the Portrait Painter; whom you will find at Baltimore or Philadelphia—at Col. Rogers's if in the former—and at the Stadt House, if at the latter.

Be so good as to take his rect for the money—but, previous to paying it, ask if this Sum has not been offered by Mr Jno. F: Mercer. This Gentlemen is owing me money &, out of it, was requested to pay the above sums whilst Mr Pine was at Annapolis; but having no acct of the compliance it is questionable, his having done it.[1]

The bearer will delive[r] you the above sums—I wish you a pleasant journey & safe return—and, with esteem & regard—am Sir Yr Most Obedt Servt

Go: Washington

ALS, ViMtV.

1. William Hunter, Jr. (1731–1792), a Scot, was a successful merchant in Alexandria who at this time dined fairly often at Mount Vernon. See GW to Robert Edge Pine, 26 February.

Letter not found: from Wakelin Welch, 27 Feb. 1786. GW wrote to Welch, July 1786, acknowledging the receipt of his letter "of the 27th of Febry."

From Tench Tilghman

Dear Sir   Baltimore 1st March 1786

I have recd your favr of the 22d ulto in consequence of which I sent for Rawlins and have prevailed upon him to go down to Mount Vernon, as I found him incapable of giving such directions in writing as would have been intelligible—The Expences of this journey are certainly provided for in the Agreement, which you have inclosed.[1] I did not hint at a doubt of this, as I knew if I gave Rawlins the least opening to make it an extra matter, he would take advantage of you.

No Horse has been imported here lately from England. The last that I remember belonged to a Mr Hall of Prince Georges County—what Freight he paid I cannot learn.[2]

I must beg the favor of you to make the Compliments of Mrs Tilghman and myself to Mrs Washington—I am with very sincere Regard Dear Sir Yr most obt & most humble Servt

Tench Tilghman

ALS, DLC:GW.

1. The enclosed articles of agreement, dated 25 Feb., made with John Rawlins, "Stucco Worker" of Baltimore, by Tilghman on behalf of GW provided that Rawlins would "on or before the fifteenth Day of April next at furthest begin to work upon a Certain Room at Mount Vernon . . . distinguished by the Name of the New Room" and would "truly and diligently continue to do and perform the Stucco Work of the said Room until he shall have finished the same, according to the Plan which hath been agreed upon . . . in a true workman like manner." Rawlins was to "provide all necessary Workmen and

Tools for the carrying on the said Work." In return, Tilghman agreed that GW would "upon the finishing of the Room aforesaid, pay" Rawlins £168, plus £13.10 for traveling expenses, Maryland currency. Also, if "Rawlins shall require it," Tilghman on behalf of GW would advance him "any sum of Money, not exceeding the sum of fifty Pounds Maryland Currency." Tilghman also agreed that GW would "at his own expence and in the manner most convenient to himself, transport the necessary Workmen and Tools" provided by Rawlins from Baltimore to Mount Vernon and back again. GW also would "be at the expence of transporting by Water . . . such of the Stucco as it shall be necessary to mould at Baltimore and . . . furnish . . . Rawlins as well as his Workmen with proper Board and Lodging while they are employed at Mount Vernon." Finally, Tilghman agreed that GW would "at his own expence furnish and provide the Matterials necessary to compleat the work." Tilghman and Rawlins both posted performance bonds of £500.

2. This may be Benjamin Hall of Francis (d. 1803), who lived at Pleasant Hill in Prince George's County, Md., or his brother Richard Bennett Hall (1760–1805), who lived at Partnership in Prince George's County.

From John Jay

Dr Sir   N[ew] York 2 March 1786
at & for some time after the arrival of your kind and friendly Letter by mr Taylor, official Business obliged me to postpone writing the Letters due to my private Correspondents.[1] In Decr a young Man under the Influence of more important advisors, made an attack in the Papers, which rendered the Publication of my Correspondence with him expedient. The first Edition being replete with Errors of the Press, a second became indispensable; and from the moment of the attack I concluded to delay answering your Letter until I could transmit with it a proper State of Facts. a new Edition has *just* been compleated, and I have the Honor of enclosing a copy of it with this.[2]

now my dear Sir let me tell you, and very sincerely, that no Letter, since my Return, has given me more pleasure than yours. as civilities like true and counterfiet Coins, are sometimes difficult to distinguish, and as Commendation, having no intrinsic Value, borrows the Chief of its worth from the merit of those who bestow it, I feel on this occasion all the Satisfaction which can result from approbation under the most advantageous Circumstances.

an apprehension that this Letter may not reach the post office in Time, presses me not to enlarge at present. Mrs Jay whose best wishes you enjoy, disires me to tell you so, and with me requests the favor of you to present the like to mrs Washington—with perfect Esteem & attachmt I am Dear Sir your most obt & very hble Servt

John Jay

ALS, DLC:GW.

1. GW sent a letter to Jay dated 27 Sept. 1785 by George Taylor, Jr.

2. For Jay's controversy with Lewis Littlepage, see Lafayette to GW, 6 Feb., n.10. See also Henry Lee, Jr., to GW, 2 Mar., n.4.

From Henry Lee, Jr.

My dear Genl   March 2d n[ew] york. 1786

I did myself the honor to write to you some days past:[1] since which an Arabian stud horse has arrived in this City & has been announced in the gazettes a present to you, from his Catholic Majesty.

I consider it not improper to inform you that the printers have mistaken the matter, the horse being sent to Mr Jay.

Our fœderal distresses gather fast to a point. New Jersey has refused the requisition, and will grant not a shilling, till New york accedes to the impost.

Pe[r]haps this intemperance in Jersey may bring this state to acquiesce in a system of finance long ago approved by ten states & whose operation might have saved the difficultys which impend over the Union.

I intended to have sent you Mr Ramsays late publication, entitled the "revolution of So. Carolina" but am anticipated by the Author who forwarded you a sett by a vessel from this port to Alexandria.[2]

Gordons history has not yet made its appearance & Many hope never may; as the character & genius of the writer illy correspondents with the subject.[3]

I hope your lady enjoys her health & beg to be presented to her. I have the honor to be dear sir your most aff. h. sert

Henry Lee Junr

Mr Jays narrative of his late altercation with Mr Littlepage accompanys this.[4]

ALS, DLC:GW.

1. Lee wrote on 16 February.

2. See David Ramsay to GW, 22 February.

3. For the public criticism of William Gordon, see Gordon to GW, 9 April, n.2.

4. Lee may have enclosed John Jay's letter of this date and Jay's "State of Facts." See Lafayette to GW, 6 Feb., n.10.

From Edmund Randolph

Dear sir   Richmond March 2. 1786.

The delay, which has hitherto occurred in transmitting to you the inclosed proceedings, will be ascribed, I hope, to its true causes; one of which will be found in my last letter, and the other in the daily expectation of Mr Ross's visit to Mount-Vernon, in pursuance of our resolution of the 8th of december 1785.

You may possibly be surprized, that a work, which has already expended a considerable sum of money, should be delineated in so few words, as the copies now sent contain, But I beg leave to inform you, that We have detailed in the execution almost the whole of the resolutions.[1]

For example: We have procured the ascertainment of a precise point, to which the navigation is to be extended; Crow's ferry being now established, as such.[2]

We are authorized to borrow money at six per cent, and to extend the number of shares.

Unexperienced as we were, we yet conceived that our duty called for an examination of the ground between Richmond and Westham. The difficulties seemed greater than we at first apprehended. As soon as the report is prepared by a more skilful hand, than we affect to be, it shall be forwarded to you.

The old books of subscriptions are not compleat, as I supposed, when I wrote to you last. Seven shares are still unoccupied; of which we shall reserve the five, which you wished for yourself.[3]

It was impossible to engage any other labour, than that of blacks: and this necessity has obliged us to bring the labourers into actual service, earlier perhaps than we should have done, in the present state of our imperfect knowledge of canals. But the subscribers would have been dissatisfied, had we not begun in the course of this Year, and negroes, you know, sir, must be hired in January at farthest.

Concerning our progress in this great business, our plans, and future expectations, we beg you to enquire of James Harris, our manager, who will deliver this letter. He is a quaker, of good character, as a man, and a mechanic, formed by nature for the management of water, when applied to mills. He has added nothing to his natural turn, by the view of any very great works. We therefore request, if you see no impropriety, that you would give him such a passport to the Potowmack works, as will enable him to get a thorough insight, into what is there projected. You perceive that Mr Ross was originally intended to be sent to Mount Vernon for this purpose; but he has been for a length of time under a severe disease, and is not yet restored. The office of subordinate manager, mentioned in one of the resolutions, does not exist; it being swallowed up in that of Mr Harris.

It is not improbable, that Mr Harris may continue his journey to the Susquehanna canal. If so, we shall thank you, to furnish him with a certificate of being employed by the James River company in any manner, which may appear most likely to introduce him into an acquaintance with those of that scheme, who may be most intelligent.[4]

Thus, my dear sir, I have written to you at the desire of my brethren in office a tedious account of our operations. Permit me therefore to return to the contemplation of private friendship, and to assure you, that I am always with the greatest respect and esteem your mo. affte and obliged humble serv.

Edm: Randolph

ALS, DLC:GW.

1. Randolph appended the proceedings of the James River Company for the period from 20 Aug. to 22 Dec. 1785 to his letter: "At the public buildings on the 20th day of august 1785. At a meeting of subscribers to the opening of the navigation of James river 287 shares Appeared.

"Resolved unanimously that General Washington be appointed president for three years.

"Resolved that John Harvie, David Ross, William Cabell, and Edmund Randolph be appointed directors for three years.

"James Buchanan laid before the meeting the state of the Subscription in his hands.

"Resolved that it be an instruction to the president and directors to take fit measures by application to the assembly, for vesting a general meeting with power to ascertain some precise point to which the navigation of James River is to be extended or, if this object cannot be obtained, to adopt any other expedient for ascertaining such point.

"Resolved that it be an instruction to the president and directors to prepare and report to the general meeting such amendments, as it may seem expedient to make in the Act for clearing and improving the navigation of James River: and to petition the assembly to make the same, if no meeting should be held on the first day of October next."

"At a meeting of John Harvie, David Ross [1736–1817; of Petersburg] and Edmund Randolph directors at Richmond.

"27 Septr 1785. A letter from the president was read.

"Resolved that we will to morrow visit the ground between tide water and Ballendine dam at Westham.

"Note: that it appears from the return of William Cabell and Charles Irving commissioners, that they have received subscriptions to the amount of fifty three shares, and of George Clendinen that he has received subscriptions of 35 Shares.

"Septr 28. The directors aforesaid viewed the Ground.

"Septr 29. At a meeting of the said directors at Richmond.

"Resolved that it appears adviseable to use slaves in the common labour.

"Resolved that an advertisement be inserted in the public gazettes for three weeks successively, inviting some person to be manager in general: but whose *present* business shall be to hire and superintend such a number of slaves as he may be instructed.

"Resolved that contracts be opened without delay for the purchase of such lands and other interests as may be necessary for the accomplishment of the objects of our institution; it being our wish not to resort to any step of coercion without unavoidable necessity.

"Resolved that each share pay on or before the 1st day of december 1785 £3 and on or before the first day of april 1786 the farther sum of £2.

"Resolved that as it is as yet uncertain, what sums may be necessary for our purchases of land or other interests of the like nature, it be recommended to the subscribers to hold themselves in readiness for further payments.

"Resolved that James Buchanan be treasurer."

"At a meeting of the subscribers at Richmond on Saturday the 1st of October 1785.

"The Proceedings of the directors were read."

"At a meeting of the directors: i.e. David Ross, John Harvie & E. Randolph Decr 8th 1785.

"A memorial to the general assembly was agreed to in the following words.

"Resolved that the allowance of the temporary and subordinate manager be £100 Per Annum and his expences—If the directors are satisfied with his exertions, they will add £50 pr Annum.

"Resolved that David Ross wait upon General Washington and request his communication of such ideas, as he may think useful to the work: and particularly inform him of the aid which we hope to receive from the skill of an engineer employed by the Potowmac company.

"Resolved that the said David Ross be impowered to bind the company for any expence, which he may think proper, for obtaining the aid of the said engineer; or for any cooperation, which may be established between the two companies."

"Decr 22d 1785. At a meeting of the directors.

"Resolved that James Harris, who appears to be highly recommended be appointed manager, with a salary of £250 per annum and support for himself and family; with liberty to the directors to remove him at pleasure.

A true copy
Edm: Randolph"

2. The Virginia assembly in its recent session passed "An act to amend an act, intituled, An act for clearing and improving the navigation of James river," which included the provision "That Crow's ferry, at the mouth of Loony's creek, shall be forever taken and deemed to be the highest place practicable within the meaning of the above recited act" (12 Hening 116–17). Looney Creek empties into the James in Botetourt County.

3. See John Hopkins to GW, 1 May.

4. James Harris, manager of the James River Company, arrived at Mount Vernon with Randolph's letter on 11 Mar. (*Diaries*, 4:292).

From Smith & Douglass

Sir   Alexandria March 4th 1786

We acknowledge your Excelencys goodness in the Indulgence we have had in makeing our remittencess for the last year and also Return you thanks for your kind offer on tuesday Last but have Since thought proper to decline for this year.

We have in your fish house A number of Hhds we wish to dispose of they possibly may answer your purpose if So we wait your Answer to detirmine us concerning them.[1] With every Sentiment of respect we are your Excelencys Most Obt & Humble Servts

Smith & Douglass

LS, DLC:GW.

1. The preceding spring, on 6 April 1785, GW has this entry in his diary: "Sent my Shad Sein and Hands to the Ferry to commen⟨ce⟩ Fishing for Mssrs. Douglas & Smith who had engaged to take all the Shad & Herring I can catch in the Season—the first at 15/. a hundred, and the other at 4/. a thousand" (*Diaries*, 4:114). After receiving this letter from Smith & Douglass, GW wrote the Alexandria firm of John Murray & Co. on 6 Mar. about buying

his fish but on 8 Mar. rejected Murray's offer to take "two or three hundred" barrels of herring (John Murray & Co. to GW, 6 Mar.; GW to John Murray & Co., 8 Mar.). On 10 Mar. another merchant in Alexandria, George Gilpin, wrote GW that having learned that Smith & Douglass had "declined fishing this season," he was offering to supply GW with as many as 150 fish barrels. Also on 10 Mar., both John Murray & Co. and Smith & Douglass wrote GW from Alexandria, the first noting that on that day GW had agreed to take 200 fish barrels from the company and the other stating: "We shall give ourselves no further trouble about the casks but request it of you to have them counted the half casks to be half price" (DLC:GW). After all of this to-do, GW reported on 7 April that George Augustine Washington "went to Alexandria and engaged 100,000 Herrings to Smith and Douglas (if caught) at 5/ pr. thousand" (*Diaries*, 4:305). The account with Smith & Douglass in Ledger B, 225, shows that they purchased from GW on 10 May 118,280 herrings at five shillings per thousand for £29.11.4 and 1,342 shad at twenty shillings per hundred for £13.8.9. It also shows the company in return supplying GW on 6 May with 84 hogsheads, 1 pipe, 16 half pipes, and 2 tierces and, on 15 May, paying him in cash £19.9.1, the balance due on the total value of the fish (£43.0.1). There is nothing in GW's ledger to indicate that GW bought fish barrels in 1786 from either John Murray & Co. or George Gilpin. The partnership of Smith & Douglass was dissolved later in the year.

Letter not found: to William Hartshorne, 6 Mar. 1786. On 6 Mar. Hartshorne wrote: "Your favor of this day I recd."

From William Hartshorne

Sir   Alexandria March 6. 1786

Your favor of this day I recd and shall forward your Letter to Mr Mercer tomorrow & if he will pay the money my assistant will bring it, or should Mr Mercer be returned to Virginia, bring back the Letter.[1]

I have a Letter from Capt. Pearce of the 26th Janry wherein he says he has wrote you respecting his acct for Freight of the Jack Ass and that you might Settle with me as you pleased and that he should be Perfectly pleased with what Suited you—I observe the uncertainty you are in about this accot being paid as mentioned in your Letter of the 20th Ulto—Mr Pearce writes me he had sent you a Letter on the Subject[2]—if the matter has not been cleared up to your Satisfaction Please to informe me as I owe you money for Flour which should have been paid before, but I was in hopes this accot would have been deducted, but I will now pay as soon as I can get the money which expect will be in a few days[3]—I am very Respectfully Yours

Wm Hartshorne

ALS, DLC:GW.
   1. GW's letter to Hartshorne has not been found. His letter to John Francis Mercer of this date is printed below.
   2. See David Pearce to GW, 22 January.
   3. GW's response to this of 21 Mar. has not been found, but see Hartshorne's letter of 25 March.

To John Francis Mercer

Dr Sir,   Mount Vernon 6th March 1786.
   The Treasurer of the Potomack Company being desired by the Directors of it to send a careful hand to Annapolis for the advance due on the State subscription; I pray you to pay the Bearer (who will be that person) the £200—for which you requested me to draw on you at that place.[1] I am Dr Sir &c.

G: Washington

P.S. Since writing to you the 30th of Jany on this subject—I have myself sent the 20 guineas &c. to Mr Pine.

LB, DLC:GW.
   1. See GW to Mercer, 20 Dec. 1785, n.1.

Letter not found: to John Murray & Co., 6 Mar. 1786. John Murray & Co. wrote GW on 6 Mar. "in reply to your favor of this date."

From John Murray & Co.

Sir   Alexandria March 6th 1786
   In reply to your favr of this date[1] we have to say that we have already contracted for a quantity of herring at Eighteen Shillings pr bbl & give salt in excha. at three Shillings pr bus., 2/9 in Coarse & 1/3 in Liverpool Salt, on which terms we are willing to engage for two or three hundred bbls more, the fine Salt to be ⟨dld⟩ either here or at Dumfries, the Coarse either at the landing where the fish are caught or in this harbor, as may be most convenient, by this we mean, if a Vessel of our own should bring it, we would deliver it where most convenient to the pur-

chaser, if freighted it must be receiv'd at the port of delivery; if those terms which are the only we can offer, suit, you will be kind enough to let us know as soon as convenient.

I hourly expect a Vessel from New York, which we suppose has been out about ten days, she has on board some freight for Your Excellency & should she come to an anchor near Mount Vernon, the Captn will deliver it if at hand upon shewing him the inclosed order.[2] Very respectfully we are Sr Your most obedt Servants

John Murray & Co.

P.S. It is most likely we shall want the early fish.

LS, DLC:GW.
   1. Letter not found.
   2. See GW's response, 8 March.

From Samuel Purviance, Jr.

Sir   Baltimore 6th March 1786

I took the liberty of troubling you in 1779 with some Queries relative to a parcel of Lands which were offerd to me near the mouth of the Great Kanhaway[1]—My Brother & I became Purchasers thereof, to the Amount of Fourteen thousand Acres, besides some other parcels in which We have become interested, upon Elk River a branch of the Kanhaway—This having interested Me so much in that Quarter, I am anxiously desirous to procure some authentic information whether any Settlements have yet begun, or are like to take place in that part of Virginia: And altho I have been at some pains to inform myself, the only certain Account which I have yet obtained, is, that Colo. Lewis had begun a Settlement at the mouth of the Kanhaway, which if it succeeds, must probably have a considerable effect on the Value of Lands in that Vicinity—Knowing that you had a considerable property near that place, I conceived that you coud probably inform me better than any Person to whom I coud apply, of what is done or doing towards the furtherance of any new Settlements upon the Kanhaway: for without the Execution of some such Measures, it is evident, that Property there can neither have any present nor encreasing Value—If I coud be assured that any effectual Steps were taken to promote or further such Settlements, I shoud gladly use every endeavour in my power to promote the design—It is with this intention that I now take the liberty of addressing You, and requesting that you will oblige Me with the best information you can give, how Matters are situated in that part of your State, And what probability there is of any effective Settlements being made there.

Permit Me also to request if it is in your power, to gratify me with any tollerable description of the Great Kanhaway and the principal branches of it, as all my Enquiries hitherto upon that Subject have been very imperfectly answerd—My Son who returned from Kentucky in August, informs Me that the Kanhaway where he crossed it, which I suppose to be the branch called New River, is a very large navigable Stream, And that James River where he crossed it, is also a fine navigable Stream of Two to three hundred Yards across—This with every other Account I have had of those Rivers, excite my Wishes to know whether the State of Navigation in the former, is such as can Establish a Communication between James River & the Western Waters, and whether such design is comprised in the Scheme now carrying on to improve the Navigation of James River. So various & contradictory have been all the Informations I coud ever collect, about either the quality or quantity of Lands on the Kanhaway, as well as of the different Falls in that River, that I coud form no certain Judgement on those Subjects—The Accounts which I have had of Elk River, are, that it is the lowest principal branch on the Northside, emptying into the Kanhaway about 40 Miles above its mouth, and considerably below the lowest Falls on that River, that it extends across towards the Little Kanhaway, And the Lands on it are said to be very rich, but Not very level.[2]

The noble design which you have taken such pains to promote, of establishing a Communication between the Eastern & Western Waters thro' Potomack I heartily wish to see atempted thro every other Channel that promises Success to such Undertakings: And it appears to Me that if the Navigation of the Kanhaway is practicable, a Communication between it & James River is more likely to be of extensive utility to your State, than that thro Potomack. I flatter myself that if the Susquehanna Canal is once compleated, it will unite the Views of Pensylvania & Maryland in opening a Communication between the Waters of Susq[uehann]a & the Allegeney, which is generally thought very practicable—The Secretary of our Corporation of the Susqa Canal is now here, and informs Me that Mr Brindley our Engineer has now compleated about two Miles of the upper End of the Canal, in which distance were included all the principal difficulties of that Undertaking, and of which three Quarters of a Mile were One continued & solid body of Rock, thro part of which they had to cut about Sixteen feet deep[3]—This being got over, there seems not a remaining doubt of our being able to effect the residue of that Undertaking, most of which is supposed to be not more difficult than an ordinary Mill Race—I shall be glad to learn that you find equal hopes of Success in the Potomack Scheme.

Mr Neilson the Bearer of this, my Nephew, having Occasion to go to Dumfries, I have directed him to forward my letter to you as he goes down, & to return by your House, in hopes you may find time for a Reply when he comes up—And as he is to proceed to Louisville immediately after his return here, and to go to Pitsburg or Wheelan, he will readily take charge of your Commands shoud you have any in his route—As he will have Occasion to call at Col. Pentecosts in Washington County, he can carry any Letters which you want to convey to that Quarter. I will also direct him to stop at Colo. Lewis's Place at the Kanhaway in order to procure information how affairs go on there, as One tract of the Lands which We purchasd, is adjoining to Colo. Lewis's.[4]

Presuming on your Goodness to excuse this trouble, I remain with every possible Sentiment of Gratitude & Respect, and with the most Affectionate Wishes for you & Mrs Washingtons' Wellfare Sir Your most Obededient And Very hble Servant

Saml Purviance

ALS, DLC:GW; ADfS, NcD: Purviance-Courtenay Papers.

Purviance's father, Samuel Purviance, Sr. (1715–1781), emigrated in the 1750s with his family from Ireland to Philadelphia, where he became a merchant. Two of his sons, Samuel (d. 1788) and Robert (c.1732–1806), settled in Baltimore during the 1760s and built a rum distillery, engaged in West Indian trade, became leading merchants in the town, and during the Revolution began speculating on a large scale in western lands. In 1787 before disappearing after his capture by the Indians in the Ohio country in March 1788, Samuel Purviance, Jr., declared bankruptcy (*Biographical Dictionary of the Maryland Legislature*, 2:667–69).

1. Purviance wrote GW on 13 July 1779 of his intention to buy two tracts of

land near the Great Kanawha, one of 5,000 acres and another of 6,000, both of which were part of the survey under the terms of Dinwiddie's Proclamation of 1754 and were originally claimed by George Muse. For Muse's Kanawha tracts, see Agreement with George Muse, 3 Aug. 1770, n.1, Petition to Lord Dunmore and the Virginia Council, c.4 Nov. 1772, n.3; GW to George Muse, 29 Jan. 1774, GW to Samuel Lewis, 1 Feb. 1784, source note, and, especially, Muse to GW, 3 Mar. 1784, n.1.

2. Purviance may be referring to his son Henry who later studied law with Henry Clay and died in Kentucky in 1811. See GW's reply of 10 March.

3. See James Rumsey to GW, 29 Mar., n.1.

4. Neilson may be Robert Neilson who died in Baltimore County in 1799. Dorsey Pentecost was a Virginian who lived at his place, Greenway, in the forks of the Youghiogheny River in Washington County, Pennsylvania. Thomas Lewis (1754–1824), Col. Andrew Lewis's second son, who had settled near the mouth of the Great Kanawha, had little success in attracting settlers to the area (see Lewis to GW, 27 Aug. 1788).

From Warner Washington

Dear Sir   March 7th 1786

In the Month of March, I do not recollect the Year, one William Bartlett took a Lease of 125 acres of your Land in the Barrens of Bullskin, Bartlett has been dead some few Years & the Widow continued on the Lease till last Summer or Fall was twelve Month. Mr John Bryan who has the management of my Business took possession of the above Lease by your permission. I will be his Security for the punctual payment of the Rent & that every Article of the Lease shall be complyd with[1]—A Dwelling house according to the dimentions has been built, also a Well of good Water, some Peach trees have been planted and about four Acres laid down in English Clover but it is now over run with blue Grass which will be broke up in the Fall & laid down with Clover—I am Dear Sir Your most Obedt Servt

Warner Washington

ALS, CSmH.

1. See Lists of Tenants, 18 Sept. 1785, n.5. Warner Washington lived at Fairfield in Frederick County.

To John Murray & Co.

Gentn   Mount Vernon 8th March 1786.

Your letter of the 6th in answer to mine of the same date,[1] is before me; but from the present view I have of the subject, I do not conceive that *my* entering into a Contract for Herrings on the terms offered by *you*, would be eligible; 1st because in my judgment, you estimate them too low—lower than they usually sell for at the landings—2dly because your Salt is rated higher than, I believe it is to be bought for—more than I have lately given. 3dly because Liverpool Salt is inadequate to the saving of Fish, & therefore useless in this business—4thly because I would not, on any terms, go to Dumfries for this article; and fifthly, because it does not suit me to receive Salt *alone* in paymt.

Moreover, if your coarse salt is allum or lump Salt, I conceive it must be reduced by pounding, before it can be applied—which would add to the expence of curing. Lisbon is the proper kind of Salt for Fish.

From these considerations I must decline contracting to furnish Herring unless you are disposed to offer more favourable terms.[2] I am &c. &c.

G: Washington

LB, DLC:GW.
1. GW's letter of 6 Mar. has not been found.
2. See Smith & Douglass to GW, 4 Mar., n.1.

To Battaile Muse

Sir,   Mt Vernon 8th March 1786

I have Just received your letter of the 20th of last Month, & only request that you will proceed as you have begun; that is, to do equal & impartial Justice to the Tennants, & myself, I want no improper advantage of them on the one hand—On the other, where leases are clearly forfeited by a manifest intention on the part of the Tennant to neglect all the Covenants in them, that were inserted for my Benefit; & their Sole aim has been to make Traffick of the land, I shall have no Scruple in Setting them aside, & Beginning a fresh, upon the best Rents I can get, for 10 years. At any rate it is my wish that you would be as attentive to the other Covenants of the leases as to that which exacts the Rent. Particularly to those which require a Certain Proportion of Woodland to be left Standing in One Place—to Orchards, to Meadows, & to Buildings. These were as much objects with me as the Rent—Nay more, because to these I looked to have the Value of my lands enhanced, whilst I was, in the first instance, Contenting myself with low rents. If therefore these have Passed off unnoticed by the Tennants, it Should be Punished equally with the nonpayment of Rents. I mention these things because it is my wish, they Should be strictly complied with. There is another matter or Two, which in Renting my lands I am desirous you Should always keep in View. 1st To lease to no Person who has lands of his own adjoining them; & 2d to no One who does not Propose to live on the Premises. My reasons are these; in the first case, my land will be cut down, worked, & Destroyed to Save his own; whilst the latter will receive all the Improvements. In the Second case, If the Tennant does not live thereon, it will not meet a much better fate, & Negroe Quarters, & Tobacco Pens, will Probably be the best edifices on the Tenement. One Grigg (I think his name is) an Overseer to Colo. John Washington, must be an exception, because at the instance of my Brother, I consented to the Purchase he has made.[1]

Inclosed you have a letter for Mr Robt Rutherford, of whome you will endeavour to receive the Amount of the Within. If you Should Succeed in this, you may carry it to my Credit, & draw a Commission thereon, as If Collected for Rent.[2] I also Send you an Accot against a Capt. David Kennedy (I believe of Winchester,[)] to receive if you can on the Same terms, I put this Accot about 18 Mos. ago into the hands of Genl Morgan, to whome Kennedy had, I believe, made Sale of a Lott, in Winchester, but know not to what effect. It may be well to enquire of Morgan concerning it, previous to an application to the former.[3] I am Sir Yr Very Hble Servt

Go: Washington

LS, in the hand of William Shaw, PWacD: Sol Feinstone Collection, on deposit PPAmP; LB, DLC:GW.

1. This was Thomas Griggs who rented lot 4 in Berkeley County. See Lists of Tenants, 18 Sept. 1785, n.4. See also GW to John Augustine Washington, 27 Mar. 1786.

2. GW's letter not found. See Robert Rutherford to GW, 28 Mar., and the source note of that document.

3. David Kennedy, who rose to the rank of lieutenant in GW's Virginia Regiment in the 1750s and in 1758 served as its quartermaster, between 1766 and 1773 rented for £28 per annum a tract of land on Bullskin Run belonging to GW. When he gave up the place, Kennedy owed GW £28, which remained unpaid. In September 1784 GW enlisted the help of Gen. Daniel Morgan to collect Kennedy's debt (GW to Morgan, 4 Sept. 1784; Morgan to GW, 30 Sept. 1784). On 3 April 1786 Morgan wrote GW to explain why he had been unable to collect from Kennedy and to say that he would turn over to Muse "the accompt and order at our court." The account that GW enclosed in this letter to Muse shows Kennedy still owing GW £28, and it includes GW's order to Kennedy: "Sir, Please to pay the above Balle to Mr Battaile Muse and his rect shall be a discharge from Yr Obt Servt Go: Washington" (ADS, NjP). Muse reported on 20 Nov. 1786 that Kennedy would not pay and asked whether he should sue him. GW's instructions of 4 Dec. 1786 were for Muse to obtain security from Kennedy to pay the debt within six or twelve months. On 17 April 1787 Muse got Kennedy's copy of GW's account on which Kennedy acknowledged his debt. Three times by letter in 1787, on 20 Jan., 4 Feb., and 15 Mar., Muse assured GW that Kennedy was not able to pay. Two years later, on 12 Mar. 1789, GW wrote Muse enclosing "a bond of Kennedy's and Speake's . . . to put in suit immediately if there is any propect of recovering either from the principal or Security." Muse replied on 21 Mar. 1789 that he did not know Speake but that he had "applyed & thretned Kennady at Least Ten Times," that Kennedy still was "not able to Pay," and furthermore that Kennedy was now "Liveing in the Prison Bounds." GW's account with Kennedy in Ledger B, 22, has as its final, undated entry the notation that the account was settled by GW's agent.

Letter not found: to Robert Rutherford, 8 Mar. 1786. On 28 Mar. Rutherford wrote: "I am hond by your excellency's letter of the 8th instant."

From Rochambeau

My Dear Général,   Paris March the 9th 1786.
    it comes to have, in the parliament of England, a scene of a great Concern. The question was to Know if they Should fortify the harbours of the Kingdom, having at their head M. Pitt and the Duc of Richmond that were for the affirmative. The house of parliament has been divided, and the voice of the Speaker has decided for the negative. So much the worse, I believe, because the Enormous Sums that they Should have Spent at this fortifications, having the Lord Richmond at the head of this Kind of works, whereof he is a Virtuoso, this Sums, I Say, instead

of being needless Spent there, Shall turn to the benefit of their navy and clearing of their debts.

Lord Cornwallis comes to be appointed Général Governor of the Bengal, his taste for travelling Shall not be disputed to him, and this last voyage will be more lucrative than that of america, tho' I believe he will behave with much more power than any of his predecessors.

I have Successively received, my Dear Général, your letters of the 7th of September and of the first of December ultime—I think as you that the Doctor francklin has undertaken too havy and ungrateful a task for his old-age, and your Existence is much more noble than his own, and without title you enjoy of all the consideration owing to your person and So much deserved by the distinguished services that you have rendered to your country which ought never forget them.

The health of the King of Prussia has been very weak all this Winter, but if Germany comes to lose him, I do not believe that Event will bring war. he has prepared every thing that his Successor may be able to make revive him. they do already his Epitaph in Latin that I find handsome by its laconism *hic Cineres, ubique nomen*. that is all what remains to the Greatest man, my Dear Général, but what is to last as long as I live, is the inviolable and Respectful attachment with which I have the honour to be my Dear Général, Your most obedient and Very humble servent.

le cte de rochambeau

LS, DLC:GW.

From George Gilpin

Dear Sir   March 10th 1786

Smith and Duglass inform'd me that they declined fishing this season which made me take my people from gitting Staves to other business, but it will be in my power to deliver Seventy five fish barrels on or before the fifteenth and seventy five more by the last day of April next in Alexandria, the barrels Shall be good my price is 4/6 ⅌ barrel, it will be convenient for me to wait Untill the fishing Season is ended, a line from you within one week will fix this matter as you may choose.[1] I am Dr sir with the greatest regard your most obedient Servt

George Gilpin

ALS, DLC:GW.
   1. See Smith & Douglass to GW, 4 Mar., n.1.

Letter not found: to John Murray & Co., 10 Mar. 1786. On 10 Mar. a letter from John Murray refers to "yours of this date."

From John Murray & Co.

Sir   Alexandria Mar. 10, 1786

By yours of this date[1] we find you conclude to take the two hundred fish barrels at five Shillings each. Should we want fish in payment we shall apply for them as you wish, otherwise we are content to wait for the Amot untill the end of the fishing season[2]—Very respectfully we remain Sir Your most obedt Servants

John Murray & Co.

LS, DLC:GW.
   1. Letter not found.
   2. See Smith & Douglass, 4 Mar., n.1.

To Samuel Purviance, Jr.

Sir,   Mount Vernon March 10th 1786

Your letter of the 6th instt is this moment put into my hands. was it in my power, I would, chearfully, answer your quæries respecting the Settlements on the Kanhawa—the nature of the water—and quality of the Soil. But of the first, I only know from information, that Colonl Lewis *is* settled there—from his own mouth I learnt that it was *his intention* to do so; and to establish a town in the Fork of the two Rivers where he proposed to fix families in the vicinity on his own Lands[1]—Of the 2d I never could obtain any distinct acct of the Navigation. It has been variously represented; favourably by some; extremely difficult by others in its passage through the Gauley Mountain (which I presume is the Laurel hill), but the uncertainty of this matter will now soon be at an end, as there are Commissioners appointed by this State to explore the navigation of that river, & the communication between it and James River with a view to a Passage[2]—This, equally with the extention of the Potomack navigation, was part of my original plan; and equally urged, by me, to our Assembly. for my object was to communicate the Western and Eastern (or Atlantic States) together by strong commercial ties. I am a friend therefore on this principle to every channel that can be opened and wish the people to have a choice of them—The Kanhawa and James river, if the obstacles in the former are not great, are certainly the shortest and best for the Settlers thereon—for those on the Ohio below—above, perhaps as high as the little Kanhawa, and for the Country immediately West of it. The Monongalia & Yohiogania with the Potomack, are most convenient for all the Settlers from the little Kanhawa inclusively, to Fort Pitt, and upwards; & West as far as the Lakes. Susquehanna, and the Aligany above Fort Pitt some distance, will accomodate a third district of Country; & may, for ought I know, be equally convenient to the trade of the Lakes. all of them therefore have my best wishes; for as I have observed already my object, and my great aim are political. If we cannot bind those people to us by interest and it is no otherwise to be effected but by a commercial knot, we shall be no more to them, after a while than G. Britain or Spain are; and thus *may* be as closely linked with one or other of those powers as we wish them to be with us; and in that event they may be a severe thorn in our sides. With respect to the nature of the Soil on the Kanhawa—the bottoms are fine, but the lands adjoining are broken. in some places the hills are very rich, in others piney, & extremely poor—but the principal reason, as I conceive, why the settlement has not progressed more, is, that the greater part, if not all the good land on the main rivers is in hands who do not incline to reside there themselves and possibly hold them too high for others; as there is a surrounding Country open to them—this I take to be my own case. and might be an inducement to concur in any well concerted measures to further a settlement that might, ultimately (not at too remote a distance) subserve my interest in that quarter. The Great Kanhawa is a long river, with very little interruption for a considerable distance. No very large Waters empty into it, I believe; Elk River,

Coal river, & a Creek called Pokitellico, below the Falls—and Green Brier above them are the most considerable—I am glad to hear that the Susquehanna Canal is so well advanced. I thank you for the offer of Mr Neilsons Services in the Western Country. and am with very great esteem and regard Dr Sir Yr Most Obedt Hble Servt

Go: Washington

ALS (photocopy), on deposit ViU; LB, DLC:GW.
   1. See Purviance to GW, 6 Mar., n.4.
   2. See Edmund Randolph to GW, 2 Mar., n.1.

To Tench Tilghman

Dear Sir, Mount Vernon 10th March 1786

Mr Rawlins has this momt presented me with your favor of the 1st instt, enclosing a counterpart of the agreement with him; for your trouble in this business I pray you to accept my thanks. Your advances to him shall be reimbursed at any moment.

It was with concern I learnt from him that you were much indisposed (tho' he could not tell with what) when he left Baltimore. I hope the cause, ere this, is removed—& that you are perfectly restored—Mrs Washington unites in best wishes for Mrs Tilghman and your self with Dr Sir Yr Most Obedt and Affecte Hble Servt

Go: Washington

P.S. Since writing the foregoing, I have seen an advertisement (in the Baltimore Advertiser) of Messrs Nicholas Owings, Brother & Co. of Seeds for sale; and would be much obliged to you for sending me, if they are reputed fresh and good—1 Bushel, or more if they do not hold it high, of Siberian Wheat; 20 lbs. of Sainfain; 10 lbs. of Burnett; 10 lbs. of yellow Clover; 1 lb. of rib. Grass; and 4 oz. of *Turnip* Cabbage Seed if they have of *that* kind of the Cabbage—and if they have Carrot seed I should be glad to get some of that also, as I mean to try a little of it in field Culture. I need not add that, if you procure these Seeds they should be sent by the first conveyance, that the Season may be properly embraced. Pray inform me whether their Pease and Beans are for the field or Garden, & the price of them; as also the price of his vetches & Clovers—Information of what you get would be satisfactory, as I could be preparing the ground previous to their arrival. Yrs &ca Go: W.

ALS, RPJCB.

Letter not found: from Patrick Henry, 11 Mar. 1786. The Mercury Stamp Co., Inc. catalog of the Theodore Sheldon Collection, 5 June 1970 sale, lists this letter, which introduces to GW M. Charton and M. Savary who "propose to settle (a large body of land, on the waters of Ohio near to some of yours) by white people, chiefly from Europe." See *Diaries*, 4:295.

From Bancroft Woodcock

Respected Friend   Wilmington Delaware State
George Washington   11—3 Mo. 1786

As I understand thou art a Lover of Regularity & Order, I take the Freedom to sugjest to thee, (hopeing it will not offend) that from what a person from Allexandra told me, (on seeing his & another Street-Commissioner, laying out the Fronts of Lots, to prevent the Masons from Incroaching on the Streets or on their neighbours) I understand that they are not Building that Town with that Accuracy that we are, & which we have found by Experience to be Absolutely Necessary to prevent Contention & even Lawsuits.

Our Mode is approved & admited by Rittenhous & Lukins, in Preferrence to theirs of Philadelphia.[1] In the year 84 we were Appointed to Run our Streets over again, which with an Instrument I Constructed & an Accromattic glass,[2] we adjusted & Corrected the Irregularities into which the former Commissioners had Inevitablity run, for want of such Machine, we have now placed Stones from one to Four Hundred weight with a Hole in them in the Center of the Intersections of the Streets, from which all Frunts of Houses, Party Walls & Partition Fences within the Corporation are to be Adjusted & Govern'd according to an Act of Assembly. This Mode I would have Allexandra Addopt, & the sooner the better to prevent Irregularities & Disputes.

If my Assistance will be acceptable, I will bring my Instrument & assist the Street Commissioners of Allexandra, for Tenn Shillings pr Day & my Accomodations.

And my Esteem'd Friend, suffer me to Request of thee, What I have often Pourd out my Tears & put up my Supplycations to the God of my Life for thee as for my self, when I have had to Remember thee, that as the curtain of our Evening Closes, & (metaphorically) our shadows Lengthens, thou & I may Dayly Experience more or less ⟨*mutilated*⟩ a Well grounded Hope, that when the auful Period arrives, wh⟨en⟩ we must forever be Seperated from all Mundine enjoyments, we may be Admited to Join the Heavenly Hoste, in the full Fruition of that Joy, the foretaste of which was so Delightful to the Soul, whilst in these Houses of Clay. That this may be Favourably received is the Desire of thy Friend

Bancroft Woodcock

ALS, DLC:GW.

Bancroft Woodcock, "Delaware's foremost eighteenth century silversmith," was born into a Quaker family in Wilmington, Del., in 1732. He in the 1760s was working as a silversmith in Wilmington with an apprentice, in 1784 was disowned by the Wilmington Meeting of the Society of Friends, and by 1786 owned a considerable amount of real estate in Wilmington and was speculating in lands located in western Pennsylvania. At the end of 1794, Woodcock moved to his land in Bedford County, Pa , and died there in 1817. The fact, however, that another Bancroft Woodcock was buried in 1825 at the Wilmington Friends Meeting House raises the possibility that it was not the clearly very prosperous silversmith, no longer a member of the Society of Friends and 53 years old in 1786, who wrote this letter offering to come to Alexandria and help resurvey its streets for ten shillings a day and keep (David B. Warren, "Bancroft Woodcock: Silversmith, Friend, and Landholder" [*Delaware Antiques Show Catalog*, 1967]).

1. David Rittenhouse (1732–1796), the famed astronomer and mathematician, was also a noted surveyor and instrument maker. John Lukens, surveyor general of colonial Pennsylvania, assisted Rittenhouse in his famous observation of the transit of Venus in 1769. Rittenhouse's most recent, and final, surveying was done in 1785 when Congress appointed him to take part in running the long-disputed New York–Massachusetts boundary line (Hindle, *Pursuit of Science*, 338).

2. This is an achromatic lens or telescope.

From David Hoar

[Concord, Mass., 12 March 1786]

State of Massachusetts. March 12, Independence ten.
May it Please your Excellency,

Your established character as a warrior, entitles you to all the respect that can be due to the occupation relative to material defence and resistance. This exercise was a very necessary and agreeable Study in ancient times; but mankind has nearly outgrown these childish plays. We are now come to years of discretion, and may quarrel in a manner much more entertaining and less toilsome.

The Gospel acquaints us with a method of overcoming our fellow-creatures, by the Subtilty of mental operations, without exposing ourselves to fatigue or the conquered to injury. We have only to reverse the mistaken ideas of personal right and the medium of Social concord; our Subjects are then forever happy, and their Governors counted honourable So far as we extend our dominion.

We are contemplating in profound Solemnity, these simple questions. What is it in the human constitution, that gives the unmolested possession of property? And what that insures Social unity of Sentiment? We consult nature, reason and revelation, which all agree in one: they plainly discover, that men have not been learned enough in any former aera or dispensation, to answer the important enquiry. The present Situation of our understanding, and the peculiar condition of America, ordain this to be the time, and place, wherein So divine a Science must be opened.

We ought not to be So impolite, as to declare our result in too blunt a tone, but are ready to communicate this inestimable Secret, to any person, State or Kingdom, who can wisely concede to the annexed preliminaries. The proposed primary immunities, must be exhibited in an incontestible theory, clearly intelligible, conclusive and practicable; that no member of the respective community, may ever be exposed to loss, trouble or danger.

preliminary first. Human being is Sufficient to solve these momentous concerns.

preliminary Second. The person and society in whom the so-
lution originates, owe no allegiance to any inferior jurisdiction.

Sir, With unfeigned respect I am yours,

David Hoar

president of the Independent Society in Concord for the culture, and propagation of learning and good manners.

ALS, DLC:GW.

David Hoar published in Boston his pamphlet entitled: *The Natural Principles of Liberty, Moral Virtue, Learning, Society, Good Manners, and Human Happiness, or, the Everlasting Gospel of the Kingdom, Offer'd, with Due Respect, to the Legislature of the State of Massachusetts, in New England, with All Others on This Continent
and Elsewhere, Whom It May Concern to Provide Peace and Union, Harmony and Concord.* Hoar later sent GW a "precept for calling a general judiciary assembly"
to "convene at the house of David Hoar on the Sixteenth day of May next, to
express their mind relating to the Gospel church character, the right of Supreme Legislation, and the Sacred institution of property" (DLC:GW). Written
in Hoar's hand, the announcement was dated "September 12, Year of Independence eleven," or 12 Sept. 1786. Hoar enclosed a printed, one-page *Circular Memorial* addressed to Gov. James Bowdoin and the Massachusetts legislature from Hoar, dated 28 Sept., which ends with the reminder: "It is God only
who makes law and authorizes governours." GW docketed Hoar's letter and
the announcement, but no indication has been found that he acknowledged
either.

Letters not found: from Thomas Newton, 13 Mar. 1786. On 9 April GW
wrote Newton: "I have been favored with your letters of . . . 13th of
March—the last of which speaks of a letter written by you to me of the
same date—this letter has never got to hand."

From James Taylor

Sir   Norfo[lk] 13 March 1786.

I had the Honor of yours of 22d febry[1] & agreeable to your
request have forwarded the pipe of Wine by a ship, the Captain
of whom promises to deliver it safe at your own door[2]—Mr
Newton says he will pay the freight, Duty & charges as below—
I presume the House in Madeira mentioned their having drawn
a Bill for the amount of this Wine, which I have in possession, &
shall wait your Directions respecting it.[3] I have the Honor to be
Sir Your most obed. hbl. Servt

Jas Taylor

ALS, DLC:GW.

1. Letter not found. See 22 February.

2. See Lamar, Hill, Bisset, & Co., 6 Dec. 1785, and notes. Taylor appended the following account of charges:

1786 His Excelley Genl Washington To James Taylor Deb.

febry 1	To Cash pd freight of wine 30/ Sterlg	£2. 2.
	To Do pd Duty Do	1.13.4
	To Do Dray, landg & storage	. 7.
		£4. 2.4

3. On 22 Mar. aboard the "Ship Bristol off & from Philadelphia," John Earle wrote GW: "The Inclosed Letters, are from Gentlemen in Norfolk, who apply'd to me to forward a pipe of Wine to you[r] Excelly which I have on board—As my Boats are not all together Callculated for landing such a Cask I have Sent my Yawl with an Officer to know if you have any Boat Sutiable for the purpose—If not my long Boat shall proceed to the Landing of it as soon as I receive your Ansr by my Officr" (DLC:GW).

Letter not found: from Wakelin Welch, 13 Mar. 1786. GW wrote Welch, July 1786, about receiving his letter of "13th of March."

From Benjamin Lincoln

My dear General   Boston March 15h 1786

Immediately on the receipt of your Excellencys favor of the 6th Ulto I wrote to Mr Lear, who lives at Portsmouth New Hampshire, on the subject of joyning your family and requested to know the terms, ℔ Year, he would perform the several duties pointed out The following is an extract from his letter in answer to mine "Two hundred dollars ℔ annum will be satisfactory on my [part] for the services which I shall render his Excellency in the capacity of a preceptor to the Children and private secretary to him. The advantages which I think must accrue to me from a connexion with that exalted Character and the company which resorts to the House will have a greater weight than any pecuniary considerations. My leisure hours I shall devote to the study of the law: And one or more I think, by method, I can call my own every day without neglecting the duties I am to perform, unless, when some pressing circumstances require particular dispatch" Mr Lear writes a good hand & has obtained a pretty good knowledge of the most exact method of book-keeping—It is *now* said little may be expected from, the supposed invention, of extracting fresh from salt water. With sentiments of the highest esteem I have the honor of being your Excellency's most Obedient servt

B. Lincoln

ALS, DLC:GW.

Letter not found: from Clement Biddle, 16 Mar. 1786. On 18 May GW wrote Biddle: "Your favors of . . . 16th & 19th March, are before me."

From John Jay

Dear Sir   New York 16 March 1786

Under the same cover with my Letter to You of 2 Instant, I transmitted a Pamphlet, in which I have since remarked the Errors mentioned in the inclosed printed Paper.

altho' you have wisely retired from public Employments, and calmly view from the Temple of Fame, the various Exertions of the Sovereignty and Independence which Providence has enabled You to be so greatly & gloriously instrumental in securing to your country; yet I am persuaded you cannot view them with the Eye of an unconcerned Spectator.

Experience has pointed out Errors in our national Government, which call for Correction, and which threaten to blast the Fruit we expected from our "Tree of Liberty." The convention proposed by Virginia may do some good and would perhaps do more, if it comprehended more Objects[1]—an opinion begins to prevail that a general convention for revising the articles of Confederation would be expedient. Whether the People are yet ripe for such a Measure, or whether the System proposed to be attained by it, is only to be expected from Calamity & Commotion, is difficult to ascertain. I think we are in a delicate Situation, and a Variety of Considerations and Circumstances give me uneasiness. It is in Contemplation to take measures for forming a general convention—the Plan is not matured—if it should be well concerted and take Effect, I am fervent in my Wishes, that it may comport with the Line of Life you have marked out for yourself, to favor your country with your counsels on such an important & single occasion. I suggest this merely as a Hint for

Consideration, and am with the highest Respect & Esteem Dear
Sir your most obt & very hble Servant

John Jay

ALS, DLC:GW.

1. On the last day of its session, 21 Jan. 1786, the house of delegates appointed five commissioners, including James Madison and Edmund Randolph, to "meet such commissioners as may be appointed by the other States in the Union, at a time and place to be agreed on, to take into consideration the trade of the United States; to examine the relative situations and trade of the said States; to consider how far a uniform system in their commercial regulations may be necessary to their common interest and their permanent harmony; and to export to the several States, such an act relative to this great object, as, when unanimously ratified by them, will enable the United States in Congress effectually to provide for the same." The Virginia delegates were to "immediately transmit to the several States, copies of the preceding resolution, with a circular letter requesting their concurrence therein, and proposing a time and place for the meeting aforesaid" (*House of Delegates Journal, 1781–1785*). The meeting was called for Annapolis in September. Twelve delegates from only five states, Virginia, Delaware, Pennsylvania, New Jersey, and New York, attended, and met from 11 to 14 September. The report of the delegates to the legislatures of the five states, drafted by Alexander Hamilton, is in Syrett, *Hamilton Papers*, 3:686–90.

To George Savage

Sir　　　　　　　　　　　　Mount Vernon March 17th 1786

I have received your letter of the 18th ulto, & one thousand bushels of Indian corn, and six bushels of peas, which your Schooner Molly and Betsey took in, on my acct at a Plantn of the deceased Mr Custis on Pamunky.

I have paid Mr Whitney, the skipper, twenty five pounds three shillings for freight of the same and taken his receipt therefor.[1]
I am Sir ⟨Your⟩ Most Obed. Servt

Go: Washington

ALS, owned (1970) by Mr. Randolph P. Barton, Salem, Massachusetts.

1. For GW's correspondence regarding the purchase of corn, see GW to Savage, 8 Feb., n.2. The receipt "for the freight of one thousand Bushels of Indian Corn and six Bushels of Peas, brought from the Plantation of the decd Mr. Custis on Pamunky River . . . ," signed by John Whitney and John Fairfax, was offered for sale by Carnegie Book Shop, catalog 315, item 510, 1969.

From Cheiza D'Artaignan

My General   Alexa[ndria] 18 March 86
    The Count De Cheiza D'artaignan, has the Honour to Inform
you of his being arriv'd at Alexa. for these Four Days; having
Come from Cape François St Dominicque, He Proposes to Pay
his very Humble Rispects & duty which he Owes to your Rank &
Illustrious merite, He hopes that His General will Grant him the
Permission to Pay his Court (or to Pay his Respects) & the Honour of his Protection (or Patronage[)]. He has the Honour to be
with very High respect My Genl Yours &c.

                                        Cheiza Darteignan
                                Officer of the French Guards

Translation, DLC:GW; ALS, in French, DLC:GW.
    GW had this to say about the comte de Cheiza d'Artaignan: "A Gentleman
calling himself the Count de Cheiza D'arteignan Officer of the French Guards
came here to dinner; but bringing no letters of introduction, nor any authentic
testemonials of his being either; I was at a loss how to receive, or treat him.
He stayed dinner and the evening" (*Diaries*, 4:296).

Letter not found: from Clement Biddle, 19 Mar. 1786. GW wrote Biddle
on 18 May: "Your favors of . . . 16th & 19th March, are before me."

From Tench Tilghman

Dear sir   Balt[imore], 19th March 1786
    Inclosed is an account of the seeds which I have procured for
you & which shall be forwarded by next Wednesdays Stage to
Alexanda to the Care of Colo. Fitzgerald.[1] They should have
been sent to morrow, had there been Time sufficient to get them
ready before the setting out of the Stage—There was no turnip
Cabbage, nor Carrot seed. All the Clover, except a little of the
White, which is 2/6 ⅌ lb., had been disposed of, as also were the
Peas Beans & Vetches. There is every reason to believe that these
Seeds are fresh & good, as they were brought from England by
a Gentleman for his own use, & were parted, with by him, because it would not have been in his Power to have sown them at
a proper season.
    I have been confined upwards of a Fortnight in great meas-
ure, to my bed, by the return of a Complaint in my side with

which I was troubled some time ago. I recover but very slowly, but I hope that as soon as I am able to enjoy the favorable Season which is approaching I shall soon get recruited. I remain Dear Sir Yr affe hble Servt

Tench Tilghman

ALS, DLC:GW.

1. The account for the seed, this date, that Tilghman purchased for GW is in DLC:GW. See GW to Tilghman, 10 March.

Letter not found: to James Rumsey, 20 Mar. 1786. On 29 Mar. Rumsey wrote GW: "I Receivd your fovor of the 20th."

Letter not found: to William Hartshorne, 21 Mar. 1786. On 25 Mar. Hartshorne wrote GW: "Your favor of the 21st inst. came."

From Tench Tilghman

Dear sir   Baltimore 23d March 1786

I hope you have ere this recd the Bag of seeds which I sent by the last Stage to Alexanda By to morrow's Stage, I shall forward a Cask of Seed which was sent to my Care by Mr Clemt Biddle of Philada It will be directed to the Care of Colo. Fitzgerald.[1]

I am still unable to leave my Chamber, tho I think I am rather better than when I wrote to you last.[2] I remain Dr Sir very sincerely, yr obt Servt

Tench Tilghman

ALS, DLC:GW.

1. See GW to Clement Biddle, 10 Feb. and 18 May.

2. This was Tilghman's last letter to GW. He died on 18 April. See Thomas Ringgold Tilghman to GW, 22 April.

From Battaile Muse

Honourable Sir,   March 24th 1786

Your Favour date the 8th of this Month I have received I shall attend Perticularly To your Instructions with the Tenants and the renting of your Lands, and it gives me Pleasure To Find their is one Man in this Country that will have Obligations Com-

plied with and attended To; their is but Very Few that has Complyed with their Leases but the Greater part Seem To be much
allarmed at my Stricktness and Promises To do Every thing as
Quick as Possable to Fullfill their Lease.

I have not rerented the Vacant Lots in Fauquier I was on the
Lands the first of this month Two days but Could not Procure
Such Tenants as I wished for I go down again Next week To See
what Can ⟨be⟩ done. I have seen Mr R. Rutherford He sayes He
Cannot Pay untill next Fall[1]—I Shall Call on Genl Morgan
on my way To Fauquier To Enquire Inconsequence of Cap. Ken-
nadyes Debt—the badness of the roads has prevented the Tenants From raiseing Money To Pay up So Fully as was Expected—
I have Pushed the whole of them, and have reasoned the necessity of their Paying as well for their benifitt as yours.

I expect the roads wil soon Get better and that they will Pay
up as Far as Possable the Fauquier Tenants are Too Poore To
Pay up Fully this year. My wheat shall be sent down as Fast as
the weather & roads will permitt & I expect To Collect as much
money as will Pay for it. I am with every Sentiment of Obedience
you Very Humble Servant

Battaile Muse

P.S. I do not Expect you will hear from me untill I appear at
Mountvernon the Last of april.

ALS, NcD: Battaile Muse Papers.

1. See Robert Rutherford to GW, 28 March.

To William Drayton

Sir,   Mt Vernon 25th Mar: 1786.

The Letter which you did me the honor to write to me on the
23d of November last, came safely; tho' not at so early a period
as might have been expected from the date of it—I remark this
by way of apology for my silence 'till now.

I feel very sensibly, the honor conferred on me by the South
Carolina Society for promoting & improving agriculture &
other rural concerns, by unanimously electing me the first honorary member of that Body; & I pray you Sir, as Chairman, to
offer my best acknowledgements & thanks for this mark of its

attention. To you, for the flattering terms in which the desires of the Society have been communicated, my thanks are particularly due.

It is much to be wished that every State in the Union would establish a Society similar to this; & that these Societies would correspond with, & fully & regularly impart to each other, the result of the experiments actually made in husbandry, together with such other useful discoveries as have stood, or are likely to stand the test of investigation. Nothing in my opinion would contribute more to the welfare of these States, than the proper management of our Lands; and nothing, in this State particularly, seems to be less understood. The present mode of cropping practised among us, is destructive to landed property; & must, if persisted in much longer, ultimately ruin the holders of it. I have the honor to be &c.

G: Washington

LB, DLC:GW.

From William Hartshorne

Sir   Alexandria March 25. 1786

Your favor of the 21st inst. came while I was from home[1]— having no other information respecting Capt. Pearce's account than what I before mentioned to you, I have only to say, that I am willing to recive the Same Sum from you for the Freight of the Jack & his Keeper from Spain that Mr Cushing paid for the other, as I see no reason why they should not be both at the same Freight, but for my justification I must request you will please send me a Copy of the account sent you by Mr Cushing— this I wish to come soon, that I may Credit Capt. Pearce for the Amot as I intend to draw on him for the Ballance of his accot— as to the Cash it may be sent at your Convenience.[2]

I have again enquired of Mr Thompson about the Seed who informs me, that no Waggons have come yet from his Fathers, since he wrote about it at my request, but as the roads are getting better I expect it will come next week—when it arrives, I will inform you as soon as possible.[3] I am very Respectfully Yours

Wm Hartshorne

ALS, DLC:GW.

1. Letter not found.

2. For David Pearce's account with GW, see Hartshorne to GW, 26 Nov. 1785, n.1. No account with Thomas Cushing has been found, but see Cushing to GW, 7 Oct., n.2, and 9 Nov. 1785.

3. See Hartshorne to GW, 10 February.

From Nicholas Pike

Newbury Port. State of Massachusetts.

Highly respected Sir. March 25. 1786

To address a Person of your exalted Rank upon a Subject for my own emolument, only, wou'd require something more than an Apology; but, when your Excellency is informed that the interests of the Public are jointly connected with the Request I have to make, my knowledge of the readiness you have ever exhibited to cherish even the smallest Effort towards the Prosperity of these Infant-States, emboldens me to expect a Pardon.

With much Labor, I have, at the request of my Friends, composed what I conceive to be a complete System of Arithmetic. The frequent complaints of the insufficiency of those now in use, joined to the sollicitations of my friends, induced me, tho' with diffidence, to undertake what I have found to be an arduous Task, and which cannot be brought forth to View, the work being so large, & costing me double to common printing, unless Subscribers, to the number of twenty three or twenty four hundred can be obtained.

The Approbation of the Gentlemen to whom my Performance has been submitted, which I enclose, cannot but be pleasing to me, more especially as they rank among the first in the New England States for Mathematical Learning, and I think will induce your Excellency to grant me the honor I wish.[1]

My Request to your Excellency is, that I may be permitted to dedicate my first Performance to the Gentleman, who, under Providence, has been the Saviour of his Country and so great & liberal an Encourager & Promoter of the Arts & Sciences in general & to hope every Attempt to promote and diffuse knowledge under your Patronage may be as successful as your Exertions in the late Contest have been glorious.[2] Shou'd the proposal I have suggested to your Excellency fall in with your Idea of propriety,

I will thank you to forward a Line to Mr Samuel Purvyance at Baltimore, which will be received by Mr Mccall, who, if any one, will print my Book & whom I send to the Southward for the express purpose of obtaining Subscriptions, & who will probably be there in the latter part of May.

I have only to add my Wishes that the Evening of your Days may receive every Pleasure which can flow from the Reflexion of a Life spent in such laudable persuits, which have so honorably terminated, and that the Infant, yet unborn, may lisp your Name, not only as po⟨*mutilated*⟩ and victorious in War; but; as the ⟨prot⟩ector, & cherisher of all useful Arts & Sciences in Peace. With Sentiments of the highest Esteem & Respect, I beg Leave to subscribe myself, your Excellency's most obliged, affectionate & grateful hble Servt

Nicolas Pike

P.S. Shou'd Gentlemen in Virginia be disposed to encourage this Work, the Book shall be sent (if published) to any Gentleman in Baltimore, whom they will point out to me.

Shou'd the Publication succeed & be approved of, I will, at any time, after the Books are out, supply the Virginia Booksellers, to be left with whom they shall direct in Baltimore at one dollar ℔ Book in sheets by the quantity, or one dollar & a third by the quantity neatly bound & lettered, so that they may have a handsome Profit. Three Bookbinders in Boston have taken 600 in Sheets at one Dollar. I am your Excellency's hble Servt ut supra.

ALS, DLC:GW.

Nicholas Pike (1743–1819), a native of New Hampshire and a graduate of Harvard College, was a schoolmaster in Newburyport who gained nationwide recognition after the publication of his *A New and Complete System of Arithmetic, Composed for the Use of the Citizens of the United States*, first published in 1788 and sold by J. McCall in Newburyport, followed by many subsequent editions.

1. The broadside that Pike enclosed, which is dated 22 Mar. 1786, is entitled: "Proposals for publishing a complete SYSTEM OF ARITHMETIC, more comprehensive, plain and Intelligible than any extant, with Demonstrations of the several Rules, & other useful matters, as the *method of making Taxes, &c.*" It describes the contents of the work that is to be printed and includes a letter recommending the work signed by Joseph Willard, president of Harvard College, and by two professors. The whole in turn is endorsed by James Bowdoin, governor of Massachusetts.

2. GW politely declined the honor on 20 June.

Letter not found: to Richard Thomas, 25 Mar. 1786. On 25 July Thomas wrote GW about his letter of "25th March 86."

To John Augustine Washington

Dear Brother: Mount Vernon, March 27, 1786

Your letter of the 17th did not reach me till yesterday afternoon.[1] Whence your overseers apprehensions proceed, I know not; for if I recollect right, I gave him, myself, assurances of the plan when I was in Berkeley in the fall of 1784; and since, have informed Mr. Muse that he was to receive a confirmation of the lease. It is true that, being a nonresident on the Lott he would have been excluded, had it not been for the communication of your wishes, that he might have it, antecedant to the above period; because, for reasons which will readily occur to you, I had established it as a maxim to accept no Tenants that did not mean to reside on the Land; or who had land of their own adjoining to it, not expecting, in either case, much improvement on, or much justice to mine under these circumstances.[2]

At the time I sent you the flour that was manufactured at my Mill, I requested to be informed if you could tell me where corn was to be had in your parts, or within your knowledge; but having received no answer to that letter, nor any one from you since, till the one above acknowledged; I sent to York River for 200 Barr., which I have just landed. I do not therefore stand in need of that at the little Falls Quarter.

Herewith you will receive an Alexandria Gazette containing a demd. upon the subscribers to the Potomack Navigation for two other dividends for carrying on the work, which the directors mean to do with spirit; and they hope to good effect this summer. It also contains an address from Mr. Stoddart to Messrs. Washington & Co. the first of whom I hope has, 'ere this, seen the impropriety of hazarding a valuable estate upon so precarious a tenure as trade and either has, already, or soon will withdraw himself from it. I beg when you see him, that you will give my love and thanks to him, for the fruit trees he sent me, which came safe, and were a very valuable present.[3]

All here join most cordially, in every good wish for you, my sister and family, and with every sentiment of regard and affection I am ever yrs.

Fitzpatrick, *Writings of Washington*, 28:395–96.

1. Letter not found.

2. See GW to Battaile Muse, 8 Mar. 1786.

3. The Potomac River Company's advertisement ran in the *Virginia Journal and Alexandria Advertiser* on 23 Mar.; Benjamin Stoddert's "address" may have appeared in either or both the missing issues of 9 or 16 March. In 1785 GW had dealings with Stoddert, a Georgetown merchant, regarding the support of GW's nephews, George Steptoe Washington and Lawrence Augustine Washington (Stoddert to GW, 21 June 1785). On 22 Mar. GW notes in his diary planting "in three Rows 177 of the wild, or Cherokee plumb; (sent me by Mr. Geo. A. Washington)" (*Diaries*, 4:297).

Letter not found: to Jean Le Mayeur, 28 Mar. 1786. On 10 April Le Mayeur wrote GW of having "the honour of your Excellency's favour of the 28th march."

From Robert Rutherford

Dear Sir   Berkeley County March 28th 1786

I am hond by your excellency's letter of the 8th instant,[1] and am very unhappy in not Complying with your utmost wish, & at the Same time to have acted up to the warm & grateful dictates of my own heart on the occasion. The very great & unequal loss of at least £10,000 Specie Value Sustained by the Continental money not to mention the entire neglect of every domestic Concern, the whole time of the late important Contest, by which the remnant of my fortune (to use a forced term) became a perfect wreck at the Close of the war has embarrassed me much, but as I am determined (however painful the Idea) to Sell 1000 Acres of my paternal Estate, I hope to pay off each Pressing demand in the Course of the year. Please to be assured that I Consider it as a very pleasing Circumstance in my life to have had your patronage, and must Still put myself upon that Condescension & goodness of heart often evinced in my favour, and intreat a recall of the note into the hand which obliged me, and into which I am anxious to return it. indeed it would distress me beyond expression to be hardly pressed for what I Consider myself bound by every tie of honor & gratitude. Most Sincerely do I wish that it may ever be in my power to render any return of good offices, and I pray you Command me freely, if Such occasion require. May you with amiable Lady, long injoy every temporal blessing. I beg pardon for being thus prolix, and have the honour to be, with every sentiment of grateful affection My Dear Genl your Most obt And Very Hble Sert

R. Rutherford

ALS, DLC: Rochambeau Papers.

Robert Rutherford (1728–1803), with whom GW formed a friendship when Rutherford was captain of a company of rangers in the 1750s, was a member of the House of Burgesses for Frederick County from 1766 to 1771. On 20 May 1769 GW lent Rutherford £5 "in Williamsburg," and on 20 Aug. 1770 he lent him £20 "at Colchester" (Ledger A, 202). An undated entry in Ledger B, 16, indicates that Rutherford paid £25 to Battaile Muse. See also GW to Muse, 8 March.

1. Letter not found.

From James Rumsey

Dr General.   Great falls March 29th 1786

This will be handed to you by Mr Brindley, we have had the pleasure of his, and Mr Harris's Company Since yesterday, and they Boath approve of what is Done and proposed Here.[1]

On Sunday Evening the 26th of this Inst. I Receivd your fovor of the 20th Respecting The Conduct of the people working here,[2] It Distress me that you had Accation to Write on Such a Subject. what follows is as near what has hapened Since I Came Down as I am Able to Relate.

On my way Down I heared great Complaints Against the people of the falls, But as Such Complaints has been frccquent when no outrages Has bee Cammited, I thought But Little of them, I was But a Short time at the falls before I Set Out for alexandria, and Mr Stuart with me for Baltimore During which time they Behaved themselves Very well, On my Return from alexandria to This place the Complaints that was made to me was Shocking, that no person Could Come on their Lawfull Buisness But what got Abused, and that Officers of Justice durst not go on the ground to Execute their Office—In Consequence of these Complaints I Immediately Set up adertisments Leting the Neighbours know that they Should be treated well when they Came to the place, and the Officers that they Should be protected In the Execution of their office, for which I pledged myself to them[.][3] notwithstanding these advertisements, The

Officer that had Mr Jacksons warrants Summined fifty men to
Come here on monday Last to aid and assist him, This Expede-
tion was Intended private which was the Reason your Letter was
not Handed to me Sooner, But I was Luckey enough to Meet
with Mr Stanhope at Mr Wheelers on Sunday and he Informed
me of it and where they ware To meet I Sett out on monday and
met them, all Armed, within a mile of the falls. I beged them to
Stop, Expostulated withem for Sum time, and gave them Every
ashorance in my power that if they would Stop I would take the
officer alone and Bring any men they would name they at first
agreed to it But Soon Changed their minds and the most of
them moved on again I Beged them to Listen to me and more
Expressed my Desire to Convince them that the men was Under
good Diciplin, and at Lenth By the Exertions of Mr Stanhope &
Mr Gunnel I Carryed my point So far that they the Justises and
the officer was to go with me to the works while the Rest was To
go to the Buildings where I was to perade the Hole of the men,
I had preveous to my Seting out Let the men know that an officer was to Be with them that Day to take a number of them, and
I Charged them to Behave well—when we Came on the works,
they accordingly Did, I ordered them all To the House and
made them form in a Line untill the officer Called out what he
wanted, all this was Done without a murmer, the number taken
was About Sixteen they ware then Caryed off and put upon tryal
which I attended and Mr Stuart Returned Before it was Over,
The Hole of Mr Jacksons afair amounted to this, that his Son
was In Company with a number of them at a Mr Conns that
they threatened Sumbodey Very hard that he beleived It to be
him, that he Borrowed a horse and rode home for his gun and
Returned Shortly with it and presented it and Swore that
he would kill The first man that afended him, on which they
⟨to⟩ok after him, and Doged him Sum time, and finaly ⟨th⟩at
he made his Excape, the men was Sentenced to have Sum
Lashes, that Mr Stanhope, Coleman, and Gunnel, prevailed
with mr Jackson after the Judgment was passed to Remit the
Hole punishement which he Did with a great Deal of Reluctance
There was tow Servants got five Lashes apeace for Sum offence
to a woman that Lives at Mrs Bauguses, I Shall Endeavor, and
I make no Doubt But the men Can Be kept in good order[4]

I am Sir With Sincere Regard your most Obt and Very Hbl.
Servt

James Rumsey

ALS, DLC:GW.

1. GW wrote William Moultrie on 25 May: "Mr [James] Brindley, nephew
to the celebrated person of that name [James Brindley; 1716–1772] who conducted the work of the Duke of Bridgewater [Francis Egerton, 3d duke of
Bridgewater; 1736–1803] & planned many others in England, possesses, I
presume, more *practical* knowledge of Cuts & Locks for the improvement of
inland navigation, than any man among us, as he was an executive officer (he
says) many years under his uncle in this particular business: but he is, I know,
engaged with the Susquehanna company, who are I believe (for I saw Mr
Brindley about six weeks ago) in a critical part of their work." Moultrie wrote
the engineer of the Susquehanna Company in August 1786 asking him to
come to South Carolina for consultation, and Brindley went down from
Pennsylvania in early 1787, visiting Mount Vernon en route (see Moultrie to
GW, 7 Aug. 1786, and *Diaries*, 5:92). See also Samuel Purviance, Jr., to GW,
6 March.

2. Letter not found.

3. Rumsey's advertisement, dated 25 Mar., reads: "Whereas a Great number
of the Inhabitants of this Neighbourhood Has Made Complaint to me—that
they have been Insulted and ill treated When they come to this Place About
their Lawful Business and that Officers of Justice has been so Intemidated by
threats that they Do not think it Safe to come to the Place to Execute their
Office—

"I therefore think it my Duty as Superintendent of the Business to Pledge
myself that all Persons for the future may Come hear unmolested to do their
Lawfull Business of what Ever kind it may be And that all Persons that Conceive that they have been Injured Shall have Redress upon Making it Clearly
Appear" ("Letters of James Rumsey," 21).

4. Most of the people to whom Rumsey refers in this account of the outcome
of the fracas involving his Potomac River Company workers at Great Falls and
a young inhabitant of the area named Jackson are difficult to identify with
certainty. Mr. Stuart is Richardson Stewart, the assistant manager of the Potomac River Company who was soon to replace Rumsey as manager. John Jackson, who probably was the John Jackson who rented land from Bryan Fairfax
in 1772 (*Diaries*, 3:110), now owned part of the John Semple tract in Loudoun
County at the Great Falls and land in Fairfax County on Difficult Run which
flows into the Potomac south of the Great Falls (Mitchell, *Beginning at a White
Oak*, 198). He in 1798 was a trustee of the town of Turbeville in Fairfax County
near the Little Falls of the Potomac. Mr. Gunnell was probably one of the sons
or grandsons of the William Gunnell who in 1730 secured a grant of 966 acres
on Difficult Run in Fairfax County. He left the lands to his sons, William and
Henry, who remained in the area as did the Grinnells of the next generation
(ibid., 185–86). This may be Henry Gunnell who was a trustee of Turbeville

along with Jackson in 1798. Mr. Stanhope may have been William Stanhope who witnessed duels for William Grinnell in 1790 and became a justice for Fairfax County in 1798 and sheriff in 1800. Samuel Wheeler lived on a plantation in Fairfax County on the road to Difficult Run bridge. James Coleman owned land on Difficult Run; Mr. Conn may be Hugh Conn who in 1790 bought 110 acres of the Semple tract near Great Falls (ibid., 149, 135). Mrs. Bauguses may be Mary Boggess who in 1783 contested the will of Henry Boggess, the owner of land in Fairfax County and across the line in Loudoun County.

To Edward Newenham

Dear Sir,   Mount Vernon Mar. 30th 1786
Having had cause, lately, to apprehend a miscarriage of the letter of which the inclosed is a duplicate, I do myself the honor of forwarding this copy, as the best apology I can make for a silence that might, otherwise, be ascribed to motives of inattention; wch would give me pain; as I have pleasure in your corrispondence, and would wish to keep up a friendly intercourse with you by letter.[1]
As your last letters gave me hopes of seeing you in Virginia this Spring, & nothing since has contradicted it, I think I may shortly look for that pleasure, and therefore shall add nothing more in this letter than my best wishes for the pleasantness of your voyage, and assurances of the happiness I shall derive from saluting you under my own roof; being with every sentiment of esteem & regard Dear Sir Yr most Obedt and Very Hble servant
                                      Go: Washington

ALS, NNPM; LB, DLC:GW.
   1. See GW to Newenham, 25 Nov. 1785.

To John Fitzgerald and George Gilpin

Gentn   Mount Vernon Mar. 31st[–2 April] 1786
Yesterday Mr Brindley, in company with a Mr Harris (Manager for the James River company, and sent by the Directors thereof for the former) left this on their way to Richmond: from whence Mr Brindley expected to be returned as far as Alexandria, by the 4th of next Month.

I have engaged him to call upon Colo. Gilpin on his rout back.

Mr Brindley and Mr Harris took the Great Falls in their way down, and both approve of the present line for our Canal. The first very much, conceiving that 9/10th of the expence which must have been incurred in the one first proposed, will be saved in the second—the work be altogether as secure—and the discharge into the river below, by no means unfavourable. He thinks however, that a good deal of attention and judgment is requisite to fix the Locks there; the height of which, he observes, must be adapted to the ground, there being no precise rule for their construction; Locks running, frequently, from 4 to 18 feet—& sometimes as high as 24—The nature, & declension of the ground, according to him, is alone to be consulted, and where these will admit of it, he thinks the larger the locks are, the better, because more convenient.

With respect to this part of the business, I feel, and always have professed, an incompetency of judgment; nor do I think that theoretical knowledge alone, is adequate to the undertaking. Locks upon the *best digested plan* will certainly be expensive—& if not properly constructed, & judiciously placed, may be altogether useless. It is for these reasons I have frequently suggested, though no decision has been had, the propriety of employing a professional man. Whether the expence of importing one has been deemed altogether unnecessary; or, that the advantages resulting therefrom are considered as unequal to the cost, I know not; but, as it is *said* no person in this Country has *more practical* knowledge than Mr Brindley, I submit it for consideration, whether it is not advisable to engage him to take the Falls on his way home—examine—level—& digest a plan for locks at that place. If it shall appear a good one, and his reasons in support of the spots for, and sizes of the locks are conclusive, they will justify the adoption of it—if on the other hand, they are palpably erroneous, we are under no obligation to follow him. and the expence, in that case, is the only evil that can result from it. this, for the chance of a probable benefit, I am not only willing, but desirous of encountering; and if Colo. Gilpin has not already made the trip to that place which he proposed at our last visit, & disappointment there, it would give me great pleasure if it could be so timed as for him to accompany

Mr Brindley. This would not only give countenance to the latter, but afford him aid also; and might be a mean of preventing the little jealousies which, otherwise might arise in the minds of our own Managers. Taking Mr Brindley to the works *now*, may, ultimately, save expence; at the sametime, having a plan before us, it would enable us at all convenient times, to be providing materials for its execution. I am Gentn—Yr Most Obedt Servt

Go: Washington

If my proposition is acceded to, it might be well to fix, at once, what shall be given to Mr Brindley—I will readily subscribe to what you two Gentlemen may agree to give him on this occasion.

G. W——n

April 2d

This letter I intended to have sent up by a Gentleman, now here, on friday last, but his remaining & the bad weather yesterday have detained it till now.[1]

ALS, owned (1971) by Dr. Gilbert C. Norton, Endicott, N.Y.; LB, DLC:GW.

1. A Mr. Wallace from Ireland visited Mount Vernon from 30 Mar. to 2 April.

From Noah Webster

Sir.   New York March 31st 1786

I am happy in the opportunity, which Mr Lee's politeness has offered, of presenting Your Excellency a copy of Mr Dwights Poem. Whatever faults may be found in this performance, its merit cannot fail to recommend it to every friend of America & of virtue.[1]

I flatter myself that in three or four weeks I shall be able to furnish you with an Instructor, as several Gentlemen will assist me in procuring a man of worth.[2]

Reading Lectures in several towns has detained me longer than I expected; but I am encouraged, by the prospect of rendering my country some service, to proceed in my design of refining the language & improving our general system of education. Dr Franklin has extended my views to a very simple plan of reducing the language to perfect regularity: Should I ever attempt it, I have no doubt that I should be patronized by many distinguished characters. Please to present my respects & Compliments to Mrs Washington—to the Major & his Lady ⟨&⟩ to Mr Shaw, if in your family—& believe me with perfect respect Your Excellencys most obliged & most obedient Servant

Noah Webster jun.

ALS, DLC:GW.

1. Timothy Dwight sent GW a copy of *The Conquest of Canaan* in October 1785 (Dwight to GW, October 1785). Arthur Lee brought this letter and poem to GW on 15 April (GW to Webster, 17 April; *Diaries*, 4:311).

2. See Webster to GW, 16, 18 Dec. 1785, and GW to Webster, 18 Dec. 1785.

From John Wilton

Sir   Common Farm Somerset [England] March the 31 1786
peruseing the Bath peaper of this week I saw A Letter of your Exelencesees Adress to Mrs Mackauley Where you seemes to Desier to heave A Engelish farmer Ingeaged, to Come to America, Wich has been long my Desier, Not only to Come to America but to bee A Real subject of that Cunterye, I am A young man twenty Six years of Age Never was from my father, who was all his life a farmer, and Rents five hundred pr Anum, pastuer & Arable I understands Everry branch of husbuntery in the Engelish Stile, but to Comepleate our bussenniss I think would Bee to Engeage two Engelish Rusticks, wich Can bee Done Very Reasenable, I dont Understand Aney thing of the law Nothing Better than A scool Education wich I supose not Capable to Undertake A Stuerdship But thear is pleanty of that Class heare, If I Come I shall Expect my pleace to bee worth one hundered pr Annum my pasige and all Other Expences paid beefore I leaves Engeland. I am Your Execlls Most Devoted Huml. Servant

Jno. Wilton

N.B. Should Bee Glad to heave a ansser as soon as posable as I Shall Not Engeage In Anny thing till I heave.
P.S. please to Direct Jno Wilton Common farm to Bee Left at the three Cups Bath Somerset Old England.

ALS, DLC:GW.

Index

NOTE: Identifications of persons, places, and things in previous volumes are noted within parentheses.

Nancy (slave at Muddy Hole): cross plowing, 403

Nanny (slave at Muddy Hole): sick, 399; harrowing, 405

Nat (slave at River plantation): plowing, 400; id., 409

Neilson, Robert, 587, 595; id., 588

Nelson, Nathaniel: id., 241

Nelson, Thomas (1715–1787; *see* 1:80), 531; id., 532

Nelson, Thomas (1738–1789; *see* 1:80), 531; id., 241, 532

Nelson, William (*see* 1:80): and resignation from council, 376

Nesbit, John Maxwell: and Potomac River Company, 244

Neufville, Dr. ——, 445

Neufville, Jean de (*see* 1:18–19), 182; and Dismal Swamp Company, 294, 568; and letter for, 312; *letters to:* from GW, 238–40

Neufville, Leonard de (*see* 1:19), 238; id., 239–40

Neville, Presley (*see* 1:305), 555; id., 278; and Monongahela road, 278, 325

New (City, Smith's) Tavern, 186

Newenham, Grace Anna, Lady: compliments to, 388

Newenham, Edward (*see* 1:440), 425, 442, 443; package from, 329; *letters from:* to GW, 17, 145; *letters to:* from GW, 386–88, 614

Newland, James: as GW's tenant, 264

Newport (R.I.): and Masonic lodges, 487

New Room. *See* Mount Vernon

Newton, Thomas, Jr. (*see* 1:80; 2:260): and John Tucker, 130; as GW's agent, 226–27; *letters from:* to GW, 516, 572, 599; *letters to:* from GW, 225–26, 464

Nicholas Owings Brother & Co. (firm): and seed for sale, 595–96

Noailles, Emmanuel-Marie-Louis, marquis de, 540; id., 546

Nokes, Tom. *See* Tom Nokes

Nourse, James (*see* 1:70): death of, 68

Nourse, Joseph, 231

Odelucq, Monsieur ——, Sr., 361–62

O'Donnell, John (shipmaster): and cargo from Far East, 188, 204–6, 213–14, 249, 306; id., 206; invited to Mount Vernon, 208

Ogden, Uzal: *An Address to Those Persons at Elizabeth-Town, and Newark . . . Who Have Lately Been Seriously Impressed with a Desire to Obtain Salvation,* 269; id., 269; *A Sermon Delivered at Morris-Town,* 269; *letters from:* to GW, 269

Ogle, Benjamin: and fawns for GW, 192; *letters from:* to Benjamin Tasker Dulany, 187; to GW, 192; *letters to:* from GW, 187

Ogle, Henrietta Margaret Hill: compliments from, 187

Oglethorpe, James, 51

Ohio lands. *See* Lands of GW

Oilliamson, Marie-Gabriel-Eléanor, comte d' (Doilliamson): gives GW hounds, 216, 218, 502, 543; *letters to:* from GW, 218

Oliphant, John: as GW's tenant, 257, 263

Oliphant, Samuel: as GW's tenant, 264

Otis, Samuel Allyne: id., 231

Otis & Andrews (firm): and Otis & Henley, 231

Otis & Henley (firm): as purchasing agents, 230–31

Otto, Louis-Guillaume, comte de Mosloy: id., 230; arrival of in New York, 288–89; *letters from:* to GW, 288–89; *letters to:* from GW, 433

Oxnard, Thomas (Francis Axnard): and Masonic lodge, 485–86; id., 487

Packard, —— (shipmaster), 210, 229

Page, Frances Burwell: ill health of, 240, 293; id., 241

Page, John (*see* 2:170): and convention of Episcopal church, 240; id., 241; as agriculturist, 572, 573; *letters from:* to GW, 240–41; *letters to:* from GW, 293–94